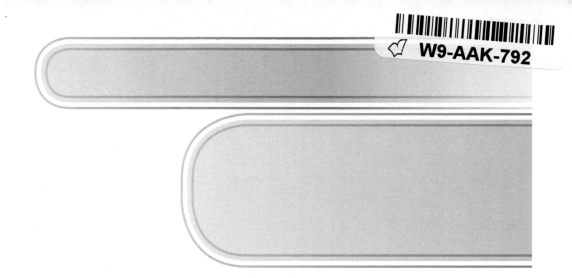

# MONEY, BANKING, AND FINANCIAL MARKETS

## THIRD EDITION

STEPHEN G. CECCHETTI
*Bank for International Settlements*

KERMIT L. SCHOENHOLTZ
*New York University*
*Stern School of Business*

## CUSTOM EDITION FOR DePAUL UNIVERSITY

**Learning Solutions**

Boston   Burr Ridge, IL   Dubuque, IA   New York   San Francisco   St. Louis
Bangkok   Bogotá   Caracas   Lisbon   London   Madrid
Mexico City   Milan   New Delhi   Seoul   Singapore   Sydney   Taipei   Toronto

Money, Banking, and Financial Markets, Third Edition
Custom Edition for DePaul University

This book is a McGraw-Hill Learning Solutions textbook and contains select material from *Money, Banking, and Financial Markets*, Third Edition by Stephen G. Cecchetti and Kermit L. Schoenholtz. Copyright © 2011, 2008, 2006 by The McGraw-Hill Companies, Inc. Reprinted with permission of the publisher. Many custom published texts are modified versions or adaptations of our best-selling textbooks. Some adaptations are printed in black and white to keep prices at a minimum, while others are in color.

1 2 3 4 5 6 7 8 9 0  RJO RJO  14 13 12

ISBN-13: 978-0-07-776616-0
ISBN-10: 0-07-776616-4

*Learning Solutions Consultant: Bridget Hannenberg*
*Production Editor: Nina Meyer*
*Cover Designer: Caitlin Anderson*
*Printer/Binder: R.R. Donnelley*
*Cover Photo Credits: © 2012 JupiterImages Corporation*

# Dedication

To my father, Giovanni Cecchetti, who argued tirelessly that financial markets are not efficient; and to my grandfather Albert Schwabacher, who patiently explained why inflation is destructive.

*Stephen G. Cecchetti*

To my parents, Evelyn and Harold Schoenholtz, and my wife, Elvira Pratsch, who continue to teach me what is true, good, and beautiful.

*Kermit L. Schoenholtz*

# About the Authors

**Stephen G. Cecchetti** is the Economic Adviser and Head of the Monetary and Economic Department at the Bank for International Settlements in Basel, Switzerland. Before joining the BIS in 2008, he was the Barbara and Richard M. Rosenberg Professor of Global Finance at the Brandeis International Business School. Previously, Dr. Cecchetti taught at the New York University Stern School of Business and, for approximately 15 years, was a member of the Department of Economics at The Ohio State University.

In addition to his other appointments, Cecchetti served as Executive Vice President and Director of Research, Federal Reserve Bank of New York (1997–1999); Editor, *Journal of Money, Credit, and Banking* (1992–2001); Research Associate, National Bureau of Economic Research (1989–present); and Research Fellow, Centre for Economic Policy Research (2008–present), among others.

He has consulted for various central banks around the world, including the European Central Bank, the Bank of England, the Central Bank of Bolivia, the Bank of Israel, and the Reserve Bank of Australia.

Cecchetti's research interests include inflation and price measurement, monetary policy, macroeconomic theory, economics of the Great Depression, and financial economics. His initial work concentrated on the theoretical basis and empirical plausibility of new Keynesian models of the business cycle that are based on nominal rigidities. More recently, he has developed new measures of core inflation and examined how monetary policy can be used to control aggregate price movements.

He has published more than 75 articles in academic and policy journals and since 2000 has been a regular contributor to the *Financial Times*. See www.brandeis.edu/global/news_cecchetti_articles.php for an archive of his recent newspaper columns.

Cecchetti received an SB in Economics from the Massachusetts Institute of Technology in 1977 and a PhD in Economics from the University of California at Berkeley in 1982.

**Kermit L. Schoenholtz** is an adjunct professor in the Department of Economics of New York University's Leonard N. Stern School of Business. Schoenholtz was Citigroup's global chief economist from 1997 until 2005. After a year's leave, he served until 2008 as senior advisor and managing director in the Economic and Market Analysis (EMA) department at Citigroup.

Schoenholtz joined Salomon Brothers in 1986, working in their New York, Tokyo, and London offices. In 1997, he became chief economist at Salomon, after which he became chief economist at Salomon Smith Barney and later at Citigroup.

Schoenholtz has published extensively for the professional investment community about financial, economic, and policy developments; more recently, he has contributed to policy-focused scholarly research in economics. He has served as a member of the Executive Committee of the London-based Centre for Economic Policy Research and is a panel member of the U.S. Monetary Policy Forum.

From 1983 to 1985, Schoenholtz was a Visiting Scholar at the Bank of Japan's Institute for Monetary and Economic Studies. He received an MPhil in economics from Yale University in 1982 and an AB from Brown University in 1977.

# Preface

The worldwide financial crisis of 2007–2009 was the most severe since that of the 1930s, and the recession it triggered was by far the most widespread and costly since the Great Depression. Around the world, it cost tens of millions of workers their jobs. In the United States, millions of families lost their homes and their wealth. To stem the crisis, governments and central banks took aggressive and, in many ways, unprecedented actions.

As a result, change will be sweeping through the world of banking and financial markets for years to come. Some of the ways in which people borrowed—to buy a home or a car or to pay for college—have become difficult or unavailable. Some of the largest financial firms have failed, while others—even larger—have risen. Some financial markets have disappeared, but new institutions are surfacing that aim to make markets less vulnerable in the future. And governments everywhere are working on new rules to make future crises both less likely and less damaging.

Just as the crisis is transforming the financial system and government policy, it is transforming the study of money and banking. Some old questions are surfacing with new intensity: Why do such costly crises occur? How can they be prevented? How can we limit their impact? How will these changes affect the financial opportunities and risks that people face?

Against this background, students who memorize the operational details of today's financial system are investing in a short-lived asset. Our purpose in writing this book is to focus on the basic functions served by the financial system while deemphasizing its current structure and rules. Learning the economic rationale behind current financial tools, rules, and structures is much more valuable than concentrating on the tools, rules, and structures themselves. It is an approach designed to give students the lifelong ability to understand and evaluate whatever financial innovations and developments they may one day confront.

## The Core Principles Approach

Toward that end, the entire content of this book is based on five *core principles*. Knowledge of these principles is the basis for learning what the financial system does, how it is organized, and how it is linked to the real economy.

1. Time has value.
2. Risk requires compensation.
3. Information is the basis for decisions.
4. Markets determine prices and allocate resources.
5. Stability improves welfare.

These five core principles serve as a framework through which to view the history, current status, and future development of money and banking. They are discussed in detail in Chapter 1; throughout the rest of the text, marginal icons remind students of the principles that underlie particular discussions.

Focusing on core principles has created a book that is both concise and logically organized. This approach does require some adjustments to the traditional methodology used to teach money and banking, but for the most part they are changes in emphasis only. That said, some of these changes have greatly improved both the ease of teaching and the value students draw from the course. Among them are the emphasis on risk and on the lessons from the financial crisis; use of the term *financial instrument*; parallel presentation of the Federal Reserve and the European Central Bank; a streamlined, updated section on monetary economics; and the adoption of an integrated global perspective.

# Innovations in This Text

In addition to the focus on core principles, this book introduces a series of innovations designed to foster coherence and relevance in the study of money and banking, in both today's financial world and tomorrow's.

## Impact of the Crisis

The effects of the financial crisis of 2007–2009 are transforming money, banking, and financial markets. Accordingly, from beginning to end, the book integrates the issues raised by the crisis and by the response of policymakers.

The concept of a liquidity crisis surfaces in Chapter 2, and the risks associated with leverage and the rise of shadow banking are introduced in Chapter 3. Issues specific to the 2007–2009 crisis—including securitization, rating agencies, subprime mortgages, over-the-counter trading, and complex financial instruments like credit-default swaps—are included in the appropriate intermediate chapters of the text. More broadly, the sources of threats to the financial system as a whole are identified throughout the book, and there is a focused discussion on regulatory initiatives to limit such systemic threats. Finally, we present—in a logical and organized manner—the unconventional monetary policy tools that became so prominent in the policy response to the crisis.

## Early Introduction of Risk

It is impossible to appreciate how the financial system works without understanding risk. In the modern financial world, virtually all transactions transfer some degree of risk between two or more parties. These risk trades can be extremely beneficial, as they are in the case of insurance markets. But there is still potential for disaster. In 2008, risk-trading activity at some of the world's largest financial firms threatened the stability of the international financial system.

Even though risk is absolutely central to an understanding of the financial system, most money and banking books give very little space to the topic. In contrast, this book devotes an entire chapter to defining and measuring risk. Chapter 5 introduces the concept of a risk premium as compensation for risk and shows how diversification can reduce risk. Because risk is central to explaining the valuation of financial instruments, the role of financial intermediaries, and the job of central bankers, the book returns to this concept throughout the chapters.

## Emphasis on Financial Instruments

Financial instruments are introduced early in the book, where they are defined based on their economic function. This perspective leads naturally to a discussion of the uses of various instruments and the determinants of their value. Bonds, stocks, and derivatives all fit neatly into this framework, so they are all discussed together.

This approach solves one of the problems with existing texts, use of the term *financial market* to refer to bonds, interest rates, and foreign exchange. In its conventional microeconomic sense, the term *market* signifies a place where trade occurs, not the instruments that are traded. This book follows standard usage of the term *market* to mean a place for trade. It uses the term *financial instruments* to describe virtually all financial arrangements, including loans, bonds, stocks, futures, options, and insurance contracts. Doing so clears up the confusion that can arise when students arrive in a money and banking class fresh from a course in the principles of economics.

## Parallel Presentation of the Federal Reserve and the European Central Bank

To foster a deeper understanding of central banking and monetary policy, the presentation of this material begins with a discussion of the central bank's role and objectives. Descriptions of the Federal Reserve and the European Central Bank follow. By starting on a theoretical plane, students gain the tools they need to understand how all central banks work. This avoids focusing on institutional details that may quickly become obsolete. Armed with a basic understanding of what central banks do and how they do it, students will be prepared to grasp the meaning of future changes in institutional structure.

Another important innovation is the parallel discussion of the two most important central banks in the world, the Federal Reserve and the European Central Bank (ECB). Students of the 21st century are ill-served by books that focus entirely on the U.S. financial system. They need a global perspective on central banking, the starting point for which is a detailed knowledge of the ECB.

## Modern Treatment of Monetary Economics

The discussion of central banking is followed by a simple framework for understanding the impact of monetary policy on the real economy. Modern central bankers think and talk about changing the interest rate when inflation and output deviate from their target objectives. Yet traditional treatments of monetary economics employ aggregate demand and aggregate supply diagrams, which relate output to the price level, and discuss inflation in terms of shifts in the AD and AS curves. The resulting development is lengthy and difficult. Because this book skips the ISLM framework, its presentation of monetary economics is several chapters shorter. Only those topics that are most important in a monetary economics course are covered: long-run money growth and inflation and short-run monetary policy and business cycles. This streamlined treatment of monetary theory is not only concise, but more modern and more relevant than the traditional approach. It helps students to see monetary policy changes as part of a strategy, rather than a one-off event, and it gives them a complete understanding of business-cycle fluctuations.

## Integrated Global Perspective

Technological advances have dramatically reduced the importance of a bank's physical location, producing a truly global financial system. Twenty years ago money and banking books could afford to focus primarily on the U.S. financial system, relegating international topics to a separate chapter that could be considered optional. But in today's financial world, even a huge country like the United States cannot be treated in isolation. The global financial system is truly an integrated one, rendering separate discussion of a single country's institutions, markets, or policies impossible. This book incorporates the discussion of international issues throughout the text, emphasizing when national borders are important to bankers and when they are not.

# Organization

This book is organized to help students understand both the financial system and its economic effects on their lives. That means surveying a broad series of topics, including what money is and how it is used; what a financial instrument is and how it is valued; what a financial market is and how it works; what a financial institution is and why we need it; and what a central bank is and how it operates. More important, it means showing students how to apply the five core principles of money and banking to the evolving financial and economic arrangements that they inevitably will confront during their lifetimes.

**Part I: Money and the Financial System.**   Chapter 1 introduces the core principles of money and banking, which serve as touchstones throughout the book. Chapter 2 examines money both in theory and in practice. Chapter 3 follows with a bird's-eye view of financial instruments, financial markets, and financial institutions. (Instructors who prefer to discuss the financial system first can cover Chapters 2 and 3 in reverse order.)

**Part II: Interest Rates, Financial Instruments, and Financial Markets.**   Part II contains a detailed description of financial instruments and the financial theory required to understand them. It begins with an explanation of present value and risk, followed by specific discussions of bonds, stocks, derivatives, and foreign exchange. Students benefit from concrete examples of these concepts. In Chapter 7 (The Risk and Term Structure of Interest Rates), for example, students learn how the information contained in the risk and term structure of interest rates can be useful in forecasting. In Chapter 8 (Stocks, Stock Markets, and Market Efficiency), they learn about stock bubbles and how those anomalies influence the economy. And in Chapter 10 (Foreign Exchange), they study the Big Mac index to understand the concept of purchasing power parity. Throughout this section, two ideas are emphasized: that financial instruments transfer resources from savers to investors, and that in doing so, they transfer risk to those best equipped to bear it.

**Part III: Financial Institutions.**   In the next section, the focus shifts to financial institutions. Chapter 11 introduces the economic theory that is the basis for our understanding of the role of financial intermediaries. Through a series of examples, students see the problems created by asymmetric information as well as how financial intermediaries can mitigate those problems. The remaining chapters in Part III put theory into practice. Chapter 12 presents a detailed discussion of banking, the bank balance sheet, and the risks that banks must manage. Chapter 13 provides a brief overview of the financial industry's structure, and Chapter 14 explains financial regulation, including a discussion of regulation to limit threats to the financial system as a whole.

**Part IV: Central Banks, Monetary Policy, and Financial Stability.** Chapters 15 through 19 survey what central banks do and how they do it. This part of the book begins with a discussion of the role and objectives of central banks, which leads naturally to the principles that guide central bank design. Chapter 16 applies those principles to the Federal Reserve and the European Central Bank. Chapter 17 presents the central bank balance sheet, the process of multiple deposit creation, and the money supply. Chapters 18 and 19 cover operational policy, based on control of both the interest rate and the exchange rate. Chapter 18 also introduces the monetary transmission mechanism and presents a variety of unconventional monetary policy tools that gained prominence during the financial crisis of 2007–2009. The goal of Part IV is to give students the knowledge they will need to cope with the inevitable changes that will occur in central bank structure.

**Part V: Modern Monetary Economics.** The last part of the book covers modern monetary economics. While most books cover this topic in six or more chapters, this one does it in four. This streamlined approach concentrates on what is important, presenting only the essential lessons that students truly need. Chapter 20 sets the stage by exploring the relationship between inflation and money growth. Starting with inflation keeps the presentation simple and powerful, and emphasizes the way monetary policymakers think about what they do. A discussion of aggregate demand, aggregate supply, and the determinants of inflation and output follows. Chapter 21 presents a complete macroeconomic model with a dynamic aggregate demand curve that integrates monetary policy directly into the presentation, along with short- and long-run aggregate supply curves. In Chapter 22 the model is used to help understand the sources of business cycles, as well as a number of important applications that face monetary policymakers in the world today. Each application stands on its own and the applications are ordered in increasing difficulty to allow maximum flexibility in their use.

For those instructors who have the time, we recommend closing the course with a rereading of the first chapter and a review of the core principles. What is the future likely to hold for the six parts of the financial system: money, financial instruments, financial markets, financial institutions, regulatory agencies, and central banks? How do students envision each of these parts of the system 20 or even 50 years from now?

# Learning Tools

In a sense, this book is a guide to the principles students will need to critically evaluate and use what they read in the financial press. Reading the newspaper and applying the information it contains require some basic knowledge. Supplying that knowledge is the purpose of the five types of inserts that complement the chapters, providing a break from the more technical material in the body of the text:

**Your Financial World** inserts provide students with practical information that is based on lessons covered in the chapter. Most chapters contain two of these boxes, each of which examines a personal finance problem that everyone faces. These boxes show students that the concepts taught in the money and banking course are relevant to their everyday lives. Among the topics covered are the importance of saving for retirement, the risk in taking on a variable-rate mortgage, the desirability of owning stocks, and techniques for getting the most out of the financial news.

**Applying the Concept** sections show how ideas introduced in the chapter can be applied to the world around us. Most describe historical episodes or examine issues relevant to the public policy debate. Subjects include how debt problems in emerging-market countries can create an increase in the demand for U.S. Treasury debt; why Long-Term Capital Management nearly caused a collapse of the world financial system; and what monetary policymakers learned from the Great Depression of the 1930s. Some chapters contain two of these applications.

**Lessons from the Crisis** inserts explain concepts or issues in a chapter that were integral to the financial crisis of 2007–2009. Most chapters contain at least one such insert. One goal of these inserts is to provide students a framework for understanding the crisis and how it transformed the world of money, banking, and financial markets. Another goal is to show how the crisis demonstrates the relevance and power of the ideas in the book. The topics range from specific aspects of the crisis such as shadow banks, asset-backed securities, and the evolution of the money supply to broad concepts like liquidity, leverage, securitization, and systemic risk.

**In the News** boxes present articles drawn from *The New York Times, The Wall Street Journal, The Financial Times, The Economist,* the *Washington Post, Los Angeles Times, Bloomberg News,* and *BusinessWeek.* These readings show how concepts introduced in the chapter are applied in the financial press. Each article is accompanied by a brief analysis that reinforces key concepts. One In the News box appears in nearly every chapter.

**Tools of the Trade** boxes teach useful skills, including how to read bond and stock tables, how to read charts, and how to do some simple algebraic calculations. Some provide brief reviews of material from the principles of economics course, such as the relationship between the current account and the capital account in the balance of payments. Most chapters contain one of these boxes.

Finally, the end-of-chapter material is divided into three sections:

**Key Terms** A listing of all the technical terms introduced and defined in the chapter. The key terms are defined in full in the glossary at the end of the book.

**Chapter Lessons** A list of the key lessons in the chapter. Other textbooks summarize a small number of points at length. This book summarizes a larger number of points, each of them short, clear, and couched in the form of an outline that matches the chapter headings—a format designed to aid student comprehension and retention.

**Problems** Each chapter contains at least 18 conceptual and analytical problems of varying levels of difficulty. These problems are designed to reinforce the lessons in the chapter.

# Organizational Alternatives

While this book greatly streamlines the traditional approach to money and banking, it remains flexible enough to be used in a broad variety of courses; 16 to 19 of the book's 23 chapters can be assigned in the following courses:

*General Money and Banking Course.* Chapters 1–8, 11, 12, 15, 16, the first section of 17 (through page 433), 18, and 20–22
This course covers the primary material needed to appreciate the connections between the financial system and the economy.

*General Money and Banking Course with International Emphasis.* Chapters 1–8, 10–12, 15–19, and 20
This alternative to the general money and banking course substitutes chapters on foreign exchange and exchange-rate policy for the macroeconomic model included in courses with less international emphasis.

*Financial Markets and Institutions.* Chapters 1–9, 11–18
The traditional financial markets and institutions course covers money, financial instruments and markets, financial institutions, and central banking. The focus is on Parts II and III of the book.

*Monetary Economics and Monetary Policy.* Chapters 1–7, 10–12, 15–23
A course called monetary economics and monetary policy uses the material in Parts II and III as a foundation for understanding the material in Parts IV and V. A half-semester course for students with a background in financial instruments and institutions might cover only Chapters 1–3 and 15–23.

# What's New in the Third Edition?

Many things have happened since the last edition. For that reason, all of the figures and data have been updated to reflect the most recent available information. In addition, Stephen Cecchetti and his new co-author, Kermit Schoenholtz, have made numerous, vital changes to enhance the Third Edition of *Money, Banking, and Financial Markets* as outlined here.

## New Topics in the Integrated Global Perspective

The Third Edition has been revised extensively in light of the global financial crisis, which began shortly after the Second Edition went to press. Throughout the Third Edition, the authors have integrated key developments and relevant insights from the crisis. New topics introduced or discussed in much greater detail include:

- Crises of liquidity and deleveraging
- Shadow banking
- Systemic risk
- Complex financial instruments
- Centralized counterparties
- Too big to fail
- Macro-prudential regulation
- Paying interest on reserves

- The zero bound
- Unconventional monetary policy tools
- Impact of the crisis on Fed independence

The most extensive changes are in Chapter 14, which now includes a treatment of systemic regulation, and in Chapter 18, which has been updated with coverage of the unconventional monetary policy approaches adopted during the financial crisis.

## Improved End-of-Chapter Problems

Many of the End-of-Chapter problem sets have been updated to highlight lessons from the financial crisis of 2007–2009.

## Changes at the Federal Reserve

The discussion of the Federal Reserve now highlights the use of unconventional policy tools in addressing the financial crisis (Chapter 18) and the impairment of the monetary transmission process during the crisis (Chapter 23). It also reflects the challenge to Fed independence in the aftermath of the crisis (Chapter 15).

## Updated Coverage of Current Events

Through new and updated Learning Tools inserts, the authors have captured developments since the Second Edition in the key areas of the financial crisis and monetary policy. Here is a complete list of the new features:

**Lessons from the Crisis**
Market Liquidity, Funding Liquidity, and Making Markets (Chapter 2)
Leverage (Chapter 3)
Interbank Lending (Chapter 3)
Shadow Banks (Chapter 3)
Risk Taking and the Search for Yield (Chapter 4)
Systemic Risk (Chapter 5)
Rating Agencies (Chapter 7)
Asset-Backed Commercial Paper (Chapter 7)
Subprime Mortgages (Chapter 7)
Centralized Counterparties and Systemic Risk (Chapter 9)
Currency Risk and Rollover Risk (Chapter 10)
Information Asymmetry and Securitization (Chapter 11)
Insufficient Bank Capital (Chapter 12)
Should the Lender of Last Resort Also Supervise? (Chapter 14)
Threats to Fed Independence (Chapter 15)
Government Funding in the Euro Area (Chapter 16)
The Impact on Money Supply (Chapter 17)

**In the News**
Dad, Can You Text Me $200? (Chapter 2)
Lessons of the Financial Crisis—One Year Later (Chapter 3)
How to Achieve Effective Portfolio Diversification (Chapter 5)
Revival in "Private-Label" Mortgage Securities? (Chapter 6)
Banks Decline Yield Curve Invitation to Party On (Chapter 7)

Efficient Market Theory and the Crisis (Chapter 8)
AIG Still Faces Billions in Credit Losses (Chapter 9)
U.S. in Standoff with Beijing over Chinese Currency (Chapter 10)
In a Tight Market, Borrowers Turn to Peers (Chapter 11)
Rogue Flight: Société Générale's Kerviel Tags Leeson (Chapter 12)
Fed's Tarullo Says Dividing Banks May Not Curb Too Big to Fail (Chapter 13)
New Bank Rules Sink Stocks (Chapter 14)
Beware the Result of Outrage (Chapter 15)
Fed Adopts De Facto Inflation Target (Chapter 16)
Fed May Take Chance End to Debt Purchases Won't Hurt Housing (Chapter 18)
As Budget Deficit Grows, So Do Doubts on Dollar (Chapter 19)
Independence Day for the Fed (Chapter 21)
Inflation Worry Limits Fed Flexibility (Chapter 22)
Bernanke's How-To on Rate Increase Lacks a When (Chapter 23)

**Applying the Concept**
Securitization (Chapter 6)
The Madoff Scandal (Chapter 11)
The Fed's Balance Sheet: Impact of the Crisis (Chapter 17)
Implications of China's Exchange-Rate Regime (Chapter 19)

**Tools of the Trade**
Some Unconventional Policy Tools (Chapter 18)

# Supplements for Students

## Online Learning Center Web Site

The book's Web site, revised by Matthew Alford (Southeastern Louisiana University), www.mhhe.com/cecchetti3e, includes a variety of free content for students, including multiple-choice chapter quizzes, PowerPoint slides, and interactive graphs with related exercises. Instructors may access all the book's major supplements using a special password.

# Supplements for Instructors

## Instructor's Resources and Solutions Manual

Tori Knight (Carson-Newman College) has collected a broad array of materials for instructors. This manual includes chapter overviews, outlines, and a discussion of how the core principles apply to each chapter. It also addresses concepts students often find difficult, including suggestions for alleviating confusion. Solutions are provided to the end-of-chapter problems by Roisin O'Sullivan (Smith College).

## Test Bank

Kenneth Slaysman (York College of Pennsylvania) and Tori Knight have revised the test bank of 2,500 multiple-choice and 600 short-answer and essay questions. The test bank can be used both as a study guide and as a source for exam questions. It has been computerized to allow for both selective and random generation of test questions.

## PowerPoint Slides

PowerPoint slides for classroom use, updated by Marie Reymore (Marion University), are available with the Third Edition. The slides outline the main points in each chapter and reproduce major graphs and charts. This handy, colorful supplement will help to maintain students' interest during lecture sessions.

# McGraw-Hill *Connect Economics*

## Less Managing. More Teaching. Greater Learning.

McGraw-Hill *Connect Economics* is an online assignment and assessment solution that connects students with the tools and resources they'll need to achieve success.

McGraw-Hill *Connect Economics* helps prepare students for their future by enabling faster learning, more efficient studying, and higher retention of knowledge.

## McGraw-Hill *Connect Economics* Features

*Connect Economics* offers a number of powerful tools and features to make managing assignments easier, so faculty can spend more time teaching. With *Connect Economics*, students can engage with their coursework anytime and anywhere, making the learning process more accessible and efficient. *Connect Economics* offers you the features described below.

**Simple Assignment Management.** With *Connect Economics*, creating assignments is easier than ever, so you can spend more time teaching and less time managing. The assignment management function enables you to:

- Create and deliver assignments easily with selectable end-of-chapter questions and test bank items.
- Streamline lesson planning, student progress reporting, and assignment grading to make classroom management more efficient than ever.
- Go paperless with the eBook and online submission and grading of student assignments.

**Smart Grading.** When it comes to studying, time is precious. *Connect Economics* helps students learn more efficiently by providing feedback and practice material when they need it, where they need it. When it comes to teaching, your time also is precious. The grading function enables you to:

- Have assignments scored automatically, giving students immediate feedback on their work and side-by-side comparisons with correct answers.
- Access and review each response; manually change grades or leave comments for students to review.
- Reinforce classroom concepts with practice tests and instant quizzes.

**Instructor Library.** The *Connect Economics* Instructor Library is your repository for instructor ancillaries and additional resources to improve student engagement in and out of class. You can select and use any asset that enhances your lecture.

**Student Study Center.** The *Connect Economics* Student Study Center is the place for students to access additional resources. The Student Study Center:

- Offers students quick access to lectures, practice materials, eBooks, and more.
- Provides instant practice material and study questions, easily accessible on the go.
- Gives students access to the Self-Quiz and Study described below.

**Self-Quiz and Study.** The Self-Quiz and Study (SQS) connects each student to the learning resources needed for success in the course. For each chapter, students:

- Take a practice test to initiate the Self-Quiz and Study.
- Immediately upon completing the practice test, see how their performance compares to content by sections within chapters.
- Receive a Study Plan that recommends specific readings from the text, supplemental study material, and practice work that will improve their understanding and mastery of each section.

**Student Progress Tracking.** *Connect Economics* keeps instructors informed about how each student, section, and class is performing, allowing for more productive use of lecture and office hours. The progress-tracking function enables you to:

- View scored work immediately and track individual or group performance with assignment and grade reports.
- Access an instant view of student or class performance relative to section headings.
- Collect data and generate reports required by many accreditation organizations, such as AACSB.

**Lecture Capture.** Increase the attention paid to lecture discussion by decreasing the attention paid to note taking. For an additional charge Lecture Capture offers new ways for students to focus on the in-class discussion, knowing they can revisit important topics later. Lecture Capture enables you to:

- Record and distribute your lecture with a click of button.
- Record and index PowerPoint presentations and anything shown on your computer so it is easily searchable, frame by frame.
- Offer access to lectures anytime and anywhere by computer, iPod, or mobile device.
- Increase intent listening and class participation by easing students' concerns about note taking. Lecture Capture will make it more likely you will see students' faces, not the tops of their heads.

**McGraw-Hill *Connect Plus Economics*.** McGraw-Hill reinvents the textbook learning experience for the modern student with *Connect Plus Economics*. A seamless integration of an eBook and *Connect Economics*, *Connect Plus Economics* provides all of the *Connect Economics* features plus the following:

- An integrated eBook, allowing for anytime, anywhere access to the textbook.
- Dynamic links between the problems or questions you assign to your students and the location in the eBook where that problem or question is covered.
- A powerful search function to pinpoint and connect key concepts in a snap.

In short, *Connect Economics* offers you and your students powerful tools and features that optimize your time and energies, enabling you to focus on course content, teaching, and student learning. *Connect Economics* also offers a wealth of content resources for both instructors and students. This state-of-the-art, thoroughly tested system supports you in preparing students for the world that awaits.

For more information about Connect, go to **www.mcgrawhillconnect.com**, or contact your local McGraw-Hill sales representative.

## Tegrity Campus: Lectures 24/7

Tegrity Campus is a service that makes class time available 24/7 by automatically capturing every lecture in a searchable format for students to review when they study and complete assignments. With a simple one-click start-and-stop process, you capture all computer screens and corresponding audio. Students can replay any part of any class with easy-to-use browser-based viewing on a PC or Mac.

Educators know that the more students can see, hear, and experience class resources, the better they learn. In fact, studies prove it. With Tegrity Campus, students quickly recall key moments by using Tegrity Campus's unique search feature. This search helps students efficiently find what they need, when they need it, across an entire semester of class recordings. Help turn all your students' study time into learning moments immediately supported by your lecture.

To learn more about Tegrity watch a 2-minute Flash demo at **http://tegritycampus .mhhe.com**.

## Assurance of Learning Ready

Many educational institutions today are focused on the notion of *assurance of learning*, an important element of some accreditation standards. *Money, Banking, and Financial Markets* is designed specifically to support your assurance of learning initiatives with a simple, yet powerful solution.

Each test bank question for *Money, Banking, and Financial Markets* maps to a specific chapter heading listed in the text. You can use our test bank software, EZ Test and EZ Test Online, or in *Connect Economics* to easily query for chapter headings and topic tags that directly relate to your course. You can then use the reporting features of EZ Test to aggregate student results in similar fashion, making the collection and presentation of assurance of learning data simple and easy.

## AACSB Statement

The McGraw-Hill Companies is a proud corporate member of AACSB International. Understanding the importance and value of AACSB accreditation, *Money, Banking, and Financial Markets*, 3/e recognizes the curricula guidelines detailed in the AACSB standards for business accreditation by connecting selected questions in the text and test bank to the six general knowledge and skill guidelines in the AACSB standards.

The statements contained in *Money, Banking, and Financial Markets*, 3/e are provided only as a guide for the users of this textbook. The AACSB leaves content coverage and assessment within the purview of individual schools, the mission of the school, and the faculty. While *Money, Banking, and Financial Markets,* 3/e and the teaching package make no claim of any specific AACSB qualification or evaluation, we have within *Money, Banking, and Financial Markets,* 3/e labeled selected questions according to the six general knowledge and skills areas.

# McGraw-Hill Customer Care Contact Information

At McGraw-Hill, we understand that getting the most from new technology can be challenging. That's why our services don't stop after you purchase our products. You can e-mail our Product Specialists 24 hours a day to get product-training online. Or you can search our knowledge bank of Frequently Asked Questions on our support website. For Customer Support, call **800-331-5094**, e-mail **hmsupport@mcgraw-hill.com,** or visit **www.mhhe.com/support**. One of our Technical Support Analysts will be able to assist you in a timely fashion.

# Acknowledgments

I owe thanks to many more people than I can possibly list, including a large number of academics, central bankers, and financial market participants around the world. A few of these deserve special mention. I would like to thank Robert M. Solow, who set me on the path doing economics as a 20-year-old undergraduate; George A. Akerlof, whose inspiration still guides me, even more than 25 years after he signed my dissertation; William J. McDonough, who gave me the opportunity to watch and ask questions from inside the Federal Reserve; and Peter R. Fisher, who was my day-to-day guide to what I was seeing at the Fed.

Of my numerous collaborators and colleagues over the years, Nelson Mark (now at the University of Notre Dame) is the most important. His encouragement, counsel, and friendship have guided me for more than 15 years. In addition, Michael Bryan of the Federal Reserve Bank of Cleveland has been a constant source of help and encouragement, as have numerous friends throughout the central banking world.

Among all of the professional colleagues who took the time to read early versions of the manuscript, I would like to single out Jim Fackler for his insight and patience. This book is much better for the time he generously devoted to correcting my logical mistakes.

Without all the people at McGraw-Hill/Irwin this book would never have been written. Gary Burke and Paul Shensa first convinced me that I could write this book, and then taught me how. Erin Strathmann worked tirelessly (and daily) to improve the book. Betty Morgan made my sentences and paragraphs readable. And all of the people in production and design turned the words and charts into a beautiful, readable book. Gregg Forte made a notable contribution to this Third Edition through his skilled editing of the manuscript.

Without students, universities would not exist. And without a class in money and banking to teach, I would not have written this book. I owe a debt to every student who has sat in a classroom with me. Not surprisingly, some students helped more than others. The ones that deserve special mention for the time and effort they put in to helping with the manuscript are: Margaret Mary McConnell of the Federal Reserve Bank of New York, Roisin O'Sullivan of Smith College, Stefan Krause of Emory University, Lianfa Li of Peking University, Craig Evers of the Federal Reserve Board, Anne LePard formerly of Brandeis University, and Georgios Karras of the University of Illinois at Chicago.

And finally, there is my family; my wife Ruth and our sons Daniel and Ethan. For three years they have put up with my daily routine of writing, rewriting, and rewriting again and again. To them I owe the biggest thanks.

**Stephen G. Cecchetti**
**Bank for International Settlements**

There is not enough space here to thank the many people who taught me about financial markets and institutions during my more than two decades of work as a market economist, but a few deserve special mention. Hugh Patrick was an inspiration in graduate school and remains a friend and guide. In the financial markets, I benefited especially from the wisdom of Henry Kaufman and the economists he gathered at Salomon Brothers in the 1980s—Richard Berner, Robert DiClemente, John Lipsky, and Nicholas Sargen. The economics team that I was privileged to lead at Salomon (and later at Citi) continued my education, including (among many others) Lewis Alexander, Robert DiClemente, Don Hanna, Michael Saunders, Christopher Wiegand, and Jeffrey Young. Of course, my greatest debt is to my wife, Elvira Pratsch. I also thank my parents, Harold and Evelyn, as well as my sister and brother, Sharon and Andy.

**Kermit L. Schoenholtz**
**New York University Leonard N. Stern School of Business**

# Reviewers

Thank you to the following contributing reviewers for this and previous editions.

Burton Abrams
*University of Delaware*

Abdiweli Ali
*Niagara University*

Thomas Martin Allen
*Texas A&M University*

Harjit Arora
*Lemoyne College*

Foued Ayari
*Bernard M. Baruch College*

Raymond Batina
*Washington State University*

Clare Battista
*California Polytechnic State University*

Larry Belcher
*Stetson University*

Robert Boatler
*Texas Christian University*

Christa Bouwman
*Case Western Reserve University*

Latanya Brown
*Bowie State University*

James Butkiewicz
*University of Delaware*

Douglas Campbell
*University of Memphis*

Giorgio Canarella
*California State University at Los Angeles*

Bolong Cao
*Ohio University, Athens*

Tina Carter
*Florida State University at Tallahassee*

Matthew S. Chambers
*Towson University*

Dong Cho
*Wichita State University*

Nan-Ting Chou
*University of Louisville*

Isabelle Delalex
*Pace University*

Mamit Deme
*Middle Tennessee State University*

Seija Doolittle
*Delaware Technical Community College
at Wilmington*

David Doorn
*University of Minnesota at Duluth*

Demissew Ejara
*William Patterson University*

Paul Emberton
*Texas State University*

Robert Eyler
*Sonoma State University*

Gregory Fallon
*College of Saint Joseph*

Richard Froyen
*University of North Carolina at
Chapel Hill*

Craig Furfine
*University of Chicago*

William Gavin
*Washington University*

Ronald Gilbert
*Texas Tech University*

Lance Girton
*University of Utah*

Stuart Glosser
*University of Wisconsin at Whitewater*

William L. Goffe
*Oswego State University of New York*

Stephan F. Gohmann
*University of Louisville*

Elias Grivoyannis
*Yeshiva University*

Joanne Guo
*Pace University*

David Hammes
*University of Hawaii at Hilo*

Scott Hein
*Texas Tech University*

Ying Huang
*Manhattan College*

Owen Irvine
*Michigan State University at East Lansing*

Aaron Jackson
*Bentley College*

Yongbok Jeon
*University of Utah at Salt Lake City*

George Jouganatos
*California State University at Sacramento*

Chris Kauffman
*University of Tennessee at Knoxville*

Andrew Kayanga
*Dillard University*

Kathy Kelly
*University of Texas, Arlington*

Kent Kimbrough
*Duke University*

Paul Kubik
*DePaul University*

Pamela Labadie
*George Washington University*

Larry Landrum
*Virginia Western Community College*

Tom Lee
*California State University at Northridge*

Serpil Leveen
*Montclair State University*

Melissa Lind
*University of Texas, Arlington*

Mark Longbrake
*Ohio State University at Columbus*

Fiona Maclachlan
*Manhattan College*

Michael Madaris
*William Carey University*

Ellie Mafi-Kreft
*Indiana University*

Vincent Marra
*University of Delaware*

Ralph May
*Southwestern Oklahoma State University*

Robert McAuliffe
*Babson College*

Chris McHugh
*Tufts University*

Alice Melkumian
*Western Illinois University*

Alla Melkumian
*Western Illinois University*

Jianjun Miao
*Boston University*

Peter Mikek
*Wabash College*

Ossama Mikhail
*University of Central Florida*

Kyoko Mona
*Bernard M. Baruch College*

Ray Nelson
*Brigham Young University*

James Nguyen
*Southeastern Louisiana University*

David O'Dell
*McPherson College*

Roisin O'Sullivan
*Smith College*

Dennis O'Toole
*Virginia Commonwealth University*

Daniel Owens
*University of North Dakota*

Hilde Patron-Boenheim
*University of West Georgia*

Robert Pennington
*University of Central Florida*

Dennis Placone
*Clemson University*

Ronald Ratti
*University of Western Sydney, Australia*

Rupert Rhodd
*Florida Atlantic University at Davie*

Kevin Salyer
*University of California, Davis*

Julia Sampson
*Malone College*

Drew Saunders
*Purdue University*

Timothy J. Schibik
*University of Southern Indiana*

Sherrill Shaffer
*University of Wyoming*

Anna Shostya
*Bernard M. Baruch College*

Harindar Singh
*Grand Valley State University*

Robert Sonora
*Fort Lewis College*

Souren Soumbatiants
*Franklin University*

Herman Stekler
*George Washington University*

Mark Strazicich
*Appalachian State University*

William Stronge
*Florida Atlantic University*

Scott Sumner
*Bentely College*

Philip Tew
*University of Mississippi*

Sven N. Thommesen
*Auburn University*

Mark Toma
*University of Kentucky at Lexington*

Kudret Topyan
*Manhattan College*

Brian Trinque
*University of Texas at Austin*

Rubina Vohra
*New Jersey City University*

William Walsh
*University of St. Thomas*

Dale Warmingham
*Rutgers University at New Brunswick*

Chao Wei
*George Washington University*

Mark Weinstock
*Pace University*

Niklas Westelius
*Hunter College*

Eugene White
*Rutgers University at New Brunswick*

Ruhai Wu
*Florida Atlantic University*

King-Yuen Yik
*University of Michigan at Ann Arbor*

Derek Yonai
*Campbell University*

# Feature Walkthrough

### YOUR FINANCIAL WORLD
#### Pay Off Your Credit Card Debt as Fast as You Can

Credit cards are extremely useful. They make buying things easy—sometimes too easy. While we all plan to pay off our credit card balances every month, sometimes we just don't have the resources. So take advantage of the loans the card issuers offer and pay off only part of what we owe. Suddenly we find ourselves deeply in debt.

How fast should you pay off your credit card balance? All the bank or finance company that issued the card will tell you is the minimum you have to pay. You get to decide whether to pay more, and your decision makes a big difference. We can use the present-value concept to figure out your alternatives.

Let's take a typical example. You have a balance of $2,000 and can afford to pay at least $50 per month. How many monthly payments will you need to pay off the full debt? What if you pay $60 or $75 per month? To find the answer, use equation (8) for the present value of a fixed series of payments. In this case, the present value is the loan amount, $2,000; the fixed monthly payment is $50, $60, or $75; and the interest rate is whatever your credit card company charges per month—10 to 20 percent a year. (The average rate is around 13 percent.) We need to figure out the number of payments, or n in equation (8).*

Table 4.4 shows the number of months needed to pay off your $2,000 balance at various interest rates and payment amounts. The first entry tells you that if your credit card company is charging a 10 percent annual interest rate (which is comparatively low), and you pay $50 per month, then you will need to make payments for 48.4 months—just over four years.

Looking at the entire table, you can see the advantage of making big payments. Assume you're paying 15 percent, which is realistic. The table shows that increasing your payment from $50 to $60 will allow you to finish paying off your debt in 42.5 months rather than 54.3 months. In other words, paying $10 more a month will allow you to finish paying off the loan one full year sooner. And if you can manage to pay $75 a month, you'll be finished 10 months before that.

*The most straightforward way to do this is to use a spreadsheet to add up the payments until their present value equals the credit card balance. You can also use equation (A5) in the appendix of this chapter, which can be solved using logarithms.

How fast should you pay off your credit card balance?

Looking more closely, you can see that making large payments is much more important than getting a low interest rate. The lesson is: Pay off your debts as fast as you possibly can. Procrastination is expensive.

| Table 4.4 | Number of Months to Pay Off a $2,000 Credit Card Debt | | |
|---|---|---|---|
| Annual Interest Rate | Monthly Payment | | |
| | $50 | $60 | $75 |
| 10% | 48.4 | 38.9 | 30.1 |
| 12% | 50.5 | 40.3 | 30.9 |
| 15% | 54.3 | 42.5 | 32.2 |
| 20% | 62.4 | 47.0 | 34.5 |

## Your Financial World

These boxes show students that the concepts taught in the text are relevant to their everyday lives. Among the topics covered are the importance of saving for retirement, the risk in taking on a variable rate mortgage, the desirability of owning stocks, and techniques for getting the most out of the financial news.

---

For a complete listing of titles of chapter features and their page references, refer to the information found on the inside front cover of this text.

## Lessons from the Crisis

These boxes explain concepts or issues that are both integral to the chapter and central to understanding how the financial crisis of 2007–2009 transformed the world of money, banking, and financial markets. The topics range from specific aspects of the crisis to broad concepts like liquidity, leverage, and systemic risk.

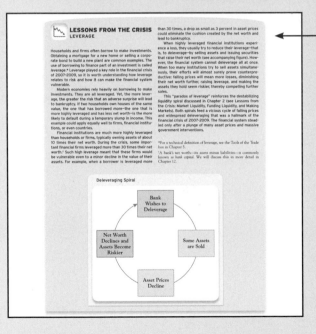

### LESSONS FROM THE CRISIS
#### LEVERAGE

Households and firms often borrow to make investments. Obtaining a mortgage for a new home or selling a corporate bond to build a new plant are common examples. The use of borrowing to finance part of an investment is called *leverage*. Leverage played a key role in the financial crisis of 2007–2009, so it is worth understanding how leverage relates to risk and how it can make the financial system vulnerable.

Modern economies rely heavily on borrowing to make investments. They are all leveraged. Yet, the more leverage, the greater the risk that an adverse surprise will lead to bankruptcy. If two households own houses of the same value, the one that has borrowed more—the one that is more highly leveraged and has less net worth—is the more likely to default during a temporary slump in income. This example could apply equally well to firms, financial institutions, or even countries.

Financial institutions are much more highly leveraged than households or firms, typically owning assets of about 10 times their net worth. During the crisis, some important financial firms leveraged more than 30 times their net worth. Such high leverage meant that these firms would be vulnerable even to a minor decline in the value of their assets. For example, when a borrower is leveraged more than 30 times, a drop as small as 3 percent in asset prices could eliminate the cushion created by the net worth and lead to bankruptcy.

When highly leveraged financial institutions experience a loss, they usually try to reduce their leverage—that is, to deleverage—by selling assets and issuing securities that raise their net worth (see accompanying figure). However, the financial system cannot deleverage all at once. When too many institutions try to sell assets simultaneously, their efforts will almost surely prove counterproductive: falling prices will mean more losses, diminishing their net worth further, raising leverage, and making the assets they hold seem riskier, thereby compelling further sales.

This "paradox of leverage" reinforces the destabilizing liquidity spiral discussed in Chapter 2 (see Lessons from the Crisis: Market Liquidity, Funding Liquidity, and Making Markets). Both spirals feed a vicious cycle of falling prices and widespread deleveraging that was a hallmark of the financial crisis of 2007–2009. The financial system steadied only after a plunge of many asset prices and massive government interventions.

*For a technical definition of leverage, see the Tools of the Trade box in Chapter 5.
†A bank's net worth—its assets minus liabilities—is commonly known as bank capital. We will discuss this in more detail in Chapter 12.

**Deleveraging Spiral**

Bank Wishes to Deleverage → Some Assets are Sold → Asset Prices Decline → Net Worth Declines and Assets Become Riskier → (back to Bank Wishes to Deleverage)

## Applying the Concept

These sections showcase history and examine issues relevant to the public policy debate. Subjects include how debt problems in emerging market countries can create an increase in the demand for U.S. Treasury debt; why Long-Term Capital Management caused a near collapse of the world financial system; and what monetary policymakers learned from the Great Depression of the 1930s.

---

### APPLYING THE CONCEPT
#### THE MADOFF SCANDAL

Fraud is the most extreme version of moral hazard. Even so, the fraud perpetrated by Bernard Madoff stands out. Thousands of investors lost billions of dollars, making it among the largest scams in history.* The swindle went undetected for decades and affected wealthy individuals and financial firms from around the world with extensive experience in finance.

Yet, Madoff's fraud was nothing more than a classic *Ponzi scheme*. Named after Charles Ponzi, who conducted a similar sting in the United States just after World War I, a Ponzi scheme is a fraud in which an intermediary collects funds from new investors, but instead of investing them, uses the funds to pay off earlier investors. Money has to flow in at least as fast as it flows out. When that flow reverses, the fraud unravels and the final investors become big losers.

How do such frauds succeed at different times in different places? How can they last so long and become so damaging?

The answer is that investors fail to screen and monitor the managers who receive their funds (such as Madoff or Ponzi). Screening and monitoring are costly. The appearance of satisfied early investors discourages new investors

from paying such costs. Many investors assume that others have already done the monitoring needed.

A facade of public respectability contributes to the success of a Ponzi scheme, and Madoff was a master at burnishing his reputation in the public eye. He had been the chairman of a major stock exchange (Nasdaq; see Chapter 8) and of the organization of U.S. securities dealers (NASD). He also was a philanthropist.

The U.S. government agency responsible for overseeing Madoff's firm, the Securities and Exchange Commission (SEC), also failed to detect the scheme. One whistleblower warned the oversight agency about possible fraud as early as 2000. Yet, the swindle ended in 2008 only because the financial crisis had prompted withdrawals from many firms, including Madoff's. Otherwise, the scam might still be going on.

With the benefit of hindsight, there were red flags that warned of a problem. Yet, everyone acted as if someone else was monitoring, so they could enjoy the *free ride* (see page 272 for a definition of a free rider). The Madoff scam is a painful reminder that there is no such free ride.

*As of October 2009, the government-appointed trustee responsible for returning investors' stolen money estimated the losses at more than $21 billion.

## In the News

One article per chapter from major media such as *The New York Times*, *The Economist*, *The Financial Times*, *The Wall Street Journal*, and *BusinessWeek* is featured. These readings show how concepts introduced in the chapter are applied in the financial press. A brief analysis of the article, called "Lessons," reinforces key concepts.

## Financial Markets

MARKETS

Financial markets are the places where financial insti... They are the economy's central nervous system, relayin... quickly, allocating resources, and determining prices... enable both firms and individuals to find financing for... working well, new firms can start up and existing fir... don't have sufficient savings can borrow to purchase ca... resources are available to those who can put them to t... costs of transactions as low as possible, these markets... When financial markets cease to function properly, rea...

## Core Principle Marginal Icons

The entire text discussion is organized around the following five core principles: Time has value; risk requires compensation; information is the basis for decisions; markets set prices and allocate resources; and stability improves welfare. Exploring these principles is the basis for learning what the financial system does, how it is organized, and how it is linked to the real economy. They are discussed in detail in Chapter 1; throughout the rest of the text, marginal icons remind students of the principles that underlie particular discussions.

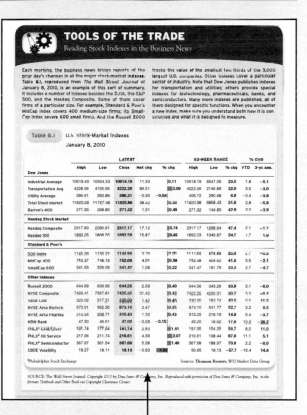

## Tools of the Trade

These boxes teach useful skills, including how to read bond and stock tables, how to read charts, and how to do some simple algebraic calculations. Some provide brief reviews of material from the principles of economics course, such as the relationship between the current account and the capital account in the balance of payments.

# Brief Contents

# Contents

## Part *III*   Financial Institutions   257

Why study money and banking?  What are the elements of the discipline that we should be highlighted? Adam Smith's "Invisible Hand" coordinates the actions of the economic agents pursuing personal gain to "promote an end which was in no part his intention," the achievement of higher levels of output and prosperity for society as a whole.  <u>Financial markets and institutions play a key role in this "Invisible Hand" process through the function of facilitating the flow of funds between savers and spending units and the allocation of capital to productive uses.</u>

The purpose of the introductory Money and Banking course is to analyze the role of financial institutions and markets in facilitating the flow of funds between savers and spending units and the characteristics and structures of financial institutions and markets that make this possible.   While the essence of money, banking and financial markets has not changed over the years, the tools we use have seen profound changes as a result of technology and financial innovation. In a similar manner, our understanding of the role of government both as the manager of monetary policy and the regulator of financial institutions and markets has changed over time as a consequence of financial crises.

The course will examine the emergence of <u>money</u> and its <u>key functions:  unit of exchange,  means of payment and source of wealth</u>, as well as the evolution of money from <u>commodity</u> money to <u>e-money</u>. The functioning of the financial and banking markets depends on the offering of investment vehicles-i.e <u>securities</u>. Next, it will look at the characteristics of <u>financial securities</u> and the <u>markets</u> in which they are traded.

The financial system as a whole and the banking system in particular are important to facilitate the flow of funds between the sources of surplus funds (savers) and those in needs of funds (spending units).  In the process, the banks, acting <u>intermediaries</u>, perform <u>maturity transformation</u> by funding longer-term assets with short-term deposits.

The intermediation function of banking is based on its ability to mitigate the problems of <u>asymmetric information that can lead to</u> <u>adverse selection</u> and <u>moral hazard issues</u>.   At the <u>micro-financial level</u>, banks perform essential functions for the <u>depositors</u> and allow for the smooth flow of credit to spending units.  At the <u>macro-financial</u> level, the stability of the financial system is a key element of long-term economic stability. Both levels are based on trust, and this is where the government comes in to provide peace of mind to the depositors and <u>regulate</u> and <u>supervise</u> the behavior of the financial institutions to maintain this "trust" contract.  This regulatory and supervisory function is all the more important because of the implicit <u>too-big-to-fail</u> guarantee offered to the banks and other financial institutions by regulatory agencies can lead the financial institutions to take excessive risks, thus putting the entire financial system at risk.

The financial system and markets also perform several other key functions.  They offer tools of <u>risk management</u>: <u>derivatives</u> and <u>insurance</u>.  They provide liquidity in <u>trading</u> financial securities. They facilitate global trade and capital flows through the provision of <u>foreign exchange</u>.

Furthermore, as the financial system is based on leverage, it needs adequate levels of both <u>capital</u> and <u>liquidity</u>. Capital levels and liquidity are the buffers that allow the banking system to withstand cyclical downturns and financial shocks.  However, it is important to distinguish between the two, as capital or (net worth, on the right-hand side of the balance sheet) is a buffer against <u>unexpected losses from the asset side of a firm's balance sheet</u>, while liquidity (cash reserves and the ability to liquefy assets, both on the left-hand side of the balance sheet) is needed to satisfy unanticipated <u>deposit withdrawals and other funding shortfalls.</u>

Moreover, in fulfilling its role, the financial system needs to manage different kinds of identifiable risks through the establishment of risk management systems. Finally, since the government provides a "<u>safety net</u>" by standing as the guarantor of deposits and lender of last resort, it needs to <u>regulate and supervise</u> the system to prevent, or at least to mitigate, <u>financial crises</u>.

 The fact that financial crises happen regularly means that the financial system is a dynamic and complex one. Two main factors lie at the source of financial crises<u>: innovation and the credit cycle</u>. As identified by Minsky, there are five phases to the credit cycle: displacement, boom, euphoria, profit-taking, and panic.[1] At that point, we see a reverse-Minsky as the ensuing credit crunch and liquidity shortage leads to a vicious cycle of economic retrenchment, <u>contagion</u> and widespread financial failure. This crisis mechanism was amplified in the 2008 financial crisis by the spread of financial innovations such as <u>credit default swaps</u>, <u>subprime mortgages</u> and <u>collateralized debt obligations</u> and the rise of <u>shadow-banking system.</u>

The bridges between providers and users of funds in financial markets are <u>interest rates and other rates of return</u>, which are set by the supply of and demand for financial instruments. The course will analyze the setting of market interest rates in the <u>bond markets</u>, as well as the <u>risk structure</u> and the term <u>(maturity) structure</u> of interest rates.

Last, but not least, given the essential role of financial markets and money as the lifeblood of a modern economy, the role of the central banks in setting the parameters of <u>monetary policy</u> needs to be analyzed.

**In a course like Money and Banking, the terms reserves and capital are often misused and poorly understood.**

Consider the following statements that appeared in the popular press.

- "Capital is the stable money banks sit on... Think of it as an expanded rainy day fund." ("A piece-by-piece guide to new financial overhaul law," *AP* July 21, 2010).

- "Every dollar of capital is one less dollar working in the economy" (Steve Bartlett, Financial Services Roundtable, reported by Floyd Norris in "A Baby Step Toward Rules on Bank Risk," *New York Times*, Sep. 16, 2010).

- "The British Bankers' Association ... calculated that demands by international banking regulators in Basle that they bolster their capital will require the UK's banking industry to hold an extra

---

[1] See Hyman P. Minsky, "The Financial-Instability Hypothesis: Capitalist processes and the behavior of the economy," in *Financial Crises: Theory, History, and Policy*, edited by Charles P. Kindleberger and Jean-Pierre Laffargue, 1982, New York: Cambridge University Press.

£600bn of capital that might otherwise have been deployed as loans to businesses or households."
*The Observer* (July 11, 2010).

Statements like these suggest that capital represents money that banks must set aside and keep idle, and it cannot be used productively. When you complete this course, you will to able to interpret these statements as distortions of the truth.

**Reserves:** When we refer to <u>reserve requirements</u> we are referring to a policy of the Federal Reserve System that mandates depository institutions to maintain a fixed percentage of each dollar of their deposits in a cash account with a Federal Reserve Bank or in depository institutions' vaults as vault cash. This mandate is written in the Act of the Federal Reserve System as <u>Regulation D</u> of the Federal Reserve System. Minimum reserve requirements are used to strengthen monetary policy. Specifically, setting minimum ratio of liquid reserve assets to deposits limits the ability of banks to expand lending and enhances the Federal Reserve System's ability to control the flow of money and credit. In this context, requirements that depository institutions hold minimum ratios of liquid assets to deposits allow the Federal Reserve System to gain greater control over the money supply and bank credit and their growth as part of its overall macro-control objectives.

When we refer to <u>reserves for possible loan losses</u> we are referring to a special account created on banks' balance sheets against which they can write off bad loans.

**Capital:** A firm capital is referred to as the owners' equity stake in it and the economic definition of this is the difference between the market value of the firm's assets and its liabilities. We called this <u>economic net worth</u>! Regulators use <u>book value capital</u> on net worth based on historic or original book values of assets and liabilities. The book value usually comprises the following four components in banking:

- *Par value of shares.* The face value of the common stock shares issued by the bank (the par value is usually $1 per share) times the number of shares outstanding.
- *Surplus value of shares* The difference between the price of the public paid for common stock or shares when originally offered (e.g., $5 per share) and their par values (e.g., $1 per share) times the number of shares outstanding.
- *Retained earnings.* The accumulated value of past profits not yet paid out in dividends to shareholders. Since these earnings could be paid out in dividends, they are part of the equity owners' stake in the bank.
- *Loan loss reserve.* A special account set aside out of retained earnings to meet expected and actual losses on the portfolio.

The <u>function</u> of capital is to absorb unanticipated losses with enough margin to inspire confidence and enable the bank to continue as a going concern. The second function of capital is to protect uninsured creditors in the event of an insolvency and liquidation. The third function of capital is to protect the insurance fund and the taxpayer. The fourth function of capital is to allow a bank to acquire the plant and other real investments necessary to provide financial services.

**More key terms that are often used that should become part of a student's vocabulary:**

**Asymmetric Information**: Situation when one party to a contract knows more about its own circumstances/conditions than the other party. Such a situation occurs for example in lending, where without further research, the lender will know less than the borrower about the latter's ability to repay the loan.

**Adverse selection:** Asymmetric information leads to adverse selection, an ex ante problem, where in the absence of sufficient information, one party (the lender) will assume that the other party (borrower) is average, and offer average lending terms. This will dissuade better-than-average borrowers to apply for a loan, leading only to worse-than-average ones in the bidding.

**Moral hazard:** an ex-post problem, reflecting the fact that once the contract is signed, in the absence of monitoring by the other party, one party can take actions contrary to the contract conditions, damaging the interests of the other party. For example, once the loan is made, the borrower could use the proceeds of the loan in a risky venture, leading to loan problems and potential default

**Shadow Banks:** According to the New York Federal Reserve Bank, "[s]hadow banks are financial intermediaries that conduct maturity, credit, and liquidity transformation without access to central bank liquidity or public sector credit guarantees. Examples of shadow banks include finance companies, asset-backed commercial paper (ABCP) conduits, limited-purpose finance companies, structured investment vehicles, credit hedge funds, money market mutual funds, securities lenders, and government-sponsored enterprises." These entities are not regulated by the traditional banking regulators, are generally lightly-capitalized and engage in significant financial engineering. They are interconnected through long funding chains and as such present significant contagion risks to the financial system

**Credit Default Swaps (CDS):** A CDS is a protection against default, a contract between two parties, in which one party pays a periodical premium (spread) to the other in exchange for protection against a default by a "reference obligor", typically an issuer of debt. However, these products are not subject to insurance industry regulators. In addition, any entity can buy or sell CDS, without even owning the "reference" asset underlying the CDS contract

**Collateralized Debt Obligation (CDO):** A CDO is a structured asset-backed security backed by a pool of underlying assets. The CDO is divided in different sections (tranches), super-senior, mezzanine and junior, with the senior tranche getting first call on the cash flow, while the junior one bears all the risk. Because of different risk characteristics, each tranche has a different risk rating. Because of the high degree of sensitivity of the distribution "cascade" to the quality of the underlying assets and default risk, the CDOs represent highly risky investments, and with the CDS, were the main culprits behind the 2008 financial crisis.

# Part *I*

## Money and the Financial System

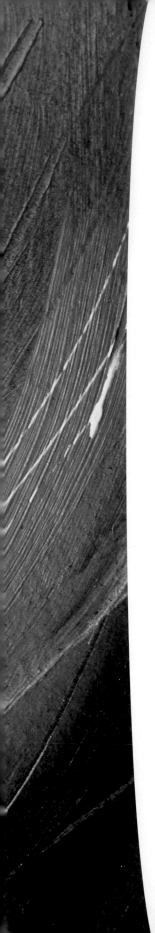

# Chapter 1

## An Introduction to Money and the Financial System

This morning, a typical American college student bought coffee at the local café, paying for it with an ATM card. Then she jumped into her insured car, and drove to the university, which she attends thanks to her student loan. She may have left her parents' home, which is mortgaged, a few minutes early to avoid construction work on a new dormitory, financed by bonds issued by the university. Or perhaps she needed to stop at the bookstore to purchase this book, using her credit card, before her first money and banking class began.

Beneath the surface, each financial transaction in this story—even the seemingly simple ones—is quite complicated. If the café owner and the student use different banks, paying for the coffee will require an interbank funds transfer. The company that insures the student's car has to invest the premiums she pays until they are needed to pay off claims. The student's parents almost surely obtained their home mortgage through a mortgage broker, whose job was to find the cheapest mortgage available. And the bonds the university issued to finance construction of the new dormitory were created with the aid of an investment bank.

This brief example hints at the complex web of interdependent institutions and markets that is the foundation for our daily financial transactions. The system is so large, so efficient, and generally speaking so well run that most of us rarely take note of it. But a financial system is like air to an economy: If it disappeared suddenly, everything would grind to a halt.

In the autumn of 2008, we came closer to such a financial meltdown than at any time since the 1930s. In the earlier episode, the collapse of the banking system led to the Great Depression. In the recent crisis, some of the world's largest financial institutions failed. Key markets stopped functioning. Credit dried up, even for healthy borrowers. As a result, vibrant companies that relied on short-term loans to pay their employees and buy materials faced potential ruin. Even some fundamental ways that we make payments for goods and services were threatened.

Gasping for air in this financial crisis, the global economy during 2008 and 2009 sank into the deepest, broadest, and longest downturn since World War II. Around the world, tens of millions of people lost their jobs. In the United States, millions lost their homes and their life's savings. Others became unable to borrow to buy a home or go to college. The chances are good that you know someone—in your neighborhood, your school, or your family—whose life was changed for the worse by the crisis.

So, what happens in the financial system—whether for good or for bad—matters greatly for all of us. To understand the system—both its strengths and its vulnerabilities—let's take a closer look.

## The Six Parts of the Financial System

The **financial system** has six parts, each of which plays a fundamental role in our economy. Those parts are money, financial instruments, financial markets, financial institutions, government regulatory agencies, and central banks.

We use the first part of the system, **money**, to pay for our purchases and to store our wealth. We use the second part, **financial instruments**, to transfer resources from savers to investors and to transfer risk to those who are best equipped to bear it. Stocks, mortgages, and insurance policies are examples of financial instruments. The third part of our financial system, **financial markets**, allows us to buy and sell financial instruments quickly and cheaply. The New York Stock Exchange is an example of a financial market. **Financial institutions**, the fourth part of the financial system, provide a myriad of services, including access to the financial markets and collection of information about prospective borrowers to ensure they are creditworthy. Banks, securities firms, and insurance companies are examples of financial institutions. Government **regulatory agencies** form the fifth part of the financial system. They are responsible for making sure that the elements of the financial system—including its instruments, markets, and institutions—operate in a safe and reliable manner. Finally, **central banks**, the sixth part of the system, monitor and stabilize the economy. The **Federal Reserve System** is the central bank of the United States.

While the essential functions that define these six categories endure, their form is constantly evolving. Money once consisted of gold and silver coins, which were eventually replaced by paper currency, which today is being eclipsed by electronic funds transfers. Methods of accessing means of payment have changed dramatically as well. As recently as 1970, people customarily obtained currency from bank tellers when they cashed their paychecks or withdrew their savings from the local bank. Today, they can get cash from practically any ATM anywhere in the world. To pay their bills, people once wrote checks and put them in the mail, then waited for their monthly bank statements to make sure the transactions had been processed correctly. Today, payments can be made automatically, and account holders can check the transactions at any time on their bank's Web site.

*Financial instruments* (or securities, as they are often called) have evolved just as much as currency. In the last few centuries, investors could buy individual stocks through stockbrokers, but the transactions were costly. Furthermore, putting together a portfolio of even a small number of stocks and bonds was extremely time consuming; just collecting the information necessary to evaluate a potential investment was a daunting task. As a result, investing was an activity reserved for the wealthy. Today, financial institutions offer people with as little as $1,000 to invest the ability to purchase shares in *mutual funds*, which pool the savings of a large number of investors. Because of their size, mutual funds can construct portfolios of hundreds or even thousands of different stocks and/or bonds.

The markets where stocks and bonds are sold have undergone a similar transformation. Originally, *financial markets* were located in coffeehouses and taverns where individuals met to exchange financial instruments. The next step was to create organized markets, like the New York Stock Exchange—trading places specifically dedicated to the buying and selling of stocks and bonds. Today, much of the activity that once occurred at these big-city financial exchanges is handled by electronic networks. Buyers and sellers obtain price information and initiate transactions from their desktop computers or from handheld devices. Because electronic networks have reduced the cost of processing financial transactions, even small investors can afford to participate in them. Just as important, today's financial markets offer a much broader array of financial instruments than those available even 50 years ago.

*Financial institutions* have changed, as well. Banks began as vaults where people could store their valuables. Gradually, they developed into institutions that accepted deposits and made loans. For hundreds of years, in fact, that was what bankers did. Today, a bank is more like a financial supermarket. Walk in and you will discover

"This is Fluffy, my pet money."

SOURCE: © Danny Shanahan/The New Yorker Collection/www.cartoonbank.com.

a huge assortment of financial products and services for sale, from access to the financial markets to insurance policies, mortgages, consumer credit, and even investment advice.

The activities of government regulatory agencies and the design of **regulation** have been evolving and have entered a period of more rapid change, too. In the aftermath of the financial crisis of 1929–1933, when the failure of thousands of banks led to the Great Depression, the U.S. government introduced regulatory agencies to provide wide-ranging financial regulation—rules for the operation of financial institutions and markets—and **supervision**—oversight through examination and enforcement. The U.S. agencies established in the 1930s to issue and enforce these financial rules still operate.

Yet, the evolution of financial instruments, institutions, and markets has led to many changes in the ways that regulatory agencies work. A bank examiner used to count the money in the cash drawers and call borrowers to see if the loans on a bank's books were real. They might even visit workplaces to see if the loans were used as designed to buy equipment or build a factory. Today, banks engage in millions of transactions, many of which are far more complex and difficult to understand than a loan or a mortgage. So, a government examiner also looks at the systems that a bank uses to manage its various risks. In doing so, regulators try to encourage best practices throughout the financial industry. However, the failure of regulators in the United States and elsewhere around the world to anticipate or prevent the financial crisis of 2007–2009 has led many governments to consider more far-reaching changes to financial regulation and the regulatory agencies. Such changes likely will affect the financial system for years to come.

Finally, *central banks* have changed a great deal. They began as large private banks founded by monarchs to finance wars. For instance, King William of Orange created the Bank of England in 1694 for the express purpose of raising taxes and borrowing to finance a war between Austria, England, and the Netherlands on one side and Louis XIV's France on the other. Eventually, these government treasuries grew into the modern central banks we know today. While only a few central banks existed in 1900, now nearly every country in the world has one, and they have become one of the most important institutions in government. Central banks control the availability of money and credit to ensure low inflation, high growth, and the stability of the financial system. Because their current mission is to serve the public at large rather than land-hungry monarchs, their operating methods have changed as well. Once the central bank's decisions were shrouded in mystery, but today's policymakers strive for transparency in their operations. Officials at the **European Central Bank** and the U.S. Federal Reserve—two of the most important central banks in the world—go out of their way to explain the rationale for their decisions.

Though the changing nature of our financial system is a fascinating topic, it poses challenges for both students and instructors. How can we teach and learn about money and banking in a way that will stand the test of time, so that the knowledge we gain won't become outmoded? The answer is that we must develop a way to understand

and adapt to the evolutionary structure of the financial system. That means discussing money and banking within a framework of core principles that do not change over time. The next section introduces the five core principles that will guide our studies throughout this book.

# The Five Core Principles of Money and Banking

Five core principles will inform our analysis of the financial system and its interaction with the real economy. Once you have grasped these principles, you will have a better understanding not only of what is happening in the financial world today but of changes that will undoubtedly occur in the future. The five principles are based on **Time, Risk, Information, Markets,** and **Stability.**

## Core Principle 1: Time Has Value

The first principle of money and banking is that *time has value*. At some very basic level, everyone knows this. If you take a job at the local supermarket, you will almost surely be paid by the hour. An hour's worth of work equals a certain number of dollars. Literally, your time has a price.

On a more sophisticated level, **time** affects the value of financial transactions. Most loan contracts allow the borrower to spread out the payments over time. If you take out an auto loan, for example, the lender will allow you to make a series of monthly payments over three, four, or even five years. If you add up the payments, you'll discover that the total exceeds the amount of the loan. At an interest rate of 6 percent, a four-year, $10,000 car loan will require 48 monthly payments of $235 each. That means you will repay a total of $11,280 (48 times $235). The reason your repayments total more than the loan amount is that you are paying interest to compensate the lender for the time during which you use the funds. That is, the resources you borrowed have an opportunity cost to the lender so you have to pay rent on them.

Interest payments are fundamental to a market economy. In Chapter 4, we will develop an understanding of interest rates and how to use them. Then, throughout the remainder of Part II, we will apply the principle that time has value in our discussion of the valuation of bonds, stocks, and other financial instruments involving future payments. How much should you be willing to pay for a particular stock or bond? Figuring out what alternative investments are worth, and comparing them, means valuing payments made on different future dates. The same principle applies to the question of how much you must invest today to achieve a particular financial objective in the future. How much of your salary, for example, do you need to save each month to meet your goal of buying a house? The length of time your savings will be earning interest is a key to answering this question.

## Core Principle 2: Risk Requires Compensation

The world is filled with uncertainty. More events, both good and bad, *can* happen than *will* happen. Some of the possibilities, such as the likelihood of your home doubling in value after you buy it, are welcome. Other possibilities, such as the chance that you might lose your job and not be able to make your car payments, are distinctly unwelcome. Dealing effectively with **risk** requires that you consider the full range of possibilities in order to eliminate some risks, reduce others, pay someone to assume particularly onerous risks, and just live with what's left. Needless to say, no one will assume your risks for free, which brings us to the second core principle of money and banking: *Risk requires compensation.* In the financial world, compensation is made in the form of explicit payments. That is, investors must be paid to assume risk; the higher the risk, the bigger the required payment.

Car insurance is a common example of paying someone else to shoulder a risk you don't want to take. If your car is wrecked in an accident, you will want to be able to repair it. But beyond that, auto insurance shelters drivers from the possibility of losing all their wealth in the event that they cause an accident in which someone is seriously injured. Although the chances of causing such an accident are quite small, the results can be so serious that, even if the government didn't require it, most of us would voluntarily purchase auto insurance. Driving without it just isn't worth the risk. The insurance company pools the premiums that policyholders pay and invests them. Even though some of the premiums will be spent to settle claims when cars are stolen or damaged by collisions, the chance to make a profit is good. So both the insurance company and the drivers who buy policies are ultimately better off.

Bearing in mind that time has value and risk requires compensation, we can begin to see the rationale behind the valuation of a broad set of financial instruments. For example, a lender will charge a higher interest rate on a loan if there is a chance that the borrower will not repay. In Chapters 6 and 7, we will use this principle when we examine the interest rates on bonds. As we will see, a company that is on the verge of bankruptcy may still be able to issue bonds (called *junk bonds*), but it will have to pay an extremely high interest rate to do so. The reason is that the lender must be compensated for the substantial risk that the company will not repay the loan. Risk requires compensation.

## Core Principle 3: Information Is the Basis for Decisions

Most of us collect **information** before making decisions. The more important the decision, the more information we gather. Think of the difference between buying a $5 sandwich and a $10,000 car. You will surely spend more time comparing cars than comparing sandwiches.

What's true for sandwiches and cars is true for finance as well. That is, *information is the basis for decisions.* In fact, the collection and processing of information is the foundation of the financial system. In Chapter 11, we will learn how financial institutions like banks funnel resources from savers to investors. Before a bank makes a loan, a loan officer will investigate the financial condition of the individual or firm seeking it. Banks want to provide loans only to the highest-quality borrowers. Thus, they spend a great deal of time gathering the information needed to evaluate the creditworthiness of loan applicants.

To understand the problem faced by the two parties to any financial transaction, think about a home mortgage. Before making the loan, the mortgage broker examines the applicant's finances and researches the home's value to make sure the applicant can afford the monthly payments and the property is more valuable than the loan.

And before the broker transfers the funds to the seller, the new homeowner must purchase fire insurance. All these requirements arise from the fact that the lender doesn't know much about the borrower and wants to make sure the loan will be repaid. When lenders fail to assess creditworthiness properly, they end up with more borrowers who are unable to repay their loans in the future. Large mistakes like these were a key factor in the wave of U.S. mortgage delinquencies and defaults that preceded the financial crisis of 2007–2009.

Information plays a key role in other parts of the financial system as well. In Chapters 2 and 3, we'll see that many types of transactions are arranged so that the buyer doesn't need to know anything about the seller. When merchants accept cash, they don't need to worry about the customer's identity. When stocks change hands, the buyer doesn't need to know anything about the seller, or vice versa. Stock exchanges are organized to eliminate the need for costly information gathering, facilitating the exchange of securities. In one way or another, information is the key to the financial system.

## Core Principle 4: Markets Determine Prices and Allocate Resources

**Markets** are the core of the economic system. They are the place, physical or virtual, where buyers and sellers meet, where firms go to issue stocks and bonds, and where individuals go to purchase assets. Financial markets are essential to the economy, channeling its resources and minimizing the cost of gathering information and making transactions. In fact, well-developed financial markets are a necessary precondition for healthy economic growth. The better developed a country's financial markets, the faster the country will grow.

The reason for this connection between markets and growth is that *markets determine prices and allocate resources*. Financial markets gather information from a large number of individual participants and aggregate it into a set of prices that signals what is valuable and what is not. Thus, markets are sources of information. By attaching prices to different stocks or bonds, they provide a basis for the allocation of capital.

To see how prices in the financial markets allocate capital, think about a large firm wishing to finance the construction of a new factory costing several hundred million dollars. To raise the funds, the firm can go directly into the financial markets and issue stocks or bonds. The higher the price investors are willing to pay in the market, the more appealing the idea will be, and the more likely it is that the firm will issue securities to raise the capital for the investment.

We will refer to the financial markets throughout much of this book. While our primary focus in Part II will be the nature of financial instruments, we will also study the markets in which those instruments are traded. Chapters 6 through 10 describe the markets for bonds, stocks, derivatives, and foreign currencies.

Importantly, financial markets do not arise by themselves—at least, not the large, well-oiled ones we see operating today. Markets like the New York Stock Exchange, where billions of shares of stock change hands every day, require rules in order to work properly, as well as authorities to police them. Otherwise, they will not function. For people to be willing to participate in a market, they must perceive it as fair. As we will see, this creates an important role for the government. Regulators and supervisors of the financial system make and enforce the rules, punishing people who violate them. When the government protects investors, financial markets work well; otherwise they don't.

Finally, even well-developed markets can break down. When they do—as some did during the financial crisis of 2007–2009—the financial system as a whole can be at risk. So today, governments must also play a role in promoting the healthy operation of markets.

## Core Principle 5: Stability Improves Welfare

Most of us prefer stable to variable incomes. We like getting raises, but the prospect of a salary cut is not a pleasant one. This brings us to the fifth core principle of money and banking: *Stability improves welfare*. **Stability** is a desirable quality, not just in our personal lives but in the financial system as a whole. As we saw at the start of this chapter, financial instability in the autumn of 2008 brought us closer to a collapse of the system than at any time since the 1930s, triggering the worst global downturn since the Great Depression.

If you are wondering whether this principle is related to Core Principle 2 (risk requires compensation), you are right. Because volatility creates risk, reducing volatility reduces risk. But while individuals can eliminate many risks on their own (we'll see how when we study financial instruments in Part II), some risks can only be reduced by government policymakers. Business cycle fluctuations are an example of the sort of instability individuals can't eliminate on their own. And though "automatic stabilizers" like unemployment insurance and the income tax system reduce the burden of recessions on individuals, they cannot eliminate an economic slowdown. Monetary policymakers can moderate these downswings by carefully adjusting interest rates. In stabilizing the economy as a whole, they eliminate risks that individuals can't, improving everyone's welfare in the process.

As we will learn in Part IV of this book, stabilizing the economy is a primary function of central banks like the Federal Reserve and the European Central Bank. Officials of these institutions are charged with controlling inflation and reducing business cycle fluctuations. That is, they work to keep inflation low and stable and to keep growth high and stable. When they are successful, they reduce both the risk that individuals will lose their jobs and the uncertainty that firms face in making investment decisions. Not surprisingly, a stable economy grows faster than an unstable economy. Stability improves welfare.

Throughout the book you will notice icons like this in the margin at various points. These will guide you to the core principle that provides the foundation for what is being discussed at that point in the text.

# Special Features of This Book

Every chapter of this book contains a series of important elements, beginning with an introduction. The introduction presents real-world examples that lead to the big questions the chapter is designed to answer: What is money? What do banks do? How does the bond market work? What does the Federal Reserve do to prevent or limit financial crises?

The text of each chapter presents the economic and financial theory you need to understand the topics covered. Each chapter also contains a series of inserts that apply the theory. There are five types of inserts: Your Financial World, Applying the Concept, Lessons from the Crisis, In the News, and Tools of the Trade. Here are some guidelines for using them.

## Your Financial World

When most people decide to make a major purchase, they begin by collecting information. If they are considering buying a car, they will first try to decide which model

## YOUR FINANCIAL WORLD

### Guard Your Identity

There is a television commercial in which a middle-aged man is sitting in his living room drinking a beer. Out of the man's mouth comes the voice of a woman describing some very expensive clothing she just bought. She didn't care how much the clothes cost because she wasn't paying— she used a credit card that was in the man's name. The ad catches viewers' attention because it is funny. But its primary purpose is to serve as a warning about identity theft, in which one person takes on the identity of another to do things like make credit card purchases.

It is important to realize that someone who has a few pieces of key information about you can get a credit card in your name. To prevent this, you need to protect personal information. Do your best to never tell anyone your birth date and birthplace, your address, or your mother's maiden name. Most importantly, guard your Social Security number. Because it is unique, it is the key to identity theft. Give out your Social Security number only when absolutely necessary—on tax forms, for employment records,

and to open bank accounts. If your driver's license has your Social Security number on it, ask that it be removed. If a business requests it, ask if some alternative number can be used. Importantly, if you get a telephone call or an e-mail from someone you don't know asking for personal data, don't provide it.

Beyond protecting access to personal information, you need to monitor your financial statements closely, looking for things that shouldn't be there. Be on the lookout for unauthorized charges. This means maintaining careful records so that you know what should be on your bank and credit card statements.

Identity theft is a crime, and governments work hard to find and prosecute the offenders. Even so, millions of people are victims each year. Don't be one of them. For more information about identity theft and how to avoid being a victim, see the U.S. Department of Justice's Web site: www.justice.gov/criminal/fraud/websites/idtheft.html.

---

is best for them and then work hard to pay the lowest price possible. Even for smaller purchases, like clothes or groceries, people first gather information and then buy.

Financial transactions should be no different from consumer purchases. Become informed first, and then buy. If you're thinking, "That's easier said than done," you're right. The problem is that most people have very little knowledge of the financial system, so they don't know how to start or what kind of information to collect.

That's where Your Financial World comes in. These inserts provide basic guidelines for applying economic theory to the bread-and-butter financial decisions you make nearly every day. Your Financial World answers questions about:

- Banking and Payments
  - What's the difference between credit and debit cards?
  - How should you pick a bank?
- Investments
  - Should you own stocks or bonds or gold?
  - Should you invest in the company you work for?
- Credit, Loans, and Mortgages
  - What do you need to know when you shop for a mortgage?
  - What is your credit score and why is it important?
- Insurance
  - How much life insurance do you need?
  - How much car insurance do you need?
- Saving and Retirement
  - How big an emergency saving reserve should you have?
  - Is your retirement savings insured?

## Applying the Concept

Each chapter in this book contains a series of applications called Applying the Concept, which show how to put theory into practice. These inserts provide real-world examples of the ideas introduced in the chapter, drawn primarily from history or from relevant public policy debates. Here are some of the questions examined in Applying the Concept:

- Why do interest rates rise when inflation goes up?
- Why does a country's exchange rate suddenly plummet?
- Why do large-scale frauds that damage investors occur repeatedly?
- Why is it important for central banks to be free of political influence?
- Can monetary policy be used to stabilize the economy?
- What determines inflation?
- What are the implications of China's exchange rate policy?

## Lessons from the Crisis

These inserts cover episodes from the financial crisis of 2007–2009. One goal is to give you a framework for understanding the crisis and how it is transforming the world of finance. Another goal is to highlight the relevance and power of the ideas in the book more generally. Along the way, the various Lessons from the Crisis offer you insight into the sources and effects of financial instability. They also address the means that governments—including regulators and central bankers—use to counter financial instability. Most chapters contain one such insert.

The topics range from specific aspects of the crisis to key issues that have wide application. Here are some of the questions examined in Lessons from the Crisis:

- What factors led to the financial crisis of 2007–2009?
- What made financial institutions especially vulnerable in this period?
- Why do financial markets sometimes stop functioning?
- How do threats to the financial system differ from threats to specific financial institutions?
- When a crisis erupts, what can central banks do to prevent another Great Depression?

## In the News

One of the primary purposes of this textbook is to help you understand the business and financial news. Critically evaluating what you read, hear, and see means developing a clear understanding of how the financial system works, as well as reading the news regularly. Like many other skills, critical reading of newspapers and magazines takes practice. You can't just pick up a newspaper and skim through it quickly and efficiently; you need to learn how. Your instructor will make suggestions about what you should read. See Table 1.1 for a list of reliable sources of information on the economy and the financial system.

Given your need to become a skilled consumer of financial information, each chapter in this book closes with an article drawn from the financial press. These stories from *The Wall Street Journal*, the *Financial Times*, *The Economist*, *BusinessWeek*, and

**Table 1.1**   Sources of Economic and Financial News and Data

**Sources of Daily News**

*The Wall Street Journal* **and www.wsj.com**

Published six days a week, and available both in print and on the Internet, *The Wall Street Journal* provides news, as well as comprehensive coverage of business and finance.

*Financial Times* **and www.ft.com**

The *Financial Times* offers reporting, analysis, and commentary on major business, political, financial, and economic events. The *FT* is written from a distinctly European perspective, and includes detailed coverage of non-U.S. business and financial news.

*Bloomberg.com*

*Bloomberg* offers a wide range of financial market services, including news. A wide variety of news and data can be found on the free portion of their Web site.

**Sources of Weekly News**

*The Economist* **and www.economist.com**

*The Economist* covers global politics, economics, business, finance, and science. It not only reports the facts, but analyzes them and draws policy conclusions. The Finance and Economics section, located roughly three-quarters of the way into each issue, is of particular interest.

*BusinessWeek* **and www.businessweek.com**

*BusinessWeek* is a U.S.-based publication that offers fair and balanced reporting and analysis of top economic, financial, business, and technological issues.

**Economic and Financial Data**

The Bureau of Labor Statistics supplies data on prices, employment and unemployment at www.bls.gov.

The Bureau of Economic Analysis provides information on gross domestic product, consumption, investment and other macroeconomic data at www.bea.gov.

The Federal Reserve Board Web site www.federalreserve.gov provides a variety of banking, monetary, interest rate, and exchange rate data.

The Federal Reserve Bank of St. Louis maintains a comprehensive data base called ALFRED (**A**rchive of **F**ederal **R**eserve **E**conomic **D**ata) that you can access by going to www.stls.frb.org.

**Personal Finance Information**

Many financial Web sites offer a variety of personal finance resources, including financial calculators to help you with mortgages, auto loans, and insurance. They are:

- www.choosetosave.org
- www.dinkytown.net
- www.wsj.com (go to "personal finance" then "family finances" and look for "tools")

other sources are reproduced under the heading In the News. Each provides an example of how the concepts introduced in the chapter are discussed in the real world, and each is followed by a brief summary.

## Tools of the Trade

Many chapters in this book include an insert called Tools of the Trade that concentrates on practical knowledge relevant to the chapter. Some of these inserts cover basic skills, including how to read bond and stock tables, how to read charts, and how to do some simple algebraic calculations. Others provide brief reviews of material from principles of economics classes, such as the relationship between the current account and the capital account in the balance of payments. Still other Tools of the Trade inserts address questions such as:

- What is leverage, and how does it affect risk?
- What are hedge funds?
- What tools did the Fed use to address the financial crisis?
- How is a recession defined?

# The Organization of This Book

This book is organized into five sections. Each one employs core principles to illuminate a particular part of the financial system and applies economic theory to the world around us. The next two chapters will continue our overview of the financial system. First, we'll study money—what it is and how it is used. We'll see that currency allows transactions to be made anonymously, which reduces the need to gather information. This advantage of currency is related to Core Principle 3: Information is the basis for decisions. In Chapter 3, we'll take a bird's-eye view of financial instruments, financial markets, and financial institutions. At various points in that chapter, we'll refer to the first four core principles.

Part II includes detailed descriptions of financial instruments. We'll study bonds, stocks, and derivatives, as well as exchange rates for foreign currency. The valuation of financial instruments requires a comparison of payments made on different dates as well as an estimate of the risk involved in each instrument. Thus, these chapters focus on Core Principles 1 and 2: Time has value and Risk requires compensation.

Throughout Part II and continuing in Part III, we'll discuss financial markets, whose purpose is to facilitate the buying and selling of financial instruments. No one would buy stocks or bonds if they could not be resold cheaply and easily. Financial markets also provide the information necessary to understand the value and risk that are associated with particular financial instruments. Core Principles 3 and 4 (Information is the basis for decisions and Markets determine prices and allocate resources) are both relevant to our discussion of markets.

Part III covers financial institutions, especially banks and their regulation. Earlier in this chapter (pages 6–7), we emphasized that financial institutions spend a great deal of time collecting and processing information. Without that information, many financial transactions could not take place. This dependence of banks on information is an example of Core Principle 3: Information is the basis for decisions. Financial regulation is driven by Core Principle 5: Stability improves welfare.

Part IV describes central banks, especially the Federal Reserve and the European Central Bank. These institutions exist to stabilize the real economy as well as the financial system. Thus, like financial regulators in Part III of the book, they embody Core Principle 5: Stability improves welfare. We'll see how central banks manipulate interest rates and other less conventional policy tools to stabilize the economy.

Finally, Part V brings together material covered in the first four sections to explain how the financial system influences the real economy. We'll use a macroeconomic model to analyze the mechanism through which central banks influence the economy, paying particular attention to the role of the financial system in determining inflation and growth.

Learning money and banking is going to be hard work. Reading and working through the remaining 22 chapters of this book will take lots of time and energy. But when you are done, you will be armed with the tools you need to understand how the financial system works and why it changes as it does. You will know how to be an informed reader of the financial and economic news and how to put the financial system to use for you. You will understand the various ways that you can pay for your morning coffee and how each one of them works. You will understand the usefulness of bonds and stocks as well as what financial institutions do and how central banks work. You will know how to make sound financial decisions for the rest of your life. You will understand how financial crises arise, how they threaten economic stability, and what can be done to prevent and contain them. Regardless of the career you choose to follow, a solid background in money, banking, and financial markets will help you make sound financial decisions from now on.

## Terms

central bank, 3

European Central Bank, 4

Federal Reserve System, 3

financial institution, 3

financial instrument, 3

financial market, 3

financial system, 2

information, 6

markets, 7

money, 3

regulation, 4

regulatory agencies, 3

risk, 6

stability, 8

supervision, 4

time, 5

## Chapter Lessons

1. A healthy and constantly evolving financial system is the foundation for economic efficiency and economic growth. It has six parts:
   a. Money is used to pay for purchases and to store wealth.
   b. Financial instruments are used to transfer resources and risk.
   c. Financial markets allow people to buy and sell financial instruments.
   d. Financial institutions provide access to the financial markets, collect information, and provide a variety of other services.

e. Government regulatory agencies aim to make the financial system operate safely and reliably.

f. Central banks stabilize the economy.

2. The core principles of money and banking are useful in understanding all six parts of the financial system.

a. Core Principle 1: Time has value.

b. Core Principle 2: Risk requires compensation.

c. Core Principle 3: Information is the basis for decisions.

d. Core Principle 4: Markets determine prices and allocate resources.

e. Core Principle 5: Stability improves welfare.

# Conceptual Problems

1. Try to list the financial transactions you have engaged in over the past week. How might each one have been carried out 50 years ago?

2. Can you think of any examples of how you, or your family or friends, were affected by the failure of the financial system to function normally during the financial crisis of 2007–2009?

3. Describe the links among the six components of the financial system and the five core principles of money and banking.

4. Socialists argue that, to reduce the power exerted by the owners of capital, the state should control the allocation of resources. Thus, in a socialist system, the state allocates investment resources. In a market-based capitalist system, financial markets do that job. Which approach do you think works better, and why? Relate your answer to the core principle that markets determine prices and allocate resources.

5. Financial innovation has reduced individuals' need to carry cash. Explain how.

6.* Many people believe that, despite ongoing financial innovations, cash will always be with us to some degree as a form of money. What core principle could justify this view?

7. When you apply for a loan, you are required to answer a lot of questions. Why? Why is the set of questions you must answer standardized?

8. Merchants that accept Visa or MasterCard pay the issuer of the card a percentage of the transaction. For example, for each $100 charged on Visa cards, a merchant might receive only $98. Explain why Visa charges the fee and why the merchant pays it. (You should be able to use at least two core principles in your answer.)

9. Suppose central bankers have figured out a way to eliminate recessions. What financial and economic changes would you expect to see? Relate these changes to the core principle that stability improves welfare.

10.* Why do you think the global financial system has become more integrated over time? Can you think of any downside to this increased integration?

11. The government is heavily involved in the financial system. Explain why.

*Indicates more difficult problems

# Analytical Problems

12. If offered the choice of receiving $1,000 today or $1,000 in one year's time, which option would you choose, and why?

13. If time has value, why are financial institutions often willing to extend you a 30-year mortgage at a lower annual interest rate than they would charge for a one-year loan?

14. Using Core Principle 2, under what circumstances would you expect a job applicant to accept an offer of a low base salary and an opportunity to earn commission over one with a higher base salary and no commission potential?

15. Suppose medical research confirms earlier speculation that red wine is good for you. Why would banks be willing to lend to vineyards that produce red wine at a lower interest rate than before?

16.* If the U.S. Securities and Exchange Commission eliminated its requirement for public companies to disclose information about their finances, what would you expect to happen to the stock prices for these companies?

17. If 2 percent growth is your break-even point for an investment project, under which outlook for the economy would you be more inclined to go ahead with the investment: (1) A forecast for economic growth that ranges from 0 to 4 percent, or (2) a forecast of 2 percent growth for sure, assuming the forecasts are equally reliable? What core principle does this illustrate?

18.* Why are large, publicly listed companies much more likely than small businesses to sell financial instruments such as bonds directly to the market, while small businesses get their financing from financial institutions such as banks?

19.* During the financial crisis of 2007–2009, some financial instruments that received high ratings in terms of their safety turned out to be much riskier than those ratings indicated. Explain why markets for other financial instruments might have been adversely affected by that development.

20. Suppose financial institutions didn't exist but you urgently needed a loan. Where would you most likely get this loan? Using core principles, identify an advantage and a disadvantage this arrangement might have over borrowing from a financial institution.

# Appendix to Chapter 1

## Measuring Economic Activity, Prices, and the Inflation Rate

## Measuring Economic Activity

*Gross Domestic Product* (GDP) is the most commonly used measure of economic activity. In order to see if the economy is improving, you can look at whether GDP is growing (or shrinking) and the rate of that growth. And to compare well-being in two countries, you can look at the GDP per person in each country—*per capita GDP*.

The definition of GDP is *the market value of final goods and services produced in a country during a year*. Let's look at the pieces of this definition:

- **Market value:** In order to add together production of cars, corn flakes, and computers, we take the market price of each and multiply it times the quantity of each that is produced, and sum the products together. That is, add up (market price of cars × quantity of cars produced) plus (market price of corn flakes × quantity of corn flakes produced), and so on.

- **Final goods and services:** We take only the price of the final product purchased by the person who uses it. For example, when a consumer buys a car, the car is considered a final good so it's included. But when the automobile manufacturer buys steel from a steel company in order to build the car, the steel is an intermediate product so it is not included.

- **In a country:** Only production within the country counts. This means that if a U.S. company owns a factory in China, the production of the factory is included in China's GDP.

- **During a year:** To measure production we need to specify a time period, and the time period is usually one year.

So, to compute U.S. GDP in 2010, for example, we sum the quantity of goods and services produced in the United States in 2010 times their 2010 prices. In an economy with only cars and corn flakes, the calculation would look like this:

GDP in 2010 = (2010 price of cars × quantity of cars produced in 2010)
         + (2010 price of corn flakes × quantity of corn flakes produced in 2010)

Note that we could always measure incomes rather than production. That is, instead of measuring total production, we can measure the total payments made to factors used to produce the output—the payments to labor, capital, and land. Because the revenue from selling all of the goods and services produced must always go to the people responsible for making them—the workers and the owners—total income equals GDP as well.

# Real versus Nominal GDP

It is essential when measuring the level of economic activity to distinguish changes in prices from changes in quantities. As defined so far, GDP confuses the two changes. For example, U.S. GDP rose from $14.078 trillion in 2007 to $14.441 trillion in 2008. Computing the annual growth rate, the percentage change from one year to the next, means that the U.S. economy grew by 2.58 percent.

$$\text{GDP growth rate from 2007 to 2008} = \frac{\$14.441\,trillion - \$14.078\,trillion}{\$14.078\,trillion} \times 100$$

$$= 2.58\%$$

This number alone only tells us the sum of the growth in the quantity of output produced (something that is beneficial) and the change in prices (which is not so good). To see the point, look back at the computation for the car and corn flakes economy and note that GDP can rise either because quantities rise or because prices go up.

Separating changes in the quantities from changes in the prices requires computing *real* GDP. To do this, government statisticians fix the prices at a base-year level and then calculate the sum of the quantities times these base-year prices. Currently, real GDP in the United States is reported in year-2005 dollars. That is, statisticians sum up the value of all production in the United States during a year measured at the prices at which the goods and services were sold in the year 2005. This procedure isolates the part of change in GDP that is due to growth in the quantity produced from the part that came from changes in prices.

For the car and corn flakes economy, the formula looks like this:

Real GDP in 2010 = (2005 price of cars × quantity of cars produced in 2010)
    + (2005 price of corn flakes × quantity of corn flakes produced in 2010)

To see what this means for the United States as a whole, we can look at www.bea.gov and find that, in 2007, real GDP (in year-2005 dollars) was $13.254 trillion. In 2008, real GDP (again in year-2005 dollars) had increased to $13.312 trillion. That's an increase of 0.44 percent.

$$\text{Real GDP growth rate from 2007 to 2008} = \frac{\$13.312\,trillion - \$13.254\,trillion}{\$13.254\,trillion} \times 100$$

$$= 0.44\%$$

# The GDP Deflator and the Inflation Rate

It should come as no surprise that from nominal and real GDP we get a measure of prices on average in the economy as a whole. We can start by thinking about nominal GDP as the product of real GDP times a measure of prices in the economy as a whole. That is:

$$\textit{Nominal GDP} = \textit{Prices} \times \textit{Real GDP}$$

Looking at this expression, you can see that by taking the ratio of nominal GDP to real GDP we get a measure of prices. This is what's called the GDP *deflator*, and using the data from 2007, we get:

$$\text{GDP deflator in 2007} = \frac{\text{Nominal GDP in 2007}}{\text{Real GDP in 2007}} = \frac{\$14.078\,trillion}{\$13.254\,trillion} = 1.0621$$

The same computation for 2008 tells us that the GDP deflator in 2008 is 1.0848.

No one spends much time worrying about the level of the GDP deflator. Instead, we are concerned with the rate at which the index is changing. The inflation rate is defined as the rate of growth in the price level. Using the GDP deflator from 2007 to 2008, we get an inflation rate of 2.14 percent.

$$\text{Inflation rate} = \frac{(1.0848 - 1.0621)}{1.0621} \times 100 = 2.14\%$$

This result makes sense. Since real GDP is designed to strip out the effect of price changes, the inflation rate should equal the growth rate of nominal GDP minus the growth rate of real GDP. And it does: $2.14 = 2.58 - 0.44$.

While it is the easiest to explain and compute, the GDP deflator is unfortunately not the most commonly used price index. The Consumer Price Index, or CPI, designed to measure the changes in the cost of living, lays claim to that title. We will learn more about the CPI throughout this book, starting with the Tools of the Trade in Chapter 2.

# Chapter 2

## Money and the Payments System

Parker Brothers' bestselling board game.

The makers of the board game Monopoly print about $50 billion of Monopoly money every year—coincidentally about the same as the amount of new U.S. currency issued in 2008. Every game has bills totaling 15,140 Monopoly dollars. At a cost of about 13 U.S. dollars per set, this "money" would be a good deal if you could buy things other than Boardwalk and Park Place with it. Unfortunately, attempts to pay for groceries, books, or rent with this particular form of money have been unsuccessful. And that's probably a good thing. Since the mid-1930s, Parker Brothers has sold more than 200 million Monopoly games, containing more than 3 trillion Monopoly dollars.[1]

When we pay for our purchases in the real world, we have lots of choices: crisp new $20 bills, credit cards, debit cards, checks, or more complicated electronic methods. Regardless of the choice we make, we are using *money* to buy our food and clothes and pay our bills. To make sure we can do it, thousands of people work through every night, for the payments system really never sleeps. And the volume of payments is astounding. The Federal Reserve reports that in 2006 there were 93 billion noncash payments made in the United States, 33 percent of which were paper checks. That means something like 120 million paper checks and 250 million electronic payments were processed on an average business day. And, regardless of how you choose to pay, the path that the payment follows is pretty complicated.

To understand why money is so important to the smooth functioning of the economy and how it improves everyone's well-being, we need to understand exactly what money is. Just why is a $20 bill issued by the U.S. government much more useful than $20 in Monopoly money? Furthermore, to quantify the impact of money on the economy, we need to be able to measure it. Those are the goals of this chapter: to understand what money is, how we use it, and how we measure it.

[1]For more fun facts about Monopoly, see www.monopoly.com.

# Money and How We Use It

When people use the word *money* in conversation, they mean many different things. Someone who "makes lots of money" has a high income; a person who "has lots of money" is wealthy. We will use the word *money* in a narrower, specialized sense to mean anything that can readily be used to make economic transactions. Formally defined, **money** is *an asset that is generally accepted as payment for goods and services or repayment of debt.* Income, in contrast, is a flow of earnings over time. **Wealth** is the value of assets minus liabilities. Money is one of those assets, albeit a very minor one.

Money, in the sense we are talking about, has three characteristics. It is (1) a means of payment, (2) a unit of account, and (3) a store of value. The first of these characteristics is the most important. Anything that is used as a means of payment must be a store of value and thus is very likely to become a unit of account. Let's see why this is so.

## Means of Payment

The primary use of money is as a **means of payment**. Most people insist on payment in money at the time a good or service is supplied because the alternatives just don't work very well. Barter, in which a good or service is exchanged directly for another good or service, requires that a plumber who needs food find a grocer who needs a plumbing repair. Relying on this "double coincidence of wants" surely causes the economy to run less smoothly. The plumber could pay for his breakfast cereal with a "promise" of plumbing services, which the grocer could then transfer to someone else. But while it would be possible to certify the plumber's trustworthiness, certainly taking payment in money is easier. Money finalizes payments so that buyers and sellers have no further claim on each other. That is money's special role. In fact, so long as a buyer has money, there is nothing more the seller needs to know.

As economies have become more complex and physically dispersed, reducing the likelihood that a seller will have good information about a buyer, the need for money has grown. The increase in both the number of transactions and the number of potential buyers and sellers (the vast majority of whom may never even have seen one another) argues for something that makes payment final and whose value is easily verified. That something is money.

INFORMATION

*"I suppose mere promises would not suffice."*

## Unit of Account

Just as we measure length using feet and inches, we measure value using dollars and cents. Money is the **unit of account** that we use to quote prices and record debts. We could also refer to it as a standard of value.

Having a unit of account is an incredible convenience. Remember from microeconomics that prices provide the information consumers and producers use to ensure that resources are allocated to their best uses. What matters are the *relative* prices of goods and services. When the price of one

## YOUR FINANCIAL WORLD
### Debit Cards versus Credit Cards

When you go shopping, should you pay with a credit card or a debit card? To decide, you need to understand the difference between the two. First make sure you know which one of your cards is which. Usually an ATM card (the one that you got from the bank when you opened your checking account) is a debit card. But check to make sure.

What's the real difference, from the shopper's point of view? A debit card works just like a check, only faster. When you write a paper check, it usually takes a day or two to go through the system. A debit card transaction goes through right away. The electronic message gets to your bank on the same day, and your account is debited immediately. So, if you want to use your debit card, your account balance has to be higher than the payment you want to make.

A credit card creates a deferred payment. The issuer agrees to make the payment for you, and you repay the debt later. That sounds good, but there's a catch. If you're late paying, there's a late fee. And if you don't pay the entire debt every month, you pay interest on the balance—at what is usually a very high interest rate. If you do pay the entire debt every month, however, there is no late fee and no interest charge. And because you don't pay right away, you get an interest-free loan from the time you make the purchase to the time you pay the balance. If you can pay off your credit cards in full and on time, it's to your advantage to use them.

Credit cards have another advantage over debit cards. They help you to build a credit history, which you'll need when the time comes to buy a car or a house. Because debit cards are just extensions of your bank account, they don't show potential lenders that you are creditworthy. In fact, some businesses, like car rental companies, require their customers to use credit cards for this reason.

product is higher than the price of another, that product is worth more to both producers and consumers. Using dollars makes these comparisons easy. Imagine what would happen if we needed to compute relative prices for each pair of goods. With two goods, we would need only one price. With three goods, we would need three prices. But with 100 goods, we would need 4,950 prices, and with 10,000 goods (substantially less than the 70,000 products in a typical supermarket), we would need nearly 50 million prices.[2] Using money as a yardstick and quoting all prices in dollars certainly is easier.

## Store of Value

For money to function as a means of payment, it has to be a **store of value**, too. That is, if we are going to use money to pay for goods and services, then it must retain its worth from day to day. Sellers are much less likely to accept things that are perishable, like milk or lettuce. So the means of payment has to be durable and capable of transferring purchasing power from one day to the next. Paper **currency** does degrade with use ($1 bills have an average lifetime of 21 months in circulation), but regardless of its physical condition, it is usually accepted at face value in transactions.

Of course, money is not the only store of value. We hold our wealth in lots of other forms—stocks, bonds, houses, even cars. Many of these are actually preferable to money as stores of value. Some, like bonds, pay higher interest rates than money. Others, like stocks, offer the potential for appreciation in nominal value, which money does not. Still others, like houses, deliver other services over time. Yet we all hold

[2]The general formula is that for $n$ goods we need $n(n - 1)/2$ prices, so for 10,000 goods, the number would be 10,000 (9,999)/2 = 49,995,000.

them. In the United States, the Civil War put pressure on government finances and the two warring parties had little choice but to issue paper money to pay for salaries and supplies. Beginning in 1862, both the Confederate and the Union governments printed and used paper money with no explicit backing. The North's "greenbacks" are still legal tender in the United States, but collectors are the only people who value the Confederate currency.

After the Civil War, the United States reverted to the use of gold as money. Both gold coins and notes backed by gold circulated well into the 20th century. Today, though, we use paper money—high-quality paper, nicely engraved, with lots of special security features. This type of currency is called **fiat money**, because its value comes from government decree, or *fiat*. Some countries print notes that are durable and attractive, bearing famous works of art in multiple colors. The Australians make their notes out of plastic. But in all cases the money has very little intrinsic worth, and the cost of production is only a small fraction of the face value. The U.S. Treasury's Bureau of Engraving and Printing pays less than 7 cents to print a note, regardless of whether it's a $1 or a $100 bill.

Why are we willing to accept these bills as payment for goods or in settlement of debts? There are two reasons. First, we take them because we believe we can use them in the future; someone else will take them from us. Second, the law says we must accept them. That is, the U.S. government stands behind its paper money. Since the first greenbacks were issued in 1862, all U.S. currency has borne the short and simple phrase "This note is legal tender for all debts, public and private." In practice, this means that private businesses must accept dollar bills as payment. More important, the U.S. government is committed to accepting the currency it has issued in settlement of debts. We will always be able to pay our taxes in dollars. As long as the government stands behind its paper money and doesn't issue too much of it, we will use it. In the end, money is about trust.

## Checks

Checks are another way of paying for things. Unlike currency, the checks you use to pay your rent and electric bill are not legal tender. In fact, they aren't money at all. A **check** is just an instruction to the bank to take funds from your account and transfer them to the person or firm whose name you have written in the "Pay to the order of" line. Thus, when you give someone a check in exchange for a good or service, it is not a final payment—at least, not in the same sense as currency. Instead, your check sets in motion a series of transactions that eventually lead to the final payment.

Here are the steps. You hand the check over to a merchant, who then takes it to the bank. Depending on the arrangement, the bank will credit the amount of the check to the merchant's account either immediately or with a short lag. At the end of the day, the bank sends the check (or an electronic image) through the check-clearing system along with the other millions of checks to be processed that night by shipping them to a check-processing center run by the Federal Reserve or to a private check clearinghouse. (The first check clearinghouses were pubs where bank employees met to have a drink and exchange checks.) At the center, the check is transferred from the bank that sent it in to the bank on which it is written—your bank. The account of the bank presenting the check is credited, and the account of

**Figure 2.1**   The Path of a Paper Check

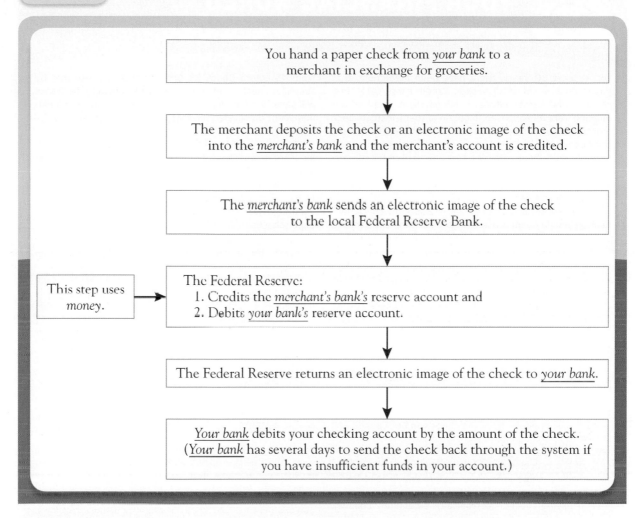

the bank on which the check is written is debited (see Figure 2.1). This is the step that uses *money*.

Finally, on receipt of the check, your bank debits your account. (If the balance in your account is insufficient to cover the check, your bank has a few days to return it to the sending bank, so the transaction isn't actually final until that period has passed.) In the past all paper checks were returned to the people who originally wrote them. Today, they are scanned and customers can view electronic images on their bank's Web sites. (See Your Financial World: Paper Checks Become Digital Images.)

Recently check volumes have fallen, but paper checks are still with us for several reasons. A canceled check is legal proof of payment and, in many states, laws require banks to return checks to customers. Then there is force of habit. Over time, people may get used to receiving bank statements without their checks, but so

# YOUR FINANCIAL WORLD
## Paper Checks Become Digital Images

For at least 30 years, there have been predictions that paper checks would disappear. Credit cards, ATM machines, debit cards, automatic bill payment, and Internet banking were all supposed to get rid of them. Instead, each month millions of people received thick envelopes from their banks that included canceled checks along with their monthly statements. Paper checks accounted for 60 percent of payments in 2000. But no more! On October 28, 2004, Check 21—the Check Clearing for the 21st Century Act—went into effect.

Banks are thrilled. Until the fall of 2004, the check verification and payment process required commercial banks to transport all paper checks to and from a Federal Reserve Bank, and eventually back to the people who wrote them. Paper checks were legal proof of payment, so customers wanted them back. But transporting tons and tons of checks around the country was an expensive headache for banks.

Check 21 gives banks the leeway to process checks electronically. Instead of shipping paper across the country, banks transmit digital images of each check that was written. These images create "substitute checks," and have the same legal standing as the original checks.

Payments in long-distance transactions are now much less complicated. Before Check 21, if someone living in Houston sent a check to make a payment to a business in Chicago, the piece of paper had to go from Texas to Illinois, and then back again. Now, the check can be scanned and shredded in Chicago and the image is saved and transmitted. If the person who wrote it in Houston wants a paper copy of the canceled check, their bank can print a substitute check. A check processing system that used to take a few days now takes a few hours.

Processing checks electronically is definitely cheaper. With the volume of paper checks dwindling and most checks now clearing electronically, the Federal Reserve has reduced the number of its processing centers to 1—down

from 45 before Check 21. And, experts estimate that by scanning checks and transmitting the images, the banks will save $2 billion a year. These savings include $250 million spent on courier services to move checks around the country.

In fact, reducing the risks of physically transporting checks was one of the big reasons for the passage of Check 21. For several days following the September 11, 2001, terrorist attacks, only military planes were allowed to fly in U.S. airspace and that disrupted the check transportation system eventually grounding $47 billion worth of paper checks.

Speeding up paper check processing does have one downside: People can't write checks with the expectation that they will have a day or two to make a deposit to cover it. There is no more float. The new rules shrink the time between when a check is written and when the account is debited, especially for out-of-town checks.*

By speeding up the processing of paper checks, Check 21 provides a further incentive for individuals to use debit cards, credit cards, or other forms of electronic payments. Nevertheless, billions of checks are likely to be written for years to come.

For more details on Check 21, payments system development and policies, see the Federal Reserve Board's payment system Web site http://www.federalreserve.gov/paymentsys.htm.

---

*Just because banks are able to move checks through the clearing system more quickly doesn't mean that they are going to offer the depositor more timely access to the funds. In an attempt to reduce fraud, banks restrict access to funds from so-called high-risk checks, such as those for more than $5,000 that are deposited into newly opened accounts, for as long as 11 business days. If you have to shift large quantities of funds and use them quickly, it is important to find out the policies of the financial intermediaries involved before you do it.

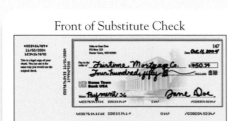
Front of Substitute Check

Back of Substitute Check

The front of the substitute check includes the following: "This is a legal copy of your check. You can use it the same way you would use the original check."

far not many people have chosen the option. Finally, new electronic mechanisms for clearing checks have lowered costs and kept checks as an attractive means of payment.

## Electronic Payments

The third and final method of payment is electronic. We are all familiar with credit cards and debit cards. A less well-known form of payment is electronic funds transfers. While there are a large number of credit and debit card transactions, electronic funds transfers account for the bulk of the $35 trillion worth of noncash, noncheck payments made each year in the United States.

What is the difference between debit cards and credit cards? A **debit card** works the same way as a check in that it provides the bank with instructions to transfer funds from the cardholder's account directly to a merchant's account. There is usually a charge for this; the processor of the payment takes a fee based on the size of the transaction.

A **credit card** is a promise by a bank to lend the cardholder money with which to make purchases. When a shopper buys a pair of shoes with a credit card, the shoe store's bank account receives payment immediately, but the money that is used for payment does not belong to the buyer. Instead, the bank that issued the credit card makes the payment, creating a loan the cardholder must repay. For this reason, credit cards do not represent money; rather, they represent access to someone else's money.

**Electronic funds transfers** are movements of funds directly from one account to another. These transactions are used extensively by banks and are becoming increasingly popular for individuals as well. For individuals, the most common form is the **automated clearinghouse transaction (ACH)**, which is generally used for recurring payments such as paychecks and utility bills. Some merchants use them for one-time transactions as well. ACH transactions are just like checks except that they are entirely electronic. Your bank account is debited or credited automatically, and you receive periodic notifications of the activity in your account.

Banks use electronic transfers to handle transactions among themselves. The most common method is to send money through a system maintained by the Federal Reserve, called Fedwire. The volume and value of payments made through this system are substantial. On a typical day in 2009, the system completed 495,000 transactions with a total value of about $2.5 trillion.

Retail businesses, together with their banks, are experimenting with a variety of new methods of electronic payment. One is the **stored-value card**, which looks like a credit or debit card except that it doesn't bear your name. To use one, you go to the bank or ATM machine and put the card into an electronic device that transfers funds from your checking account to your card. Then you take the card to a merchant who has a reader that is capable of deducting funds from the card and depositing them directly into the store's account. The stuff on the card is in fact money, and the system can be set up so that if you lose your card, its current value can be canceled.

So far, these cards have limited usefulness. The New York City Metropolitan Transit Authority and other city transit systems sell stored-value cards, but it's hard to buy anything with them other than subway and bus rides. The same is true of long-distance phone cards and gift cards sold by chain stores like Barnes & Noble.

## LESSONS FROM THE CRISIS
### MARKET LIQUIDITY, FUNDING LIQUIDITY, AND MAKING MARKETS

A "market maker" in stocks, bonds, or other securities is usually a financial institution that buys and sells securities on behalf of clients. If buy orders at a market maker exceed sell orders for a particular security, the market maker must be able to act as the seller to clear the market. Therefore, market makers usually hold inventories of the specific financial instruments in which they trade, and they borrow to maintain inventories at adequate levels.

*Market liquidity*—the ability to sell assets—and *funding liquidity*—the ability to borrow money—are both needed to make financial markets function smoothly. If a loss of funding liquidity prevents market makers from holding adequate inventories, trading and market liquidity suffer. Conversely, if market liquidity for some financial instruments declines, the prices of those instruments will fall as they become less attractive to investors; resulting concerns about the safety of the market makers that hold the assets with falling prices may reduce their ability to borrow.

A sudden loss of liquidity was central to the 2007-2009 financial crisis. Before the crisis, many financial institutions relied on short-term borrowing to hold long-term financial instruments because their managers believed that funding liquidity would remain readily available. They also believed that markets would always be liquid—that is, they would always be able to sell the securities and loans that they held. They were wrong on both counts.

In the summer of 2007, investors began to doubt the value of a wide class of securities. As a result, market liquidity for those instruments disappeared, and financial institutions that held them faced large potential losses. In turn, funding liquidity for these institutions evaporated as the potential losses caused their lenders to worry about their safety.

This double "liquidity shock" led many financial institutions to increase cash holdings that they might otherwise have lent to others. Reduced loan supply intensified the vicious spiral of dwindling liquidity and falling securities prices. The financial system as a whole could not provide sufficient market liquidity or funding liquidity to satisfy heightened demands.

One lesson from the financial crisis is clear: Liquidity is a highly valuable resource that can disappear when it is most needed, so it should not be taken for granted. Even large and seemingly wealthy financial firms can fail if liquidity evaporates.

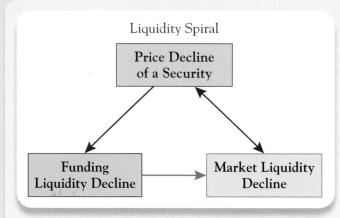

In the accompanying figure, a decline of the price of a security makes it more costly for a financial institution to make a market in that security, resulting in a decline of market liquidity. That decline makes the security less attractive to investors, further reducing its price. If the price falls sufficiently, concern about the well-being of market makers diminishes their funding liquidity, advancing a vicious cycle.

Attempts to implement the stored-value card more broadly haven't worked very well because most merchants lack the hardware to read the cards. And few of us know how to use them.

**E-money** is another new method of payment. It can be used to pay for purchases on the Internet. You open an account by transferring funds to the issuer of the e-money. Then, when you are shopping online, you instruct the issuer to send your e-money to the merchant.

E-money is really a form of private money. It is not issued or guaranteed by the government, so you can't use it to pay your taxes. It's hard to even define what the term *e-money* means. One definition that seems helpful is "monetary value, as represented by a claim on the issuer, which is (a) stored on an electronic device, (b) issued on receipt of funds, and (c) accepted as a means of payment by persons other than the issuer."[4]

But at this point, e-money is questionable at best. Will individuals develop enough trust in e-money to be willing to use it? Will merchants install the expensive equipment to handle it? Who will be allowed to issue e-money? Still, the day may come when you can park your car and pay the parking meter by simply punching a series of numbers into your cell phone that transfers e-money issued by your phone provider to the city government that owns the parking meter.

# The Future of Money

Let's speculate about what might happen to money and each of its three functions in the future. As a *means of payment,* it has already undergone big changes. The time is rapidly approaching when safe and secure systems for payment will use virtually no money at all.

We will always need money as a *unit of account* in which to quote values and prices; the efficiency of quoting prices in commonly understood terms isn't going to change. But the question is, how many units of account will we need? Today, many countries have their own currencies, which give rise to their own units of account. In the future, though, there will be little reason to maintain different units of account across different countries. Price systems will be more like systems of weights and measures. Today, there are two commonly used systems of weights and measures: English ounces and yards and metric grams and meters. We will likely see a similar sort of standardization of money and a dramatic reduction in the number of units of account.

Finally, money as a *store of value* is clearly on the way out. With the advances in financial markets, many financial instruments have become highly liquid. They are easily bought and sold and can be converted into a means of payment quickly and cheaply. These instruments and the financial markets in which they trade are the subject of the next chapter. For now, though, we can conclude that in the future, there will almost surely be less and less money.

One caution is in order. As we look into the future and try to discern what will happen to money, we should remember that 150 years ago there was virtually no paper currency in circulation. The first credit card was issued in the early 1950s; the first ATM was installed around 1970. Not until the mid-1990s could we shop via the Internet. Forecasting most of these developments, as well as any other trend in technology, is nearly impossible. After all, who could have predicted even 10 years ago that today we would be able to check our bank balances, buy and sell stocks, and pay our utility bills 24 hours a day, seven days a week from the comfort of our homes? (See In the News: Dad, Can You Text Me $200?)

---

[4]This definition comes from Directive 2000/46 of the European Parliament and the Council of 18 September 2000, "On the Taking Up, Pursuit and Prudential Supervision of the Business of Electronic Money Institutions," *Official Journal of the European Communities*, 275/39, 27 October 2000.

## IN THE NEWS
### Dad, Can You Text Me $200?

**THE WALL STREET JOURNAL.**
WSJ.com

**by Jonnelle Marte**

**June 23, 2009**

Parents, used to receiving kids' requests for money via email and cellphone, are now able to send that money via text message, email or cell.

A new service by CashEdge Inc., which provides online banking services for financial institutions, would let users send money to friends and family through a text message or email—further cutting down on our need to stop at ATMs or write checks when we owe people money.

"Paper transactions are shrinking and electronic transactions are growing and this just seems to be the next step along that path," said Steve Kenneally of the American Bankers Association.

The new service, called POPmoney, will let consumers "Pay Other People" through their bank's online or mobile banking application by providing the recipient's email address, cell phone number or account number.

Once users enter their friends' information online, they would be able to send the person-to-person payments directly from their cell phones.

"You will be using your mobile phone to do small transfers over dinner" and to make other quick payments to friends or relatives, says CashEdge president Sanjeev Dheer.

OMG, plz txt me $!

## Measuring Money

Changes in the amount of money in the economy are related to changes in interest rates, economic growth, and most important, **inflation**. Inflation is the rate at which prices in general are increasing over time—and the **inflation rate** is a measure of that process.[5] With inflation, you need more units of money to buy the same basket of goods you bought a month or a year ago. Put another way, inflation makes money less valuable. And the primary cause of inflation is the issuance of too much money. When the Continental Congress issued too much currency to finance the Revolutionary

---

[5]The terms "inflation" and "inflation rate" are often used interchangeably. We will refer to inflation as the process of prices rising, and inflation rate as the measurement of the process. The relationship between these terms is analogous to that between "heat" and "temperature." The second is the measure of the first.

Recipients at participating banks will be able to accept the cash deposits through their own online banking accounts. They can also automatically deposit payments from specific users. For example, college students could have payments from mom and dad automatically deposited into their checking accounts or vice versa.

The service will likely come with a fee, which Mr. Dheer says will be set by the financial institutions. A demo transaction showed a standard transfer, which could take a few days, costing $2 and an express one costing $10.

The concept isn't completely new. Mobile banking apps already let people check their balances and transfer money from one account to another by pushing a few buttons. PayPal, which most online shoppers know well, lets consumers send money electronically to friends using their email address. Zoompass, a service recently launched in Canada, lets users send, receive and request money from their mobile phones to an intermediary account—similar to PayPal—linked to their bank accounts.

But POPmoney's key feature is that it will allow users to send money directly from one bank account to another.

"This is a function that people should be able to do within their banks and not have to sign up for another service," says Mr. Dheer.

Those with banks that don't offer the service will be able to sign on to an online payment hub where they can provide their bank account information in order to receive the money.

Larger transactions will have added security measures, said Mr. Dheer. For instance, the person sending money will have to give both an email and phone number for the recipient, who would be required to submit a code sent to them via text before they could accept the money.

At first, consumers will only have the option to send and accept cash, not to request it, but CashEdge is hoping to offer that feature in later releases, said Mr. Dheer. POPmoney will likely be up and running around September, after banks integrate the service into their online banking hubs, says Mr. Dheer.

SOURCE: *The Wall Street Journal Online.* "Dad, Can You Text Me $200?" by Jonnelle Marte, June 23, 2009. Copyright 2009 by Dow Jones & Company, Inc. Reproduced with permission of Dow Jones & Company, Inc. in the formats Textbook and Other Book via Copyright Clearance Center.

## LESSONS OF THE ARTICLE

Technological advances are constantly creating new methods of payment. While their adoption depends on many things, one thing is for certain: Someone will always be searching for easier and cheaper ways for us to pay for things. And as the payments system evolves, so will the assets that we need to hold. As our cell phones transform into a part of the payments sytem, we will need to carry less and less cash.

War, the number of continentals people needed to purchase food and shelter rose dramatically. Continentals slowly became less valuable. So the value of the means of payment depends on how much of it is circulating.

To use the insight that money growth is somehow related to inflation, we must be able to measure how much money is circulating. This is no easy task. Let's start with money's primary function, as a means of payment. If that were the definition of money, we would measure the quantity of money as the quantity of currency in circulation—an unrealistically limited measure, since there are many ways to complete transactions (effect final payment) without using currency.

A reasonable alternative would be to consider the functionality of a broad category of financial assets and sort them by their degree of liquidity. That is, we could sort them by the ease with which they can be converted into a means of payment, arranging them along a spectrum from the most liquid (currency) to the least liquid (art,

### Figure 2.2 The Liquidity Spectrum

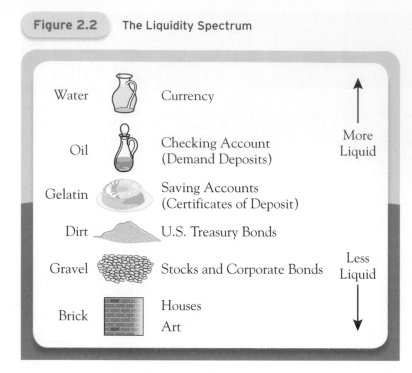

| | | |
|---|---|---|
| Water | Currency | |
| Oil | Checking Account (Demand Deposits) | More Liquid |
| Gelatin | Saving Accounts (Certificates of Deposit) | |
| Dirt | U.S. Treasury Bonds | |
| Gravel | Stocks and Corporate Bonds | Less Liquid |
| Brick | Houses Art | |

Liquidity is the ease with which you can turn an asset into a means of payment without loss of value.

antique cars, and the like). Figure 2.2 shows what our liquidity spectrum would look like.

Once we have our list, we could draw a line and include everything on one side of the line in our measure of money. Over the years, figuring out just where to draw the line has proven very difficult, especially since the introduction of new types of checking accounts. There really is no perfect solution. Instead, we have drawn the line in a number of different places and computed several measures of money, called the **monetary aggregates**: M1 and M2.[6]

Table 2.1 shows the components of the two monetary aggregates as defined by the Federal Reserve, along with the size of each as of January 2010. Let's go through each one to understand how it is constructed. **M1**, the narrowest definition of money, includes only currency and various deposit accounts on which people can write checks. These are the most liquid assets in the financial system. The components of M1 include *currency in the hands of the public*, which is the quantity of dollar bills outstanding excluding the ones in the vaults of banks; *travelers' checks* issued by travel companies, banks, and credit card companies, which are guaranteed by the issuer and usually work just like cash; **demand deposits** at commercial banks, which are standard checking accounts that pay no interest; and other checkable deposits, which are deposits in checking accounts that pay interest.

**M2** equals all of M1 plus assets that cannot be used directly as a means of payment and are difficult to turn into currency quickly. These assets in M2 include small-denomination **time deposits** (less than $100,000) that cannot be withdrawn without advance notice; *savings deposits*, including *money-market deposit accounts*, which pay interest and offer limited check-writing privileges; *retail money-market mutual fund shares*, or shares in funds that collect relatively small sums from individuals, pool them together, and invest them in short-term marketable debt issued by large corporations. Money-market mutual fund shares can be issued by nonbank financial intermediaries, such as brokerage firms. They do carry check-writing privileges. M2 is the most commonly quoted monetary aggregate, since its movements are most closely related to interest rates and economic growth.

To clarify what the monetary aggregates mean, let's compare their size to the size of the economy. In winter 2010, nominal U.S. **gross domestic product (GDP)** was

---

[6]On March 23, 2006, the Federal Reserve Board ceased collection and publication of a third monetary aggregate, M3. In announcing their decision, officials wrote: "M3 does not appear to convey any additional information about economic activity that is not already embodied in M2 and has not played a role in the monetary policy process for many years."

| Table 2.1 | The Monetary Aggregates |
|-----------|-------------------------|

| Monetary Aggregates | | | Value as of January 2010 (US$ billions) |
|---|---|---|---|
| M1 | = | Currency in the hands of the public | 861.1 |
| | + | Traveler's Checks | 5.1 |
| | + | Demand Deposits | 435.0 |
| | + | Other Checkable Deposits | 375.3 |
| | | **Total M1** | **1676.5** |
| M2 | = | M1 | |
| | + | Small-denomination time deposits | 1139.8 |
| | + | Savings Deposits and Money Market Deposit Accounts | 4856.5 |
| | + | Retail Money Market Mutual Fund Shares | 790.7 |
| | | **Total M2** | **8463.5** |

SOURCE: *Board of Governors of the Federal Reserve.*

$14.5 trillion. Putting that number into the same units as those in Table 2.1, that's $14,500 billion. So GDP is nearly nine times as large as M1 and about 70 percent larger than M2.

Which one of the Ms should we use to understand inflation? That's a difficult question whose answer has changed over time. Until the early 1980s, economists and policymakers looked at M1. But with the introduction of substitutes for standard checking accounts, especially money-market mutual fund shares, M1 became less useful than M2. These innovations enabled people to shift their balances out of the noninterest-bearing accounts in M1 and into accounts that paid interest. As Table 2.1 shows, demand deposits and other checkable deposits in M1 total about $810 billion, which represents less than 6 percent of GDP. By comparison, the savings deposits, money-market deposit accounts, and retail money-market mutual fund shares in M2 total over $6.7 trillion, representing nearly one-half of GDP. M1 is no longer a useful measure of money.

Looking at Figure 2.3 on page 35, you can see that from 1960 to 1980 the growth rates of the two measures of money moved together. After 1980, however, M1 behaved very differently from M2. Here's what happened. In the late 1970s and early 1980s, inflation climbed to over 10 percent for a few years. Needless to say, people who had money in zero-interest checking accounts were upset. Their money was losing value at a rapid rate. They went looking for ways to get checking services along with interest. Soon financial firms began to offer "money market" accounts that compensated depositors at least in part for inflation. These accounts are part of M2. The movement of funds into the non-M1 portion of M2 meant that the two measures no longer moved together. At the same time, the new money market accounts made M2 accounts more liquid. Analysts stopped looking at M1 and began to look at M2.

# TOOLS OF THE TRADE

## The Consumer Price Index

Understanding how to measure inflation is central to understanding economics and finance. Most of us keep a close eye on measures like the Consumer Price Index (CPI) to help gauge the value of our salary increases or the purchasing power of the money we hold. And adjusting interest rates for inflation is critical for making investment decisions. (See Chapter 4.)

The CPI is designed to answer the following question: How much more would it cost for people to purchase today the same basket of goods and services that they actually bought at some fixed time in the past?

To calculate the CPI, every few years statisticians at the Bureau of Labor Statistics (BLS) survey people to find out what they bought. This gives us the basket of goods and services bought by the typical consumer. Next, every month the BLS collects information on the prices of thousands of goods and services—everything from breakfast cereal to gasoline to washing machines to the cost of cable television. Combining the expenditure and price surveys allows statisticians to compute the current cost of the basket. Finally, this current cost is compared to a benchmark to yield an index. And the percentage change in this index is a measure of inflation.

To see how this works, let's look at an example. Assume people spend 25 percent of their income on food, 50 percent on housing and 25 percent on transportation. That's the survey information. Examples of the prices are in Table 2.2. Importantly, these are the prices of exactly the same bundle of food, the same size and quality of housing, and the same transportation for each year.

Using the numbers in Table 2.2 we can compute the cost of the basket of goods in each year:

**Cost of the basket in 2010**

$= 0.25 \times$ **Price of food** $+ 0.5 \times$ **Price of housing**
$+ 0.25 \times$ **Price of transportation**

$= 0.25 \times \$100 + 0.5 \times \$200 + 0.25 \times \$100$

$= \$150$

And for 2011, we get $165. Choosing 2010 as the base year, the index level in each year equals

$$\text{CPI} = \frac{\text{Cost of the basket in current year}}{\text{Cost of the basket in base year}} \times 100$$

The result of this computation is the fifth column of the table.

Finally, we can use the index number to compute the inflation rate from the previous year. From 2010 to 2011, this means that

$$\text{Inflation Rate 2011} = \frac{\text{CPI in 2011} - \text{CPI in 2010}}{\text{CPI in 2010}} \times 100$$

Using the numbers from Table 2.2 to compute the inflation rate in 2011, we get that

$$\frac{110 - 100}{100} \times 100 = 10\%$$

and for 2012 the result is

$$\frac{120 - 110}{110} \times 100 = 9.1\%$$

(These numbers are just for illustration. The U.S. inflation rate is closer to 2 percent.)

Inflation measured using the CPI tells us how much more money we need to give someone to restore the purchasing power they had in the earlier period when the survey was done. But adjustments in wages based on fixed-expenditure-weight inflation indices like the CPI are known to overcompensate people in an unintended way. This overstatement of inflation comes from what is known as *substitution bias*. Because inflation is not uniform, the prices of some products will increase by more than the prices of others. People can escape some of the inflation by *substituting* goods and services that have sustained less inflation for those that have sustained more. By assuming that any substitution makes people worse off, the index *overstates* the impact of price changes. To address this problem, and take into account changes in spending patterns, the Bureau of Labor Statistics now changes the weights every two years. As a result, today's CPI is a much more accurate measure of inflation than the one published a decade ago.

| Table 2.2 | Computing the Consumer Price Index |
|-----------|-------------------------------------|

| Year | Price of Food | Price of Housing | Price of Transportation | Cost of the Basket | Consumer Price Index |
|------|---------------|------------------|-------------------------|--------------------|----------------------|
| 2010 | $100 | $200 | $100 | $150 | 100 |
| 2011 | 110 | 205 | 140 | 165 | 110 |
| 2012 | 120 | 210 | 180 | 180 | 120 |

## APPLYING THE CONCEPT
### WHERE ARE ALL THOSE $100 BILLS?

A quick look at the Federal Reserve's Web site, www.federalreserve.gov, tells us that during the winter of 2009, the public held about $880 billion in United States currency. That's a huge amount. To get some sense of the size of this number, you can divide it by the U.S. population, 310 million, to get roughly $2,800 per person. For a household of four, that's an average of more than $11,000 in cash. What's even more absurd is that nearly 80 percent of the $880 billion is held in the form of $100 bills, meaning that there must be twenty-two $100 bills for each United States resident. Clearly, we do not hold all this cash in our wallets or our homes, nor does it fill the cash registers of local businesses. Where are all those $100 bills?

Not in the United States. In many countries, people do not trust their governments to protect the value of the currency they print. They fear the authorities will print too much, creating inflation. And because money is all about trust, if you don't have confidence in your government, you don't want to hold your wealth in the government's money. In many cases, the lack of faith has been warranted. When the Soviet Union collapsed in the early 1990s, the currency issued by the old regime became nearly worthless. The same thing happened in Argentina in the 1980s.

When people stop trusting the local currency, they look for substitutes. The most sought-after is the U.S. dollar bill. With the stability of the constant addition of new security features, and the stability of the government, everyone seems to have faith in it.* The U.S. Treasury estimates that between two-thirds and three-quarters of U.S. currency is held outside the United States. That's around $600 billion—and most of it is in hundreds!

*For a guide to the security features in U.S. currency, go to www.moneyfactory.gov. This constant redesign has been successful in thwarting counterfeiting. Estimates are that the total quantity [of counterfeit bills] is less than 10,000 bills outstanding. This is definitely not something that anyone should worry about.

### Figure 2.3   Growth Rates of Monetary Aggregates, 1960-2009

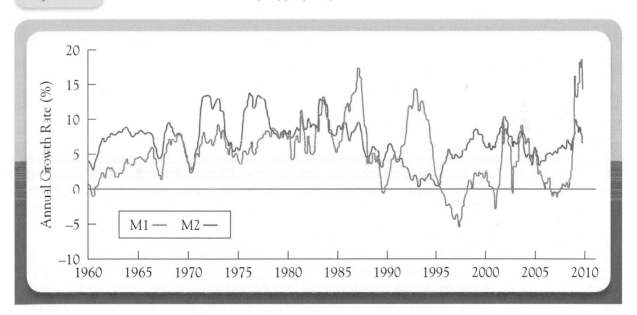

SOURCE: *Board of Governors of the Federal Reserve System, Release H.6.*

How useful is M2 in tracking inflation? We already know that when the quantity of money grows quickly, it produces very high inflation. A cross-country analysis of money growth supports this conclusion. In Turkey, Venezuela, and Ukraine, where in the last half of the 1990s the inflation rate ranged from 30 to 75 percent per year, the

**Figure 2.4** Money Growth and Inflation, Monthly 1960–2009

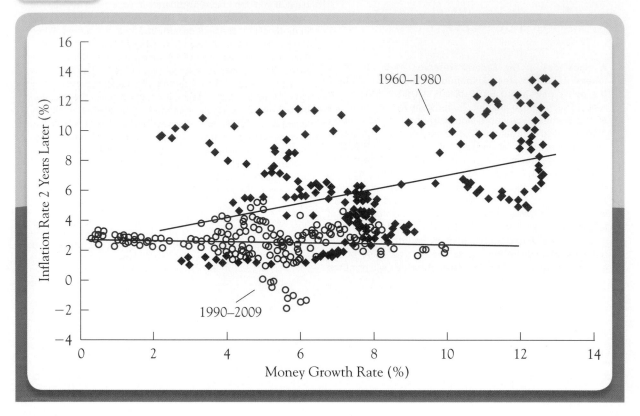

Money growth measured as the 12-month change in M2, and inflation measured as the 12-month change in the Consumer Price Index.

SOURCE: Board of Governors of the Federal Reserve System and Bureau of Labor Statistics.

money supply grew at comparable rates.[7] By contrast, in the United States, Canada, and Europe, the inflation rate averaged only about 2 percent, and the money growth rate stayed in the range of 6 to 7 percent. Because high money growth means high inflation, controlling inflation means controlling the money supply. Imagine how much inflation there would be if people could spend the $3 trillion in Monopoly dollars Parker Brothers has printed over the past seven decades!

How useful is money growth in helping us to control moderate inflation? We will address this question in detail in Chapter 20 of this book. For now, though, let's look at whether money growth helps to forecast inflation.

Figure 2.4 shows the inflation rate on the vertical axis and M2 growth *two years earlier* on the horizontal axis, both for the United States. The solid red diamonds represent data from 1960 to 1980. Note that, while the relationship is far from perfect

[7]From 1995 to 2000, inflation averaged 74 percent, 42 percent, and 30 percent, respectively, in Turkey, Venezuela, and Ukraine. At the same time, a measure of money that is close to U.S. M2 grew at 86, 33, and 36 percent per year. Data for these comparisons come from the International Monetary Fund's *International Financial Statistics*.

in those years, higher money growth was clearly associated with higher inflation two years later. In fact, the correlation was over 0.5.[8] But look at what has happened to the relationship more recently. The hollow blue dots represent data from 1990 to 2009, when there was virtually no relationship at all between the two measures. (The correlation was slightly negative.) Growth in M2 stopped being a useful tool for forecasting inflation.

There are two possible explanations for the fact that M2 no longer predicts inflation. One is that the relationship between the two applies only at high levels of inflation. Figure 2.4 shows that during the period 1960–1980, the inflation rate often rose higher than 5 percent, but from 1990 to 2009, it rarely did. Maybe the relationship between money growth and inflation doesn't exist at low levels of inflation, or it shows up only over longer periods of time. All we really know is that at low levels of money growth, inflation is likely to stay low.

An alternative explanation is that we need a new measure of money that takes into account recent changes in the way we make payments and use money. Once economists have identified the right measure, we'll be able to predict inflation again.

---

[8]Correlation is a measure of how closely two quantities are related, or change together. The numerical value ranges from +1 to −1. A positive correlation signifies that the two variables move up and down together, while a negative correlation means that they move in opposite directions.

## Terms

automated clearinghouse transaction (ACH), 27
check, 24
credit card, 27
currency, 21
debit card, 27
demand deposits, 32
electronic funds transfer, 27
e-money, 28
fiat money, 24
funding liquidity, 22
gross domestic product (GDP), 32
inflation, 30
inflation rate, 30

liquidity, 22
market liquidity, 22
M1, 32
M2, 32
means of payment, 20
monetary aggregates, 32
money, 20
payments system, 22
store of value, 21
stored-value card, 27
time deposits, 32
unit of account, 20
wealth, 20

# Chapter Lessons

1. Money is an asset that is generally accepted in payment for goods and services or repayment of debts.
   a. Money has three basic uses:
      i. Means of payment
      ii. Unit of account
      iii. Store of value
   b. Money is liquid. Liquidity is the ease with which an asset can be turned into a means of payment.
   c. For financial institutions, market liquidity is the ease with which they can sell a security or loan for money. Funding liquidity is the ease with which they can borrow to acquire a security or loan.

2. Money makes the payments system work. The payments system is the web of arrangements that allows people to exchange goods and services. There are three broad categories of payments, all of which use money at some stage.
   a. Cash
   b. Checks
   c. Electronic payments

3. In the future, money will be used less and less as a means of payment.

4. To understand the links among money, inflation, and economic growth, we need to measure the quantity of money in the economy. There are two basic measures of money.
   a. M1, the narrowest measure, includes only the most liquid assets.
   b. M2, a broader measure, includes assets not usable as means of payment.
   c. Countries with high money growth have high inflation.
   d. In countries with low inflation, money growth is a poor forecaster of inflation.

# Conceptual Problems

1. The country of Brieonia has an economy that is based largely on farming and agricultural products. The inhabitants of Brieonia use cheese as their money.
   a. Not surprisingly, the Brieonians complain bitterly about the problems that their commodity money creates. What are they?
   b. Modern medical science arrives in Brieonia, and doctors begin giving the Brieonians cholesterol tests. The results lead to the recommendation that the Brieonians reduce the amount of cheese they eat. What is the impact of this recommendation on their economy?
   c. As the economy of Brieonia becomes industrialized, what changes in the monetary system would you expect to see, and why?

2. Describe at least three ways you could pay for your morning cup of coffee. What are the advantages and disadvantages of each?

3. Explain how money encourages specialization, and how specialization improves everyone's standard of living.

4.* Could the dollar still function as the unit of account in a totally cashless society?

5. Explain why a security for which there is a financial institution acting as a market maker would be more attractive to an investor.

6. As of March 2010, 16 of the 27 countries of the European Union have adopted the euro. The remaining 11 countries, including Great Britain, Denmark, and Sweden, have retained their own currencies. What are the advantages of a common currency for someone who is traveling through Europe?

7. Using the current level of M2 from the Federal Reserve's Web site, compute the quantity of money divided by the (approximate) population of the United States. Do you think that your answer is large? Why?

8. Using data from the Federal Reserve's Web site, compute the annual percentage change in M1 and M2 since 1980. Use the data to reproduce Figure 2.3. Comment on the pattern over the last five years. Would it matter which of the two monetary aggregates you looked at?

9. Despite the efforts of the United States Treasury and the Secret Service, someone discovers a cheap way to counterfeit $100 bills. What will be the impact of this discovery on the economy?

10.* You have decided to issue your own currency and use your computer to produce some impressive looking notes. What could you do to increase the chances of these notes being accepted as a means of payment?

11. Over a nine-year period in the 16th century, King Henry VIII reduced the silver content of the British pound to one-sixth its initial value. Why do you think he did so? What do you think happened to the use of pounds as a means of payment? If you held both the old and new pounds, which would you use first, and why?

## Analytical Problems

12. Under what circumstances might you expect barter to reemerge in an economy that has fiat money as a means of payment? Can you think of an example of a country where this has happened recently?

13. You visit a tropical island that has only four goods in its economy—oranges, pineapples, coconuts, and bananas. There is no money in this economy.
    a. Draw a grid showing all the prices for this economy. (You should check your answer using the $n(n - 1)/2$ formula where $n$ is the number of goods.)
    b. An islander suggests designating oranges as the means of payment and unit of account for the economy. How many prices would there be if her suggestion was followed?
    c. Do you think the change suggested in part b is worth implementing? Why or why not?

14. Consider again the tropical island described in question 13. Under what circumstances would you recommend the issue of a paper currency by the government of the island? What advantages might this strategy have over the use of oranges as money?

*Indicates more difficult problems

15. What factors should you take into account when considering using the following assets as stores of value?
    a. Gold
    b. Real estate
    c. Stocks
    d. Government bonds

16.* Under what circumstances might money in the form of currency be the best option as a store of value?

17. Suppose a significant fall in the price of certain stocks caused the market makers in those stocks to worry about their funding liquidity. Under what circumstances might that development lead to liquidity problems in markets for other assets?

18.* Consider an economy that only produces and consumes two goods—food and apparel. Suppose the inflation rate based on the consumer price index is higher during the year than that based on the GDP deflator. Assuming underlying tastes and preferences in the economy stay the same, what can you say about food and apparel price movements during the year?

19. Assuming no interest is paid on checking accounts, what would you expect to see happen to the relative growth rates of M1 and M2 if interest rates rose significantly?

20. If money growth is related to inflation, what would you expect to happen to the inflation rates of countries that join a monetary union and adopt a common currency such as the euro?

# Chapter 3

## Financial Instruments, Financial Markets, and Financial Institutions

Long before formal financial institutions and instruments became common, there were times when people lacked the resources to meet their immediate needs. In the terminology of introductory economics, people's incomes were exceeded by their necessary consumption. When a harvest was poor, they would dip into the reserves stored from previous years or exchange assets like land and livestock for food. But often those measures were insufficient, so communities developed informal financial arrangements that allowed people to borrow or lend among themselves. After a poor harvest, those people with relatively good yields would help those with relatively poor ones. When the tables were turned, help would flow the other way. In some societies, families spread out geographically to facilitate these arrangements. For example, in rural Indian communities, households deliberately married off their daughters to families in different regions to increase the chance that their in-laws would be able to respond in a time of crisis.[1] These informal insurance arrangements ensured that everyone had enough to eat.

While family members and friends still make loans among themselves, the informal arrangements that were the mainstay of the financial system centuries ago have given way to the formal financial instruments of the modern world. Today, the international financial system exists to facilitate the design, sale, and exchange of a broad set of contracts with a very specific set of characteristics. As shown in Figure 3.1 we obtain the financial resources we need through this system in two ways: directly from markets and indirectly through institutions.

In **indirect finance**, an institution like a bank stands between the lender and the borrower, borrowing from the lender and then providing the funds to the borrower. Most of us do our borrowing and lending indirectly. If we need a loan to buy a car, we get it from a bank or finance company—that's indirect finance. Once we get the loan, the car becomes one of our assets, and the loan becomes our liability. We all have assets and liabilities. Your **assets** probably include things of value like a bank account and a computer. If you have a student loan or credit card debt, those are your **liabilities**.

In **direct finance**, borrowers sell securities directly to lenders in the financial markets. Governments and corporations finance their activities in this way. These securities become assets for the lenders who buy them and liabilities to the government or corporation that initially sells them.

Financial development is inextricably linked to economic growth. A country's financial system has to grow as its level of economic activity rises, or the country will stagnate. The role of the financial system is to facilitate production, employment, and

[1]See M. R. Rosenzweig, "Risk, Implicit Contracts, and the Family in Rural Areas of Low-Income Countries," *Economic Journal* 98 (December 1988).

**Figure 3.1** Funds Flowing through the Financial System

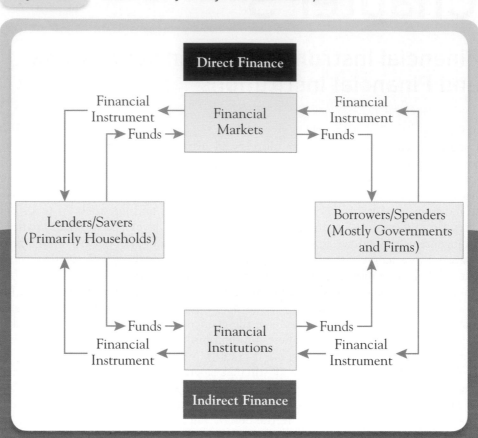

The financial system channels funds from lenders to borrowers in two ways: directly and indirectly. In **direct finance,** borrowers obtain resources by selling financial instruments like bonds and stocks in financial markets directly to lenders. In **indirect finance,** a financial institution like a bank takes the resources from the lender in the form of a deposit (or something like it) and then provides them to the borrower in the form of a loan (or the equivalent).

consumption. In a prosperous economy, people have the means to pay for things, and resources flow to their most efficient uses. Savings are funneled through the system so that they can finance investment and allow the economy to grow. The decisions made by the people who do the saving direct the investment.

In this chapter, we will survey the financial system in three steps. First, we'll study *financial instruments,* or *securities,* as they are often called. Stocks, bonds, and loans of all types are financial instruments, as are more exotic agreements like options and insurance. Exactly what are these financial instruments, and what is their role in our economy? Second, we'll look at *financial markets,* such as the New York Stock Exchange and the Nasdaq (National Association of Securities Dealers Automatic Quotations), where investors can buy and sell stocks, bonds, and various other instruments. And finally, we'll look at *financial institutions*—what they are and what they do.

# Financial Instruments

A **financial instrument** is the *written legal obligation of one party to transfer something of value, usually money, to another party at some future date, under certain conditions*. Let's dissect this definition to understand it better. First, a financial instrument is a *written legal obligation* that is subject to government enforcement. That is, a person can be compelled to take the action specified in the agreement. The enforceability of the obligation is an important feature of a financial instrument. Without enforcement of the specified terms, financial instruments would not exist.[2]

Second, a financial instrument obligates *one party to transfer something of value, usually money, to another party*. By *party*, we mean a person, company, or government. Usually the financial instrument specifies that payments will be made. For example, if you get a car loan, you are obligated to make monthly payments of a particular amount to the lender. And if you have an accident, your insurance company is obligated to fix your car, though the cost of the repair is left unspecified.

Third, a financial instrument specifies that payment will be made *at some future date*. In some cases, such as a car loan that requires payments, the dates may be very specific. In others,

SOURCE: © Wayne Bressler/The New Yorker Collection/www.cartoonbank.com.

such as car insurance, the payment is triggered when something specific happens, like an accident.

Finally, a financial instrument *specifies certain conditions* under which a payment will be made. Some agreements specify payments only when certain events happen. That is clearly the case with car insurance and with stocks as well. The holder of a stock owns a small part of a firm and so can expect to receive occasional cash payments, called *dividends*, when the company is profitable. There is no way to know in advance, however, exactly when such payments will be made. In general, financial instruments specify a number of possible contingencies under which one party is required to make a payment to another.

## Uses of Financial Instruments

Stocks, loans, and insurance are all examples of financial instruments. Taking them as a group, we can see that they have three functions (see Table 3.1). Financial instruments can act as a means of payment, and they can also be stores of value. Thus, they offer two of the three uses of money. (Remember from Chapter 2 that money is a means of payment, a unit of account, and a store of value.) But financial instruments have a third function that can make them very different from money: They allow for the transfer of risk.

---

[2]A myriad of financial arrangements that exist outside the legal system, like loan sharking, are also enforced, but those sorts of obligations are not part of the formal financial system.

**Table 3.1**   Uses of Financial Instruments

**Means of Payment:** Purchase of goods or services.

**Store of Value:** Transfer of purchasing power into the future.

**Transfer of Risk:** Transfer of risk from one person or company to another.

Recall that a means of payment is something that is generally accepted as payment for goods and services or repayment of a debt. It is possible to pay for purchases with financial instruments, even if they don't look much like money. An example is the willingness of employees to accept a company's stock as payment for working. (This means of payment was very popular in the late 1990s, when the stock market was booming.) While we cannot yet pay for groceries with shares of stock, the time may come when we can. For now, although some financial instruments may function as means of payment, they aren't terribly good ones.

Having a store of value means that your consumption doesn't need to exactly match your income. For days, months, and years, if necessary, you can spend more than you make, repaying the difference later. Even though most of us are paid weekly or monthly, we eat every day. As stores of value, financial instruments like stocks and bonds are thought to be better than money. Over time, they generate increases in wealth that are bigger than those we can obtain from holding money in most of its forms. These higher payoffs are compensation for higher levels of risk, because the payoffs from holding most financial instruments are generally more uncertain than those that arise from holding money. Nevertheless, many financial instruments can be used to transfer purchasing power into the future.

RISK

The third use of a financial instrument lies in its ability to *transfer risk* between the buyer and the seller. Most financial instruments involve some sort of risk transfer. For example, think of wheat farmers. If only one farm has a huge harvest, that farmer does very well. But if everyone's harvest is huge, then prices can plummet and individual farms can lose money. The risk that the harvest will be too good, resulting in low grain prices, is a risk that most individual farmers do not want to take. A *wheat futures contract* allows the farmer to transfer that risk to someone else. A wheat futures contract is a financial instrument in which two parties agree to exchange a fixed quantity of wheat on a prearranged future date at a specified price. By fixing the price at which the crop will be sold well in advance of the harvest, the farmer can forget about what happens in the wheat market because the risk has been transferred to someone else.

Insurance contracts are another example of a financial instrument that transfers risk—in this case, from individuals to an insurance company. Because a car accident can be financially catastrophic, we buy car insurance and transfer the risk to an insurance company. Because insurance companies make similar guarantees to a large group of people, they have the capacity to shoulder the risk. While the timing of an individual automobile accident is impossible to forecast, a predictable percentage of a large group of drivers will experience accidents over a given period.

## Characteristics of Financial Instruments: Standardization and Information

As is obvious from the definition of a financial instrument, these sorts of contracts can be very complex. If you don't believe it, take a look at the fine print in a car insurance policy, a student loan, or even a credit card agreement. Complexity is costly. The more complicated something is, the more it costs to create and the more difficult it is to

## LESSONS FROM THE CRISIS
### LEVERAGE

Households and firms often borrow to make investments. Obtaining a mortgage for a new home or selling a corporate bond to build a new plant are common examples. The use of borrowing to finance part of an investment is called *leverage.** Leverage played a key role in the financial crisis of 2007-2009, so it is worth understanding how leverage relates to risk and how it can make the financial system vulnerable.

Modern economies rely heavily on borrowing to make investments. They are all leveraged. Yet, the more leverage, the greater the risk that an adverse surprise will lead to bankruptcy. If two households own houses of the same value, the one that has borrowed more—the one that is more highly leveraged and has less net worth—is the more likely to default during a temporary slump in income. This example could apply equally well to firms, financial institutions, or even countries.

Financial institutions are much more highly leveraged than households or firms, typically owning assets of about 10 times their net worth. During the crisis, some important financial firms leveraged more than 30 times their net worth.† Such high leverage meant that these firms would be vulnerable even to a minor decline in the value of their assets. For example, when a borrower is leveraged more than 30 times, a drop as small as 3 percent in asset prices could eliminate the cushion created by the net worth and lead to bankruptcy.

When highly leveraged financial institutions experience a loss, they usually try to reduce their leverage—that is, to *deleverage*—by selling assets and issuing securities that raise their net worth (see accompanying figure). However, the financial system cannot deleverage all at once. When too many institutions try to sell assets simultaneously, their efforts will almost surely prove counterproductive: falling prices will mean more losses, diminishing their net worth further, raising leverage, and making the assets they hold seem riskier, thereby compelling further sales.

This "paradox of leverage" reinforces the destabilizing liquidity spiral discussed in Chapter 2 (see Lessons from the Crisis: Market Liquidity, Funding Liquidity, and Making Markets). Both spirals feed a vicious cycle of falling prices and widespread deleveraging that was a hallmark of the financial crisis of 2007-2009. The financial system steadied only after a plunge of many asset prices and massive government interventions.

*For a technical definition of leverage, see the Tools of the Trade box in Chapter 5.

†A bank's net worth—its assets minus liabilities—is commonly known as *bank capital.* We will discuss this in more detail in Chapter 12.

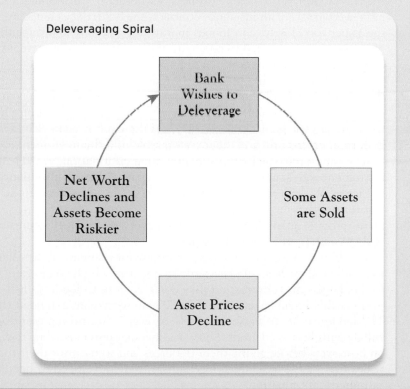

Deleveraging Spiral

understand. As a rule, people do not want to bear these costs. Yes, the owner of an oil tanker may be willing to go to the expense of negotiating a specific insurance contract for each voyage a ship makes. The same owner may agree to make premium payments based on the load carried, the distance traveled, the route taken, and the weather expected. But for most of us, the cost of such custom contracts is simply too high.

In fact, people on both sides of financial contracts shy away from specialized agreements. Instead, they use standardized financial instruments to overcome the potential costs of complexity. Because of *standardization,* most of the financial instruments that we encounter on a day-to-day basis are very homogeneous. For example, most mortgages feature a standard application process and offer standardized terms. Automobile insurance contracts generally offer only certain standard options.

Standardization of terms makes sense. If all financial instruments differed in critical ways, most of us would not be able to understand them. Their usefulness would be severely limited. If the shares of Microsoft stock sold to one person differed in a crucial way from the shares sold to someone else, for instance, potential investors might not understand what they were buying. Even more important, the resale and trading of the shares would become virtually impossible, which would certainly discourage anyone from purchasing them in the first place. From this, we conclude that arrangements that obligate people to make payments to one another cannot all be one-of-a-kind arrangements.

**INFORMATION**

Another characteristic of financial instruments is that they communicate *information,* summarizing certain essential details about the issuer. How much do you really want to learn about the original issuer of a financial instrument? Or if you are purchasing an existing instrument, how much do you want to have to know about the person who is selling it to you? Surely, the less you feel you need to know to feel secure about the transaction, the better. Regardless of whether the instrument is a stock, a bond, a futures contract, or an insurance contract, the holder does not want to have to watch the issuer too closely; continuous monitoring is costly and difficult. Thus, financial instruments are designed to eliminate the expensive and time-consuming process of collecting such information.

A number of mechanisms exist to reduce the cost of monitoring the behavior of the counterparties to a financial arrangement. A **counterparty** is the person or institution on the other side of a contract. If you obtain a car loan from your local bank, then you are the bank's counterparty and the bank is yours. In the case of a stock or bond, the issuing firm and the investors who hold the instrument are counterparties.

The solution to the high cost of obtaining information on the parties to a financial instrument is to standardize both the instrument and the information provided about the issuer. We can also hire a specialist whom we all trust to do the monitoring. The institutions that have arisen over the years to support the existence of financial instruments provide an environment in which everyone can feel secure about the behavior of the counterparties to an agreement.

In addition to simply summarizing information, financial instruments are designed to handle the problem of *asymmetric information,* which comes from the fact that borrowers have some information they don't disclose to lenders. Instead of buying new ovens, will a bread baker use a $50,000 loan to take an extended vacation in Tahiti? The lender wants to make sure the borrower is not misrepresenting what he or she will do with borrowed funds. Thus, the financial system is set up to gather information on borrowers before giving them resources and to monitor their use of the resources afterwards. These specialized mechanisms were developed to handle the problem of asymmetric information.

## Underlying versus Derivative Instruments

There are two fundamental classes of financial instruments. The first, **underlying instruments** (sometimes called *primitive securities*), are used by savers/lenders to transfer resources directly to investors/borrowers. Through these instruments, the financial system improves the efficient allocation of resources in the real economy.

The primary examples of underlying securities or instruments are stocks and bonds that offer payments based solely on the issuer's status. Bonds, for example, make payments depending on the solvency of the firm that issued them. Stocks sometimes pay dividends when the issuing corporation's profits are sufficient.

The second class of financial instruments is known as **derivative instruments**. Their value and payoffs are "derived" from the behavior of the underlying instruments. The most common examples of derivatives are futures and options. In general, derivatives specify a payment to be made between the person who sells the instrument and the person who buys it. The amount of the payment depends on various factors associated with the price of the underlying asset. The primary use of derivatives is to shift risk among investors. We will see some examples in a moment; Chapter 9 discusses derivatives in detail.

## A Primer for Valuing Financial Instruments

Why are some financial instruments more valuable than others? If you look at *The Wall Street Journal*, you'll see the prices of many bonds and stocks. They are quite different from each other. Not only that, but from day to day, the prices of an individual bond or stock can vary quite a bit. What characteristics affect the price someone will pay to buy or sell a financial instrument?

Four fundamental characteristics influence the value of a financial instrument (see Table 3.2): (1) the *size* of the payment that is promised, (2) *when* the promised payment is to be made, (3) the *likelihood* that the payment will be made, and (4) the *circumstances* under which the payment is to be made. Let's look at each one of these traits.

First, people will pay more for an instrument that obligates the issuer to pay the holder $1,000 than for one that offers a payment of $100. Regardless of any other conditions, this simply must be true: *The bigger the promised payment, the more valuable the financial instrument.*

Second, if you are promised a payment of $100 sometime in the future, you will want to know when you will receive it. Receiving $100 tomorrow is different from receiving $100 next year. This simple example illustrates a very general proposition: *The sooner the payment is made, the more valuable is the promise to make it.* Time has

TIME

---

**Table 3.2**   What Makes a Financial Instrument Valuable?

**Size:** Payments that are larger are more valuable.

**Timing:** Payments that are made sooner are more valuable.

**Likelihood:** Payments that are more likely to be made are more valuable.

**Circumstances:** Payments that are made when we need them most are more valuable.

value because of opportunity cost. If you receive a payment immediately, you have an opportunity to invest or consume it right away. If you don't receive the payment until later, you lose that opportunity.

**RISK**

The third factor that affects the value of a financial instrument is the odds that the issuer will meet the obligation to make the payment. Regardless of how conscientious and diligent the party who made the promise is, there remains some possibility that the payment will not be made. Because risk requires compensation, the impact of this uncertainty on the value of a financial instrument is clear: *The more likely it is that the payment will be made, the more valuable the financial instrument.*

Finally, the value of a financial instrument is affected by the conditions under which a promised payment is to be made. Insurance is the best example. We buy car insurance to receive a payment if we have an accident, so we can repair the car. No one buys insurance that pays off when good things happen. *Payments that are made when we need them most are more valuable than other payments.*[3]

## Examples of Financial Instruments

We'll have quite a bit to say about financial instruments in Part II of the book. For now, let's take a look at some of the most common varieties. The best way to organize them is by whether they are used primarily as stores of value or for trading risk.

### Financial Instruments Used Primarily as Stores of Value

1. **Bank loans.** A borrower obtains resources from a lender immediately in exchange for a promised set of payments in the future. The borrower, who can be either an individual or a firm, needs funds to make an investment or purchase, while the lender is looking for a way to store value into the future.

2. **Bonds.** Bonds are a form of loan. In exchange for obtaining funds today, a corporation or government promises to make payments in the future. While bond payments are often stated in fixed dollars, they need not be. Unlike most bank loans, most bonds can be bought and sold in financial markets. Like bank loans, bonds are used by the borrower to finance current operations and by the lender to store value.

3. **Home mortgages.** Most people who wish to purchase a home need to borrow some portion of the funds. A mortgage is a loan that is used to purchase real estate. In exchange for the funds, the borrower promises to make a series of payments. The house is collateral for the loan. **Collateral** is the term used to describe specific assets a borrower pledges to protect the lender's interests in the event of nonpayment. If the payments aren't made, the lender can take the house, a process called *foreclosure*.

4. **Stocks.** The holder of a share of a company's stock owns a small piece of the firm and is entitled to part of its profits. The owner of a firm sells stock as a way of raising funds to enlarge operations as well as a way of transferring the risk of ownership to someone else. Buyers of stocks use them primarily as stores of wealth.

---

[3]This conclusion is related to the principle of declining marginal utility, which you may recall from your study of microeconomics. The idea is that the satisfaction obtained from consumption declines as the level of consumption increases. Each succeeding candy bar brings less pleasure than the last one. Thus, a financial instrument that pays off when marginal utility is high is worth more than one that pays off when marginal utility is low. This means that payoffs that are made when income and wealth are low are more valuable than payoffs that are made when income and wealth are high.

## YOUR FINANCIAL WORLD
### Disability Income Insurance

People insure their houses so they can rebuild them if they burn down. They insure their cars so they can repair them if they have an accident. And they insure their lives so their families will be financially secure if they die prematurely. But few people insure their most important asset: their ability to produce an income. The biggest risk all of us face is that we will become disabled and lose our earning capacity. Insuring it should be one of our highest priorities.

If you think this advice is alarmist, just look at a few numbers. The odds of a man becoming disabled for 90 days or longer between the ages of 20 and 60 are one in five. For women they're somewhat lower, more like one in seven. In fact, the chance you'll become disabled during your working life is far higher than the chance of your house burning down—which over 40 years is about 1 in 30.*

Fortunately, you may already have some disability insurance. The government provides some through Social Security; your employer may insure you; and if you're injured on the job and can't work, there is always workers' compensation insurance. But is that enough? You should evaluate what your needs are likely to be. If the disability insurance you already have is not enough, you should buy more. While it isn't very pleasant to think about what would happen if you became disabled, you need to do it. Surely this is one risk you should transfer to someone else.

*The chance of any particular house burning down is 1 in 1,200 in a given year. So there is a 1,199 chance in 1,200 of a house *not* burning down in a particular year. This means that the probability of a house *not* burning down in 40 years is $(1{,}199/1{,}200)^{40} = 0.967$. So the probability of the house burning down is 0.033, which is 1 in 30.

5. **Asset-backed securities.** Asset-backed securities are shares in the returns or payments arising from specific assets, such as home mortgages, student loans, credit card debt, or even movie box-office receipts. Investors purchase shares in the revenue that comes from these underlying assets. The most prominent of these instruments are **mortgage-backed securities**, which bundle a large number of mortgages together into a pool in which shares are then sold. Securities backed by *subprime* mortgages—loans to borrowers who are less likely to repay than borrowers of conventional mortgages—played an important role in the financial crisis of 2007–2009 (see Chapter 7, Lessons from the Crisis: Subprime Mortgages). The owners of these securities receive a share of the payments made by the homeowners who borrowed the funds. Asset-backed securities are an innovation that allows funds in one part of the country to find productive uses elsewhere. Thus, the availability of some sorts of financing no longer depends on local credit conditions.[4]

## Financial Instruments Used Primarily to Transfer Risk

1. **Insurance contracts.** The primary purpose of insurance policies is to assure that payments will be made under particular, and often rare, circumstances. These instruments exist expressly to transfer risk from one party to another.

2. **Futures contracts.** A futures contract is an agreement between two parties to exchange a fixed quantity of a commodity (such as wheat or corn) or an asset (such as a bond) at a fixed price on a set future date. A futures contract always specifies the *price* at which the transaction will take place. A futures contract is a

---

[4]For an introduction to how asset-backed securities work, see Andreas Jobst, "What is Securitization?" *Finance and Development*, International Monetary Fund, September 2008.

type of derivative instrument, since its value is based on the price of some other asset. It is used to transfer the risk of price fluctuations from one party to another.

3. **Options.** Like futures contracts, options are derivative instruments whose prices are based on the value of some underlying asset. Options give the holder the right, but not the obligation, to buy or sell a fixed quantity of the underlying asset at a predetermined price either on a specified date or at any time during a specified period.

These are just a few examples of the most prominent financial instruments. Together, they allow people to buy and sell almost any sort of payment on any date under any circumstances. Thus, they offer the opportunity to store value and trade risk in almost any way that one might want.[5] When you encounter a financial instrument for the first time, try to figure out whether it is used primarily for storing value or for transferring risk. Then try to identify which characteristics determine its value.

# Financial Markets

MARKETS

**Financial markets** are the places where financial instruments are bought and sold. They are the economy's central nervous system, relaying and reacting to information quickly, allocating resources, and determining prices. In doing so, financial markets enable both firms and individuals to find financing for their activities. When they are working well, new firms can start up and existing firms can grow; individuals who don't have sufficient savings can borrow to purchase cars and houses. By ensuring that resources are available to those who can put them to the best use, and by keeping the costs of transactions as low as possible, these markets promote economic efficiency. When financial markets cease to function properly, resources are no longer channeled to their best possible use, and we all suffer.[6]

In this section, we will look at the role of financial markets and the economic justification for their existence. Next, we will examine the structure of the markets and how they are organized. Finally, we will look at the characteristics that are essential for the markets to work smoothly.

## The Role of Financial Markets

Financial markets serve three roles in our economic system (see Table 3.3). They offer savers and borrowers *liquidity*; they pool and communicate *information*; and they allow *risk sharing*. We encountered the concept of liquidity in our discussion of money, where we defined it as the ease with which an asset can be turned into money without loss of value. Without financial markets and the institutional structure that supports them, selling the assets we own would be extremely difficult. Thus, we cannot overstate the importance of liquidity for the smooth operation of an economy. Just think what would happen if the stock market were open only one day a month. Stocks would surely become less attractive investments. If you had an emergency and needed

---

[5]An important exception is the common desire to borrow using future income as collateral. While young people with good career prospects might wish to spend their future earnings now, lenders worry that such loans will diminish the borrower's incentive to work and repay.

[6]An example demonstrates the point. Following the September 11, 2001, terrorist attacks, the New York Stock Exchange became inaccessible, and other markets were not functioning properly. Alarmed government officials took measures to ensure that markets would open as soon as possible so that trading could proceed. Without these efforts to get the financial markets up and running, the financial system might quickly have come to a standstill.

money immediately, you probably would not be able to sell your stocks in time. Liquidity is a crucial characteristic of financial markets.

Related to liquidity is the fact that financial markets need to be designed in a way that keeps transactions costs—the cost of buying and selling—low. If you want to buy or sell a stock, you have to hire someone to do it for you. The process is complex, and we need not go into it in detail, but you must pay a broker to complete the purchase or sale on your behalf. While this service can't be free, it is important to keep its cost relatively low. The very high trading volumes that we see in the stock market—several billion shares per day in the United States—is evidence that U.S. stock markets have low transactions costs as well as being liquid. (One market in which transactions costs are high is the market for housing. Once you add together everything you pay agents, bankers, and lawyers, you have spent almost 10 percent of the sale price of the house to complete the transaction. The housing market is not very liquid.)

| Table 3.3 | The Role of Financial Markets |
|---|---|

**Liquidity:** Ensure that owners of financial instruments can buy and sell them cheaply and easily.

**Information:** Pool and communicate information about the issuer of a financial instrument.

**Risk Sharing:** Provide individuals with a place to buy and sell risks, sharing them with others.

Financial markets pool and communicate information about the issuers of financial instruments, summarizing it in the form of a price. Does a company have good prospects for future growth and profits? If so, its stock price will be high; if not, its stock price will be low. Is a borrower likely to repay a bond? The more likely repayment is, the higher the price of the bond. Obtaining the answers to these questions is time consuming and costly. Most of us just don't have the resources or know-how to do it. Instead, we turn to the financial markets to summarize the information for us so that we can look it up in the newspaper or on the Internet.

Finally, while financial instruments are the means for transferring risk, financial markets are the place where we can do it. The markets allow us to buy and sell risks, holding the ones we want and getting rid of the ones we don't want. As we will see in Chapter 5, a prudent investor holds a collection of assets called a **portfolio**, which includes a number of stocks and bonds as well as various forms of money. A well-designed portfolio has a lower overall risk than any individual stock or bond. An investor constructs it by buying and selling financial instruments in the marketplace. Without the market, we wouldn't be able to share risk.

## The Structure of Financial Markets

There are lots of financial markets and many ways to categorize them. Just take a look at any source of business news. You will see charts and tables for domestic stocks, global stocks, bonds and interest rates, the dollar exchange rate, commodities, and more. Keep going and you will find references to stock markets, bond markets, credit markets, currency trading, options, futures, new securities, and on and on. Grasping the overall structure of all of these financial markets requires grouping them in some sort of meaningful way—but how?

There are three possibilities (see Table 3.4 on page 54). First, we can distinguish between markets where new financial instruments are sold and those where they are resold, or traded. Second, we can categorize the markets by the way they trade financial instruments—whether on a centralized exchange or not. And third, we can group them based on the type of instrument they trade—those that are used primarily as a store of value or those that are used to transfer risk. We'll use the vocabulary that is

# TOOLS OF THE TRADE
Trading in Financial Markets

Trading is what makes financial markets work. No one would ever buy a stock or bond if he or she couldn't sell it. Let's take a brief look at how trading works. For this example, we will focus on the stock market.

Placing an order in a stock market is a bit like going to a fast-food restaurant or a coffee shop. You have to enter your order and wait to be served. Not only that, but the order can be very complicated, and how long you wait depends on both what you ordered and on how many other people are waiting to be served.

If you place an order, it will have a number of important characteristics.

- The stock you wish to trade.
- Whether you wish to buy or sell.
- The size of the order—how many shares you wish to trade.
- The price at which you would like to trade.

You can place either a *market order*, in which case your order is executed at the most favorable price currently available on the other side, or a *limit order*, which places a maximum on the price you wish to pay to buy or a minimum on the price you will accept to sell. Placing a market order means you value speed over price; you want the trade to occur as soon as possible and are willing to pay for the privilege. By contrast, you can specify a time at which the limit order is canceled if it hasn't been filled.

Executing the trade requires finding someone to take the other side. To do this, you can ask a broker to do it, or your broker can provide "direct access" to electronic trading networks. Even though IBM is traded on the New York Stock Exchange, you are not required to send an order to buy 100 shares of IBM to the floor of the exchange. Instead, you can request execution through an electronic communication network (ECN) like Arca (that is part of the NYSE) or Instinet (that is part of Nasdaq).

Electronic networks operate in a very simple way. If you want to buy, you enter a bid. If your bid is better than everyone else's, and there is someone willing to sell at or below the price you bid, then you trade immediately. Otherwise, your bid goes into an order book to wait for a seller. On a network like Arca or Instinet, customer orders interact automatically following a set of priority rules established by the network, but with no one acting as an intermediary in the transaction. The liquidity in the market is provided by the customers.

For a stock like IBM or GE, the New York Stock Exchange is an alternative place to send the order. A NYSE order may be satisfied electronically, through Arca. On the NYSE, liquidity provided by customer orders is supplemented by designated market makers (DMMs). A DMM is the person on the floor of the Stock Exchange charged with making a market, ensuring that it is liquid so that people can both buy and sell and that prices aren't overly volatile. Electronic mechanisms match the orders as they come in, keeping track of orders that are outstanding. To make the system work, DMMs often buy and sell on their own account.*

On the next page is a portion of the screen from an independent ECN known as BATS. The screen shows outstanding bids and offers for the common stock of General Electric (GE)

common as of this writing. Bear in mind that there are no hard and fast rules for the terminology used to describe these markets, so it may change.

## Primary versus Secondary Markets

A **primary financial market** is one in which a borrower obtains funds from a lender by selling newly issued securities. Businesses use primary markets to raise the resources they need to grow. Governments use them to finance ongoing operations. Most of the action in primary markets occurs out of public view. While some companies that want to raise funds go directly to the financial markets themselves, most use an investment bank. The bank examines the company's financial health to determine whether the proposed issue is sound Assuming that it is, the bank will determine a price and then purchase the securities in preparation for resale to clients. This activity, called *underwriting,* is usually very profitable. Since small investors are not customers of large investment banks, most of us do not have access to these new securities.

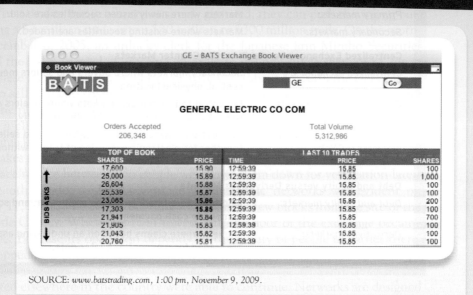

at 1:00 pm on November 9, 2009. The system shows more than 100,000 limit orders on each side of the market (bids in blue; asks in pink) within a few cents of the most recent execution price ($15.85). The system combines the sell (buy) orders of different customers at each price, so we see the aggregate supply (demand) for the stock at that price. If a market sell order for 100 shares were to arrive, the system would match that order with the highest bid ($15.85). If a market buy order for 100 shares were to arrive, the system would match that order with the lowest offer ($15.86). More than 5,000,000 GE shares already had traded that day.

*For a description of designated market makers, see http://www. nyse.com/pdfs/fact_sheet_dmm.pdf.

Everyone knows about **secondary financial markets**. Those are the markets where people can buy and sell existing securities. If you want to buy a share of stock in IBM or Microsoft, you won't get it from the company itself. Instead, you'll buy it in a secondary market from another investor. The prices in the secondary markets are the ones we hear about in the news.

**Centralized Exchanges, Over-the-Counter Markets, and Electronic Communication Networks**    Buying a stock or bond is not like buying a new pair of shoes. You can't just go into a store, ask for the stock you want, pay for it with your credit card, and walk out with it in a bag. Instead, you can either ask a broker to buy the stock for you or you can do it yourself on an electronic exchange. In both cases, the transaction is in a secondary market. The organization of secondary financial markets is changing rapidly. Historically there have been two types. Some organizations, like the New York Stock Exchange and the large exchanges in London

**IN THE NEWS**

Lessons of the Financial Crisis—One Year Later

## THE WALL STREET JOURNAL.
WSJ.com

### by Gregory Zuckerman

**August 30, 2009**

The numbers hardly tell the story.

Today, the Dow Jones Industrial Average stands roughly 2000 points below where it was on this end-of-summer weekend one year ago. No one knew then, of course, but the U.S. stock market and the world economy were just days from historic calamity, unprecedented in the lives of anyone born in the last 80 years.

And today? We are nearly six months into one of the most impressive bull markets in memory. . . .

Go figure. It's been a year of horrors and opportunities for investors.

The troubles began in 2007 with rising defaults among "subprime" mortgage borrowers and a market slowly drifting downward from an all-time high set that October.

But then critical mass was reached over a stunning two-week period last September. The U.S. government rapidly took over mortgage-lending giants Fannie Mae and Freddie Mac, along with huge insurer American International Group.

Onetime Wall Street power Lehman Brothers filed for bankruptcy, wounded brokerage giant Merrill Lynch rushed into the arms of Bank of America, and federal regulators seized Washington Mutual in the largest bank failure in U.S. history.

At one point, panicked investors offered to buy U.S. Treasury bills without asking for any return on their investment, hoping to simply find somewhere safe to put their money.

By early 2009, when the stock market hit what looks like its post-crisis bottom, the collapse had vaporized more than $30 trillion, a decade's worth of investment gains.

Yet, almost as stunning as the fall, has been the stock market's recovery. Although still well below 2007 levels, the market has defied horrible levels of unemployment, a housing market that is still barely breathing, and an economy bound in recession.

There are ample signs that the worst is over, of course, and a recovery may already be under way. (Yes, but tell that to the millions who have lost jobs, business owners who have shut down their companies, or the legions whose retirement nest eggs may not recover in time. Their personal recessions may never be over.)

So what have investors learned from all this? With a full year of hindsight, here are some lessons of the crisis:

Diversification doesn't always work. Financial advisers have drilled into investors the need for diversification. But the past year has taught that spreading money around the globe and into different asset classes sometimes results in less safety than one would expect. The lesson isn't to put more eggs in a single basket, but to acknowledge the limits of diversification.

Markets are more interlocked than ever before. When the U.S. markets began to fall, investors pulled money from foreign stocks, almost every kind of bond and even investments that sometimes are sold as a way to protect a portfolio, such as commodities and hedge funds. Even gold, a traditional haven, experienced some rough periods as investors raised cash by selling almost anything they could get rid of.

Understand every investment. Even the most sophisticated investors can be fooled by complicated investments.

In October of last year, Chuck Prince, Citigroup's CEO [chief executive officer], said "we expect to return to a more normal earnings environment as the year progresses," while UBS CEO Marcel Rohner said "we expect positive investment bank performance." But Citigroup and UBS turned into two of the biggest losers from the crisis, as the seemingly safe collateralized debt obligations on their books led to billions of dollars in losses.

Just as banks need to make sure they understand the risks and downsides of their holdings, so do individual investors.

Make sure your portfolio is as liquid as you need it to be. Some of the biggest mistakes were made by investors who thought their holdings were more "liquid," or easy to exit without incurring big cost, than they actually were.

Even university endowments run by some of the most sophisticated investors were surprised to find that their hedge funds, private equity and other holdings were difficult to exit in the heat of the crisis. They've vowed to do a better job of matching their needs and their investments.

Government works. The aggressive steps by the government seem to have helped avert an even deeper recession, or even a depression, suggesting that big government can sometimes be a friend of business.

But questions remain about whether all the spending will eventually lead to inflation or other problems, making this a qualified lesson of the period.

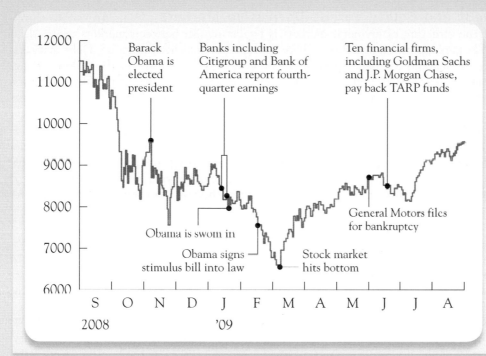

**What a Ride**
The Dow Jones Industrial Average zigged and zagged over the past year as the market reacted to economic calamity and unprecedented government involvement.

SOURCE: *WSJ Market Data Group*

Within the chart:

12000
11000
10000
9000
8000
7000
6000

Barack Obama is elected president

Banks including Citigroup and Bank of America report fourth-quarter earnings

Ten financial firms, including Goldman Sachs and J.P. Morgan Chase, pay back TARP funds

Obama is sworn in

Obama signs stimulus bill into law

Stock market hits bottom

General Motors files for bankruptcy

S O N D J F M A M J J A

2008          '09

Don't let financial companies become too big to fail. It's not clear if regulators fully understand this lesson of the fiasco. For years, critics said companies like Fannie Mae and Freddie Mac had grown too large, and that firms like Lehman Brothers carried too much debt. Today, firms like Goldman Sachs and J.P. Morgan Chase are growing and might end up too big to be allowed to crumble, some analysts say.

Factor into any investment equation a worst-case scenario. Too many investors piled into housing-related investments, confident that real estate never had dropped on a national basis or that investment-grade mortgage investments never defaulted. They would have been better served to examine potential holes in their bullish stance.

Don't get too gloomy. Like the old saying goes, in every crisis is an opportunity. As nations around the globe confronted the crisis and pumped huge sums into their economies, the economy stabilized. And even as the recession looked its worst, the stock market began to sense that a recovery was coming.

SOURCE: *The Wall Street Journal Online.* "Lessons of the Financial Crisis—One Year Later" by Gregory Zuckerman, August 30, 2009. Copyright 2009 by Dow Jones & Company, Inc. Reproduced with permission of Dow Jones & Company, Inc. in the formats Textbook and Other Book via Copyright Clearance Center.

## LESSONS OF THE ARTICLE

The article highlights the large swings in financial markets during the financial crisis of 2007-2009. Before the crisis, professional investors had made their own institutions and the overall financial system vulnerable by taking on too much risk (see Lessons from the Crisis: Leverage, earlier in this chapter). When the crisis hit, they faced a shortfall of liquidity (see Chapter 2, Lessons from the Crisis: Market Liquidity, Funding Liquidity, and Making Markets). At the height of the crisis, panic purchases of Treasury bills constituted a classic "flight to safety" by investors seeking the most liquid assets. Liquidity swings caused many financial markets—including the stock market—to plunge and rebound together.

erupted. Exchanges seem inclined to take advantage of their technologies and customer relationships by linking across borders to lower costs and speed transactions. Whether these economies of scale and scope lead to further international consolidation will depend both on performance *and* on the attitudes of various governments toward foreign ownership and operation of national exchanges.

**Debt and Equity versus Derivative Markets** A useful way to think of the structure of financial markets is to distinguish between markets where *debt and equity* are traded and those where *derivative instruments* are traded. **Debt markets** are the markets for loans, mortgages, and bonds—the instruments that allow for the transfer of resources from lenders to borrowers and at the same time give investors a store of value for their wealth. **Equity markets** are the markets for stocks. For the most part, stocks are traded in the countries where the companies are based. U.S. companies' stocks are traded in the United States, Japanese stocks in Japan, Chinese stocks in China, and so on. Derivative markets are the markets where investors trade instruments like futures and options, which are designed primarily to transfer risk. To put it another way, in debt and equity markets, actual claims are bought and sold for immediate cash payment; in derivative markets, investors make agreements that are settled later.

Looking at debt instruments in more detail, we can place them in one of two categories, depending on the length of time until the final payment, called the loan's maturity. Debt instruments that are completely repaid in less than a year (from their original issue date) are traded in **money markets**, while those with a maturity of more than a year are traded in **bond markets**. *Money market instruments* have different names and are treated somewhat differently from *bond market instruments*. For example, the United States Treasury issues Treasury bills, which have a maturity of less than one year when they are issued and are traded in the money market. U.S. Treasury bonds, which are repaid over 10 years or more, are traded in the bond markets. The same distinction can be made for large private corporations, which issue commercial paper when borrowing for short periods and corporate bonds when borrowing for long periods.

## Characteristics of a Well-Run Financial Market

Well-run financial markets exhibit a few essential characteristics that are related to the role we ask them to play in our economies. First, these markets must be designed to keep transaction costs low. Second, the information the market pools and communicates must be both accurate and widely available. If analysts do not communicate accurate assessments of the firms they follow, the markets will not generate the correct prices for the firms' stocks. The prices of financial instruments reflect all the information that is available to market participants. Those prices are the link between the financial markets and the real economy, ensuring that resources are allocated to their most efficient uses. If the information that goes into the market is wrong, then the prices will be wrong, and the economy will not operate as effectively as it could.

INFORMATION

Finally, investors need protection. For the financial system to work at all, borrowers' promises to pay lenders must be credible. Individuals must be assured that their investments will not simply be stolen. In countries that have weak investor protections, firms can behave deceptively, borrowing when they have no intention of repaying the funds and going unpunished. The lack of proper safeguards dampens people's willingness to invest. Thus, governments are an essential part of financial markets,

## LESSONS FROM THE CRISIS
### INTERBANK LENDING

Interbank lending is a critical foundation of modern financial markets. In normal times, banks lend to each other in large volumes at low cost for periods ranging from overnight to a few months. These liquid, interbank loans are the marginal source of funds for many banks, and their cost guides other lending rates.

Interbank lending helps smooth the function of markets because it allows banks to satisfy temporary, localized excess demand for funding liquidity (see Chapter 2, Lessons from the Crisis: Market Liquidity, Funding Liquidity, and Making Markets). If a bank could not reliably borrow and lend each day to offset the random ebbs and flows of its deposits and loans, it would need to hold a larger volume of cash to insure itself against unanticipated payment outflows or loan demand. For the banking system as a whole, such extra cash holdings waste resources that could be lent profitably elsewhere.

Events occasionally strain the interbank market. For example, on September 11, 2001, physical disruptions and communication obstacles boosted banks' demand for funds. The Federal Reserve supplied extraordinary amounts of liquidity for a few days until efficient interbank lending was restored.

The financial crisis of 2007–2009 triggered much greater, and more prolonged, strains in interbank lending. Rather than lend out additional liquid assets, anxious banks preferred to hold them in case their own needs might rise. Banks also grew concerned about the safety of their trading partners as the level of trust and confidence plunged. The rising cost and reduced availability of interbank loans created a vicious circle of increased caution, greater demand for liquid assets, reduced willingness to lend, and higher loan rates.

The waves of the financial crisis may be seen in the accompanying figure that shows the extra cost (or *spread*) of an interbank loan over the expected federal funds rate (the interest rate that the U.S. Federal Reserve chooses to control as its primary policy tool—see Chapter 16). Beginning in August 2007, this spread jumped and remained elevated. When Lehman Brothers failed on September 15, 2008, the spread leapt above 350 basis points as panic dried up interbank lending.

Unprecedented actions by governments to add liquidity and guarantee bank debt eventually eased the record interbank lending strains in 2009, but these actions did not prevent extensive disruptions in the financial system and the global economy. The financial crisis made painfully clear to surviving financial institutions that they cannot always count on being able to borrow at a low cost when needed.

**Strains in the Interbank Market: Interbank Lending Rate *Minus* Expected Federal Reserve Policy Interest Rate, 2007–2009**

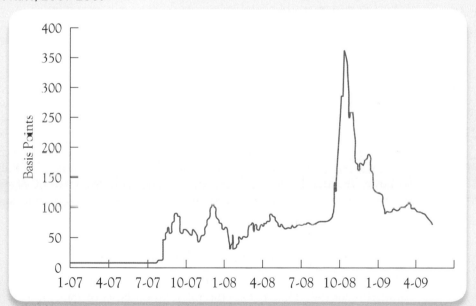

SOURCE: *www.bloomberg.com*

Note: The vertical scale is in basis points (a basis point is 0.01 percent). The figure shows the gap between two measures: (1) the cost of an interbank loan, represented by the three-month London Interbank Offered Rate (LIBOR, see Chapter 13) and (2) the expected federal funds rate (the Federal Reserve's policy interest rate), represented by a financial instrument called the overnight indexed swap (OIS). One party in an OIS pays a fixed interest rate in return for a payment from the other party equal to the average federal funds rate over the life of the swap. The OIS rate should closely reflect the expected federal funds rate.

because they set and enforce the rules of the game. While informal lending networks do develop and flourish spontaneously, they can accommodate only simple, small-scale transactions. Because modern financial markets require a legal structure that is designed and enforced by the government, countries with better investor protections have bigger and deeper financial markets than other countries.

# Financial Institutions

**Financial institutions** are the firms that provide access to the financial markets, both to savers who wish to purchase financial instruments directly and to borrowers who want to issue them. Because financial institutions sit between savers and borrowers, they are also known as *financial intermediaries*, and what they do is known as intermediation. Banks, insurance companies, securities firms, and pension funds are all financial intermediaries. These institutions are essential; any disturbance to the services they provide will have severe adverse effects on the economy.

To understand the importance of financial institutions, think what the world would be like if they didn't exist. Without a bank, individuals and households wishing to save would either have to hold their wealth in cash or figure out some way to funnel it directly to companies or households that could put it to use. The assets of these household savers would be some combination of government liabilities and the equity and debt issued by corporations and other households. All finance would be direct, with borrowers obtaining funds straight from the lenders.

Such a system would be unlikely to work very well, for a number of reasons. First, individual transactions between saver-lenders and spender-borrowers would likely be extremely expensive. Not only would the two sides have difficulty finding each other, but even if they did, writing the contract to effect the transaction would be very costly. Second, lenders need to evaluate the creditworthiness of borrowers and then monitor them to ensure that they don't abscond with the funds. Individuals are not specialists in monitoring. Third, most borrowers want to borrow for the long term, while lenders favor more liquid short-term loans. Lenders would surely require compensation for the illiquidity of long-term loans, driving the price of borrowing up.

A financial market could be created in which the loans and other securities could be resold, but that would create the risk of price fluctuations. All these problems would restrict the flow of resources through the economy. Healthy financial institutions open up the flow, directing it to the most productive investments and increasing the system's efficiency.

## The Role of Financial Institutions

Financial institutions reduce transactions costs by specializing in the issuance of standardized securities. They reduce the information costs of screening and monitoring borrowers to make sure they are creditworthy and they use the proceeds of a loan or security issue properly. In other words, financial institutions curb information asymmetries and the problems that go along with them, helping resources flow to their most productive uses.

At the same time that they make long-term loans, financial institutions also give savers ready access to their funds. That is, they issue short-term liabilities to lenders while making long-term loans to borrowers. By making loans to many different borrowers at once, financial institutions can provide savers with financial instruments

## LESSONS FROM THE CRISIS
### SHADOW BANKS

Over the past few decades, financial intermediation and leverage in the United States has shifted away from traditional banks* and toward other financial institutions that are less subject to government rules. These other intermediaries include brokerages, consumer and mortgage finance firms, insurers, investment organizations (such as hedge funds and private equity firms†), money-market mutual funds (MMMFs), and even bank-created asset-management firms, such as special investment vehicles (SIVs).

These other intermediaries have come to be known as *shadow banks* because they provide services that compete with or substitute for those supplied by traditional banks. Unlike banks, however, shadow banks do not accept deposits. In addition, the leverage and risk taking of shadow banks can be greater than that of traditional banks while being less transparent.

Beginning in the 1970s, financial innovation sped the shift of intermediation to the shadow banks and was, in turn, stimulated by it. Broader markets, plunging information costs, new profit opportunities, and government practices all encouraged the development of new financial instruments and institutions to meet customer needs at lower cost.

Over time, the rise of highly leveraged shadow banks—combined with government relaxation of rules for traditional banks—permitted a rise of leverage in the financial system as a whole, making it more vulnerable to shocks (see Lessons from the Crisis: Leverage earlier in this chapter).

Rapid growth in some new financial instruments made it easier to conceal leverage and risk-taking. Derivatives—options, futures, and the like—allow investors to transfer risks at low cost (see Chapter 9). After 2000, the use of customized derivatives that do not trade in open markets (so-called over-the-counter, or OTC, derivatives) rose dramatically. Those derivatives permitted some large financial institutions to take risks that were unknown to their investors and trading partners and to the public officials who were supposed to monitor them. The spillover from the failure of these firms during the financial crisis nearly sank the entire system.

The financial crisis transformed shadow banking. During the fateful week that began with the failure of Lehman Brothers on Monday, September 15, 2008, the largest U.S. brokerages failed, merged, or converted themselves into traditional banks in order to gain access to funding. In the same month, the loss of confidence in MMMFs required a U.S. government guarantee to halt withdrawals. Over the past two years, many SIVs failed or were reabsorbed by the banks that created them. Many hedge funds chose to shrink or close as investors fled.

The future of shadow banking remains highly uncertain. The crisis has encouraged governments to scrutinize any financial institution that could, by its risk taking, pose a threat to the financial system. Partly as a result, the scope for leverage and risk taking is lower, at least for now.

*One traditional form of bank is a commercial bank, which is defined in Chapter 12 as accepting deposits from and making loans to businesses and individuals.

†Hedge funds (defined in Chapter 13) are private, largely unregulated investment partnerships that bring together small groups of wealthy people who meet certain financial requirements. Private equity funds are investment pools that typically invest directly in private companies.

that are both more liquid and less risky than the individual stocks and bonds they would purchase directly in financial markets.

Figure 3.2 is a schematic overview of the financial system. It shows that there are two types of financial institutions: those that provide brokerage services (top) and those that transform assets (bottom). Broker institutions give households and corporations access to financial markets and direct finance. Institutions that transform assets take deposits and issue insurance contracts to households. They use the proceeds to make loans and purchase stocks, bonds, and real estate. That is their transformation function. Figure 3.3 shows what the balance sheet for such an institution would include.

## The Structure of the Financial Industry

In analyzing the structure of the financial industry, we can start by dividing intermediaries into two broad categories called depository and nondepository institutions. *Depository institutions* take deposits and make loans; they are what most people think of as banks, whether they are commercial banks, savings banks, or credit unions.

**Figure 3.2** Flow of Funds through Financial Institutions

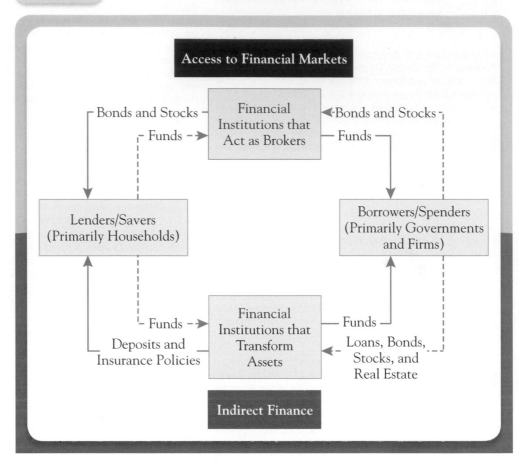

Financial institutions perform both brokerage and asset transformation services. As brokers, they provide access to financial markets, giving households and corporations access to indirect finance. Institutions transform assets by taking deposits and issuing insurance contracts to households at the same time that they make loans and purchase stocks, bonds, and real estate.

**Figure 3.3** The Simplified Balance Sheet of a Financial Institution

| Assets | Liabilities |
|---|---|
| Bonds | Deposits |
| Stocks | Insurance policies |
| Loans | |
| Real estate | |

*Nondepository institutions* include insurance companies, securities firms, mutual fund companies, hedge funds, finance companies, and pension funds. Each of these serves a very different function from a bank. Some screen and monitor borrowers; others transfer and reduce risk. Still others are primarily brokers. Here is a list of the major groups of financial institutions, together with a brief description of what they do.

1. **Depository institutions** (commercial banks, savings banks, and credit unions) take deposits and make loans.

2. **Insurance companies** accept premiums, which they invest in securities and real estate (their assets) in return for promising compensation to policyholders should certain events occur (their liabilities). Life insurers protect against

## YOUR FINANCIAL WORLD
### Shop for a Mortgage

Everyone loves a bargain. There are people who will spend hours making sure they pay the lowest price they can for virtually anything they buy. Borrowing shouldn't be any different. When the time comes to buy a house, most of us need to borrow. That is, we need to get a mortgage. Because the mortgage payment will almost surely be your biggest monthly expense, getting the cheapest mortgage you can will save you more than a year's worth of bargain hunting in stores.

There are a number of ways to shop for a mortgage. Any real estate agent can hand you a list of mortgage providers in your area. You can also find Web sites that publish quotes for mortgages. As you look through these lists, you'll notice that many of the firms on them are not banks. Instead, they are *mortgage brokers,* firms that have access to pools of funds earmarked for use as mortgages.

Say, for instance, that a financial firm raises a large amount of financing to be used to make mortgages. A pool of $100 million can finance a thousand $100,000 mortgages. Shares in these pools are sold to investors. If you get a mortgage from one of these firms, it will go into the pool. In 2009, half of the nearly $15 trillion in mortgages in the United States was in these mortgage pools.

Should you care whether you get your mortgage from a traditional bank or a mortgage broker? Should you care if your mortgage is pooled and sold off? The answer is no; it should make no difference to you. In fact, chances are that regardless of which option you choose—bank or mortgage broker—you'll make your payments to a company that does nothing but collect them and monitor your compliance. From your point of view, a mortgage is a mortgage. Get the one that suits you best. But shop before you sign on the dotted line. And if you let the various brokers know that you are shopping around, they may start competing for your business and give you a better deal.

the risk of untimely death. Property and casualty insurers protect against personal injury loss and losses from theft, accidents, and fire.

3. **Pension funds** invest individual and company contributions in stocks, bonds, and real estate (their assets) in order to provide payments to retired workers (their liabilities).

4. **Securities firms** include brokers, investment banks, underwriters, and mutual-fund companies. Brokers and investment banks issue stocks and bonds for corporate customers, trade them, and advise customers. All these activities give customers access to the financial markets. Mutual-fund companies pool the resources of individuals and companies and invest them in portfolios of bonds, stocks, and real estate. Hedge funds do the same for small groups of wealthy investors. Customers own shares of the portfolios, so they face the risk that the assets will change in value. But portfolios are less risky than individual securities, and individual savers can purchase smaller units than they could if they went directly to the financial markets.

5. **Finance companies** raise funds directly in the financial markets in order to make loans to individuals and firms. Finance companies tend to specialize in particular types of loans, such as mortgage, automobile, or certain types of business equipment. While their assets are similar to a bank's, their liabilities are debt instruments that are traded in financial markets, not deposits.

6. **Government-sponsored enterprises** are federal credit agencies that provide loans directly for farmers and home mortgagors. They also guarantee programs that insure loans made by private lenders. The government also provides retirement income and medical care to the elderly through Social Security and Medicare. Pension funds and insurance companies perform these functions privately.

As we continue our study of the relationship between the financial system and the real economy, we will return to the importance of financial institutions, the conduits that channel resources from savers to investors. These intermediaries are absolutely essential to the operation of any economy. When they cease to function, so does everything else. Recall from Chapter 2 that the measures of money (M1 and M2) include checking deposits, savings deposits, and certificates of deposit, among other things. These are all important liabilities of banks. Because they are very liquid, they are accepted as a means of payment. Clearly, the financial structure is tied to the availability of money and credit. But we are getting ahead of ourselves. Before we study financial institutions, we need to look more closely at financial instruments and financial markets, the subjects of Part II of this book.

# Terms

asset, 41

asset-backed security, 49

bond market, 58

centralized exchange, 54

collateral, 48

counterparty, 46

debt market, 58

derivative instrument, 47

direct finance, 41

electronic communications networks (ECNs), 54

equity market, 58

financial institutions, 60

financial instrument, 43

financial markets, 50

indirect finance, 41

liability, 41

money market, 58

mortgage-backed security, 49

over-the-counter (OTC) market, 54

portfolio, 51

primary financial market, 52

secondary financial market, 53

underlying instrument, 47

# Chapter Lessons

1. Financial instruments are crucial to the operation of the economy.
   a. Financial arrangements can be either formal or informal. Industrial economies are dominated by formal arrangements.
   b. A financial instrument is the written legal obligation of one party to transfer something of value, usually money, to another party at some future date, under certain conditions.
   c. Financial instruments are used primarily as stores of value and means of trading risk. They are less likely to be used as means of payment, although many of them can be.
   d. Financial instruments are most useful when they are simple and standardized.

   e. There are two basic classes of financial instruments: underlying and derivative.
      i. Underlying instruments are used to transfer resources directly from one party to another.
      ii. Derivative instruments derive their value from the behavior of an underlying instrument.
   f. The payments promised by a financial instrument are more valuable
      i. The larger they are.
      ii. The sooner they are made.
      iii. The more likely they are to be made.
      iv. If they are made when they are needed most.
   g. Common examples of financial instruments include
      i. Those that serve primarily as stores of value, including bank loans, bonds, mortgages, stocks, and asset-backed securities.
      ii. Those that are used primarily to transfer risk, including futures and options.

2. Financial markets are essential to the operation of our economic system.
   a. Financial markets
      i. Offer savers and borrowers liquidity so that they can buy and sell financial instruments easily.
      ii. Pool and communicate information through prices.
      iii. Allow for the sharing of risk.
   b. There are several ways to categorize financial markets.
      i. Primary markets that issue new securities versus secondary markets, where existing securities are bought and sold.
      ii. Physically centralized exchanges, dealer-based electronic systems (over-the-counter markets), or electronic networks.
      iii. Debt and equity markets (where instruments that are used primarily for financing are traded) versus derivative markets (where instruments that are used to transfer risk are traded).
   c. A well-functioning financial market is characterized by
      i. Low transactions costs and sufficient liquidity.
      ii. Accurate and widely available information.
      iii. Legal protection of investors against the arbitrary seizure of their property.

3. Financial institutions perform brokerage and asset transformation functions.
   a. In their role as brokers, they provide access to financial markets.
   b. In transforming assets, they provide indirect finance.
   c. Indirect finance reduces transaction and information costs.
   d. Financial institutions, also known as financial intermediaries, help individuals and firms to transfer and reduce risk.

# Conceptual Problems

1. As the end of the month approaches, you realize that you probably will not be able to pay the next month's rent. Describe both an informal and a formal financial instrument that you might use to solve your dilemma.

2.* While we often associate informal financial arrangements with poorer countries where financial systems are less developed, informal arrangements often coexist

*Indicates more difficult problems

with even the most developed financial systems. What advantages might there be to engaging in informal arrangements rather than utilizing the formal financial sector?

3. If higher leverage is associated with greater risk, explain why the process of deleveraging (reducing leverage) can be destabilizing.

4. The Chicago Mercantile Exchange has announced the introduction of a financial instrument that is based on rainfall in the state of Illinois. The standard agreement states that for each inch of rain over and above the average rainfall for a particular month, the seller will pay the buyer $1,000. Who could benefit from buying such a contract? Who could benefit from selling it?

5. Consider an annuity that makes monthly payments for as long as someone lives. Describe what happens to the purchase price of the annuity as (1) the age of the purchaser goes up, (2) the size of the monthly payment rises, and (3) the health of the purchaser improves.

6. Consider the investment returns to holding stock. Which of the following would be more valuable to you: Stocks that rise in value when your income rises or stocks that rise in value when your income falls? Why?

7. *The Wall Street Journal* has a daily listing of what are called "Money Rates" or interest rates on short-term securities. Locate it either in a recent issue of the newspaper by looking at the index on page 1 of the Money and Investing section, or in the Market Data Center of www.wsj.com. The most important money rates are the prime rate, the federal funds rate, and the Treasury bill rate. Describe each of these and report the current rate quoted in the paper.

8. You are asked for advice by the government of a small, less developed country interested in increasing its rate of economic growth. You notice that the country has no financial markets. What advice would you give?

9. The design and function of financial instruments, markets, and institutions are tied to the importance of information. Describe the role played by information in each of these three pieces of the financial system.

10. Suppose you need to take out a personal loan with a bank. Explain how you could be affected by problems in the interbank lending market such as those seen during the 2007–2009 financial crisis.

11.* Advances in technology have facilitated the widespread use of credit scoring by financial institutions in making their lending decisions. Credit scoring can be defined broadly as the use of historical data and statistical techniques to rank the attractiveness of potential borrowers and guide lending decisions. In what ways might this practice enhance the efficiency of the financial system?

## Analytical Problems

12. For each pair of instruments below, use the criteria for valuing a financial instrument to choose the one with the highest value.
   a. A U.S. Treasury bill that pays $1,000 in six months or a U.S. Treasury bill that pays $1,000 in three months.
   b. A U.S. Treasury bill that pays $1,000 in three months or commercial paper issued by a private corporation that pays $1,000 in three months.

    c. An insurance policy that pays out in the event of serious illness or one that pays out when you are healthy, assuming you are equally likely to be ill or healthy.

Explain each of your choices briefly.

13. Consider a situation where there is a huge influx of inexperienced, reckless drivers into your area. Assuming this increase is large enough to influence the market in which your insurance company operates, explain why the price of your car insurance policy will go up even though your driving record hasn't changed.

14. Suppose Joe and Mike purchase identical houses for $200,000. Joe makes a down payment of $40,000, while Mike only puts down $10,000. Assuming everything else is equal, who is more highly leveraged? If house prices in the neighborhood immediately fall by 10 percent (before any mortgage payments are made), what would happen to Joe's and Mike's net worth?

15.* Everything else being equal, which would be more valuable to you—a derivative instrument whose value is derived from an underlying instrument with a very volatile price history or one derived from an underlying instrument with a very stable price history? Explain your choice.

16. Explain why a person starting up a small business is more likely to take out a bank loan than to issue bonds.

17. Splitland is a developing economy with two distinct regions. The northern region has great investment opportunities, but the people who live there need to consume all of their income to survive. Those living in the south are better off than their northern counterparts and save a significant portion of their income. The southern region, however, has few profitable investment opportunities and so most of the savings remain in shoeboxes and under mattresses. Explain how the development of the financial sector could benefit both regions and promote economic growth in Splitland.

18. Suppose the U.S. government decided to abolish the Securities and Exchange Commission. What would you expect to happen to investment and growth in the economy?

19. Use Core Principle 3 from Chapter 1 to suggest some ways in which the problems associated with the shadow banking sector during the 2007–2009 financial crisis could be mitigated in the future.

20. What risks might financial institutions face by funding long-run loans such as mortgages to borrowers (often at fixed interest rates) with short-term deposits from savers?

21.* As the manager of a financial institution, what steps could you take to reduce the risks referred to in question 20?

# Part *II*

## Interest Rates, Financial Instruments, and Financial Markets

# Chapter 4

## Future Value, Present Value, and Interest Rates

Lenders have been despised for most of history. They make borrowers pay for loans, while just sitting around doing nothing. No wonder people have been vilified for charging interest. No wonder that for centuries, clerics pointed to biblical passages damning interest. Even philosophers like Aristotle weighed in against the practice, calling the "breeding of money from money" unnatural.

After scorning lenders for millennia, today we recognize their service as a fundamental building block of civilization. Credit is one of the critical mechanisms we have for allocating resources. Without it, our market-based economy would grind to a halt. Even the simplest financial transaction, like saving some of your paycheck each month to buy a car, would be difficult, if not impossible. And corporations, most of which survive from day to day by borrowing to finance their activities, would not be able to function. Credit is so basic that we can find records of people lending grain and metal from 5,000 years ago. Credit probably existed before common measures of value, and it predates coinage by 2,000 years.

Despite its early existence and its central role in economic transactions, credit was hard to come by until the Protestant Reformation. By the 16th century, views had changed, and interest payments were tolerated if not encouraged, so long as the rate charged was thought to be reasonable. Some historians even point to this shift as a key to the development of capitalism and its institutions. Protestant European countries did develop faster than Catholic ones, at least at first.[1] Since then, credit has exploded, facilitating extraordinary increases in general economic well-being. Yet even so, most people still take a dim view of the fact that lenders charge interest. Why?

The main reason for the enduring unpopularity of interest comes from the failure to appreciate the fact that lending has an opportunity cost. Think of it from the point of view of the lender. People who offer credit don't need to make loans. They have alternatives, and extending a loan means giving them up. While lenders can eventually recoup the sum they lend, neither the time that the loan was outstanding nor the opportunities missed during that time can be gotten back. So interest isn't really "the breeding of money from money," as Aristotle put it; it's more like a rental fee that borrowers must pay lenders to compensate them for lost opportunities.

It's no surprise that in today's world, interest rates are of enormous importance to virtually everyone—individuals, businesses, and governments. Quoted as a percentage of the amount borrowed, interest rates link the present to the future, allowing us to compare payments made on different dates. Interest rates also tell us the future reward for lending today, as well as the cost of borrowing now and repaying later. To make sound financial decisions, we must learn how to calculate and compare different rates

---

[1]Max Weber makes this argument in his classic work *The Protestant Ethic and the Spirit of Capitalism*, first published in 1905.

on various financial instruments. In this chapter, we'll explore interest rates using the concepts of future value and present value and then apply those concepts to the valuation of bonds. Finally, we'll look at the relationship between interest rates and inflation.

# Valuing Monetary Payments Now and in the Future

To compare the value of payments made on different dates, we need a set of tools called *future value* and *present value*. We'll use them to see how and why the promise to make a payment on one date is more or less valuable than the promise to make a payment on a different date. For example, we already know that if you want to borrow $100 today, your repayment needs to be bigger if you promise to make it in a year than if you promise to make it in a month. But how much more will you have to pay? The answer depends on both the date of payment and the interest rate. For the time being, we're going to assume that we know for sure that you will repay the loan. We'll get to the possibility of default when we study risk in the next chapter.

## Future Value and Compound Interest

**TIME**

What is the future value of one dollar deposited in an interest-bearing account today? To answer this question, let's start with a definition: **Future value** *is the value on some future date of an investment made today.* Say that today you invest $100 in a savings account that guarantees 5 percent interest per year. After one year, you'll have $105 (the investment at its present value of $100 plus $5 in interest). So the future value of $100 one year from now at an interest rate of 5 percent is $105. We could also say that the $100 investment yields $5, which explains why an interest rate is sometimes called a **yield**. Notice that the same calculation works for a simple loan in which you borrow $100 for one year at 5 percent interest. The amount you will need to repay is $105. Remember Core Principle 1: Time has value.

To generalize this concept so that we can handle different interest rates and initial investments of any size, we can express it mathematically. First we need to convert the percentage interest rate into a decimal, so that 5 percent becomes 0.05. *Note that in this expression, as in all mathematical manipulations in this chapter, the interest rate is expressed in decimal terms.* Now we can express future value as an equation. If the present value of your initial investment is $100 and the interest rate is 5 percent, then the *future value* one year from now is:

$$\$100 + \$100 \times (0.05) = \$105$$

Present value of the investment + Interest = Future value in one year

It is essential to convert all interest rates to decimals before doing any computation. This is consistent with the fact that we quote interest rates as "parts per 100," so 5 percent means 5 parts per 100, or 0.05.

This expression shows us immediately that the higher the interest rate, the higher the future value. If the interest rate were to rise to 6 percent, then the future value of $100 would be

$$\$100 + \$100 \,(0.06) = \$106$$

In general, the future value, $FV$, of an investment with a present value, $PV$, invested at an interest rate $i$ is:

$$FV = PV + PV \times i$$
$$= PV \times (1 + i) \qquad (1)$$

Future value in one year

= Present value of the investment today $\times$ (one plus the interest rate)

We can see right away that the higher the interest rate or the amount invested, the higher the future value.

But this example is too simple. Most financial instruments don't make single payments in exactly one year, so we need to figure out what happens when the time to repayment varies. Computing the future value of an investment to be repaid two years from now is straightforward, so let's do that first. But since we quote interest rates on a yearly basis, we need to be careful. Using one-year interest rates to compute the value of an investment that will be repaid more than one year from now requires applying the concept of **compound interest**, *which is interest on the interest.* If you leave an investment in an interest-bearing account for two years, during the second year you will receive interest not only on your initial investment but also on the interest you earned for the first year (because they both have an opportunity cost).

Getting back to our example, let's say that you leave your $100 deposit in the bank for two years at 5 percent interest per year. The future value of this investment has four parts. The first three are straightforward. They are the initial investment of $100, the interest on that investment in the first year, and the interest on it in the second year. But because you left the interest from the first year in the bank during the second year, it is as if you made a new deposit at the beginning of the second year, and that earns interest too. So the fourth part of the future value is the interest you receive during the second year on the interest you received in the first year. That's compounding. With an initial deposit of $100 and an interest rate of 5 percent, we can add up these four parts to compute your investment's future value in two years.

$$\$100 + \$100(0.05) + \$100(0.05) + \$5(0.05) = \$110.25$$

Present value of the initial investment

+ Interest on the initial investment in first year

+ Interest on the initial investment in second year

+ Interest on the interest from first year in second year

= Future value in two years

We can use a small amount of algebra to show that this equals

$$\$100(1.05)(1.05) = \$100(1.05)^2$$

Extending it to three years, four years, or more just means multiplying by (1.05) over and over again. The multiplication takes care of the compounding. Table 4.1 shows the calculations. The final line shows that after 10 years, a deposit with a present value of $100 becomes $162.89. That is, it earns $62.89 in interest. If we had ignored compounding and just multiplied 5 percent by 10 years to get 50 percent, the answer would have been $150. Compounding produced an additional $12.89 in interest over 10 years. To put it as clearly as possible, multiplying the number of years times the annual interest rate gives the *wrong* answer!

| Table 4.1 | Computing the Future Value of $100 at 5 Percent Annual Interest |

| Years into Future | Computation | Future Value |
|:---:|:---:|:---:|
| 1 | $100(1.05) | $105.00 |
| 2 | $100(1.05)$^2$ | $110.25 |
| 3 | $100(1.05)$^3$ | $115.76 |
| 4 | $100(1.05)$^4$ | $121.55 |
| 5 | $100(1.05)$^5$ | $127.63 |
| 10 | $100(1.05)$^{10}$ | $162.89 |

Using the computations in Table 4.1, we can derive a general formula for future value.

$$FV_n = PV \times (1 + i)^n \tag{2}$$

Future value in $n$ years = Present value of the investment

$\times$ (One plus the interest rate) raised to $n$

*So to compute future value, all we need to do is calculate one plus the interest rate (measured as a decimal) raised to the nth power and multiply it by the present value.*

Before we go any further, we should stop to consider an important problem. What if you want to put your $100 into a bank for six months, or 2½ years, or any amount of time that is not a round number of years? The answer is that the formula still works. You can compute the future value using equation (2) regardless of whether $n$ is a whole number. There is one pitfall, however. *In computing future value, both the interest rate and n must be measured in the same time units.* We have been measuring interest rates as the percentage per year, so we were careful to measure $n$ in years as well. So, if we want the future value in half of one year, $n$ would be ½; if we wanted it in one month, $n$ would be 1/12; and if we wanted the future value in one day, $n$ would be 1/365.

As you can see, taking advantage of the future-value formula requires an understanding of the transformations needed to convert time from years to months or vice versa. Converting $n$ from years to months is easy—everyone knows there are 12 months in a year—but converting the interest rate is harder. If the annual interest rate is 5 percent, what is the interest rate for one month? To figure out the answer, we'll start with the future-value formula, but in months. Remember that compounding means you *cannot* just multiply the monthly interest rate by 12 to get the annual interest rate. Instead, if $i^m$ is the one-month interest rate and $n$ is the number of months, then a deposit made for one year will have a future value of $100(1 + i^m)^{12}$. We know that this amount equals $100(1.05), so figuring out the answer means equating the two amounts,

$$(1 + i^m)^{12} = (1.05)$$

and raising each side to the one-twelfth power:

$$(1 + i^m) = (1.05)^{1/12} = 1.0041$$

## YOUR FINANCIAL WORLD
### How Long Does Your Investment Take to Double?

You invest $100 at 5 percent interest. How long will you need to wait until you have $200? That may seem like a simple question, but compounding makes it difficult. The straightforward (some people would call it "brute force") way to find the answer is to take out your calculator and multiply $100 times 1.05 over and over again counting how many times it takes to get to an answer that is close to $200. If you did that, you would find that after the 14th time, you had reached $197.99. And multiplying once more, you would have $207.89. You would conclude that, at 5 percent interest, your investment takes between 14 and 15 years to double.

While the brute force technique works—you can multiply over and over again—it's clumsy. Fortunately, there is a simpler way called the **rule of 72**. If you want to compute the number of years it takes an investment to double, divide the annual interest rate measured as an integer into 72.* So at an interest rate of 5 percent, we would expect an investment to double in $72/5 = 14.4$ years (we can check and see that $1.05^{14.4} = 2.02$). If the interest rate were 8 percent, we would estimate 9 years ($1.08^9 = 2.00$).

The rule of 72 shows the power of compounding. It shows that when the interest rate doubles, the time a $100 investment takes to become $200 is cut in half. That is, while it takes 14.4 years to double at 5 percent interest, it takes only 7.2 years at 10 percent ($72/10 = 7.2$ and $1.10^{7.2} = 1.99$). This rule works for anything that is growing at a constant rate. So, if you want to estimate how long it will take a country's population or company's sales to double, just divide the annual growth rate measured as a percentage per year into 72.

*The rule of 72 is an approximation of the solution to an algebraic problem that requires the use of logarithms. Consider the formula for compound interest, in which the future value after $n$ years is equal to $FV = PV (1 + i)^n$. Setting the present value $PV$ equal to 1 and the future value $FV$ equal to 2 and taking logarithms, we get $n = ln(2)/ln(1 + i)$. This formula is exact. Next, we use the approximation that $ln(1 + i) \approx i$ for small $i$. Substituting this into the equation gives us $n = ln(2)/i$. The $ln(2) = 0.693$, so it might seem that we should be using the rule of 69.3. For very low interest rates, we should, but that approximation isn't that useful with real-world interest rates. In the range of interest rates that we normally see (2 to 15 percent), 72 works better.

Converting from decimals to a percentage, the one-month interest rate is 0.41 percent. We can handle any mismatch between the time units of $i$ and $n$ in a similar way (see Tools of the Trade: Computing Compound Annual Rates on page 78).

These fractions of percentage points, like 0.41 percent, are so important in discussing interest rates that they have their own name, basis points. A **basis point** is one one-hundredth of a percentage point. That is, one basis point equals 0.01 percent.

You're probably wondering how useful all this discussion of future value really is. To see, consider the following question: If you put $1,000 per year into the bank at 4 percent interest, how much would you have saved after 40 years? The answer is $98,826—more than twice the $40,000 you deposited. Figuring out the exact answer is complicated since we need to add up the future values of forty $1,000 deposits, each made in a different year, but doing so uses the concept of future value. The first $1,000 is deposited for 40 years, so its future value is

$$\$1,000(1.04)^{40} = \$4,801.02$$

the second $1,000 is deposited for 39 years, so its future value is

$$\$1,000(1.04)^{39} = \$4,616.37$$

and so on. The practical implication of this calculation is that buying one less soda or candy bar per day isn't just good for your physical health; it's good for your financial health, too.

## Present Value

It's easy to see why future value is important. We often want to know what savings and investments will be worth in the future. But that isn't the only thing we need to know. There is another, somewhat different task that we face with some regularity. We need to be able to figure out how much a payment promised in the future is worth today. Say you agree to make a $225 loan, and the borrower offers to repay you either $100 a year for three years or $125 a year for two years. Which offer should you take? Answering this question means figuring out the current value of the promised payments on the dates when they will be made. To do that, we'll use the concept of present value, sometimes referred to as *present discounted value*.

TIME

**The Definition** In our discussion of future value, we used the term *present value* to mean the initial amount invested or deposited. The way we used the term suggests its technical definition: **Present value** *is the value today (in the present) of a payment that is promised to be made in the future.* Put another way, present value is the amount that must be invested today in order to realize a specific amount on a given future date. Financial instruments promise future cash payments, so we need to know how to value those payments. Present value is an integral component of the computation of the price of all financial instruments.

To understand the calculation of present value, go back to future value. Remember that at a 5 percent interest rate, the future value one year from now of a $100 investment today is $105. It follows that at this same 5 percent interest rate, the present value of $105 one year from now is $100. *All we did was invert the future value calculation.*

Reversing the calculation in general terms is just as easy. Start with the fact that the future value of a payment equals the current investment times one plus the interest rate: $FV = PV \times (1 + i)$ (equation 1). Divide both sides of this expression by $(1 + i)$ to get an expression for how much we need to invest today to realize the future value one year from today. The result is

$$PV = \frac{FV}{(1 + i)} \qquad (3)$$

Present value = Future value of the payment divided by (One plus the interest rate)

In our example, we see that

$$\frac{FV}{(1 + i)} = \frac{\$105}{(1.05)} = \$100$$

so the present value of $105 one year from now, at a 5 percent interest rate, is indeed $100.

While future value tells us what today's investment will be worth in the future, present value tells us what promised future payments are worth today. This means that the properties of present value mirror those of future value. In the same way that future value *rises* as the interest rate rises, present value *falls* as the interest rate rises. To see this, first look at the calculation of the present value of $105 in one year at an interest rate of 6 percent. The answer is

$$\frac{\$105}{1.06} = \$99.06$$

## LESSONS FROM THE CRISIS
### RISK TAKING AND THE SEARCH FOR YIELD

Core Principle 2 teaches us that risk requires compensation. But to secure proper compensation, investors must understand the risks of what they buy.

The present-value analysis of this chapter helps us understand the risk of bonds with different maturities. If interest rates rise, the losses on a long-term bond will exceed the losses on a short-term bond. The reason is that the further in the future the promised payment, the more the present value falls when interest rates rise. As a result, long-term bonds are more sensitive to the risk that interest rates will change. Unsurprisingly, buyers of long-term bonds usually insist on an extra reward as compensation for such *interest-rate risk* (see discussion of the yield curve in Chapter 7).

In some circumstances, many investors underestimate the risks of particular assets. For example, investors lacking sufficient regard for risk typically seek higher-yield bonds even if those bonds are riskier (due to longer maturities or higher default probabilities).

What can prompt the underestimation of risk? Experience suggests that some investors extrapolate from recent patterns and pay less attention to the more distant past. For example, if interest rates have been low and stable for some time, investors may expect this pattern to persist even if rates tended to be higher and more volatile in earlier periods.

Extrapolation of recent experience also can lead investors to misjudge default risk. For example, business defaults are relatively infrequent during economic expansions. Because such booms are long and recessions are short, investors can become accustomed to unsustainably low levels of corporate default. Again, naively projecting recent experience underestimates the default risks for which investors should be compensated when buying corporate securities.

Investors also may underestimate risk if their professional investment managers take risks that are not evident or are purposely concealed. For example, when market interest rates are low, some investment managers may try to generate high interest payments to clients by taking greater risks—a so-called search for yield. Until events compel the manager to reduce payments, the investor may think that the manager is unusually skillful rather than lucky and prone to risk.

The search for yield can bid up the prices of risky securities and depress the market compensation for risk below a sustainable level. Eventually, when the risk comes to fruition (say, defaults increase), the prices of riskier securities fall disproportionately, potentially triggering large financial losses. During the financial crisis of 2007–2009, the plunge of corporate and mortgage security prices highlighted how forcefully markets can reprice risk when the search for yield has gone too far.

---

less than the $100 needed when the interest rate is only 5 percent. *Present value falls as the interest rate rises.*

What happens if the payment is going to be made in two years instead of one? What is the present value of $105 in two years at an interest rate of 5 percent? Again, we can compute the answer using the future-value formula by asking what present value has a future value of $105 in two years at an interest rate of 5 percent. This is the solution to

$$\$105 = PV(1.05)^2$$

The answer is

$$PV = \frac{\$105}{1.05^2} = \$95.24$$

We can generalize this process by looking at the future value in $n$ years of an investment today: $FV_n = PV(1 + i)^n$. Dividing both sides of this expression by $(1 + i)^n$, we get the general formula for present value:

$$PV = \frac{FV_n}{(1 + i)^n} \tag{4}$$

Present value = Future value of a payment made in $n$ years divided
by (One plus the interest rate) raised to $n$

From this simple expression, we can deduce three important properties of present value. Present value is higher

1. The higher the future value of the payment, $FV_n$.
2. The shorter the time until the payment, $n$.
3. The lower the interest rate, $i$.

We're going to use equation (4) over and over again. *It is the single most important relationship in our study of financial instruments.* Once we can figure out the present value of any future payment, then we understand the fundamentals of mortgages, credit cards, car loans, and even stocks.

We will spend the rest of this chapter looking at how present value changes when we change the various components of the formula, and how to use it more generally. But before we do, it is important to note one final similarity between present value and future value. Recall that to calculate future value, $n$ need not be measured in years. We can do the computation even when $n$ is the number of months, so long as the interest rate is measured in months as well. The same is true of present value. So long as we measure $n$ and $i$ in the same time unit, and the interest rate is expressed as a decimal, the formula works.

**How Present Value Changes**    It is useful to go through each of the three properties of present value, looking at the impact of changing each one: the size of the future payment ($FV_n$), the time until the payment is made ($n$), and the interest rate ($i$). Starting with $FV_n$, we see that *doubling the future value of the payment, without changing the time of the payment or the interest rate, doubles the present value.* For example, at a 5 percent interest rate, a $100 payment made in two years has a present value of $90.70. Doubling the payment to $200 doubles the present value to $181.40. In fact, increasing or decreasing $FV_n$ by any percentage will change $PV$ by the same percentage, in the same direction.

We have already seen that *the sooner a payment is to be made, the more it is worth.* How much more? To see, let's return to the example of a $100 payment at 5 percent interest. How sensitive is the present value of this payment to the time until it is made?

Plugging some numbers into the general present-value formula [equation (4)], and allowing the time to go from 0 to 30 years, we can construct Figure 4.1, which shows that the present value of the payment is worth $100 if it is made immediately but declines gradually to $23 for a payment made in 30 years.

The rate of decline in the present value is related to the same phenomenon that gives us the rule of 72 (described in Your Financial World: How Long Does Your Investment Take to Double? on page 73). Consider this question: At a 5 percent interest rate, how long into the future must a payment of $100 be made for it to be worth the same as $50 received today? The answer is 14.4 years. That is, at 5 percent interest, the present value of $100 paid in 14.4 years is $50. Note that 14.4 equals 72 divided by 5, so it is also the number of years an investment takes to double in value when the return is 5 percent per year. We can

"I'm just glad we got out before interest rates went up again."

SOURCE: © Mick Stevens/The New Yorker Collection/www.cartoonbank.com.

repeat the computation to see that the investment takes 28.8 years to double twice, which tells us that the present value of $100 paid 28.8 years from now is $25. These two points are highlighted in Figure 4.1.

The interest rate is the third important determinant of the present value of a future payment. To see how important it is, let's look at the present value of a $100 payment made 1, 5, 10, and 20 years from now at various interest rates. The general formula [equation (4)] allows us to do this series of computations. Table 4.2 shows the numerical results. Note what happens as the interest rate increases—that is, as you read down a column in the table or move to the right in the figure. You can see immediately that *higher interest rates are associated with lower present values, no matter what the size or timing of the payment.* Conversely, lower interest rates are associated with higher present values.

Note, too, that *at any fixed interest rate, an increase in the time until a payment is made reduces its present value.* Read across any row of the table and you will see that as the time increases from 1 to 5 to 10 to 20 years, the present value goes down.

The final lesson to take away from these calculations has to do with how present value changes with both time and the interest rate. Table 4.2 shows what happens to the present value of a payment as the interest rate increases. You can see that if the payment is to be made in one year (column 2), as the interest rate increases from 1 percent to

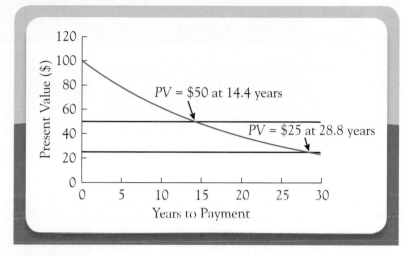

**Figure 4.1**   Present Value of $100 at 5 Percent Interest

PV = $50 at 14.4 years

PV = $25 at 28.8 years

**Table 4.2**   Present Value of a $100 Payment

| Interest Rate | Payment due in | | | |
|---|---|---|---|---|
| | 1 Year | 5 Years | 10 Years | 20 Years |
| 1% | $99.01 | $95.15 | $90.53 | $81.95 |
| 2% | $98.04 | $90.57 | $82.03 | $67.30 |
| 3% | $97.09 | $86.26 | $74.41 | $55.37 |
| 4% | $96.15 | $82.19 | $67.56 | $45.64 |
| 5% | $95.24 | $78.35 | $61.39 | $37.69 |
| 6% | $94.34 | $74.73 | $55.84 | $31.18 |
| 7% | $93.46 | $71.30 | $50.83 | $25.84 |
| 8% | $92.59 | $68.06 | $46.32 | $21.45 |
| 9% | $91.74 | $64.99 | $42.24 | $17.84 |
| 10% | $90.91 | $62.09 | $38.55 | $14.86 |
| 11% | $90.09 | $59.35 | $35.22 | $12.40 |
| 12% | $89.29 | $56.74 | $32.20 | $10.37 |
| 13% | $88.50 | $54.28 | $29.46 | $ 8.68 |
| 14% | $87.72 | $51.94 | $26.97 | $ 7.28 |
| 15% | $86.96 | $49.72 | $24.72 | $ 6.11 |

5 percent, the present value falls from $99.01 to $95.24. This is a drop of $3.77, or just under 4 percent. In fact, for the single payment made in one year, the percentage change in the present value is approximately equal to the percentage point change in the interest rate: A rise of 4 percentage points in the interest rate has caused a decline in present value of 4 percent.

Now look at the present value of a payment that will be made in 10 years (column 4 of Table 4.2). As the interest rate goes from 1 to 5 percent, the present value of

## TOOLS OF THE TRADE
### Computing Compound Annual Rates

Comparing changes over days, months, years, and decades can be very difficult. If someone tells you that an investment grew at a rate of 1/2 percent last month, what should you think? You're used to thinking about growth in terms of years, not months. The way to deal with such problems is to turn the monthly growth rate into a *compound-annual rate*. Here's how you do it.

An investment whose value grows 1/2 percent per month goes from 100 at the beginning of the month to 100.5 at the end of the month. Remembering to multiply by 100 to convert the decimal into a percentage, we can verify this:

$$100\left(\frac{100.5 - 100}{100}\right) = 100\left[\left(\frac{100.5}{100}\right) - 1\right] = 0.5\%$$

To convert this monthly rate to an annual rate, we need to figure out what would happen if the investment's value continued to grow at a rate of 1/2 percent per month for the next 12 months. We can't just multiply 0.5 times 12. Instead, we need to compute a 12-month compound rate by raising the one-month rate to the 12th power. Assuming that our index starts at 100 and increases by 1/2 percent per month, we can use the expression for a compound future value to compute the index level 12 months later. Remembering to convert percentages to their decimal form, so that 0.5 percent is 0.005, we find the result is

$$FV_n = PV(1 + i)^n = 100\,(1.005)^{12} = 106.17$$

an increase of 6.17 percent. That's the compound annual rate, and it's obviously bigger than the 6 percent result we

get from just multiplying 0.5 by 12. The difference between the two answers—the one you get by multiplying by 12 and the one you get by compounding—grows as the interest rate grows. At a 1 percent monthly rate, the compounded annual rate is 12.68 percent.

Another use for compounding is to compute the percentage change per year when we know how much an investment has grown over a number of years. This rate is sometimes referred to as the *average annual rate*. Say that over five years an investment has increased 20 percent, from 100 to 120. What annual increase will give us a 20 percent increase over five years? Dividing by 5 gives the wrong answer because it ignores compounding; the increase in the second year must be calculated as a percentage of the index level at the end of the first year. What is the growth rate that after five years will give us an increase of 20 percent? Using the future-value formula,

$$FV_n = PV(1 + i)^n$$
$$120 = 100(1 + i)^5$$

Solving this equation means computing the following:

$$i = \left[\left(\frac{120}{100}\right)^{1/5} - 1\right] = 0.0371$$

This tells us that five consecutive annual increases of 3.71 percent will result in an overall increase of 20 percent. (Just to check, we can compute $(1.0371)^5 = 1.20 = 120/100$.)

a $100 payment 10 years from now falls from $90.53 to $61.39. This is a decline of $29.14, or more than 30 percent. *Not only does the present value of a future payment fall with the interest rate; the further in the future the promised payment is to be made, the more the present value falls.* As a result, a change in interest rates has a much greater impact on the present value of a payment made far in the future than it has on one to be made soon. Remember this principle because it will be extremely important when we discuss bonds in the next section.

## Applying Present Value

All of our examples thus far have focused on computing the present value of a single payment on a given future date. Thinking of present value in this way gives us enormous flexibility. It means that we can compute the present value not just of a single payment but also of any group of payments made on any number of dates. As we saw

## YOUR FINANCIAL WORLD

### Should You Buy a New Car Now or Wait?

For a long time you've wanted to buy a new car and you know you'll need a loan to do it. You have $4,000 in savings and figure you can afford a monthly payment of $300. A quick check on the Internet tells you that you can get a four-year loan at 6¾ percent interest. Payments are $237 a month for each $10,000 you borrow. That is, $10,000 is the present value of $237 per month for 48 months at a monthly interest rate of 0.54581 percent (the monthly rate that equals 6¾ percent per year). Because you can afford a $300 payment, you can get a loan of up to $12,658, or (300/237) × $10,000. With a $4,000 down payment, you can afford a car that costs $16,658.

You don't have to buy the car right away, however. You could wait and drive your old car a while longer. What if you wait a year to buy the car? Waiting means you should put $300 per month into the bank along with the $4,000 you already have. At 4 percent interest, at the end of a year you will have $7,838—the future value of the $4,000 plus 12 monthly contributions of $300 each.

For the sake of comparison, let's keep the out-of-pocket cost at $300 per month for 4 years, so that at the end of the year you look for a three-year loan with a $300 payment. At 6¾ percent interest, you can now afford to borrow $9,781. Adding this amount to your savings, you can spend a total of $7,837 + $9,781, or $17,618. So by waiting a year, you'll be able to afford a car that costs about $1,000 more. (That's approximately the 4 percent interest you earned on your $4,000 down payment plus the 6¾ percent interest you didn't pay on a $12,658 loan: $160 + $854 = $1,014.)

Should you buy the new car now or wait? It depends on how you feel about the extra $1,000 you will have available to spend if you wait and how much you'll have to pay to repair your old car in the meantime.*

*In addition, there is always the possibility that the price of the car will change. It could go up because of general inflation or down as a result of increases in the efficiency of production. If you have reason to believe that the price may change in a particular direction, factor that into your computation.

earlier, to use present value in practice, we need to look at sequences, or streams of payments. And valuing a stream of payments means summing their present values. That is, the value of the whole is the sum of the value of its parts. *Present value is additive.* To see how present value is applied to a stream of payments, we will look at two applications: internal rate of return and the valuation of bonds.

## Internal Rate of Return

Imagine that you run a sports equipment factory. As part of your strategic planning, you are considering buying a new machine that makes tennis rackets. The machine costs $1 million and can produce 3,000 rackets a year. If you can sell the rackets for $50 apiece (wholesale), the machine will generate $150,000 in revenue each year. To simplify the analysis, we will assume that the machine is the only necessary input in the production of tennis rackets; that we know the exact amount of revenue it will produce (in reality, that has to be estimated); and that the machine will last for exactly 10 years, during which time it will work perfectly, without requiring any maintenance. At the end of the 10 years, the machine will abruptly cease to operate and will have no resale value. Should you buy the machine?

The answer is: It depends. If you borrow the $1 million to pay for the machine, will the revenue from the machine, $150,000 per year, be enough to cover the payments on the loan? If so and you have something left over, then buying the machine may be a good idea. But if you can't make the payments, then buying the machine is a losing proposition. So you need to figure out whether the machine's revenue will be high enough to cover the payments on the loan you would need to buy it. We'll do this in two steps: First, we'll compute the internal rate of return on your investment in the machine, and second, we'll compare that return to the cost of buying the machine. If the cost is less than the return, then you should buy the machine.

The **internal rate of return** *is the interest rate that equates the present value of an investment with its cost.* For the tennis racket machine, it is the interest rate at which the present value of the revenue from the tennis rackets, $150,000 per year for 10 years, equals the $1 million cost of the machine. To find the internal rate of return, we take the sum of the present value of each of the yearly revenues (we can't take the present value of the total revenue) and equate it with the machine's cost. Then we solve for the interest rate, $i$:

$$\$1,000,000 = \frac{\$150,000}{(1+i)^1} + \frac{\$150,000}{(1+i)^2} + \ldots + \frac{\$150,000}{(1+i)^{10}} \quad (5)$$

You can solve this equation using a financial calculator or spreadsheet. The answer, 8.14 percent, is the internal rate of return on your investment. That is, the annual rate of return for investing $1 million in the machine is 8.14 percent. But is that rate of return high enough to justify your investment? That depends on the cost of the $1 million you need to buy the machine.

There are two ways you can come up with the $1 million. You can use your company's retained earnings—the funds you've saved from your past profits. Or you can borrow. In the first case, you need to figure out if the machine is more profitable than other ways you might use the funds, just as you might compare interest-bearing investments. The other main use for the retained earnings is to lend it to someone at the same rate at which you could borrow. That is the opportunity cost of your investment. If you borrow the money to buy the machine, you need to know whether you will have a profit left after paying off the loan. Let's assume you're considering borrowing.

Table 4.3 shows the payments you will have to make if you borrow $1 million at various interest rates. To keep the example fairly simple, we'll assume that the loan requires 10 equal payments, one for each year. This type of loan is called a **fixed-payment loan**, and it is exactly the same as a car loan or a mortgage. Using the present-value formula (equation 4), we know that the amount of the loan must equal the present value of the 10 payments. If the interest rate is $i$, then

**Table 4.3**  Fixed Annual Payments on a 10-Year, $1 Million Loan

| Interest Rate | Payment |
|---|---|
| 5% | $129,505 |
| 6% | $135,868 |
| 7% | $142,378 |
| 8% | $149,030 |
| 9% | $155,820 |
| 10% | $162,745 |

$$\$1,000,000 = \frac{Fixed\ payment}{(1+i)} + \frac{Fixed\ payment}{(1+i)^2} + \ldots + \frac{Fixed\ payment}{(1+i)^{10}} \quad (6)$$

$1,000,000 = Present value of 10 equal annual payments at interest rate $i$.

Using this relationship (and the methods described in the appendix to this chapter), we can compute your loan payment at various interest rates, as shown in Table 4.3. As we would expect, when the interest rate rises, the payments rise too.

At what interest rate can you afford a loan to buy the tennis racket machine? Recall that you have $150,000 a year in revenue, and your internal rate of return is 8.14 percent. So as long as the interest rate is 8 percent or less, you know you can cover the payments. But we can answer this question with more precision. To see

## APPLYING THE CONCEPT
### EARLY RETIREMENT

Many people want to retire early. They would love to quit work when they turn 40 (that's less than 20 years of work after college) and spend the next 40 years doing whatever they want. In the late 1990s, it looked as if lots of dot-com millionaires had managed to pull it off—at least for a while. But when the Internet bubble burst in 2000, some early retirees discovered that they really couldn't afford retirement. Some had to go back to work.

How expensive is early retirement anyway? The answer is, very expensive. Here's the problem. Assume that you're going to live to be exactly 85 years old. Though you're rich, you are willing to live modestly (for a rich person) and spend only $100,000 a year. Remember that you're going to be on vacation 365 days a year and you'll want to put your kids through college, buy new cars, and so on. And you'll still need to pay income taxes, so you won't see all of your income. Assuming you have no other retirement plan, and no Social Security payments (you can't get those for at least 20 years anyway), you'll need $100,000 a year for 45 years.

To figure out how much you need to save by age 40, you can use the present value concept. Think of the amount you need to invest today to have $100,000 in five years. That is:

$$\$100{,}000 = PV(1 + i)^5$$

Assuming a 4 percent interest rate on your investment (that may seem conservative, but you can't count on much more than that), the answer is

$$PV = \frac{\$100{,}000}{(1.04)^5} = \$82{,}193$$

To retire at 40, you need to do this for *each* of the 45 years of your retirement. That is, you need a sequence of $100,000 payments:

$$\frac{\$100{,}000}{(1.04)^1} + \frac{\$100{,}000}{(1.04)^2} + \cdots + \frac{\$100{,}000}{(1.04)^{44}} + \frac{\$100{,}000}{(1.04)^{45}} = \$2{,}072{,}004$$

Retiring at 40 with an income of $100,000 a year means accumulating about $2 million in assets (not counting your house). You can see how someone who retired at age 40 with a few million dollars worth of Internet stocks might have had to go back to work when the bubble burst, reducing his or her wealth by 75 percent or more.

The point of this discussion is that retirement, especially early retirement, is expensive. Even if you are willing to work until you are 65, and live on only $50,000 a year (plus Social Security), you'll need to amass around $700,000. As a rule of thumb, people in their mid-20s should be putting away 10 percent of their income toward retirement in order to retire at the same preretirement standard of living by age 65. It takes significant savings to live without a paycheck.

why, notice that the internal rate of return equation 5 is virtually identical to the loan equation 6. In fact, the internal rate of return is the interest rate at which $150,000 a year for 10 years will exactly cover the loan. So we really needed to do this computation only once to answer the question. You should buy the tennis racket machine if its internal rate of return exceeds the interest rate on the loan you would need to finance it. In general, *an investment will be profitable if its internal rate of return exceeds the cost of borrowing.*

Before we go on, we can use the concept of internal rate of return to answer the question at the beginning of the present-value section on page 74: If you agree to make a $225 loan, and the borrower offers to repay either $100 a year for three years or $125 a year for two years, which should you take? The first step in figuring out what to do is to compute the internal rate of return of the two payment streams. For the series of three $100 payments, we need to find the interest rate $i$ that solves

$$\$225 = \frac{\$100}{(1 + i)} + \frac{\$100}{(1 + i)^2} + \frac{\$100}{(1 + i)^3}$$

The answer is $i = 0.159$, or 15.9 percent.

Turning to the alternative, we need to calculate the interest rate that solves

$$\$225 = \frac{\$125}{(1 + i)} + \frac{\$125}{(1 + i)^2}$$

The answer here is $i = 0.073$, or 7.3 percent.

## IN THE NEWS
### Economic Scene: Pentagon Shows That It Doesn't Always Pay to Take the Money and Run

### The New York Times

by Alan B. Krueger

May 24, 2001

Suppose your employer hands you a pink slip and offers you a choice: an annual payment of $8,000 a year for 30 years or a lump sum of $50,000 today. Which would you choose?

This is not just a hypothetical exercise. When it downsized in the early 1990s, the Defense Department offered many military personnel a similar choice. The military also provided pamphlets and counseling to explain how to make the choice wisely. To the surprise of most economists, the affected personnel rarely followed the military's sound advice.

The decision should depend, of course, on how much one values money received today versus tomorrow. A bird in the hand is worth more today than tomorrow, but how much more? The difference between the value an individual places on a dollar received today as opposed to a year from now is called the discount rate.*

Standard economic theory says that if capital markets work perfectly, people will borrow or lend until their discount rate equals the market rate for borrowing or lending. Someone with a low discount rate will save and accumulate interest; someone with a high discount rate will borrow and accumulate debt. This should continue to the point where their personal discount rates equal the market rate.

Thus, with some justification, the military's pamphlet provided calculations of the present value of the annuity payment using a 7 percent discount rate, the interest rate on money-market funds at the time. If the annuity's present value exceeds the value of the lump sum, the annual payment is a better deal.

Mounting evidence indicates that most people put excessive weight on a bird in the hand. That $8,000 annual payment is worth more than $106,000 if future income is discounted at 7 percent a year—more than double the value of the lump sum. If the discount rate is 10 percent, as high as the interest rate on 30-year fixed-rate mortgages has been the last decade, the promised $8,000 payment is still worth $83,000. The annual payment is a better deal for anyone who can borrow from a bank.

Yet when the military offered essentially this package, three-quarters of enlisted personnel selected the lump sum, according to an article by John Warner of Clemson University and Saul Pleeter of the Defense Department in *The American Economic Review*. The authors also examined a number

This means that if you choose the three $100 payments, you will earn 15.9 percent interest on the loan, while if you accept the two $125 payments, the interest rate will be 7.3 percent. Clearly, the three payments are better for you as the lender, but we had to do quite a bit of work to figure it out.

## Bonds: The Basics

One of the most common uses of the concept of present value is in the valuation of bonds. A **bond** is a promise to make a series of payments on specific future dates. It is issued as part of an arrangement to borrow. In essence, the borrower, or seller, gives an IOU to the lender, or buyer, in return for some amount of money. Both governments and corporations need to borrow, so both issue bonds. Because bonds create obligations, they are best thought of as legal contracts that (1) require the borrower to make payments to the lender and (2) specify what happens if the borrower fails to do so.

of other separation packages. The break-even discount rate—or rate that makes the lump sum and annuity payment equivalent—varied from 17 to 20 percent, depending on years of service and salary. Over all, 92 percent of enlisted personnel and 51 percent of officers chose the lump sum.

Because the government could borrow at 7 percent at the time, Mr. Warner and Mr. Pleeter calculate that the Treasury saved $1.7 billion by offering the lump-sum option.

Using a sample of 65,000 departing members of the armed forces, they estimate that the average personal discount rate, taking taxes into account, exceeded 25 percent. Discount rates were higher for the less educated, the young, minorities, and those with dependents; they were lower for officers.

Recognition of this fact helps to explain a number of other phenomena. For instance, the public's penchant for holding high credit card debt—more than $6,000 per household with a credit card—at interest rates near 15 percent a year is also consistent with high discount rates, as are low savings rates. (Indeed, one wonders why the government, which borrows at 5 percent, doesn't offer a credit card to every man, woman, and child at an interest rate of, say, 10 percent. This would help reduce the debt and quench individuals' thirst for fast cash.)

SOURCE: Copyright © 2001 by *The New York Times Co.* Reprinted with permission.

### LESSONS OF THE ARTICLE

This article examines a common problem faced by people who are retiring. Should they take a single lump-sum payment or a series of annual payments? Answering this question requires using the concept of present value. The article also describes how most people are extremely impatient, behaving as if their own personal discount rate is extraordinarily high, and how that explains the willingness to borrow at very high interest rates.

*The author is using the term *discount rate* in the same way that we use the term *interest rate* in the present-value calculation. Computing present value requires that we reduce the future payments to their equivalent value today—that is, we need to *discount* them. We all have our own personal discount rate, or interest rate, that is a measure of how patient or impatient we are.

---

Because there are many different kinds of bonds, to focus our discussion, we'll look at the most common type, a **coupon bond**. Say a borrower who needs $100 "issues" or sells a $100 coupon bond to a lender. The bond issuer is required to make annual payments, called **coupon payments**. The annual amount of those payments (expressed as a percentage of the amount borrowed) is called the **coupon rate**. If the coupon rate is 5 percent, then the borrower/issuer pays the lender/bondholder $5 per year per $100 borrowed. The yearly coupon payment equals the coupon rate times the amount borrowed. The bond also specifies when the issuer is going to repay the initial $100 and the payments will stop, called the **maturity date** or *term to maturity*. The final payment, a repayment of the initial $100 loan, is often referred to as the **principal, face value,** or **par value** of the bond.

Before the advent of computers, an investor buying a bond would receive a certificate with a number of dated coupons attached. To claim the coupon payments, the investor would cut off the coupons and mail them to the bond issuer. At maturity, the

TIME

A coupon bond issued by the Reading Railroad Company on May 1, 1945. Some of the coupons are still attached to the bond.

investor would redeem the certificate for the final payment. The Reading Railroad Company bond pictured nearby still has some coupons attached.[2]

You can see that the borrower who issues a bond is promising to make a series of regular interest payments over the life of the bond, plus a final payment on the maturity date. How much should someone be willing to pay for such a contract? The answer comes directly from present value: *The price of a bond is the present value of its payments*. To see how to value a bond, we'll start with repayment of the principal; then we'll add the coupon payments.

### Valuing the Principal Payment

Valuing the bond's principal, or final payment, is a straightforward application of present value. Let's look at a bond that promises a principal payment of $100 on its maturity date $n$ years in the future. The present value of this payment is

---

[2]The bond in the picture is a $1,000 face value 50-year 3½ percent coupon bond issued on May 1, 1945. It promised 100 payments of $17.35, to be made every six months beginning on November 1, 1945, plus a $1,000 final payment on May 1, 1995. The vast majority of bonds pay interest biannually.

$$P_{BP} = \frac{F}{(1+i)^n} = \frac{\$100}{(1+i)^n} \tag{7}$$

Present value of bond principal $(P_{BP})$ =

Principal payment $(F)$ divided by (One plus the interest rate) raised to $n$.

We can see immediately that the value of the principal payment varies with both the time to maturity and the interest rate. The longer the time until the payment is made—the higher the $n$—the lower the value of the payment. And the higher the interest rate, $i$, the lower the value of the payment.

To see how this works, let's start with an interest rate of 6 percent and a final payment of $1,000 to be made in 30 years. If the interest rate is 6 percent, the present value of the final payment is

$$P_{BP} = \frac{\$1000}{(1.06)^{30}} = \$174.11$$

Not surprisingly, this promise to make a payment that far in the future is worth only a fraction of the $1,000 principal. Lowering the interest rate, say to 4 percent, would increase the present value of the principal payment to $308.32, but it would still be much less than half of the payment itself.

**Valuing the Coupon Payments**   What about the coupon payments? This series of equal payments resembles the loan payments we examined in our discussion of internal rate of return. There we computed the sum of a series of equal payments by adding up the present value of each payment. Let's look at this process in more detail, starting with two $10 payments made in consecutive years. Assuming an interest rate of 6 percent, the value of these two payments is

$$\frac{\$10}{1.06} + \frac{\$10}{1.06^2} = \$9.43 + \$8.90 = \$18.33$$

Adding additional payments simply means adding more terms. So for five $10 payments made over five consecutive years, the present value is

$$\frac{\$10}{1.06} + \frac{\$10}{1.06^2} + \frac{\$10}{1.06^3} + \frac{\$10}{1.06^4} + \frac{\$10}{1.06^5} = \$9.43 + \$8.90 + \$8.40 + \$7.92 + \$7.47 = \$42.12$$

This example highlights two important properties of periodic fixed payments. First, the longer the payments go on—the more of them there are—the higher their total value. Even though the additional payments fall further into the future, the overall present value still grows. Because a long-term bond (one that lasts for 30 years, for instance) has more payments than a short-term maturity bond (one whose final payment is made, say, in five years), the coupon payments on the long-term bond will be worth more than the coupon payments on the short-term bond.

Second, as is always the case in present-value calculations, the higher the interest rate, the lower the present value. Raising the interest rate from 6 to 7 percent, for example, lowers the total value of the five future payments on our short-term bond from $42.12 to $41.00.

We can use the present-value expression to write a general formula for a string of yearly coupon payments made over $n$ years. It is simply the sum of the present value of the payments for each year from one to $n$ years:

$$P_{CP} = \frac{C}{(1+i)^1} + \frac{C}{(1+i)^2} + \frac{C}{(1+i)^3} + \cdots + \frac{C}{(1+i)^n} \tag{8}$$

**Figure 4.2** The Nominal Interest Rate, the Inflation Rate, and the Real Interest Rate

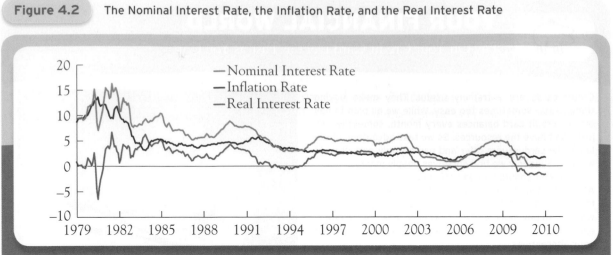

SOURCE: *Three-month Treasury bill rates from the Federal Reserve Board and 12-month inflation rates computed from the Bureau of Labor Statistics Consumer Price Index Research Series. The real interest rate is the nominal rate minus the inflation rate.*

power of the dollars you will use to repay the loan. But neither of you knows what that rate is going to be, so you need to forecast it to conclude your agreement. That is, the nominal interest rate you agree on must be based on *expected inflation* over the term of the loan, plus the real interest rate you agree on.

Writing this statement down in the form of an equation is helpful. The nominal interest rate, $i$, equals the real interest rate, $r$, plus expected inflation, $\pi^e$:[3]

$$i = r + \pi^e \tag{10}$$

This is called the *Fisher equation* after the early 20th-century economist Irving Fisher. It shows that in general, the nominal interest rate is positively related to expected inflation. The higher expected inflation, the higher the nominal interest rate. As we can see in Figure 4.2, the data bear this out. While the relationship is not a tight one, higher nominal interest rates are usually associated with higher inflation rates. In 1980 and 1981, for example, U.S. interest rates were sky high; the U.S. Treasury had to pay more than 15 percent for its short-term borrowing. By 1986, interest rates had dropped to more reasonable levels, close to 5 percent. That's a 10-percentage point move in just five years! The figure shows that as inflation fell, nominal interest rates also fell. In fact, the declines were almost identical. Real interest rates didn't change much during this period.

[3]This equation is an approximation that works only at low levels of inflation and the real interest rate. The exact relationship among the nominal interest rate, real interest rate, and the inflation rate is $(1 + i) = (1 + r)(1 + \pi^e)$, which equals $(1 + i) = 1 + r + \pi^i + r\pi^e$. The approximation, $i = r + \pi^e$, ignores the cross-term $r\pi^e$, which is usually small. For example, if the real interest rate and the inflation rate are both 5 percent, then $r\pi^e = 0.05 \times 0.05 = 0.0025$, or 0.25 percent. But when inflation is very high, this cross-term becomes important. If the real interest rate is 5 percent, at zero inflation, a nominal interest rate of 5 percent means that a $100 investment yields $105. But if the inflation rate rises to 100 percent, an investor will require $210 to make the same investment a year later, so the nominal interest rate that results in a 5 percent real return at 100 percent inflation is $(1 + i) = (1 + 0.05)(1 + 1) = 2.1$, which implies an interest rate of 110 percent, not 105 percent. The 5 percent difference comes from the part of the equation that we ignore in the approximation.

**APPLYING THE CONCEPT**
HIGH INTEREST RATES,
LOW INTEREST RATES

Once we realize that the nominal interest rate moves with expected inflation, big swings in interest rates become less of a mystery. And the fact that the Japanese interest rate is close to zero while the Russian interest rate is nearly 9 percent is easier to understand. All we need to do to understand these differences is look at differences in inflation. In 2010, for example, Japanese prices were *falling* at a rate of about 2 percent a year, while the Russian inflation rate was an uncomfortable 8 percent per year. This 10-percentage-point difference in inflation

rates accounts for more than the 9-percentage-point difference in the nominal interest rates.

Figure 4.3 shows the nominal interest rate and the inflation rate in 35 countries and the euro area in early 2010. Note first that higher inflation is associated with higher nominal interest rates. Second, more than half of the points are above the 45-degree line, meaning that in these countries, the nominal interest rate is higher than the inflation rate. Yet, on average, the ex post real interest rate was close to zero—a low level that reflects the weakness of the global economy following the financial crisis of 2007–2009. Note that, with few exceptions, the distance of these points from the 45-degree line, which represents the real interest rate, does not vary nearly as much as their distance from the horizontal axis, which represents the nominal interest rate.

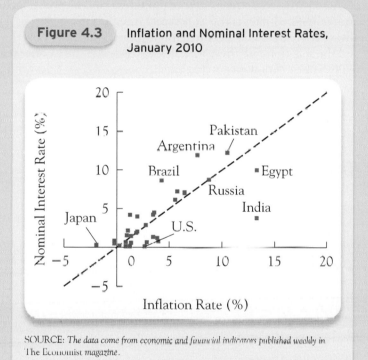

**Figure 4.3**    Inflation and Nominal Interest Rates, January 2010

SOURCE: *The data come from economic and financial indicators published weekly in The Economist magazine.*

 

The term *real interest rate* can cause confusion. The financial markets quote nominal interest rates, the ones that appear in the newspaper and on bank statements.[4] They are "real" in the sense that they are real-life interest rates. When people use the term *interest rate* without qualification, they are referring to the *nominal* interest rate, the one they see every day. We will follow this convention, using the term *interest rate* to mean the nominal rate and the term *real interest rate* to refer to the nominal rate less expected inflation.

[4]One exception is certain bonds whose interest rates are quoted in real, inflation-adjusted terms. We will examine these *inflation-indexed* bonds in detail in Chapter 6.

Unlike the nominal rates, we cannot directly observe the real interest rate; we have to estimate it. The easiest way to do that is to turn the Fisher equation around, rewriting it as

$$r = i - \pi^e \tag{11}$$

Because we know the nominal interest rate, $i$, measuring the real interest rate means subtracting forecasted inflation. There are a number of sources for these forecasts. Twice a year the Federal Reserve Bank of Philadelphia publishes professional forecasts. Once a month, the Survey Research Center of the University of Michigan computes consumer inflation expectations.

But because forecasts are often wrong, our estimate will usually differ from the real interest rate that occurs. Someone who is making an economically important decision will do so based on the expected real interest rate. Some time later, that person will look back and compute the real interest rate actually paid or received. The first of these is known as the *ex ante* real interest rate, meaning "before the fact." The second, or realized rate, is the *ex post* real interest rate, meaning "after the fact." We can always compute the ex post real interest rate, since we know the nominal interest rate and the inflation rate there actually was. But it is the ex ante real interest rate that we really want to know.

## Terms

| | |
|---|---|
| basis point, 73 | internal rate of return, 80 |
| bond, 82 | maturity date, 83 |
| compound interest, 71 | nominal interest rate, 86 |
| coupon bond, 83 | par value, 83 |
| coupon payment, 83 | present value, 74 |
| coupon rate, 83 | principal, 83 |
| face value, 83 | real interest rate, 86 |
| fixed-payment loan, 80 | rule of 72, 73 |
| future value, 70 | yield, 70 |

## Chapter Lessons

1. The value of a payment depends on when it is made.
   a. Future value is the present value of an initial investment times one plus the interest rate for each year you hold it. The higher the interest rate, the higher the future value.
   b. Present value is equal to the value today of a payment made on a future date.
      i. The higher the payment, the higher the present value at a given interest rate.
      ii. The higher the interest rate, the lower the present value of a given payment.

www.mhhe.com/cecchetti3e

iii. The longer the time until the payment is made, the lower the present value of a given payment at a given interest rate.

iv. For a given increase in the interest rate, the present value of a promised payment falls more the farther into the future the payment is to be made.

v. When computing present value, the interest rate and the time until the payment is to be made must be measured in the same time units.

2. Present value can be used to value any stream of future payments.

a. The internal rate of return is the interest rate that equates the present value of the future payments or profits from an investment with its current cost.

b. A coupon bond is a promise to make periodic interest payments and a final principal payment on specific future dates.

i. The present value of a bond depends on its coupon rate, date of maturity, and the current interest rate.

ii. The higher the coupon rate, given the maturity and the interest rate, the higher the present value of the bond.

iii. The price of a bond is inversely related to the interest rate. The higher the price, the lower the interest rate that equates the price with the present value of the promised payments.

3. The real interest rate is the nominal interest rate minus expected inflation. It expresses the interest rate in terms of purchasing power rather than current dollars.

# Conceptual Problems

1. Compute the future value of $100 at an 8 percent interest rate 5, 10, and 15 years into the future. What would the future value be over these time horizons if the interest rate were 5 percent?

2. Compute the present value of a $100 investment made 6 months, 5 years, and 10 years from now at 4 percent interest.

3. Assuming that the current interest rate is 3 percent, compute the value of a five-year, 5 percent coupon bond with a face value of $1,000. What happens when the interest rate goes to 4 percent? What happens when the interest rate goes to 2 percent?

4.* Given a choice of two investments, would you choose one that pays a total return of 30 percent over five years or one that pays 0.5 percent per month for five years?

5. A financial institution offers you a one-year certificate of deposit with an interest rate of 5 percent. You expect the inflation rate to be 3 percent. What is the real return on your deposit?

6. Explain why choosing an investment manager based purely on his or her recent performance in terms of generating high yields might not necessarily be the best idea.

*Indicates more difficult problems

7. You decide you would like to retire at age 65, and expect to live until you are 85 (assume there is no chance you will die younger or live longer). You figure that you can live nicely on $50,000 per year.
   a. Describe the calculation you need to make to determine how much you must save to purchase an annuity paying $50,000 per year for the rest of your life. Assume the interest rate is 7 percent.
   b. How would your calculation change if you expected inflation to average 2 percent for the rest of your life?

8. Most businesses replace their computers every two to three years. Assume that a computer costs $2,000 and that it fully depreciates in 3 years, at which point it has no resale value whatsoever and is thrown away.
   a. If the interest rate for financing the equipment is equal to $i$, show how to compute the minimum annual cash flow that a computer must generate to be worth the purchase. Your answer will depend on $i$.
   b. Suppose the computer did not fully depreciate, but still had a $250 value at the time it was replaced. Show how you would adjust the calculation given in your answer to part $a$.
   c. What if financing can only be had at a 10 percent interest rate? Calculate the minimum cash flow the computer must generate to be worth the purchase using your answer to part $a$.

9. Some friends of yours have just had a child. Thinking ahead, and realizing the power of compound interest, they are considering investing for their child's college education, which will begin in 18 years. Assume that the cost of a college education today is $125,000; there is no inflation; and there are no taxes on interest income that is used to pay college tuition and expenses.
   a. If the interest rate is 5 percent, how much money will your friends need to put into their savings account today to have $125,000 in 18 years?
   b. What if the interest rate were 10 percent?
   c. The chance that the price of a college education will be the same 18 years from now as it is today seems remote. Assuming that the price will rise 3 percent per year, and that today's interest rate is 8 percent, what will your friends' investment need to be?
   d. Return to part $a$, the case with a 5 percent interest rate and no inflation. Assume that your friends don't have enough financial resources to make the entire investment at the beginning. Instead, they think they will be able to split their investment into two equal parts, one invested immediately and the second invested in five years. Describe how you would compute the required size of the two equal investments, made five years apart.

10. You are considering buying a new house, and have found that a $100,000, 30-year fixed-rate mortgage is available with an interest rate of 7 percent. This mortgage requires 360 monthly payments of approximately $651 each. If the interest rate rises to 8 percent, what will happen to your monthly payment? Compare the percentage change in the monthly payment with the percentage change in the interest rate.

11.* Use the Fisher equation to explain in detail what a borrower is compensating a lender for when he pays her a nominal rate of interest.

# Analytical Problems

12. If the current interest rate increases, what would you expect to happen to bond prices? Explain.

13. Which would be most affected in the event of an interest rate increase—the price of a five-year coupon bond that paid coupons only in years 3, 4, and 5 or the price of a five-year coupon bond that paid coupons only in years 1, 2, and 3, everything else being equal? Explain.

14. Under what circumstances might you be willing to pay more than $1,000 for a coupon bond that matures in three years, has a coupon rate of 10 percent and a face value of $1,000?

15.* Approximately how long would it take for an investment of $100 to reach $800 if you earned 5 percent? What if the interest rate were 10 percent? How long would it take an investment of $200 to reach $800 at an interest rate of 5 percent? Why is there a difference between doubling the interest rate and doubling the initial investment?

16. Suppose two investors (A and B) are thinking about purchasing the same long-term bond. When deciding what price he would be willing to pay for the bond, investor A takes into account the behavior of interest rates over the previous 10 years, noting a period of interest-rate volatility before the low and stable interest rates of the most recent two years. Investor B only looks at the past two years when making his decision. Everything else being equal, which investor do you think would be willing to pay a higher price for the bond?

17. Recently, some lucky person won the lottery. The lottery winnings were reported to be $85.5 million. In reality, the winner got a choice of $2.85 million per year for 30 years or $46 million today.
    a. Explain briefly why winning $2.85 million per year for 30 years is not equivalent to winning $85.5 million.
    b. The evening news interviewed a group of people the day after the winner was announced. When asked, most of them responded that, if they were the lucky winner, they would take the $46 million up-front payment. Suppose (just for a moment) that you were that lucky winner. How would you decide between the annual installments or the up-front payment?

18. You are considering going to graduate school for a one-year master's program. You have done some research and believe that the master's degree will add $5,000 per year to your salary for the next 10 years of your working life, starting at the end of this year. From then on, after the next 10 years, it makes no difference. Completing the master's program will cost you $35,000, which you would have to borrow at an interest rate of 6 percent. How would you decide if this investment in your education were profitable?

19. Assuming the chances of being paid back are the same, would a nominal interest rate of 10 percent always be more attractive to a lender than a nominal rate of 5 percent? Explain.

20.* Suppose two parties agree that the expected inflation rate for the next year is 3 percent. Based on this, they enter into a loan agreement where the nominal interest rate to be charged is 7 percent. If the inflation rate for the year turns out to be 2 percent, who gains and who loses?

# Appendix to Chapter 4

## The Algebra of Present-Value Formulas

In this short appendix, we will derive a formula for computing present value. To do it we need to use some algebra, but the result is worth the trouble. The formula is useful in computing the present value of any series of payments, such as a car loan, a mortgage, or a coupon bond, and the internal rate of return on an investment.

Imagine that you are going to buy a house. You would like to borrow $PV$ dollars at interest rate $i$ and agree to make $n$ equal mortgage payments. How large will your payment be? It will be just big enough so that the present value of all your payments, discounted at interest rate $i$, equals the amount of the loan.

To compute the payment, we will use the present-value formula. If we call the size of the monthly payments C, then we need to solve the following formula:

$$PV = \frac{C}{(1+i)^1} + \frac{C}{(1+i)^2} + \frac{C}{(1+i)^3} + \ldots + \frac{C}{(1+i)^n} \tag{A1}$$

Each term in expression (A1) is the present value of a payment C made on a future date. To simplify (A1), we multiply it by $[1/(1+i)]$ to get

$$\frac{1}{(1+i)}PV = \frac{1}{(1+i)}\left[\frac{C}{(1+i)^1} + \frac{C}{(1+i)^2} + \frac{C}{(1+i)^3} + \ldots + \frac{C}{(1+i)^n}\right]$$

$$= \frac{C}{(1+i)^2} + \frac{C}{(1+i)^3} + \frac{C}{(1+i)^4} + \ldots + \frac{C}{(1+i)^n} + \frac{C}{(1+i)^{n+1}} \tag{A2}$$

Now subtract (A2) from (A1):

$$PV - \frac{1}{(1+i)}PV = \frac{C}{(1+i)^1} + \frac{C}{(1+i)^2} + \frac{C}{(1+i)^3} + \ldots + \frac{C}{(1+i)^n}$$

$$- \frac{C}{(1+i)^2} - \frac{C}{(1+i)^3} - \ldots - \frac{C}{(1+i)^n} - \frac{C}{(1+i)^{n+1}} \tag{A3}$$

to get

$$\frac{i}{(1+i)}PV = \frac{C}{(1+i)^1} - \frac{C}{(1+i)^{n+1}} \tag{A4}$$

Simplifying this result yields the following formula:

$$PV = \left(\frac{C}{i}\right)\left[1 - \frac{1}{(1+i)^n}\right] \tag{A5}$$

To see how to use this formula, suppose you're taking out a $100,000 mortgage that you agree to repay over 30 years at an interest rate of 8 percent. Remember that the interest rate must be quoted in decimal form and at the same frequency as the payments. For example, if you are going to make monthly payments, then $i$ must be a monthly interest rate. To figure out your annual payment (in reality you would make 360 *monthly* payments), just solve the following formula for C:

$$\$100,000 = \left(\frac{C}{0.08}\right)\left[1 - \frac{1}{(1.08)^{30}}\right] \qquad (A6)$$

Simplifying the right-hand side gives us

$$\$100,000 = 11.258C \qquad (A7)$$

So your annual payment will be $8,882.57. We can do the same calculation for 360 monthly payments using a monthly interest rate of 0.6434 percent, which annualizes to 8 percent.

Formula (A5) is very useful in computing the fixed payments due on a loan, the coupon payments on a bond, or the internal rate of return on an investment. Notice that as the number of payments increases (as $n$ gets bigger), the term $[1/(1 + i)^n]$ grows smaller. If the payments never end, so that $n$ represents infinity, then $[1/(1 + i)^n]$ shrinks to zero. Thus, the present value of a stream of fixed payments that never ends is $[C/i]$.

# Chapter 6

## Bonds, Bond Prices, and the Determination of Interest Rates

Virtually any financial arrangement involving the current transfer of resources from a lender to a borrower, with a transfer back at some time in the future, is a form of bond. Car loans, home mortgages, even credit card balances all create a loan from a financial intermediary to an individual making a purchase—just like the bonds governments and large corporations sell when they need to borrow.

When companies like Ford, IBM, or General Electric need to finance their operations, they sell bonds. When the U.S. Treasury or a state government needs to borrow, it sells bonds. And they do it billions of dollars at a time. In 2009, following the financial crisis, U.S. corporations tried to reduce their debt, but their bonds outstanding remained above $11 trillion. Federal, state, and local American governments have more than $10 trillion in outstanding debt as well.[1] The ease with which individuals, corporations, and governments borrow is essential to the functioning of our economic system. Without this free flow of resources through the bond markets, the economy would grind to a halt.

Historically, we can trace the concept of using bonds to borrow to monarchs' almost insatiable appetite for resources. To maintain lavish lifestyles, fight wars, and explore the globe, kings, princes, and other rulers drew on every available source of financing. Even with these incentives, after thousands of years of civilization only a few possibilities had been developed: outright confiscation; taxation, which is a mild form of confiscation; debasement of currency, in which people are required to exchange their coins for ones that weigh less—in effect, a tax on currency; and borrowing. Monarchs who borrowed directly from international bankers frequently defaulted or failed to make the loan payments they had promised.[2]

Between 1557 and 1696, the various kings of Spain defaulted 14 times. With that track record, it's no wonder they had to pay interest rates close to 40 percent.

The Dutch invented modern bonds to finance their lengthy war of independence against those same Spanish kings who defaulted on loans in the 16th and 17th centuries. Over the next two centuries, the British refined the use of bonds to finance government activities. The practice then spread to other countries. Alexander Hamilton, the first Secretary of the U.S. Treasury and the man whose face appears on the $10 bill, brought bonds to the United States. One of Hamilton's first acts after the formation of the U.S. Treasury in 1789 was to consolidate all the debt remaining from the Revolutionary War. This resulted in the first U.S. government bonds. While

---

[1]These numbers come from the *Flow of Funds Accounts of the United States*, published quarterly by the Federal Reserve Board.

[2]For a detailed analysis of such sovereign defaults, see Carmen M. Reinhart and Kenneth S. Rogoff, *This Time Is Different: Eight Hundred Years of Financial Folly* (Princeton, NJ: Princeton University Press, 2009).

*"The name's Bond. Duane Bond."*

SOURCE: © Michael Crawford/The New Yorker Collection/
www.cartoonbank.com.

the depth and complexity of bond markets have increased in modern times, many of their original features remain.

If we want to understand the financial system, particularly the bond market, we must understand three things. The first is the relationship between bond prices and interest rates (yet another application of present value). The second is that supply and demand in the bond market determine bond prices. The third is why bonds are risky. Let's get started.

# Bond Prices

A standard bond specifies the fixed amounts to be paid and the exact dates of the payments. *How much should you be willing to pay for a bond?* The answer depends on the bond's characteristics. We will look at four basic types:

1. *Zero-coupon bonds*, which promise a single future payment, such as a U.S. Treasury bill.
2. *Fixed-payment loans*, such as conventional mortgages.
3. *Coupon bonds*, which make periodic interest payments and repay the principal at maturity. U.S. Treasury bonds and most corporate bonds are coupon bonds.
4. *Consols*, which make periodic interest payments forever, never repaying the principal that was borrowed. (There aren't many examples of these.)

Let's see how each of these bonds is priced. To keep the analysis simple, we'll ignore risk for now.

## Zero-Coupon Bonds

**U.S. Treasury bills** (commonly known as **T-bills**) are the most straightforward type of bond. Each T-bill represents a promise by the U.S. government to pay $100 on a fixed future date. There are no coupon payments, which is why T-bills are known as **zero-coupon bonds**. They are also called *pure discount bonds* (or just discount bonds), since the price is less than their face value—they sell at a discount. This isn't a discount in the sense of a markdown at a clothing store, however. If a $100 face value T-bill sells for $96, the $4 difference is the interest, the payment to the lender for making the loan.

Because a Treasury bill makes a single payment on a future date, its price is just the present value of that payment:

$$\text{Price of \$100 face value zero-coupon bond} = \frac{\$100}{(1 + i)^n} \qquad (1)$$

where *i* is the interest rate expressed in decimal form and *n* is the time until the payment is made, measured in the same time units as the interest rate. Suppose the annual interest rate is 5 percent. What is the price of a one-year T-bill? To figure out the answer, take the present value formula, set $i$ at 0.05 and $n$ at 1, and then compute the price:

$$\text{Price of one-year Treasury bill} = \frac{\$100}{(1 + 0.05)} = \$95.24$$

The U.S. Treasury doesn't issue T-bills with a maturity of more than one year; six-month T-bills are much more common. At an annual interest rate of 5 percent, what is the price of such a zero-coupon bond? We can use the present-value formula, again, but this time we have to be careful. Recall that we need to measure $i$ and $n$ in the same time units. Because $i$ is the interest rate for one year, we need to measure $n$ in years, and since six months is half a year,

TIME

$$\text{Price of a six-month Treasury bill} = \frac{\$100}{(1 + 0.05)^{1/2}} = \$97.59$$

As you can see, the price of a six-month Treasury bill is higher than that of a one-year T-bill. The shorter the time until the payment is made, the more we are willing to pay for it now. If we go on to compute the price of a three-month T-bill, setting $n$ at 0.25 (one-fourth of a year), we find the answer is $99.02.

Equation (1) shows that for a zero-coupon bond, the relationship between the price and the interest rate is the same as the one we saw in our discussion of present value. When the price moves, the interest rate moves with it, albeit in the opposite direction. Thus, we can compute the interest rate from the price using the present-value formula. For example, if the price of a one-year T-bill is $95, then the interest rate is $i = (\$100/\$95) - 1 = 0.0526$, or 5.26 percent.

## Fixed-Payment Loans

Home mortgages and car loans are called *fixed-payment loans* because they promise a fixed number of equal payments at regular intervals. These loans are *amortized*, meaning that the borrower pays off the principal along with the interest over the life of the loan. Each payment includes both interest and a portion of the principal. Pricing these sorts of loans is straightforward using the present-value formula: The value of the loan today is the present value of all the payments. If we assume that the annual interest rate is $i$ (measured as a decimal) and that the loan specifies $n$ payments, then

$$\text{Value of a fixed-payment loan} = \frac{\text{Fixed payment}}{(1 + i)} + \frac{\text{Fixed payment}}{(1 + i)^2} + \ldots + \frac{\text{Fixed payment}}{(1 + i)^n} \quad (2)$$

Using this formula is complicated, so we won't go any further. But when lenders figure out your monthly payment for a car loan or home mortgage, this is how they do it.

## Coupon Bonds

Recall from Chapter 4 that the issuer of a coupon bond promises to make a series of periodic interest payments called coupon payments, plus a principal payment at maturity. So we can value a coupon bond using (you guessed it) the present-value formula. The price of the coupon bond is

$$P_{CB} = \left[ \frac{\text{Coupon payment}}{(1 + i)^1} + \frac{\text{Coupon payment}}{(1 + i)^2} + \ldots + \frac{\text{Coupon payment}}{(1 + i)^n} \right] + \frac{\text{Face value}}{(1 + i)^n} \quad (3)$$

## YOUR FINANCIAL WORLD
Know Your Mortgage

Survey evidence tells us that a large number of people with adjustable-rate mortgages underestimate how much their monthly payments can change.* Don't be one of these people! When you buy a home and get a mortgage, know what can happen.

There are two basic types of mortgages: conventional fixed-rate and adjustable-rate, also known as ARMs. Fixed-rate mortgages are the easiest to understand since the payments, like the interest rate, are fixed. That means you make the same monthly payment for the entire term of the mortgage, for most people that is 30 years. (You can also get 10, 15, and 20 year fixed-rate mortgages.) Since the payments don't change, fixed-rate borrowers are not exposed to the risks of interest rates increases.

ARMs are more complicated, since the interest rate changes. This means that the payments change, too. Getting an adjustable-rate mortgage means knowing about things like interest-rate indexes, margins, discounts, caps, negative amortization, and convertibility:†

- On what interest-rate index is the mortgage rate based? How much does that index move around?
- How big is the mortgage rate margin above the interest-rate index on which it is based?
- How frequently is the rate adjusted?

- Does the ARM have an initial interest rate that will almost surely rise? If so, when and by how much?
- What is the cap for the mortgage rate? What is the maximum for a single adjustment and what is the highest the interest rate can ever go?
- Does the ARM include a payment cap? If you hit the payment cap, will the principal of the loan start to increase? (That's negative amortization.)
- Can you convert the ARM into a fixed-rate mortgage?

This list may seem long, but it is really only the beginning. Getting the right mortgage may be the most important financial decision you ever make, so it is worth spending some time figuring it out. And once you have it, don't forget how your mortgage works.

*In "Do Homeowners Know Their House Values and Mortgage Terms?", Federal Reserve Board Finance and Economics Discussion Paper 2006–3, January 2006, Brian Bucks and Karen Pence estimate that nearly half of people with adjustable-rate mortgages don't know how much the interest rate can move at one time, the maximum rate, or the index to which the mortgage rate is tied.

†The Federal Reserve Board's *Consumer Handbook on Adjustable Rate Mortgages* is a great place to start learning about mortgages.

The right side of this equation has two parts. The first part, in brackets, looks just like the fixed-payment loan—and it is, with the important exception that it represents only the interest. The second part, on the far right, looks just like a zero-coupon bond, and it is. It represents the value of the promise to repay the principal at maturity.

## Consols

Another type of bond offers only periodic payments. That is, the borrower pays only interest, never repaying the principal. These loans, called **consols** or **perpetuities**, are like coupon bonds whose payments last forever. Because governments are really the only borrowers that can credibly promise to make payments forever, there are no privately issued consols. The British government has a number of consols currently outstanding, the oldest of which was issued in 1853. The U.S. government sold consols once in 1900. The bonds had a special provision allowing the Treasury to buy them back starting in 1930. The Treasury bought back all the consols so you would not be able to find one today.

You won't be surprised to learn that the price of a consol is the present value of all the future interest payments. The fact that the number of payments is infinite complicates things. But we can derive a formula for the price of a consol that makes a coupon payment every year forever.[3] At interest rate $i$,

$$P_{Consol} = \frac{\text{Yearly coupon payment}}{i} \qquad (4)$$

The price of a consol equals the annual coupon payment divided by the interest rate. So at an interest rate of 5 percent, a consol that promises $1 per year forever would sell for $20. If the interest rate changes to 4 percent, the price rises to $25. Again, the interest rate and the price move in opposite directions.

# Bond Yields

Now that we know how to calculate a bond price given the interest rate, we need to move in the other direction and calculate the interest rate, or the return to an investor, implicit in the bond's price. Doing so means combining information about the promised payments with the price to obtain what is called the *yield*—a measure of the cost of borrowing and the reward for lending. When people talk about bonds they use the terms *yield* and *interest rate* interchangeably, so we will too.

## Yield to Maturity

The most useful measure of the return on holding a bond is called the **yield to maturity**, or the yield bondholders receive if they hold the bond to its maturity when the final principal payment is made. Take a $100 face value 5 percent coupon bond with one year to maturity. At maturity, the owner of this bond receives a coupon payment of $5 plus a principal payment of $100.[4] Using the formula from equation (3), we know that the price of the bond is

$$\text{Price of one-year 5 percent coupon bond} = \frac{\$5}{(1+i)} + \frac{\$100}{(1+i)} \qquad (5)$$

The value of $i$ that solves this equation is the *yield to maturity*. Remembering that present value and interest rates move in opposite directions, we can conclude the following:

1. If the price of the bond is $100, then the yield to maturity equals the coupon rate. (Recall from Chapter 4 that the coupon rate is the ratio of the annual coupon payments to the face value of the bond.)

---

[3]You may find it troubling that you can add up an infinite number of payments and get a finite number. To see why this works, notice that as the number of years at which the terminal payment occurs increases, $1/(1+i)^n$ grows very small. After 100 years, at an interest rate of 5 percent, it is 0.008. So the present value of $1 promised in 100 years is less than one cent. We could just ignore the payments that come after this and get virtually the same answer. To derive the expression for the price of a consol, use the techniques from Appendix 4. Start by calling C the coupon payment and writing the price as the sum of the present value of the (infinite) number of payments $P_{Consol} = \frac{C}{(1+i)} + \frac{C}{(1+i)^2} + \frac{C}{(1+i)^3} + \dots$. Next, multiply this expression by $[1/(1+i)]$ to get $\frac{1}{(1+i)} P_{Consol} = \frac{C}{(1+i)^2} + \frac{C}{(1+i)^3} + \frac{C}{(1+i)^4} + \dots$. Then subtract this expression from the original, which gives $P_{Consol} - \frac{1}{(1+i)} P_{Consol} = \frac{C}{(1+i)}$. Solving for the price yields equation (4).

[4]Most bonds offer two semiannual payments, each equal to half the annual coupon. We will ignore this complication.

2. Because the price rises as the yield falls, when the price is *above* $100, the yield to maturity must be *below* the coupon rate.
3. Because the price falls as the yield rises, when the price is *below* $100, the yield to maturity must be *above* the coupon rate.

Looking at the one-year 5 percent coupon bond, we can see right away that if the yield to maturity is 5 percent, then

$$\frac{\$5}{(1 + 0.05)} + \frac{\$100}{(1 + 0.05)} = \frac{\$105}{1.05} = \$100$$

That's the first point. Now look at what happens when yield to maturity falls to 4 percent. The price becomes

$$\frac{\$5}{(1 + 0.04)} + \frac{\$100}{(1 + 0.04)} = \frac{\$105}{1.04} = \$100.96$$

That's the second point. If the yield to maturity rises to 6 percent, then the price falls to

$$\frac{\$5}{(1 + 0.06)} + \frac{\$100}{(1 + 0.06)} = \$99.06$$

That's the third point. You can try this process with a more complicated bond—say, one with 10 years to maturity that makes more than just one coupon payment—and get exactly the same results.

The fact that the return on a bond depends on the price you pay for it really isn't that mysterious. If you pay $95 for a $100 face value bond, for example, you will receive both the interest payments and the increase in value from $95 to $100. This rise in value, referred to as a **capital gain**, is part of the return on your investment. So when the price of the bond is below the face value, the return is above the coupon rate. When the price is above the face value, the bondholder incurs a **capital loss** and the bond's yield to maturity falls below its coupon rate.

## Current Yield

**Current yield** is a commonly used, easy-to-compute measure of the proceeds the bondholder receives for making a loan. It is the yearly coupon payment divided by the price:

$$\text{Current yield} = \frac{\text{Yearly coupon payment}}{\text{Price paid}} \tag{6}$$

Looking at this expression, we can see that the current yield measures that part of the return from buying the bond that arises solely from the coupon payments. It ignores the capital gain or loss that arises when the price at which the bond is purchased differs from its face value. So if the price is below par, the current yield will be below the yield to maturity.

Let's return to the one-year 5 percent coupon bond and assume that it is selling for $99. The current yield is easy to calculate as

$$\frac{5}{99} = 0.0505$$

or 5.05 percent. The yield to maturity for this bond is the solution to

$$\frac{\$5}{(1 + i)} + \frac{\$100}{(1 + i)} = \$99$$

which is 6.06 percent. The yield to maturity is higher because, if you buy the bond for $99, one year later you get not only the $5 coupon payment but also a guaranteed $1 capital gain for a total of $6.

   We can repeat these calculations for a case in which the bond is selling for $101. Then the current yield is

$$\frac{5}{101} = 0.0495$$

or 4.95 percent, and the yield to maturity is

$$\frac{\$5}{(1 + i)} + \frac{\$100}{(1 + i)} = \$101$$

or 3.96 percent.

   Putting all this together, we see the relationship between the current yield and the coupon rate. Again, it comes from the fact that current yield moves in the opposite direction from the price: it falls when the bond's price goes up and rises when the price goes down. So when the price equals the face value of the bond, the current yield and coupon rate are equal. When the price rises above the face value, the current yield falls below the coupon rate. And when the price falls below the face value, the current yield rises above the coupon rate.

   Table 6.1 summarizes the relationships among the price, coupon rate, current yield, and yield to maturity. We know that when the bond price is less than face value, the current yield and the yield to maturity are both higher than the coupon rate. But since the yield to maturity takes account of the capital gain the bondholder receives, while the current yield does not, the yield to maturity must be even higher than the current yield. When the price is above the face value, the yield to maturity is lower than the current yield, which is lower than the coupon rate.

## Holding Period Returns

We have emphasized that if you buy a bond whose yield to maturity deviates from the coupon rate, the price will not be the face value. Similarly, the return from holding a bond need not be the coupon rate. For example, if you pay $95 for a one-year 6 percent coupon bond, one year later you will get both the $6 coupon payment and the $5 difference between the purchase price and the $100 face value at maturity. But

**Table 6.1**   Relationship among a Bond's Price and Its Coupon Rate, Current Yield, and Yield to Maturity

*Bond price < Face value:* Coupon rate < Current yield < Yield to maturity
*Bond price = Face value:* Coupon rate = Current yield = Yield to maturity
*Bond price > Face value:* Coupon rate > Current yield > Yield to maturity

this example is really too simple, since it assumes that the investor holds the bond to maturity. Most holders of long-term bonds plan to sell them well before they mature. And since the price of the bond may change between the time of the purchase and the time of the sale, the return to buying a bond and selling it before it matures—the **holding period return**—can differ from the yield to maturity.

Take an example in which you pay $100 for a 10-year, 6 percent coupon bond with a face value of $100. You intend to hold the bond for one year. That is, you are going to buy a 10-year bond and then a year later, you'll sell a 9-year bond. What is your return from holding this bond? If the interest rate doesn't change (that is, it stays at 6 percent) your return will be $6/$100 = 0.06, or 6 percent. But if the interest rate changes, calculating your return becomes more complicated. Say that over the year you hold the bond, the interest rate falls from 6 to 5 percent. That is, the yield to maturity falls to 5 percent. Using equation (3), we can figure out that you have bought a 10-year bond for $100 and sold a 9-year bond for $107.11. What is your one-year holding period return on the initial $100 investment? It has two parts: the $6 coupon payment and the $7.11 capital gain (the difference between the price at which you bought the bond and the price at which you sold it). So the holding period return is

$$\text{One-year holding period return} = \frac{\$6}{\$100} + \frac{\$107.11 - \$100}{\$100} = \frac{\$13.11}{\$100} = 0.1311$$

$$= 13.11 \text{ percent}$$

Obviously, bond prices can go down as well as up. Consider what happens if the yield to maturity rises to 7 percent so that the price falls to $93.48. Now the one-year holding period return is

$$\text{One-year holding period return} = \frac{\$6}{100} + \frac{\$93.48 - \$100}{\$100} = \frac{-\$.52}{\$100} = -0.0052$$

$$= -0.52 \text{ percent}$$

The coupon payment still represents a 6 percent return, but the capital loss from the price movement is 6.52 percent. The one-year holding period return is negative, as overall there is a small loss.[5]

To generalize these examples, notice that the one-year holding period return is the sum of the yearly coupon payment divided by the price paid for the bond, and the change in the price (price sold minus price paid) divided by the price paid:

$$\text{Holding period return} = \frac{\text{Yearly coupon payment}}{\text{Price paid}} + \frac{\text{Change in price of bond}}{\text{Price paid}} \quad (7)$$

The first part on the right-hand side of this equation is the current yield (equation 6). The second part is the capital gain. So the holding period return is

$$\text{Holding period return} = \text{Current yield} + \text{Capital gain} \quad (8)$$

[5]The multiyear case is somewhat more complex. Say that an investor purchased the same 10-year 6 percent coupon bond at par, and then held it for *two* years. If the interest rate were to rise from 7 percent, the price of the now 8-year bond would fall to $94.03 per $100 of face value. This means that the investor would receive $12 in coupon payments plus a capital loss of $5.97, for a total payoff of $106.03. To simplify, let us assume that the first-year coupon cannot be reinvested. Then, using the methods described in the Tools of the Trade on page 78 of Chapter 4, we can compute the annual-rate return as $\left[\left(\frac{106.03}{100}\right)^{1/2} - 1\right] = 0.0297$, or 2.97%. If instead the interest rate were to fall to 4 percent, the price of the bond would rise to $106.46, the total payoff would be $118.46, and the annual-rate return would be 8.84 percent.

Whenever the price of a bond changes, there is a capital gain or loss. The greater the price change, the more important a part of the holding period return the capital gain or loss becomes. The potential for interest-rate movements and changes in bond prices creates risk. The longer the term of the bond, the greater those price movements and the associated risk can be, as we'll see in more detail in the last section of this chapter.

# The Bond Market and the Determination of Interest Rates

Now that we understand the relationship between bond prices and various measures of interest rates, we need to figure out how bond prices are determined and why they change. The best way to do that is to look at bond supply, bond demand, and equilibrium prices in the bond market. Once we understand how the bond market determines bond prices, we can figure out why the prices change.

To keep the analysis simple, we need to make a few choices about how to proceed. First, we'll restrict the discussion to the quantity of bonds outstanding, called the *stock of bonds*. (We could look at what causes the changes in the quantity of bonds outstanding—the *flow*—but that would complicate matters.) Second, we are going to talk about *bond prices* rather than interest rates. Because a bond's price, together with its various characteristics, determines its yield, it really doesn't matter whether we talk about yields (interest rates) or bond prices. Once we know the price, we know the yield. Finally, we're going to consider the *market for a one-year zero-coupon bond* (one that makes no coupon payments) with a face value of $100.

If we assume the investor is planning to purchase a one-year bond and hold it to maturity—they have a one-year **investment horizon**—then the holding period return equals the bond's yield to maturity, and both are determined directly from the price. The present-value formula shows that the relationship between the price and the yield on such a bond is simply $P = \$100/(1 + i)$, so $i = [(\$100 - P)/P]$.

For example, if a bond sells for $95, then the yield is $i = \$5/\$95 = 0.0526$, or 5.26 percent.

"Your pot o'gold is doing nothing for you sitting at the end of the rainbow. At the very least, you should put it in a no-risk interest-bearing account."

SOURCE: © Michael Maslin/The New Yorker Collection/www.cartoonbank.com.

## Bond Supply, Bond Demand, and Equilibrium in the Bond Market

How are bond prices (and bond yields) determined? Not surprisingly, by supply and demand. Some investors are supplying bonds, while others are demanding them. The *bond supply curve* is the relationship between the price and the quantity of bonds people

# TOOLS OF THE TRADE
Reading the Bond Page

Every day *The Wall Street Journal* lists the previous day's closing yields for a wide variety of bonds that serve as standards—or benchmarks—for comparison with other financial instruments. Table 6.2 shows some representative data on global government bonds published on January 14, 2010, while Table 6.3 presents some data on corporate bonds. Let's see what we can learn from reading these tables.

## Global Government Bonds

Governments issue hundreds of bonds. At the beginning of 2010, the U.S. Treasury alone had more than 200 different coupon-bearing instruments outstanding. But investors often focus on the most liquid bonds at key maturities to summarize the evolution of the entire bond market. Table 6.2 uses a two-year bond yield to represent relatively short-term issues and a 10-year bond yield to represent the longer term. In Chapter 7, we'll see how the *term structure of*

*interest rates* relates the level of bond yields to the maturity of the bonds.

The table highlights several points. First, the yields on government bonds change significantly over time. For example, on January 14, 2010, the "latest" 10-year U.S. Treasury bond yield (that is, the yield at the close of the market on January 13) was 3.783 percent. The table also shows that the latest yield exceeded the day-earlier (January 12, or "previous") level of 3.721 percent and was markedly higher than the "year ago" level of 2.298 percent. Assuming that the representative bond had exactly 10 years to maturity on each date, then, as the yield rose, its price fell from $109.57 on January 13, 2009, to $96.63 on January 13, 2010. Similarly, the 10-year Australian yield climbed during the year from 3.967 percent to 5.582 percent, lowering the Australian dollar price of the bond from $104.36 to $91.79.

### Table 6.2 Government Bonds

Yields and spreads over or under U.S. Treasurys on benchmark two-year and 10-year government bonds in selected other countries; arrows indicate whether the yield rose(△) or fell (▼) in the latest session

| Coupon (%) | Country/ Maturity, in years | Latest (●) | 0 | 1.5 | 3 | 4.5 | 6 | 7.5 | 9 | Previous | Month ago | Year ago | SPREAD UNDER/OVER U.S. TREASURYS, in basis points Latest | Chg from prev | Year ago |
|---|---|---|---|---|---|---|---|---|---|---|---|---|---|---|---|
| 1.000 | U.S. 2 | 0.956 △ | ● | | | | | | | 0.916 | 0.817 | 0.751 | | | |
| 3.375 | 10 | 3.783 △ | | ● | | | | | | 3.721 | 3.548 | 2.298 | | | |
| 5.750 | Australia 2 | 4.435 | | | ● | | | | | 4.435 | 4.563 | 2.734 | 347.9 | −4.0 | 198.3 |
| 4.500 | 10 | 5.582 ▼ | | | | ● | | | | 5.685 | 5.577 | 3.967 | 179.9 | −16.5 | 166.9 |
| 1.250 | Canada 2 | 1.288 | ● | | | | | | | 1.288 | 1.255 | 1.024 | 33.2 | −4.0 | 27.3 |
| 3.750 | 10 | 3.588 △ | | ● | | | | | | 3.554 | 3.387 | 2.717 | −19.5 | −2.8 | 41.9 |
| 1.250 | Germany 2 | 1.220 ▼ | ● | | | | | | | 1.226 | 1.260 | 1.506 | 26.4 | −4.6 | 75.5 |
| 3.250 | 10 | 3.313 △ | | ● | | | | | | 3.312 | 3.206 | 2.987 | −47.0 | −6.1 | 68.9 |
| 0.200 | Japan 2 | 0.168 | ● | | | | | | | 0.168 | 0.180 | 0.385 | −78.8 | −4.0 | −36.6 |
| 1.300 | 10 | 1.345 ▼ | | ● | | | | | | 1.352 | 1.286 | 1.242 | −243.8 | −6.9 | −105.6 |
| 5.500 | Sweden 2 | 1.635 △ | | ● | | | | | | 1.634 | 1.795 | 1.376 | 67.9 | −3.9 | 62.5 |
| 5.000 | 10 | 3.397 △ | | ● | | | | | | 3.384 | 3.367 | 2.607 | −38.6 | −4.9 | 30.9 |
| 2.750 | Switzerland 2 | 0.618 ▼ | ● | | | | | | | 0.625 | 0.388 | 0.514 | −33.8 | −4.7 | −23.7 |
| 2.250 | 10 | 2.051 ▼ | | ● | | | | | | 2.099 | 1.910 | 2.216 | −173.2 | −11.0 | −8.2 |
| 3.250 | U.K. 2 | 1.226 △ | ● | | | | | | | 1.191 | 1.230 | 1.596 | 27.0 | −0.5 | 84.5 |
| 4.500 | 10 | 3.957 △ | | ● | | | | | | 3.932 | 3.852 | 3.204 | 17.4 | −3.7 | 90.6 |

Source: Thomson Reuters

## Table 6.3   Corporate Bonds

**Investment-grade spreads that tightened the most . . .**

| Issuer | Symbol | Coupon (%) | Maturity | SPREAD*, in basis points | | STOCK PERFORMANCE | | |
| | | | | Current | One-day change | Last week | Close ($) | % chg |
|---|---|---|---|---|---|---|---|---|
| Prologis | PLD | 6.625 | May 15, '18 | 269 | −52 | 325 | 13.95 | 2.65 |
| BHP Billiton Finance | BHP | 5.125 | March 29, '12 | 37 | −37 | n.a. | ... | |
| American Express | AXP | 7.300 | Aug. 20, '13 | 160 | −33 | 193 | 42.15 | 0.31 |
| Chemtura | CEM | 6.875 | June 1, '16 | 231 | −30 | 147 | ... | ... |

**. . . And spreads that widened the most**

| Issuer | Symbol | Coupon (%) | Maturity | SPREAD*, in basis points | | STOCK PERFORMANCE | | |
| | | | | Current | One-day change | Last week | Close ($) | % chg |
|---|---|---|---|---|---|---|---|---|
| Digicel | DLLTD | 8.875 | Jan. 15, '15 | 716 | 38 | n.a. | ... | ... |
| Citigroup | C | 5.000 | Sept.15, '14 | 321 | 32 | 286 | 3.50 | −0.57 |
| Daimler North America | DAIGR | 7.300 | Jan. 15, '12 | 134 | 29 | 131 | ... | ... |
| Tyco Electronics S.A. | TEL | 6.000 | Oct. 1, '12 | 217 | 27 | n.a. | 25.52 | 3.15 |

*Estimated spread over 2-year, 3-year, 5-year, 10-year or 30-year hot-run Treasury; 100 basis points = one percentage pt., change in spread shown is for Z-spread. Note: Data are for the most active issue of bonds with maturities of two years or more

Sources: MarketAxess Corporate Bond Ticker; WSJ Market Data Group.

Second, the yields on government bonds differ substantially across countries. The "latest" 10-year U.S. Treasury yield was much lower than the yield on 10-year Australian bonds, but far above the 1.345 percent yield on 10-year Japanese bonds. The difference across countries is also portrayed by the bars in the third column from the right, which show the latest *yield spread* versus 10-year U.S. Treasuries. The difference between the two yields was 179.9 basis points (a basis point is one one-hundredth of a percentage point) for Australian bonds and −243.8 basis points for Japanese bonds. Recall from Figure 4.3 that the difference between interest rates in different countries mostly reflects differences in expected inflation.

Third, the latest 10-year yield exceeded the latest two-year yield in every country shown in the table. When we study the term structure of interest rates in Chapter 7, we'll learn why this pattern of higher long-term yields is common but does not always hold.

Finally, the yield on each bond differs from its coupon rate (shown in the first column). As noted elsewhere in this chapter, when the yield is higher (lower) than the coupon, the price of the bond is below (above) the par value of 100.

## Corporate Debt

Thousands of corporations in the United States issue bonds, and the bonds vary significantly in default risk (see the discussion of default risk on pages 144–146). In line with Core

Principal 2, investors expect to be compensated for those risks. Table 6.3 captures a measure of that compensation—the yield spread over Treasury securities.

The table shows the levels and one-day changes of yield spreads on actively traded corporate bond yields compared to a similar-maturity U.S. Treasury yield. For the American Express bond, which matures on August 20, 2013, the "current" spread of 160 basis points is the amount by which its previous-day yield exceeded that on the most recent three-year Treasury issue.

Narrower corporate bond spreads over U.S. Treasuries are associated with lower default risk. Hence, spreads are as diverse as corporate default risks. The narrowest spread shown in the table is 37 basis points, for BHP Billiton Finance; the widest is 716, for Digicel. Spreads can change significantly from day-to-day: The table shows that the largest swings in spreads on January 13 were the 52-basis-point tightening for Prologis and the 38-basis-point widening for Digicel. Presumably, these day-to-day changes reflect changing perceptions of each company's default risk.

The last two columns of the table show the stock price level and change for those bond issuers that also issue shares. Note that a gain (loss) in the price of a company's stock, which normally indicates greater (lesser) confidence in the prospects for a company, is not always accompanied by similar change in the yield spread of that company's bond.

are willing to sell, all other things being equal. The higher the price of a bond, the larger the quantity supplied will be for two reasons. From investors' point of view, the higher the price, the more tempting it is to sell a bond they currently hold. From the point of view of companies seeking finance for new projects, the higher the price at which they can sell bonds, the better. Taking our example of a $100 one-year zero-coupon bond, the quantity supplied will be higher at $95 per bond than it will be at $90 per bond, all other things being equal. This means that *the bond supply curve slopes upward*.

The *bond demand curve* is the relationship between the price and quantity of bonds that investors demand, all other things being equal. As the price falls, the reward for holding the bond rises, so the demand goes up. That is, the lower the price potential bondholders must pay for a fixed-dollar payment on a future date, the more likely they are to buy a bond. Again, think of the zero-coupon bond promising to pay $100 in one year. That bond will attract more demand at $90 than it will at $95 per bond, all other things being equal. Thus, *the bond demand curve slopes downward*. Since the price of bonds is inversely related to the yield, the demand curve implies that the higher the demand for bonds, the higher the yield.

Equilibrium in the bond market is the point at which supply equals demand—point $E$ in Figure 6.1. As is always the case with supply and demand analysis, we need to explain how the market adjusts when the price deviates from the price that equates supply and demand—point $P_0$ in Figure 6.1. Let's look briefly at the two possibilities: either the price is too high or the price is too low. If bond prices start out above the equilibrium point, somewhere greater than $P_0$, quantity supplied will exceed quantity demanded. That is, excess supply means that suppliers cannot sell the bonds they want to at the current price. To make the sale, they will start cutting the price. The excess supply will put downward pressure on the price until supply equals demand.

When the price is below the equilibrium point, quantity demanded will exceed quantity supplied. Those people who wish to buy bonds cannot get all they want at the prevailing price. Their reaction is to start bidding up the price. Excess demand continues to put upward pressure on the price until the market reaches equilibrium.

So far, so good. But to really understand how bond prices (and bond yields) change over time, we need to learn what determines the location of the supply and demand curves. Over time they shift around, leading to changes in the equilibrium prices. As we discuss the causes of such shifts in the following section, make sure you remember the distinction between moving *along* a supply or demand curve and *shifting* a curve. When the quantity demanded or quantity supplied changes because of a change in the price, it produces a movement along the curve. But when the quantity demanded or supplied at a given price changes, it shifts the entire curve. More important, in the bond market, a shift in either the supply or the demand curve changes the price of bonds, so it changes the yield as well.

**MARKETS**

**Figure 6.1**   Supply, Demand, and Equilibrium in the Bond Market

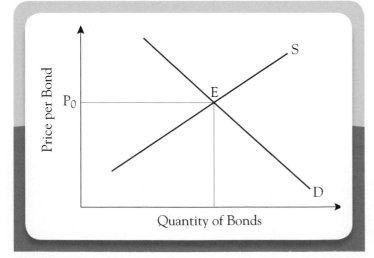

The supply of bonds from borrowers slopes up and the demand for bonds from lenders slopes down. Equilibrium in the bond market is determined by the intersection of supply and demand.

# Factors That Shift Bond Supply

What changes the quantity of bonds *supplied* at a given price, shifting the supply curve? We can identify three factors: changes in government borrowing, in general business conditions, and in expected inflation. Let's look at these one at a time.

**Changes in Government Borrowing**   The government's need to issue bonds affects the supply of bonds out there. Both changes in tax policy and adjustments in fixed spending can affect a government's need to borrow. Regardless of the reason, *any increase in the government's borrowing needs increases the quantity of bonds outstanding, shifting the bond supply curve to the right.* The result is an increase in quantity of the bonds supplied at every price (see Figure 6.2). Because the demand curve stays where it is (remember, we're holding everything else constant), the increase in supply drives the price down. The added supply of U.S. government bonds has reduced prices, raising interest rates.

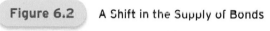

**Figure 6.2**    A Shift in the Supply of Bonds

**Changes in General Business Conditions**   During business-cycle expansions, when general business conditions are good, investment opportunities abound, prompting firms to increase their borrowing. As the amount of debt in the economy rises, the quantity of bonds outstanding goes up. So *as business conditions improve, the bond supply curve shifts to the right,* forcing bond prices down and interest rates up. Again, Figure 6.2 shows what happens. This connection between general business conditions and the supply of bonds also helps explain how weak economic growth can lead to rising bond prices and lower interest rates.

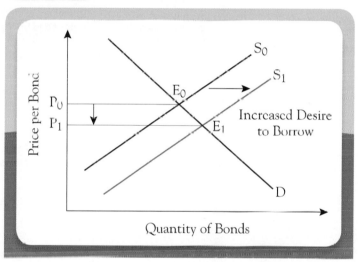

When borrowers' desire for funds increases, the bond supply curve shifts to the right, lowering bond prices and raising interest rates.

**Changes in Expected Inflation**   Bond issuers care about the *real cost of* borrowing—the cost of the loan taking inflation into account. At a given *nominal* interest rate, higher expected inflation means a lower *real* interest rate. And at a lower real interest rate, fewer real resources are required to make the payments promised by a bond. So when expected inflation rises, the cost of borrowing falls and the desire to borrow rises. Figure 6.2 shows that *an increase in expected inflation shifts the bond supply curve to the right.* Higher expected inflation increases the bond supply, reducing bond prices and raising the nominal interest rate.

Table 6.4 summarizes the factors that increase the quantity of bonds supplied at every price, shifting the bond supply curve to the right. Before moving on to shifts in the demand for bonds, we should mention that there is one other factor that shifts the bond supply: changes in corporate taxation. Because such changes in the tax code require government legislation, they don't occur very often. But when they do, they can affect the economywide supply of bonds. Corporations pay taxes on their profits, just as individuals pay taxes on their income, so they are concerned with after-tax profits.

**Table 6.4**  Factors That Shift Bond Supply to the Right, Lower Bond Prices, and Raise Interest Rates

| Change | Effect on Bond Supply, Bond Prices, and Interest Rates | Shift in Bond Supply |
|---|---|---|
| An increase in the government's desired expenditure relative to its revenue | Bond supply shifts to the right, bond prices ↓, and interest rates ↑ | |
| An improvement in general business conditions | Bond supply shifts to the right, bond prices ↓, and interest rates ↑ | |
| An increase in expected inflation, reducing the real cost of repayment | Bond supply shifts to the right, bond prices ↓, and interest rates ↑ | |

Governments often create special tax subsidies that make corporate investments less costly. These tax incentives increase the supply of bonds because they raise the after-tax profitability of investing in new equipment purchased with funds raised from selling bonds. Like the other three factors we have considered, government tax incentives increase bond supply, shift the supply curve to the right, and lower the price of bonds.

## Factors That Shift Bond Demand

Now we move on to bond demand. Six factors shift the *demand* for bonds at a given price: wealth, expected inflation, the expected return on stocks and other assets, expected interest rates, risk, and the liquidity of bonds (see Table 6.5).

**Wealth**   The more rapidly the economy grows, the wealthier individuals become. As their wealth increases, they increase their investment in stocks, bonds, real estate, and art. Thus, *increases in wealth shift the demand for bonds to the right*, raising bond

**Table 6.5**    Factors That Shift Bond Demand to the Right, Raise Bond Prices, and Lower Interest Rates

| Change | Effect on Bond Demand | Shift in Bond Demand |
|---|---|---|
| An increase in wealth increases demand for all assets including bonds. | Bond demand shifts to the right, bond prices $\uparrow$, and interest rates $\downarrow$ | |
| A reduction in expected inflation makes bonds with fixed nominal payments more desirable. | Bond demand shifts to the right, bond prices $\uparrow$, and interest rates $\downarrow$ | |
| A decrease in the expected future interest rate makes bonds more attractive. | Bond demand shifts to the right, bond prices $\uparrow$, and interest rates $\downarrow$ | |
| An increase in the expected return on the bond relative to the expected return on alternatives makes bonds more attractive. | Bond demand shifts to the right, bond prices $\uparrow$, and interest rates $\downarrow$ | |
| A fall in the riskiness of the bond relative to the riskiness of alternatives makes bonds more attractive. | Bond demand shifts to the right, bond prices $\uparrow$, and interest rates $\downarrow$ | |
| An increase in the liquidity of the bond relative to the liquidity of alternatives makes bonds more attractive. | Bond demand shifts to the right, bond prices $\uparrow$, and interest rates $\downarrow$ | |

# YOUR FINANCIAL WORLD
## Understanding the Ads in the Newspaper

You're drinking your coffee and as you read the business news, something catches your eye. An investment company is advertising that their bond mutual funds returned 13½ percent over the last year. But you remember that interest rates have been pretty low—7 percent at most. And a quick check of the numbers in the business section you're holding tells you that your recollection is correct. How could the ad be right?

The answer is that the advertisement is about last year's holding period return, when interest rates were falling. When interest rates fall, bond prices rise and the holding period return is higher than the interest rate. And the longer the term of the bond, the bigger the price movements for a given interest rate change. To see what can happen,

take an example of a 20-year, 7 percent coupon bond with a face value of $100. If the interest rate is initially 7 percent, this bond sells for $100. But if the interest rate falls by even one-half of one percentage point to 6½ percent, the price will rise to about $106.50 giving the owner a 6½ percent capital gain. Adding this to the 7 percent coupon payments, we get a one-year holding period return of 13½ percent.

So the ad isn't really much of a mystery once you think about it. But the implication of the ad, that these are great investments, is something you ought to think about. Remember, if interest rates go back up, things won't be so pretty. When it says at the bottom of the ad that "Past Performance is No Indication of Future Returns" you should take the statement very seriously.

prices and lowering yields (see Figure 6.3). This is what happens in a business-cycle expansion. In a recession, as wealth falls, the demand for bonds falls with it, lowering bond prices and raising interest rates.

**Expected Inflation** Changes in expected inflation alter investors' willingness to purchase bonds promising fixed-dollar payments. A decline in expected inflation means that the payments promised by the bond's issuer have a higher value than borrowers originally thought, so the bond will become more attractive. *This fall in expected inflation shifts the bond demand curve to the right,* increasing demand at each price and lowering the yield, as shown in Figure 6.3. In short, the higher real return on the bond increases the willingness of would-be lenders to buy it at any given price. Note that the decline in expected inflation has reduced the nominal interest rate that investors require in order to make a loan.

**Expected Returns and Expected Interest Rates** An investor's desire to hold any particular financial instrument depends on how its return compares to those of alternative instruments. Bonds are no different. *If the return on bonds rises relative to the return on alternative investments, the quantity of bonds demanded at every price will rise shifting the bond demand curve to the right.* This leads us to conclude that bond prices are connected to the stock market. Investors see bonds as an alternative to stocks, so when the stock market drops, they shift their portfolios into bonds, increasing demand, driving prices up and interest rates down.

**Figure 6.3** A Shift in the Demand for Bonds

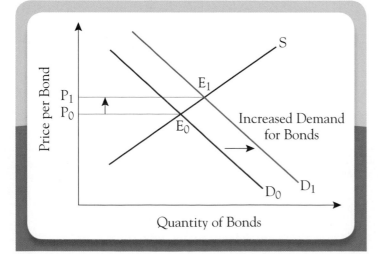

When there is an increase in investors' willingness to hold bonds, the bond demand curve shifts to the right, increasing bond prices and reducing interest rates.

Similarly, when interest rates are expected to change in the future, bond prices adjust immediately. Recall that the holding period return on a bond depends on the coupon payment plus the capital gain or loss. When interest rates fall, bond prices rise, creating a capital gain. Whenever interest rates are expected to fall, then bond prices are expected to rise, creating an expectation of a capital gain. This makes bonds more attractive. Knowing that bonds are a good investment, investors increase their demand immediately, driving bond prices up. So *an increase in the expected return on a bond, relative to the return on alternatives, shifts bond demand to the right.*

**Risk Relative to Alternatives**   On May 13, 2002, a headline in *The Wall Street Journal* read "Japan Gets Irate at Having Its Risk Compared to Botswana." What's going on here? Japan is the second largest economy in the world, with a population of more than 125 million and a GDP in excess of $5 trillion. Botswana is a landlocked country in Southern Africa with a population of 2 million people and a GDP of $26.5 billion.

The problem was that investors had two reasons to question Japan's budget outlook. First, the fiscal deficit was a very high 7 percent of GDP. Second, over the next few decades, the Japanese government would have to find a way to meet its promises to make pension payments to the growing number of retirees. Together these created the perception that Japan's bonds were risky, which meant that investors would be less interested in holding them.

Remember that investors require compensation for risk, which means that when a bond becomes more or less risky, the demand for the bond changes. The less risky the bond, the higher the price investors are willing to pay for it, all other things being equal. From this we can conclude that *if a bond becomes less risky relative to alternative investments, the demand for the bond shifts to the right.* The reason Japan was irate was because the price of its bonds would be lower, so its borrowing costs would be higher.

**Liquidity Relative to Alternatives**   Liquidity measures how easily and cheaply investors can convert one financial instrument into another. A liquid asset is something investors can sell without a large loss in value. Investors like liquidity; the more liquid a bond, the higher the demand for it, all other things being equal. So if a bond's liquidity changes, demand for it changes, too.

During the financial crisis in the fall of 1998, for example, the bonds issued by emerging-market governments in Latin America and Eastern Europe became virtually impossible to sell. The same thing happened to some U.S. mortgage-related bonds during the crisis of 2007–2009. For all practical purposes, the market for them disappeared. When a buyer could be found, prices were severely depressed. Who wants to buy a bond that is difficult to sell? Liquidity matters. The less liquid a bond is, the lower the demand for it, and the lower the price. So *when a bond becomes more liquid relative to alternatives, the demand curve shifts to the right.*

## Understanding Changes in Equilibrium Bond Prices and Interest Rates

Before we continue, let's look again at how bond prices and interest rates move in response to changes in expected inflation and a change in general business conditions. Recall that expected inflation affects both bond supply and bond demand. An increase in expected inflation reduces the real cost of borrowing, shifting bond *supply* to the *right*. But at the same time, this increase in expected inflation lowers the real return on lending, shifting bond *demand* to the *left*. These two effects reinforce each

**Figure 6.4** Equilibrium in the Bond Market: The Effect of an Increase in Expected Inflation

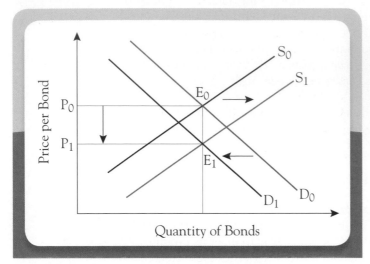

An increase in expected inflation increases bond supply from $S_0$ to $S_1$ by lowering the real cost of borrowing. At the same time, it reduces bond demand from $D_0$ to $D_1$ by reducing the real interest rate bondholders receive. These two effects reinforce each other, lowering the bond's price from $P_0$ to $P_1$ and increasing the interest rate.

**Figure 6.5** Equilibrium in the Bond Market: The Effect of a Business-Cycle Downturn

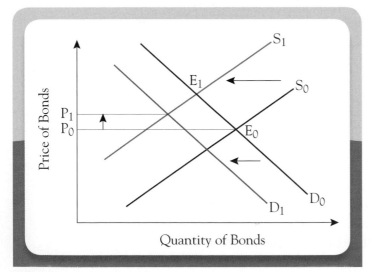

Interest rates tend to fall during business-cycle downturns. The combination of reduced investment opportunities for businesses, which shifts the bond supply curve to the left from $S_0$ to $S_1$, and a decline in household wealth, which shifts the bond demand curve to the left from $D_0$ to $D_1$, causes an increase in bond prices and a drop in the interest rate.

other, lowering the price of the bond and raising the interest rate (see Figure 6.4).

We also saw that changes in business conditions affect both the supply and the demand for bonds. A business-cycle downturn reduces business investment opportunities, shifting the bond *supply* to the left, and reduces wealth, shifting bond *demand* in the same direction. When both curves shift in the same direction, the price can rise or fall. The theory does not give us an unambiguous prediction. In cases like this, we can look for regular movements in the data to help resolve the question. In this case we know that in recessions, interest rates tend to fall, so prices should increase (see Figure 6.5).

# Why Bonds Are Risky

"Bonds Look Attractive Now but They Come with Risks"

—*The Wall Street Journal*, July 26, 2002

How can bonds be risky? They are promises to make fixed payments on future dates. Where is the risk in that? The fact is that the return an investor receives for holding a bond is far from riskless. Bondholders face three major risks (see Table 6.6). **Default risk** is the chance that the bond's issuer may fail to make the promised payment. **Inflation risk** means an investor can't be sure of what the real value of the payments will be, even if they are made. And **interest-rate risk** arises from a bondholder's investment horizon, which may be shorter than the maturity of the bond. If, for example, the interest rate were to rise between the time the bond is purchased and the time it is sold, the investor would suffer a capital loss.[6]

[6]Beyond these three primary sources of risk, the buyer of a bond faces a number of more subtle risks. For example, liquidity risk is the possibility that the investor will experience difficulty selling a bond before it matures. An investor who buys a bond denominated in a foreign currency faces the risk of changes in the exchange rate. A bond may promise payments in euros, say, which must be converted into dollars before they can be used or reinvested.

## APPLYING THE CONCEPT
### WHEN RUSSIA DEFAULTED

The idea that risk matters to bond investors is not just a textbook theory. On numerous occasions, investors' concerns about increased risk in certain areas of the globe have led to a significant shift in demand for U.S. Treasury bonds. A noteworthy example occurred in August 1998, when the Russian government failed to make the payments on some bonds held by foreign investors. That is, the Russian government defaulted. Suddenly, no one wanted to hold Russian debt. More important, people lost confidence in the debt issued by all emerging market countries, including Brazil, Argentina, Turkey, and Thailand. After dumping anything that they thought at all risky, investors went looking for a safe place to put the proceeds.

Since the safest assets around are U.S. Treasury bonds, that is what they bought. The perception during this episode was that the riskiness of U.S. Treasury bonds had fallen relative to the riskiness of virtually everything else. The result was an increase in the price of U.S. Treasury bonds and a decline in their yield. At the same time, the prices of the more risky alternatives fell and their yields rose.

The data in Figure 6.6 show what happened. After the default (at the vertical line in the figure), the price of U.S. Treasury bonds rose by roughly 10 percent while the price of Brazilian bonds fell by more than one-third. Even though it was a half a world away from Russia, investors' demand for Brazilian bonds plummeted. Meanwhile, demand for the safe U.S. Treasury debt went up.

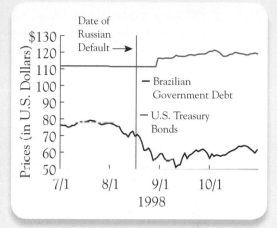

**Figure 6.6** Prices of Brazilian Government Debt and U.S. Treasury Bonds, July 1998 to October 1998

One bond index is for five- to seven-year U.S. Treasury bonds and the other is for Brazilian government bonds. The indexes, which show the movement in the prices of the bonds, were constructed by Lehman Brothers and supplied by Datastream.

SOURCE: *Data compiled from Thompson Datastream.*

**Table 6.6**   What Makes Bonds Risky?

| | |
|---|---|
| 1. *Default risk:* | The issuer may not make the promised payments. |
| 2. *Inflation risk:* | Inflation may turn out to be higher than expected, reducing the real return on holding the bond. |
| 3. *Interest-rate risk:* | Interest rates may rise between the time a bond is purchased and the time it is sold reducing the bond's price. |

We'll look at each of these sources of risk separately, using the tools for understanding risk introduced in Chapter 5. Remember that risk arises from the fact that an investment has many possible payoffs during the horizon for which it is held. So in looking at the risk a bondholder faces, we need to ask what the possible payoffs are and how likely each one is to occur. As we do, we will be looking at the impact of risk on the bond's return relative to the risk-free rate. That is, we will try to figure out how certain risks affect the premium investors require over the risk-free return. Once again, *risk requires compensation*.

## Default Risk

There is no guarantee that a bond issuer will make the promised payments. While we might ignore default risk in thinking about U.S. Treasury bonds, we cannot do so when discussing bonds issued by private corporations. When corporations fail to meet their payments, what happens to the price of their bonds?

To figure out the answer, let's list all the possibilities and payoffs that might occur, along with their probabilities. We can then calculate the expected value of the promised payments, from which we can compute the bond's price and yield. Suppose, for example, that the one-year risk-free interest rate is 5 percent. Flim.com, an Internet firm hoping to market its own brand of e-cash called "Flam,"[7] has issued one-year, 5 percent coupon bonds with a face value of $100. This represents a promise to pay $105 in one year. What is the price of this bond?

If Flim.com were risk free, and lenders were certain they would be paid back, the price of the bond would be computed as the present value of the $105 payment, calculated using the 5 percent risk-free interest rate.

$$\text{Price of Flim.com bond if it is risk free} = \frac{\$100 + \$5}{1.05} = \$100$$

But unlike the U.S. Treasury, Flim.com may not make the payments. People might be unwilling to use Flam, so Flim.com could default. Suppose there is a 0.10 probability (1 chance in 10) that Flim.com will go bankrupt before paying bondholders their $105. To simplify the example, we will assume that in the case of default, the bondholders get nothing. This means that there are two possible payoffs, $105 and $0 (see Table 6.7).

Table 6.7 shows that the expected value of the payment on this bond is $94.50. But even if the payment is made, it will be made one year from now, which means that the price we would be willing to pay for the bond today must be the present value of the future payment. Using the risk-free interest rate for this computation, we find that

$$\text{Expected present value of Flim.com bond payment} = \frac{\$94.50}{1.05} = \$90$$

**Table 6.7**   Expected Value of Flim.com Bond Payment

| Possibilities | Payoff | Probability | Payoff × Probabilities |
|---|---|---|---|
| Full payment | $105 | 0.90 | $94.50 |
| Default | $0 | 0.10 | $0 |
| Expected Value = Sum of Payoffs times Probabilities = $94.50 | | | |

[7]This example is not farfetched. In the 1990s a company called flooz.com tried to issue e-money called "flooz."

**APPLYING THE CONCEPT**
SECURITIZATION

*Securitization* is the process by which financial institutions pool various assets (such as residential mortgages) that generate a stream of payments and transform them into a bond that gives the bondholder a claim on those payments (instead of a fixed coupon). The resulting bond trades in open markets.

Securitization has grown sharply over the past 30 years and now encompasses more than half of U.S. mortgages (see Table 6.8). *Mortgage-backed securities* (MBS) are just one form of securitized debt. Other commonly securitized debts are student loans, auto loans, and credit card debt. However, any stream of payments can be used to create a bond, even movie box-office receipts or sales of music recordings.

What are the benefits of securitization? Securitization uses the efficiency of markets to lower the cost of borrowing. It does so by (1) facilitating diversification of risks, (2) making assets liquid, (3) allowing greater specialization in the business of finance, (4) broadening markets, and (5) fostering innovation.

- *Diversification* or *risk-spreading*. Owning a security that provides a claim on a tiny portion of the payments from several thousand mortgages is less risky than owning a few mortgages in their entirety. By spreading the total risk of thousands of mortgages among many investors, diversification lowers the cost of funding to home buyers.*

- *Liquidity*. Securitization makes the underlying assets liquid by creating a market for them in the form of a bond. Borrowers thus face lower costs because lenders can sell the assets more easily.

- *Specialization*. Some financial institutions are effective in *originating* (creating) the underlying assets (such as a residential mortgage), while others are more proficient at collecting these assets and issuing and *distributing* the securities. By allowing these institutions to specialize, securitization lowers the cost of funds to borrowers. Because origination and distribution are often separated, this pattern of financial activity is called the *originate-to-distribute* model of securitization.

- *Broadening markets*. Home buyers in a small town need not depend on the ability of a small, local bank to bear the entire risk of holding their long-term mortgages. Instead, securitization gives that small group of home buyers access to investors across the globe who can afford to buy a tiny portion of those mortgages in the form of a marketable security.

- *Innovation*. Financial firms seeking to lower the cost of funds to borrowers can broaden the range of assets that are transformed into securities. They can also develop securities that better fit the preferences of the ultimate buyers.

| Table 6.8 | U.S. Mortgages Outstanding (Trillions of Dollars), 1980–2009 | | | |
|---|---|---|---|---|
| | 2009 | 2000 | 1990 | 1980 |
| Mortgages | 14.3 | 6.8 | 3.8 | 1.5 |
| Pools and ABS | 7.6 | 3.1 | 1.1 | 0.1 |

SOURCE: *Federal Reserve Board*, Flow of Funds Accounts of the United States.

*Chapter 11 makes a similar argument with regard to risk-pooling by banks: each depositor owns a very small stake in the thousands of loans made by bank.

So the bond will sell for $90. What yield to maturity does this price imply? If the promised payment is $105, the promised yield to maturity is

$$\text{Promised yield on Flim.com bond} = \frac{\$105}{\$90} - 1 = 0.1667$$

Converting the decimal to a percentage, we get an interest rate of 16.67 percent.[8] Since the default-risk premium is the promised yield to maturity minus the risk-free rate, it is 16.67 percent − 5 percent = 11.67 percent.

[8]This set of calculations could have been done in reverse. Given the yield of 16.67 percent and the characteristics of the bond, it is straightforward to compute the probability of default as 10 percent.

# YOUR FINANCIAL WORLD

## Bonds Guaranteed to Beat Inflation

Inflation creates risk that the nominal return you receive on a bond won't be worth as much as you expected. If a bond pays a 6 percent yield but the inflation rate is also 6 percent, then the real return is zero! What can you do? You could accept the inflation risk, buy a regular bond, and hope for the best. But that's not always appealing.

Fortunately, there are alternatives. One is to buy a type of U.S. Treasury bond that compensates you for inflation. This **inflation-indexed bond** is structured so that the government promises to pay you a fixed interest rate plus the change in the consumer price index (the CPI). For instance, if you buy a $1,000 bond with an interest rate of 3 percent plus inflation, and the CPI rises 2 percent, you will get 3 + 2 = 5 percent. If the inflation rate jumps to 5 percent, then you'll get 3 + 5 = 8 percent. Regardless of what inflation turns out to be, you get 3 percent more, so there is no inflation risk. And since the U.S. Treasury issues these bonds, there is no default risk.

The U.S. Treasury sells two types of bonds that are guaranteed to beat inflation, Series I savings bonds and Treasury Inflation Protection Securities (*TIPS*). But while you can buy a savings bond with as little as $50, you'll need $1,000 to start buying TIPS. Series I savings bonds have a long list of rules about how many can be purchased and how long they need to be held. You can learn about these bonds on the Web site of the Bureau of Public Debt at www.publicdebt.treas.gov. You can buy and sell TIPS in financial markets, or you can buy them directly from the U.S. Treasury through Treasury Direct (see Your Financial World in Chapter 16).

SOURCE: *Courtesy of the Bureau of the Public Debt, U.S. Department of Treasury.*

In calculating the default-risk premium on Flim.com's bond, we computed the expected value of holding the bond—the yield at which the bond is a fair bet. But we know that risk-averse investors require some compensation for bearing risk. The more risk, the greater the compensation they demand. Only a risk-neutral investor would be willing to pay $90 for this bond. Any risk premium will drive the price down below $90 and push the yield to maturity above 16.67 percent.

This example shows that the higher the default risk, the higher the probability that the bondholders will not receive the promised payments. Risk reduces the expected value of a given promise, lowering the price an investor is willing to pay and raising the yield. The higher the default risk, the higher the yield.

## Inflation Risk

With few exceptions, bonds promise to make fixed-dollar payments. That is, a $100 face value, one-year bond at 5 percent is a promise to make a $105 payment in one year. If this promise comes from the government (and therefore is free of default risk), the bondholder can be sure of receiving the $105 payment. Still, there is a risk of inflation. Remember that what you care about is the purchasing power of the money, not the number of dollars. In other words, bondholders are interested in the *real interest rate*, not just the nominal interest rate. And they don't know what the inflation rate will be.

Let's look at an example that shows how inflation risk affects the interest rate. To begin with, think about the interest rate as having three components: the real interest

| Table 6.9 | Inflation Risk | | |

|               | Probabilities | | |
| Inflation Rate | Case I | Case II | Case III |
| --- | --- | --- | --- |
| 1 percent | 0.50 | 0.25 | 0.10 |
| 2 percent | — | 0.50 | 0.80 |
| 3 percent | 0.50 | 0.25 | 0.10 |
| Expected inflation | 2 percent | 2 percent | 2 percent |
| Standard deviation | 1.0 percent | 0.71 percent | 0.45 percent |

rate, expected inflation, and a compensation for inflation risk. Suppose the real interest rate is 3 percent but we are unsure what the inflation rate will be. It could be either 1 percent or 3 percent with equal probability (see Case I in Table 6.9). Expected inflation is 2 percent, with a standard deviation of 1.0 percent. This means the nominal interest rate should equal the 3 percent real interest rate plus the 2 percent expected inflation plus the compensation for inflation risk. The greater the inflation risk, the larger the compensation for it will be.

In Cases II and III, expected inflation is the same (2 percent) but the standard deviation is lower, since we are more certain that the inflation rate will be close to its expected value. That is, Case III is less risky than Case II, which is less risky than Case I. Because risk requires compensation, we would expect the interest rate to be highest in Case I and lowest in Case III. While we may not see this distinction much in the United States or Europe, where inflation is stable, emerging-market countries can go through periods when increases in inflation risk substantially drive up nominal interest rates.

## Interest-Rate Risk

To explain interest-rate risk, we'll focus on a U.S. Treasury bond and assume that we know how much inflation there will be, so there is no default or inflation risk. Interest-rate risk arises from the fact that investors don't know the holding period return of a long-term bond. Remember that when interest rates change, bond prices move; the longer the term of the bond, the larger the price change for a given change in the interest rate. Now think about what happens if you have a short investment horizon. If you buy a long-term bond, you will need to sell the bond before it matures, so you have to worry about what will happen if the interest rate changes.

Whenever there is a mismatch between your investment horizon and a bond's maturity, there is interest-rate risk. Because the prices of long-term bonds can change dramatically, this can be an important source of risk. For example, on January 14, 2010, the 8.75 percent coupon Treasury bond that matures on August 15, 2020, traded

# IN THE NEWS
## Revival in 'Private-Label' Mortgage Securities?

### THE WALL STREET JOURNAL.
WSJ.com

### By Ruth Simon and James R. Hagerty

**January 20, 2010**

The market for "private-label" mortgage-backed securities screeched to a halt two years ago when surging defaults ruined investors' appetite for the bonds. But is sentiment starting to shift?

The answer could come soon. According to securities analysts, some underwriters on Wall Street are discussing the possibility of bringing small amounts of private-label mortgage securities to market within a few months. The first such sales are likely to consist of securities backed by high-quality "jumbo" mortgages, those too big to be backed by government agencies.

The securitization market "for newly originated mortgage loans is getting closer to reopening" says Tom Deutsch, executive director of the American Securitization Forum, an industry group. Bryan Whalen, a managing director at Trust Co. of the West, says Wall Street dealers have been having "hypothetical" chats with investors about possible deals. Mr. Whalen estimates that the first offering could total $250 million to $500 million and debut during the first quarter of this year.

Historically, most mortgage securities were issued or backed by Fannie Mae, Freddie Mac and the Federal Housing Administration. But during the housing boom, investment banks and mortgage banks jumped into the market and began issuing their own brand of mortgage-backed securities. These private-label mortgage securities were often backed by riskier loans, including subprime mortgages and loans made to borrowers who didn't fully document their income and assets.

At the peak of the housing boom in 2006, private-label mortgage securities accounted for 56% of the $2 trillion in mortgage securities sold to investors, according to Inside Mortgage Finance, an industry publication. But the private-label market has been nearly dead since the third quarter of 2007. Virtually all mortgage securities now offered are those backed by government agencies, and demand for those securities has been so tepid that the Federal Reserve has become the biggest buyer.

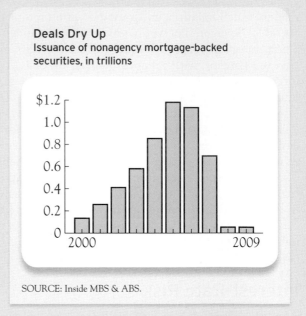

**Deals Dry Up**
Issuance of nonagency mortgage-backed securities, in trillions

SOURCE: Inside MBS & ABS.

at a price of $142.22 (per $100 face value). When it was originally issued as a 30-year bond in August 1990, its price was $98.747.[9] An investor who bought the bond when it was originally issued and sold it 20 years later on January 14, 2010, earned a capital gain of nearly 45 percent. By comparison, an investor who purchased the 2.75 percent

[9]The U.S. Treasury auctions its bonds, so the original selling price is not the exact par value of the bond. To see the original auction prices, go to the Web site of the Bureau of the Public Debt at http://www.publicdebt.treas.gov/.

But there are indications that some investors are ready to take another look. Tom Capasse, a principal with Waterfall Asset Management LLC, notes that there is a dwindling inventory of private-label securities in the secondary market that sets the stage for new issues. Any deal would mark a milestone for efforts to reduce the mortgage market's current dependence on government coverage of default risks.

. . .

Even if the market's first offering is successful, it isn't likely to trigger an immediate flood of new issues. One limiting factor is that lenders aren't originating large numbers of nongovernment-backed mortgages. The maximum size of "conforming" loans—those that can be sold to Fannie Mae or Freddie Mac—has risen to $729,750 in the priciest housing markets, up from $417,000 during the housing boom. That means that most home buyers can get a conforming loan rather than a jumbo, which carry higher interest rates. Sales of higher-end homes in many markets have been sluggish, further reducing the supply of mortgages tied to the homes.

To be eligible for purchase by many insurers, pension funds and mutual funds, any new deal would need a big slice of bonds with triple-A ratings.*

But ratings firms are still facing some key questions. One is "has there been a psychological change in the U.S. borrower that will make them more readily walk away [from their mortgage] in the future," says Huxley Somerville, a group managing director with Fitch Ratings. If borrowers are more likely to walk away, any deal would have to be structured to protect against higher expected losses. Another open question is how much more home prices are likely to decline over the next few years.

*Chapter 7 describes bond ratings and the rating agencies.

In reviewing new deals, Standard & Poor's says it will also look at the lender's past performance, management and organization. Pools will also be sampled by third-party quality-control experts.

While a triple-A rating may be necessary to get a deal off the ground, investors are also seeking more details on the quality of underlying loans. "In the old days, the ratings agencies drove the looks of those deals," said Edward Gainor, a securities lawyer in Washington, D.C. "In the post-collapse world, the investors will very much be at the table."

SOURCE: *The Wall Street Journal Online*, "Revival in 'Private-Label' Mortgage Securities?" by Ruth Simon and James R. Hagerty, January 20, 2010. Copyright 2010 by Dow Jones & Company, Inc. Reproduced with permission of Dow Jones & Company, Inc. in the formats Textbook and Other Book via Copyright Clearance Center.

### LESSONS OF THE ARTICLE

Private securitization of mortgages—securitization that does not involve government agency guarantees—surged in the U.S. housing boom from 2003 to 2006, and the securities were increasingly backed by risky mortgages (See Chapter 7, Lessons from the Crisis: Subprime Mortgages). When the boom in house prices ended, holders of the private-label securities suffered large losses, and in the resulting financial crisis that hit in 2007, private securitization of mortgages collapsed. The article reports that, as of early 2010, it had yet to rebound, and although some underwriters were seeing an opportunity to revive it, many obstacles remained.

coupon 10-year Treasury note when it was issued on February 17, 2009, at $99.41 and sold it 11 months later at its market price of $93.01 on January 14, 2010, suffered a capital loss of more than 6 percent.

The lesson is that any move in interest rates changes the price of a bond. For investors with holding periods shorter than the maturity of the bond, the potential for a change in interest rates creates risk. The more likely interest rates are to change during the bondholder's investment horizon, the larger the risk of holding a bond.

## Terms

capital gain, 130
capital loss, 130
consol or perpetuity, 128
current yield, 130
default risk, 142
holding period return, 132
inflation-indexed bonds, 146

inflation risk, 142
interest-rate risk, 142
investment horizon, 133
U.S. Treasury bill (T-bill), 126
yield to maturity, 129
zero-coupon bond, 126

## Chapter Lessons

1. Valuing bonds is an application of present value.
   a. Pure discount or zero-coupon bonds promise to make a single payment on a predetermined future date.
   b. Fixed-payment loans promise to make a fixed number of equal payments at regular intervals.
   c. Coupon bonds promise to make periodic interest payments and repay the principal at maturity.
   d. Consols (perpetuities) promise to make periodic coupon payments forever.

2. Yields are measures of the return on holding a bond.
   a. The yield to maturity is a measure of the interest rate on a bond. To compute it, set the price of the bond equal to the present value of the payments.
   b. The current yield on a bond is equal to the coupon rate divided by the price.
   c. When the price of a bond is above its face value, the coupon rate is greater than the current yield, which is higher than the yield to maturity.
   d. One-year holding period returns are equal to the sum of the current yield and any capital gain or loss arising from a change in a bond's price.

3. Bond prices (and bond yields) are determined by supply and demand in the bond market.
   a. The higher the price, the larger the quantity of bonds supplied.
   b. The higher the price, the smaller the quantity of bonds demanded.
   c. The supply of bonds rises when
      i. Governments need to borrow more.
      ii. General business conditions improve.
      iii. Expected inflation rises.
   d. The demand for bonds rises when
      i. Wealth increases.
      ii. Expected inflation falls.
      iii. The expected return, relative to other investments, rises.
      iv. The expected future interest rate falls.
      v. Bonds become less risky relative to other investments.
      vi. Bonds become more liquid relative to other investments.

4. Bonds are risky because of
   a. Default risk: the risk that the issuer may fail to pay.

b. Inflation risk: the risk that the inflation rate may be more or less than expected, affecting the real value of the promised nominal payments.

c. Interest-rate risk: the risk that the interest rate may change, causing the bond's price to change.

# Conceptual Problems

1. Consider a U.S. Treasury bill with 270 days to maturity. If the annual yield is 3.8 percent, what is the price?

2. Which of these $100 face value one-year bonds will have the highest yield to maturity and why?
   a. 6 percent coupon bond selling for $85.
   b. 7 percent coupon bond selling for $100.
   c. 8 percent coupon bond selling for $115.

3. You are considering purchasing a consol that promises annual payments of $4.
   a. If the current interest rate is 5 percent, what is the price of the consol?
   b. You are concerned that the interest rate may rise to 6 percent. Compute the percentage change in the price of the consol and the percentage change in the interest rate. Compare them.
   c. Your investment horizon is one year. You purchase the consol when the interest rate is 5 percent and sell it a year later, following a rise in the interest rate to 6 percent. What is your holding period return?

4.* Suppose you purchase a 3-year, 5 percent coupon bond at par and hold it for two years. During that time, the interest rate falls to 4 percent. Calculate your annual holding period return.

5. In a recent issue of *The Wall Street Journal* (or on www.wsj.com or an equivalent financial Web site), locate the prices and yields on U.S. Treasury issues. For one bond selling above par and one selling below par (assuming they both exist), compute the current yield and compare it to the coupon rate and the ask yield printed in the paper.

6. In a recent issue of *The Wall Street Journal* (or on www.wsj.com), locate the yields on government bonds for various countries. Find a country whose 10-year government bond yield was above that on the U.S. 10-year Treasury bond and one whose 10-year yield was below the Treasury yield. What might account for these differences in yields?

7. A 10-year zero-coupon bond has a yield of 6 percent. Through a series of unfortunate circumstances, expected inflation rises from 2 percent to 3 percent.
   a. Compute the change in the price of the bond.
   b. Suppose that expected inflation is still 2 percent, but the probability that it will move to 3 percent has risen. Describe the consequences for the price of the bond.

8. As you read the business news, you come across an advertisement for a bond mutual fund—a fund that pools the investments from a large number of people and then purchases bonds, giving the individuals "shares" in the fund. The company

*Indicates more difficult problems

claims their fund has had a return of 13½ percent over the last year. But you remember that interest rates have been pretty low—5 percent at most. A quick check of the numbers in the business section you're holding tells you that your recollection is correct. Explain the logic behind the mutual fund's claim in the advertisement.

9. You are sitting at the dinner table and your father is extolling the benefits of investing in bonds. He insists that as a conservative investor he will only make investments that are safe, and what could be safer than a bond, especially a U.S. Treasury bond? What accounts for his view of bonds, and explain why you think it is right or wrong?

10.* Consider a one-year, 10 percent coupon bond with a face value of $1,000 issued by a private corporation. The one-year risk-free rate is 10 percent. The corporation has hit on hard times, and the consensus is that there is a 20 percent probability that it will default on its bonds. If an investor were willing to pay $775 for the bond, is that investor risk neutral or risk averse?

# Analytical Problems

11. If, after one year, the yield to maturity on a multiyear coupon bond that was issued at par is higher than the coupon rate, what happened to the price of the bond during that first year?

12. Use your knowledge of bond pricing to explain under what circumstances you would be willing to pay the same price for a consol that pays $5 a year forever and a 5 percent, 10-year coupon bond with a face value of $100 that only makes annual coupon payments for 10 years.

13.* You are about to purchase your first home and receive an advertisement regarding adjustable-rate mortgages (ARMs). The interest rate on the ARM is lower than that on a fixed-rate mortgage. The advertisement mentions that there would be a payment cap on your monthly payments and you would have the option to convert to a fixed-rate mortgage. You are tempted. Interest rates are currently low by historical standards and you are anxious to buy a house and stay in it for the long term. Why might an ARM not be the right mortgage for you?

14. Use the model of supply and demand for bonds to illustrate and explain the impact of each of the following on the equilibrium quantity of bonds outstanding and on equilibrium bond prices and yields:
   a. A new Web site is launched facilitating the trading of corporate bonds with much more ease than before.
   b. Inflationary expectations in the economy fall evoking a much stronger response from issuers of bonds than investors in bonds.
   c. The government removes tax incentives for investment and spends additional funds on a new education program. Overall, the changes have no effect on the government's financing requirements.
   d. All leading indicators point to stronger economic growth in the near future. The response of bond issuers dominates that of bond purchasers.

15. Suppose sustainable peace is reached in Iraq and Afghanistan, reducing military spending by the U.S. government. How would you expect this development to affect the U.S. bond market?

16. Use the model of supply and demand for bonds to determine the impact on bond prices and yields of expectations that the real estate market is going to weaken.

17.* Suppose there is an increase in investors' willingness to hold bonds at a given price. Use the model for the demand and supply of bonds to show that the impact on the equilibrium bond price depends on how sensitive the quantity supplied of bonds is to the bond price.

18. Under what circumstances would purchasing a Treasury Inflation Protected Security (TIPS) from the U.S. government be virtually risk free?

19. In the wake of the financial crisis of 2007–2009, negative connotations often surrounded the term "mortgage-backed security." What arguments could you make to convince someone that she may have benefited from the growth in securitization over the past 30 years?

# Chapter 7

## The Risk and Term Structure of Interest Rates

On October 5, 1998, William McDonough, president of the Federal Reserve Bank of New York, declared "I believe that we are in the most serious financial crisis since World War II."[1] Since August 17, when the Russian government had defaulted on some of its bonds, deteriorating investor confidence had increased volatility in the financial markets. Bond markets were the hardest hit; as lenders re-evaluated the relative risk of holding different bonds, some prices plummeted while others soared. This simultaneous increase in some interest rates and decline in others—a rise in what are called **interest-rate spreads**—was a clear sign to McDonough that the substantial stress the financial markets were experiencing could easily spread to the wider economy, affecting everyone.

Changes in bond prices, and the associated changes in interest rates, can have a pronounced effect on borrowing costs corporations face. The experience of Ford and General Motors (GM), the American automobile manufacturers, provides an instructive example. Like virtually every large company, the two car makers borrow to maintain and expand their businesses. And the amounts are very large. By 2005, Ford's borrowing exceeded $150 billion while GM's was nearly twice that. The two companies produce more than half of the cars and trucks Americans buy. And they buy quite a few—more than 10 million even in the slump of 2009. But for years the fortunes of U.S. automakers have been declining. Plummeting sales in the recession of 2007–2009 triggered massive losses that eventually led to the bankruptcy of GM. Even before GM's failure, the perceived riskiness of Ford and GM's bonds led to a decline in the price investors were willing to pay for them. A fall in bond prices means an increase in interest rates and a corresponding rise in the cost the auto companies have to pay to borrow.

These examples highlight the need to understand the differences among the many types of bonds that are sold and traded in financial markets. What was it about the movement in the prices of different bonds that Mr. McDonough found so informative? How did information about profitability affect investors' willingness to lend to GM and Ford? To answer these questions, we will study the differences among the multitude of bonds issued by governments and private corporations. As we will see, these bonds differ in two crucial respects: the identity of the issuer and the time to maturity. The purpose of this chapter is to examine how each of these affects the price of a bond, and then to use our knowledge to interpret fluctuations in a broad variety of bond prices.

---

[1]Mr. McDonough's job was to monitor financial market developments for the Federal Reserve System, to devise government reaction to such financial crises, and to formulate policies that prevented crises. As we will see in our discussion of the structure of the Federal Reserve System in Chapter 16, the Federal Reserve Bank of New York is the largest of the 12 district banks in the Federal Reserve System. The president of that bank plays a special role as the eyes and ears of the government in world financial markets.

# Ratings and the Risk Structure of Interest Rates

Default is one of the most important risks a bondholder faces. Not surprisingly, the risk that an issuer will fail to make a bond's promised payments varies substantially from one borrower to another. The risk of default is so important to potential investors that independent companies have come into existence to evaluate the creditworthiness of potential borrowers. These firms, sometimes called rating agencies, estimate the likelihood that a corporate or government borrower will make a bond's promised payments. The first such ratings began in the United States more than 100 years ago. Since 1975, the U.S. government has acknowledged a few firms as "nationally recognized statistical rating organizations" (NRSROs), a designation that has encouraged investors and governments worldwide to rely on their ratings. In 2010, legislative proposals sought to counter excessive reliance on ratings agencies by limiting the special status accorded to NRSROs. Let's look at these companies and the information that they produce.

## Bond Ratings

The best-known bond rating services are Moody's and Standard & Poor's.[2] These companies monitor the status of individual bond issuers and assess the likelihood that a lender/bondholder will be repaid by a borrower/bond issuer. Companies with good credit—those with low levels of debt, high profitability, and sizable amounts of cash assets—earn high bond **ratings**. A high rating suggests that a bond issuer will have little problem meeting a bond's payment obligations.

SOURCE: *Courtesy of Standard & Poor's.*

Table 7.1 reports the rating systems of Moody's and Standard & Poor's. As you can see, they are very similar. Both systems are based on letters and bear a broad similarity to the rankings in minor-league baseball. Firms or governments with an exceptionally strong financial position carry the highest ratings and are able to issue the highest-rated bonds, Triple A. The U.S. government, ExxonMobil, and Microsoft are all examples of entities with Aaa bond ratings.

The top four categories, Aaa down to Baa in the Moody's scheme, are considered **investment-grade bonds**, meaning they have a very low risk of default. These ratings are reserved for most government issuers as well as corporations that are among the most financially sound.[3] Famously, these top ratings also were awarded to many risky mortgage-backed securities (see Lessons from the Crisis: Subprime Mortgages on page 157) that later plunged in value, triggering the financial crisis of 2007–2009 (see Lessons from the Crisis: Rating Agencies on page 158). Table 7.1 gives examples of companies that had various ratings in the spring of 2009.

The distinction between investment-grade and speculative, noninvestment-grade bonds is an important one. A number of regulated institutional investors, among them some insurance companies, pension funds, and commercial banks, are not allowed to invest in bonds that are rated below Baa on Moody's scale or BBB on Standard & Poor's scale.[4]

---

[2]Duff & Phelps, Fitch IBCA is a third, less well-known bond rating company. In addition to the big three, seven small agencies also now enjoy the U.S. government's NRSRO designation.

[3]Government debt ratings are important, as they generally create a ceiling on the ratings for private companies in that country.

[4]Restrictions on the investments of financial intermediaries, such as insurance companies, are a matter for state regulators. There is no comprehensive reference for all of the legal restrictions that force financial firms to sell bonds whose ratings fall below Baa. In many cases, such as those of bond mutual funds, the restrictions are self-imposed.

RISK

## The Impact of Ratings on Yields

Bond ratings are designed to reflect default risk: The lower the rating, the higher the risk of default. We know investors require compensation for risk, so everything else held equal, the lower a bond's rating, the lower its price and the higher its yield. From Chapter 6 we know that we can think about changes in risk as shifts in the demand for bonds. Increases in risk will reduce investor demand for bonds at every price, shifting the demand curve to the left, decreasing the equilibrium price and increasing the yield (see Figure 7.1).

The easiest way to understand the quantitative impact of ratings on bond yields is to compare different bonds that are identical in every way except for the issuer's credit rating. U.S. Treasury issues are the natural standard of comparison because they are the closest to being risk free. This is why they are commonly referred to as **benchmark bonds**, and the yields on other bonds are measured in terms of the **spread over Treasuries**. (Remember from the definition in Chapter 5: Risk is measured relative to a benchmark. For bonds the benchmark is U.S. Treasury bonds.)

We can think of any bond yield as the sum of two parts: the yield on the benchmark U.S. Treasury bond plus a default-risk premium, sometimes called a **risk spread**.

$$\text{Bond yield} = \text{U.S. Treasury yield} + \text{Default risk premium} \qquad (1)$$

If bond ratings properly reflect the probability of default, then the lower the rating of the issuer, the higher the default-risk premium in equation (1). This way of thinking about bond yields provides us with a second insight: When Treasury yields move, all other yields move with them.

These two predictions—that interest rates on a variety of bonds will move together and that lower-rated bonds will have higher yields—are both borne out by the data. To see this, let's look at a plot of the **risk structure of interest rates**. Panel A of Figure 7.2 shows the yield to maturity for long-term bonds with three different ratings: 10-year U.S. Treasury, Moody's Aaa rated, and Moody's Baa long-term bonds. As you can see from the figure, all of these yields move together. When the U.S. Treasury yield goes up or down, the Aaa and Baa yields do too. While the default-risk premiums do fluctuate—rising particularly in periods of financial stress—changes in the U.S. Treasury yield account for most of the movement in the Aaa and Baa bond yields. Furthermore, the yield on the higher-rated U.S. Treasury bond is consistently the lowest. In fact, over the years from 1971 to 2009, the 10-year U.S. Treasury bond yield has averaged almost a full percentage point below the average yield on Aaa bonds and two percentage points below the average yield on Baa bonds.

| Figure 7.1 | The Effect of an Increase in Risk on Equilibrium in the Bond Market |

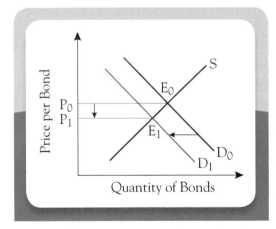

Increased risk reduces the demand for the bond at every price, shifting the demand curve to the left from $D_0$ to $D_1$. The result is a decline in the equilibrium price and quantity in the market. Importantly, the price falls from $P_0$ to $P_1$, so the yield on the bond must rise.

How important is one or two percentage points in yield? To see, we can do a simple computation. At an interest rate of 5 percent, the present value of a $100 payment made 10 years from now is $61.39. If the interest rate rose to 7 percent, the value of this same promise would decline to $50.83. So a two-percentage point increase in the yield, from 5 percent to 7 percent, lowers the value of the promise of $100 in 10 years by $10.56, or 17 percent!

| Figure 7.2 | The Risk Structure of Interest Rates |

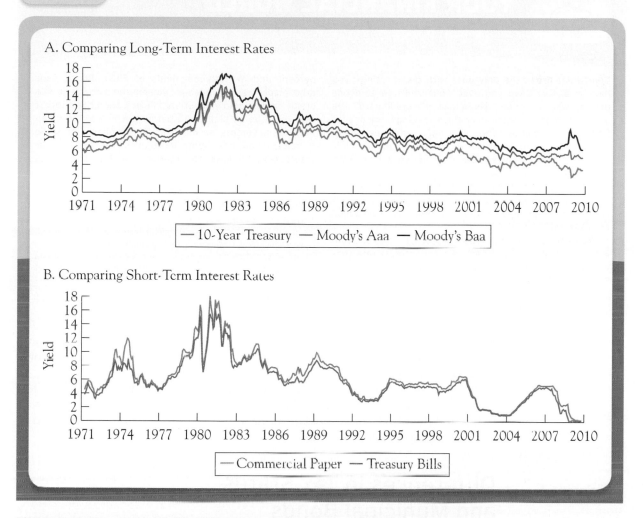

A. Comparing Long-Term Interest Rates

— 10-Year Treasury — Moody's Aaa — Moody's Baa

B. Comparing Short-Term Interest Rates

— Commercial Paper — Treasury Bills

SOURCE: Board of Governors of the Federal Reserve System.

From the viewpoint of the borrower, an increase in the interest rate from 5 percent to 7 percent means paying $7 rather than $5 per year for each $100 borrowed. That is a 40 percent difference. Clearly, ratings are crucial to corporations' ability to raise financing. Whenever a company's bond rating declines, the cost of funds goes up, impairing the company's ability to finance new ventures.[9]

What is true for long-term bond yields is true for short-term bond yields; they move together, and lower ratings imply higher yields. Compare the yields on three-month U.S. Treasury bills with those on A-1/P-1 commercial paper of the same maturity (see Panel B of Figure 7.2). The two yields clearly move together, and the U.S. Treasury bill yield is always lower than the yield on commercial paper. From 1971 to 2009, the

[9]The same is true for individuals. Consider the impact on the monthly payments required to service a thirty-year, $100,000 mortgage. At an interest rate of 5 percent, payments would be approximately $530 per month. If the interest rate were to increase to 7 percent, the required monthly payments would rise to more than $650. You can compute these amounts using the formulas in the Appendix to Chapter 4.

## YOUR FINANCIAL WORLD
### Your Credit Rating

Companies aren't the only ones with credit ratings; you have one, too. Have you ever wondered how someone decides whether to give you a loan or a credit card? The answer is that there are companies keeping track of your financial information. They rate your creditworthiness, and they know more about you than you might think. Credit-rating companies know all about your credit cards, your car loan or mortgage (if you have one), and whether you pay your bills on time. All of this information is combined in something called a *credit score*. If you have low levels of debt and pay your bills on time, you have a high credit score.

You care about your credit score; here's why. Lenders use credit scores to calculate the interest rate they charge on a loan. With a top credit score, a four-year, $10,000 car loan might have an interest rate of 6¾

percent and monthly payments of $237. But if your credit score was low, because you missed a payment on a credit card or paid your utility bill late, then the interest rate could be as high as 16 percent, which would mean monthly payments as much as $50 higher. The same principle applies to home mortgages; the better your credit score, the lower the interest rate. It pays to pay all your bills on time.*

*Ironically, someone who has never had a credit card and never owed anyone any money has no credit history at all and so will have a low credit score. You cannot start too soon in creating a record as a good credit risk. And you are entitled to a free annual credit report from each of the credit-rating companies. To find out how to get it, go to www.annualcreditreport.com.

spread of commercial paper over U.S. Treasury bills averaged about six-tenths of one percentage point, or roughly 60 *basis points*. (Recall from Chapter 6 that a basis point is one one-hundredth of a percentage point, or 0.01 percent.)

The lesson is clear; investors must be compensated for assuming risk. The less creditworthy the borrower, the higher the risk of default, the lower the borrower's rating, and the higher the cost of borrowing. And the lower the rating of the bond or commercial paper, the higher the yield.

## Differences in Tax Status and Municipal Bonds

Default risk is not the only factor that affects the return on a bond. The second important factor is taxes. Bondholders must pay income tax on the interest income they receive from owning privately issued bonds. These are **taxable bonds**. In contrast, the coupon payments on bonds issued by state and local governments, called **municipal** or **tax-exempt bonds**, are specifically exempt from taxation.[10]

The general rule in the United States is that the interest income from bonds issued by one government is not taxed by another government, although the issuing government may tax it. The interest income from U.S. Treasury securities is taxed by the federal government, which issued them, but not by state or local governments. In the same way, the federal government is precluded from taxing interest on municipal bonds. In an effort to make their bonds even more attractive to investors, however,

---

[10]Municipal bonds come in two varieties. Some are general-obligation bonds backed by the taxing power of the governmental issuer. Others are revenue bonds issued to fund specific projects; these are backed by revenues from the project or operator.

## LESSONS FROM THE CRISIS
### ASSET-BACKED COMMERCIAL PAPER

Asset-backed commercial paper (ABCP) is a short-term liability with a maturity of up to 270 days. Unlike most commercial paper, which is unsecured, ABCP is collateralized by assets that financial institutions place in a special portfolio. As we saw in Chapter 3, collateral is something of value that is pledged to pay a loan (in this case, CP) in the event that the borrower does not make the required payments. ABCP has existed for decades, but it played a special role in the housing boom that preceded the financial crisis of 2007-2009.

To lower their costs and limit their own asset holding, some large banks created firms (a form of *shadow bank*) that issued ABCP and used the money to buy mortgages and other loans (see Chapter 3, Lessons from the Crisis: Shadow Banks). The payment stream generated by the loans was used to compensate the holders of the ABCP. This off-balance-sheet financing also allowed banks to boost leverage and take more risk. When mortgage volume surged in the housing bubble, these shadow banks issued more ABCP to finance their rapid expansion.

The mismatch between the long-term maturity of the assets (mortgages) and the short-term maturity of the liabilities (ABCP) posed an underappreciated threat to the ABCP issuers. When the ABCP matures, the issuers have to borrow (or to sell the underlying assets) to be able to return the principal to the ABCP holders. The risk was that the issuers would be unable to borrow—that is, they faced *rollover* risk. If they were also unable to sell the long-term assets easily, these shadow banks would face failure.

ABCP rollover risk played an early role in the financial crisis of 2007-2009. When the value of some mortgages became highly uncertain in 2007, purchasers of ABCP grew anxious that the assets backing their commercial paper might plunge in value. Because they had erroneously viewed ABCP as a very low risk security, the sudden awareness of risk caused a virtual halt to ABCP purchases. Outstanding ABCP began to plunge in the third quarter of 2007.

Firms that had issued ABCP faced an immediate threat to their survival. Unable to sell their assets or to obtain other funding, some failed. In other cases, banks chose to rescue their shadow banks to limit legal risks and reputational damage. As a result, those banks faced heightened liquidity needs and pressures to sell assets precisely when the cost of funds had surged and asset prices were plunging. The risk that they had sought to shift off balance sheet returned at the worst possible time—in the midst of a crisis.

state and local governments usually choose not to tax the interest on their own bonds, exempting it from all income taxes.

How does a tax exemption affect a bond's yield? Bondholders care about the return they actually receive, after tax authorities have taken their cut. If investors expect to receive a payment of $6 for holding a bond but know they will lose $1.80 of it in taxes, they will act as if the return on the investment is only $4.20. That is, investors base their decisions on the *after-tax yield*.

Calculating the tax implications for bond yields is straightforward. Consider a one-year $100 face value taxable bond with a coupon rate of 6 percent. This is a promise to pay $106 in one year. If the bond is selling at par, at a price of $100, then the yield to maturity is 6 percent. From the point of view of the government issuers, the bondholder receives $6 in taxable income at maturity. If the tax rate is 30 percent, the tax on that income is $1.80, so the $100 bond yields $104.20 after taxes. In other words, at a 30 percent tax rate, a 6 percent taxable bond yields the equivalent of 4.2 percent.

This same calculation works for any interest rate and any bond, which allows us to derive a relationship between the yields on taxable and tax-exempt bonds. The rule is that the yield on a tax-exempt bond equals the taxable bond yield times one minus the tax rate:

$$\text{Tax-exempt bond yield} = (\text{Taxable bond yield}) \times (1 - \text{Tax rate}) \quad (2)$$

For an investor with a 30 percent tax rate, then, we can compute the tax-exempt yield on a 10 percent bond by multiplying 10 percent times $(1 - 0.3)$, or 7 percent. Overall, the higher the tax rate, the wider the gap between the yields on taxable and tax-exempt bonds.

# The Term Structure of Interest Rates

A bond's tax status and rating aren't the only factors that affect its yield. In fact, bonds with the same default rate and tax status but different maturity dates usually have different yields. Why? The answer is that long-term bonds are like a composite of a series of short-term bonds, so their yield depends on what people expect to happen in years to come. In this section, we will develop a framework for thinking about *future interest rates*.

The relationship among bonds with the same risk characteristics but different maturities is called the **term structure of interest rates**.

In studying the term structure of interest rates, we will focus our attention on Treasury yields; see Figure 7.3. Comparing information on 3-month (the green line) and 10-year (the orange line) Treasury issues, we can draw three conclusions:

1. *Interest rates of different maturities tend to move together.* The bulk of the variation in short- and long-term interest rates is in the same direction. That is, the orange and green lines clearly move together.
2. *Yields on short-term bonds are more volatile than yields on long-term bonds.* The green line moves over a much broader range than the orange line.
3. *Long-term yields tend to be higher than short-term yields.* The orange line usually, *but not always*, lies above the green line.

Default risk and tax differences cannot explain these relationships. What can? We will examine two explanations, the expectations hypothesis and the liquidity premium theory.

## The Expectations Hypothesis

Over the years, economists have proposed and discarded numerous theories to explain the term structure of interest rates. We can benefit from their hard work and ignore all the ones they found wanting. The first one we will focus on, called the **expectations**

**Figure 7.3**    The Term Structure of Treasury Interest Rates

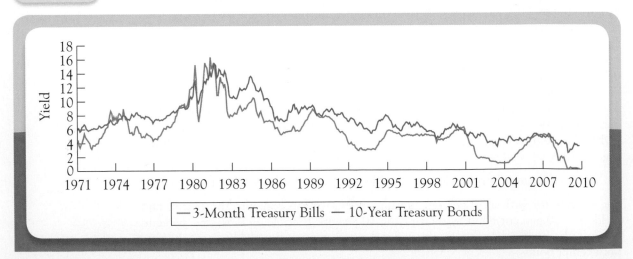

SOURCE: *Board of Governors of the Federal Reserve System.*

**hypothesis of the term structure**, is straightforward and intuitive. If we think about yields as the sum of a risk-free interest rate and a risk premium, the expectations hypothesis focuses on the first of those elements. It begins with the observation that the risk-free interest rate can be computed, assuming there is no uncertainty about the future. That is, we know not just the yield on bonds available today but the yields that will be available on bonds next year, the year after that, and so on.

To understand the implications of this statement, think about an investor who wishes to purchase a bond and hold it for two years. Because there is no uncertainty, the investor knows the yield today on a bond with two years to maturity, as well as the yields on a one-year bond purchased today and on a second one-year bond purchased one year from now. Being sure about all of these, the investor will be indifferent between holding the two-year bond and holding a series of two one-year bonds. *Certainty means that bonds of different maturities are perfect substitutes for each other.* This is the essence of the expectations hypothesis.

To see how this works, assume that the current one-year interest rate is 5 percent. The expectations hypothesis implies that the current two-year interest rate should equal the average of 5 percent and the one-year interest rate one year in the future. If that future interest rate is 7 percent, then the current two-year interest rate will be $(5 + 7)/2 = 6\%$.

According to the expectations hypothesis, then, when interest rates are expected to rise in the future, long-term interest rates will be higher than short-term interest rates. This means that the **yield curve**, which plots the yield to maturity on the vertical axis and the time to maturity on the horizontal axis, will slope up. (*The Wall Street Journal's* Credit Market column often includes a plot of a yield curve for U.S. Treasury issues like the one shown in Figure 7.4.) Analogously, the expectations hypothesis implies that if interest rates are expected to fall, the yield curve will slope down. And if interest rates are expected to remain unchanged, the yield curve will be flat. (See Figure 7.5.)

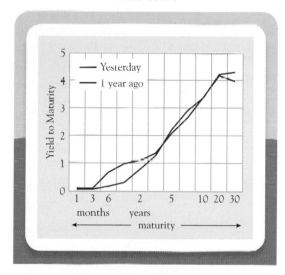

**Figure 7.4**   The U.S. Treasury Yield Curve

The figure plots the yields on Treasury bills and bonds for November 19, 2009.

SOURCE: *Board of Governors of the Federal Reserve System.*

**Figure 7.5**   The Expectations Hypothesis and Expectations of Future Short-term Interest Rates

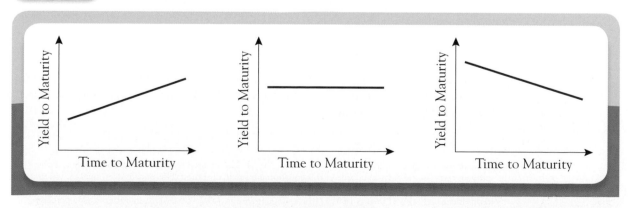

Interest rates are expected to **rise**.      Interest rates are expected to **remain unchanged**.      Interest rates are expected to **fall**.

If bonds of different maturities are perfect substitutes for each other, then we can construct investment strategies that must have the same yields. Let's look at the investor with a two-year horizon. Two possible strategies are available to this investor:

A. Invest in a two-year bond and hold it to maturity. We will call the interest rate associated with this investment $i_{2t}$ ("$i$" stands for the interest rate, "2" for two years, and "$t$" for the time period, which is today). Investing one dollar in this bond will yield $(1 + i_{2t})(1 + i_{2t})$ two years later.

B. Invest in two one-year bonds, one today and a second when the first one matures. The one-year bond purchased today has an interest rate of $i_{1t}$ ("1" stands for one year). The one-year bond purchased one year from now has an interest rate of $i^e_{1t+1}$, where the "$t+1$" stands for one time period past period $t$, or next year. The "$e$," which stands for *expected*, indicates that this is the one-year interest rate investors *expect* to obtain one year ahead. Since we are assuming that the future is known, this expectation is certain to be correct. A dollar invested using this strategy will return $(1 + i_{1t})(1 + i^e_{1t+1})$ in two years.

The expectations hypothesis tells us that investors will be indifferent between these two strategies. (Remember, the bonds are perfect substitutes for each other.) Indifference between strategies A and B means that they must have the same return, so

$$(1 + i_{2t})(1 + i_{2t}) = (1 + i_{1t})(1 + i^e_{1t+1}) \qquad (3)$$

Expanding equation (3) and taking an approximation that is very accurate, we can write the two-year interest rate as the average of the current and future expected one-year interest rates:[11]

$$i_{2t} = \frac{i_{1t} + i^e_{1t+1}}{2} \qquad (4)$$

For a comparison between a three-year bond and three one-year bonds, we get

$$i_{3t} = \frac{i_{1t} + i^e_{1t+1} + i^e_{1t+2}}{3} \qquad (5)$$

where the notation $i_{3t}$ stands for a three-year interest rate and $i^e_{1t+2}$ for the expected one-year interest rate two years from now.

The general statement of the expectations hypothesis is that the interest rate on a bond with $n$ years to maturity is the average of $n$ expected future one-year interest rates:

$$i_{nt} = \frac{i_{1t} + i^e_{1t+1} + i^e_{1t+2} + \ldots + i^e_{1t+n-1}}{n} \qquad (6)$$

What are the implications of this mathematical expression? Does the *expectations hypothesis of the term structure of interest rates* explain the three observations we started with? Let's look at each one.

---

[11]Expanding (3) gives us $2i_{2t} + i^2_{2t} = i_{1t} + i^e_{1t+1} + (i_{1t})(i^e_{1t+1})$. The squared term on the left-hand side and the product term on the right-hand side of this equation are small, and their difference is even smaller. Using the example of 5 percent and 7 percent for the one-year interest rates, we can see that ignoring the two product terms means ignoring $((.06)^2 - (.05^*.07))/2 = (0.0036 - 0.0035)/2 = 0.00005$, an error of 0.005 percentage points.

**The Expectations Hypothesis of the Term Structure:**

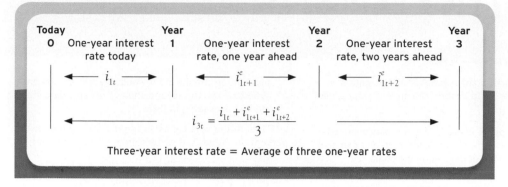

Three-year interest rate = Average of three one-year rates

If the one-year interest rate today is $i_{1t} = 5\%$, one-year interest rate, one year ahead is $i^e_{1t+1} = 6\%$, and the one-year interest rate two years ahead, $i^e_{1t+2} = 7\%$, then the expectation hypothesis tells us that the three-year interest rate will be $i_{3t} = (5\% + 6\% + 7\%)/3 = 6\%$.

1. The expectations hypothesis tells us that long-term bond yields are all averages of expected future short-term yields—the same set of short-term interest rates—so *interest rates of different maturities will move together*. From equation (6) we see that if the current one-year interest rate, $i_{1t}$, changes, all the yields at higher maturities will change with it.

2. The expectations hypothesis implies that *yields on short-term bonds will be more volatile than yields on long-term bonds*. Because long-term interest rates are averages of a sequence of expected future short-term rates, if the current 3-month interest rate moves, it will have only a small impact on the 10-year interest rate. Again, look at equation (6).[12]

3. The expectations hypothesis *cannot* explain why *long-term yields are normally higher than short-term yields*, since it implies that the yield curve slopes upward only when interest rates are expected to rise. To explain why the yield curve normally slopes upward, the expectations hypothesis would suggest that interest rates are normally expected to rise. But as the data in Figure 7.3 show, interest rates have been trending downward for nearly 30 years, so anyone constantly forecasting interest-rate increases would have been sorely disappointed.

The expectations hypothesis has gotten us two-thirds of the way toward understanding the term structure of interest rates. By ignoring risk and assuming that investors view short- and long-term bonds as perfect substitutes, we have explained why yields at different maturities move together and why short-term interest rates are more volatile than long-term rates. But we have failed to explain why the yield curve normally slopes upward. To understand this, we need to extend the expectations hypothesis to include risk. After all, we all know that long-term bonds are riskier than short-term bonds. Integrating this observation into our analysis will give us the *liquidity premium theory* of the term structure of interest rates.

---

[12]Take a simple example in which the one-year and two-year interest rates, $i_{1t}$ and $i_{2t}$, are both 5 percent. If the one-year interest rate increases to 7 percent, then the two-year interest rate will rise to 6 percent. The two move together, and the short-term rate is more volatile than the long-term rate.

# TOOLS OF THE TRADE
## Reading Charts

A picture can be worth a thousand words, but only if you know what it represents. To decode charts and graphs, use these strategies:

1. *Read the title of the chart.* This point may seem trivial, but titles are often very descriptive and can give you a good start in understanding a chart.

2. *Read the label on the horizontal axis.* Does the chart show the movements in a stock price or in the interest rate over minutes, hours, days, weeks, months, or years? Are the numbers spaced evenly?

Look at Figure 7.6, a sample of the Treasury yield curve that appears in *The Wall Street Journal* every day. The horizontal axis extends from three months to 30 years, but the increments are not evenly spaced. In fact, a distance that starts out as three months on the left-hand corner becomes over 10 years at the far right. The axis is drawn in this way for two reasons. First, it focuses the reader's eye on the shorter end of the yield curve. Second, the telescoped axis narrows so that it takes up less space.

Interestingly, this particular yield curve shows a slight downward slope from three months to one year, followed by a steep upward slope. This pattern suggests that investors expected interest rates to decline sharply for the next year and then rise after that, which is exactly what happened.

3. *Read the label on the vertical axis.* What is the range of the data? This is a crucial piece of information, since most charts are made to fill the space available. As a result, small movements can appear to be very large. Compare Panel A and Panel B of Figure 7.7 on page 169 on inflation. The first shows the

percentage change in the consumer price index from 1960 to 2010; the second shows the same data starting 25 years later, in 1985.

In Panel A, the vertical axis ranges from −2 percent to 16 percent; in Panel B, it covers only −2 to 7 percent. To

### Figure 7.6    Treasury Yield Curve

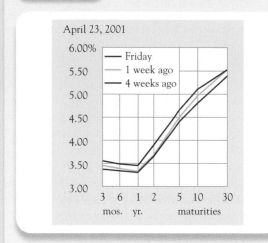

April 23, 2001

SOURCE: *The Wall Street Journal.* Copyright 2001 by Dow Jones & Company, Inc. Reproduced with permission of Dow Jones & Company, Inc. in the formats Textbook and Other Book via Copyright Clearance Center.

## The Liquidity Premium Theory

Throughout our discussion of bonds, we emphasized that even default-free bonds are risky because of uncertainty about inflation and future interest rates. What are the implications of these risks for our understanding of the term structure of interest rates? The answer is that risk is the key to understanding the usual upward *slope* of the yield curve. Long-term interest rates are typically higher than short-term interest rates because long-term bonds are riskier than short-term bonds. Bondholders face both inflation and interest-rate risk. The longer the term of the bond, the greater both types of risk.

The reason for the increase in inflation risk over time is clear-cut. Remember that bondholders care about the purchasing power of the return—the *real* return—they receive from a bond, not just the nominal dollar value of the coupon payments. Computing the real return from the nominal return requires a forecast of future inflation, or fill the second panel visually, the artist changed the vertical scale.

Taking only a superficial look at these two charts can be misleading. Without noticing the difference in their vertical scales, we could conclude that the decline of inflation from 2008 to 2009 was as dramatic as the decline of inflation from 1980 to 1983. But, on closer inspection, inflation fell from 5.4 percent to −1.9 percent in the recent episode, while in the 1980-1983 period, it dropped from 14.6 percent to 2.4 percent. A proper reading of the charts leads to the correct conclusion that the earlier decline was nearly twice as large as the recent one.

### Figure 7.7    U.S. Consumer Price Inflation

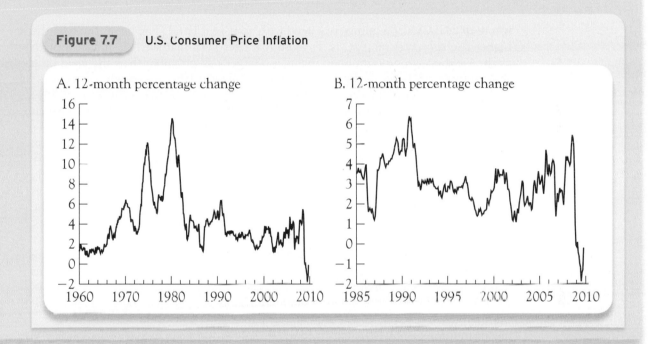

*expected* future inflation. For a three-month bond, an investor need only be concerned with inflation over the next three months. For a 10-year bond, however, computation of the real return requires a forecast of inflation over the next decade.

In summary, uncertainty about inflation creates uncertainty about a bond's real return, making the bond a risky investment. The further we look into the future, the greater the uncertainty about inflation. We are more uncertain about the level of inflation several years from now than about the level of inflation a few months from now, which implies that *a bond's inflation risk increases with its time to maturity*.

What about interest-rate risk? Interest-rate risk arises from a mismatch between the investor's investment horizon and a bond's time to maturity. Remember that if a bondholder plans to sell a bond prior to maturity, changes in the interest rate (which cause bond prices to move) generate capital gains or losses. The longer the term of the bond, the greater the price changes for a given change in interest rates and the larger the potential for capital losses.

Because some holders of long-term bonds will want to sell their bonds before they mature, interest-rate risk concerns them. These investors require compensation for the risk they take in buying long-term bonds. As in the case of inflation, the risk increases with the term to maturity, so the compensation must increase with it.

What are the implications of including risk in our model of the term structure of interest rates? To answer this question, we can think about a bond yield as having two parts, one that is risk free and another that is a risk premium. The expectations hypothesis explains the risk-free part, and inflation and interest-rate risk explain the risk premium. Together they form the **liquidity premium theory of the term structure** of interest rates. Adding the risk premium to equation (6), we can express this theory mathematically as

$$i_{nt} = rp_n + \frac{i_{1t} + i^e_{1t+1} + i^e_{1t+2} + \ldots + i^e_{1t+n-1}}{n} \tag{7}$$

where $rp_n$ is the risk premium associated with an $n$-year bond. The larger the risk, the higher the risk premium, $rp_n$, is. Because risk rises with maturity, $rp_n$ increases with $n$, the yield on a long-term bond includes a larger risk premium than the yield on a short-term bond.

To get some idea of the size of the risk premium $rp_n$, we can look at the average slope of the term structure over a long period. From 1985 to 2009, the difference between the interest rate on a 10-year Treasury bond and that on a 3-month Treasury bill has averaged a bit over 1½ percentage points. It is important to keep in mind that this risk premium will vary over time. For example, if inflation is very stable or the variability of the real interest rate were to fall, then the 10-year bond risk premium could easily fall below one percentage point.

Can the liquidity premium theory explain all three of our conclusions about the term structure of interest rates? The answer is yes. Like the expectations hypothesis, the liquidity premium theory predicts that *interest rates of different maturities will move together* and that *yields on short-term bonds will be more volatile than yields on long-term bonds*. And by adding a risk premium that grows with time to maturity, it explains why *long-term yields are higher than short-term yields*. Because the risk premium increases with time to maturity, the liquidity premium theory tells us that the yield curve will normally slope upward; only rarely will it lie flat or slope downward. (A flat yield curve means that interest rates are expected to fall; a downward-sloping yield curve suggests that the financial markets are expecting a significant decline in interest rates.)

# The Information Content of Interest Rates

The risk and term structure of interest rates contain useful information about overall economic conditions. These indicators are helpful in evaluating both the present health of the economy and its likely future course. Risk spreads provide one type of information, the term structure another. In the following sections we will apply what we have just learned about interest rates to recent U.S. economic history and show how forecasters use these tools.

## Information in the Risk Structure of Interest Rates

When the overall growth rate of the economy slows or turns negative, it strains private businesses, increasing the risk that corporations will be unable to meet their

**APPLYING THE CONCEPT**
THE FLIGHT TO QUALITY

Standing in the middle of an open field during a thunderstorm is a good way to get hurt, so few people do it. Instead, they take shelter. Investors do exactly the same thing during financial storms; they look for a safe place to put their investments until the storm blows over. In practical terms, that means selling risky investments and buying the safest instruments they can: U.S. Treasury bills, notes, and bonds. An increase in the demand for government bonds coupled with a decrease in the demand for virtually everything else is called a **flight to quality**. When it happens, there is a dramatic increase in the difference between the yields on safe and risky bonds—the *risk spread rises.*

When the government of Russia defaulted on its bonds in August 1998, the shock set off an almost unprecedented flight to quality. Yields on U.S. Treasuries plummeted, while those on corporate bonds rose. Risk spreads widened quickly; the difference between U.S. Treasury bills and commercial paper rates more than doubled, from its normal level of half a percentage point to over one percentage point. The debt of countries with emerging markets was particularly hard hit.

This flight to quality was what William McDonough called "the most serious financial crisis since World War II" (see the opening of this chapter). Because people wanted to hold only U.S. Treasury securities, the financial markets had ceased to function properly. McDonough worried that the problems in the financial markets would spread to the economy as a whole. They didn't in the 1998 episode, but they did in the much larger financial crisis of 2007–2009.

financial obligations. The immediate impact of an impending recession, then, is to raise the risk premium on privately issued bonds. Importantly, though, an economic slowdown or recession does not affect the risk of holding government bonds.

The increased risk of default is not the same for all firms. The impact of a recession on companies with high bond ratings is usually small, so the spread between U.S. Treasuries and Aaa-rated bonds of the same maturity is not likely to move by much. But for issuers whose finances were precarious prior to the downturn, the effect is quite different. Those borrowers who were least likely to meet their payment obligations when times were good are even less likely to meet them when times turn bad. There is a real chance that they will fail to make interest payments. Of course, firms for whom even the slightest negative development might mean disaster are the ones that issue low-grade bonds. The lower the initial grade of the bond, the more the default-risk premium rises as general economic conditions deteriorate. The spread between U.S. Treasury bonds and junk bonds widens the most.

Panel A of Figure 7.8 shows annual GDP growth over four decades superimposed on shading that shows the dates of recessions. (We'll learn more about recession dating in Chapter 22.) Notice that during the shaded periods, growth is usually negative. In Panel B of Figure 7.8, GDP growth is drawn as the red line and the green line is the spread between yields on Baa-rated bonds and U.S. Treasury bonds. Note that the two lines move in opposite directions. (The correlation between the two series is −0.55.) That is, when the risk spread rises, output falls. The risk spread provides a good measure of general economic activity, and since financial markets operate every day, this information is available well before GDP data, which is published only once every three months. During the financial crisis of 2007–2009, the spread reached its widest level since the Great Depression of the 1930s.

## Information in the Term Structure of Interest Rates

Like information on the risk structure of interest rates, information on the term structure—particularly the slope of the yield curve—helps us to forecast general economic conditions. Recall that according to the expectations hypothesis, long-term interest rates contain information about expected future short-term interest rates.

**Figure 7.8**   The Risk Spread and GDP Growth

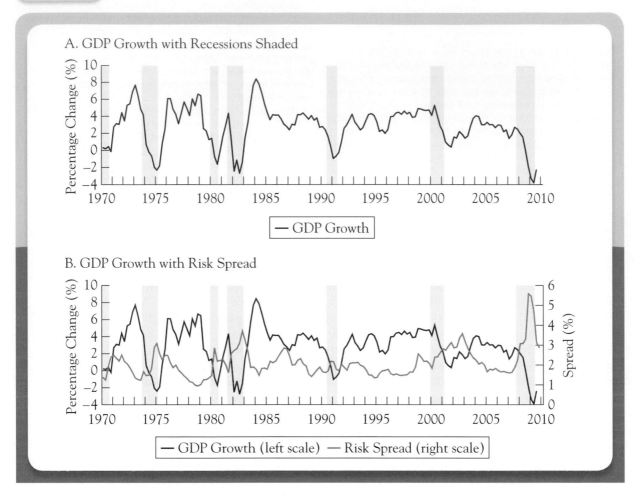

SOURCE: *Bureau of Economic Analysis and Board of Governors of the Federal Reserve System. GDP growth is the percentage change from the same quarter of the previous year, while the yield spread is the difference between the average yield on Baa and 10-year U.S. Treasury bonds during the quarter. Shaded periods denote recessions.*

And according to the liquidity premium theory, the yield curve usually slopes upward. The key term in this statement is *usually*. On rare occasions, short-term interest rates exceed long-term yields. When they do, the term structure is said to be *inverted*, and the yield curve slopes downward.

An **inverted yield curve** is a valuable forecasting tool because it predicts a general economic slowdown. Because the yield curve slopes upward even when short-term yields are expected to remain constant—it's the average of expected future short-term interest rates plus a risk premium—an inverted yield curve signals an expected fall in short-term interest rates. If interest rates are comparatively high, they serve as a brake on real economic activity. As we will see in Part IV, monetary policymakers adjust short-term interest rates in order to influence real economic growth and inflation. When the yield curve slopes downward, it indicates that policy is *tight* because policymakers are attempting to slow economic growth and inflation.

| Figure 7.9 | The Term Spread and GDP Growth |
| --- | --- |

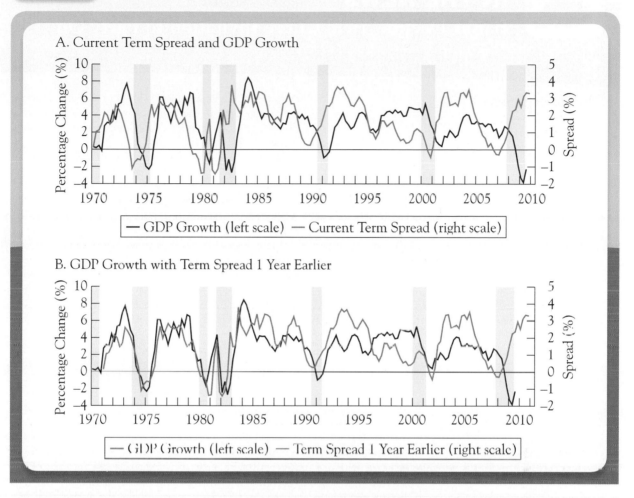

A. Current Term Spread and GDP Growth

— GDP Growth (left scale) — Current Term Spread (right scale)

B. GDP Growth with Term Spread 1 Year Earlier

— GDP Growth (left scale) — Term Spread 1 Year Earlier (right scale)

SOURCE: *Bureau of Economic Analysis and Board of Governors of the Federal Reserve System. GDP growth is the percentage change from the same quarter of the previous year, while the term spread is the difference between the average yield on 10-year U.S. Treasury bond and a 3-month U.S. Treasury bill during the quarter. In Panel B, the spread is lagged one year. Shaded periods denote recessions.*

Careful statistical analysis confirms the value of the yield curve as a forecasting tool.[13] Figure 7.9 shows GDP growth and the slope of the yield curve, measured as the difference between the 10-year and 3-month yields—what is called a **term spread**. Panel A of Figure 7.9 shows GDP growth (as in Figure 7.8) together with the contemporaneous term spread (the growth and the term spread at the same time). Notice that when the term spread falls, GDP growth tends to fall somewhat later. In fact, when the yield curve becomes inverted, the economy tends to go into a recession roughly a year later. Panel B of Figure 7.9 makes this clear. At each point, GDP growth in the current year (e.g., 1990) is plotted against the slope of the yield curve *one year earlier*

[13]See Arturo Estrella and Frederic S. Mishkin, "The Yield Curve as a Predictor of U.S. Recessions," Federal Reserve Bank of New York, *Current Issues in Economics and Finance* 2, no. 7 (June 1996).

## IN THE NEWS
### Banks Decline Yield Curve Invitation to Party On

**Bloomberg.com**

**By Caroline Baum**

January 7, 2010

If you were to stop the average person on the street and ask him about the Treasury yield curve, he'd probably look at you with a blank stare.

"What's a yield curve and why should I care about it?" our passer-by might say.

I'm sure lots of people are wondering the same thing, now that the yield curve is garnering headlines.

The yield curve, or the "term structure of interest rates" in economists' parlance, is the pictorial representation of two points connected by a line.

Not any two points, mind you. One point is a short-term interest rate that is either pegged by the central bank (the federal funds rate) or influenced by it (the yield on the three-month Treasury bill). The other point is some long-term interest rate, the yield on the 10- or 30-year Treasury, whose price is determined by the marketplace.

What's so important about these two particular points?

Simple. These two points, in relationship to one another, succinctly describe the stance of monetary policy....

When short-term rates are below long-term rates, banks have an incentive to go out and lend. "Borrow short, lend long" is the first rule of banking. That's why a steep yield curve is expansionary. It's a means to an end, the end being money and credit creation. The central bank provides the raw material in the form of bank reserves. Depository institutions do—or don't do, in the present situation—the rest.

When the yield curve is inverted, with short rates higher than long rates, bank lending screeches to a halt.

The current ultra-steep yield curve is reminiscent of the early 1990s. Back then, banks were saddled with—what else?—bad real estate loans. History repeats itself with increased frequency.

Courtesy of what was at the time an unheard-of low level for the funds rate (3 percent) and a vertical yield curve, banks bought boatloads of U.S. government securities, which carry a zero risk-based capital weighting. The profit went right to the bottom line. Banks healed themselves, then got back to the business of allocating capital to the private sector.

People who are up in arms about the banks getting free money from the Fed and buying Treasuries should relax. That's how it always works. Banks lend to Uncle Sam so they can lend to you. During recessions, there's never much private-sector credit demand, so the Treasury's appetite satisfies the banks' need for high-quality assets.

As a devout believer in the predictive powers of the spread, I have always challenged those who try to deconstruct it, to mold its meaning to fit the current fashion. History shows the "what" matters more than the "why."

An inverted yield curve is one of the most reliable harbingers of recession. Yet when the curve inverted in 2006 and stayed that way through 2007, the protests went out:

(e.g., 1989). The two lines clearly move together; their correlation is +0.48. What the data show is that when the term spread falls, GDP growth tends to fall one year later. The yield curve is a valuable forecasting tool.

An example illustrates the usefulness of this information. In the left-hand panel of Figure 7.10, we can see that on January 23, 2001, the yield curve sloped downward from 3 months to 5 years, then upward for maturities to 30 years. This pattern indicated that interest rates were expected to fall over the next few years. Eight months later, after monetary policy had eased and the U.S. economy had slowed substantially, the Treasury yield curve sloped upward again (see the right-hand panel of Figure 7.10). At that point, growth was at a virtual standstill, and policymakers were

This time is different! An influx of foreign capital—the "savings glut"—is depressing long-term rates. The inverted yield doesn't mean what it usually means.

It wasn't different. It just took longer.

So what is the spread telling us now? All systems are go. With the funds rate close to zero and 10-year Treasuries yielding about 3.8 percent, there's a lot of carry in the curve.

Yet money and credit aren't growing. The M2 money supply, which includes savings and time deposits and money market mutual funds in addition to M1's currency and demand deposits, rose an annualized 1.2 percent from May to November, according to the Fed. The three-month annualized increase of 4.2 percent is encouraging if it continues.

On the other side of the balance sheet, bank credit fell an annualized 5 percent in the same six-month period. Loans and leases plunged 9.2 percent at an annual rate.

"Banks aren't lending," says Paul Kasriel, chief economist at the Northern Trust Corp. in Chicago.

At least not to non-government entities. Bank purchases of U.S. Treasury and agency securities rose an annualized 21 percent from May to November. The next step is a return to private lending.

. . .

For all its allure, the yield curve isn't acting as a transmission mechanism just yet. That doesn't mean that it won't. When the financial system is impaired, it takes a steeper curve for a longer period of time to produce an expansion in money and credit—just as it did in the early 90s. The invitation to party stands. Banks have yet to RSVP.

With time, the spread will translate into more borrowing and lending. It's the Fed's job to prevent a trickle from becoming a cascade, fanning what would be the third bubble in two decades.

## LESSONS OF THE ARTICLE

The slope of the yield curve can help predict the direction and speed of economic growth. At the beginning of 2010, the yield curve was unusually steep, pointing to a strong economic expansion (see Figure 7.9B, where the steep slope in 2010 is shown as a high value for the term spread). However, in the aftermath of the financial crisis of 2007-2009, lenders were especially cautious about extending credit to risky borrowers, even though risk spreads had narrowed sharply from crisis peaks (see Figure 7.8B). The author argues that it is only a matter of time until the steep yield curve encourages lenders to start lending again. However, the ability and willingness to lend will depend on how quickly intermediaries can repair the damage to their balance sheets incurred by the crisis and gain confidence that borrowers will repay.

doing everything they could to get the economy moving again. They had reduced interest rates by more than 3 percentage points over a period of less than nine months. Thus, investors expected little in the way of short-term interest-rate reductions. This prediction turned out to be wrong, however; interest rates kept falling after the terrorist attacks of September 11, 2001. They continued to fall through the remainder of 2001 as the economy went into a mild recession.

The yield curve did *not* predict the depth or duration of the recession of 2007–2009. One- and two-year market rates did not anticipate the persistent plunge of overnight rates. As financial institutions weakened in the crisis, the widening risk spread signaled a severe economic downturn, providing a more useful predictor in this episode.

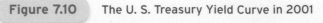

**Figure 7.10**     The U. S. Treasury Yield Curve in 2001

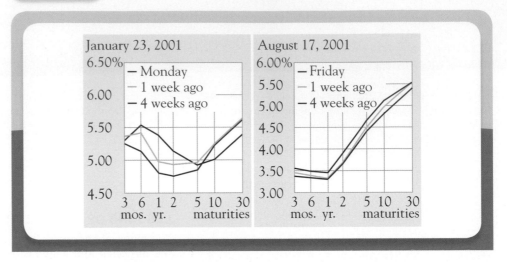

SOURCE: *Board of Governors of the Federal Reserve System.*

We started this chapter by asking why different types of bonds have different yields and what it is we can learn from those differences. After a bit of work, we can now see that differences in both risk and time to maturity affect bond yields. The less likely the issuer is to repay or the longer the time to maturity, the riskier a bond and the higher its yield. Even more importantly, both increases in the risk spread and an inverted yield curve suggest troubled economic times ahead.

# Terms

# Chapter Lessons

1. Bond ratings summarize the likelihood that a bond issuer will meet its payment obligations.
   a. Highly rated investment-grade bonds are those with the lowest risk of default.
   b. If a firm encounters financial difficulties, its bond rating may be downgraded.
   c. Commercial paper is the short-term version of a privately issued bond.
   d. Junk bonds are high-risk bonds with very low ratings. Firms that have a high probability of default issue these bonds.
   e. Investors demand compensation for default risk in the form of a risk premium. The higher the risk of default, the lower a bond's rating, the higher its risk premium, and the higher its yield.

2. Municipal bonds are usually exempt from income taxes. Because investors care about the after-tax returns on their investments, these bonds have lower yields than bonds whose interest payments are taxable.

3. The term structure of interest rates is the relationship between yield to maturity and time to maturity. A graph with the yield to maturity on the vertical axis and the time to maturity on the horizontal axis is called the yield curve.
   a. Any theory of the term structure of interest rates must explain three facts:
      i. Interest rates of different maturities move together.
      ii. The yields on short-term bonds are more volatile than the yields on long-term bonds.
      iii. Long-term yields are usually higher than short-term yields.
   b. The expectations hypothesis of the term structure of interest rates states that long-term interest rates are the average of expected future short-term interest rates. This hypothesis explains only the first two facts about the term structure of interest rates.
   c. The liquidity premium theory of the term structure of interest rates, which is based on the fact that long-term bonds are riskier than short-term bonds, explains all three facts in 3a.

4. The risk structure and the term structure of interest rates both signal financial markets' expectations of future economic activity. Specifically, the likelihood of a recession will be higher when
   a. The risk spread, or the range between low- and high-grade bond yields, is wide.
   b. The yield curve slopes downward, or is inverted, so that short-term interest rates are higher than long-term interest rates.

# Conceptual Problems

1. Suppose your marginal federal income tax rate is 36 percent. What is your after-tax return from holding a one-year corporate bond with a yield of 9 percent? What is your after-tax return from holding a one-year municipal bond with a yield of 5 percent? How would you decide which bond to hold?

2. Why do you think the amount of commercial paper outstanding fell significantly during the 2007–2009 financial crisis?

3.* Taking into account your answer to question 2, how would you explain the fall in the amount of asset-backed commercial paper outstanding that began in the third quarter of 2007?

4. Go to the Federal Reserve Board's Web site (www.federalreserve.gov), and click first on *Economic Research and Data*, and then on *Statistical Releases and Historical Data*. Under the data download program, choose *Selected Interest Rates (H.15)* and build a package of data to include monthly series from 2006 for the yields on three-month nonfinancial commercial paper, three-month financial commercial paper, and the three-month Treasury bills sold on the secondary market. Compute the spread between each of the two commercial paper yields and the Treasury bill yield, and comment on the patterns you observe in the data.

5. What was the connection between house price movements, the growth in subprime mortgages, and securities backed by these mortgages—on the one hand—and—on the other hand—the difficulties encountered by some financial institutions during the 2007–2009 financial crisis?

6. Suppose that the interest rate on one-year bonds is 4 percent today, and is expected to be 5 percent one year from now and 6 percent two years from now. Using the expectations hypothesis, compute the yield curve for the next three years.

7.* According to the liquidity premium theory, if the yield on both one- and two-year bonds are the same, would you expect the one-year yield in one year's time to be higher, lower, or the same? Explain your answer.

8. You have $1,000 to invest over an investment horizon of three years. The bond market offers various options. You can buy (i) a sequence of three one-year bonds; (ii) a three-year bond; or (iii) a two-year bond followed by a one-year bond. The current yield curve tells you that the one-year, two-year, and three-year yields to maturity are 3.5 percent, 4.0 percent, and 4.5 percent, respectively. You expect that one-year interest rates will be 4 percent next year and 5 percent the year after that. Assuming annual compounding, compute the return on each of the three investments, and discuss which one you would choose.

9.* If inflation and interest rates become more volatile, what would you expect to see happen to the slope of the yield curve?

10. As economic conditions improve in countries with emerging markets, the cost of borrowing funds there tends to fall. Explain why.

11. When countries with emerging markets have financial problems, the yields on U.S. Treasury issues tend to fall. Can you explain this phenomenon? What would happen to the risk spread under such circumstances, and how would you use that information?

## Analytical Problems

12. Suppose your local government decided to tax the interest income on its own bonds as part of an effort to rectify serious budgetary woes. What would you expect to see happen to the yields on these bonds?

*Indicates more difficult problems

13.* If, before the change in tax status, the yields on the bonds described in question 12 were below the Treasury yield of the same maturity, would you expect this spread to narrow, to disappear, or to change sign after the policy change? Explain your answer.

14. Suppose the risk premium on bonds increases. How would the change affect your forecast of future economic activity, and why?

15. If regulations restricting institutional investors to investment-grade bonds were lifted, what do you think would happen to the spreads between yields on investment-grade and speculative-grade bonds?

16. Suppose a country with a struggling economy suddenly discovered vast quantities of valuable minerals under government-owned land. How might the government's bond rating be affected? Using the model of demand and supply for bonds, what would you expect to happen to the bond yields of that country's government bonds?

17. The misrating of mortgage-backed securities by rating agencies contributed to the financial crisis of 2007–2009. List some recommendations you would make to avoid such mistakes in the future.

18. How do you think the abolition of investor protection laws would affect the risk spread between corporate and government bonds?

19. You and a friend are reading *The Wall Street Journal* and notice that the Treasury yield curve is slightly upward sloping. Your friend comments that all looks well for the economy but you are concerned that the economy is heading for trouble. Assuming you are both believers in the liquidity premium theory, what might account for your difference of opinion?

20. Do you think the term spread was an effective predictor of the recession that started in December 2007? Why or why not?

21.* Given the data in the accompanying table, would you say that this economy is heading for a boom or for a recession? Explain your choice.

| | 3-month Treasury-bill | 10-year Treasury bond | Baa corporate 10-year bond |
|---|---|---|---|
| January | 1.00% | 3.0% | 7.0% |
| February | 1.05 | 3.5 | 7.2 |
| March | 1.10 | 4.0 | 7.6 |
| April | 1.20 | 4.6 | 8.0 |
| May | 1.25 | 5.0 | 8.2 |

www.mhhe.com/cecchetti3e

# Chapter 9

## Derivatives: Futures, Options, and Swaps

Derivatives played a central role in the financial crisis of 2007–2009. One of the key events during the crisis was the fall of AIG, the world's largest insurance company. Through the use of derivatives contracts, AIG had taken enormous risks that it was able to conceal from the view both of government officials and its trading partners. Each contract was arranged over the counter (OTC)—that is, directly between AIG and a single counterparty—rather than through an organized exchange. In the crisis, these hidden risks threatened the entire financial system.

Leading up to the crisis, the tight but largely unseen links that OTC derivatives created among the largest, most important global financial institutions made the entire system vulnerable to the weakest of those institutions. Partly as a result of the *systemic vulnerabilities* posed by OTC derivatives, phrases like "too interconnected to fail" and "too big to fail" filled newspapers and the media (see Chapter 5, Lessons from the Crisis: Systemic Risk). Warren Buffett, the famed investor, called derivatives "weapons of financial mass destruction."

Even in the years before the financial crisis, stories detailing the abuse of derivatives filled the pages of the business press. Derivatives were at the bottom of the scandal that engulfed Enron immediately after it declared bankruptcy in November 2001. As we have learned since then, Enron engaged in a variety of financial transactions whose express purpose was to give the appearance of low debt, low risk, and high profitability. This sleight of hand kept the stock price high and made shareholders happy, so no one complained. In fact, no one even looked. But eventually the day of reckoning came, and the company collapsed.

Financial derivatives were also linked to the collapse of Long-Term Capital Management (LTCM), a Connecticut-based hedge fund, in fall 1998. On a single day in August 1998, LTCM lost an astounding $553 million. By late September, the fund had lost another $2 billion. That left LTCM with more than $99 billion in debt and $100 billion in assets. With loans accounting for 99 percent of total assets, repayment was nearly impossible. LTCM also had significant derivatives positions that did not show up on the balance sheet as assets or liabilities. These off-balance-sheet arrangements, which carried even more risk, were the primary cause of the fund's stunningly swift losses.

If derivatives are open to abuse, why do they exist? The answer is that when used properly, derivatives are extremely helpful financial instruments. They can be used to reduce risk, allowing firms and individuals to enter into agreements that they otherwise wouldn't be willing to accept. Derivatives can also be used as insurance. For example, in winter 1998, a snowmobile manufacturer named Bombardier offered a $1,000 rebate to buyers should snowfall in 44 cities total less than half what it had averaged over the preceding three years. Sales rose 38 percent. The existence of "weather derivatives" enabled Bombardier to undertake this risky marketing strategy. Paying the rebates would have bankrupted the company, but Bombardier purchased

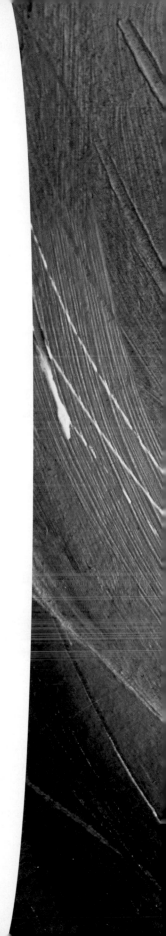

derivatives that would pay off if snowfall were low. By using this unorthodox form of insurance, Bombardier transferred the risk to someone else.

What exactly are derivatives, and why are they so important? Though they play a critical role in our financial well-being, most people barely know what they are. This chapter will provide an introduction to the uses and abuses of derivatives.

# The Basics: Defining Derivatives

To understand what derivatives are, let's begin with the basics. A **derivative** is a financial instrument whose value depends on—is *derived* from—the value of some other financial instrument, called the *underlying asset*. Some common examples of underlying assets are stocks, bonds, wheat, snowfall, and stock-market indexes like the S&P 500.

A simple example of a derivative is a contractual agreement between two investors that obligates one to make a payment to the other, depending on the movement in interest rates over the next year. This type of derivative is called an interest-rate *futures contract*. Such an arrangement is quite different from the outright purchase of a bond for two reasons. First, derivatives provide an easy way for investors to profit from price declines. The purchase of a bond, in contrast, is a bet that its price will rise.[1] Second, and more important, in a derivatives transaction, one person's loss is always another person's gain. Buyer and seller are like two people playing poker. How much each player wins or loses depends on how the game progresses, but the total amount on the table doesn't change.

While derivatives can be used to *speculate*, or gamble on future price movements, the fact that they allow investors to manage and reduce risk makes them indispensable to a modern economy. Bombardier used a derivative to hedge the risk of having to pay rebates in the event of low snowfall (we discussed hedging in Chapter 5). As we will see, farmers use derivatives regularly, to insure themselves against fluctuations in the market prices of their crops. Risk can be bought and sold using derivatives. Thus, *the purpose of derivatives is to transfer risk from one person or firm to another*.

When people have the ability to transfer risks, they will do things that they wouldn't do otherwise. Think of a wheat farmer and a bread baker. If he or she cannot insure against a decline in the price of wheat, the farmer will plant fewer acres of wheat. And without a guarantee that the price of flour will not rise, the baker will build a smaller bakery. Those are prudent responses to the risks created by price fluctuations. Now introduce a mechanism through which the farmer and the baker can guarantee the price of wheat. As a result the farmer will plant more and the baker will build a bigger bakery. Insurance is what allows them to do it! Derivatives provide

"At the Hawescroft School we've de-emphasized singing and drawing and emphasized stocks and derivatives."

SOURCE: © Peter Steiner/The New Yorker Collection/www.cartoonbank.com.

[1]Investors can bet that prices will fall using a technique called *short selling*. The investor borrows an asset from its owner for a fee, sells it at the current market price, and then repurchases it later. The short seller is betting that the price of the asset will fall between the time it is sold and the time it is repurchased.

that insurance. In fact, by shifting risk to those willing and able to bear it, derivatives increase the risk-carrying capacity of the economy as a whole, improving the allocation of resources and increasing the level of output.

While derivatives allow individuals and firms to manage risk, they also allow them to conceal the true nature of certain financial transactions. In the same way that stripping a coupon bond separates the coupons from the principal payment, buying and selling derivatives can unbundle virtually any group of future payments and risks. A company that hesitates to issue a coupon bond for fear analysts will frown on the extra debt can instead issue the coupon payments and the principal payment as individual zero-coupon bonds, using derivative transactions to label them something other than borrowing. Thus, if stock-market analysts penalize companies for obtaining funding in certain ways, derivatives (as we will see) allow the companies to get exactly the same resources at the same risk but under a different name.

Derivatives may be divided into three major categories: forwards and futures, options, and swaps. Let's look at each one.

# Forwards and Futures

Of all derivative financial instruments, forwards and futures are the simplest to understand and the easiest to use. A **forward**, or **forward contract**, *is an agreement between a buyer and a seller to exchange a commodity or financial instrument for a specified amount of cash on a prearranged future date.* Forward contracts are private agreements between two parties. Because they are customized, forward contracts are very difficult to resell to someone else.

To see why forward contracts are difficult to resell, consider the example of a year-long apartment lease, in which the renter agrees to make a series of monthly payments to the landlord in exchange for the right to live in the apartment. Such a lease is a sequence of 12 forward contracts. Rent is paid in predetermined amounts on prearranged future dates in exchange for housing. While there is some standardization of leases, a contract between a specific renter and a specific landlord is unlike any other rental contract. Thus, there is no market for the resale or reassignment of apartment rental contracts.

*In contrast, a* **future**, *or* **futures contract**, *is a forward contract that has been standardized and sold through an organized exchange.* A futures contract specifies that the seller—who has the *short position*—will deliver some quantity of a commodity or financial instrument to the buyer— who has the *long position*—on a specific date, called the *settlement* or *delivery* date, for a predetermined price. No payments are made initially when the contract is agreed to. The seller/short position benefits from declines in the price of the underlying asset, while the buyer/long position benefits from increases.[2]

Trading pit at the New York Mercantile Exchange in New York City that appeared in the movie *Trading Places* with Eddie Murphy and Dan Aykroyd.

Take the U.S. Treasury bond futures contract that trades on the Chicago Board of Trade. The contract specifies the delivery of $100,000 face value worth of 10-year, 6 percent coupon U.S. Treasury bonds at

---

[2]The term *short* refers to the fact that one party to the agreement is obligated to deliver something, whether or not he or she currently owns it. The term *long* signifies that the other party is obligated to buy something at a future date.

**Table 9.1** Interest-Rate Futures

| | (1) | (2) | (3) | (4) | (5) | (6) | (7) |
|---|---|---|---|---|---|---|---|
| | | Open | High | Low | Settle | Chg | Open Interest |
| **Interest Rate Futures** | | | | | | | |
| Treasury Bonds (cbt)-$100,000; pts 32nds of 100% | | | | | | | |
| | March | 117-31 | 118-27 | 117-23 | 118-20 | 21 | 653,111 |
| | June | 116-08 | 117-08 | 116-08 | 117-04 | 21 | 1,220 |

This table reports information on a contract for delivery of $100,000 face value worth of 10-year 6 percent coupon U.S. Treasury bonds.

*Column 1* reports the month when the contract requires delivery of the bonds from the short position/seller to the long position/buyer.

*Column 2.* "Open" is the price quoted when the exchange opened on the morning of January 21, 2010. This need not be the same as the price at the preceding afternoon's close. The price in the first row, 117-31, is quoted in 32nds and represents the cost of $100 face value worth of the 10-year 6 percent coupon U.S. Treasury bonds.

*Columns 3 and 4.* "High" and "Low" are the highest and lowest prices posted during the trading day.

*Column 5.* "Settle" is the closing or settlement price at the end of the trading day. This is the price used for *marking to market*.

*Column 6.* "Change" is the change in the closing price, measured in 32nds, from the preceding day's closing price.

*Column 7.* "Open Interest" is the number of contracts outstanding, or open. For contracts near expiration, this number is often quite large. Most of the time, contract sellers repurchase their positions rather than delivering the bonds, a procedure called *settlement by offset*.

SOURCE: *The Wall Street Journal.* Copyright 2010 by Dow Jones & Company, Inc. Reproduced with permission of Dow Jones & Company, Inc. in the formats Textbook and Other Book via Copyright Clearance Center.

any time during a given month, called the *delivery* month.[3] Table 9.1 shows the prices and trading activity for this contract on January 21, 2010. The fact that the contract is so specific means there is no need for negotiation. And the existence of the exchange creates a natural place for people who are interested in a particular futures contract to meet and trade. Historically, exchanges have been physical locations, but with the Internet came online trading of futures. In recent years, firms have created virtual futures markets for a wide variety of products, including energy, bandwidth, and plastics.

One more thing is needed before anyone will actually buy or sell futures contracts: assurance that the buyer and seller will meet their obligations. In the case of the U.S. Treasury futures contract, the buyer must be sure that the seller will deliver the bond,

[3]A bond issued by the U.S. Treasury with an original maturity of 10 years or less is officially called a "Treasury note," but we use the term "Treasury bond" in this chapter for simplicity. The seller of a U.S. Treasury bond futures contract need not deliver the exact bond specified in the contract. The Chicago Board of Trade maintains a spreadsheet of conversion factors to use in adjusting the quantity (face value) when delivery of some other bond is made. While these particular futures allow for delivery at any time during the delivery month, other futures may require delivery on a specific day. Specifications of the contract are available at: http://www.cmegroup.com/trading/interest-rates/us-treasury/10-year-us-treasury-note_contract_specifications.html

and the seller must believe that the buyer will pay for it. Market participants have found an ingenious solution to this problem. Instead of making a bilateral arrangement, the two parties to a futures contract each make an agreement with a *clearing corporation*. The clearing corporation, which operates like a large insurance company, is the counterparty to both sides of a transaction, guaranteeing that they will meet their obligations. This arrangement reduces the risk buyers and sellers face. The clearing corporation has the ability to monitor traders and the incentive to limit their risk taking (see Lessons from the Crisis: Centralized Counterparties and Systemic Risk).

## Margin Accounts and Marking to Market

To reduce the risk it faces, the clearing corporation requires both parties to a futures contract to place a deposit with the corporation itself. This practice is called posting **margin** in a *margin account*. The margin deposits guarantee that when the contract comes due, the parties will be able to meet their obligations. But the clearing corporation does more than collect the *initial margin* when a contract is signed. It also posts daily gains and losses on the contract to the margin accounts of the parties involved.[4] This process is called *marking to market*, and it is done daily.

Marking to market is analogous to what happens during a poker game. At the end of each hand, the amount wagered is transferred from the losers to the winner. In financial parlance, the account of each player is marked to market. Alternative methods of accounting are too complicated, making it difficult to identify players who should be excused from the game because they have run out of resources. For similar reasons, the clearing corporation marks futures accounts to market every day. Doing so ensures that sellers always have the resources to make delivery and that buyers always can pay. As in poker, if someone's margin account falls below the minimum, the clearing corporation will sell the contracts, ending the person's participation in the market.

An example will help you understand how marking to market works. Take the case of a futures contract for the purchase of 1,000 ounces of silver at $7 per ounce. The contract specifies that the buyer of the contract, the long position, will pay $7,000 in exchange for 1,000 ounces of silver. The seller of the contract, the short position, receives the $7,000 and delivers the 1,000 ounces of silver. We can think about this contract as guaranteeing the long position the ability to buy 1,000 ounces of silver for $7,000 and guaranteeing the short position the ability to sell 1,000 ounces of silver for $7,000. Now consider what happens when the price of silver changes. If the price rises to $8 per ounce, the seller needs to give the buyer $1,000 so that the buyer pays only $7,000 for the 1,000 ounces of silver. By contrast, if the price falls to $6 an ounce, the buyer of the futures contract needs to pay $1,000 to the seller to make sure that the seller receives $7,000 for selling the 1,000 ounces of silver. Marking to market is the transfer of funds at the end of each day that ensures the buyers and sellers get what the contract promises.

## Hedging and Speculating with Futures

Futures contracts allow the transfer of risk between buyer and seller. This transfer can be accomplished through hedging or speculation. Let's look at *hedging* first. Say a government securities dealer wishes to insure against declines in the value of an inventory of bonds. Recall from Chapter 5 that this type of risk can be reduced by finding

[4]On January 21, 2010, the March U.S. Treasury bond futures contract in Table 9.1 rose 21/32 per $100 face value worth of bonds. A single contract covers 1,000 times that amount, so the value of each contract rose by ($21/32)(1000) = $656.25. Marking to market means that, at the end of the day for each outstanding contract, the clearing corporation credited the long position/seller and debited the short position/buyer $656.25.

another financial instrument that delivers a high payoff when bond prices fall. That is exactly what happens with the sale of a U.S. Treasury bond futures contract: the seller/short position benefits from price declines. Put differently, the seller of a futures contract—the securities dealer, in this case—can guarantee the price at which the bonds are sold. The other party to this transaction might be a pension fund manager who is planning to purchase bonds in the future and wishes to insure against possible price increases.[5] Buying a futures contract fixes the price that the fund will need to pay. In this example, *both sides use the futures contract as a hedge*. They are both *hedgers*.[6]

Producers and users of commodities employ futures markets to hedge their risks as well. Farmers, mining companies, oil drillers, and the like are sellers of futures, taking short positions. After all, they own the commodities outright, so they want to stabilize the revenue they receive when they sell. In contrast, millers, jewelers, and oil distributors want to buy futures to take long positions. They require the commodity to do business, so they buy the futures contract to reduce risk arising from fluctuations in the cost of essential inputs.

What about *speculators*? Their objective is simple: They are trying to make a profit. To do so, they bet on price movements. Sellers of futures are betting that prices will fall, while buyers are betting that prices will rise. Futures contracts are popular tools for speculation because they are cheap. An investor needs only a relatively small amount of investment—the margin—to purchase a futures contract that is worth a great deal. Margin requirements of 10 percent or less are common. In the case of a futures contract for the delivery of $100,000 face value worth of 10-year, 6 percent coupon U.S. Treasury bonds, the Chicago Board of Trade (the clearing corporation that guarantees the contract) requires an initial margin of only $2,700 per contract. That is, an investment of only $2,700 gives the investor the same returns as the purchase of $100,000 worth of bonds. It is as if the investor borrowed the remaining $97,300 without having to pay any interest.[7]

To see the impact of this kind of leverage on the return to the buyer and seller of a futures contract, recall from footnote 4 that a rise of 21/32nds in the price of the Treasury bond futures contract meant that the long position/seller gained $656.25, while the short position/buyer lost $656.25. With a minimum initial investment of $2,700 for each contract, this represents a 24.3 percent gain to the futures contract buyer and a 24.3 percent loss to the futures contract seller. In contrast, the owner of the bond itself would have gained $656.25 on an approximately $100,000 investment, which is a return of just 0.656 percent! *Speculators, then, can use futures to obtain very large amounts of leverage at a very low cost.*

## Arbitrage and the Determinants of Futures Prices

To understand how the price of a futures contract is determined, let's start at the settlement date and work backward. On the settlement or delivery date, we know that the price of the futures contract must equal the price of the underlying asset the seller is obligated to deliver. The reason is simple: If, at expiration, the futures price were to deviate from the asset's price, then it would be possible to make a risk-free profit by engaging in offsetting cash and futures transactions. If the current market price of

---

[5]Recall from Chapters 4 and 6 that bond prices and interest rates move in opposite directions. That means the bond dealer who sells the futures contract is insuring against interest rate increases.

[6]Hedgers who buy futures are called *long hedgers* and hedgers who sell futures are called *short hedgers*.

[7]It is even possible to arrange a margin account so that the balance earns interest.

## LESSONS FROM THE CRISIS
### CENTRALIZED COUNTERPARTIES AND SYSTEMIC RISK

We know that a loss of liquidity and transparency can threaten the financial system as a whole (see Chapter 5, Lessons from the Crisis: Systemic Risk). Lack of liquidity can make trading impossible, while lack of transparency can make traders unwilling to trust one another. Both can cause markets to seize up and trigger a cascade of failures. Transparent, liquid financial markets are less prone to such systemic disruptions.

How can we make markets more robust? One way is to shift trading from over-the-counter (OTC) markets, where products tend to be customized, to transactions with a **centralized counterparty (CCP)** in standardized financial instruments.*

OTC trading is bilateral, that is, directly between buyer and seller, rather than through an intermediary. By contrast, a CCP is an entity that interposes itself between the two sides of a transaction, becoming the buyer to every seller and the seller to every buyer. Trading on most stock, futures, and options exchanges goes through CCPs. As a result, when you buy or sell a stock, you neither know nor care who the ultimate seller or buyer is because you are trading with the CCP of the exchange.

When trading OTC with many partners, a firm can build up excessively large positions without other parties being aware of the risk it is acquiring. In contrast, a CCP has the *ability*, as well as the *incentive*, to monitor the riskiness of its counterparties. Because all trades occur with the CCP, it can see whether a trader is taking a large position on one side of a trade. Standardization of contracts also facilitates CCP monitoring. If it finds itself trading with a risky counterparty, a CCP can insist on a risk premium to protect itself. A CCP also can refuse to trade with a counterparty that may not be able to pay. And it can insist on frequent marking of prices to market to measure and control risks effectively.

A CCP also limits its own risk through economies of scale. Most of the trades that a CCP conducts can be offset against one another. Therefore, the volume of net payments that must occur on any given day are only a small fraction of the gross value of the trades, sharply lowering the risk of nonpayment.

The history of CCPs reveals their practical benefits. Since 1925, when all U.S. futures contracts began trading through a CCP, no contract has failed despite many subsequent financial disruptions, including the Great Depression. CCPs have helped markets function well even when traders cannot pay. For example, when one large energy futures trader (Amaranth) failed in 2006, the futures market adjusted smoothly because the CCP could use the trader's collateral to satisfy its contracts with other firms. In contrast, systemic threats and disruptions have arisen repeatedly with OTC contracts: in 1998, when the possible demise of the hedge fund LTCM threatened numerous counterparties of its OTC interest-rate swaps; and again, during the financial crisis of 2007-2009, with a number of firms active in OTC derivatives, including Bear Stearns, Lehman Brothers, and AIG.

*For more details on CCPs, see Stephen G. Cecchetti, Jacob Gyntelberg, and Marc Hollanders, "Central Counterparties for Over-the-Counter Derivatives," *BIS Quarterly Review*, September 2009, pp. 45–58.

a bond were below the futures contract price, someone could buy a bond at the low price and simultaneously sell a futures contract (take a short position and promise to deliver the bond on a future date). Immediate exercise of the futures contract and delivery of the bond would yield a profit equal to the difference between the market price and the futures price. Thinking about this example carefully, we can see that the investor who engages in these transactions has been able to make a profit without taking on any risk or making any investment.

The practice of simultaneously buying and selling financial instruments in order to benefit from temporary price differences is called **arbitrage**, and the people who engage in it are called *arbitrageurs*. Arbitrage means that two financial instruments with the same risk and promised future payments will sell for the same price. If, for example, the price of a specific bond is higher in one market than in another, an arbitrageur can buy at the low price and sell at the high price. The increase in demand in the market where the price is low drives the price up there, while the increase in supply in the market where the price is high drives the price down there, and the process continues until prices are equal in the two markets. As long as there are arbitrageurs, on the day when a futures contract is settled, the price of a bond futures contract will be the same as the market price—what is called the *spot price*—of the bond.

So we know that on the settlement date, the price of a futures contract must equal the spot price of the underlying asset. But what happens before the settlement date? The principle of arbitrage still applies. The price of the futures contract depends on the fact that someone can buy a bond and sell a futures contract simultaneously. Here's how it's done. First, the arbitrageur borrows at the current market interest rate. With the funds, the arbitrageur buys a bond and sells a bond futures contract. Now the arbitrageur has a loan on which interest must be paid, a bond that pays interest, and a promise to deliver the bond for a fixed price at the expiration of the futures contract. Because the interest owed on the loan and received from the bond will cancel out, this position costs nothing to initiate.[8] As before, if the market price of the bond is below the futures contract price, this strategy will yield a profit. *Thus, the futures price must move in lockstep with the market price of the bond.*

To see how arbitrage works, consider an example in which the spot price of a 6 percent coupon 10-year bond is $100, the current interest rate on a 3-month loan is also 6 percent (quoted at an annual rate), and the futures market price for delivery of a 6 percent, 10-year bond is $101. An investor could borrow $100, purchase the 10-year bond, and sell a bond future for $101 promising delivery of the bond in three months. The investor could use the interest payment from the bond to pay the interest on the loan and deliver the bond to the buyer of the futures contract on the delivery date. This transaction is completely riskless and nets the investor a profit of $1—without even putting up any funds. A riskless profit is extremely tempting, so the investor will continue to engage in the transactions needed to generate it. Here that means continuing to buy bonds (driving the price up) and sell futures (forcing the price down) until the prices converge and no further profits are available.[9]

Table 9.2 summarizes the positions of buyers and sellers in the futures market.

**Table 9.2**   Who's Who in Futures

| | Buyer of a Futures Contract | Seller of a Futures Contract |
|---|---|---|
| This is called the | *Long* position | *Short* position |
| Obligation of the party | Buy the commodity or asset on the settlement date | Deliver the commodity or asset on the settlement date |
| What happens to this person's margin account after a *rise* in the market price of the commodity or asset? | *Credited* | *Debited* |
| Who takes this position to *hedge?* | The *user* of the commodity or *buyer* of the asset who needs to insure against the price *rising* | The *producer* of the commodity or owner of the asset who needs to insure against the price *falling* |
| Who takes this position to *speculate?* | Someone who believes that the market price of the commodity or asset will *rise* | Someone who believes that the market price of the commodity or asset will *fall* |

[8]Unlike you and me, the arbitrageur can borrow at an interest rate that is close to the one received from the bond. There are two reasons for this. First, the arbitrageur is likely to be a large financial intermediary with a very high credit rating; second, the loan is collateralized by the bond itself.

[9]In a commodity futures contract, the futures price will equal the present value of the expected spot price on the delivery date, discounted at the risk-free interest rate.

# Options

Everyone likes to have options. Having the option to go on vacation or buy a new car is nice. The alternative to having options, having our decisions made for us, is surely worse. Because options are valuable, people are willing to pay for them when they can. Financial options are no different; because they are worth having, we can put a price on them.

Calculating the price of an option is incredibly complicated. In fact, no one knew how before Fischer Black and Myron Scholes figured it out in 1973. Traders immediately programmed their famous Black-Scholes formula into the computers available at the time, and the options markets took off. By June 2000, the market value of outstanding options was in the neighborhood of $500 billion. Today, millions of options contracts are outstanding, and millions of them change hands every day.

Before we learn how to price options, we'll need to master the vocabulary used to describe them. Once we have the language, the next step is to move on to how to use options and how to value them.

## Calls, Puts, and All That: Definitions

Like futures, options are agreements between two parties. There is a seller, called an *option writer*, and a buyer, called an *option holder*. As we will see, option writers incur obligations, while option holders obtain rights. There are two basic options, *puts* and *calls*.

A **call option** is the right to buy—"call away"—a given quantity of an underlying asset at a predetermined price, called the **strike price** (or *exercise price*), on or before a specific date. For example, a January 2011 call option on 100 shares of IBM stock at a strike price of 90 gives the option holder the right to buy 100 shares of IBM for $90 apiece prior to the third Friday of January 2011. The writer of the call option *must* sell the shares if and when the holder chooses to use the call option. The holder of the call is *not required* to buy the shares; rather, the holder has the option to buy and will do so only if buying is beneficial. When the price of IBM stock exceeds the option strike price of 90, the option holder can either call away the 100 shares from the option writer by *exercising* the option or sell the option to someone else at a profit. If the market price rose to $95, for example, then exercising the call would allow the holder to buy the stock from the option writer for $90 and reap a $5 per share profit. Whenever the price of the stock is above the strike price of the call option, exercising the option is profitable for the holder, and the option is said to be *in the money* (as in "I'm in the money!"). If the price of the stock exactly equals the strike price, the option is said to be *at the money*. If the strike price exceeds the market price of the underlying asset, it is termed *out of the money*.

A **put option** gives the holder the right but not the obligation to sell the underlying asset at a predetermined price on or before a fixed date. The holder can "put" the asset in the hands of the option writer. Again, the writer of the option is obliged to buy the shares should the holder choose to exercise the option. Returning to the example of IBM stock, consider a put option with a strike price of 90. This is the right to sell 100 shares at $90 per share, which is valuable when the market price of IBM stock falls below $90. If the price of a share of IBM stock were $80, then exercising the put option would yield a profit of $10 per share.

The same terminology that is used to describe calls—in the money, at the money, and out of the money—applies to puts as well, but the circumstances in which it is used are reversed. Since the buyer of a put obtains the right to sell a stock, the put is *in the money* when the option's strike price is *above* the market price of the stock. It is *out of the money* when the strike price is *below* the market price.

While it is possible to customize options in the same way as forward contracts, many are standardized and traded on exchanges, just like futures contracts. The mechanics of trading are the same. A clearing corporation guarantees the obligations embodied in the option—those of the option writer. And the option writer is required to post margin. Because option holders incur no obligation, they are not required to post margin.

There are two types of calls and puts: American and European. **American options** can be exercised on any date from the time they are written until the day they expire. As a result, prior to the expiration date, the holder of an American option has three choices: (1) continue to hold the option, (2) sell the option to someone else, or (3) exercise the option immediately. **European options** can be exercised only on the day that they expire. Thus, the holder of a European option has two choices on a date prior to expiration: hold or sell. The vast majority of options traded in the United States are American.

## Using Options

Who buys and sells options, and why? To answer this question, we need to understand how options are used. *Options transfer risk* from the buyer to the seller, so they can be used for both hedging and speculation. Let's take hedging first. Remember that a hedger is buying insurance. For someone who wants to purchase an asset such as a bond or a stock in the future, a call option ensures that the cost of buying the asset will not rise. For someone who plans to sell the asset in the future, a put option ensures that the price at which the asset can be sold will not go down.

To understand the close correspondence between options and insurance, think of the arrangement that automobile owners have with their insurance company. The owner pays an insurance premium and obtains the right to file a claim in the event of an accident. If the terms of the policy are met, the insurance company is obligated to pay the claim. If no accident occurs, then there is no claim and the insurance company makes no payment; the insurance premium is lost. In effect, the insurance company has sold an American call option to the car's owner where the underlying asset is a working car and the strike price is zero. This call option can be exercised if and only if the car is damaged in an accident on any day before the policy expires.

Options can be used for speculation as well. Say that you believe that interest rates are going to fall over the next few months. There are three ways to bet on this possibility. The first is to purchase a bond outright, hoping that its price will rise as interest rates fall. This is expensive, because you will need to come up with the resources to buy the bond. A second strategy is to buy a futures contract, taking the long position. If the market price of the bond rises, you will make a profit. As we saw in the last section, this is an attractive approach, since it requires only a small investment. But it is also very risky, because the investment is highly leveraged. Both the bond purchase and the futures contract carry the risk that you will take a loss, and if interest rates rise substantially, your loss will be large.

The third strategy for betting that interest rates will fall is to buy a call option on a U.S. Treasury bond. If you are right and interest rates fall, the value of the call option will rise. But if you are wrong and interest rates rise, the call will expire worthless and

## YOUR FINANCIAL WORLD
### Should You Believe Corporate Financial Statements?

Corporations work hard to appear as profitable as possible. They employ squadrons of accountants and financial wizards to dress up their financial statements so that reported profits are as high and stable as possible. While financial statements must meet exacting accounting standards, that does not mean they accurately reflect a company's true financial position. The problem is that the standards are so specific they provide a road map for the creation of misleading statements. Remember that derivatives render the names attached to particular risks and payoffs arbitrary and irrelevant. But accounting regulations are all about names. That is the way the system works, and there is nothing illegal about it.

So what are investors supposed to do? First, never trust an accounting statement that doesn't meet the standards set forth by financial regulators. In recent years, especially during the Internet boom of the late 1990s, firms published so-called pro forma financial statements based on their own definitions of revenue and costs. To look profitable, these companies had to make their own accounting rules. Such tinkering implies that a firm has something to hide.

Second, the more open a company is in its financial accounting, the more likely that it is honest. One of the lasting effects of Enron's collapse is that investors now punish companies that publish opaque financial statements. Honesty really is the best policy; the more information a firm makes public, the more credible it will be with investors.

Finally, remember that diversification reduces risk. If you own shares in many different companies, you are better protected against the possibility that some of them will be less than honest in their disclosures.

your losses will be limited to the price you paid for it. This bet is both highly leveraged and limited in its potential losses.

In the same way that purchasing a call option allows an investor to bet that the price of the underlying asset will rise, purchasing a put option allows the investor to bet that the price will fall. Again, if the investor is wrong, all that is lost is the price paid for the option. In the meantime, the option provides a cheap way to bet on the movement in the price of the underlying asset. The bet is highly leveraged, because a small initial investment creates the opportunity for a large gain. But unlike a futures contract, a put option has a limited potential loss.

So far we have discussed only the purchase of options. For every buyer there must be a seller. Who is it? After all, an option writer can take a large loss. Nevertheless, for a fee, some people are willing to take the risk and bet that prices will not move against them. These people are simply speculators. A second group of people who are willing to write options are insured against any losses that may arise. They are primarily dealers who engage in the regular purchase and sale of the underlying asset. These people are called *market makers* because they are always there to make the market. Because they are in the business of buying and selling, market markers both own the underlying asset so that they can deliver it and are willing to buy the underlying asset so that they have it ready to sell to someone else. If you own the underlying asset, writing a call option that obligates you to sell it at a fixed price is not that risky. These people write options to obtain the fee paid by the buyer.

Writing options can also generate clear benefits. To see how, think about the case of an electricity producer who has a plant that is worth operating only when electricity prices exceed a relatively high minimum level. Such peak-load plants are relatively common. They sit idle most of the time and are fired up only when demand is so high that prices spike. The problem is that when they are not operating—which is the normal state of affairs—the owner must pay maintenance charges. To cover these charges, the producer might choose to write a call option on electricity. Here's how the strategy works. For a fee, the plant owner sells a call option with a strike price that is higher than the price at which the plant will be brought on line. The buyer of the call might be someone who uses electricity and wants insurance against a spike in prices. The option fee will cover the producer's maintenance cost while the plant is shut down. And, because the producer as option writer owns the underlying asset here—electricity—he or she is hedged against the possibility that the call option will pay off. As the price of electricity rises, the plant's revenue goes up with it.

Options are very versatile and can be bought and sold in many combinations. They allow investors to get rid of the risks they do not want and keep the ones they do want. In fact, options can be used to construct synthetic instruments that mimic the payoffs of virtually any other financial instrument. For example, the purchase of an at-the-money call and simultaneous sale of an at-the-money put gives the exact same payoff pattern as the purchase of a futures contract. If the price of the underlying asset rises, the call's value increases just as a futures contract does, while the put remains worthless. If the price falls, the put seller loses, just as a futures contract does, while the call is out of the money. Finally, options allow investors to bet that prices will be volatile. Buy a put and a call at the same strike price, and you have a bet that pays off only if the underlying asset price moves up or down significantly.

In summary, options are extremely useful. Remember the example at the beginning of the chapter, in which the snowmobile manufacturer Bombardier purchased insurance so it could offer its customers a rebate? What it bought were put options with a payoff tied to the amount of snow that fell. The puts promised payments in the event of low snowfall. This hedged the risk the company incurred when it offered rebates to the purchasers of its snowmobiles. The providers of this insurance, the sellers of the snowfall options, may have been betting that snowfall would not be low. That is, they may have been speculating—but not necessarily. After all, there are many companies whose sales and profits rise during warm weather and who are well positioned to take such a risk. Insurance companies, for instance, have lower expenses during warm winters, since there are fewer accident claims when there is less snow. If there is little snow, the insurance company has the funds to make the payments, while if there is lots of snow they can use the price they were paid to write the put to help pay the cost of the claims they face.[10]

Table 9.3 provides a summary of what options are, who buys and sells them, and why they do it.

## Pricing Options: Intrinsic Value and the Time Value of the Option

An option price has two parts. The first is the value of the option if it is exercised immediately, and the second is the fee paid for the option's potential benefits. We will refer to the first of these, the value of the option if it is exercised immediately, as the *intrinsic value*. The second, the fee paid for the potential benefit from buying the option, we will call the **time value of the option** to emphasize its relationship to the time of the option's expiration. This means that

$$\textit{Option price} = \textit{Intrinsic value} + \textit{Time value of the option}$$

---

[10]Bombardier purchased its snowfall insurance from Enron (prior to that company's bankruptcy). As it turned out, there was sufficient snowfall, so no payments were made either from Bombardier to the buyers of the snowmobiles or from Enron to Bombardier.

Table 9.3    A Guide to Options

| | Calls | Puts |
|---|---|---|
| Buyer | *Right* to *buy* the underlying asset at the strike price prior to or on the expiration date.<br><br>"Hey, send it over!" | *Right* to *sell* the underlying asset at a fixed price prior to or on the expiration date.<br><br>"Here it is; it's yours now!" |
| Seller (Writer) | *Obligation* to *sell* the underlying asset at the strike price prior to or on the expiration date. | *Obligation* to *buy* the underlying asset at the strike price prior to or on the expiration date. |
| Option is *in the money* when | Price of underlying asset is *above* the strike price of the call. | Price of underlying asset is *below* the strike price of the put. |
| Who *buys* one | Someone who<br><br>• Wants to *buy* an asset in the future and insure the price paid will not *rise*.<br><br>• Wants to bet that the price of the underlying asset will rise. | Someone who<br><br>• Wants to *sell* an asset in the future and insure the price paid will not fall.<br><br>• Wants to bet that the price of the underlying asset will fall. |
| Who *sells* (writes) one | Someone who<br><br>• Wants to bet that the market price of the underlying asset will *not* rise.<br><br>• A broker who is always willing to sell the underlying asset and is paid to take the risk. | Someone who<br><br>• Wants to bet that the market price of the underlying asset will *not* fall.<br><br>• A broker who is always willing to buy the underlying asset and is paid to take the risk. |

As an example, before we launch into a discussion of option valuation in general, let's apply what we know about present value and risk analysis. Consider the example of an at-the-money European call option on the stock of XYZ Corporation that expires in one month. Recall that a European option can be exercised only at expiration and that an at-the-money option is one for which the current price equals the strike price. In this case, both equal $100. So, to start with, the intrinsic value of this call option is zero. To the extent that it has any value at all, that value resides entirely in the option's time value. Assume that, over the next month, the price of XYZ Corporation's stock will either rise or fall by $10 with equal probability. That is, there is a probability of ½ the price will go up to $110, and there is a probability of ½ it will fall to $90. What is the value of this call option?

To find the answer, we can compute the expected present value of the payoff. Let's assume that the interest rate is so low that we can ignore it. (If the payoff were postponed sufficiently far into the future or the interest rate were high enough, we could not ignore the present-value calculation but would have to divide by one plus the interest rate.) Now notice that the option is worth something only if the price goes up. In the event that XYZ's stock price falls to $90, you will allow the option to expire without exercising it. For a call option, then, we need to concern ourselves with the upside, and the expected value of that payoff is the probability, ½, times the payoff, $10, which is $5. This is the time value of the option.

Now think about what happens if, instead of rising or falling by $10, XYZ's stock will rise or fall by $20. This change increases the standard deviation of the stock price. In the terminology used in options trading, the stock price *volatility* has increased. Doing the same calculation, we see that the expected payoff is now $10. As the volatility of the stock price rises, the option's time value rises with it.

**General Considerations**   In general, calculating the price of an option and how it might change means developing some rules for figuring out its intrinsic value and time value. We can do that using the framework from Chapter 3. Recall that the value of any financial instrument depends on four attributes: the size of the promised payment, the timing of the payment, the likelihood that the payment will be made, and the circumstances under which the payment will be made.[11] As we consider each of these, remember that the most important thing about an option is that the buyer is not obligated to exercise it. An option gives the buyer a choice! What this means is that someone holding an option will never make any additional payment to exercise it, so its value cannot be less than zero.

Because the options can either be exercised or expire worthless, we can conclude that the intrinsic value depends only on what the holder receives if the option is exercised. The intrinsic value is the difference between the price of the underlying asset and the strike price of the option. This is the *size of the payment* that the option represents, and it must be greater than or equal to zero—the intrinsic value cannot be negative. For an in-the-money call, or the option to buy, the intrinsic value to the holder (the long position) is the market price of the underlying asset minus the strike price. If the call is at the money or out of the money, it has no intrinsic value. Analogously, the intrinsic value of a put, or the option to sell, equals the strike price minus the market price of the underlying asset, or zero, whichever is greater.

At expiration, the value of an option equals its intrinsic value. But what about prior to expiration? To think about this question, consider an at-the-money option—one whose intrinsic value is zero. Prior to expiration, there is always the chance that the price of the underlying asset will move so as to make the option valuable. This potential benefit is represented by the option's time value. *The longer the time to expiration, the bigger the likely payoff when the option does expire and, thus, the more valuable it is.* Remember that the option payoff is asymmetric, so what is important is the chance of making profit. In the last example, think about what will happen if the option expires in three months instead of one and the stock price has an equal probability of rising or falling $10 each month. The expected payoff of the call option rises from $5 after one month and to $7.50 after three. (After three months, the stock can either rise by $30 with probability ⅛, rise by $10 with probability ⅜, fall by $10 with probability ⅜ or fall by $30 with probability ⅛. When the price falls, the call option is not exercised, so the expected value of the three-month call is ⅛ × $30 + ⅜ × $10 = $7.50.)

*The likelihood that an option will pay off depends on the volatility, or standard deviation, of the price of the underlying asset.* To see this, consider an option on IBM stock that is currently at the money—one with a strike price that equals the current price of the stock. The chance of this option being in the money by the time it expires increases with the volatility of IBM's stock price. Think about an option on an asset whose price is simply fixed—that is, whose standard deviation is zero. This option will never

---

[11]Because the pricing of European options is easier to understand, we will talk about options as if they can be exercised only at the expiration date. The principles for pricing American options are the same, however.

## YOUR FINANCIAL WORLD

### Should You Accept Options as Part of Your Pay?

What if someone offers you a job in return for a salary and stock options? Should you take it? Before you do, ask questions! Let's look at what you need to know. Many firms that offer options on their own stock to employees view the options as a substitute for wages. Employees receive call options that give them the right to purchase the company's stock at a fixed price. The strike price is usually set at the current market price of the stock, so that when employees receive the options, they are at the money. Normally, the expiration date is from one to 10 years in the future. Because the options are long-term, they will have substantial value, as measured by the option's time value. But there is a catch. Employees generally are not allowed to sell them and may need to remain with the firm to exercise them.

Nevertheless, the price of the company's stock could skyrocket, so the options may bring a substantial payoff. To take an extreme example, from January 1991 to January 2000, Microsoft's stock price rose from $2 to $116 per share. An employee with 1,000 options to purchase the stock at $2 would have made $114,000 by exercising them. Though Microsoft employees were winners, there are many losers in the options game. Employees holding options to purchase stock in General Motors or Lehman, both of which went bankrupt in 2008, got nothing.

So what should you do? If taking the options means accepting a lower salary, then you are paying for them, and you should think hard before you take the offer. Stock options are almost like lottery tickets, but with a drawing that may not occur for years. They give you a small chance to make a large profit. But investing in the same company that pays your salary is a risky business. If the company goes broke or you lose your job, the options will be worthless to you. So think hard before you trade a high-paying job for a lower-paying job with options.

pay off, so no one would be willing to pay for it. Add some variability to the price, however, and there is a chance that the price will rise, moving the option into the money. That is something people will pay for. Thus, the option's time value increases with the volatility of the price of the underlying asset. Taking this analysis one step further, we know that regardless of how far the price of the underlying asset falls, the holder of a call option cannot lose more. In contrast, whenever the price rises higher, the call option increases in value. Increased volatility has no cost to the option holder, only benefits.

We have emphasized that options provide insurance, allowing investors to hedge particular risks. The bigger the risk being insured, the more valuable the insurance, and the higher the price investors will pay. Thus, *the circumstances under which the payment is made* have an important impact on the option's time value. As with futures, however, both writers and holders of options may be hedging risks, so it is impossible to know exactly how risk will affect the option price. Table 9.4 summarizes the factors that affect the value of options.

## The Value of Options: Some Examples

To see how options are valued, we can examine a simple example. The daily news reports the prices of options that are traded on organized exchanges. Table 9.5 shows the prices of IBM puts and calls on January 22, 2010, as reported on the Web site of *The Wall Street Journal*. Panel A shows the prices of options with different strike prices but the same expiration date, April 2010. Panel B shows the prices of options with different expiration dates but the same strike price. From the top of the table we can see that the price of IBM stock, the underlying asset on which these options were written, was $125.50 per share at the close of that day.

**Table 9.4**  Factors Affecting the Value of Options

*Option Value = Intrinsic Value + Time Value*

| Increase in one factor, holding all others fixed | Call (the right to buy) | Put (the right to sell) |
|---|---|---|
| Increase in the strike price | Decrease (intrinsic value falls) | Increase (intrinsic value rises) |
| Increase in the market price of the underlying asset | Increase (intrinsic value rises) | Decrease (intrinsic value falls) |
| Increase in the time to expiration | Increase (time value rises) | Increase (time value rises) |
| Increase in the volatility of the underlying asset price | Increase (time value rises) | Increase (time value rises) |

**Table 9.5**  Prices of IBM Puts and Calls

At the close on Friday, January 22, 2010
IBM Stock Price at close = $125.50

**A. April Expiration**

| | Calls | | | Puts | | |
|---|---|---|---|---|---|---|
| Strike Price | Call Price | Intrinsic Value | Time Value of Call | Put Price | Intrinsic Value | Time Value of Put |
| $110 | $16.79 | $15.50 | $1.29 | $1.04 | $0.00 | $1.04 |
| 120 | 8.33 | 5.50 | 2.83 | 3.00 | 0.00 | 3.00 |
| 125 | 5.08 | 0.50 | 4.58 | 5.10 | 0.00 | 5.10 |
| 130 | 2.85 | 0.00 | 2.85 | 7.85 | 4.50 | 3.35 |
| 135 | 1.46 | 0.00 | 1.46 | 11.30 | 9.50 | 1.80 |
| 140 | 0.67 | 0.00 | 0.67 | 15.35 | 14.50 | 0.85 |

**B. Strike Price of 120**

| | Calls | | | Puts | | |
|---|---|---|---|---|---|---|
| Expiration Month | Call Price | Intrinsic Value | Time Value of Call | Put Price | Intrinsic Value | Time Value of Put |
| Feb | 6.35 | 5.50 | 0.85 | 1.11 | 0.00 | 1.11 |
| Apr | 8.33 | 5.50 | 2.83 | 3.00 | 0.00 | 3.00 |
| Jul | 10.25 | 5.50 | 4.75 | 5.20 | 0.00 | 5.20 |

Intrinsic value of a call = Stock price − Strike price, or zero, whichever is larger.
Intrinsic value of a put = Strike price − Stock price, or zero, whichever is larger.
Time value of the option = Option price − Intrinsic value.

By examining the table, we can discover the following:

- At a given price of the underlying asset and time to expiration, the higher the strike price of a call option, the lower its intrinsic value and the less expensive the option. That is, as you read down the column labeled "Strike Price" in Panel A, the intrinsic value under "Calls" (IBM stock price minus the strike price) falls. For example, as the strike price goes from $120 to $125, the intrinsic value falls from $5.50 to $0.50.

- At a given price of the underlying asset and time to expiration, the higher the strike price of a put option, the higher the intrinsic value and the more expensive the option. (See the "Intrinsic Value" column for Puts in Panel A.) As the strike price rises from $130 to $135, the intrinsic value of the IBM put (the strike price minus the IBM stock price) rises from $4.50 to $9.50.

- The closer the strike price is to the current price of the underlying asset, the larger the option's time value. (See the two columns in Panel A labeled "Time Value of Call" and "Time Value of Put.") For a call option with a strike price of $125 and an intrinsic value of $0.50, the time value is $4.58. As the strike price goes down to $120, the time value falls to $2.83.

- Deep in-the-money options have lower time value (see the time value of the calls in Panel A). Because a deep in-the-money call option is very likely to expire in the money, buying one is much like buying the stock itself. Note that the call with a strike price of $110 and an intrinsic value of $15.50 has a time value of only $1.29, much less than the $4.58 time value of a call with an intrinsic value of $0.50.

- The longer the time to expiration at a given strike price, the higher the option price. Looking at the prices of both puts and calls in Panel B of Table 9.5, you can see that as you read down those columns and the time to expiration rises, the price goes up with it. That is because the option's time value is going up. A $120 IBM call that expires in April sells for $8.33, while the price of one that expires three months later sells for $10.25. The same rule applies to puts.

# Swaps

Like other derivatives, swaps are contracts that allow traders to transfer risks. Swaps come in numerous varieties. We will study two types: *Interest-rate swaps* allow one swap party—for a fee—to alter the stream of payments it makes or receives. Interest-rate swaps have been used widely for decades to synchronize receipts and payments. *Credit-default swaps* (CDS) are more recent. CDS are a form of insurance that allow a buyer to own a bond or mortgage without bearing its default risk. We will see that CDS played an important role in the financial crisis of 2007–2009.

## Interest-Rate Swaps

Government debt managers—the people at the U.S. Treasury who decide when and how to issue U.S. Treasury bonds, notes, and bills—do their best to keep public borrowing costs as low as possible. That means (a) selling bonds at the lowest interest rates possible and (b) ensuring that government revenues will be available when payments must be made. Because of the structure of financial markets, keeping interest costs low usually is not a problem. Demand for long-term government bonds is high.

## APPLYING THE CONCEPT
### WHAT WAS LONG-TERM CAPITAL MANAGEMENT DOING?

From mid-August to late September 1998, Long-Term Capital Management (LTCM), a *hedge fund* based in Greenwich, Connecticut, lost more than $2.5 billion, placing itself in danger of default. (For a detailed description of hedge funds, see the Tools of the Trade box in Chapter 13.) The prospect of LTCM's failure struck fear into world financial markets, prompting the Federal Reserve Bank of New York to form a group of 14 banks and investment companies to purchase the company. How did so much wealth disappear so fast, and why did so many people care? Until the crisis of 2007-2009, there was no comparable case in which the financial community was so desperate to avoid a bankruptcy.

The answer is that LTCM had engaged in a large number of complex speculative transactions, including interest-rate swaps and options writing, which all failed simultaneously. One of the bets LTCM had made was based on the belief that interest-rate spreads would shrink. Following the Russian government bond default on August 17, 1998, financial market participants' willingness to take on risk declined dramatically, so the risk premium exploded. (Recall the discussion of this episode in Chapter 6.) As a result, the spread between corporate bonds and U.S. Treasury bonds grew in a way that had never before occurred. By relying on historical data, LTCM lost billions. While the interest-rate spread did eventually shrink, so that the bets

LTCM had made paid off in the long run, marking to market drove the fund bankrupt.

The really scary part of this episode was that many of the transactions LTCM had engaged in involved instruments that could not easily be resold. The most amazing discovery was the $1¼ trillion (yes, trillion) in interest-rate swaps. Granted, this was a notional principal of all the transactions added together, but the problem is that swaps are individualized, bilateral transactions. The fact that LTCM was willing to make a swap agreement with a particular counterparty was no guarantee that some other party would. Thus, a normal bankruptcy settlement, in which assets are sold off in the marketplace and the proceeds given to the failed company's creditors, was not an option. LTCM's failure would mean it could not honor its side of the agreements, which would mean the counterparties would not be able to honor their own agreements, creating a cascade of failure. Its collapse would jeopardize the entire financial system. Large banks, insurance companies, pension funds, and mutual-fund companies with whom LTCM did business were at risk of being bankrupted themselves.

In short, while one person's derivatives loss is another's gain, the system works only if the winners can collect. In this case, the Federal Reserve had no choice but to step in and ensure that the financial system remained sound. LTCM was essentially sold to its creditors—the banks from which it had borrowed—and then closed down about a year later.*

*For a detailed history of the rise and fall of Long-Term Capital Management, see Roger Lowenstein, *When Genius Failed* (New York: Random House, 2000).

(They are used as collateral in many financial transactions.) Thus, government debt managers can sell them at relatively high prices.

Managing government revenues is more of a challenge. Revenues tend to rise during economic booms and fall during recessions. Even if tax revenues fall, the government must still make its bond payments. Short-term interest rates, like tax revenues, tend to move with the business cycle, rising during booms and falling during recessions. (Improvements in general business conditions raise the corporate bond supply, lowering bond prices and raising interest rates.) Ensuring that future interest expenses match future tax revenues might be easier if government borrowers issued short-term bonds.

This difficulty leaves the public debt manager in a quandary. Which is more important, keeping interest costs down by issuing long-term debt or matching costs with tax revenues by issuing short-term debt? Fortunately, derivatives allow government debt managers to meet both these goals using a tool called an interest-rate swap.

RISK

### Understanding Interest-Rate Swaps
**Interest-rate swaps** are agreements between two counterparties to exchange periodic interest-rate payments over some future period, based on an agreed-upon amount of principal—what's called the **notional principal**. The term *notional* is used here because the principal of a **swap** is not borrowed, lent, or exchanged; it just serves as the basis for calculation of the

**Figure 9.1**   An Interest-Rate Swap Agreement

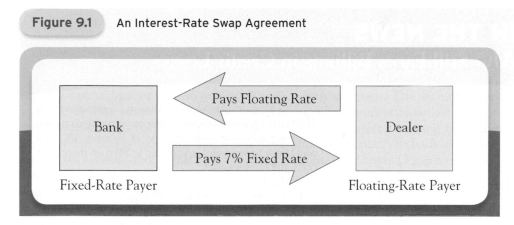

The bank agrees to pay a fixed rate to the swap dealer in exchange for payments based on a floating rate. The fixed-rate payments match the bank's loan income, while the floating-rate payments match the payments promised to the bank's deposit holders.

periodic cash flows between the counterparties to the swap. In the simplest type of interest-rate swap, one party agrees to make payments based on a fixed interest rate, and in exchange the counterparty agrees to make payments based on a floating interest rate. The effect of this agreement is to transform fixed-rate payments into floating-rate payments and vice versa.

Figure 9.1 shows a typical interest-rate swap. A bank agrees to make payments to a swap dealer at a fixed interest rate, say, 7 percent, in exchange for payments based on a floating rate determined in the market.[12] Both payments are based on the same agreed-upon principal, say $100 million. That is, the notional principal on the swap is $100 million. The bank is the **fixed-rate payer** and the swap dealer is the **floating-rate payer**. Put slightly differently, the two parties enter into a series of forward agreements in which they agree today to exchange interest payments on a series of future dates for the life of the swap. As in a futures contract, no payment is made at the outset.

Now let's return to the government debt manager's problem. Remember that the government can issue long-term debt cheaply but its revenues tend to fluctuate with the short-term interest rate, going up when short-term interest rates rise and down when they fall. The solution is to sell long-term bonds and then enter into an interest-rate swap. The government becomes the floating-rate payer for the term of the bonds.

**Pricing and Using Interest-Rate Swaps**   Pricing interest-rate swaps means figuring out the fixed interest rate to be paid. To do so, financial firms begin by noting the market interest rate on a U.S. Treasury bond of the same maturity as the swap, called the *benchmark*. The rate to be paid by the fixed-rate payer, called the *swap rate*, will be the benchmark rate plus a premium. The difference between the benchmark rate and the swap rate, called the **swap spread**, is a measure of risk. In recent years, the swap spread has attracted substantial attention as a measure of systematic

---

[12]The floating rate is the interest rate at which banks make loans to each other. Specifically, it is the London Interbank Offered Rate (LIBOR), the rate at which banks in London make short-term loans to each other.

event that the underlying loan or security defaults and the seller is unable to pay. The collateral for a CDS varies with the credit rating of the seller and buyer.

The market for CDS expanded astronomically in the years before the financial crisis of 2007–2009 but then shrank rapidly. The volume of CDS (based on the initial value of the underlying assets), which was about $6 trillion at the end of 2004, soared to $58 trillion at the end of 2007 before plunging to $33 trillion two years later.

CDS contributed to the financial crisis in three important ways: (1) fostering uncertainty about who bears the credit risk on a given loan or security, (2) making the leading CDS sellers mutually vulnerable, and (3) making it easier for sellers of insurance to assume and conceal risk.

Financial institutions do not report the amount of their CDS purchases and sales, so their depositors or investors do not know how much risk they bear. This loss of transparency makes the financial system more vulnerable to a shock that threatens trust in counterparties.

Because CDS contracts are traded over the counter (OTC), even traders cannot identify others who take on concentrated positions on one side of a trade. As a result, CDS dealers—typically the largest financial institutions—are collectively exposed to a failure by any weak dealer, much like a train can go off the tracks when one flimsy car derails. When you read the phrase "too interconnected to fail" in the financial news, think of the mutual—but hidden—vulnerabilities of the large CDS vendors. So long as CDS trading lacks transparency, the lingering worry is that a failure of one institution could bring down the financial system as a whole (see Lessons from the Crisis: Centralized Counterparties and Systemic Risk on page 211).

# Terms

# Chapter Lessons

1. Derivatives transfer risk from one person or firm to another. They can be used in any combination to unbundle risks and resell them.

2. Futures contracts are standardized contracts for the delivery of a specified quantity of a commodity or financial instrument on a prearranged future date, at an

agreed-upon price. They are a bet on the movement in the price of the underlying asset on which they are written, whether it is a commodity or a financial instrument.

a. Futures contracts are used both to decrease risk, which is called hedging, and to increase risk, which is called speculating.

b. The futures clearing corporation, as the counterparty to all futures contracts, guarantees the performance of both the buyer and the seller.

c. Participants in the futures market must establish a margin account with the clearing corporation and make a deposit that ensures they will meet their obligations.

d. Futures prices are marked to market daily, as if the contracts were sold and repurchased every day.

e. Since no payment is made when a futures contract is initiated, the transaction allows an investor to create a large amount of leverage at a very low cost.

f. The prices of futures contracts are determined by arbitrage within the market for immediate delivery of the underlying asset.

3. Options give the buyer (option holder) a right and the seller (option writer) an obligation to buy or sell an underlying asset at a predetermined price on or before a fixed future date.

a. A call option gives the holder the right to buy the underlying asset.

b. A put option gives the holder the right to sell the underlying asset.

c. Options can be used both to reduce risk through hedging and to speculate.

d. The option price equals the sum of its intrinsic value, which is the value if the option is exercised, plus the time value of the option.

e. The intrinsic value depends on the strike price of the option and the price of the underlying asset on which the option is written.

f. The time value of the option depends on the time to expiration and the volatility in the price of the underlying asset.

4. Interest-rate swaps are agreements between two parties to exchange a fixed for a variable interest-rate payment over a future period.

a. The fixed-rate payer in a swap pays the U.S. Treasury bond rate plus a risk premium.

b. The flexible-rate payer in a swap normally pays the London Interbank Offered Rate (LIBOR).

c. Interest-rate swaps are useful when a government, firm, or investment company can borrow more cheaply at one maturity but would prefer to borrow at a different maturity.

d. Swaps can be based on an agreed-upon exchange of any two future sequences of payments.

5. Credit-default swaps (CDS) are a form of insurance in which the buyer of the insurance makes payments (like insurance premiums) to the seller, who in turn agrees to pay the buyer if an underlying loan or security defaults.

a. A CDS agreement often lasts several years and requires that collateral be posted to protect against the inability to pay of the seller or the buyer of insurance.

b. Because financial institutions do not report CDS sales and purchases, it is not clear who bears credit risk on a given loan or security.

c. Because CDS are traded over the counter, even traders cannot identify others who take on concentrated risks on one side of a trade.

www.mhhe.com/cecchetti3e

6. Derivatives allow firms to arbitrarily divide up and rename risks and future payments, rendering their actual names irrelevant.

## Conceptual Problems

1. An agreement to lease a car can be thought of as a set of derivative contracts. Describe them.

2. In spring 2002, an electronically traded futures contract on the stock index, called an E-mini future, was introduced. The contract was one-fifth the size of the standard futures contract, and could be traded on the 24-hour CME Globex electronic trading system. Why might someone introduce a futures contract with these properties?

3. A hedger buys a futures contract, taking a long position in the wheat futures market. What are the hedger's obligations under this contract? Describe the risk that is hedged in this transaction, and give an example of someone who might enter into such an arrangement.

4. A futures contract on a payment of $250 times the Standard & Poors' 500 Index is traded on the Chicago Mercantile Exchange. At an index level of $1,000 or more, the contract calls for a payment of over $250,000. It is settled by a cash payment between the buyer and the seller. Who are the hedgers and who are the speculators in the S&P 500 futures market?

5. Explain why trading derivatives on centralized exchanges rather than in over-the-counter markets helps reduce systemic risk.

6. What are the risks and rewards of writing and buying options? Are there any circumstances under which you would get involved? Why or why not? (Hint: Think of a case in which you own shares of the stock on which you are considering writing a call.)

7. Suppose XYZ Corporation's stock price rises or falls with equal probability by $20 each month, starting where it ended the previous month. What is the value of a three-month at-the-money European call option on XYZ's stock if the stock is priced at $100 when the option is purchased?

8.* Why might a borrower who wishes to make fixed interest rate payments and who has access to both fixed- and floating-rate loans still benefit from becoming a party to a fixed-for-floating interest-rate swap?

9. Concerned about possible disruptions in the oil stream coming from the Middle East, the chief financial officer (CFO) of American Airlines would like to hedge the risk of an increase in the price of jet fuel. What tools could the CFO use to hedge this risk?

10.* How does the existence of derivatives markets enhance an economy's ability to grow?

11. Credit-default swaps provide a means to insure against default risk and require the posting of collateral by buyers and sellers. Explain how these "safe-sounding" derivative products contributed to the 2007–2009 financial crisis.

*Indicates more difficult problems

# Analytical Problems

12. Of the following options, which would you expect to have the highest option price?
    a. A European three-month put option on a stock whose market price is $90 where the strike price is $100. The standard deviation of the stock price over the past five years has been 15 percent.
    b. A European three-month put option on a stock whose market price is $110 where the strike price is $100. The standard deviation of the stock price over the past five years has been 15 percent.
    c. A European one-month put option on a stock whose market price is $90 where the strike price is $100. The standard deviation of the stock price over the past five years has been 15 percent.

13. What kind of an option should you purchase if you anticipate selling $1 million of Treasury bonds in one year's time and wish to hedge against the risk of interest rates rising?

14. You sell a bond futures contract and, one day later, the clearinghouse informs you that it had credited funds to your margin account. What happened to interest rates over that day?

15. You are completely convinced that the price of copper is going to rise significantly over the next year and want to take as large a position as you can in the market but have limited funds. How could you use the futures market to leverage your position?

16. Suppose you have $8,000 to invest and you follow the strategy you devise in question 15 to leverage your exposure to the copper market. Copper is selling at $3 a pound and the margin requirement for a futures contract for 25,000 pounds of copper is $8,000.
    a. Calculate your return if copper prices rise to $3.10 a pound.
    b. How does this compare with the return you would have made if you had simply purchased $8,000 worth of copper and sold it a year later?
    c. Compare the risk involved in each of these strategies.

17.* The table below shows the yields on the fixed and floating borrowing choices available to three firms. Firms A and B want to be exposed to a floating interest rate while Firm C would prefer to pay a fixed interest rate. Which pair(s) of firms (if any) should borrow in the market they do not want and then enter into a fixed-for-floating interest-rate swap?

|        | Fixed Rate | Floating Rate    |
|--------|------------|------------------|
| Firm A | 7%         | LIBOR + 50 bps   |
| Firm B | 12%        | LIBOR + 150 bps  |
| Firm C | 10%        | LIBOR + 150 bps  |

Note: LIBOR, which stands for London Interbank Offered Rate, is a floating interest rate.

www.mhhe.com/cecchetti3e

18. Suppose you were the manager of a bank that raised most of its funds from short-term variable-rate deposits and used these funds to make fixed-rate mortgage loans. Should you be more concerned about rises or falls in short-term interest rates? How could you use interest-rate swaps to hedge against the interest-rate risk you face?

19.* Basis swaps are swaps where, instead of one payment stream being based on a fixed interest rate, both payment streams are based on floating interest rates. Why might anyone be interested in entering a floating-for-floating interest-rate swap? (You should assume that both payment flows are denominated in the same currency.)

# Chapter 10

## Foreign Exchange

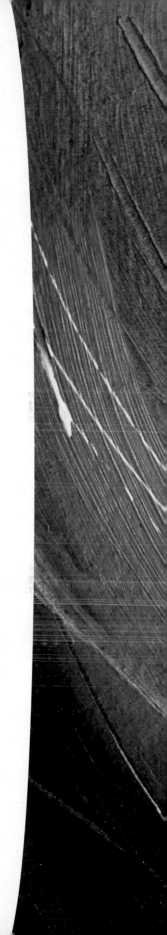

Every year, moving goods and services around the globe becomes easier. By 2009, the volume of international transactions had grown to more than $30 trillion, more than half of world GDP. Today, Americans buy shoes made in China, computers assembled in Singapore, and fruit grown in Chile. But global business deals aren't limited to goods and services. Individuals, companies, and governments also invest abroad, buying and selling stocks and bonds in financial markets around the globe. The magnitude of the international flow of goods, services, and assets is impossible to ignore. To understand the nature of these transactions, we must become familiar with a key tool that makes this trade possible: *exchange rates*.

Whenever you buy something that has been made overseas, whether it is an article of clothing, a car, a stock, or a bond, someone somewhere has exchanged dollars for the currency used where the item was made. The reason is simple: You want to use dollars to pay for an imported shirt that you buy in a local store, but the Malaysian producer wants to be paid in *ringgit*. All cross-border transactions are like this; the buyer and seller both want to use their own currency. The exchange rate, at its most basic level, is the tool we use to measure the price of one currency in terms of another.

Exchange rates have broad implications both for countries and for individuals. Take the case of South Korea in the winter of 1998. As economic and financial turmoil spread through Asia starting in the summer of 1997, output and employment plunged. In Korea, large industrial companies and financial institutions approached bankruptcy. From October 1997 to January 1998, the number of South Korean *won* needed to purchase one dollar more than doubled, rising from 900 to 1,900 (see Figure 10.1). The consequences were dramatic, both inside and outside the country. When the cost of buying won plummeted, South Korean products became much cheaper for foreigners to buy. As the value of the won dropped, the U.S. prices of Hyundai cars and Samsung televisions fell with it. At the same time, U.S.-made products became extremely expensive for South Koreans to buy. In fact, the crisis became so severe that many Korean students at U.S. colleges and universities had to go home. The price of a U.S. education, measured in won, had doubled, and many Korean students just couldn't afford to continue.

Exchange rates go through long swings as well as sudden spikes. In 1973, the currency used in the United Kingdom, the **British pound** or "pound sterling," was worth $2.50. Over the next 36 years, its value declined by 35 percent, so that by late 2009 one pound was worth $1.62 (see Figure 10.2). Nevertheless, Americans visiting Great Britain during the summer of 2009 did not return thinking that their vacations had been inexpensive. At an exchange rate of $1.62, a low-priced hotel room in London cost about the same as a fairly expensive room in New York, and even a trip to McDonald's was more expensive than in the United States.

How are foreign exchange rates determined, and what accounts for their fluctuation over days, months, years, and decades? This chapter provides an introduction to foreign exchange rates and exchange markets.

**Figure 10.1**   South Korean Won–Dollar Exchange Rate, 1997–1999

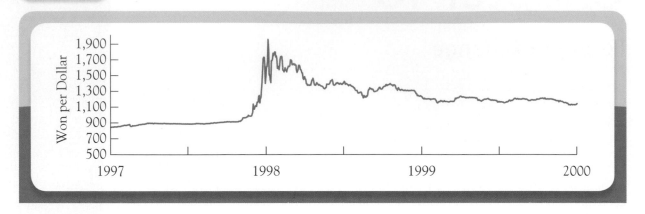

**Figure 10.2**   Dollar–Pound Exchange Rate, 1971–2009

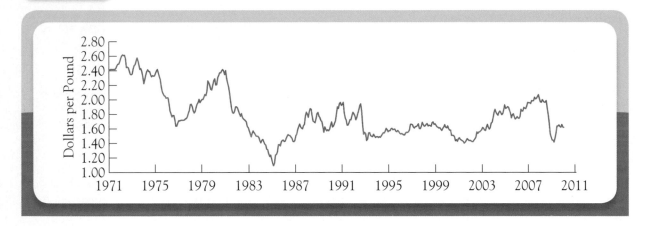

# Foreign Exchange Basics

After graduation, you are planning to travel to Europe. You would like to see the Eiffel Tower in Paris, the Colosseum in Rome, and the Parthenon in Athens. As you pack, you worry a little about paying your hotel bills and the tab for all that great food you expect to eat. The waiters in French, Italian, and Greek restaurants aren't interested in your dollar bills; they want to be paid in their own currency. But you are fortunate, for while the French, Italians, and Greeks speak different languages, they all use the same coins and bills. In fact, buying anything in Europe—at least in the countries that are members of the European Monetary Union—means exchanging your dollars for **euros**. So when you get to Europe, you will care about the rate of exchange between the dollar and the euro. The price of one euro in dollars is called the dollar–euro exchange rate.

## The Nominal Exchange Rate

Exchanging dollars for euros is like any other economic transaction: you are using your money to buy something—in this case, money to spend in another country. The price you pay for this currency is called the nominal exchange rate, or simply the *exchange rate*. Formally defined, the **nominal exchange rate** *is the rate at which one can exchange the currency of one country for the currency of another country.* The dollar–euro exchange rate is the number of dollars you can get for each euro. In January 2010, one euro (the symbol for the euro is €) would buy $1.41. So an American who went to Europe in January 2010 paid $141 for €100.

Exchange rates change every day. Figure 10.3 shows the dollar–euro exchange rate over the first years of the euro's circulation, from January 1999 to January 2010. The figure plots the number of dollars per euro, which is the conventional way to quote the dollar–euro exchange rate. When the euro was introduced, it was worth $1.17. But by October 2000, less than two years later, it could be exchanged

"When did your dad first explain foreign-currency exchange rates to you?"

SOURCE: © Michael Maslin/The New Yorker Collection/www.cartoonbank.com.

for only 83 cents. Such a decline in the value of one currency relative to another is called a **depreciation** of the currency that is falling in value. During the first 22 months of the euro's existence, it depreciated nearly 30 percent relative to the dollar. Later in this chapter, we will consider the reasons for large movements in exchange rates.

At the same time that the euro was falling in value, the dollar was rising. After all, if you can buy fewer dollars with one euro, you can get more euros for one dollar. The rise in the value of one currency relative to another is called an **appreciation** of the currency that is rising in value. During 1999 and 2000, the euro's depreciation was matched by the dollar's appreciation; they are really one and the same. When one currency goes up in value *relative to another*, the other currency must go down.

**Figure 10.3**   Dollar-Euro Exchange Rate, 1999-2010

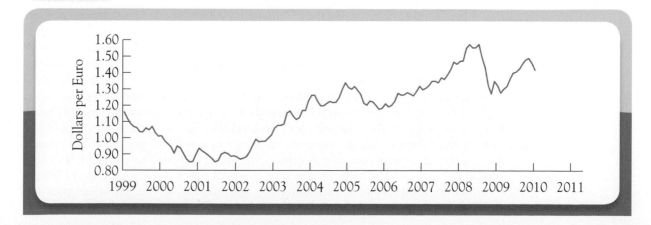

A 20-euro note used in the countries that participate in the European Monetary Union.

Note that, theoretically, exchange rates can be quoted in units of either currency—for example, as the number of dollars needed to buy one euro or as the number of euros needed to buy one dollar. The two prices are equivalent; one is simply the reciprocal of the other. In practice, however, each currency has its convention. The price of the British pound is quoted in the same way as the euro, so that people talk about the number of dollars that can be exchanged for one pound (£). The price of the Japanese **yen** (¥) is quoted as the number of yen that can be purchased with one dollar.

Unfortunately, there is no simple rule for determining which way a particular exchange rate should be quoted. Most rates tend to be quoted in the way that yields a number larger than one. The fact that €1 equaled $1.17 when the euro was created on January 1, 1999, is the likely explanation for why we talk about the number of dollars needed to purchase one euro. Ever since, people have quoted dollars per euro, even though there have been significant periods of time when the number was less than one. If you need to guess which way to quote an exchange rate, the best guess is that it is the way that yields a number larger than one. But the real solution is always to state the units explicitly, to avoid confusion.

## The Real Exchange Rate

While it may be interesting to know that one euro is worth $1.41, you are interested in more than just the rate at which one country's currency can be exchanged for another. What you really want to know when you travel to Europe is how much you can buy with that euro. When all is said and done, will you return home thinking that your trip was cheap or expensive?

Because nominal exchange rates do not provide an answer to this question, we now turn to the concept of a **real exchange rate**, *the rate at which one can exchange the goods and services from one country for the goods and services from another country.* It is the cost of a basket of goods in one country *relative* to the cost of the same basket of goods in another country. To grasp this concept, we will start with the real exchange rate between two cups of espresso, one American and the other Italian. The local Starbucks charges $1.65 for an espresso; in Florence, Italy, a cup of espresso costs €1.00. (Yes, the Italian version is better and espresso is a luxury in the United States, but for the sake of the example, let's pretend they're the same.) To simplify the arithmetic, imagine that the nominal exchange rate is $1.50 per euro. This means that to buy an espresso on your European vacation, you need to spend $1.50. More important, you can exchange one cup of Starbucks espresso for 1.1 cups of Italian espresso. This is the *real* exchange rate. You will return from your European vacation thinking that espresso was very cheap in Italy.

There is a simple relationship between the real exchange rate and the nominal exchange rate, which we can infer from our espresso calculation. To compute the real exchange rate, we took the euro price of an espresso in Italy and multiplied it by the nominal exchange rate, the number of dollars per euro. Then we divided it into the dollar price of a cup of espresso in the United States:

*Real coffee exchange rate*

$$= \frac{\text{Dollar price of espresso in the U.S. (\$1.65)}}{\text{Euro price of espresso in Italy (€1.00)} \times \text{Dollars per euro (\$1.50/€)}} \quad (1)$$

$$= \frac{\text{Dollar price of espresso in the U.S. (\$1.65)}}{\text{Dollar price of espresso in Italy (€1.00)} \times (\$1.50/€)}$$

$$= \frac{\$1.65}{\$1.50}$$

$$= 1.10$$

At these prices and exchange rate, one cup of Starbucks espresso buys 1.1 cups of Italian espresso. Note in equation (1) that the units of measurement cancel out. In the denominator, we multiplied the price in euros times the nominal exchange rate (measured as dollars per euro) to get an amount stated in dollars. Then we divided that number into the numerator, also expressed in dollars. The real exchange rate has no units of measurement.

In summary, to figure out the real coffee exchange rate in equation (1), we divided the dollar price of coffee in the United States by the dollar price of coffee in Italy. We can use the same procedure to compute the real exchange rate more broadly by comparing the prices of a set of goods and services that are commonly purchased in any country. If we can transform a basket of goods and services produced in the United States into more than one basket produced in Europe, as in the coffee example, then we are likely to return from a trip to Paris, Rome, and Athens thinking that the cost of living there is relatively cheap. Using this idea, we can write the real exchange rate as

$$\text{Real exchange rate} = \frac{\text{Dollar price of domestic goods}}{\text{Dollar price of foreign goods}} \quad (2)$$

From this definition of the real exchange rate, we can see that whenever the ratio in equation (2) is more than one, foreign products will seem cheap.

The real exchange rate, then, is much more important than the nominal exchange rate. It is the rate that measures the relative price of goods and services across countries, telling us where things are cheap and where they are expensive. The real exchange rate is the guiding force behind international transactions. When foreign goods are less expensive than domestic goods, their prices create an incentive for people to buy imports. Competing with foreign imports becomes more difficult for local producers. Think about what would happen if you could ship cups of espresso to the United States from Italy and sell them in an import shop. Starbucks would lose business. Obviously, you can't do that with freshly brewed coffee, but you can do it with clothing, electronics, cars, airplanes, and a wide variety of other goods and services. As a result, the competitiveness of U.S. exports depends on the real exchange rate. *Appreciation* of the real exchange rate makes U.S. exports more expensive to foreigners, reducing their competitiveness, while *depreciation* of the real exchange rate makes U.S. exports seem cheaper to foreigners, improving their competitiveness.

# TOOLS OF THE TRADE
## Following Exchange Rates in the News

Exchange rates are reported in the business news. *The Wall Street Journal* carries a daily Foreign Exchange column that describes events in the markets, as well as a table reporting the most recent nominal exchange rates between the U.S. dollar and various foreign currencies. (Because the rates quoted are generally for transactions of $1 million or more, they normally are not available to tourists.) The column and the table, one of which is reprinted here, appear in both the print and online versions of the paper. Let's run through Table 10.1 to see how to read it.

*Column 1:* The name of the country together with the name of its currency.

*Column 2:* The number of dollars that could be purchased per unit of foreign currency at the close of business on Thursday, January 21, 2010. Looking at the entry for "**UK** pound" we can see that on that date, one British pound purchased $1.6199.

*Column 3:* The numbers of units of foreign currency needed to purchase one dollar at the close of business on Thursday, January 21, 2010. Looking at the entry for "**Japan** yen" we can see that on that date, you could exchange 90.41 Japanese yen for one dollar.*

*Column 4:* The year to date change in the U.S. dollar equivalent. That is, the change since January 1, 2010, in the units of foreign currency that could be purchased per dollar, so positive values mean that the dollar has appreciated relative to a particular currency, while negative values imply a depreciation of the dollar. In some cases, the exchange rate hasn't moved, so the entry reads "unch" for "unchanged." To see how it works, notice that the "**Euro area** euro" in this column is 1.6 percent. This means that during the first three weeks of 2010 the dollar appreciated against the euro, rising by 1.6 percent from roughly €0.6983 per dollar to €0.7095 per dollar.

For large foreign currency markets, like Britain's and Japan's, the table quotes the forward as well as the spot rates. *Spot rates* are the rates for an immediate exchange (subject to a two-day settlement period). *Forward rates* are the rates at which foreign currency dealers are willing to commit to buying or selling a currency in the future, so they give some indication of whether market participants expect currencies to appreciate or depreciate over time.

In thinking about foreign exchange rates, be sure to keep track of whether you are quoting the number of U.S. dollars that can be exchanged for one unit of foreign currency, as in column 2 of the table, or the number of units of foreign currency that can be purchased with one dollar. They are easy to confuse. If you went to Europe and confused $1.4094 per euro with €0.7095 per dollar, you would think everything was less expensive than it really is, and you end up buying something for more than you originally planned to pay.

*Note the reciprocal nature of the rates in columns 2 and 3. For any entry, the value in column 2 times the value in column 3 equals 1, so either value divided into 1 equals the other value.

## Foreign Exchange Markets

The volume of foreign exchange transactions is enormous. On an average day in 2007, $3.2 trillion in foreign currency was traded in a market that operates 24 hours a day.[1] To get a sense of how huge this number is, compare it to world output and trade. The International Monetary Fund estimates that in 2007, world GDP (at market prices) was roughly $55 trillion, and international trade transactions (measured as exports plus imports) accounted for $17 trillion of that amount. But these are annual numbers. If there are 260 business days in a normal year, the volume of foreign exchange transactions is about $830 trillion per year—15 times world GDP and nearly 50 times world trade volume.

[1]This estimate comes from a triennial survey by the Bank for International Settlements in Basel, Switzerland. The complete survey is available at www.bis.org.

### Table 10.1    Currencies

#### U.S.-dollar foreign-exchange rates in late New York trading, January 21, 2010

| (1) Country/currency | (2) ——Thurs—— in US$ | (3) per US$ | (4) US$ vs, YTD chg (%) | (1) Country/currency | (2) ——Thurs—— in US$ | (3) per US$ | (4) US$ vs, YTD chg (%) |
|---|---|---|---|---|---|---|---|
| **Americas** | | | | **Europe** | | | |
| Argentina peso* | .2627 | 3.8066 | 0.2 | Czech Rep. koruna | .05394 | 18.539 | 0.6 |
| Brazil real | .5545 | 1.8034 | 3.5 | Denmark krone | .1894 | 5.2798 | 1.6 |
| Canada dollar | .9511 | 1.0514 | unch | Euro area euro | 1.4094 | .7095 | 1.6 |
| 1-mos forward | .9511 | 1.0514 | unch | Hungary forint | .005179 | 193.09 | 2.2 |
| 3-mos forward | .9511 | 1.0514 | unch | Norway krone | .1720 | 5.8140 | 0.3 |
| 6-mos forward | .9509 | 1.0516 | unch | Poland zloty | .3445 | 2.9028 | 1.2 |
| Chile peso | .001995 | 501.25 | −1.2 | Russia ruble‡ | .03360 | 29.762 | −1.8 |
| Colombia peso | .0005058 | 1977.07 | −3.2 | Sweden krona | .1381 | 7.2411 | 1.2 |
| Ecuador US dollar | 1 | 1 | unch | Switzerland franc | .9596 | 1.0421 | 0.6 |
| Mexico peso* | .0772 | 12.9618 | −0.9 | 1-mos forward | .9598 | 1.0419 | 0.0 |
| Peru new sol | .3509 | 2.850 | −1.4 | 3-mos forward | .9601 | 1.0416 | 0.6 |
| Uruguay peso† | .05120 | 19.53 | unch | 6-mos forward | .9607 | 1.0409 | 0.7 |
| Venezuela b. fuerte | .232845 | 4.2947 | 100.0 | Turkey lira** | .6722 | 1.4877 | −0.6 |
| **Asia-Pacific** | | | | UK pound | 1.6199 | .6173 | −0.2 |
| Australian dollar | .9022 | 1.1084 | −0.4 | 1-mos forward | 1.6195 | .6175 | −0.2 |
| China yuan | .1465 | 6.8269 | unch | 3-mos forward | 1.6188 | .6177 | −0.2 |
| Hong Kong dollar | .1287 | 7.7717 | 0.2 | 6-mos forward | 1.6178 | .6181 | −0.2 |
| India rupee | .02163 | 46.232 | −0.4 | **Middle East/Africa** | | | |
| Indonesia rupiah | .0001077 | 9285 | −1.5 | Bahrain dinar | 2.6526 | .3770 | unch |
| Japan yen | .011061 | 90.41 | −2.9 | Egypt pound* | .1837 | 5.4451 | −0.7 |
| 1-mos forward | .011062 | 90.40 | −2.9 | Israel shekel | .2683 | 3.7272 | −1.7 |
| 3-mos forward | .011065 | 90.38 | −2.9 | Jordan dinar | 1.4139 | .7073 | −0.1 |
| 6-mos forward | .011073 | 90.31 | −2.8 | Kuwait dinar | 3.4803 | .2873 | 0.1 |
| Malaysia ringgit§ | .2968 | 3.3693 | −1.6 | Lebanon pound | .0006656 | 1502.40 | unch |
| New Zealand dollar | .7119 | 1.4047 | 1.9 | Saudi Arabia riyal | .2666 | 3.7509 | unch |
| Pakistan rupee | .01182 | 84.602 | 0.3 | South Africa rand | .1317 | 7.5930 | 2.5 |
| Philippines peso | .0218 | 45.977 | −1.1 | UAE dirham | .2723 | 3.6724 | unch |
| Singapore dollar | .7122 | 1.4041 | −0.1 | | | | |
| South Korea won | .0008734 | 1144.95 | −1.8 | SDR†† | 1.5550 | .6431 | 0.8 |
| Taiwan dollar | .03131 | 31.939 | −0.2 | | | | |
| Thailand baht | .03033 | 32.971 | −1.2 | | | | |
| Vietnam dong | .00005413 | 18474 | unch | | | | |

*Floating rate   †Financial   §Government rate   ‡Russian Central Bank rate   **Rebased as of Jan 1, 2005   ††Special Drawing Rights (SDR); from the International Monetary Fund; based on exchange rates for U.S., British and Japanese currencies.   Note: Based on trading among banks of $1 million and more, as quoted at 4 p.m. ET by Reuters.

Because of its liquidity, the U.S. dollar is one side of roughly 85 percent of these currency transactions.[2] That means that someone who wishes to exchange Thai baht for Japanese yen is likely to make two transactions, the first to convert the baht to

[2]The liquidity of the market for dollars creates a premium, driving up the dollar's value in the same way that liquidity increases the price of a bond.

dollars and the second to convert the dollars to yen. Most likely these transactions will take place in London, because the United Kingdom is home to more than one-third of foreign exchange trades—about twice the volume in New York. Other significant foreign exchange trading takes place in Singapore, Tokyo, and Zurich (each about 6 percent).

# Exchange Rates in the Long Run

How are exchange rates determined? To answer this question, we will divide our discussion into two parts. This section will look at the determination of the long-run exchange rate and the forces that drive its movement over an extended period, such as a year or more. The next section will consider what causes exchange rates to vary over the short term—a few days or months.

## The Law of One Price

The starting point for understanding how long-run exchange rates are determined is *the law of one price*. The **law of one price** is based on the concept of *arbitrage*—the idea that identical products should sell for the same price. Recall from our discussion in Chapter 9 that two financial instruments with the same risk and promised future payments will sell for the same price. We might refer to this phenomenon as financial arbitrage. If we extend the concept of arbitrage from financial instruments to goods and services, we can conclude that identical goods and services should sell for the same price regardless of *where* they are sold. Identical televisions or cars should cost the same whether they are sold in St. Louis or Philadelphia. When they don't, someone can make a profit.

**MARKETS**

For instance, if a specific model television were cheaper in St. Louis than in Philadelphia, someone could buy it in St. Louis, drive to Philadelphia, and sell it at a profit. This opportunity to profit from arbitrage would increase demand for televisions in St. Louis, where the price is low, and increase the supply of televisions in Philadelphia, where the price is high. Higher demand drives prices up, while a larger supply forces them down. The process will continue until the television sells for the same price in both cities. Of course, complete price equalization occurs only in the absence of transportation costs. If it costs $10 to transport the television 900 miles from the Mississippi River to the East Coast, then arbitrage will continue until the price in St. Louis is within $10 of the price in Philadelphia.

We can extend the law of one price from cities in the same country to cities in different countries. Instead of St. Louis and Philadelphia, think of Detroit, Michigan, and Windsor, Ontario—two cities separated by the Detroit River and the Canadian border. The river can be crossed by bridge or tunnel in roughly one minute. Ignoring transportation costs, then, once we have converted a price from U.S. to Canadian dollars, the cost of a television should be the same in both cities. If a TV costs $500 in the United States, at a nominal exchange rate of 1.05 Canadian dollars per U.S. dollar (see Table 10.1), the Canadian price should be $(500 \times 1.05) = 525$ Canadian dollars. That is, the law of one price tells us that

$$\begin{array}{l} \text{Canadian dollar price of a} \\ \text{TV in Windsor, Ontario} \end{array} = \begin{array}{l} \text{(U.S. dollar price of a TV in Detroit)} \\ \times \text{ (Canadian dollars per U.S. dollar)} \end{array} \quad (3)$$

This example shows once again the importance of using the correct units when working with exchange rates. In converting the U.S. dollar price to Canadian dollars,

## YOUR FINANCIAL WORLD
Investing Overseas

More diversification is always better. Increasing the number of independent risks in a portfolio by spreading investments across a broader set of stocks and bonds can reduce risk without decreasing the expected return. That is the rationale behind investing in mutual funds and the reason for investing abroad as well. In the same way that someone living in Kansas would not hesitate to invest in an Ohio company, there is no reason why someone who lives in the United States should hesitate to invest outside the United States.

For many years, some financial advisors have been telling their clients in the United States to hold a portion of their equity portfolios in foreign stocks. But you don't need an investment advisor to heed this advice. As soon as you begin to save for your retirement—which should be as soon

as you get a steady job—you should diversify your investments internationally. So long as the returns on stocks in other countries do not move in lockstep with the U.S. stock market, holding them will reduce the risk in your investment portfolio. The data indicate that the returns on other countries' stock markets move somewhat independently of the U.S. stock market. And the benefits of diversification are not counteracted by exposure to the risk of exchange rate fluctuations. True, buying British stock means trading dollars for pounds and then changing back to dollars at a later date. In the meantime, the exchange rate could move. But the evidence shows us that holding foreign stocks reduces risk without sacrificing returns, despite the risk of exchange rate fluctuations.

we multiply by the number of Canadian dollars needed to buy one U.S. dollar. That is, we compute (U.S. dollars) times (Canadian dollars/U.S. dollar) equals Canadian dollars. This is the same calculation we did earlier to figure out the U.S. dollar price of an Italian cup of coffee. There, we multiplied (euros) times (U.S. dollars/euro) to get U.S. dollars.

Returning to the law of one price, we can see immediately that it fails almost all the time. The fact is that the same commodity or service sells for vastly different prices in different countries. Why? Transportation costs can be significant, especially for heavy items like marble or slate. Tariffs—the taxes countries charge at their borders—are high sometimes, especially if a country is trying to protect a domestic industry. And technical specifications can differ. A television bought in Paris will not work in St. Louis because it requires a different input signal. A car sold in Great Britain cannot be used in the United States or continental Europe because its steering wheel is on the right. Moreover, tastes differ across countries, leading to different pricing. Finally, some things simply cannot be traded. A haircut may be cheaper in New Delhi than in Philadelphia, but most Americans simply can't take advantage of that price difference.

## Purchasing Power Parity

Since the law of one price fails so often, why do we bother with it? Because even with its obvious flaws, the law of one price is extremely useful in explaining the behavior of exchange rates over long periods, like 10 or 20 years. To see why, we need to extend the law from a single commodity to a basket of goods and services. The result is the theory of **purchasing power parity (PPP)**, which means that one unit of U.S. domestic currency will buy the same basket of goods and services anywhere in the world. This idea may sound absurd, but let's look at its implications.

According to the theory of purchasing power parity, the dollar price of a basket of goods and services in the United States should be the same as the dollar price of a basket of goods and services in Mexico, Japan, or the United Kingdom. In the case of the United Kingdom, this statement means that

$$\text{Dollar price of basket of goods in U.S.} = \text{Dollar price of basket of goods in U.K.} \qquad (4)$$

Rearranging this expression gives us

$$\frac{\text{Dollar price of basket of goods in U.S.}}{\text{Dollar price of basket of goods in U.K.}} = 1 \qquad (5)$$

The left-hand side of equation (5) is familiar: It is the real exchange rate [see equation (2) on page 235]. Thus, *purchasing power parity implies that the real exchange rate is always equal to one*. The implication of this conclusion is straightforward. It is that the purchasing power of a dollar is always the same, regardless of where in the world you go.

This idea must seem doubly absurd. If a dollar doesn't even buy the same number of cups of coffee in Italy and the United States, how can it have the same purchasing power all the time, everywhere in the world? On any given day, it doesn't. But over the long term, exchange rates do tend to move, so this concept helps us to understand changes that happen over years or decades. To see how, remember that the dollar price of a foreign basket of goods is just the foreign currency price of the basket of goods times the number of dollars per unit of foreign currency. This means that if we quote the price of a basket of goods in the United Kingdom in pounds instead of dollars, then

$$\frac{\text{Dollar price of basket of goods in U.S.}}{(\text{Pound price of basket of goods in U.K.}) \times (\text{Dollars per pound})} = 1 \qquad (6)$$

so

$$\frac{\text{Dollar price of basket of goods in U.S.}}{\text{Pound price of basket of goods in U.K.}} = (\text{Dollars per pound}) \qquad (7)$$

That is, purchasing power parity implies that when prices change in one country but not in another, the exchange rate should change as well. When prices rise within a country, the effect is called inflation. If inflation occurs in one country but not in another, the change in prices creates an international inflation differential. So purchasing power parity tells us that changes in exchange rates are tied to differences in inflation from one country to another. Specifically, the currency of a country with high inflation will depreciate.

To see this point, think about what would happen if there were no inflation in the United Kingdom, but prices in the United States doubled. We would not expect the dollar–pound exchange rate to stay the same. Instead, we would predict that one dollar would now buy half as many British pounds as it did before (that is, twice as many dollars would be needed to purchase one pound).[3] There is strong evidence to support this conclusion, but the data must be drawn over fairly long periods, and the relationship is not perfect.

---

[3]It is possible to show this mathematically. If $P$ represents the domestic (U.S.) currency price of a basket of goods, $P^f$ the foreign currency price of the foreign (British) basket of goods, and $e$ the nominal exchange rate, expressed as the domestic currency price of foreign currency (dollars per pound), then purchasing power parity tells us that $(P/eP^f) = 1$ (eq. 5), so $e = (P/P^f)$ (eq. 7). This expression immediately implies that the change in the exchange rate equals the difference between domestic and foreign inflation.

Take, for instance, the U.S. dollar–British pound exchange rate plotted in Figure 10.2 (page 232). Recall that in 1973, one pound was worth around $2.50. By May 2010, a pound was worth $1.44—a decline of 42 percent, or nearly 1.5 percent per year for 37 years. Over the same period, U.S. prices increased an average of 4.45 percent per year, while British prices increased an average of 6.44 percent per year—a difference of 1.99 percent per year. While the relationship between the inflation and exchange rates is not perfect, it surely explains much of the movement in the dollar–pound exchange rate over the 37-year period.

What is true for the United Kingdom is true for the rest of the world. To confirm it, we can look at a plot of (a) the historical difference between inflation in other countries and inflation in the United States against (b) the percentage change in the number of units of other countries' currencies required to purchase one dollar—that is, the average annual depreciation of the exchange rate.

Figure 10.4 presents data for 71 countries drawn from files maintained by the International Monetary Fund. Each point represents a country. The difference between its average annual inflation and that of the U.S. is on the horizontal axis, and the average annual percentage change in the exchange rate between the country's currency and the U.S. dollar is on the vertical axis. Points further to the right represent countries with higher levels of inflation, and points higher up are countries whose dollar-exchange rate experienced more depreciation over the 25-year period of the sample. The solid line is a 45-degree line that is consistent with the theoretical prediction of purchasing power parity. On the 45-degree line, exchange rate movements exactly equal differences in inflation. Granted, the points don't all lie exactly on the line, but the pattern is clearly there. The higher a country's inflation, the greater the depreciation in its exchange rate.

**Figure 10.4**    Exchange Rate Movements and Inflation Differentials, 1980–2005

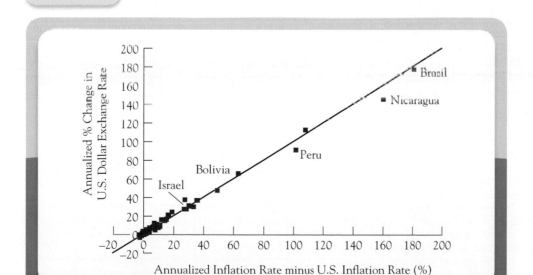

SOURCE: *The International Monetary Fund*

# APPLYING THE CONCEPT
## THE BIG MAC INDEX

By the close of the 20th century, the Big Mac was available to consumers in 121 countries. Regardless of where it was sold, a Big Mac was defined as "two all-beef patties, special sauce, lettuce, cheese, pickles, onions on a sesame seed bun." Needless to say, every McDonald's restaurant requires payment in the local currency. In 1986, the staff of *The Economist* magazine realized that this presented an opportunity. Together, the market exchange rate and the price of a Big Mac would allow them to estimate the extent to which a country's currency deviates from the level implied by purchasing power parity.

Twice a year, under headlines like "Big MacCurrencies" and "Burgernomics," *The Economist* publishes a table showing Big Mac prices in about 50 countries. Figure 10.5 is based on Big Mac prices from *The Economist* edition of July 16, 2009, but shows exchange rates as of March 10, 2010 from http://www.oanda.com/currency/big-mac-index. Using Big Mac prices as a basis for comparison, it shows the extent to which each country's currency was undervalued or overvalued relative to the U.S. dollar. As you look at the table, you will realize that with the exception of the pound and the euro, all exchange rates are quoted as the number of units of local currency required to purchase one dollar. The pound and the euro are exceptions—they are quoted as the number of dollars required to purchase one pound or one euro.

To see how the **Big Mac index** works, take the case of Denmark. The Danish currency is called the *krone* (which means "crown") and in mid-2009, a Big Mac cost DKr29.5 in Copenhagen. At an exchange rate of 5.48, that's equivalent to $5.39. To figure out the purchasing power parity value of one dollar in krone, we can use the relationship in equation (7), which tells us to divide the price of a Big Mac in krone by the dollar price: 29.5 krone per Big Mac/$3.57 per Big Mac = 8.26 krone per dollar. If the theory of purchasing power parity holds, then 8.26 krone should buy one dollar. But instead, the price of one dollar in the currency markets was 5.48 krone, which means that the Danish krone was *overvalued* by 51 percent. For the Chinese *yuan*, the same calculation implies an *undervaluation* of roughly −49 percent.

Figure 10.5 A feast of burgernomics
The Big Mac index

*The Purchasing Power Parity (PPP) rate is the local Big Mac price divided by its price in the United States. Prices and their corresponding implied PPP rates are the latest figures available from The Economist. †The Over/Under valuation against the dollar is calculated as follows using OANDA's latest rates: 100 × (PPP − Exchange Rate) / Exchange Rate ††Average of New York, Atlanta, Chicago and San Francisco ‡Dollars per pound §Weighted average of prices in euro area **Dollars per euro

| Country | Big Mac prices — In local currency | In U.S. dollars | Implied PPP* of the dollar | Actual dollar exchange rate Mar 10 | Under(−)/over(+) valuation against the dollar, %† |
|---|---|---|---|---|---|
| United States†† | $3.57 | 3.57 | — | 1.00 | — |
| Argentina | Peso 11.5 | 2.98 | 3.22 | 3.86 | −17 |
| Australia | A$4.34 | 3.95 | 1.22 | 1.10 | 11 |
| Brazil | Real 8.03 | 4.48 | 2.25 | 1.79 | 25 |
| Britain | £2.29 | 3.43 | 1.56‡ | 1.50‡ | −4 |
| Canada | C$3.89 | 3.78 | 1.09 | 1.03 | 6 |
| Chile | Peso 1,750 | 3.36 | 490 | 521 | −6 |
| China | Yuan 12.5 | 1.83 | 3.50 | 6.84 | −49 |
| Colombia | Peso 7,000 | 3.64 | 1,961 | 1,923 | 2 |
| Costa Rica | Colones 2,000 | 3.60 | 560 | 555 | 1 |
| Czech Republic | Koruna 67.9 | 3.60 | 19.0 | 18.9 | 1 |
| Denmark | DKr29.5 | 5.39 | 8.26 | 5.48 | 51 |
| Estonia | Kroon 32.0 | 2.78 | 8.96 | 11.5 | −22 |
| Egypt | Pound 13.0 | 2.36 | 3.64 | 5.51 | −34 |
| Euro area§ | €3.31 | 4.50 | 1.08** | 1.36** | 26 |
| Hong Kong | HK$13.3 | 1.71 | 3.73 | 7.76 | −52 |
| Hungary | Forint 720 | 3.66 | 202 | 197 | 3 |
| Iceland | Kronur 640 | 4.98 | 179 | 129 | 39 |
| Indonesia | Rupiah 20,900 | 2.27 | 5,854 | 9,208 | −36 |
| Israel | Shekel 15.0 | 3.98 | 4.20 | 3.77 | 11 |
| Japan | ¥320 | 3.56 | 89.6 | 89.9 | nil |
| Latvia | Lats 1.55 | 2.96 | 0.43 | 0.52 | −18 |
| Lithuania | Litas 7.1 | 2.79 | 1.99 | 2.54 | −22 |
| Malaysia | Ringgit 6.77 | 2.03 | 1.90 | 3.34 | −43 |
| Mexico | Peso 33.0 | 2.60 | 9.24 | 12.7 | −27 |
| New Zealand | NZ$4.90 | 3.43 | 1.37 | 1.43 | −4 |
| Norway | Kroner 40.0 | 6.76 | 11.2 | 5.92 | 89 |
| Pakistan | Rupee 190 | 2.22 | 53.2 | 85.6 | −38 |
| Peru | New Sol 8.06 | 2.79 | 2.26 | 2.88 | −22 |
| Philippines | Peso 99.4 | 2.17 | 27.8 | 45.9 | −39 |
| Poland | Zloty 7.60 | 2.66 | 2.13 | 2.85 | −25 |
| Russia | Rouble 67.0 | 2.25 | 18.8 | 29.8 | −37 |
| Saudi Arabia | Riyal 11.0 | 2.93 | 3.08 | 3.76 | −18 |
| Singapore | S$4.22 | 3.01 | 1.18 | 1.40 | −16 |
| South Africa | Rand 18.0 | 2.42 | 5.03 | 7.43 | −32 |
| South Korea | Won 3,400 | 2.99 | 952 | 1,135 | −16 |
| Sri Lanka | Rupee 210 | 1.84 | 58.8 | 114 | −49 |
| Sweden | SKr39.0 | 5.45 | 10.9 | 7.15 | 52 |
| Switzerland | SFr6.50 | 6.04 | 1.82 | 1.08 | 69 |
| Taiwan | NT$75.0 | 2.36 | 21.0 | 31.8 | −34 |
| Thailand | Baht 64.5 | 1.96 | 18.1 | 32.8 | −45 |
| Turkey | Lire 5.65 | 3.67 | 1.58 | 1.54 | 3 |
| UAE | Dirhams 10.0 | 2.72 | 2.80 | 3.67 | −24 |
| Ukraine | Hryvnia 14.0 | 1.73 | 3.92 | 8.11 | −52 |
| Uruguay | Peso 61.0 | 3.04 | 17.1 | 20.1 | −15 |

The Big Mac index is a clever idea, and it works surprisingly well considering that it is based on a single commodity that is not tradeable, and whose local price surely depends on costs like wages, rent, and taxes.

Take the extreme example of Bolivia. From 1980 to 2005, Bolivia's inflation minus U.S. inflation averaged 63 percent per year, and the Bolivian currency (originally the bolivar, now the boliviano) depreciated at an average annual rate of 66 percent. Putting that into perspective, the 2005 Bolivian price level was more than 340,000 times the 1980 Bolivian price level, and the exchange rate depreciated by roughly the same multiple. That means purchasing one dollar in the foreign exchange market required 330,000 times as many bolivianos in 2005 as in 1980. Importantly, Figure 10.4 shows that there are no countries with high inflation differentials and small exchange rate changes or big exchange rate changes and low inflation differentials. All of the points lie close to the 45-degree line.

The data in Figure 10.4 tell us that purchasing power parity held true over a 25-year period. Even if we look at a decade, the connection between movements in the exchange rate and differences in inflation across countries holds up to scrutiny. But the same exercise applied to periods of a few weeks, months, or even years would be a total failure. We know that from examining the plots of the Korean won–U.S. dollar exchange rate in Figure 10.1 and the dollar–euro exchange rate in Figure 10.3. Recall that the Korean won went through a sudden, steep depreciation, falling from 900 to 1,900 won to the dollar in just a few months, at the end of 1997. The pattern of Korean inflation at the time, a relatively steady 7½ percent versus 1½ percent in the United States, simply cannot explain this sudden change.

Similarly, from the euro's inception in January 1999, the dollar–euro rate fell steadily for two years, dropping more than 25 percent (see Figure 10.3). At the same time, inflation in the euro area ran a full percentage point *below* U.S. inflation. Examples like these are the norm, not the exception. Over weeks, months, and even years, nominal exchange rates can deviate substantially from the levels implied by purchasing power parity. So, while the theory can help us to understand long swings in exchange rates, it provides no explanation for the short-term movements we see all the time. Fortunately, we do have some equipment in our tool kit that we can use to explain short-term movements in exchange rates.

Before continuing, we should note the meaning of two additional terms. We often hear currencies described as **undervalued** or **overvalued**. When people use these terms, they have in mind a current market rate that deviates from what they consider to be purchasing power parity. For example, a person who thinks that one dollar should purchase one euro—that is, that one to one is somehow the "correct" long-run exchange rate—would say that if one dollar purchases only €0.90, it is *undervalued* relative to the euro, or the euro is *overvalued* relative to the dollar.

# Exchange Rates in the Short Run

While purchasing power parity helps us to understand movements in nominal exchange rates over decades, it cannot explain the weekly, monthly, or even yearly movements we see. What can? What sorts of phenomena are responsible for the nearly constant movement in exchange rates? To explain short-run changes in nominal exchange rates, we turn to an analysis of the supply of and demand for currencies. Because, in the short run, prices don't move much, these nominal exchange rate movements represent changes in the real exchange rate. That is, a 1 or 2 percent change in the *nominal* dollar–euro exchange rate over a day or week creates a roughly equivalent change in the *real* dollar–euro exchange rate.

## The Supply of Dollars

As is always the case in discussing foreign exchange, we need to pick a home country and stick to it. The most natural choice for us is the United States, so we'll use the U.S. dollar as the domestic currency. Consistent with this, we will discuss the number of units of foreign currency that it takes to purchase one dollar. For example, we will talk about the number of euros per dollar.

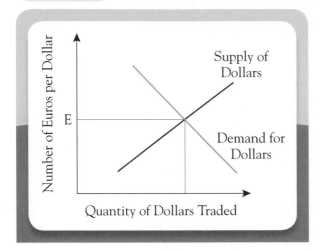

**Figure 10.6**  The Dollar–Euro Market

Who supplies dollars to the foreign exchange markets? People who have them, of course—primarily people in the United States. There are two reasons why someone who is holding dollars would want to exchange them for euros or yen: (1) to purchase goods and services produced abroad, like a Japanese television set, dinner in Paris, or tuition at a foreign university; and (2) to invest in foreign assets, such as bonds issued by the German telecommunications company Deutsche Telekom, or shares in Honda, the Japanese manufacturer of cars and motorcycles.

Figure 10.6 shows the **supply of dollars** in the dollar–euro market. Just like any other supply curve, it slopes upward. The higher the price a dollar commands in the market, the more dollars are supplied. And the more valuable the dollar, the cheaper are foreign-produced goods and foreign assets *relative to domestic ones* in U.S. markets.

To see why, suppose you are planning to buy a car. You have narrowed your options to a German-made Volkswagen Jetta and an American-made Ford Focus. Price is important to you. Because the Volkswagen is manufactured abroad, a change in the value of the dollar will affect your decision. As the dollar increases in value, the price of the Jetta falls and you become more likely to buy the Jetta. If you do, you will be supplying dollars to the foreign exchange market. What is true for your car purchase is true for everything else. The more valuable the dollar, the cheaper foreign goods, services, and assets will be and the higher the supply of dollars in the dollar–euro market. Thus, *the supply curve for dollars slopes upward*, as shown in Figure 10.6.

## The Demand for Dollars

Foreigners who want to purchase American-made goods, assets, or services need dollars to do so. Suppose a European student would like to attend college in the United States. The school will accept payment only in dollars, so paying the tuition bill means exchanging euros for dollars. The lower the dollar–euro exchange rate—the fewer euros needed to buy one dollar—the cheaper the tuition bill will be from the viewpoint of a European student. At a given dollar price, the fewer euros needed to purchase one dollar, the cheaper are American-made goods and services. And the cheaper a good or service, the higher the demand for it. The same is true of investments. The cheaper the dollar—the lower the dollar–euro exchange rate—the more attractive are U.S. investments and the higher is the

# YOUR FINANCIAL WORLD
## Don't Bet on Exchange Rates

Lots of people have an opinion about the likely course of exchange rates. Should you listen to them to try to turn a profit on changes in the exchange rate? The answer is surely no. To see why, let's look at a recent episode in economic history. In 2008, U.S. imports exceeded exports by nearly 5 percent of GDP (that's a really big current account deficit); the economy was faltering; the stock market was declining; but still the dollar was strong. Moreover, the Japanese yen remained strong after more than a decade of stagnation and record low interest rates. Anyone who followed such matters would tell you that both the dollar and the yen should have depreciated. But having a good sense of what will happen over the long run doesn't help much in the short run. What the experts can't tell you is when the dollar will depreciate.

So how can you get a forecast of the future exchange rate? You can look at the *forward markets* for the major currencies. In these markets, foreign currency dealers agree today to a price at which they will sell euros (or yen or other major currencies) three months from now. Since they don't want to incur losses, the dealers will use

all the information available to them (including interest rates) to make the most accurate forecast they can for the exchange rate on the day they agree to make the transaction. But if you look at the newspaper, you will discover that forward rates are virtually always within 1 or 2 percent of the current spot rate. In other words, the best forecast is that the exchange rate won't change much. (Take a look at the "Exchange Rates" column in the business section of a newspaper like *The Wall Street Journal* to confirm this claim.) This tendency holds true even if the Big Mac index or more sophisticated calculations based on purchasing power parity tell us that the exchange rate should move significantly in one direction or another.

The problem is that, in the short run, exchange rates are inherently unpredictable. No one has any idea what is going to happen over the next week, month, or even year. In short, the best forecast of the future exchange rate is usually today's exchange rate. Because you really can't do any better than that, betting on exchange rates is a bad idea.

**demand for dollars** with which to buy them. Thus, *the demand curve for dollars slopes downward* (see Figure 10.6).

## Equilibrium in the Market for Dollars

MARKETS

The equilibrium exchange rate, labeled $E$ in Figure 10.6, equates the supply of and demand for dollars. Because the values of all the major currencies of the world (including the dollar, the euro, the yen, and the pound) float freely, they are determined by market forces. As a result, fluctuations in their value are the consequence of shifts in supply or demand.

## Shifts in the Supply of and Demand for Dollars

Shifts in either the supply of or the demand for dollars will change the *equilibrium exchange rate*. Let's begin with *shifts in the supply of dollars*. Remember that Americans wanting to purchase products from abroad or to buy foreign assets will supply dollars to the foreign exchange market. Anything that increases their desire to import goods and services from abroad, or their preference for foreign stocks and bonds, will increase the supply of dollars, leading to a depreciation of the dollar. Figure 10.7 shows the mechanics of this process.

What causes Americans' preferences for foreign goods, services, and assets to increase, prompting them to supply more dollars to the foreign exchange market shifting the supply of dollars to the right? This question has many answers. The list includes the following possibilities:

*A rise in the supply of dollars Americans use to purchase foreign goods and services can be caused by*

- *An increase in Americans' preference for foreign goods.* For instance, a successful advertising campaign might convince American consumers to buy more imported olive oil. To fill the new orders, U.S. importers would exchange dollars for euros, shifting the dollar supply curve to the right.

*A rise in the supply of dollars Americans use to purchase foreign assets can be caused by*

- *An increase in the real interest rate on foreign bonds (relative to U.S. bonds).* With U.S. real interest rates holding steady, an increase in the return on foreign bonds would make them a more appealing investment. Because buying German bonds means exchanging dollars for euros, a rise in the desire to purchase foreign bonds shifts the supply curve for dollars to the right. (Remember that the real interest rate is the nominal interest rate minus expected inflation, so real interest rates increase either when the nominal interest rate rises and expected inflation holds steady or when expected inflation falls and the nominal interest rate remains the same.)

- *An increase in American wealth.* Just as an increase in income raises consumption of everything, an increase in wealth raises investment in everything. The wealthier we are, the more foreign investments we will make, and the more dollars we will exchange for euros, shifting the supply of dollars to the right.

- *A decrease in the riskiness of foreign investments relative to U.S. investments.* Lower-risk bonds are always more desirable than others, regardless of their country of origin. If the risk associated with foreign investments falls, Americans will want more of them. To get them, they will increase the supply of dollars in the foreign exchange market.

**Figure 10.7** Effect of an Increase in the Supply of Dollars in the Dollar–Euro Market

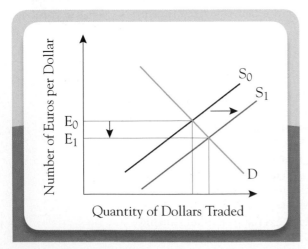

Quantity of Dollars Traded

**Figure 10.8** Effect of an Increase in the Demand for Dollars in the Dollar–Euro Market

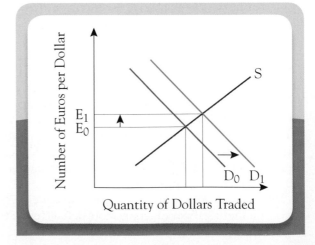

Quantity of Dollars Traded

- *An expected depreciation of the dollar.* If people think the dollar is going to lose value, possibly because of inflation, they will want to exchange it for foreign currency. To see why, assume that the euro is currently worth €0.66 per dollar and that you expect it to move to €0.60/$1 over the next year. If you exchange $100 for euros today, you will get €66. Reversing the transaction a year later, you will be left with $110: a 10 percent return. The point is simple: If investors think the dollar will decline in value—it will depreciate—they will sell dollars, increasing the supply of dollars in the foreign exchange market.

To understand *shifts in the demand for dollars,* all we need to do is review the list just presented, this time from the point of view of a foreigner. Anything that increases the desire of foreigners to buy American-made goods and services, or to invest in U.S. assets, will increase the demand for dollars and shift the demand curve to the right. Increases in demand come about when foreigners prefer more American-made goods, when the real yield on U.S. bonds rises (relative to the yield on foreign bonds), when foreign wealth increases, when the riskiness of American investments falls, and when the dollar is expected to appreciate. All these events increase demand, shifting the demand curve to the right and causing the dollar to appreciate (see Figure 10.8). Table 10.2 summarizes all the events that increase the supply of and demand for dollars in the foreign exchange market.

## Explaining Exchange Rate Movements

The supply and demand model of the determination of exchange rates helps to explain short-run movements in currency values. Let's return to the 30 percent appreciation of the dollar relative to the euro that occurred between January 1999 and October 2000 (see Figure 10.3 on page 233). Over this period, the number of euros required to purchase one dollar increased. Our model allows us to conclude that the cause was either a decrease in the dollars supplied by Americans or an increase in the dollars demanded by foreigners. The first would shift the supply curve to the left

| **Table 10.2** | Causes of an Increase In the Supply of and Demand for Dollars |

| **Increased Supply Shifts Supply Curve to the Right**<br>(Leads to a fall in the value of the dollar) | **Increased Demand Shifts Demand Curve to the Right**<br>(Leads to a rise in the value of the dollar) |
|---|---|
| Increase in American preference for foreign goods | Increase in foreign preference for American goods |
| Increase in real interest rate on foreign bonds (relative to U.S. bonds) | Increase in real interest rate on U.S. bonds (relative to foreign bonds) |
| Increase in American wealth | Increase in foreign wealth |
| Reduction in riskiness of foreign investment (relative to U.S. investment) | Reduction in riskiness of U.S. investment (relative to foreign investment) |
| Expected depreciation of the dollar | Expected future dollar appreciation |

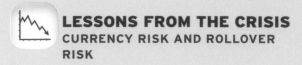

## LESSONS FROM THE CRISIS
### CURRENCY RISK AND ROLLOVER RISK

During the crisis of 2007–2009, some non-U.S. banks faced a sudden threat to their survival: When the interbank market dried up, they found it difficult to borrow the U.S. dollars needed to fund their dollar loans and securities (see Chapter 3, Lessons from the Crisis: Interbank Lending).*

When a bank lends in a foreign currency, it typically borrows in that currency, too. Banks face *currency risk* if they borrow in one currency and lend in another. If the currency in which they lent appreciates relative to the currency in which they borrowed, they benefit. If the opposite occurs, so the currency in which they borrowed rises in value relative to the currency in which they lend, they lose. The larger the mismatch between lending and borrowing in a currency, the greater the currency risk.

But simply matching the currencies of assets and liabilities does not eliminate all the risks the bank faces. Because loans usually have a longer maturity than borrowings, banks still face a danger that funding liquidity in the foreign currency will dry up. This danger is called *rollover risk*. If a bank is unable to "roll over" its short-term foreign currency borrowing (that is, renew at maturity), it must either sell the foreign-currency assets it has purchased or accept increased currency risk by borrowing in domestic currency. A crisis may eliminate even these options and thus threaten the bank's survival.

To see the relationship between currency risk and rollover risk, consider the balance sheet of a hypothetical Japanese bank (Table 10.3). The bank has borrowed short term and made long-term loans in both U.S. dollars and Japanese yen. But because of the way it did this, it has a currency mismatch of $100 million. This is the gap between its lending and borrowing in the foreign currency. At an initial exchange rate of ¥100/US$, in yen this gap equals ¥10 billion. What is the bank's currency risk? If the yen appreciates to ¥99/US$—so instead of taking 100 yen to purchase 1 dollar, it now only takes 99—the bank loses ¥100 million. If the yen depreciates to ¥101/US$, the bank gains ¥100 million. The bank also has rollover risk in dollars. If it cannot roll over its $100 million liability, the bank must repay it by selling dollar loans or by borrowing in yen. The latter adds to its currency risk.

In the financial crisis of 2007–2009, the rollover risk facing internationally active banks became acute and posed a threat to the financial system as a whole. From a policy perspective, the goal was not just to create an adequate supply of dollars, but to deliver it to the banks that needed it. Only the central bank of the United States (the Federal Reserve) can create dollars, but the Fed is not in a position to know all about non-U.S. private banks in need of dollar funding.

So, to limit its credit exposure, the U.S. central bank arranged a series of extraordinary dollar swaps with 10 other central banks, who accepted the currency and credit risks of lending these newly created dollars to their domestic banks. Unprecedented cooperation among central banks allowed for an aggressive and successful policy response to the threat of a currency-driven meltdown.

| Table 10.3 | Simple Balance Sheet of a Hypothetical Japanese Bank | |
|---|---|---|
| **Assets** **Long Term** | | **Liabilities** **Short Term** |
| ¥10 billion US$200 million | | ¥20 billion US$100 million |

*We defined funding liquidity in Chapter 2 as the ease with which a financial institution can borrow to buy securities or make loans.

and the second would shift the demand curve to the right, increasing the equilibrium exchange rate and making dollars more valuable. To figure out which of these is right, we need to look for other evidence.

Looking at the statistics on the supply of dollars, we see that the U.S. current account deficit—exports minus imports—increased from $200 billion at the end of 1998 to $450 billion by the close of 2000. That is, Americans increased their purchases of foreign goods during this period, *raising* the supply of dollars shifting the supply curve to the right. But at the same time, investment funds were pouring into the United States from abroad. Fall 1998 was a time of extreme financial stress, and during times of crisis, investors tend to shift into the safest place, which they view as the United States. Moreover, 1999 was the peak of the U.S. stock-market bubble. Foreign capital streamed toward the dot-com companies, especially those on the Nasdaq (see the discussion at the end of Chapter 8). As a result, foreigners' demand for dollars skyrocketed, outstripping the increased supply of dollars and driving up the "price"—the exchange rate. That is, the demand for dollars shifted to the right by more than the supply for dollars did. In the long run, however, such a move was unsustainable, so the dollar eventually depreciated, returning to a level more consistent with the theory of purchasing power parity.

# Government Policy and Foreign Exchange Intervention

The more a country relies on exports and imports, the more important its exchange rate. Currency appreciation drives up the price foreigners pay for a country's exports as it reduces the price residents of the country pay for imports. This shift in foreign versus domestic prices hurts domestic businesses. Companies with big export businesses suffer the most, along with businesses whose products compete with imported goods. They often respond by pressuring elected officials to reduce the value of the currency. After all, government policymakers may control the prices of lots of goods and services. Milk, rent, and electric power are just a few possibilities. Why not exchange rates too?

Government officials can intervene in foreign exchange markets in several ways. Some countries adopt a fixed exchange rate and act to maintain it at a level of their choosing. We will discuss the implications of this approach in Chapter 19. For now, all we need to know is that exchange rates can be controlled if policymakers have the resources available and are willing to take the necessary actions.

Large industrialized countries and common currency zones like the United States, Europe, and Japan generally allow currency markets to determine their exchange rate. Even so, there are occasions when officials in these countries try to influence the currency values. Sometimes they make public statements in the hope of influencing currency traders. But talk is cheap, and such statements rarely have an impact on their own. At other times, policymakers will buy or sell currency in an attempt to affect demand or supply. This approach is called a *foreign exchange intervention*.

Some countries hardly ever attempt to influence their exchange rates in this way, while others intervene in the markets frequently. Between 1997 and 2009, the United States intervened only twice; both times it was pressured to do so by other allies. Among the major industrialized countries, the Japanese are the most frequent participants in foreign exchange markets. The spring of 2002 provides a good example of their approach.

In the latter half of the 1990s, the Japanese economy was stagnant; real GDP grew at a rate of about 1 percent. In 2001, the economic situation worsened and output fell 2 percent. After trying almost every other approach imaginable to resuscitate the economy, Japanese officials decided to see if depreciating the yen would help. The idea was to help Japanese exporters increase their foreign sales by reducing the prices foreigners paid for Japanese products. In late May 2002, Japan's Ministry of Finance sold yen in exchange for dollars, hoping to drive down the price by increasing the supply of yen. While the yen did depreciate very modestly as a result of intervention, by the end of the month its price was higher than it had been before the intervention.

## IN THE NEWS
### U.S. in Standoff with Beijing over Chinese Currency

**Los Angeles Times**

**By Reducing the Value of the Yuan in Lock Step with the Declining Dollar, China is Making it Difficult for American Exporters to Gain Ground in Overseas Markets.**

### By Don Lee and David Pierson

November 19, 2009

As President Obama's trip to Beijing proved, the days when U.S. leaders could jawbone China into making major changes in economic policy appear to be gone. Not only did the Chinese brush off Obama's appeals this week, they harangued the United States for its own shortcomings.

...

The immediate issues in Beijing centered on highly technical matters of currency valuation and import-export policy.

...

Obama was not alone in asking Beijing to reconsider its economic strategy. Other developed nations and some emerging economies in Asia have made similar appeals. The head of the International Monetary Fund, Dominique Strauss-Kahn, was in Beijing making the same pitch during Obama's visit. He contended that change was in China's interest, as well as the world's.

All the appeals seemed to be turned away politely.

...

In the case of China, that means that, at least well into next year, it's likely to stick to a policy of using government authority to peg the value of its currency to the dollar instead of raising the yuan and gradually letting it fluctuate freely in response to independent market forces, as other major currencies do.

Since mid-2008, Beijing has kept the exchange rate fixed at about 6.8 yuan to the dollar.

China's policy of mandating a set relationship with the dollar helps the Chinese economy even as it hobbles efforts in the U.S. to create jobs and return to prosperity by stepping up American exports.

Theoretically, with the dollar falling in value, American products should be cheaper and more competitive in overseas markets.

But China, by reducing the value of the yuan in lock step with the declining dollar, makes it hard for U.S. companies to gain ground. China's already cheaper products remain cheaper.

One result is huge deficits for the U.S. in its trade with China. Even though the trade deficit has eased, it was still running at $165.8 billion in the first nine months of [2009].

Much the same is true of some other countries, including some of China's neighbors, that are still struggling with the effects of the global financial crisis.

China's party line throughout has been that it seeks greater currency flexibility, but on its own timetable, not someone else's.

In part, China's refusal to bend reflects a growing nationalism.

---

Why did the Japanese government's policy fail? Shouldn't an increase in the supply of yen, regardless of where it comes from, lead to a depreciation? The primary reason the intervention didn't work was that, while the Japanese Ministry of Finance was selling yen, the Bank of Japan was buying them. We'll study the details when we get to Chapter 19, but here is a quick version of the story. The Bank of Japan is in charge of monetary policy in Japan, which means controlling a particular short-term interest rate. Operationally, the result was that, within a few days, the Bank of Japan reversed the Ministry's foreign exchange intervention. If it hadn't, the interest rate it wished to control would have changed. Thus, foreign exchange interventions will be ineffective unless they are accompanied by a change in the interest rate. That is the reason countries like the United States rarely intervene in the foreign exchange markets.

Behind the scenes, it also masks a split between two powerful groups—its central bank and China's huge job- and tax-generating manufacturing sector, supported by the Ministry of Commerce.

Officials of China's central bank have been warning political leaders that keeping the yuan artificially low could ultimately hurt China too by exacerbating the country's trade imbalance problem and bringing in a flood of so-called hot money, or speculative funds from investors.

To keep the yuan pegged to the dollar, "the central bank has to intervene enormously," said Michael Pettis, a professor of finance at Peking University. It's why China holds a record of nearly $2.3 trillion in foreign reserves as of September [2009], most of it in dollar-denominated assets.

The central bank's position is getting a determined push-back from manufacturers and exporters—especially along China's wealthy coast—who stand to reap significant gains in the short term. If the yuan were to rise in value, China's exports would become more expensive relative to goods in the U.S. and other foreign markets.

"It's not the right time for the [yuan] to appreciate," said Wu Haoliang, general secretary of the Foshan Textile Assn., which represents about 3,000 manufacturers in Guangdong province in southeast China.

"Exports are not looking optimistic at all. We're continuing to decline," he added.

...

Twice a year, a small group of association leaders like Wu, usually no more than 20 people, get together with government officials to air their concerns. Wu said they last met over the summer, and sitting in was an official from the central government's National Development and Reform Commission, an important policymaking body.

"They pay attention," Wu said. "But most of the time they can't give you a direct answer. They have to go back to Beijing and discuss policy."

Aside from lobbying or sniping between ministries and other groups over the currency, any movement on the subject would be deliberated by the Politburo, the inner sanctum of the Chinese Communist Party, said Arthur Kroeber, managing director of Dragonomics, a Beijing economic research firm.

...

SOURCE: Don Lee and David Pierson, *Los Angeles Times*, Copyright © 2009. Reprinted with Permission.

## LESSONS OF THE ARTICLE

In 2009, most analysts viewed the Chinese yuan as undervalued, and many firms complained that an overly cheap yuan was putting Chinese producers at an unfair advantage. In response, other governments sought to convince China to allow their currency to appreciate. But Chinese exporters, preferring a weak yuan, successfully prevailed upon Chinese policymakers to continue to keep the yuan weak. As a by-product of this policy, China accumulated a record volume of currency reserves—in excess of $2 trillion—and became the largest holder of U.S. Treasury debt. It remains to be seen how long China can delay a rise of the yuan.

# Terms

# Chapter Lessons

1. Different areas and countries of the world use different currencies in their transactions.
   a. The nominal exchange rate is the rate at which the currency of one country can be exchanged for the currency of another.
   b. A decline in the value of one currency relative to another is called depreciation.
   c. An increase in the value of one currency relative to another is called appreciation.
   d. When the dollar appreciates relative to the euro, the euro depreciates relative to the dollar.
   e. The real exchange rate is the rate at which the goods and services of one country can be exchanged for the goods and services of another.
   f. More than $3 trillion worth of currency is traded every day in markets run by brokers and foreign exchange dealers.

2. In the long run, the value of a country's currency is tied to the price of goods and services in that country.
   a. The law of one price states that two identical goods should sell for the same price, regardless of location.
   b. The law of one price fails because of transportation costs, differences in taxation and technical specifications, and the fact that some goods cannot be moved.
   c. The theory of purchasing power parity applies the law of one price to international transactions; it states that the real exchange rate always equals one.
   d. Purchasing power parity implies that countries with higher inflation than other countries will experience exchange rate depreciation.
   e. Over decades, exchange rate changes are approximately equal to differences in inflation, implying that purchasing power parity holds.

3. In the short run, the value of a country's currency depends on supply of and demand for the currency in foreign exchange markets.
   a. When people in the United States wish to purchase foreign goods and services or invest in foreign assets, they must supply dollars to the foreign exchange market.
   b. The more foreign currency that can be exchanged for one dollar, the greater will be the supply of dollars. That is, the supply curve for dollars slopes upward.
   c. Foreigners who wish to purchase American-made goods and services or invest in U.S. assets will demand dollars in the foreign exchange market.
   d. The fewer units of foreign currency needed to buy one dollar, the higher the demand for dollars. That is, the demand curve for dollars slopes downward.
   e. Anything that increases the desire of Americans to buy foreign-made goods and services or invest in foreign assets will increase the supply of dollars (shift the supply curve for dollars to the right), causing the dollar to depreciate.
   f. Anything that increases the desire of foreigners to buy American-made goods and services or invest in U.S. assets will increase the demand for dollars (shift the demand curve for dollars to the right), causing the dollar to appreciate.

4. Some governments buy and sell their own currency in an effort to affect the exchange rate. Such foreign exchange interventions are usually ineffective.

# Conceptual Problems

1.  If the U.S. dollar–British pound exchange rate is $1.50 per pound, and the U.S. dollar–euro rate is $0.90 per euro:
    a.  What is the pound per euro rate?
    b.  How could you profit if the pound per euro rate were above the rate you calculated in part *a*? What if it were lower?

2.  If a computer game costs $30 in the United States and £26 in the United Kingdom, what is the real "computer game" exchange rate? Look up the current dollar–pound exchange rate in a newspaper or an online source, and compare the two prices. What do you conclude?

3.  Suppose the euro–dollar exchange rate moves from $0.90 per euro to $0.92 per euro. At the same time, the prices of European-made goods and services rise 1 percent, while prices of American-made goods and services rise 3 percent. What has happened to the real exchange rate between the dollar and the euro? Assuming the same change in the nominal exchange rate, what if inflation were 3 percent in Europe and 1 percent in the United States?

4.  The same television set costs $500 in the United States, €450 in France, £300 in the United Kingdom, and ¥100,000 in Japan. If the law of one price holds, what are the euro–dollar, pound–dollar, and yen–dollar exchange rates? Why might the law of one price fail?

5.*  What does the theory of purchasing power parity predict in the long run regarding the inflation rate of a country that fixes its exchange rate to the U.S. dollar?

6.*  Why is it not a good idea to speculate on short-term exchange rate movements using the predictions of purchasing power parity?

7.  You need to purchase Japanese yen and have called two brokers to get quotes. The first broker offered you a rate of 125 yen per dollar. The second broker, ignoring market convention, quoted a price of 0.0084 dollars per yen. To which broker should you give your business? Why?

8.  During the 1990s, the U.S. Secretary of the Treasury often stated, "a strong dollar is in the interest of the United States."
    a.  Is this statement true? Explain your answer.
    b.  What can the Secretary of the Treasury actually do about the value of the dollar relative to other currencies?

9.  Your investment advisor calls to suggest that you invest in Mexican bonds with a yield of 8.5 percent, 3 percent above U.S. Treasury rates. Should you do it? What factors should you consider in making your decision?

# Analytical Problems

10.  If the price (measured in a common currency) of a particular basket of goods is 10 percent higher in the United Kingdom than it is in the United States, which country's currency is undervalued, according to the theory of purchasing power parity?

*Indicates more difficult problems

11.* You hear an interview with a well-known economist who states that she expects the U.S. dollar to strengthen against the British pound over the next five to ten years. This economist is known for her support of the theory of purchasing power parity. Using an equation to summarize the relationship predicted by purchasing power parity between exchange-rate movements and the inflation rates in the two countries, explain whether you expect inflation in the United States to be higher or lower on average compared with that in the U.K. over the period in question.

12. Using the model of demand and supply for U.S. dollars, what would you expect to happen to the U.S. dollar exchange rate if, in light of a worsening geopolitical situation, Americans viewed foreign bonds as more risky than before? (You should quote the exchange rate as number of units of foreign currency per U.S. dollar.)

13. In recent times, the Chinese central bank has been buying U.S. dollars in the market in an effort to keep its own currency, the yuan, weak. Use the model of demand and supply for dollars to show what the immediate effect would be on the yuan–dollar exchange rate of a decision by China to allow its currency to float freely.

14. Consider again the situation described in question 13, where China decided to allow the yuan to float. What would you expect to happen to
   a. U.S. exports to China?
   b. U.S. imports from China?
   c. The U.S. trade deficit with China?
   Explain your answers.

15. Impressed with the magnificent scenery from Vancouver during the coverage of the Winter Olympics, French and German tourists flock to the west coast of Canada. Use the model of demand and supply for Canadian dollars to illustrate and explain the impact this would have on the euro–Canadian dollar exchange rate in the short run.

16. Suppose consumers across the world (including in the United States), driven by a wave of national pride, decided to buy home-produced products where possible. How would demand and supply for dollars be affected? What can you say about the impact on the equilibrium dollar exchange rate?

17. Suppose an Italian bank has short-term borrowings of 400 million euros and 100 million U.S. dollars and made long-term loans of 300 million euros and 250 million U.S. dollars. The euro–dollar exchange rate is initially $1.50 per euro.
   a. Draw up a simple balance sheet for this bank.
   b. List the risks that this bank faces.
   c. If the euro–dollar exchange rate moved to $1.60 per euro, would the bank gain or lose? Provide calculations to support your answer.

18.* Suppose government officials in a small open economy decided they wanted their currency to weaken in order to boost exports. What kind of foreign exchange market intervention would they have to make to cause their currency to depreciate? What would happen to domestic interest rates in that country if its central bank doesn't take any action to offset the impact on interest rates of the foreign exchange intervention?

19. Suppose the interest rate on a one-year U.S. bond were 10 percent and the interest rate on an equivalent Canadian bond were 8 percent. If the interest-rate parity condition holds (see Appendix to Chapter 10), is the U.S. dollar expected to appreciate or depreciate relative to the Canadian dollar over the next year? Explain your choice.

# Appendix to Chapter 10

## Interest-Rate Parity and Short-Run Exchange Rate Determination

There is another way to think about the determinants of exchange rates in the short run. Rather than focus on the supply of and demand for currency, we can look at exchange rates from an investor's point of view. If the bonds issued in different countries are perfect substitutes for one another, then arbitrage will equalize the returns on domestic and foreign bonds. And since investing abroad means exchanging currencies, the result is a relationship among domestic interest rates, foreign interest rates, and the exchange rate. From this intuition, we can develop an understanding of the short-run movements in exchange rates.

Let's take the example of an American investor with a one-year investment horizon and $1,000 to invest in either a one-year U.S. Treasury bond or a one-year German government bond. Since the investor is from the United States, we will assume that at the end of the year when the bonds mature, she wants to receive dollars. The question is: Which investment is more attractive? To find the answer, we need to compute the dollar return on buying a one-year $1,000 U.S. Treasury bond and compare it to the dollar return on converting $1,000 to euros, buying a German government bond, and converting the proceeds back to dollars after one year. The value of the first investment is easy to find. If the one-year U.S. Treasury interest rate is $i$, then one year later an initial investment of $1,000 is worth $1,000 \times (1 + i)$. But the currency conversion complicates the calculation of the return to the foreign investment.

Computing the return to investing $1,000 in a one-year German bond requires a series of steps. First, the investor needs to take the $1,000 and convert it to euros. If $E$ is the dollar–euro exchange rate measured as the number of euros per dollar, then $1,000 purchases $E \times 1,000$ euros. Next, the investor purchases the German bond. If the one-year German bond rate is $i^f$, a $1,000 investment yields $E \times 1,000 \times (1 + i^f)$ euros in one year. Finally, at the end of the year, the investor must exchange the euros for dollars. If we call $E^e$ the expected future exchange rate—the number of euros per dollar expected in a year's time—then the dollar return to a $1,000 investment in foreign bonds is

$$\text{Value of \$1,000 invested in foreign bonds after one year} = \frac{\$1,000 E(1 + i^f)}{E^e} \qquad \text{(A1)}$$

Looking at this equation, we can see that for the U.S. investor, the return to holding the German bond has two parts: (1) the interest income and (2) the expected change in the exchange rate. By doing a little algebra and using an approximation, we can rewrite equation (A1) to divide the return into these two parts. The result is

$$\text{Value of \$1,000 invested in foreign bonds after one year} = \$1,000(1 + i^f)\left(1 - \frac{\Delta E^e}{E}\right) \quad \text{(A2)}$$

where $\Delta E^e$ is the expected change in the exchange rate.

This expression tells us that the return on the foreign bond is the foreign interest rate minus the expected percentage change in the dollar–euro exchange rate.

To see why the return depends on the change in the exchange rate, take an example in which the dollar–euro rate is €1/$1 at the start of the year and €1.05/$1 at the end of the year. That is, at the start of the year, you exchange one dollar for one euro, but at the end of the year the dollar is worth 1.05 euros—an appreciation of 5 percent in the value of the dollar. If the German interest rate is 6 percent, then a $1,000 investment will yield $1,000 × (1.06/1.05) = $1,010. Because the dollar has appreciated by 5 percent, the return on a 6 percent German bond is only 6 percent −5 percent = 1 percent.

Returning to our comparison of a domestic and a foreign bond, we know that if the investor is indifferent between the two, their returns must be the same. That must be the case for the two bonds to be perfect substitutes. The implication is that

Value of $1,000 invested in U.S. Treasury bonds for one year

$$= \text{Value of \$1,000 invested in foreign bonds after one year} \quad \text{(A3)}$$

This means that

$$\$1,000(1 + i) = \$1,000(1 + i^f)\left(1 - \frac{\Delta E^e}{E}\right) \quad \text{(A4)}$$

or using an approximation

$$i = i^f - \frac{\Delta E^e}{E}$$

This equation, called the *interest parity condition,* tells us that the U.S. interest rate equals the German interest rate minus the dollar's expected appreciation. (These calculations ignore the risk of exchange rates moving in an unexpected way.)

If the interest parity condition did not hold, people would have an incentive to shift their investments until it did. For instance, if the U.S. interest rate exceeded the German interest rate minus the expected depreciation in the dollar, then foreign and domestic investors would sell German bonds and buy U.S. Treasury bonds. Their action would drive down the price of German bonds and drive up the price of U.S. bonds, raising the foreign interest rate and lowering the domestic rate until the relationship held.

Because we know the current U.S. and German interest rates, the interest parity condition tells us what the current dollar–euro exchange rate should be for a given expected future dollar–euro exchange rate. The interest rate parity condition tells us that the current value of the dollar will be higher

1. the higher U.S. interest rates,
2. the lower German interest rates, and
3. the higher the expected future value of the dollar.

These are the same conclusions we arrived at using supply and demand theory.

# Part *III*

## Financial Institutions

# Chapter 11

## The Economics of Financial Intermediation

The financial crisis of 2007–2009 alerted everyone that general economic well-being is closely tied to the health of the financial institutions that make up the financial system. The financial system is a lot like plumbing. When it's working well, we pay little attention. But its failure almost inevitably leads to a costly economic mess. The breadth, depth, and persistence of financial disruptions in the recent crisis brought us closer to a second Great Depression than at any time since the first one, in the 1930s.

As described in Chapter 1, our financial system is made up of six components: money, financial instruments, financial markets, financial institutions, government regulatory agencies, and the central bank. In Parts I and II we covered the first three of these components. In Part III we focus on the fourth, financial institutions, and the fifth, government regulatory agencies. In this chapter, we examine financial institutions' purpose, which is known as *financial intermediation*. As we learned in Chapter 3, financial institutions intermediate between savers and borrowers, and so their assets and liabilities are primarily financial instruments. Various sorts of banks, brokerage firms, investment companies, insurance companies, and pension funds all fall into this category. These are the institutions that pool funds from people and firms who save and lend them to people and firms who need to borrow, transforming assets and providing access to financial markets. They funnel savers' surplus resources into home mortgages, business loans, and investments.

As we discussed briefly at the end of Chapter 3, financial intermediaries are involved in both direct finance—in which borrowers sell securities directly to lenders in the financial markets—and indirect finance, in which a third party stands between those who provide funds and those who use them. Intermediaries investigate the financial condition of the individuals and firms who want financing to figure out which have the best investment opportunities. As providers of indirect finance, banks want to make loans only to the highest-quality borrowers. When they do their job correctly, financial intermediaries increase investment and economic growth at the same time that they reduce investment risk and economic volatility.

Ensuring that the best investment opportunities and highest-quality borrowers are funded is extremely important. Any country that wants to grow must ensure that its financial system works. When a country's financial system crumbles, its economy fails with it. That is what happened in the United States in the Great Depression of the 1930s, when a series of bank closings was followed by an increase in the unemployment rate to over 25 percent and a fall of nearly one-third in the level of economic activity (measured by GDP). The Asian crisis of 1997, in which the banking systems of Thailand and Indonesia collapsed, is a more recent example. And the deep, prolonged economic plunge of 2008–2009 highlights how a financial crisis, once started, can spread devastation across the global economy, triggering a spiral of economic and financial decline that is difficult to halt. Without a stable, smoothly functioning financial system, no country can prosper.

| Figure 11.1 | Financial and Economic Development |

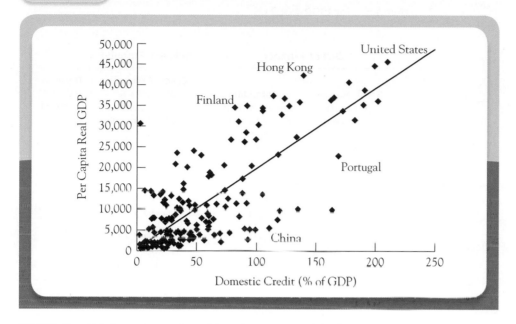

SOURCE: *Financial development is measured as total financial system credit extended to the private sector. World Development Indicators, the World Bank. All data are for 2007. www.worldbank.org.*

The strong relationship between financial development and economic development is clearly apparent from the data. Figure 11.1 plots a commonly used measure of financial activity—the ratio of credit extended to the private sector (both through financial intermediaries and markets) to gross domestic product (GDP)—against real GDP per capita. The resulting strong correlation, roughly 0.7, is no surprise. There aren't any rich countries that have very low levels of financial development.

In theory, the market system may seem neat and simple, but the reality is that economic growth is a messy, chaotic thing. The flow of information among parties in a market system is particularly rife with problems—problems that can derail real growth unless they are addressed properly. In this chapter, we will discuss some of these information problems—including several that contributed to the financial crisis of 2007–2009—and learn how financial intermediaries attempt to solve them.

# The Role of Financial Intermediaries

Markets are remarkably effective at coordinating the behavior of millions of firms and households in an economy. And financial markets are among the most important markets of all; they price economic resources and allocate them to their most productive uses. In many countries over the past 20 years, the value of stock and bond markets—the avenues of direct finance—has come to rival the value of outstanding loans through financial intermediaries—the path of indirect finance. But as we will see, intermediaries, including banks and securities firms, continue to play a key role in both these types of finance.

| Table 11.1 | The Relative Importance of Direct and Indirect Finance (Averages for 1990-2007) |
|---|---|

| | Direct Finance | | Indirect Finance | |
| Country | Stock Market Capitalization as Percent of GDP (A) | Outstanding Domestic Debt Securities as Percent of GDP (B) | Credit Extended by Banks & Other Financial Institutions as Percent of GDP (C) | Ratio of Indirect to Direct Finance C/(A+B) (D) |
|---|---|---|---|---|
| **Industrialized Countries** | | | | |
| France | 59.0 | 45.0 | 88.2 | 0.8 |
| Germany | 40.7 | 47.4 | 107.2 | 1.2 |
| Greece | 38.9 | 2.3 | 45.4 | 1.1 |
| Italy | 34.0 | 35.8 | 68.0 | 1.0 |
| Japan | 78.7 | 43.9 | 154.0 | 1.3 |
| United Kingdom | 131.1 | 15.6 | 125.4 | 0.9 |
| United States | 113.2 | 94.9 | 154.3 | 0.7 |
| **Emerging Markets Countries** | | | | |
| Argentina | 31.6 | 4.7 | 16.7 | 0.5 |
| Brazil | 34.0 | 9.8 | 34.1 | 0.8 |
| India | 38.3 | 0.9 | 27.5 | 0.7 |

Note that numbers in columns A, B, and C are as a percentage of GDP. Since these are not components of GDP, there is no reason they should add to 100.

SOURCE: *Data from Thorstein, Beck, Asli Demirguc-Kunt, and Ross Eric Levine, "A New Database on Financial Development and Structure," updated May 2009, World Bank. www.worldbank.org.*

Table 11.1 illustrates the importance of direct and indirect finance. As you look at the table, note two things. First, to make comparisons across countries of vastly different size, we measure everything relative to GDP. Second, there is no reason that the value of a country's stock market, bonds outstanding, or bank loans cannot be bigger than its GDP. In fact, we would expect it to be much larger, because the value of a company to its owners is normally quite a bit more than one year's sales. This means that when you add up all the types of financing, direct and indirect, as a percentage of GDP, the numbers will generally sum to more than 100 in an advanced economy.

To see the lessons from the table, take the example of France, in the first row. The value of the French stock market (the value of the shares of all companies listed on the exchanges) is equivalent to 59 percent of that country's GDP (column A); the value of French debt securities is 45 percent of GDP (column B). Adding columns A and B tells us that, in France, direct finance equals 104 percent of GDP. That exceeds the amount of credit extended by French banks and other intermediaries—88 percent of GDP (column C). The final column, D, reports the ratio of indirect to direct finance. For

France, the result is 0.85, which means that indirect finance is a bit smaller than direct finance. For the industrialized countries in the table, the range of that ratio is between 0.74 and 1.26, so the French case is not unusual. In many emerging markets, the ratio is somewhat lower because in recent decades their stock markets have expanded notably.

These data highlight the importance of intermediaries. Banks are still critical providers of financing around the world, although bank lending may not be the dominant source of financing that it once was. And intermediation is not limited to bank lending. Intermediaries determine which firms can access the stock and bond markets. Just as banks decide the size of a loan and the interest rate to be charged, securities firms set the volume and price of new stock and bond issues when they purchase them for sale to investors. And other intermediaries, like mutual funds, help individual investors sort among the thousands of stocks and bonds that are issued to develop a diversified portfolio with the desired risk characteristics.

Why are financial intermediaries so important? The answer has to do with information. To understand the importance of information in the role financial intermediaries play in the economy, consider the online company eBay. This virtual auction house may seem an unlikely place to start, but while eBay deals primarily with physical objects, it faces some of the same information problems as financial firms. As an online intermediary, eBay provides a mechanism through which almost anyone can auction off almost anything. At any time, upwards of 15 million items are for sale at www.ebay.com—everything from $5 dinner plates to $3 million vacation homes. And people buy them! In a single year, eBay reports total transactions valued at over $50 billion, entered into by more than 100 million active users.

While millions of items are for sale on eBay, if you look carefully you'll notice an absence of financial products. You can purchase collectible coins and paper currency on eBay, but you can't borrow. There are no listings for Samantha's student loan, Chad's car loan, Chloe's credit card balance, or Mort's mortgage—at least, not yet. And though you can buy defaulted bond certificates, like the Reading Railroad bond shown in Chapter 4 (which was purchased on eBay), you can't buy or sell bonds on which the issuer is still making payments. People are selling cars and even real estate on eBay, but no one is auctioning off checking account services. (There are hints that this may be changing. See the In the News story near the end of this chapter.)

Think for a moment about why eBay doesn't auction off mortgages. First, Mort might need a $100,000 mortgage, and not many people can finance a mortgage of that size. The people who run eBay could try to establish a system in which 100 people sign up to lend Mort $1,000, but it would be extremely complex and cumbersome. Imagine collecting the payments, figuring out how to repay the lenders, and writing all the legal contracts that go with the transaction. Just as important, before offering to finance Mort's mortgage, lenders would want to know something about Mort and the house he's proposing to buy. Is Mort accurately representing his ability to repay the loan? Does he really intend to buy a house with the loan? The questions are nearly endless, and answering them is both difficult and time consuming.

Financial intermediaries exist so that individual lenders don't have to worry about getting answers to all of these questions. Most people take for granted the ability of the financial system to shift resources from savers to investors, but when you look closely at the details, you're struck by how complicated the task is. It's amazing the enterprise works at all. Lending and borrowing involve both *transactions costs*, like the cost of writing a loan contract, and *information costs*, like the cost of figuring out whether a borrower is trustworthy. Financial institutions exist to reduce these costs.

**Table 11.2**   A Summary of the Role of Financial Intermediaries

| | |
|---|---|
| 1. *Pooling savings* | Accepting resources from a large number of small savers/lenders in order to provide large loans to borrowers. |
| 2. *Safekeeping and accounting* | Keeping depositors' savings safe, giving them access to the payments system, and providing them with accounting statements that help them to track their income and expenditures. |
| 3. *Providing liquidity* | Allowing depositors to transform their financial assets into money quickly, easily, and at low cost. |
| 4. *Diversifying risk* | Providing investors with the ability to diversify even small investments. |
| 5. *Collecting and processing information services* | Generating large amounts of standardized financial information. |

In their role as financial intermediaries, financial institutions perform five functions (see Table 11.2): (1) pooling the resources of small savers; (2) providing safekeeping and accounting services, as well as access to the payments system; (3) supplying liquidity by converting savers' balances directly into a means of payment whenever needed; (4) providing ways to diversify risk; and (5) collecting and processing information in ways that reduce information costs. As we go through these, you'll see that the first four have to do with lowering transactions costs. That is, by specializing and providing these services to large numbers of customers, a financial firm can reduce the cost of providing them to individual customers. As in other fields, experts can do a better job than others, and more cheaply at that. The fifth function on the list, collecting and processing information, is a category all by itself, so we'll consider it in more detail.

While we will not discuss international banks in any depth, it is worth mentioning that they provide an additional set of services that complements those offered by your neighborhood bank. International banks handle transactions that cross international borders. That may mean taking deposits from savers in one country and providing them to investors in another country. It may also mean converting currencies in order to facilitate transactions for customers who do business or travel abroad.

## Pooling Savings

The most straightforward economic function of a financial intermediary is to pool the resources of many small savers. By accepting many small deposits, banks empower themselves to make large loans. So, for example, Mort might get his $100,000 mortgage from a bank or finance company with access to a large group of savers, 100 of whom have $1,000 to invest (see Figure 11.2). Similarly, a government or large company that wishes to borrow billions of dollars by issuing bonds will rely on a financial intermediary to find buyers for the bonds.

To succeed in this endeavor—pooling people's savings in order to make large loans—the intermediary must attract substantial numbers of savers. This is the essence of indirect finance, and it means convincing potential depositors of the institution's soundness. Banks are particularly adept at making sure customers feel that their funds will be safe. In the past, they did so by installing large safes in imposing bank buildings.

Today, they rely on their reputations, as well as on government guarantees like deposit insurance. We'll return to this topic in Chapter 14.

## Safekeeping, Payments System Access, and Accounting

Goldsmiths were the original bankers. To keep their gold and jewelry safe, they had to construct vaults. Soon people began asking the goldsmiths to store gold for them in return for a receipt to prove it was there. It didn't take long for someone to realize that trading the goldsmith's receipts was easier than trading the gold itself. The next step came when the goldsmith noticed that there was quite a bit of gold left in the vault at the end of the day, so that some of it could safely be lent to others. The goldsmiths took the resources of those with gold to spare—the savers of the day—and channeled them to individuals who were short—the borrowers. Today, banks are the places where we put things for safekeeping—not just gold and jewelry, but our financial wealth as well. We deposit our paychecks and entrust our savings to a bank or other financial institution because we believe it will keep our resources safe until we need them.

When we think of banks, safekeeping is only one of several services that immediately come to mind. The others are automated teller machines, checkbooks, and monthly bank statements. In providing depositors with access to ATMs, credit and debit cards, checks, and monthly statements, a bank gives them access to the payments system—the network that transfers funds from the account of one person or business to the account of another. The bank provides depositors a way to get cash into their wallets and to finalize payments using credit cards, debit cards, and checks. And since banks specialize in handling payments transactions, they can offer all these services relatively cheaply. Financial intermediaries reduce the costs of financial transactions.

This is not a trivial matter. It would be a disaster if we didn't have a convenient way to pay for things. By giving us one, financial intermediaries facilitate the exchange of goods and services, promoting specialization. Remember that in efficient economies—those that manage to get the most output from a given set of inputs—people and companies concentrate on the activities at which they are best and for which their opportunity cost is lowest. This principle of

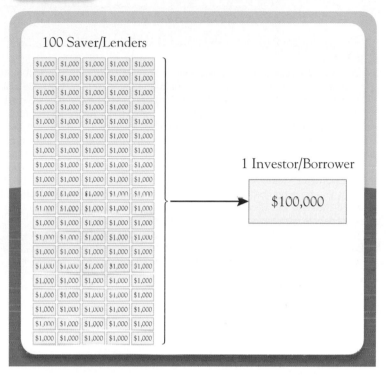

**Figure 11.2**    Financial Intermediaries Pool Savings

Financial intermediaries pool the funds of many small savers and lend them to one large borrower.

The door to the largest gold vault in the world at the Federal Reserve Bank of New York. The only entry is through a 10-foot passageway cut into a 9-foot high, 90-ton steel cylinder that rotates 90 degrees to open and close the vault. Many governments keep their gold here.

## YOUR FINANCIAL WORLD

### Your First Credit Card

Credit card interest rates are outrageous, running to more than 30 percent in some cases (really)! In Chapter 4, Your Financial World: Pay Off Your Credit Card discussed how expensive borrowing can be and demonstrated why you should pay off your credit card debt as quickly as possible. The odds are, when you get your first credit card, the interest rate will be extremely high. Why?

Unless your parent signed your credit card papers (or you worked a steady job before starting college), as a student you have no credit history, and the company that issued the card will assume the worst. So you're lumped in with people who have very poor credit, who would rather get lower-interest loans elsewhere but can't. This is adverse selection at its worst (see page 267 for a definition of adverse selection). When you get your first credit card,

the assumption is that you are in a group of people who will have a high default rate. No wonder the issuers charge high interest rates. It is compensation for the risk they are taking. And just to prove the point, this is not a very profitable business.*

You need a credit card to build up a credit history, to establish yourself as a person who repays loans promptly. After a while, you'll be able to get a new card at a lower interest rate. But in the meantime, remember that your interest rate is extremely high, so borrowing is very expensive.

*There are a number of studies of the credit card industry. Paul S. Calem and Loretta J. Mester's study "Consumer Behavior and the Stickiness of Credit-Card Interest Rates," *American Economic Review* 85, no. 5 (December 1995), pp. 1327–1336, examines the nature of the credit card industry.

**MARKETS**

*comparative advantage* leads to specialization so that each of us ends up doing just one job and being paid in some form of money. But as specialization increases, more and more trading must take place to ensure that most of us end up with the goods and services we need and want. The more trading, the more financial transactions; and the more financial transactions, the more important it is that those transactions be cheap. If getting hold of money and using it to make payments were costly, that would surely put a damper on people's willingness to specialize. Financial intermediaries, by providing us with a reliable and inexpensive payments system, help our economy to function more efficiently.

Beyond safekeeping and access to the payments system, financial intermediaries provide bookkeeping and accounting services. They help us to manage our finances. Just think about your financial transactions over the past few months. If you work, you were paid, probably more than once. If you rent an apartment or own a home, you paid the rent or mortgage and probably the electric and gas bills. You paid your phone bill. Then there's transportation. If you have a car, you may have made a loan payment. You surely paid for gasoline and possibly for a repair. You purchased food too, both at the grocery store and in various restaurants. And don't forget the movies and books you bought. As you get older, you may shoulder the expense of having children, along with saving for their education and your retirement. The point is, our financial lives are extraordinarily complex, and we need help keeping track of them. Financial intermediaries do the job: They provide us with bookkeeping and accounting services, noting all our transactions for us and making our lives more tolerable in the process.

Before we continue, we should note that providing safekeeping and accounting services, as well as access to the payments system, forces financial intermediaries to write legal contracts. Writing individualized contracts to ensure that each customer will maintain a checking account balance as required, or repay a loan as promised, would be extremely costly. But a financial intermediary can hire a lawyer to write one very high-quality contract that can be used over and over again, thus reducing the cost of each use. In fact, much of what financial intermediaries do takes advantage of what are known as *economies of scale*, in which the average cost of producing a good or service falls as the quantity produced increases. As we will see later, information is subject to economies of scale just as other goods and services are.

## Providing Liquidity

One function that is related to access to the payments system is the provision of liquidity. Recall from Chapter 2 that *liquidity* is a measure of the ease and cost with which an asset can be turned into a means of payment. When a financial asset can be transformed into money quickly, easily, and at low cost, it is said to be very liquid. Financial intermediaries offer us the ability to transform assets into money at relatively low cost. That's what ATMs are all about—converting deposit balances into money on demand.

Financial intermediaries provide liquidity in a way that is both efficient and beneficial to all of us. To understand the process, think about your bank. Two kinds of customers come through the doors: those with funds, who want to make deposits, and those in need of funds, who want to take out loans. Depositors want easy access to their funds—not just the currency they withdraw every week or so but the larger amounts they may need in an emergency. Borrowers don't want to pay the funds back for awhile, and they certainly can't be expected to repay the entire amount on short notice.

In the same way that an insurance company knows that not all its policyholders will have automobile accidents on the same day, a bank knows that not all its depositors will experience an emergency and need to withdraw funds at the same time. The bank can structure its assets accordingly, keeping enough funds in short-term, liquid financial instruments to satisfy the few people who will need them and lending out the rest. And since long-term loans usually have higher interest rates than short-term money-market instruments—for instance, commercial paper and U.S. Treasury bills—the bank can offer depositors a higher interest rate than they would get otherwise.

Even the bank's short-term investments will do better than an individual depositor's could, because the bank can take advantage of economies of scale to lower its transactions costs. It isn't much more expensive to buy a $1 million U.S. Treasury bill than it is to buy one worth only $1,000. By collecting funds from a large number of small investors, the bank can reduce the cost of their combined investment, offering each individual investor both liquidity and high rates of return. Pooling large numbers of small accounts in this way is very efficient. By doing so, an intermediary offers depositors something they can't get from the financial markets on their own.

The liquidity services financial intermediaries provide go beyond fast and easy access to account balances. Intermediaries offer both individuals and businesses lines of credit, which are similar to overdraft protection for checking accounts. A line of credit is essentially a preapproved loan that can be drawn on whenever a customer needs funds. Home equity lines of credit, credit-card cash advances, and business lines of credit are examples. Like a deposit account, the line of credit provides a customer with access to liquidity, except that in this case withdrawals may exceed deposit balances. To offer this service profitably, a financial intermediary must specialize in liquidity management. That is, it must design its balance sheet so that it can sustain sudden withdrawals.

## Diversifying Risk

If you had $1,000 or $10,000 or even $100,000 to invest, would you want to keep it all in one place? Would you be willing to lend it all to a single person or firm? By now you have read Chapter 5, so you know the answer to this question: Don't put all your eggs in one basket, it's unnecessarily risky. But even without knowing much about diversifying through hedging and spreading risk, you would sense intuitively that lending $1 to each of 1,000 borrowers is less risky than lending $1,000 to just one borrower, and putting $1 in each of 1,000 different stocks is safer than putting $1,000 in one stock. Financial institutions enable us to diversify our investments and reduce risk.

Banks mitigate risk in a straightforward way: They take deposits from thousands or even millions of individuals and make thousands of loans with them. Thus, each depositor has a very small stake in each one of the loans. For example, a bank might collect $1,000 from each of one million depositors and then use the resulting $1 billion to make 10,000 loans of $100,000 each. So each depositor has a 1/1,000,000 share in each of the 10,000 loans.

RISK

To picture this, look back at Figure 11.2 (page 263) and imagine that it shows 10,000 times as many deposits and 10,000 times as many mortgages. Next, picture each of those deposits cut up into 10,000 pieces, each assigned to a different loan. That is, each deposit contributes 10 cents to each loan. That's diversification! And since the bank specializes in taking deposits and making loans, it can minimize the cost of setting up all the necessary legal contracts to do this.

All financial intermediaries provide a low-cost way for individuals to diversify their investments. Mutual-fund companies offer small investors a low-cost way to purchase a diversified portfolio of stocks and eliminate the idiosyncratic risk associated with any single investment. Many of the mutual funds based on the Standard & Poor's 500 index (described in Chapter 8) require a minimum investment of as little as a few thousand dollars. Because the average price of each stock in the index usually runs between $30 and $40, a small investor would need more than $15,000 to buy even a single share of stock in each of the 500 companies in the index (not to mention the fees the investor would need to pay to a broker to do it). Thus, the mutual-fund company lets a small investor buy a fraction of a share in each of the 500 companies in the fund. And because mutual fund companies specialize in this activity, the cost remains low.

## Collecting and Processing Information

One of the biggest problems individual savers face is figuring out which potential borrowers are trustworthy and which are not. Most of us do not have the time or skill to collect and process information on a wide array of potential borrowers. And we are understandably reluctant to invest in activities about which we have little reliable information. The fact that the borrower knows whether he or she is trustworthy, while the lender faces substantial costs to obtain the same information, results in an *information asymmetry*. Very simply, borrowers have information that lenders don't.

By collecting and processing standardized information, financial intermediaries reduce the problems information asymmetries create. They screen loan applicants to guarantee that they are creditworthy. They monitor loan recipients to ensure that they use the funds as they have claimed they will. To understand how this process works, and the implications it has for the financial system, we need to study information asymmetries in more detail.

# Information Asymmetries and Information Costs

Information plays a central role in the structure of financial markets and financial institutions. Markets require sophisticated information to work well; when the cost of obtaining that information is too high, markets cease to function. Information costs make the financial markets, as important as they are, among the worst functioning of all markets. The fact is, the issuers of financial instruments—borrowers who want to issue bonds and firms that want to issue stock—know much more about their business prospects and their willingness to work than potential lenders or investors—those who would buy their bonds and stocks. This **asymmetric information** is a serious hindrance to the operation of financial markets. Solving this problem is one key to making our financial system work as well as it does.

To understand the nature of the problem and the possible solutions, let's go back to eBay. Why are the people who win online auctions willing to send payments totaling $50 billion a year to the sellers? An amazing amount of trust is involved in these transactions. To bid at all, buyers must believe that an item has been described accurately. And winners must be sure that the seller will send the item in exchange for their payments, because the normal arrangement is for the seller to be paid first.

eBay's feedback rating system awards +1 point for each positive comment, 0 points for each neutral comment, and −1 point for each negative comment

How can buyers be sure they won't be disappointed by their purchases when they arrive, assuming they arrive at all? The fact that sellers have much more information about the items they are selling and their own reliability creates an information asymmetry. Aware of this problem, the people who started eBay took two steps. First, they offered insurance to protect buyers who don't receive their purchases. Second, they devised a feedback forum to collect and store information about both bidders and sellers. Anyone can read the comments posted in the forum or check an overall rating that summarizes their content. Sellers who develop good reputations in the feedback forum command higher prices than others; buyers who develop bad reputations can be banned from bidding. Without this means of gathering information, eBay probably could not have been successful. Together, the buyers' insurance and the feedback forum make eBay run smoothly.[1]

The two problems eBay faced arise in financial markets, too. In fact, information problems are the key to understanding the structure of our financial system and the central role of financial intermediaries. Asymmetric information poses two important obstacles to the smooth flow of funds from savers to investors. The first, called **adverse selection**, arises before the transaction occurs. Just as buyers on eBay need to know the relative trustworthiness of sellers, lenders need to know how to distinguish good credit risks from bad. The second problem, called **moral hazard**, occurs after the transaction. In the same way that buyers on eBay need reassurance that sellers will deliver their purchases after receiving payment, lenders need to find a way to tell whether borrowers will use the proceeds of a loan as they claim they will. The following sections will look at both these problems in detail to see how they affect the structure of the financial system.

---

[1] A low-cost, reliable payments system helps, too. The easier it is for buyers to pay sellers, the more likely both are to use the auction site. Realizing the need for a payments system, eBay users created *PayPal*, which allows buyers and sellers to set up electronic accounts through which to make and receive payments for their eBay transactions. Because many sellers are too small to take credit cards, this innovation greatly facilitated the online exchanges. Initially an independent concern, PayPal became so central to eBay's success that the auction site's owners bought it.

## APPLYING THE CONCEPT
### THE MADOFF SCANDAL

Fraud is the most extreme version of moral hazard. Even so, the fraud perpetrated by Bernard Madoff stands out. Thousands of investors lost billions of dollars, making it among the largest scams in history.* The swindle went undetected for decades and affected wealthy individuals and financial firms from around the world with extensive experience in finance.

Yet, Madoff's fraud was nothing more than a classic *Ponzi scheme*. Named after Charles Ponzi, who conducted a similar sting in the United States just after World War I, a Ponzi scheme is a fraud in which an intermediary collects funds from new investors, but instead of investing them, uses the funds to pay off earlier investors. Money has to flow in at least as fast as it flows out. When that flow reverses, the fraud unravels and the final investors become big losers.

How do such frauds succeed at different times in different places? How can they last so long and become so damaging?

The answer is that investors fail to screen and monitor the managers who receive their funds (such as Madoff or Ponzi). Screening and monitoring are costly. The appearance of satisfied early investors discourages new investors from paying such costs. Many investors assume that others have already done the monitoring needed.

A facade of public respectability contributes to the success of a Ponzi scheme, and Madoff was a master at burnishing his reputation in the public eye. He had been the chairman of a major stock exchange (Nasdaq; see Chapter 8) and of the organization of U.S. securities dealers (NASD). He also was a philanthropist.

The U.S. government agency responsible for overseeing Madoff's firm, the Securities and Exchange Commission (SEC), also failed to detect the scheme. One whistleblower warned the oversight agency about possible fraud as early as 2000. Yet, the swindle ended in 2008 only because the financial crisis had prompted withdrawals from many firms, including Madoff's. Otherwise, the scam might still be going on.

With the benefit of hindsight, there were red flags that warned of a problem. Yet, everyone acted as if someone else was monitoring, so they could enjoy the *free ride* (see page 272 for a definition of a free rider). The Madoff scam is a painful reminder that there is no such free ride.

*As of October 2009, the government-appointed trustee responsible for returning investors' stolen money estimated the losses at more than $21 billion.

# Adverse Selection

## Used Cars and the Market for Lemons

The 2001 Nobel Prize in Economics was awarded to George A. Akerlof, A. Michael Spence, and Joseph E. Stiglitz "for their analyses of markets with asymmetric information." Professor Akerlof's contribution came first, in a paper published in 1970 titled "The Market for Lemons."[2] Akerlof's paper explained why the market for used cars—some of which may be "lemons"— doesn't function very well. Here's the logic.

Suppose the used-car market has only two cars for sale, both 2007 model Honda Accords. One is immaculate, having been driven and maintained by a careful elderly woman who didn't travel much. The second car belonged to a young man who got it from his parents, loved to drive fast, and did not worry about the damage he might cause if he hit a pothole. The owners of these two cars know whether their own cars are in good repair, but used-car shoppers do not.

Let's say that potential buyers are willing to pay $15,000 for a well-maintained car, but only $7,500 for a "lemon"—a car with lots of mechanical problems. The elderly woman knows her car is a "peach." It's in good condition and she won't part with it for less than $12,500. The young man, knowing the poor condition of his car, will take $6,000 for

Used Cars: clean, reliable, and priced just right!

[2]See "The Market for 'Lemons': Quality Uncertainty and the Market Mechanism," *Quarterly Journal of Economics* (August 1970). This paper contains very little mathematics and is quite readable. You can find it through your university library using an electronic storage system called JSTOR.

it. But if buyers can't tell the difference between the two cars, without more information they will pay only the average price of $11,250. (A risk-averse buyer wouldn't even pay that much.) That is less than the owner of the good car will accept, so she won't sell her car and it disappears from the market. The problem is that if buyers are willing to pay only the average value of all the cars on the market, sellers with cars in above-average condition won't put their cars up for sale. Only the worst cars, the lemons, will be left on the market.

Information asymmetries aside, people like to buy new cars, and when they do, they sell their old cars. People who can't afford new cars, or who would rather not pay for them, are looking to buy good used cars. Together, these potential buyers and sellers of used cars provide a substantial incentive for creative people to solve the problem of adverse selection in the used-car market. Some companies try to help buyers separate the peaches from the lemons. For instance, *Consumer Reports* provides information about the reliability and safety of particular makes and models. Car dealers may try to maintain their reputations by refusing to pass off a clunker as a well-maintained car. For a fee, a mechanic will check out a used car for a potential buyer, and Internet services will provide a report on its accident history. Finally, many car manufacturers offer warranties on the used cars they have certified. We have found ways to overcome the information problems pointed out by Professor Akerlof, and as a result both good and bad used cars sell at prices much closer to their true value.

**Adverse Selection in Financial Markets**   When it comes to information costs, financial markets are not that different from the used-car market. In the same way that the seller of a used car knows more about the car than the buyer, potential borrowers know more about the projects they wish to finance than prospective lenders. And in the same way that information asymmetries can drive good cars out of the used-car market, they can drive good stocks and bonds out of the financial market. To see why, let's start with stocks.

Think about a simple case in which there are two firms, one with good prospects and one with bad prospects. If you can't tell the difference between the two firms, you will be willing to pay a price based only on their average quality. The stock of the good company will be undervalued. Because the managers know their stock is worth more than the average price, they won't issue it in the first place. That leaves only the firm with bad prospects in the market. And because most investors aren't interested in companies with poor prospects, the market is very unlikely to get started at all.

The same thing happens in the bond market. Remember that risk requires compensation. The higher the risk, the greater the risk premium. In the bond market, this relationship between risk and return affects the cost of borrowing. The more risky the borrower, the higher the cost of borrowing. If a lender can't tell whether a borrower is a good or bad credit risk, the lender will demand a risk premium based on the average risk. Borrowers who know they are good credit risks won't want to borrow at this elevated interest rate, so they will withdraw from the market, leaving only the bad credit risks. The result is the same as for used cars and stocks: Because lenders are not eager to buy bonds issued by bad credit risks, the market will disappear.

RISK

## Solving the Adverse Selection Problem

From a social perspective, the fact that managers might avoid issuing stock or bonds because they know the market will not value their company correctly is not good. It

## YOUR FINANCIAL WORLD
### Private Mortgage Insurance

If you try to buy a house with a down payment of less than 20 percent of the purchase price, the lender may require you to buy private mortgage insurance (PMI). PMI insures the lender in the event that the borrower defaults on the mortgage. This type of insurance can be expensive. For example, if you make a down payment of $10,000, or 10 percent, on a $100,000 home and finance the rest of the purchase price with a 30-year, 6 percent, fixed-rate mortgage, the required private mortgage insurance will raise your monthly payment from $530 to $570. But if you want to buy a house and you don't have savings that meet the 20 percent down payment requirement, you will have no choice but to purchase PMI.

Fortunately, you can cancel the insurance when the amount you owe on your mortgage falls to less than 80 percent of the value of your home. This can happen in two ways. The first is that you make your payments, gradually reducing the principal on the loan. (Recall from Chapter 6 that each loan payment is part interest and part repayment of principal.) But paying off the first $10,000 of a $90,000 30-year mortgage will take you at least 10 years. The second way you can cancel your PMI is if the value of your house rises, in which case you can contact the insurance provider and ask to drop the insurance. The law is on your side. So long as you have been making your mortgage payments on time, you have the right to cancel your PMI when your stake in the house—your net worth—rises above 20 percent of its value.

means that the company will pass up some good investments. And because some of the best investments will not be undertaken, the economy won't grow as rapidly as it could. Thus, it is extremely important to find ways for investors and lenders to distinguish well-run firms from poorly run firms. Well-run firms need to highlight their quality so they can obtain financing more cheaply. Investors need to distinguish between high- and low-risk investments so they can adjust their expected rates of return. The question is how to do it.

Recall how buyers and sellers in the used-car market developed ways to address the problem of distinguishing good from bad cars? The answer here is similar. First, because the problem is caused by a lack of information, we can create more information for investors. Second, we can provide guarantees in the form of financial contracts that can be written so a firm's owners suffer together with the people who invested in the company if the firm does poorly. This type of arrangement helps to persuade investors that a firm's stocks and bonds are of high quality. And as we will see later, financial intermediaries can do a great deal to reduce the information costs associated with stock and bond investments.

**Disclosure of Information**    One obvious way to solve the problem created by asymmetric information is to generate more information. This can be done in one of two ways, government-required disclosure and the private collection and production of information. In most industrialized countries, *public companies*—those that issue stocks and bonds that are bought and sold in public financial markets—are required to disclose voluminous amounts of information. For example, in the United States the Securities and Exchange Commission requires firms to produce public financial statements that are prepared according to standard accounting practices. Corporations are also required to disclose, on an ongoing basis, information that could have a bearing on the value of their firms. And since August 2000, U.S. companies have

## APPLYING THE CONCEPT
### DEFLATION, NET WORTH, AND INFORMATION COSTS

A casual reader of the business press might get the impression that **deflation**, when prices are declining on average, is a fate we would rather not contemplate. Deflation is associated with the Great Depression of the 1930s, when consumer prices and output both fell about 30 percent. It is also associated with the Japanese stagnation of the 1990s, when output remained virtually unchanged and prices fell for five years running.

Deflation is the opposite of the more familiar inflation. Inflation is when prices are going up, on average. Deflation is when they are going down. A primary reason deflation is so bad is that it aggravates information problems in ways that inflation does not. It does so by reducing a company's net worth. To see why, think about a typical firm's balance sheet. Its assets are buildings, machines, and product inventories. Its liabilities include various kinds of debt, much of it fixed

in nominal terms. That is, companies borrow fixed numbers of dollars. Now think about the consequences of a decline in the price level. When prices fall, the dollar value of the firm's liabilities remains the same. The value of the firm's assets, however, tends to fall with the price level. Deflation drives down a firm's net worth, making it less trustworthy as a borrower. Remember, net worth solves the problems of adverse selection and moral hazard, allowing firms to obtain loans. With a low net worth, firms can no longer obtain financing because lenders cannot overcome the difficulty of asymmetric information.

The connection among net worth, information, and the availability of credit to borrowers helps to explain the dynamics of the business cycle. Think about what happens at the start of a recession. The value of a firm (as measured by the present value of its expected future sales) falls, compounding lenders' information problems. Lenders, suddenly more concerned about a borrower's creditworthiness, become more reluctant to make loans. The availability of investment funds falls, pushing the economy further into recession.

---

been required to release to the public any information they provide to professional stock analysts.[3]

As we learned in 2001 and 2002, however, these requirements can go only so far in assuring that investors are well informed. Despite government regulations designed to protect investors, Enron, WorldCom, Global Crossing, and numerous other companies managed to distort the profits and debt levels published in their financial statements. With the help of some unethical accountants, company executives found a broad range of ways to manipulate the statements to disguise their firms' true financial condition. While accounting practices have changed since then and financial statements may now convey more information than they once did, everyone remains on guard. Information problems persist.

What about the private collection and sale of information? You might think that this would provide investors with what they need to solve the adverse selection problem, but unfortunately it doesn't work. While it is in everyone's interest to produce credible proof of the quality of a company's activities, such information doesn't really exist. In a limited sense there is private information collected and sold to investors. Various research services like Moody's, Value Line, and Dun and Bradstreet collect information directly from firms and produce evaluations.

These reports are not cheap. For example, Value Line charges $600 a year for its weekly publication. To be credible, the companies examined can't pay for the research themselves, so investors have to. And while some individuals might be willing to pay, in the end they don't have to and so they won't. Private information services

---

[3]Some people were concerned that Regulation FD, for "fair disclosure," might have the perverse effect of causing firms to make less information public. Fortunately, evidence shows that public corporations are now providing more information to both professional stock analysts and individual investors. Today, virtually all company conference calls—the mechanism used to disseminate information about a firm's financial performance—are open to individual investors.

face what is called a free-rider problem. A **free rider** is someone who doesn't pay the cost to get the benefit of a good or service, and free riding on stock-market analysis is easy to do. Even though these publications are expensive, public libraries subscribe to some of them. Reporters for *The Wall Street Journal* and other periodicals read them and write stories publicizing crucial information. And individual investors can simply follow the lead of people they know who subscribe to the publications. Of course, all these practices reduce the ability of the producers of private information to actually profit from their hard work.

**Collateral and Net Worth**   While government-required disclosure and private information collection are crucial, they haven't solved all the information problems that plague investors and the firms they invest in. Fortunately, other solutions exist. One is to make sure that lenders are compensated even if borrowers default. If a loan is insured in some way, then the borrower isn't a bad credit risk.

There are two mechanisms for ensuring that a borrower is likely to repay a lender: collateral and net worth. Recall from Chapter 3 that **collateral** is something of value pledged by a borrower to the lender in the event of the borrower's default. Collateral is said to *back* or *secure* a loan. Houses serve as collateral for mortgages; cars, as collateral for car loans. If the borrower fails to keep up with the mortgage or car payments, the lender will take possession of the house or car and sell it to recover the borrowed funds. In circumstances like these, adverse selection is less of a concern; that's why collateral is so prevalent in loan agreements. Loans that are made without collateral—**unsecured loans**, like credit card debt—generally involve very high interest rates. Adverse selection is the reason. (See Your Financial World: Your First Credit Card on page 264.)

**Net worth** is the owner's stake in a firm, the value of the firm's assets minus the value of its liabilities. Under many circumstances, net worth serves the same purpose as collateral. If a firm defaults on a loan, the lender can make a claim against the firm's net worth. Consider what would happen if a firm with a high net worth borrowed to undertake a project that turned out to be unsuccessful. If the firm had no net worth, the lender would be out of luck. Instead, the firm's owners can use their net worth to repay the lender.

The same is true of a home mortgage. A mortgage is much easier and cheaper to get when a homebuyer makes a substantial down payment. For the lender, the risk is that the price of the home will fall, in which case its value will not be sufficient to fully compensate the lender in the event of a default. But with a large down payment, the homeowner has a substantial stake in the house, so even if the price falls, the mortgage can likely be repaid even if the borrower defaults. From the perspective of the mortgage lender, the homeowner's equity serves exactly the same function as net worth in a business loan.

The importance of net worth in reducing adverse selection is the reason owners of new businesses have so much difficulty borrowing money. If you want to start a bakery, for example, you will need financing to buy equipment and cover the rent and payroll for the first few months. Such seed money is very hard to get. Most small business owners must put up their homes and other property as collateral for their business loans. Only after they have managed to establish a successful business, and have built up some net worth in it can they borrow without pledging their personal property.

## Moral Hazard: Problem and Solutions

The phrase *moral hazard* originated when economists who were studying insurance noted that an insurance policy changes the behavior of the person who is insured.

Examples are everywhere. A fire insurance policy written for more than the value of the property might induce the owner to arson; a generous automobile insurance policy might encourage reckless driving. Employment arrangements suffer from moral hazard, too. How can your boss be sure you are working as hard as you can if you'll get your paycheck at the end of the week whether you do or not? Moral hazard arises when we cannot observe people's actions and so cannot judge whether a poor outcome was intentional or just a result of bad luck.

Thus, a lender's or investor's information problems do not end with adverse selection. A second information asymmetry arises because the borrower knows more than the lender about the way borrowed funds will be used and the effort that will go into a project. Moral hazard plagues both equity

"It's been moved and seconded that we fly the company plane to Zurich, split the bank accounts, and go our merry ways."

SOURCE: © Henry Martin/The New Yorker Collection/ www.cartoonbank.com.

and bond financing, making it difficult for all but the biggest, best known companies to issue either stocks or bonds successfully. Let's look at each type of financing and examine the ways people have tried to solve the problem of moral hazard.

## Moral Hazard in Equity Financing

If you buy a stock, how do you know the company that issued it will use the funds you have invested in the way that is best for you? The answer is that it almost surely will not. You have given your funds to managers, who will tend to run the company in the way most advantageous to them. The separation of your ownership from their control creates what is called a *principal–agent problem*, which can be more than a little costly to stockholders. Witness the luxurious offices, corporate jets, limousines, and artwork that executives surround themselves with, not to mention the millions of dollars in salary they pay themselves. Managers gain all these personal benefits at the expense of stockholders.

A simple example will illustrate this point. Let's say that your cousin Ina, who is a whiz at writing software, has an idea for a program to speed up wireless Internet access. Together, the two of you estimate she needs $10,000 to write the program and sell it to an interested buyer. But Ina has only $1,000 in savings, so you will have to contribute $9,000. Family etiquette dictates that once you've made the investment, you won't be able to monitor Ina's progress—to tell whether she is working hard or even if she is working at all. If everything goes well, you think you can sell the program to Microsoft for $100,000, which is ten times the initial investment. But Ina had better work quickly or someone else may make it to market first and Ina's program won't be worth nearly as much.

The difficulty in this arrangement is immediately apparent. If Ina works hard and all goes according to plan, she will get 10 percent of the $100,000 (that's $10,000) and you will get the rest, a whopping $90,000. But if Ina runs into programming problems or spends part of the time surfing instead of working, someone else may output the product first, reducing the value of Ina's software to $10,000. The problem is, Ina's decision to go surfing would cost her only $9,000, but it would cost you $81,000! And because you wouldn't be able to tell why the venture failed, you're unlikely to part with your $9,000 in the first place.

Moral hazard: How can you be sure that your investment isn't being used to buy one of these vacation homes in Tahiti?

## Solving the Moral Hazard Problem in Equity Financing

Solutions to the moral hazard problem in equity finance are hard to come by. Information on the quality of management can be useful, but only if owners have the power to fire managers—and that can be extremely difficult. Requiring managers to own a significant stake in their own firm is another possibility. If Ina comes up with the entire $10,000, then there is no separation between ownership and control and no question whether Ina will behave in the owner's interest—she is the owner. But people who have good ideas don't always have the resources to pursue them. Ina doesn't have the $10,000 she needs.

During the 1990s, a concerted attempt was made to align managers' interests with those of stockholders. Executives were given stock options that provided lucrative payoffs if a firm's stock price rose above a certain level. This approach worked until managers found ways to misrepresent their companies' profitability, driving up stock prices temporarily so they could cash in their options. Accounting methods have been reformed in an attempt to reduce such abuses, but at this writing, no one has devised a foolproof way of ensuring that managers will behave in the owners' interest instead of their own.

**Moral Hazard in Debt Finance**   When the managers of a company are the owners, the problem of moral hazard in equity financing disappears. This suggests that investors should prefer debt financing to equity financing. But debt financing has its problems, too. Imagine that instead of buying a 90 percent share in your cousin Ina's software venture, you lend her $9,000 at an 11 percent annual interest rate. The debt contract specifies that she will repay you $9,990 in one year's time. This arrangement dramatically changes Ina's incentives. Now, if she works hard, she gets $90,010, but if she goes surfing, she still has to repay the $9,990, leaving her nothing at the end of the year. Surely this solves your problem.

Debt does go a long way toward eliminating the moral hazard problem inherent in equity finance, but it doesn't finish the job. Because debt contracts allow owners to keep all the profits in excess of the loan payments, they encourage risk taking. Suppose Ina decides to use some or all of the $10,000 to buy lottery tickets. That's an extremely risky thing to do. The problem is, if her lottery number comes up, she gets the winnings, but if she loses, you pay the cost. That's not a very desirable outcome for you, the lender. While in the real world the danger isn't quite that extreme, the problem still exists. Lenders need to find ways to make sure borrowers don't take too many risks. Unfortunately, borrowers' limited liability has the same effect that an insurance policy has on the insured. People with risky projects are attracted to debt finance because they get the full benefit of the upside, while the downside is limited to their collateral, if any.

**Solving the Moral Hazard Problem in Debt Finance**   To some degree, a good legal contract can solve the moral hazard problem that is inherent in debt finance. Bonds and loans often carry *restrictive covenants* that limit the amount of risk a borrower can assume. For example, a covenant may restrict the nature of the goods or services the borrower can purchase. It may require the firm to maintain a certain level of net worth, a minimum balance in a bank account, or a minimum credit rating. Home mortgages often come with restrictive covenants requiring the homeowners to purchase fire insurance or to make monthly deposits toward payment of their property

## LESSONS FROM THE CRISIS
### INFORMATION ASYMMETRY AND SECURITIZATION

This chapter highlights the importance of *screening* credit risks to limit adverse selection and of *monitoring* the recipients of funds to limit moral hazard. It also warns that *free riding* can diminish screening and monitoring. A key source of the financial crisis of 2007-2009 was insufficient screening and monitoring in the securitization of mortgages (see Chapter 6, Applying the Concept: Securitization).

Mortgage securitization problems started with the initial mortgage lenders—the *originators*—who eased standards and reduced screening to increase the volume of lending and the short-term profitability of their businesses. The result was many risky mortgages: When housing prices began to fall in 2006, defaults soared.

At the next stage of securitization, the firms that assembled these mortgages into securities for sale—the *distributors*—did little to forestall the decline of lending standards by originators. Had they wished to, they could have required that the originators demonstrate a high level of net worth and invest it in the mortgages that they sold.

When lending standards decline, securitization becomes like a game of "hot potato." Players in the game try to pass risky loans—the hot potato—along to the next player as quickly as they can, while it's still possible. The game ends when defaults soar, leaving someone with the loss.

Rating agencies might have halted the game early. Instead, they awarded their top ratings to a large share of mortgage-backed securities, severely underestimating the riskiness of the loans. In retrospect, we can now see that the agencies had little incentive to expend the resources necessary to adequately screen the underlying loans or the lenders.

Finally, many investors (and government officials responsible for overseeing intermediaries) assumed they could rely on other people—they were free riders. Rather than undertake their own costly screening efforts, they assumed the assessment of the rating agencies was accurate.

Implicitly, the participants in the process acted as if the ultimate collateral—the value of houses—would always be adequate to contain the damage from adverse selection. Had housing prices risen indefinitely, as many appeared to assume they would, the collateral would have protected investors against any damage. But, when housing prices and the value of the collateral started to plunge, the effects of adverse selection threatened the financial system as a whole.

taxes. (Failure to pay property taxes can lead the government to seize the borrower's house, complicating the mortgage company's attempt to recover its principal.)

Table 11.3 summarizes this section's discussion of how financial relationships are affected by information problems, together with a list of the various solutions used to address the problems information costs create.

### Table 11.3   The Negative Consequences of Information Costs

1. Adverse selection. Lenders can't distinguish good from bad credit risks, which discourages transactions from taking place.

   *Solutions include*

   Government-required information disclosure

   Private collection of information

   Pledging of collateral to insure lenders against the borrower's default

   Requiring borrowers to invest substantial resources of their own

2. Moral hazard. Lenders can't tell whether borrowers will do what they claim they will do with the borrowed resources; borrowers may take too many risks.

   *Solutions include*

   Requiring managers to report to owners

   Requiring managers to invest substantial resources of their own

   Covenants that restrict what borrowers can do with borrowed funds

# Financial Intermediaries and Information Costs

The problems of adverse selection and moral hazard make direct finance expensive and difficult to get. These drawbacks lead us immediately to indirect finance and the role of financial institutions. Much of the information that financial intermediaries collect is used to reduce information costs and minimize the effects of adverse selection and moral hazard. To reduce the potential costs of adverse selection, intermediaries screen loan applicants. To minimize moral hazard, they monitor borrowers. And when borrowers fail to live up to their contracts with lenders, financial intermediaries penalize them by enforcing the contracts. Let's look more closely at how financial firms screen and monitor borrowers to reduce information costs. And then we will conclude with a quick look at how firms finance growth and investment.

## Screening and Certifying to Reduce Adverse Selection

To get a loan, whether from a bank, a mortgage company, or a finance company, you must fill out an application. As part of the process, you will be asked to supply your Social Security number. The lender uses the number to identify you to a company that collects and analyzes credit information, summarizing it for potential lenders in a credit score.

Your personal credit score (described in Chapter 7 in Your Financial World: Your Credit Rating) tells a lender how likely you are to repay a loan. It is analogous to eBay's feedback forum rating or to an expert appraiser's certification of the authenticity and condition of an original painting. The credit rating company *screens* you and then *certifies* your credit rating. If you are a good credit risk with a high credit score, you are more likely than others to get a loan at a relatively low interest rate. Note that the company that collects your credit information and produces your credit score charges a fee each time someone wants to see it. This overcomes the free-rider problem.

Banks can collect information on a borrower that goes beyond what a loan application or credit report contains. By noting the pattern of deposits and withdrawals from your account, as well as your use of your debit card if you have one, they can learn more about you than you might like. Banks monitor both their individual and their business customers in this way. Again, the information they collect is easy to protect and use. The special information banks have puts them in an almost unique position to *screen* customers and reduce the costs of adverse selection. This expertise helps to explain another phenomenon, the fact that most small and medium-size businesses depend on banks for their financing.

Financial intermediaries' superior ability to screen and certify borrowers extends beyond loan making to the issuance of bonds and equity. Underwriters—large investment banks, like Goldman Sachs, JPMorgan Chase, and Morgan Stanley—screen and certify firms seeking to raise

In the financial world, Goldman Sachs, JPMorgan Chase, and Morgan Stanley have as much brand recognition as Coke does in the soft drink world.

funds directly in the financial markets. Without certification by one of these firms, companies would find it difficult to raise funds. Investment banks go to great lengths to market their expertise as underwriters; they want people to recognize their names the world over, just as everyone recognizes Coca-Cola. A can of Coke, the best-selling soft drink in the world, is instantly recognizable, whether the fine print is in English, Chinese, Arabic, or Swedish. Financial institutions have applied this concept, which marketing people call branding, to their certification of financial products. If JPMorgan Chase, a well-known commercial and investment bank, is willing to sell a bond or stock, the brand name suggests that it is a high-quality investment.

## Monitoring to Reduce Moral Hazard

If someone weren't watching over your shoulder, you might take the money you borrowed for a business project and fly off to Tahiti. To address the risk that sellers might take the money and run, eBay developed buyers' insurance. In the financial world, intermediaries insure against this type of moral hazard by monitoring both the firms that issue bonds and those that issue stocks.

Car dealers provide an interesting example of how this process works. Dealers have to finance all those shiny new cars that sit on the lot, waiting for buyers to show up. One way to do this is with a bank loan that is collateralized by the cars themselves. But the bank doesn't completely trust the dealer to use the loan proceeds properly. Every so often, the bank manager will send an associate to count the number of cars on the lot. The count tells the manager whether the dealer is using the borrowed funds properly. In monitoring the dealer this way, the bank is enforcing the restrictive covenants contained in the loan contract. Because banks specialize in this type of monitoring, they can do it more cheaply than individual borrowers and lenders.

Many financial intermediaries (other than banks) hold significant numbers of shares in individual firms. When they do, they find ways to monitor the companies' activities. For example, the California Public Employee Retirement System (CalPERS) manages around $200 billion in assets, the income from which is used to pay retired employees' pensions. About 1.1 million "members" of CalPERS depend on the fund's managers to carefully monitor its investments. Before buying a company's stock, CalPERS' managers do a significant amount of research on the firm; once they have purchased the shares, they monitor the firm's activities very closely. In some cases, they place a representative on the company's board of directors to monitor and protect CalPERS' investment firsthand.

In the case of some new companies, a financial intermediary called a *venture capital firm* does the monitoring. Venture capital firms specialize in investing in risky new *ventures* in return for a stake in the ownership and a share of the profits. To guard against moral hazard and ensure that the new company has the best possible chance of success, the venture capitalist keeps a close watch on the managers' actions.

Finally, the threat of a takeover helps to persuade managers to act in the interest of the stock- and bondholders. If managers don't do a good job of watching out for shareholders' interests, another company can buy the firm and replace them. In the 1980s, some firms specialized in such tactics. When the new owners put their own people in charge of the firm, they eliminate the moral hazard problem.

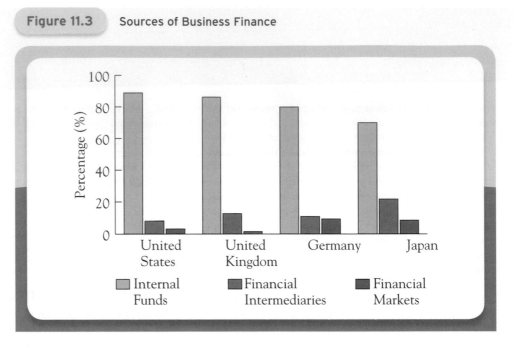

**Figure 11.3** Sources of Business Finance

SOURCE: Data are averages for 1970 to 1994, computed from Table 1 of Jenny Corbett and Tim Jenkinson, "How is Investment Financed?" *The Manchester School Supplement*, 1997, pp. 69–93. Used with permission.

## Terms

adverse selection, 267

asymmetric information, 267

collateral, 272

deflation, 271

free rider, 272

moral hazard, 267

net worth, 272

unsecured loan, 272

## Chapter Lessons

1. Financial intermediaries specialize in reducing costs by
   a. Pooling the resources of small savers and lending them to large borrowers.
   b. Providing safekeeping, accounting services, and access to the payments system.
   c. Providing liquidity services.
   d. Providing the ability to diversify small investments.
   e. Providing information services.
2. For potential lenders, investigating borrowers' trustworthiness is costly. This problem, known as asymmetric information, occurs both before and after a transaction.
   a. Before a transaction, the least creditworthy borrowers are the ones most likely to apply for funds. This problem is known as adverse selection.
   b. Lenders and investors can reduce adverse selection by
      i. Collecting and disclosing information on borrowers.
      ii. Requiring borrowers to post collateral and show sufficient net worth.

c. After a transaction, a borrower may not use the borrowed funds as productively as possible. This problem is known as moral hazard.

    i. In equity markets, moral hazard exists when the managers' interests diverge from the owners' interests.

    ii. Finding solutions to the moral hazard problem in equity financing is difficult.

    iii. In debt markets, moral hazard exists because borrowers have limited liability. They get the benefits when a risky bet pays off, but they don't suffer a loss when it doesn't.

    iv. The fact that debt financing gives managers/borrowers an incentive to take too many risks gives rise to restrictive covenants, which require borrowers to use funds in specific ways.

3. Financial intermediaries can manage the problems of adverse selection and moral hazard.

    a. They can reduce adverse selection by collecting information on borrowers and screening them to check their creditworthiness.

    b. They can reduce moral hazard by monitoring what borrowers are doing with borrowed funds.

    c. In the end, the vast majority of firms' finance comes from internal sources, suggesting that information problems are too big for even financial intermediaries to solve.

# Conceptual Problems

1. Describe the problem of asymmetric information that an employer faces in hiring a new employee. What solutions can you think of? Does the problem persist after the person has been hired? If so, how and what can be done about it? Is the problem more or less severe for employees on a fixed salary? Why or why not?

2. In some cities, newspapers publish a weekly list of restaurants that have been cited for health code violations by local health inspectors. What information problem is this feature designed to solve, and how?

3. What problem associated with asymmetric information was central to Bernard Madoff's success in cheating so many investors for so long?

4. Financial intermediation is not confined to bank lending but is also carried out by nonbank firms such as mutual fund companies. How do mutual funds help overcome information problems in financial markets?

5. In some countries it is very difficult for shareholders to fire managers when they do a poor job. What type of financing would you expect to find in those countries?

6. Define the term *economies of scale* and explain how a financial intermediary can take advantage of such economies.

7. The Internet can have a significant influence on asymmetric information problems.

    a. How can the Internet help to solve information problems?

    b. Can the Internet compound some information problems?

    c. On which problem would the Internet have a greater impact, adverse selection or moral hazard?

8. The financial sector is heavily regulated. Explain how government regulations help to solve information problems, increasing the effectiveness of financial markets and institutions.

9. One of the solutions to the adverse selection problem associated with asymmetric information is the pledging of collateral. Why did this solution not work adequately to mitigate the mortgage securitization problems associated with the financial crisis of 2007–2009?

10.* Deflation causes the value of a borrower's collateral to drop. Define deflation and explain how it reduces the value of a borrower's collateral. What is the effect on the information problems a borrower faces?

11. In 2002 the trustworthiness of corporate financial reporting was called into question when a number of companies corrected their financial statements for past years. What impact did their action have on the financial markets?

## Analytical Problems

12.* Your parents give you $2,000 as a graduation gift and you decide to invest the money in the stock market. If you are risk averse, should you purchase some stock in a few different companies through a Web site with low transaction fees or put the entire $2,000 into a mutual fund? Explain your answer.

13. Suppose a new Web site was launched providing up-to-date, credible information on all firms wishing to issue bonds. What would you expect to happen to the overall level of interest rates in the bond market?

14. Suppose two types of firms wish to borrow in the bond market. Firms of type A are in good financial health and are relatively low risk. The appropriate premium over the risk-free rate of lending to these firms is 2 percent. Firms of type B are in poor financial health and are relatively high risk. The appropriate premium over the risk-free rate of lending to these firms is 6 percent. As an investor, you have no other information about these firms except that type A and type B firms exist in equal numbers.
   a. At what interest rate would you be willing to lend if the risk-free rate were 5 percent?
   b. Would this market function well? What type of asymmetric information problem does this example illustrate?

15. Consider again the low-risk type A firm described in question 14. If you were the financial advisor to such a firm, what suggestions would you make to the firm's management about obtaining borrowed funds?

16. Consider a small company run by a manager who is also the owner. If this company borrows funds, why might a moral hazard problem still exist?

17.* The island of Utopia has a very unusual economy. Everyone on Utopia knows everyone else and knows all about the firms they own and operate. The financial system is well developed on Utopia. Everything else being equal, how would you expect the mix on Utopia between internal finance (where companies use their

*Indicates more difficult problems

own funds such as retained earnings) and external funding (where companies obtain funds through financial markets) to compare with other countries? What role would financial intermediaries play in this economy?

18. You and a friend visit the headquarters of a company and are awestruck by the expensive artwork and designer furniture that grace every office. Your friend is very impressed and encourages you to consider buying stock in the company, arguing that it must be really successful to afford such elegant surroundings. Would you agree with your friend's assessment? What further information (other than the usual financial data) would you obtain before making an investment decision?

19. Under what circumstances, if any, would you be willing to participate as a lender in a peer-to-peer lending arrangement?

# Chapter 12

## Depository Institutions: Banks and Bank Management

Banks are the most visible financial intermediaries in the economy. Most of us use the word *bank* to describe what people in the financial world call **depository institutions**. These are the financial institutions that accept deposits from savers and make loans to borrowers. What distinguishes depository institutions from **nondepository institutions** is their primary source of funds—that is, the liability side of their balance sheets. Depository institutions include commercial banks, savings and loans, and credit unions—the financial intermediaries most of us encounter in the course of our day-to-day lives.

Banking is a business. Actually, it's a combination of businesses designed to deliver the services discussed in Chapter 11. One business provides the accounting and record-keeping services that track the balances in your accounts. Another grants you access to the payments system, allowing you to convert your account balances into cash or transfer them to someone else. Yet a third business pools the savings of many small depositors and uses them to make large loans to trustworthy borrowers. A fourth business offers customers diversification services, buying and selling financial instruments in the financial markets in an effort to make a profit. Banks trade in the financial markets not just as a service to their customers but in an effort to earn a profit for their owners as well.

The intent of banks, of course, is to profit from each of these lines of business. Our objective in this chapter is to see how they do it. Not all banks make a profit. While some banks are extremely large, with hundreds of billions of dollars in loans and securities on their balance sheets, their access to funds is no guarantee of profitability. The risk that banks may fail is a problem not just for their owners and managers but for the rest of us, too. In 2009, 140 U.S. banks failed outright, and others were pushed into mergers, reflecting the most severe financial crisis since the 1930s.

We have emphasized repeatedly that financial and economic development go hand in hand. An economy that lacks the financial institutions to effectively channel resources from savers to investors is much less likely to thrive. This statement applies regardless of whether a country is rich or poor. The United States and Japan provide a striking example. By virtually any standard, both countries are well off. Yet during the 1990s, U.S. banks made substantial profits, while Japanese banks suffered prodigious losses. At the same time, Japan's economy grew at a rate of just over 1 percent, while the U.S. economy grew at a rate well over 3 percent. The financial problems of Japanese banks played an important role in Japan's poor economic performance. Banks are important; when they are poorly managed, we all suffer. Now that U.S. banks have been weakened by the financial crisis of 2007–2009, the prospects for the U.S. economy are dimmer, too, but not to the same extent as what happened in Japan.

In this chapter, we will examine the business of banking. We will see where depository institutions get their funds and what they do with them. That is, we will study the sources of banks' liabilities and learn how they manage their assets. And because banking is a risky business, we will examine the sources of risk that bankers face, as well as how those risks can be managed.

# The Balance Sheet of Commercial Banks

To focus our discussion of depository institutions, we will concentrate on what are called *commercial banks*. These institutions were established to provide banking services to businesses, allowing them to deposit funds safely and borrow them when necessary. Today, many commercial banks offer accounts and loans to individuals as well. To understand the business of commercial banking, we'll start by examining the commercial bank's balance sheet. Recall that a balance sheet is a list of a household or firm's assets and liabilities: the sources of its funds (liabilities) and the uses to which those funds are put (assets). A bank's balance sheet says that

$$\text{Total bank assets} = \text{Total bank liabilities} + \text{Bank capital} \qquad (1)$$

Banks obtain their funds from individual depositors and businesses, as well as by borrowing from other financial institutions and through the financial markets. They use these funds to make loans, purchase marketable securities, and hold cash. The difference between a bank's assets and liabilities is the bank's capital, or *net worth*—the value of the bank to its owners. The bank's profits come both from service fees and from the difference between what the bank pays for its liabilities and the return it receives on its assets (a topic we'll return to later).

Table 12.1 shows a consolidated balance sheet for all the commercial banks in the United States in January 2010. It reports the sum of all the items on all the balance sheets of the 6,800 or so commercial banks that existed in the United States at the time. The government collects these statistics in the course of supervising and regulating the financial system, to ensure bank safety and soundness. The numbers in the table are also related to the measures of money discussed in Chapter 2. Recall that the monetary aggregate M2 includes deposits, which are liabilities of the banking system.

## Assets: Uses of Funds

Let's start with the asset side of the balance sheet—what banks do with the funds they raise. Table 12.1 shows that assets are divided into four broad categories: cash, securities, loans, and all other assets. Roughly 20 percent of assets, or $2.3 trillion, is held in the form of securities; 57 percent ($6.7 trillion), in the form of loans; and the remaining 23 percent in the form of cash and "*other assets*." The last category includes mostly buildings and equipment, as well as collateral repossessed from borrowers who defaulted. In looking at consolidated figures like the ones in Table 12.1, we can get some sense of their scale by comparing them to *nominal GDP*. In the winter of 2010, U.S. nominal GDP was roughly $14.5 trillion, so total bank assets were equivalent to about 80 percent of one year's GDP.

**Cash Items**   Cash assets are of three types. The first and most important is **reserves**. Banks hold reserves because regulations require it and because prudent business practice dictates it. Reserves include the cash in the bank's vault (and the currency in its ATM machines), called **vault cash**, as well as the bank's deposits at the Federal Reserve System. Cash is the most liquid of the bank's assets; the bank holds it to meet customers' withdrawal requests.

Cash items also include what are called *cash items in process of collection*. When you deposit your paycheck into your checking account, several days may pass before your bank can collect the funds from your employer's bank. In the meantime, the uncollected funds are considered your bank's asset, since the bank is expecting to receive them.

| Table 12.1 | Balance Sheet of U.S. Commercial Banks, January 2010 |

**Assets** in billions of dollars (numbers with % sign are percentages of total assets)

| | | | | |
|---|---|---|---|---|
| Cash items | | | 1246.7 | 10.6% |
| Securities* | | | 2336.8 | 19.9% |
| U.S. government and agency | 1421.2 | 12.1% | | |
| Other securities | 915.5 | 7.8% | | |
| Loans | | | 6693.8 | 57.1% |
| Commercial and industrial | 1320.1 | 11.3% | | |
| Real estate (including mortgage) | 3794.3 | 32.4% | | |
| Consumer | 817.7 | 7.0% | | |
| Interbank | 212.4 | 1.8% | | |
| Other | 761.6 | 6.5% | | |
| Other assets | | | 1439.5 | 12.3% |
| **Total Commercial Bank Assets** | | | **11716.8** | |

**Liabilities** in billions of dollars (numbers with % sign are percentages of total liabilities)

| | | | | |
|---|---|---|---|---|
| Deposits | | | 7716.1 | 74.0% |
| Large time deposits | 1886.2 | 18.1% | | |
| Borrowings | | | 1901.6 | 18.2% |
| From banks in the U.S. | 256.3 | 2.5% | | |
| From others | 1645.4 | 15.8% | | |
| Other liabilities | | | 807.8 | 7.7% |
| **Total Commercial Bank Liabilities** | | | **10425.5** | |
| **Bank Assets − Bank Liabilities = Bank Capital** | | | **1291.3** | |

*Securities include mortgage-backed securities worth $1,195.3 billion, equivalent to 10.2% of assets.

SOURCE: *Data are for the week ending January 13, 2010, seasonally adjusted, from Board of Governors of the Federal Reserve System statistical release H.8. "Assets and Liabilities of Commercial Banks in the United States," available at www.federalreserve.gov/ releases/h8/current.*

Finally, cash includes the balances of the accounts that banks hold at other banks. In the same way that individuals have checking accounts at the local bank, small banks have deposit accounts at large banks, and those accounts are classified as cash. Over the years, the practice of holding such accounts has declined, so the total quantity of these so-called *correspondent bank* deposits has shrunk.

In January 2010, banks held more than 10 percent of their assets in cash (see Table 12.1). Up to the financial crisis of 2007–2009, that share was much smaller (in early 2007, it was about 3 percent; see Figure 12.1). Banks usually try to minimize their cash holdings because they typically earn less interest than loans or securities. However, the crisis forced them to change their strategy: A heightened possibility of bank runs, credit line takedowns, and borrower defaults prompted them to scramble for liquidity, and as market interest rates fell, the opportunity cost of holding cash plummeted.

**Securities** The second largest component of bank assets is marketable securities. While banks in many countries can hold stock, U.S. banks cannot, so this category of

**Figure 12.1**   U.S. Commercial Bank Assets, 1973-2009

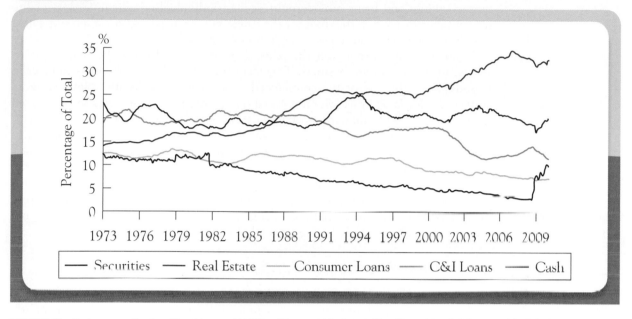

SOURCE: *Monthly data, seasonally adjusted from "Assets and Liabilities of Commercial Banks in the United States," Board of Governors of the Federal Reserve System Statistical Release H.8.*

assets includes only bonds. Banks' bond holdings are split between U.S. government and agency securities, which account for 12.1 percent of their assets, and other securities (including state and local government bonds), which account for an additional 7.8 percent.[1] Note that about half of all the securities are mortgage-backed (10.2 percent of assets). Nevertheless, a sizable proportion of the securities held by banks are very liquid. They can be sold quickly if the bank needs cash, which makes them a good backup for the bank's cash balances. For this reason securities are sometimes referred to as *secondary reserves*.

Figure 12.1 shows the trends in the composition of bank assets over the past four decades. Focusing on the line representing securities, we can see that the share of securities in bank assets has varied around 20 percent throughout the period.

**Loans**   Loans are the primary asset of modern commercial banks, accounting for well over one-half of assets. We can divide loans into five broad categories: business loans, called commercial and industrial (C&I) loans; real estate loans, including both home and commercial mortgages as well as home equity loans; consumer loans, like auto loans and credit card loans; interbank loans (loans made from one bank to another); and other types, including loans for the purchase of other securities. These types of loans vary considerably in their liquidity. Some, like home mortgages and auto loans, usually can be securitized and resold. (We discussed this process in Chapter 3, in connection with asset-backed securities.) Others, like small business loans, may be nearly impossible to resell.

---

[1] While there is nothing to prevent banks from holding corporate bonds, regulatory rules make the practice expensive. In Chapter 14, we will learn that banks are required to hold capital based on the composition of their balance sheets. The amount of capital required to extend a loan to a corporation is the same as the amount required to purchase a corporate bond. But since interest rates banks can charge on loans are generally higher than interest rates on bonds, there is no reason to purchase a bond.

The primary difference among various kinds of depository institutions is in the composition of their loan portfolios. Commercial banks make loans primarily to businesses; savings and loans provide mortgages to individuals; credit unions specialize in consumer loans. See the Tools of the Trade box on page 292 for a more detailed description of the various types of depository institutions.

Figure 12.1 shows that over the years, commercial banks have become more involved in the real estate business. This change happened gradually for a number of reasons. First, the rise of the commercial paper market made direct finance more convenient for large firms, which reduced the quantity of commercial and industrial loans demanded. (Commercial paper is described in Chapter 7.) Second, the creation of mortgage-backed securities meant that banks could sell the mortgage loans they had made. This innovation reduced the risk associated with an illiquid asset, encouraging banks to move into the business of home lending. But, as we saw earlier, risky mortgage-backed securities (MBS) played a critical role in the financial crisis of 2007–2009 (see Chapter 11, Lessons from the Crisis: Information Asymmetry and Securitization). Note, also, that real estate loans do not include MBS, which recently accounted for about one-half of securities held (see Table 12.1).

## Liabilities: Sources of Funds

To finance their operations, banks need funds. They get them from savers and from borrowing in the financial markets. To entice individuals and businesses to place their funds in the bank, institutions offer a range of deposit accounts that provide safekeeping and accounting services, access to the payments system, liquidity, and diversification of risk (see Chapter 11), as well as interest payments on the balance. There are two types of deposit accounts, transaction and nontransaction accounts. Transaction accounts are known as checkable deposits. As of December 2009, checkable deposits totaled $814 billion, or only about 10 percent of total deposits in the commercial banking system.

**Checkable Deposits**   Banks offer customers a variety of options that fall into the category of checking accounts, including NOW, super-NOW, and insured market rate accounts. A typical bank will offer half a dozen or more of these, each with slightly different characteristics. In addition to the names created by banks' marketing departments, economists use various other terms in speaking of checkable deposits. For example, some economists call them "sight deposits," since a depositor can show up to withdraw them when the bank is in sight.

Over the years, financial innovation has reduced the importance of checkable deposits in the day-to-day business of banking. As a share of total liabilities, checkable deposits plummeted from 40 percent in the 1970s to less than 10 percent in 2009. The reason for their decline is that checking accounts pay little or no interest; they are a low-cost source of funds for banks but a low-return investment for depositors. As interest rates rose through the 1970s and remained high into the 1990s, individuals and businesses realized the benefits of reducing the balances in their checking accounts and began to look for ways to earn higher interest rates. Banks obliged by offering innovative accounts whose balances could be shifted automatically when the customers' checking accounts ran low.[2] Thus, traditional deposit accounts are no longer an important source of bank funds.

[2]This is also related to a practice called *deposit sweeping,* in which banks take checking account balances and put them into savings deposits, thereby reducing the level of reserves they are required to hold. Over recent decades, deposit sweeping has lowered required reserves even as the monetary aggregates have risen markedly.

## YOUR FINANCIAL WORLD
### Choosing the Right Bank for You

Choosing the right bank takes some work. First, you should decide exactly why you need a bank and whether a particular bank will serve your needs conveniently and cheaply. Shop around for the best deal. Make sure the bank will pay a competitive interest rate on your deposit balance and you won't be paying for services you don't use. You may want to make sure the bank will give you immediate access to your deposits. The ability to reach someone either in person or on the phone during hours that are convenient for you is also important. And be sure the bank has a reputation for courteous, efficient service. Because service isn't cheap, ask what it will cost you. Will you have to pay a fee to see a teller in person? Will you have to pay a fee to cash a check? If you have friends with needs similar to yours, find out where they bank and ask whether they're happy with the cost and service.

The Internet has revolutionized banking. Traditional "bricks and mortar" banks now provide many of their services on the Internet. Using your computer, you can access your account, review and pay your bills, or transfer funds. In fact, when you decide to open a bank account, you may be tempted to give your business to an Internet bank—one without any local branches. If you do, be careful. Looking at your computer screen, you may not be able to tell where the Web site you are viewing is physically located. While many people think the irrelevance of physical location is a real benefit of the Internet, in making financial transactions, it presents a challenge. Unfortunately, U.S. laws and regulations may not protect transactions with institutions located outside the United States. Instead, the laws and regulations of a foreign bank's home country may apply. So if you choose an Internet bank, make sure that its operations are located in the United States. The easiest way to find out is to verify that the bank is a member of the *Federal Deposit Insurance Corporation (FDIC)*. You can check by going to www.fdic.gov and clicking on "Is My Bank Insured?" If a bank is listed there, it is a legitimate U.S. bank, and your deposits will be insured.

**Nontransaction Deposits**    In 2009, nontransaction deposits, including savings and time deposits, accounted for more than half of all commercial bank liabilities. Savings deposits, commonly known as *passbook savings* accounts, were popular for many decades, though they are less so today. Time deposits are *certificates of deposit* (CDs) with a fixed maturity. When you place your savings in a CD at your local bank, it is as if you are buying a bond issued by that bank. But unlike government or corporate bonds, there isn't much of a resale market for your small CD. So if you want to withdraw your funds before the CD matures, you must get them back from the bank. To discourage early withdrawals, banks charge a significant penalty.

Certificates of deposit come in two varieties: small and large. Small CDs are issued for $100,000 or less; *large certificates of deposit* exceed $100,000 in face value. Large CDs are negotiable, which means that they can be bought and sold in the financial markets, just like bonds and commercial paper. Because large CDs can be resold, they have become an important source of bank financing. When a bank needs funds, it can issue large CDs, in addition to commercial paper and more conventional bonds.

**Borrowings**    Borrowing is the second most important source of bank funds. Figure 12.2 shows that borrowing grew increasingly important over the past four decades, until the financial crisis of 2007–2009 triggered greater bank caution. Today, borrowings account for somewhat less than 20 percent of bank liabilities. Banks borrow in a number of ways. First, they can borrow from the Federal Reserve. We'll have much more to say about such **discount loans** in Part IV. For now, think of this source of funds as borrowing from the government. Banks rarely borrow in this way.

**Figure 12.2**  U.S. Commercial Bank Liabilities, 1979–2009

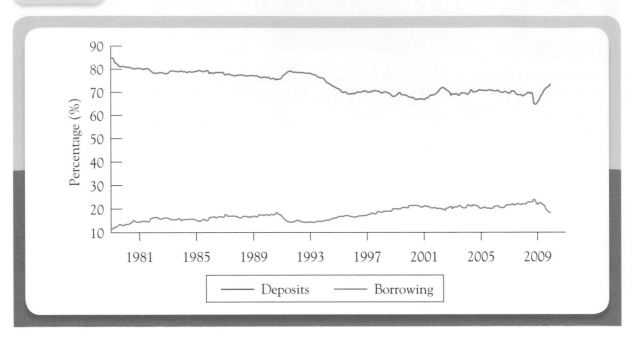

SOURCE: *Monthly data, seasonally adjusted from "Assets and Liabilities of Commercial Banks in the United States," Board of Governors of the Federal Reserve System Statistical Release H.8.*

More often, banks borrow from other banks. That is, banks with **excess reserves** will lend their surplus funds to banks that need them through an interbank market called the **federal funds market**. Loans made in the federal funds market are unsecured—they lack collateral—so the lending bank must trust the borrowing bank. Look back at the balance sheet in Table 12.1; you will see interbank loans listed as an asset and borrowings from banks in the United States listed as a liability.[3] Besides borrowing from U.S. banks in the federal funds market, commercial banks also borrow from foreign banks.

Finally, banks borrow using an instrument called a **repurchase agreement**, or **repo**, a short-term collateralized loan in which a security is exchanged for cash, with the agreement that the parties will reverse the transaction on a specific future date, as soon as the next day. For example, a bank that has a U.S. Treasury bill might need cash, while a pension fund might have cash that it doesn't need overnight. Through a repo, the bank would give the T-bill to the pension fund in exchange for cash, agreeing to buy it back—repurchase it—with interest the next day. In short, the bank gets an overnight loan and the pension fund gets some extra interest. The details are shown in Figure 12.3.

[3]An astute reader will notice that the amount of "Interbank loans" on the asset side of the balance sheet does not match the amount for "Borrowings from Banks in the U.S." on the liability side of the balance sheet. In fact, the two amounts differ by more than $40 billion. If the data in the table cover the entire banking system, shouldn't loans to banks (assets) equal borrowings from banks (liabilities)? There are two reasons why the amounts do not match. First, the data in the table are constructed from a survey that covers all large banks but only a minority of small banks. Large banks tend to be borrowers, while small banks tend to be lenders. The way in which the data are collected, then, distorts the results. Second, small banks may report their lending to large banks as deposits rather than as interbank loans. For both these reasons, the entry on the liability side of Table 12.1 is larger than the corresponding entry on the asset side.

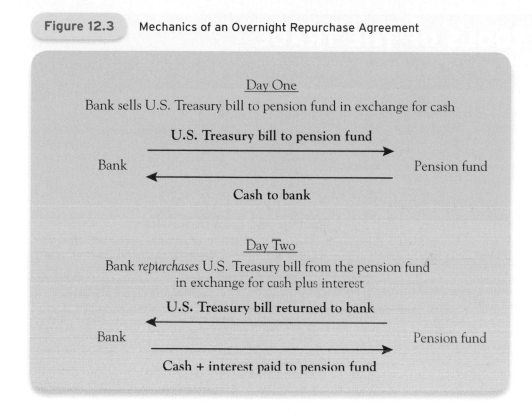

**Figure 12.3**    Mechanics of an Overnight Repurchase Agreement

<u>Day One</u>
Bank sells U.S. Treasury bill to pension fund in exchange for cash

**U.S. Treasury bill to pension fund**

Bank ─────────────────────────────────────▶ Pension fund

◀─────────────────────────────────────

**Cash to bank**

<u>Day Two</u>
Bank *repurchases* U.S. Treasury bill from the pension fund
in exchange for cash plus interest

**U.S. Treasury bill returned to bank**

Bank ◀───────────────────────────────────── Pension fund

─────────────────────────────────────▶

**Cash + interest paid to pension fund**

## Bank Capital and Profitability

Net worth equals assets minus liabilities, whether we are talking about an individual's net worth or a bank's. In the case of banks, however, net worth is referred to as **bank capital**, or *equity capital*. If the bank's owners sold all its assets (without taking a loss) and used the proceeds to repay all the liabilities, capital is what would be left. We can think of capital as the owners' stake in the bank.

Capital is the cushion banks have against a sudden drop in the value of their assets or an unexpected withdrawal of liabilities. It provides some insurance against insolvency (the inability to repay debts when a firm's liabilities exceed its assets). An important component of bank capital is **loan loss reserves**, an amount the bank sets aside to cover potential losses from defaulted loans. At some point a bank gives up hope that a loan will be repaid and the loan is *written off*, or erased from the bank's balance sheet. At that point the loan loss reserve is reduced by the amount of the loan that has defaulted.

Looking once again at the balance sheet in Table 12.1 (page 286), we can see that in January of 2010, bank capital in the U.S. commercial banking system totaled nearly $1.3 trillion. That nearly $1.3 trillion of capital was combined with $10.4 trillion worth of liabilities to purchase $11.7 trillion in assets. So the ratio of debt to equity in the U.S. banking system was about 8 to 1. That's a substantial amount of leverage, but it is nearly 25 percent below the average commercial bank leverage ratio that prevailed prior to the financial crisis of 2007–2009. As we saw in Chapter 3, Lessons from the Crisis: Leverage, the crisis compelled banks to reduce their leverage sharply. (Recall that the term *leverage* refers to the portion of an asset that is purchased using borrowed funds.)

# TOOLS OF THE TRADE
## A Catalog of Depository Institutions

*While the financial landscape is constantly shifting, it is safe to assume that depository institutions will be with us for some time. These are the financial intermediaries for whom deposits are the primary source of funds. There are three basic types of depository institution: commercial banks, savings institutions, and credit unions.*

## Commercial Banks

A commercial bank is an institution that accepts deposits and uses the proceeds to make consumer, commercial, and real estate loans. Originally established to meet the needs of businesses, many of these banks now serve individual customers as well. Commercial banks tend to specialize as community, regional and super-regional, or money center banks. As a result of mergers during the crisis of 2007–2009, roughly 40 percent of U.S. deposits are in four commercial banks: Bank of America, JPMorgan Chase, Wells Fargo, and Citigroup.

## Community Banks

Community banks are small banks—those with assets of less than $1 billion—that concentrate on serving consumers and small businesses. These are the banks that take deposits from people in the local area and lend them back to local businesses and consumers. Of the 8,000 banks and savings institutions in the United States at the end of 2009, 97 percent were community banks.

## Regional and Super-Regional Banks

Regional and super-regional banks are larger than community banks and much less local. Besides consumer and residential loans, these banks also make commercial and industrial loans. Regional banks obtain their funds through borrowing as well as from deposits. These banks can be very large. When the largest regional bank, Wachovia, faced a bank run in 2008, it was taken over by Wells Fargo.

## Money Center Banks

A few large banks—only five or six—do not rely primarily on deposit financing. These banks rely instead on borrowing for their funding. They stand at the center of the *money market*, the market for short-term debt. Citigroup and JPMorgan Chase are two examples. (Recall from Chapter 3 that money-market instruments are bonds with a maturity of less than 12 months.)

## Savings Institutions

Savings institutions are financial intermediaries that were established to serve households and individuals. They provide both mortgage and lending services and a place for households to deposit their savings. There are two types of savings institutions, S&Ls and savings banks.

## Savings and Loan Institutions

Savings and loan institutions (S&Ls) were established in the 1800s to help factory workers become homeowners. They accepted workers' savings deposits and used the funds to make loans to homebuyers, most of who were not served by traditional banks. These institutions traditionally specialized in taking short-term deposits and turning them into residential mortgages. The S&Ls that still exist today engage in a much broader range of financial activities.

## Savings Banks

Most savings banks are mutually owned. That is, the depositors are also the legal owners. These institutions specialize in residential mortgages that are funded by deposits. They are permitted to exist only in certain states. When the largest savings bank, Washington Mutual, failed during the crisis of 2007–2009, JPMorgan Chase acquired its deposits.

## Credit Unions

Credit unions are nonprofit depository institutions that are owned by people with a common bond—members of police associations, union members, and university students and employees. Credit unions specialize in making small consumer loans. They originated in the 19th century to meet the needs of people who could not borrow from traditional lenders. Before credit unions existed, many ordinary people had nowhere to turn when they faced unexpected home repairs or medical emergencies.

*Not all these depository institutions are likely to survive the financial innovations and economic upheaval of the coming decades. Commercial banks will likely remain with us, but savings institutions have already declined in importance and are at risk of disappearing altogether due to changes in the mortgage business. Whether credit unions remain viable will depend on their continuing ability to exploit their advantage in verifying members' creditworthiness.*

To put this ratio of 8 to 1 into perspective, we can compare it to the debt-to-equity ratio for nonfinancial businesses in the United States, which is only 1 to 1. Household leverage is much lower, less than ⅓ to 1.[4] Recall from Tools of the Trade in Chapter 5 that leverage increases both risk and the expected return. If you contribute half the purchase price of a house and borrow the other half, both your risk and your expected return double. If you contribute one-fifth of the purchase price and borrow the other four-fifths, your risk and expected return go up by a factor of 5 (see the Tools of the Trade box in Chapter 5). So if a bank borrows $8 for each $1 in capital, its risk and expected return increase a whopping 9 times! Banking, it seems, is a very risky business. As we will see in Chapter 14, one of the explanations for the relatively high degree of leverage in banking is the existence of government guarantees like deposit insurance, which allow banks to capture the benefits of risk taking without subjecting depositors to potential losses.

There are several basic measures of bank profitability. The first is called **return on assets (ROA)**. Return on assets equals a bank's net profit after taxes divided by the bank's total assets:

$$ROA = \frac{\text{Net profit after taxes}}{\text{Total bank assets}} \qquad (2)$$

ROA is an important measure of how efficiently a particular bank uses its assets. By looking at the different units' ROAs, for example, the manager of a large bank can also compare the performance of the bank's various lines of business. But for the bank's owners, return on assets is less important than the return on their own investment, which is leveraged at an average ratio of 9 to 1. (The leverage ratio equals total assets divided by bank capital.) The bank's return to its owners is measured by the **return on equity (ROE)**, which equals the bank's net profit after taxes divided by the bank's capital:

$$ROE = \frac{\text{Net profit after taxes}}{\text{Bank capital}} \qquad (3)$$

Not surprisingly, ROA and ROE are related to leverage. One measure of leverage is the ratio of bank assets to bank capital. Multiplying ROA by this ratio yields ROE:

$$ROA \times \frac{\text{Bank assets}}{\text{Bank capital}} = \frac{\text{Net profit after taxes}}{\text{Total bank assets}} \times \frac{\text{Bank assets}}{\text{Bank capital}} \qquad (4)$$

$$= \frac{\text{Net profit after taxes}}{\text{Bank capital}} = ROE$$

For a typical U.S. bank, prior to the financial crisis of 2007–2009, the return on assets was about 1.3 percent, while the return on equity was 10 to 12 times that high. For large banks, the return on equity tends to be higher than for small banks, which suggests greater leverage, a riskier mix of assets, or the existence of significant economies of scale in banking. The poor performance of many large banks in the crisis suggests that their higher returns at least partly reflected more leverage or a riskier asset mix.

[4]You can arrive at these figures yourself by looking at the *Flow of Funds Accounts of the United States*, which is computed by the Board of Governors of the Federal Reserve (see its Web site). The appropriate tables are L.100 for households and L.102 for nonfarm nonfinancial corporate business; both include assets, liabilities, and net worth for their parts of the U.S. economy.

## APPLYING THE CONCEPT
### GROWTH AND BANKING IN CHINA AND INDIA

China and India are experiencing phenomenal economic growth rates of 7 to 11 percent per year. As high as that is, some people think growth could be even higher if the banks in the two countries worked properly. Let's look to see why.

While the Chinese financial system is large overall, banks account for a disproportion share of intermediation there. In 2004, 75 percent of all China's capital—190 percent of GDP—was channeled through banks.* That's twice the amount in South Korea, relative to its GDP, and three times what goes through Chile's banking system. This heavy reliance on banks for financing is a sign of inadequate financial development. The solution is to encourage the development of debt and equity markets, with broad participation by small savers.

In addition to accounting for too large a proportion of China's financial system, Chinese banks are directing resources inefficiently. State-owned enterprises that account for 48 percent of China's GDP receive 73 percent of the credit. That is, banks are directing funds to government-favored firms. This fact should not be all that surprising given that the government implicitly backs loans made to the companies it owns. Improvement will require both that the government stop providing the guarantees (probably by selling the companies) and that banks learn to evaluate the creditworthiness of borrowers.

Turning to India, instead of attracting too many deposits, there banks attract too few. Overall, the Indian financial system is 1.4 times the country's GDP, half that in China, and banks attract deposits equal to only 60 percent of GDP. The problem is that the Indian people mistrust banks, holding more than half of their wealth in physical assets such as land, houses, cattle, and especially gold. Solving this problem requires finding a way to lure savers to make deposits in banks.

While private Indian firms have more access to bank financing than their Chinese counterparts, it could be better. First, Indian banks need to stop holding so many Indian government bonds—they are holding an amount equal to 46 percent of deposits. And second, the government has to stop directing banks to make at least 40 percent of loans to small borrowers in favored sectors. Reforms are needed to free banks to lend where the resources can be best used.

If Chinese and Indian banks are given the proper incentives to direct financial resources to their most economically efficient uses, it will enhance living standards in those two countries. Without a well-functioning financial system, growth will not be as high as it could be.

*These estimates, along with the information that follows, are from the McKinsey Global Institute, "Putting China's Capital to Work: The Value of Financial System Reform," May 2006; and Diana Farrell and Susan Lund, "Reforming India's Financial System," *The McKinsey Quarterly Report*, June 5, 2006.

Before continuing, it is important to introduce one more measure of bank profitability: net interest income. This measure is related to the fact that banks pay interest on their liabilities, creating interest expenses, and receive interest on their assets, creating interest income. Deposits and bank borrowing create interest expenses; securities and loans generate interest income. The difference between the two is the bank's *net interest income*.

Net interest income can also be expressed as a percentage of total assets to yield a quantity called **net interest margin**. This is the bank's **interest-rate spread**, which is the (weighted) average difference between the interest rate received on assets and the interest rate paid for liabilities. A bank's net interest margin is closely related to its return on assets. Just take the bank's fee income minus its operating costs, divide by total assets, add the result to the net interest margin, and you get its ROA. Roughly equivalent to a manufacturer or retailer's gross profits and gross profit margin, net interest income and net interest margin reveal a great deal about a bank's business.

Well-run banks have high net interest income and a high net interest margin. And since we would expect most of a bank's loans to be repaid, net interest margin tells us not just current profitability but future profitability as well; it is a forward-looking measure. If a bank's net interest margin is currently improving, its profitability is likely to improve in the future.

## Off-Balance-Sheet Activities

A financial firm's balance sheet provides only so much information. To generate fees, banks engage in numerous **off-balance-sheet activities**. Recall that banks exist to reduce

# YOUR FINANCIAL WORLD
## The Cost of Payday Loans

If you drive through the streets of most U.S. cities, you will eventually pass a store with a sign saying "Checks Cashed." These financial intermediaries provide loans to people who cannot borrow from mainstream financial institutions such as banks. In addition to their check-cashing business—they charge about 3 percent to cash a payroll or government check, more if the bearer can't produce acceptable identification—these firms offer small loans.

The most common type of loan these stores offer is a *payday loan*. To get one, you just walk into the store with an ID card, a utility or phone bill, a checkbook, and some pay stubs; you come out with cash. Why do you need all these documents? The utility bill proves where you live; the pay stubs establish that you are employed, how much you make, and when you are paid. You need the checkbook so you can write a check that the store will hold until your next payday, when it will send your check to the bank. With just these few requirements, the store will lend you up to $500 for the week or two weeks until you are paid.

The catch is that there is a fee, and it's huge. Payday lenders charge a fee equal to 15 percent of the loan's principal. So if you borrow $500, you will have to repay a minimum of $575. That's the size of the check you will need to write to get the loan. To understand what this arrangement can mean, suppose that you need to renew the loan on your next payday, so you don't want the lender to cash the check you gave him or her initially. To do this, you will have to pay the fee again. So you keep the loan for a year, paying $75 every two weeks to stay current. At the end of the year you will have paid $1,950 in "interest" (the lender calls it "fees") on a $500 loan. And you'll still owe the original $500!

Not surprisingly, at these interest rates, payday loans appeal only to people who can't get credit anywhere else. While data are hard to come by, it appears that well over half of payday borrowers fail to repay their loans, which explains the high fees. These loans, though legal, are for the truly desperate.*

*Laws are changing to prevent some of these practices. For example, in the fall of 2006 the representatives in the U.S. Congress noticed the impact of payday loans, especially on members of the armed forces. After a Pentagon report showed that the average military payday loan borrower ended up paying $834 on a $339 loan, lawmakers imposed a 36 percent annual interest-rate cap on payday loans to servicemembers and their spouses.

---

transactions costs and information costs as well as to transfer risks. When they perform these services, bankers expect to be compensated. Yet many of these activities do not appear as either assets or liabilities on the bank's balance sheet, even though they may represent an important part of a bank's profits.

For example, banks often provide trusted customers with lines of credit, which are similar to the credit limits on credit cards. The firm pays the bank a fee in return for the ability to borrow whenever necessary. When the agreement is signed, the bank receives the payment and the firm receives a *loan commitment*. However, not until a loan has actually been made—until the firm has *drawn down* the credit line—does the transaction appear on the bank's balance sheet.

In the meantime, the bank is compensated for reducing both transactions and information costs. Without the loan commitment, the firm would find credit difficult and potentially expensive to obtain on short notice (a transactions cost). And since the bank usually knows the firms to which it grants lines of credit, the cost of establishing their creditworthiness (an information cost) is negligible.

"What I'd like, basically, is a temporary line of credit just to tide me over the rest of my life."

SOURCE: © J.B. Handelsman/The New Yorker Collection/ www.cartoonbank.com.

*Letters of credit* are another important off-balance-sheet item for banks. These letters guarantee that a customer of the bank will be able to make a promised payment. For example, a U.S. importer of television sets may need to reassure a Chinese exporter that the firm will be able to pay for the imported goods when they arrive. This customer might request that the bank send a *commercial letter of credit* to the Chinese exporter guaranteeing payment for the goods on receipt. By issuing the letter of credit, the bank substitutes its own guarantee for the U.S. importer's credit risk, enabling the transaction to go forward. In return for taking this risk, the bank receives a fee.

A related form of the letter of credit is called a *standby letter of credit*. These letters, which are issued to firms and governments that wish to borrow in the financial markets, are a form of insurance. Commercial paper, even when it is issued by a large, well-known firm, must be backed by a standby letter of credit that promises the bank will repay the lender should the issuer default. What is true for large corporations is true for state and local governments as well: in most cases, they need a bank guarantee to issue debt. As with loan commitments, letters of credit expose the bank to risk in a way that is not readily apparent on the bank's balance sheet.

Because off-balance-sheet activities create risk for financial institutions, they have come under increasing scrutiny in recent years. Recall the case of Long-Term Capital Management (LTCM), which we discussed in Chapter 9. While LTCM's balance sheet carried assets worth over $100 billion when the firm got into trouble, the risky instruments that did *not* appear on its balance sheet—the $1.25 trillion in interest-rate swaps—were what scared everyone. A similar problem arose in the financial crisis of 2007–2009, when the invisible, off-balance-sheet risks taken by some of the largest banks added to doubts about their solvency (see Chapter 3, Lessons from the Crisis: Shadow Banks). By allowing for the transfer of risk, modern financial instruments enable individual institutions to concentrate risk in ways that are very difficult for outsiders to discern.

## Bank Risk: Where It Comes from and What to Do about It

Banking is risky both because depository institutions are highly leveraged and because of what they do. The bank's goal is to make a profit in each of its lines of business. Some of these are simply fee-for-service activities. For example, a financial institution might act as a broker, buying and selling stocks and bonds on a customer's behalf and charging a fee in return. Banks also transform deposit liabilities into assets such as loans and securities. In the process, they pool savings, provide liquidity services, allow for diversification of risk, and capitalize on the advantages they have in producing information. All along, the goal is to pay less for the deposits the bank receives than for the loans it makes and the securities it buys. That is, the interest rate the bank pays to attract liabilities must be lower than the return it receives on assets.

In the process of all these activities, the bank is exposed to a host of risks. They include the chance that depositors will suddenly withdraw their balances, that borrowers will not repay their loans, that interest rates will change, and that the bank's securities trading operation will do poorly. Each of these risks has a name: *liquidity risk, credit risk, interest-rate risk,* and *trading risk.* To understand how these risks arise and what can be done about them, we will look at each in detail.

## Liquidity Risk

All financial institutions face the risk that their liabilities holders (depositors) will seek to cash in their claims. The holder of a checking account can always walk into the bank and ask for the balance in cash. This risk of a sudden demand for liquid funds is called **liquidity risk**. Banks face liquidity risk on both sides of their balance sheets. Deposit withdrawal is a liability-side risk, but there is an asset-side risk as well. Recall from our discussion of off-balance-sheet activities that banks provide firms with lines of credit—promises to make loans on demand. When this type of loan commitment is claimed, or *taken down*, the bank must find the liquidity to cover it.

If the bank cannot meet customers' requests for immediate funds, it runs the risk of failure. Even if a bank has a positive net worth, illiquidity can still drive it out of business. Who would put their funds in a bank that can't always provide cash on demand? For this reason, bankers must manage liquidity risk with great care. Failure to do so in the crisis of 2007–2009 led to bank runs—such as the run on Wachovia in September 2008—and to the failures of numerous bank and nonbank intermediaries.

To fully understand liquidity risk and how banks manage it, let's look at a simplified balance sheet. Figure 12.4 shows a stripped-down version of the balance sheet of a hypothetical bank. Keep in mind that the two sides of a balance sheet must always balance. Any change in the level of assets must be mirrored by an equal change in the level of liabilities.

TIME

In Figure 12.4, bank liabilities are composed primarily of deposits, along with some borrowing and $20 million of bank capital. Liabilities total $150 million. The bank's assets include $15 million in reserves. Banking regulations require that banks hold a portion of their assets either as vault cash or as deposits at the Fed. That portion is stated as a specific percentage of the bank's deposits. If we assume that **required reserves** are 10 percent of deposits, then the $100 million in deposits shown on the balance sheet means that the bank is required to hold $10 million in reserves. The fact that the bank is holding $15 million in reserves means that it has $5 million in *excess reserves*.

To assess liquidity risk, we need to ask how the bank will handle a customer's demand for funds. What happens if a corporate customer arrives at the bank and requests a withdrawal of $5 million? Because the bank has $5 million in excess reserves, it can honor the customer's request immediately, without difficulty. Similarly, if the bank were forced suddenly to honor a $5 million loan commitment, it could do so by drawing down its reserves. In the past, this was a common way to manage liquidity risk; banks would simply hold sufficient excess reserves to accommodate customers' withdrawals. This is a passive way to manage liquidity risk.

The problem is, holding excess reserves is expensive, because it means forgoing the higher rate of interest that typically can be earned on loans or securities. Banks work

### Figure 12.4   Balance Sheet of a Bank Holding $5 Million in Excess Reserves

| Assets | | Liabilities | |
| --- | --- | --- | --- |
| Reserves | $15 million | Deposits | $100 million |
| Loans | $100 million | Borrowed funds | $30 million |
| Securities | $35 million | Bank capital | $20 million |

**Figure 12.5**     Balance Sheet of a Bank Holding No Excess Reserves

| Assets | | Liabilities | |
|---|---|---|---|
| Reserves | $10 million | Deposits | $100 million |
| Loans | $100 million | Borrowed funds | $30 million |
| Securities | $40 million | Bank capital | $20 million |

hard to find other ways to manage the risk of sudden withdrawals and drawdowns of loan commitments. There are two other ways to manage the risk that customers will require cash: The bank can adjust its assets or its liabilities. To see how it's done, let's look at Figure 12.5. This bank has $10 million in reserves to back its $100 million in deposits, so it has no excess reserves. If a customer makes a $5 million withdrawal, the bank can't simply deduct it from reserves. Instead, the bank will need to adjust another part of its balance sheet.[5]

This bank has two choices in responding to the shortfall created by the $5 million withdrawal: It can adjust either its assets or its liabilities. On the asset side, the bank has several options. The quickest and easiest one is to sell a portion of its securities portfolio. Because some of them are almost surely U.S. Treasury securities, they can be sold quickly and easily at relatively low cost. The result of this action is shown in the top panel of Figure 12.6. Note that assets and liabilities are both $5 million

**Figure 12.6**     Balance Sheet of a Bank Following a $5 Million Withdrawal and Asset Adjustment

**Withdrawal Is Met by Selling Securities**

| Assets | | Liabilities | |
|---|---|---|---|
| Reserves | $10 million | Deposits | $95 million |
| Loans | $100 million | Borrowed funds | $30 million |
| Securities | $35 million | Bank capital | $20 million |

**Withdrawal Is Met by Reducing Loans**

| Assets | | Liabilities | |
|---|---|---|---|
| Reserves | $10 million | Deposits | $95 million |
| Loans | $95 million | Borrowed funds | $30 million |
| Securities | $40 million | Bank capital | $20 million |

[5]If you're thinking that the bank can finance part of the withdrawal from reserves, because the $5 million withdrawal will reduce required reserves by $500,000, you're right. But that still leaves the bank $4.5 million short.

lower than they were prior to the withdrawal (compare Figure 12.5). Banks that are particularly concerned about liquidity risk can structure their securities holdings to facilitate such sales.

A second possibility is for the bank to sell some of its loans to another bank. This option is shown in the bottom panel of Figure 12.6. While not all loans can be sold, some can. Banks generally make sure that a portion of the loans they hold are marketable for just such purposes.

Yet another way to handle the bank's need for liquidity is to refuse to renew a customer loan that has come due. Corporate customers have short-term loans that are periodically renewed, so the bank always has the option of refusing to extend the loan again for another week, month, or year. But this course of action is not very appealing. Failing to renew a loan is guaranteed to alienate the customer and could well drive the customer to another bank. Recall from Chapter 11 that banks specialize in solving information problems by screening to find customers who are creditworthy and then monitoring them to ensure they repay their loans. The idea is to separate good customers from bad ones and develop long-term relationships with the good ones. The last thing a bank wants to do is to refuse a loan to a creditworthy customer it has gone to some trouble and expense to find.

Moreover, bankers do not like to meet their deposit outflows by contracting the asset side of the balance sheet because doing so shrinks the size of the bank. And since banks make a profit by turning liabilities into assets, the smaller their balance sheets, the lower their profits. For this reason alone, today's bankers prefer to use liability management to address liquidity risk. That is, instead of selling assets in response to a deposit withdrawal, they find other sources of funds.

There are two ways for banks to obtain additional funds. First, they can borrow to meet the shortfall, either from the Federal Reserve or from another bank. The result of such an action is shown in the top panel of Figure 12.7. As you can see, while deposits have fallen by $5 million, borrowing has made up the difference.

**Figure 12.7**   Balance Sheet of a Bank Following a $5 Million Withdrawal and Liability Adjustment

**Withdrawal Is Met by Borrowing**

| Assets | | Liabilities | |
|---|---|---|---|
| Reserves | $10 million | Deposits | $95 million |
| Loans | $100 million | Borrowed funds | $35 million |
| Securities | $40 million | Bank capital | $20 million |

**Withdrawal Is Met by Attracting Deposits**

| Assets | | Liabilities | |
|---|---|---|---|
| Reserves | $10 million | Deposits | $100 million |
| Loans | $100 million | Borrowed funds | $30 million |
| Securities | $40 million | Bank capital | $20 million |

A second way to adjust liabilities in response to a deposit outflow is to attract additional deposits. The most common way to do so is to issue large-denomination CDs (with a value over $100,000).[6] In the bottom panel of Figure 12.7, these nontransaction deposits are combined with checking accounts. As we saw earlier, large certificates of deposit have become an increasingly important source of funds for banks. Now we know why: It is because they allow banks to manage their liquidity risk without changing the asset side of their balance sheets.

In the crisis of 2007–2009, many of the usual mechanisms for managing liquidity risk failed. Banks could neither sell their illiquid assets nor obtain at a reasonable cost the funding needed to hold those assets. When the interbank lending market dried up, many banks faced a threat to their survival (see Chapter 3, Lessons from the Crisis: Interbank Lending).

## Credit Risk

Banks profit from the difference between the interest rate they pay to depositors and the interest rate they receive from borrowers. That is, the return on their assets exceeds the cost of their liabilities. At least, that's the idea. But to ensure that this profit-making process works, for the bank to make a profit, borrowers must repay their loans. There is always some risk that they won't. The risk that a bank's loans will not be repaid is called **credit risk**. To manage their credit risk, banks use a variety of tools. The most basic are diversification, in which the bank makes a variety of different loans to spread the risk, and credit risk analysis, in which the bank examines the borrower's credit history to determine the appropriate interest rate to charge.

Diversification means spreading risk, which can be difficult for banks, especially those that focus on certain kinds of lending. Since banks specialize in information gathering, it is tempting to try to gain a competitive advantage in a narrow line of business. The problem is, if a bank lends in only one geographic area or only one industry, it exposes itself to economic downturns that are local or industry-specific. It is important that banks find a way to hedge such risks.

Credit risk analysis produces information that is very similar to the bond rating systems discussed in Chapter 7. There we saw that rating agencies like Moody's and Standard & Poor's produce letter ratings for large corporations wishing to issue bonds. Banks do the same for small firms wishing to borrow, and credit rating agencies perform the service for individual borrowers (see Your Financial World: Your Credit Rating in Chapter 7). Credit risk analysis uses a combination of statistical models and information that is specific to the loan applicant. The result is an assessment of the likelihood that a particular borrower will default. When the bank's loan officers decide to make a loan, they use the customer's credit rating to determine how high an interest rate to charge. To the interest rate they must pay on their liabilities, they add a markup that will allow them to make a profit. The poorer a borrower's credit rating, the higher the interest rate they will charge.[7]

---

[6]Unlike transactions deposits such as checking accounts, CDs are not subject to a reserve requirement. Thus, a change in the composition of a bank's deposits affects the level of reserves it is required to hold and hence its balance sheet.

[7]Banks can also manage their credit risk by purchasing *credit default swaps* (CDS), a type of derivative that allows lenders to insure themselves against the chance that a borrower will default. For a discussion of CDS, see pages 225–226 of Chapter 9.

In the crisis of 2007–2009, many banks seriously underestimated the risks associated with mortgage and other household credit. They had not anticipated the first decline of nationwide housing prices since the Great Depression or the surge of unemployment to double-digit rates. Rising defaults prompted large losses and impaired their capital, although not as much as crisis-driven trading losses on mortgage-backed and related securities (see pages 304–305).

## Interest-Rate Risk

Because banks are in the business of turning deposit liabilities into loan assets, the two sides of their balance sheet do not match up. One important difference is that a bank's liabilities tend to be short term, while its assets tend to be long term. This mismatch between the maturities of the two sides of the balance sheet creates **interest-rate risk**.

To understand the problem, think of both the bank's assets and its liabilities as bonds. That is, the bank's deposit liabilities are just like bonds, as are its loan assets. (The bank must have some capital as well.) We know that a change in interest rates will affect the value of a bond; when interest rates rise, the price of a bond falls. More important, the longer the term of the bond is, the greater the change in the bond's price at any given change in the interest rate. (Refer back to Chapter 1 to refresh your memory.) Thus, when interest rates rise, banks face the risk that the value of their assets will fall more than the value of their liabilities (reducing the bank's capital). Put another way, if a bank makes long-term loans, it receives payments from borrowers that do not vary with the interest rate. But its short-term liabilities—those with variable interest rates—require the bank to make larger payments when interest rates rise. So rising interest rates reduce revenues relative to expenses, directly lowering the bank's profits.

The best way to see this point is to focus on a bank's revenue and expenses. Let's start by dividing the bank's assets and liabilities into two categories, those that are interest-rate sensitive and those that are not. The term *interest-rate sensitive* means that a change in interest rates will change the revenue produced by an asset. Because newly purchased short-term bonds always reflect a change in interest rates, short-term bonds that are constantly maturing and being replaced with new ones produce interest-rate-sensitive revenue. In contrast, when the bank purchases long-term bonds, it receives a fixed stream of revenue. Purchasing a 5 percent, 10-year bond means getting $5 per $100 of face value for 10 years, regardless of what happens to interest rates in the meantime. So the revenue stream from a long-term bond is not interest-rate sensitive.

Suppose that 20 percent of a bank's assets fall into the first category, those that are sensitive to changes in the interest rate. Another 80 percent fall into the second category, those that are not sensitive to changes in the interest rate. If the interest rate has been stable at 5 percent for some time, then for each $100 in assets, the bank receives $5 in interest.

The bank's liabilities tend to have a different structure. Let's assume that half the bank's deposits are interest-rate sensitive and half are not. In other words, half the bank's liabilities are deposits that earn variable interest rates, so the costs associated with them move with the market rate. Interest-bearing checking accounts fall into this category. The remainder of the bank's liabilities are time deposits such as certificates of deposit, which have fixed interest rates. The payment a bank makes to the holder of an existing CD does not change with the interest rate.

For the bank to make a profit, the interest rate on its liabilities must be lower than the interest rate on its assets. The difference between the two rates is the bank's net interest margin. Assuming that the interest rate on its liabilities has been 3 percent, the bank has

## LESSONS FROM THE CRISIS
### INSUFFICIENT BANK CAPITAL

The financial crisis of 2007-2009 and the recession that it triggered led to projected losses on U.S. bank assets of nearly $1 trillion.* For comparison, the total capital of U.S. depositories before the crisis began was about $1.3 trillion. Had the U.S. government not provided massive support to the banking system, many banks probably would have become *insolvent*—unable to repay their debts because their liabilities would have exceeded their assets.

What is bank capital? Why do banks hold it? Through what mechanism did the crisis erode capital?

A bank's capital is its net worth—the difference between the value of it assets and the value of its liabilities. The capital a bank holds cushions it against many risks, including declines in the market value of assets—so-called *market risk*. The larger a bank's capital cushion, the less likely that it will be made insolvent by an adverse surprise.

In the financial crisis, U.S. bank capital was insufficient to cushion against the market risks that surfaced. Put another way, banks were too leveraged: They had too many assets for each unit of capital, making them vulnerable to market risk.

How did declines in the market value of assets arise in the crisis? The process began in 2007 when surging mortgage defaults depressed the value of many mortgage-backed securities. U.S. banks were sensitive to such declines because they held more than $4 trillion in mortgages.

Even when borrowers make timely interest payments, mortgages and the securities backed by them can pose market risk. *Mark-to-market* accounting rules require banks to adjust the recorded value of the assets on their balance sheets when the market value of those assets changes. When the market price rises, the value of the assets is "written up." When the price falls, the value is "written down." Because bank capital is the difference between assets and liabilities, *writedowns* reduce a bank's capital.

Why didn't banks hold a larger capital cushion against market and other risks? The answer is that capital is costly. Financial institutions must pay for capital, compensating the investors that provide it with dividends and the like.

To boost profits, intermediaries try to reduce costs, including the amount of capital they require. They also may take more risk by increasing leverage. The more leverage, the greater the possible reward for each unit of costly capital—and the greater the risk. Highly leveraged firms are vulnerable even to modest declines in market prices. When a financial institution is leveraged 30 times—as some were before the crisis—a drop in asset prices of as little as 3 percent can wipe out the capital cushion and lead to bankruptcy. Yet, even some top-rated mortgage securities plunged in price by one-third, threatening widespread insolvency among the institutions that held them.

*See the projection in the IMF *Global Financial Stability Report*, April 2009, Table 1.15.

been paying out $3 per $100 in liabilities. Since the bank is receiving 5 percent interest on its assets, its net interest margin is 2 percent (5 minus 3). This margin is the bank's profit.

Now look at what happens if interest rates rise 1 percent for interest-sensitive assets and liabilities. For each $100 in assets, the bank's revenue goes up from $(0.05 \times \$100) = \$5$ to $[(0.05 \times \$80) + (0.06 \times \$20)] = \$5.20$. But the cost of its liabilities goes up too, from $(0.03 \times \$100) = \$3$ to $[(0.03 \times \$50) + (0.04 \times \$50)] = \$3.50$. So a one-percentage point rise in the interest rate reduces the bank's profit from $(\$5 - \$3) = \$2$ per $100 in assets to $(\$5.20 - \$3.50) = \$1.70$, a decline of $0.30, or 15 percent. This example illustrates a general principle: When a bank's liabilities are more interest-rate-sensitive than its assets are, an increase in interest rates will cut into the bank's profits.

The first step in managing interest-rate risk is to determine how sensitive the bank's balance sheet is to a change in interest rates. Managers must compute an estimate of the change in the bank's profit for each one-percentage-point change in the interest rate. This procedure is called *gap analysis*, because it highlights the gap, or difference, between the yield on interest-rate-sensitive assets and the yield on interest-rate-sensitive liabilities. In our example, the asset-liability gap is (20 percent − 50 percent) = −30. Multiplying this gap times the projected change in the interest rate yields the change in the bank's profit. A gap of −30 tells us that a one-percentage-point increase in the interest rate will reduce the bank's profit by 30 cents per $100 in assets, which is the same answer we got in the last paragraph. Gap analysis can be refined to take account of differences in the maturity of assets and liabilities, but the analysis quickly becomes complicated.[8] Table 12.2 summarizes all of these calculations.

Bank managers can use a number of tools to manage interest-rate risk. The simplest approach is to match the interest-rate sensitivity of assets with the interest-rate sensitivity of liabilities. For instance, if the bank accepts a variable-rate deposit, it then uses the funds to purchase short-term securities. A similar strategy is to make long-term loans at a floating interest rate—as in adjustable-rate mortgages (ARMs)—instead of at the fixed interest rate characteristic of a conventional mortgage. But while this

| Table 12.2 | An Example of Interest-Rate Risk |

The impact of an interest-rate increase on bank profits (per $100 of assets)

| | Assets | Liabilities |
|---|---|---|
| Interest-rate sensitive | $20 | $50 |
| *Not* interest-rate sensitive | $80 | $50 |
| Initial interest rate | 5% | 3% |
| New interest rate on interest-rate-sensitive assets and liabilities | 6% | 4% |
| | **Revenue from Assets** | **Cost of Liabilities** |
| At initial interest rate | (0.05 × $20) + (0.05 × $80) = $5.00 | (0.03 × $50) + (0.03 × $50) = $3.00 |
| After interest-rate change | (0.06 × $20) + (0.05 × $80) = $5.20 | (0.04 × $50) + (0.03 × $50) = $3.50 |
| Profits at initial interest rate: ($5.00) − ($3.00) = $2.00 per $100 in assets | | |
| Profits after interest-rate change: ($5.20) − ($3.50) = $1.70 per $100 in assets | | |

**Gap Analysis**

Gap between interest-rate-sensitive assets and interest-rate-sensitive liabilities:

(Interest-rate-sensitive assets of $20) − (Interest-rate-sensitive liabilities of $50) = (Gap of −$30)

approach reduces interest-rate risk, it increases credit risk. Rising interest rates put additional strain on floating-rate borrowers, increasing the likelihood that they will default on their payments.

While restructuring assets to better match those of liabilities can reduce risk, the fact that it also reduces potential profitability has led bankers to look for other ways to control interest-rate risk. Alternatives include the use of derivatives, specifically interest-rate swaps, to manage interest-rate risk. Recall from Chapter 9 that an interest-rate swap is an agreement in which one party promises to make fixed-interest-rate payments in exchange for floating-interest-rate payments. For a bank that is holding long-term assets and short-term liabilities, an interest-rate swap is exactly the sort of financial instrument that will transfer the risk of rising interest rates to another party.

## Trading Risk

There was a time when banks merely took deposits and made loans, holding them until they were completely paid off. Today, banks not only engage in sophisticated asset and liability management but they hire traders to actively buy and sell securities, loans, and derivatives using a portion of the bank's capital, in the hope of making additional profits for the bank's owners. But trading financial instruments is risky. If the price at which an instrument is purchased differs from the price at which it is sold, the risk is that the instrument may go down in value rather than up. This type of risk is called **trading risk**, or sometimes *market risk*.[9]

---

[8]A more sophisticated examination of interest-rate risk, called *duration analysis,* includes a measure of the interest-rate sensitivity of bond prices. A bond's duration is related to its maturity. The percentage change in the market value = −(duration of the bond) × (percentage-point change in the interest rate). Bankers compute the weighted-average duration of their liabilities and subtract it from the weighted-average duration of their assets to get a duration gap, which can be used to guide the bank's risk management strategy. For a complete treatment, see Chapter 9 in Anthony Saunders and Marcia Miller Cornett, *Financial Institutions Management: A Modern Perspective,* 6th ed. (New York: McGraw-Hill/Irwin, 2008).

[9]Because regulators in the United States won't allow banks to hold stock (equity), the traders employed by the bank can't, either. But because the traders buy and sell derivatives that are based on bonds, commodities, and foreign exchange, the rule against stock ownership doesn't restrict their ability to take risks.

# IN THE NEWS
## Rogue Flight: Societe Generale's Kerviel Tags Leeson

## Bloomberg.com

### By Peter Robison

### January 25, 2008

A rogue trader on the run. A storied bank in turmoil. Shareholders left to ask what happened.

More than a decade after former Barings Plc trader Nick Leeson provoked a worldwide manhunt with $1.4 billion in losses, the script has become familiar at modern financial institutions where traders can make fortunes on complex instruments their bosses may not understand.

Jerome Kerviel, 31, who was blamed by Societe Generale SA yesterday for causing a 4.9 billion-euro ($7.2 billion) trading loss, the largest in banking history, is at least the seventh individual singled out for unauthorized trading since 1994. Some hid, or obstructed investigators. Most were jailed.

"It's yet another argument why you want to have all derivatives trading in standardized instruments that are exchange-traded," said Martin Mayer, a guest scholar at the Brookings Institution in Washington who has written more than a dozen books on finance. "Anything else is asking for a lot of trouble, and it will keep coming back."

When Leeson, then 28, went missing from Barings's Singapore office in February 1995, the story of how a single trader brought down a 233-year-old British merchant bank caused a sensation. The memoir Leeson wrote while serving

3½ years in jail, "Rogue Trader," was made into a film starring Ewan McGregor.

Since then, financial institutions including Sumitomo Corp., Daiwa Bank and Allied Irish Banks Plc have been burned by unauthorized trading, causing billions of dollars in losses. Trading blowups are so frequent that Leeson, who now lives in Ireland, fields calls through an agent to dissect the latest financial scandals.

. . .

"I think rogue trading is probably a daily occurrence amongst the financial markets," the BBC quoted Leeson as saying. "You're still looking at a situation where the systems and controls aren't good enough."

Paris-based Societe Generale, France's second-largest bank by market value, said Kerviel set up secret positions that went beyond permitted limits on futures linked to European stock indexes. In a letter on the bank's Web site, Societe Generale Chairman Daniel Bouton said the trades were hidden "through extremely sophisticated and varied techniques."

. . .

The bank said Kerviel didn't enrich himself from the trades, which began in early 2007. He began working at Societe Generale in 2000 and made a salary and bonus of less than 100,000 euros a year, it said.

By its nature, trading tends to attract competitive people who take risks and push limits, Mayer said.

"I didn't set out to rob a bank," former Daiwa trader Toshihide Iguchi told Time magazine in a 1997 interview at

Managing trading risk is a major concern for today's banks. Some of the largest banks in the world have sustained billions of dollars in losses as a result of unsupervised risk taking by employees in their trading operations. The problem is that traders normally share in the profits from good investments, but the bank pays for the losses. Heads, the trader wins; tails, the bank loses. This arrangement creates moral hazard: Traders have an incentive to take more risk than bank managers would like.

The solution to the moral hazard problem in trading is to compute the risk the portfolios traders generate using measures like standard deviation and value at risk (see Chapter 5). The bank's risk manager then limits the amount of risk any individual trader is allowed to assume and monitors each trader's holdings closely, at least once a day. Moreover, the higher the risk inherent in the bank's portfolio, the more capital the bank will need to hold to make sure the institution remains solvent.

In the crisis of 2007–2009, some banks, especially large ones, sharply underestimated the risks associated with mortgage-backed securities and related derivatives.

a prison in Pennsylvania, where he was serving a four-year sentence for fraud and falsifying documents.

. . .

Tokyo-based Daiwa in 1995 was forced to shut its U.S. branches after disclosing a $1.1 billion loss from 11 years of unauthorized trading by Iguchi, its chief New York government bond trader. Iguchi, born in Kobe, Japan, had studied psychology at Southwest Missouri State University in Springfield, Missouri, and earlier worked in Daiwa's back office.

"To me, it was only a violation of internal rules," Iguchi told Time. "I think all traders have a tendency to fall into the same trap. You always have a way of recovering the loss."

A year later, Sumitomo disclosed a $2.6 billion loss on unauthorized copper trades. The Japanese firm blamed its chief copper trader, Yasuo Hamanaka, who was known as "Mr. Copper" in the markets because of his aggressive trading. Hamanaka was sentenced to eight years in prison in 1998. He was released in 2005.

In an interview that year with Bloomberg News at his two-story house in Kawasaki, near Tokyo, Hamanaka said he was "amazed" at today's high prices for copper and wanted to go back to work.

. . .

John Rusnak, a Baltimore-based trader for Allied Irish Banks, is serving 7½ years in prison for his role in amassing and hiding $691 million of losses over more than five years. Allied Irish Banks discovered the losses in 2002, and sold the Allfirst Financial unit where Rusnak worked to M&T Bank Corp. of Buffalo, New York.

. . .

### LESSONS OF THE ARTICLE

Trading operations are notoriously difficult to monitor, and they can go dramatically wrong. The problem is analogous to moral hazard in debt finance (discussed in Chapter 11). Traders are gambling with someone else's money, sharing the gains but not the losses from their risk taking. As a result, they are prone to taking too much risk—and in the cases discussed here, to hiding their losses when their trades turn sour. This moral hazard presents a challenge to the bank's owners, who must find ways to rein in traders' tendencies to take too much risk. The tip-off to unbridled risk taking can come when a trader makes too big a profit. Odds are that someone who is making large profits on some days will register big losses on other days. There is no way to make a large profit without taking a big risk.

As market prices on these financial instruments plunged, losses on their large holdings of these instruments seriously depleted their bank capital and threatened insolvency (see Lessons from the Crisis: Insufficient Bank Capital on page 302).

## Other Risks

Beyond liquidity, credit, interest-rate, and trading risk, banks face an assortment of other risks. A bank that operates internationally will face foreign exchange risk and sovereign risk. *Foreign exchange risk* comes from holding assets denominated in one currency and liabilities denominated in another. For example, a U.S. bank that holds dollar-denominated liabilities might purchase bonds issued by Sony Corporation or make a loan to a Japanese business. Both those assets would be denominated in yen. Thus, when the dollar–yen exchange rate moves, the dollar value of the bank's assets will change. Banks manage their foreign exchange risk in two ways. They work to attract deposits that are denominated in the same currency as their loans, thereby matching their assets with their liabilities, and they use foreign exchange futures and swaps to hedge the risk (see Chapter 10, Lessons from the Crisis: Currency Risk and Rollover Risk).

*Sovereign risk* arises from the fact that some foreign borrowers may not repay their loans, not because they are unwilling to, but because their government prohibits them from doing so. When a foreign country is experiencing a financial crisis, the government may decide to restrict dollar-denominated payments, in which case a U.S. bank would have difficulty collecting payments on its loans in the country. Such circumstances have arisen on numerous occasions. Examples include Asia in 1997, Russia in 1998, and Argentina in 2002. In all these cases governments and corporations alike had difficulty raising enough dollars to repay their dollar-denominated debts. In such crises, a bank has very little recourse in the courts and little hope of recovering the loans.

Managing sovereign risk is difficult. Banks have three options. The first is diversification, which means distributing the bank's loans and securities holdings throughout the world, carefully avoiding too much exposure in any country where a crisis might arise. Second, the bank can simply refuse to do business in a particular country or set of countries. And third, the bank can use derivatives to hedge sovereign risk.

The final risk that banks face is the risk that their computer systems may fail or their buildings burn down (or blow up), what's called **operational risk**. When terrorists destroyed the World Trade Center towers on September 11, 2001, power and communications were disrupted in a large and important part of lower Manhattan. Many financial firms located in or near the World Trade Center quickly switched to backup sites, but others couldn't. The Bank of New York, a large commercial bank, was one of those that fell victim to operational risk. The Bank of New York (now The Bank of New York Mellon) plays an important role in the U.S. financial system, handling hundreds of billions of dollars worth of transactions each day in the U.S. Treasury securities market. Prior to September 11, the bank maintained both its primary and backup operations within blocks of the World Trade Center (see Figure 12.8). Not only were power and communications to these buildings knocked out by the terrorist attack, but no one could even get to them. The bank practically shut down for several days and recovered only slowly, losing an estimated $140 million in the process. In placing the backup site so close to the bank's primary operations, managers had made an enormous mistake: They had failed to take account of a significant operational risk.[10]

These risks are serious business. One study estimates that over the 10 years ending in 2002, there were more than 100 events in which financial institutions lost a total of $100 million.[11]

In principle, managing operational risk is straightforward, but in practice it can be difficult. The bank must make sure that its computer systems and buildings are sufficiently robust to withstand potential disasters. That means both anticipating what might happen and testing to ensure the system's readiness. Forecasting the possibilities can be daunting. Who could have predicted what happened on September 11?

Table 12.3 summarizes the four major risks banks face and the recommended risk-management strategies.

---

[10]For a discussion of the problems that occurred in the U.S. financial system following the destruction of the World Trade Center towers, see the Federal Reserve Bank of New York's *Economic Policy Review*, November 2002, special issue on the economic effects of September 11. Of particular note are Michael J. Fleming and Kenneth D. Garbade, "When the Back Office Moved to the Front Burner: Settlement Fails in the Treasury Market after September 11," and James J. McAndrews and Simon Potter, "Liquidity Effects of the Event of September 11, 2001."

[11]See Patrick de Fountnouville, Virginia DeJesus-Rueff, John Jordan, and Eric Rosengren, "Capital and Risk: New Evidence on Implications of Large Operational Losses," *Journal of Money, Credit, and Banking* 38, no. 7 (October 2006), pp. 1819–1846.

**Figure 12.8**   The Bank of New York and September 11, 2001

SOURCE: *Copyright American Map Corporation, Lic. No. AMC033007.*

The two red stars show the location of the Bank of New York's primary operations and the backup site. They are both within half a mile of the center of the World Trade Center complex that was destroyed by terrorists on September 11, 2001. Because these buildings became inaccessible, the Bank of New York ceased operation for several days.

**Table 12.3**   Risks Banks Face and How They Manage Them

| Type of Risk | Source of Risk | Recommended Responses |
|---|---|---|
| *Liquidity Risk* | Sudden withdrawals by depositors or takedowns of credit lines | 1. Hold sufficient cash reserves to meet customer demand.<br>2. Manage assets—sell securities or loans (contracts the size of the balance sheet)<br>3. Manage liabilities—attract more deposits (maintains the size of the balance sheet) |
| *Credit Risk* | Default by borrowers on their loans | 1. Diversify to spread risk.<br>2. Use statistical models to screen for creditworthy borrowers.<br>3. Monitor to reduce moral hazard. |
| *Interest-Rate Risk* | Mismatch in maturity of assets and liabilities coupled with a change in interest rates | 1. Closely match the maturity of both sides of the balance sheet.<br>2. Use derivatives such as interest-rate swaps. |
| *Trading (Market) Risk* | Trading losses in the bank's own account | Closely monitor traders using risk management tools, including value at risk. |

## APPLYING THE CONCEPT
### JAPANESE AND U.S. COMMERCIAL BANKING IN THE 1990S

In 1990, of the top 15 financial firms in the world (measured by their stock market value) 13 were Japanese. By 2001, none were Japanese. In a single decade, the assets of Japanese commercial banks had fallen nearly 15 percent, while those of U.S. banks had risen 80 percent. From 1993 through 2001, Japanese banks produced a negative return, reporting cumulative losses of roughly 16.5 percent of Japan's one-year GDP.

To get some sense of what happened, we can look at the numbers in Table 12.4. Starting with net interest margin, we see that U.S. banks do very well at their traditional deposit and lending operations. By contrast, Japanese banks do not. In 2001, net interest margin in Japan was only one-third what it was in the United States. Second, note that for U.S. banks net income fell from nearly 70 percent in 1991 to less than 60 percent by 2001 (that's the last line in the table). By contrast, in Japan net interest income remained roughly 80 percent of total bank income. More recently, fee income (row B of Table 12.4) rather than interest (row A) accounts for nearly half of bank income in the United States. In Japan, the fraction remains lower.

During the 1990s, American banks found new ways to produce revenue and profits. As a result, by 2001 U.S. banks had a before-tax return on equity of 18.6 percent. Meanwhile, Japanese banks' profits had turned negative, so their return on equity was −18 percent. (At the time, the Japanese banking system had a leverage ratio of 30 to 1, well above the 11 to 1 leverage ratio in the U.S. banks.)*

There were two reasons Japanese banks performed so poorly in the 1990s. The first was loan losses. In 2001, Japan's banks reported losses of 9.4 trillion yen—more than 2 percent of their outstanding loans, and more than 1 percent of their assets. Both ratios are more than twice the level in U.S. banks. Added to these loan losses were capital losses of 2.4 trillion yen on the sale of stocks and real estate (row G in Table 12.4). Though U.S. banks are not allowed to own stock, Japanese banks are; they hold roughly 5 percent of their assets in the form of equities. From its peak in the late 1980s through 2001, the Japanese stock market fell roughly two-thirds in value, causing significant losses for banks.

As bad as the numbers are in Table 12.4, they don't tell the whole story. Japanese banks formerly were allowed to compute their financial statements using the values they paid for their assets. Given the collapse of stock and real estate values, market prices fell well below these "book" values, meaning that the value of the assets and bank capital were overstated. Added to these overstated asset values was the manner in which Japanese banks treated borrowers who could not pay off their loans. Instead of simply taking the losses, the banks increased the size of the loans and included the interest the borrowers couldn't pay as part of the principal in their new loans. This approach inflates the size of the bank's balance sheet, putting off the day of reckoning when the borrower must finally default. For these reasons, balance sheet measures overstated capital in the Japanese banking system, and understated its impairment.

The impact of these problems on the Japanese economy was nothing short of catastrophic. Because the banks need to hold capital as a buffer against unpredictable losses on their loans, they could not make new loans. Without new lending, firms cannot grow, and neither can the economy.

*For a more detailed account, see Chapter 8 of Takeo Hoshi and Anil K Kashyap, *Corporate Financing and Governance in Japan: The Road to the Future* (Cambridge Mass.: M.I.T. Press, 2001).

# Terms

| Table 12.4 | Profitability of Japanese and U.S. Commercial Banks (in yen or dollars, except for bottom four rows) | | | |

|  | Japanese banks (in trillions of yen) | | U.S. banks (in billions of dollars) | |
|---|---|---|---|---|
|  | 1991 | 2001 | 1991 | 2001 |
| A. Interest income-Interest expense (net interest income) | ¥8.9 | ¥9.8 | $121.3 | $210.8 |
| B. Other revenue* | 2.2 | 3.1 | 59.5 | 153.7 |
| C. Operating costs | 7.5 | 7.0 | 124.2 | 218.7 |
| D. Gross profit (A + B − C) | 3.5 | 5.9 | 56.5 | 145.8 |
| E. Loan losses (provisions) | 1.0 | 9.4 | 34.2 | 41.0 |
| F. Net operating profit (D − E) | 2.5 | −3.5 | 22.4 | 104.8 |
| G. Realized capital gains from sale of real estate | 0.7 | −2.4 | 3.0 | 4.4 |
| H. Net profits before taxes (F + G) | 3.3 | −5.9 | 25.4 | 109.3 |
| I. Assets | 914.4 | 772.0 | 3,120.5 | 6,454.5 |
| Net interest margin (A/I) | 1.0% | 1.3% | 3.5% | 3.3% |
| Before tax return on assets (H/I) | 0.4 | −0.8 | 0.7 | 1.7 |
| Before tax return on equity | 10.5 | −18.0 | 12.6 | 18.6 |
| Net interest income/Total income [A/(A + B)] | 80.2 | 76.0 | 67.1 | 57.8 |

*Includes fee income and profits from trading for own account.

(Numbers may not add up exactly due to rounding in the original.)

SOURCE: Table 1 in Anil K Kashyap, "Sorting Out Japan's Financial Crisis," Economic Perspectives of the Federal Reserve Bank of Chicago, 4th quarter 2002, pp. 12–55. For Japan, return on equity is computed using information from the Bank of Japan's "Financial Statements of Japanese Banks" available at http://www.boj.or.jp/en/stryo/stryo_f.htm. For U.S. banks, return on equity is computed using information from Table CB14, "Liabilities and Equity Capital FDIC-Insured Commercial Banks, United States and Other Areas, Balances at End of Year, 1934–2001," on the Federal Deposit Insurance Corporation Web site, www.fdic.gov.

# Chapter Lessons

1. Bank assets equal bank liabilities plus bank capital.
   a. Bank assets are the uses for bank funds.
      i. They include reserves, securities, and loans.
      ii. Over the years, securities have become less important and mortgages more important as a use for bank funds.
   b. Bank liabilities are the sources of bank funds.
      i. They include transaction and nontransaction deposits as well as borrowings.
      ii. Over the years, transaction deposits have become less important as a source of bank funds.

   c. Bank capital is the contribution of the bank's owners; it acts as a cushion against a fall in the value of the bank's assets or a withdrawal of its liabilities.

   d. Banks make a profit for their owners. Measures of a bank's profitability include return on assets (ROA), return on equity (ROE), net interest income, and net interest margin.

   e. Banks' off-balance-sheet activities have become increasingly important in recent years. They include
      i. Loan commitments, which are lines of credit firms can use whenever necessary.
      ii. Letters of credit, which are guarantees that a customer will make a promised payment.

2. Banks face several types of risk in day-to-day business. They include
   a. Liquidity risk—the risk that customers will demand cash immediately.
      i. Liability-side liquidity risk arises from deposit withdrawals.
      ii. Asset-side liquidity risk arises from the use of loan commitments to borrow.
      iii. Banks can manage liquidity risk by adjusting either their assets or their liabilities.

   b. Credit risk—the risk that customers will not repay their loans. Banks can manage credit risk by
      i. Diversifying their loan portfolios.
      ii. Using statistical models to analyze borrowers' creditworthiness.
      iii. Monitoring borrowers to ensure that they use borrowed funds properly.
      iv. Purchasing credit default swaps (CDS) to insure against borrower default.

   c. Interest-rate risk—the risk that a movement in interest rates will change the value of the bank's assets more than the value of its liabilities.
      i. When a bank lends long and borrows short, increases in interest rates will drive down the bank's profits.
      ii. Banks use a variety of tools, such as gap analysis, to assess the sensitivity of their balance sheets to a change in interest rates.
      iii. Banks manage interest-rate risk by matching the maturity of their assets and liabilities and using derivatives like interest-rate swaps.

   d. Trading risk—the risk that traders who work for the bank will create losses on the bank's own account. Banks can manage this risk using complex statistical models and closely monitoring traders.

   e. Other risks banks face include foreign exchange risk, sovereign risk, and operational risk.

# Conceptual Problems

1. Banks hold more liquid assets than most businesses do. Explain why.

2. Explain why banks' holdings of cash have increased significantly as a portion of their balance sheets in recent times.

3. Why are checking accounts not an important source of funds for commercial banks in the United States?

4. The volume of commercial and industrial loans made by banks has declined over the past few decades, while the volume of real estate loans has risen. Explain why this trend occurred and how it contributed to banks' difficulties during the financial crisis of 2007–2009.

5.* Why do you think that U.S. banks are prohibited from holding equity as part of their own portfolios?

6. On the Federal Reserve Board's Web site, http://www.federalreserve.gov, under Economic Research and Data, Statistical Releases, and Historical Data, you will find a weekly release called H.8, "Assets and Liabilities of Commercial Banks in the United States." For the seven consecutive months shown, look at the trends in:
   a. Banks' holdings of mortgage-backed securities (both "Treasury and Agency" and "Other").
   b. Cash assets.

   Comment on what you see.

7. Explain how a bank uses liability management to respond to a deposit outflow. Why do banks prefer liability management to asset management?

8. Banks carefully consider the maturity structure of both their assets and their liabilities. What is the significance of the maturity structure? What risks are banks trying to manage when they adjust their maturity structure?

9. A bank has issued a one-year certificate of deposit for $50 million at an interest rate of 2 percent. With the proceeds, the bank has purchased a two-year Treasury note that pays 4 percent interest. What risk does the bank face in entering into these transactions? What would happen if all interest rates were to rise by 1 percent?

10. Define operational risk and explain how a bank manages it.

11.* In response to changes in banking legislation, the past two decades have seen a significant increase in interstate branching by banks in the United States. How do you think a development of this type would affect the level of risk in the banking business?

# Analytical Problems

12. Consider the balance sheets of Bank A and Bank B. If reserve requirements were 10 percent of transaction deposits and both banks had equal access to the interbank market and funds from the Federal Reserve, which bank do you think faces the greatest liquidity risk? Explain your answer.

**Bank A**
(in millions)

| Assets | | Liabilities | |
|---|---|---|---|
| Reserves | $50 | Transaction Deposits | $200 |
| Loans | $920 | Nontransaction Deposits | $600 |
| Securities | $250 | Borrowings | $100 |

**Bank B**
(in millions)

| Assets | | Liabilities | |
|---|---|---|---|
| Reserves | $30 | Transaction Deposits | $200 |
| Loans | $920 | Nontransaction Deposits | $600 |
| Securities | $50 | Borrowings | $100 |

*Indicates more difficult problems

www.mhhe.com/cecchetti3e

13. Looking again at Bank A and Bank B, based on the information available, which bank do you think is at the greatest risk of insolvency? What other information might you use to assess the risk of insolvency of these banks?

14. Bank Y and Bank Z both have assets of $1 billion. The return on assets for both banks is the same. Bank Y has liabilities of $800 million while Bank Z's liabilities are $900 million. In which bank would you prefer to hold an equity stake? Explain your choice.

15.* You are a bank manager and have been approached by a swap dealer about participating in fixed for floating interest-rate swaps. If your bank has the typical maturity structure, which side of the swap might you be interested in paying and which side would you want to receive?

16. If lines of credit and other off-balance-sheet activities do not, by definition, directly affect the balance sheet, how can they influence the level of liquidity risk to which the bank is exposed?

17. Suppose a bank faces a gap of $-20$ between its interest-sensitive assets and its interest-sensitive liabilities. What would happen to bank profits if interest rates were to fall by 1 percentage point? You should report your answer in terms of the change in profit per $100 in assets.

18.* Duration analysis is an alternative to gap analysis for measuring interest-rate risk. (See footnote 8 on page 303.) The duration of an asset or liability measures how sensitive its market value is to a change in the interest rate: the more sensitive, the longer the duration. In Chapter 6, you saw that the longer the term of a bond, the larger the price change for a given change in the interest rate.

Using this information and the knowledge that interest-rate increases tend to hurt banks, would you say that the average duration of a bank's assets is longer or shorter than that of its liabilities?

19. Suppose you were the manager of a bank with the following balance sheet.

### Bank Balance Sheet
### (in millions)

| Assets | | Liabilities | |
|---|---|---|---|
| Reserves | $30 | Checkable Deposits | $200 |
| Securities | $150 | Time Deposits | $600 |
| Loans | $820 | Borrowings | $100 |

You are required to hold 10 percent of checkable deposits as reserves. If you were faced with unexpected withdrawals of $30 million from time deposits, would you rather
a. Draw down $10 million excess reserves and borrow $20 million from the Fed?
b. Draw down $10 million excess reserves and sell securities of $20 million?

Explain your choice.

20. Suppose you are advising a bank on the management of its balance sheet. In light of the financial crisis of 2007–2009, what arguments might you make to convince the bank to hold additional capital?

# Chapter 13

## Financial Industry Structure

Canada, a nation of 33 million people, has 22 domestic banks. If the United States had the same ratio of banks to population, there would be something like 205 banks in this country. In fact, about 6,800 commercial banks and roughly 16,000 depository institutions exist within U.S. borders, all vying to serve some 310 million Americans. While the United States and Canada are extremes, most countries' banking systems more closely resemble the Canadian structure. In Japan, for example, 127 million people depend on 148 banks; in the United Kingdom, 62 million people are served by 260 banks; and in China, there are fewer than 200 banks for 1.35 billion people!

Amazingly, the United States once had even more banks than it does today. As Figure 13.1 shows, the number peaked at nearly 15,000 in 1984 and has been falling ever since. The figure also shows an odd pattern in the structure of banks. For decades, most U.S. banks were **unit banks**, or banks without branches. Throughout the 1950s and 1960s, more than two-thirds of banks were unit banks confined to a single building. Over the last quarter of the 20th century, however, the pattern changed. Today, less than one-third of banks in the United States are unit banks. What explains this change in structure?

The decline in the total number of banks and the increase in the number of banks with branches are not the only changes the U.S. banking industry has seen in recent years. In April 1998, the Traveler's Insurance Company, together with its investment banking and brokerage subsidiary Salomon Smith Barney, merged with Citibank, then the second largest commercial bank in the country, to become Citigroup. At the time of its creation, Citigroup had $700 billion in assets and more than 100 million customers in 100 different countries. It was also illegal. But by the end of 1999, the law that forbid such combinations had been repealed, and Citigroup began buying up even more financial firms. Today, Citigroup and a few other megabanks provide a broad assortment of products offered by almost all other financial institutions. These may include the functions of an insurance company, a pension fund, a securities broker, a collection of mutual funds, a finance company and—of course—a commercial bank, all rolled into one.

The crisis of 2007–2009 has transformed the U.S. financial industry. The failure or forced merger of several large banks and other depository institutions accelerated concentration, boosting the deposit share of the top four commercial banks by about 7 percentage points, to around 40 percent of the total. In July 2008, the U.S. government placed the two massive government-sponsored enterprises (GSEs, page 63) for housing finance in conservatorship (wiping out their private shareholders, but allowing them to operate while insolvent). In September 2008, the investment banking era that had prevailed since the 1930s came to an abrupt end as the four largest independent investment banks failed, merged, or became bank holding companies. The ensuing run on money-market mutual funds (MMMFs, page 32) was stopped only by a government guarantee of MMMF liabilities. And the federal government

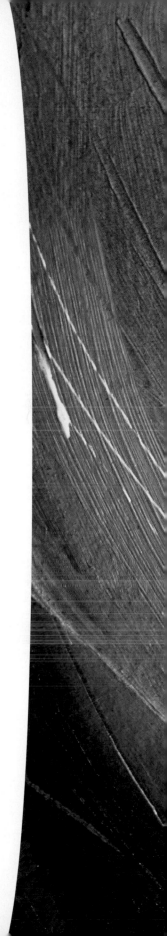

**Figure 13.1**   Number of Insured Commercial Banks in the United States, 1935-2009

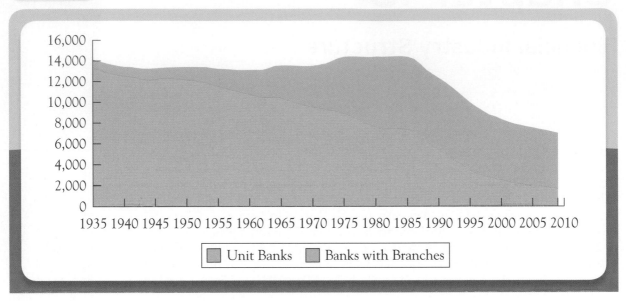

SOURCE: FDIC Historical Statistics on Banking, http://www2.fdic.gov/hsob/hsobRpt.asp.

invested several hundred billion dollars to restore the capital of the largest U.S. financial institutions. Most of those institutions have repaid the government, but in 2010 a few "private" intermediaries still had the U.S. government as their largest shareholder.

To understand the changing structure of the financial industry, we will discuss the services provided by both depository and nondepository financial institutions. Together, they provide a broad menu of services: buying and selling securities; offering loans, insurance, and pensions; and providing checking accounts, credit cards, and debit cards. Most financial institutions perform at least a few of these functions. Visit the Web site of any large bank, for instance, and you will discover that you can get not only checking and savings accounts, loans and credit cards, but insurance and stockbrokerage services. The first half of this chapter will consider current trends in the banking industry, including the tendency toward consolidation with nondepository institutions. The second half of the chapter will study the functions and characteristics of nondepository institutions.

## Banking Industry Structure

Today's banking system bears little resemblance to the one Americans knew in 1960 or 1970. Then people used their neighborhood banks. Not only did customers walk into the bank to conduct their business, but they knew the tellers and bank managers they saw there. Today most of us don't go beyond the ATM in the lobby, and if we do, we probably don't recognize the employees inside. Banks have been transformed so that location doesn't matter the way it once did. This change has occurred on both the national and the international level.

The best way to understand the structure of today's banking industry is to trace it back to its roots. That means looking at the legal history of banking. In this section we'll learn that banking legislation is the reason we have so many banks in the United States. We'll look at the trend toward consolidation that has been steadily reducing the number of banks since the mid-1980s. And we'll briefly consider the effects of globalization.

## A Short History of U.S. Banking

If you want to start a bank, you can't just rent a space, put up a sign, and open the door. You need permission in the form of a **bank charter**. Until the Civil War, all bank charters were issued by state banking authorities. Because the authors of the U.S. Constitution feared a strong central government, in the early years of the Republic the federal government was weak and sometimes ineffectual. State governments were often more powerful. Until 1863, in fact, there was no national currency. Instead, state banks issued banknotes that circulated in much the way dollar bills do today. But while the state-chartered banks usually promised to redeem their banknotes in gold, they did so only if the bearer presented them at the bank. As the bearer traveled farther and farther from the bank, the value of the notes fell. So a note issued by a New York bank was worth considerably less in Philadelphia than it was in New York.

A $10 banknote issued by the Central Bank of Tennessee in 1853.

Besides currency that did not hold its value from one place to another, the early American financial system was plagued by insufficient capital and fraud. Banks regularly failed, and when they did, their banknotes became worthless. As we saw in Chapter 2, given the license to print money, most people will print too much. With so many different banknotes circulating, telling the sound money from the unsound became inordinately confusing and inefficient. The whole point of printing money is to reduce information costs and facilitate trade. Still, reasonable people hesitated to accept banknotes issued by banks they weren't familiar with, so money was not widely accepted. In the end, the system just didn't work.

Radical change came during the Civil War, when Congress passed the National Banking Act of 1863, initiating a gradual shift in power away from the states. While the new law didn't eliminate state-chartered banks, it did impose a 10 percent tax on their issue of banknotes. At the same time, the act created a system of federally chartered banks, or *national banks*, which would be supervised by the Office of the Comptroller of the Currency, inside the U.S. Department of the Treasury. These new national banks could issue banknotes tax-free. Congress's intent was to put the state banks out of business by taking away their source of funds.

While the act did get rid of state-issued banknotes, state banks devised another way to raise funds, by creating demand deposits. This explains the origin of the **dual banking system** we have today, in which banks can choose whether to get their charters from the Comptroller of the Currency at the U.S. Treasury or from state officials. Roughly three-quarters of U.S. banks now have a state charter and the rest have a federal charter. The decision is related to a bank's profitability. State banking authorities have been more permissive than federal authorities in the types of operations they allow. Because greater flexibility in a bank's operations means a better chance of making a profit, state charters have been the overwhelming choice.

Furthermore, if the Comptroller of the Currency won't allow a bank to engage in a particular practice, the bank can always change its charter. This ability to switch back

The first national banknote issued in 1863.

and forth between state and federal charters created what amounts to regulatory competition, which has hastened innovation in the financial industry. In the 1990s, changes in banking law required federal and state agencies to coordinate their oversight of financial intermediaries. But the globalization of the financial system, together with banks' ability to move funds easily across international boundaries, means that today regulatory competition exists not so much between state and federal government regulators but between national government regulators.

The next major event in U.S. banking history occurred in 1933, in the midst of the Great Depression. From 1929 to 1933, more than a third of all U.S. banks failed; individual depositors lost $1.5 billion, or about 3 percent of total bank deposits. At the time, total personal income was less than $50 billion, or about $1 billion a week. So on average, the bank failures of the Great Depression cost depositors one and a half weeks' pay. (Today, total personal income in the United States is more than $12 trillion, or roughly $250 billion a week, so the equivalent loss would be about $375 billion.) But because failures were concentrated in small banks, small depositors bore the brunt of the collapse. Millions of small savers lost their life savings.

Congress responded to the crisis with the Glass-Steagall Act of 1933, which created the Federal Deposit Insurance Corporation (FDIC) and severely limited the activities of commercial banks. The FDIC provided insurance to individual depositors, so they would not lose their savings in the event that a bank failed. The act also restricted bank assets to certain approved forms of debt. In an effort to eliminate potential conflicts of interest that arise when an institution issues securities for one set of customers and manages assets for another, banks were forbidden from dealing in securities, providing insurance, or engaging in any of the other activities undertaken by nondepository institutions. But by separating commercial banks from investment banking, the law limited the ability of financial institutions to take advantage of economies of scale and scope that might exist in various lines of business. Nevertheless, this restriction on banks' activities remained in place until 1999, when the Gramm-Leach-Bliley Financial Services Modernization Act repealed the Glass-Steagall Act. We will return to this topic shortly. The repeal of the Glass-Steagall Act in 1999 eliminated the restrictions on banks' activities, but renewed concerns about potential mismanagement of large financial holding companies. The poor performance and outright failure of some of the largest U.S. intermediaries during the financial crisis of 2007–2009 have intensified these management concerns.

## Competition and Consolidation

None of the historical events we have discussed explains why there are roughly 6,800 commercial banks in the United States today or why that number has been shrinking since the mid-1980s. To unravel the mystery, let's return to Figure 13.1. Notice the division between banks with branches and banks that don't have branches. As we mentioned in the introduction, banks that do not have branches are called *unit banks*. The alternative, which is familiar to most of us today, is a bank with many branches spread out over a wide geographic area. Large banks like the Big Four— Bank of America, Citibank, JPMorgan Chase, and Wells Fargo—maintain branches in many cities across many states. We'll return to these banks in a moment. For now,

| Table 13.1 | Number and Assets of Commercial Banks in the United States |

| Size of Institution (Assets) | Number | Percent of Total Assets |
| --- | --- | --- |
| Less than $100 million | 2,525 | 1.2% |
| $100 million to $1 billion | 3,800 | 9.4% |
| $1 billion to $10 billion | 429 | 9.5% |
| $10 billion or more | 85 | 80.0% |
| Total | 6,839 | 100% ($11.8 trillion) |

SOURCE: FDIC *Quarterly Banking Profile, 2009, Table III-A.*

notice from the figure that in 1935, the vast majority of banks had no branches; today, nearly three-quarters of them do. In fact, if we look at the numbers, we see that in 1935 there were 14,125 commercial banks in the United States, with a total of 17,237 offices; at the end of 2009 there were 6,839 banks with a whopping 90,159 offices. Today's banks not only have branches, they have lots of them.

The number of banks and bank branches in the United States tells only part of the story; we also need to look at bank size. Table 13.1 shows that the U.S. banking system is composed of a large number of very small banks and a small number of very large ones. Roughly 1 percent of the banks hold more than 75 percent of all bank assets. In fact, the Big Four alone account for around 40 percent of assets and deposits in the U.S. commercial banking system.

The primary reason for this structure is the McFadden Act of 1927, which required that nationally chartered banks meet the branching restrictions of the states in which they were located.[1] Because some states had laws that forbade branch banking, the result was a large number of very small banks.[2] Advocates of legal limits on branching argued that they prevented concentration and monopoly in banking in the same way that antitrust laws prevented concentration in manufacturing. They feared that without such limits, a few large banks could drive small ones out of business, reducing the quality of financial services available in small communities.

*"Of course, you could try another bank, if there were any other banks."*

SOURCE: © Robert Mankoff/The New Yorker Collection/www.cartoonbank.com.

[1]The 1956 Douglas Amendment applied the same restrictions to bank holding companies, requiring that any out-of-state expansion be expressly approved by the host state.

[2]In the nation's early years, the states were starved for revenue; they could neither issue their own currency nor tax interstate trade. The fees the states earned for granting bank charters and the taxes they levied on bank profits became important sources of revenue for state government. The fees gave the state governments an incentive to create many small banks, while the taxes gave them an interest in protecting banks and ensuring they would be profitable. The result was a fragmented banking system with little competition. See R. Kroszner and P. Strahan, "What Drives Deregulation? Economics and Politics of the Relaxation of Bank Branching Restrictions," *Quarterly Journal of Economics* 114 (November 1999), pp. 1437–1467.

## YOUR FINANCIAL WORLD
Pawnshops

Contrary to their portrayal in the movies and on TV, pawnshops are not disreputable establishments frequented by criminals who are selling stolen goods. They are legitimate businesses that provide a useful service. Think of a pawnshop as a neighborhood nondepository institution that makes collateralized loans and sells a wide variety of merchandise on the side. The pawnshop's main business is to provide very small loans—smaller than a bank would consider—to people who lack access to the conventional financial system.

Say you have something valuable, like a piece of jewelry, a bicycle, or a camera. You need cash, so you take the valuable item to a pawnshop. The pawnbroker will offer you a loan on the condition that you leave the item there as collateral. When you repay the loan along with interest and fees, the pawnbroker will return your collateral. But if you don't repay the loan on time, the pawnbroker takes the collateral and sells it. The merchandise that's for sale in the pawnshop was collateral for defaulted loans.

Needless to say, the terms of the loan are favorable to the pawnbroker, not to you. The loan amount is usually less than half the value of the collateral, and the interest rate is high: 3 to 5 percent *per month* is standard. There

is also a fee that can drive up the interest rate to several hundred percent per year. While such an arrangement may seem outrageous, it is better than the payday loan described in Chapter 12. Because pawnbrokers' loans are collateralized, the interest rates charged are more reasonable than the ones on payday loans. So if you ever find yourself in dire straits, with no other source of credit, you can go to a pawnshop.

The McFadden Act produced a fragmented banking system nearly devoid of large institutions. The result was a network of small, geographically dispersed banks that faced virtually no competition—the opposite of what the act's advocates had intended. Not only that, but the system was prone to failure. In many states, more efficient and modern banks were legally precluded from opening branches to compete with the small, inefficient ones that were already there. In these states, the result was a network of small community banks that faced no competitive pressures to innovate. And because the only loan applications these banks received were from residents of their own communities, their loan portfolios were insufficiently diversified. In a farming town, the bank's fortunes depended on the weather, because its loan portfolio was composed almost entirely of agricultural loans. Aware of the problem, the bank manager would eventually stop making loans because the risk was simply too great. When credit ceased to flow into the community, farmers curtailed their operations. In the end, the bank's owners made a healthy profit because the bank was protected from competition—but everyone else in town suffered.

Some banks reacted to branching restrictions by creating **bank holding companies**. A holding company is a corporation that owns a group of other firms. In some contexts, it may be thought of as the *parent firm* for a group of subsidiaries. Bank holding companies have been around since the early 1900s. Initially, they were created not just as a way to evade branching restrictions but as a way to provide nonbank financial services in more than one state. In 1956, the U.S. Congress passed the Bank Holding

Company Act, which broadened the scope of what bank holding companies could do, allowing them to provide various nonbank financial services. Over the years, changes in laws and regulations have added asset management, investment advice, insurance, leasing, collections, and real estate services to the list of allowable activities.

Beginning in the early 1970s, technology enabled banks to borrow and lend at a distance. The combination of the U.S. mail, telephone service, and finally the Internet dramatically reduced the importance of physical location in banking. Without the need to personally visit the bank to conduct their business, people ceased to care whether a bank was chartered in the state where they lived. Today, ATMs, laptop computers, cell phones, and debit and credit cards allow depositors access to means of payment even when they are far from home. Credit companies can evaluate any individual or firm's creditworthiness, so a bank can make a loan regardless of the borrower's location. In 1976, small businesses were located an average of 16 miles from their banks. By 1992, the average distance was 64 miles. Today, the majority of small businesses use various forms of Internet banking, making the physical location of the bank even less important.

In changing the way people use the financial system, technology has eroded the value of the local banking monopoly. In the 1970s and 1980s, states responded by loosening their branching restrictions.[3] Then in 1994, Congress passed the Riegel-Neal Interstate Banking and Branching Efficiency Act. This legislation reversed the restrictions put in place almost 70 years earlier by the McFadden Act. Since 1997, banks have been able to acquire an unlimited number of branches nationwide, and the number of commercial banks has fallen nearly in half. What is more, the number of savings institutions—savings and loans plus savings banks—has fallen even more. While some banks couldn't handle the new competition and went out of business, the vast majority disappeared through mergers with other banks.

The Riegel-Neal Act allowed banks to diversify geographically. Today a bank that wants to establish operations in a new state can purchase a bank already located in that state. In doing so, it acquires the bank's customers, as well as its employees and their knowledge of the state's business and legal environment. The results have been dramatic. Banks became more profitable: their operating costs and loan losses fell; the interest rates paid to depositors rose while the interest rates charged to borrowers fell. The only people who suffered were the employees of inefficient banks, who had to work harder and were paid less as a result of the new competition. So, the deregulation of banks provided sizable benefits for the economy.[4]

Table 13.2 summarizes the key events in the evolution of the U.S. banking industry over the last century.

The financial crisis of 2007–2009 has focused attention on the costs of deregulation. Did the poor management of some megabanks reveal the limits to expanding institutional scale and scope? Have the biggest banks already outrun those economies? Has deregulation encouraged banks to take on too much risk? Has deregulation

---

[3]A number of other changes took place as well. For example, until 1980, federal law restricted the interest rate banks could pay on deposits. Under Regulation Q, they were prohibited from paying interest on checking accounts, and were limited to a maximum rate of just over 5 percent on savings deposits. As inflation and interest rates rose in the late 1970s, these restrictions became prohibitive. Many depositors withdrew their funds from banks and placed them in money-market mutual funds, whose interest rates were not restricted by law.

[4]One way to tell that deregulation improved growth is to look at what happened in different states. Separating the impact of deregulation from that of a variety of other effects on growth can be tricky. The fact that states deregulated at different times allows economists to disentangle the effects. See J. Jayaranthe and P. Strahan, "The Finance-Growth Nexus: Evidence from Bank Branch Deregulation," *Quarterly Journal of Economics* 111 (1996), pp. 639–670.

| Table 13.2 | Key Legislation Affecting the U.S. Banking Industry |
| --- | --- |
| 1927 McFadden Act | Outlawed interstate branching and required national banks to abide by the laws of the states in which they operated. |
| 1933 Glass-Steagall Act | Established federal deposit insurance and prohibited commercial banks from engaging in the insurance and securities businesses. |
| 1994 Riegel-Neal Act | Repealed the McFadden Act's prohibition of interstate branching. |
| 1999 Gramm-Leach-Bliley Act | Repealed the Glass-Steagall Act's prohibition of mergers between commercial banks and insurance companies or securities firms. |

motivated some banks to become "too big to fail" in order to secure a government bailout in the event of distress?

Addressing these complex questions is mostly an issue for government supervision, which is the subject of Chapter 14. However, scholars and policymakers also are reviewing whether the benefits of deregulation noted earlier warrant the extra risks associated with those large intermediaries that became a burden on taxpayers and the economy during the financial crisis. Some analysts argue that the crisis-induced increase in banking concentration raises both the likelihood and expected cost of a future financial crisis.[5]

## The Globalization of Banking

Toward the end of the 20th century, U.S. banking underwent not just a national but an international transformation. An explosion in international trade had increased the need for international financial services. Very simply, every time a Japanese company purchased software produced in the United States or an American bought a television set manufactured in China, payments had to be made across national boundaries. Today, the international banking system has adjusted to the needs of an interdependent, globalized world. Large U.S. banks like JPMorgan Chase and Citibank have stationed ATMs on the streets of Frankfurt, Buenos Aires, and other major capitals. In New York, keen observers can spot the foreign offices of Barclays, Deutsche Bank, and Tokyo-Mitsubishi. All told, by 2009, nearly 50 large U.S. banks had established foreign operations of one type or another, with foreign assets totaling more than $1 trillion. And more than 300 foreign banks with assets totaling more than $3 trillion had established a presence in the United States.

There are a number of ways banks can operate in foreign countries, depending on such factors as the legal environment. The most straightforward approach is to open a foreign branch that offers the same services as those in the home country. Certain legal structures also allow U.S. banks to engage in operations outside of the country, opening what looks to the casual observer like a branch (but may have a different legal status). For example, a bank can create an international banking facility (IBF), which allows it to accept deposits from and make loans to foreigners outside the country. Or the bank can create a subsidiary called an Edge Act corporation, which is established specifically to engage in international banking transactions. Alternatively, a bank

[5]See, for example, Chapter 7 of the *Annual Report* of the Bank for International Settlements, 2009.

holding company can purchase a controlling interest in a foreign bank. From our point of view, the classification of the particular enterprise is less important than the fact that U.S. banks take advantage of various methods to operate outside the country.

Foreign banks, of course, can take advantage of similar options. They can purchase an interest in a U.S. bank, open branches on U.S. soil, create a U.S. subsidiary, or open what is called an *agency office*. These alternatives differ in the spectrum of financial services they can provide.

The growth of international banking has had an economic impact similar to that of deregulation in the United States. Today, a borrower in France, Brazil, or Singapore can shop for a loan virtually anywhere in the world, and a depositor seeking the highest return can do the same. All this competition has surely made banking a tougher business. Profits are harder for bankers to come by today than they were in 1970, when depositors and borrowers were captive to small local banks. But while bankers' lives may be more difficult, on balance the improved efficiency of the financial system has enhanced growth everywhere.

MARKETS

One of the most important aspects of international banking is the eurodollar market. **Eurodollars** are dollar-denominated deposits in foreign banks. For reasons we will explain shortly, a bank in London, Zurich, or the Cayman Islands might offer its best customers the ability to make their deposits in dollars. In response, Ford Motor Corporation might convert a $1 million deposit in its New York bank to a eurodollar deposit in the bank's Cayman Islands subsidiary. After the $1 million has been deposited in Ford's Cayman Islands account, it is lent back to the New York bank. So, the account continues to provide Ford with all the same functions of the deposit at the same time that the New York bank now has a loan liability from its off-shore subsidiary.

Both Ford and the New York bank have an incentive to do this. For the bank, the Cayman Islands deposit is cheaper. It is not subject to U.S. reserve requirements, nor is the bank required to pay a deposit insurance premium on the balance. Moreover, regulatory supervision is more lax in the middle of the Gulf of Mexico than it is in the United States, which reduces the cost of compliance. Finally, profits from the offshore bank may be subject to a lower corporate income tax rate than profits originating inside the United States. These advantages allow the bank to pay Ford a higher interest rate on the deposit, and they increase the bank's net interest margin.

A number of forces conspired to create the euromarket. Originally, it was a response to restrictions on the movement of international capital that were instituted at the end of World War II with the creation of the Bretton Woods system of exchange rate management. (We will learn more about the international monetary system and capital controls in Chapter 19.) To ensure that the pound would retain its value, the British government imposed restrictions on the ability of British banks to finance international transactions. In an attempt to evade these restrictions, London banks began to offer dollar deposits and dollar-denominated loans to foreigners. The result was what we know today as the eurodollar market. The Cold War accelerated the market's development when the Soviet government, fearful that the U.S. government might freeze or confiscate them, shifted its dollar deposits from New York to London. In the United States, a combination of factors propelled the eurodollar market forward. In the 1960s, U.S. authorities tried to prevent dollars from leaving the country and made it costly for foreigners to borrow dollars in the United States for use elsewhere in the world. Then in the early 1970s, a combination of domestic interest-rate controls and high inflation rates made domestic deposits much less attractive than eurodollar deposits, which paid comparatively high interest rates.

Today, the eurodollar market in London is one of the biggest and most important financial markets in the world. And the interest rate at which banks lend each other eurodollars, called the **London Interbank Offered Rate (LIBOR)**, is the standard against which many private loan rates are measured. For example, some adjustable-rate home mortgages in the United States carry an interest rate that is pegged to LIBOR. LIBOR figured prominently in the financial crisis of 2007–2009 when the interbank lending market dried up. The gap between LIBOR and the expected Federal Reserve policy interest rate provides a key measure of the intensity and persistence of the liquidity crisis (see Chapter 3, Lessons from the Crisis: Interbank Lending).

## The Future of Banks

Today's banks are bigger, fewer in number, and more international in reach than the banks of yesteryear; they also have more to offer in the way of services. A typical large commercial bank now offers investment and insurance products as well as the more conventional deposit accounts and loans. This trend began in 1998 with Citigroup's creation (see the chapter introduction). At the time Citigroup was established, insurance companies were permitted to own investment banks, so Traveler's Insurance could merge, unchallenged, with the brokerage and investment banking businesses known as Salomon Smith Barney. But the two together could not legally purchase Citibank. They did it anyway and were given five years to sell off those businesses the law prohibited them from keeping. Instead of divesting Citibank, however, Citigroup did the opposite. Managers set to work integrating all the businesses, betting that Congress would amend the law to legalize Citigroup's innovative combination.

In November 1999, the Gramm-Leach-Bliley Financial Services Modernization Act went into effect. The new law effectively repealed the Glass-Steagall Act of 1933, allowing a commercial bank, investment bank, and insurance company to merge and form a **financial holding company**. Citigroup, with more than 100 million customers in more than 100 countries and assets in excess of $1 trillion, became legal. Since then, investment firms like JPMorgan, which once dealt only in securities, were acquired by commercial banks (in this case, Chase Manhattan), while commercial banks like Bank of America have purchased large securities dealers and retail brokers (Merrill Lynch). To serve all their customers' financial needs, bank holding companies are converting to financial holding companies.

Financial holding companies are a limited form of **universal banks**, firms that engage in nonfinancial as well as financial activities. Depending on the country, such an arrangement provides more or less separation among the banking, insurance, and securities industries. The most extreme example is Germany, where universal banks do everything under one roof, including direct investment in the shares of nonfinancial firms. In the United States, different financial activities must be undertaken in separate subsidiaries, and financial holding companies are still prohibited from making equity investments in nonfinancial companies.

The owners and managers of these large financial firms cite three reasons to create them. First, their range of activities, properly managed, permits them to be well diversified, so their profitability does not rely on one particular line of business. This reduced risk should increase the value of the firm.[6] Second, these firms are large

---

[6]Financial economists disagree on whether the reduced risk would actually increase the firm's value. Some people argue that firms should not diversify themselves but leave the choice to their stockholders. An investor can always purchase shares in two companies that would otherwise merge, in proportion to whatever risk exposure the investor desires. There also is concern that a firm with many different lines of business may not be as well managed as specialized firms.

enough to take advantage of **economies of scale**. A financial holding company needs only one CEO and one board of directors regardless of its size. Only one accounting system is required to run the company. Third, these companies hope to benefit from **economies of scope**. In the same way that a supermarket offers all sorts of food and nonfood items under one roof, financial holding companies offer customers a wide variety of services, all under the same brand name. This, too, should reduce costs—or maybe the people who run these firms are just trying to build empires.

While Citigroup was creating the first of these full-service financial firms in the United States, the rest of the financial world was not standing still. Individual firms were working to provide customers with the same services they could obtain from more traditional financial intermediaries. Money-market mutual funds competed with banks in providing liquidity services to customers. Mortgage brokers gave consumers a choice in how to borrow for the purchase of a home and then sold the mortgages in the financial marketplace. Today, people who need an auto loan or any kind of insurance can get dozens of price quotes in a few hours just by logging onto the Internet. The screening of loan applicants, which was once the job of the neighborhood banker, has been standardized and now can be done by virtually anyone. Then there are discount brokerage firms like Charles Schwab and E-Trade, which provide low-cost access to the financial markets. Unlike the banks of the past, these alternative financial intermediaries don't have balance sheets of their own. Instead, for a fee they provide their customers with access to financial markets.

In fact, thanks to recent technological advances, almost every service traditionally provided by financial intermediaries can now be produced independently, without the help of a large organization. Loan brokers can give large borrowers access to the pooled funds of many small savers. A variety of financial firms, including brokerage firms and mutual-fund companies, provides connections to the payments system, as well as the ability to transform assets into money quickly and at low cost. One of these days, even the electric company may get into the act. And many intermediaries, including mutual-fund companies and pension funds, help customers to spread, share, and transfer risk. Finally, the production of information to mitigate the problems of adverse selection and moral hazard has become a business in and of itself.

As we survey the financial industry, then, we see two trends running in opposite directions. On the one hand, large firms are working hard to provide one-stop shopping for financial services. On the other hand, the industry is splintering into a host of small firms, each of which serves a very specific purpose. Will the future be one of generalists, specialists, or both? We will have to wait and see. In the meantime, let's look more closely at the role of nondepository financial institutions. And as we do, let's think about whether their products can be provided more easily and cheaply alone or together with other financial services.

# Nondepository Institutions

A survey of the financial industry reveals a broad array of intermediaries. Besides depository institutions, there are five categories of nondepository institution: insurance companies; pension funds; securities firms, including brokers, mutual-fund companies, and investment banks; finance companies; and government-sponsored enterprises. This classification is neither exhaustive nor meant to imply that an institution's activities are restricted to a particular category. Nondepository institutions also include an assortment of alternative intermediaries, such as pawnshops (see Your Financial

| Table 13.3 | Relative Size of U.S. Financial Intermediaries, 1970–2009 |

| | Assets ($ billions) 2009 | Percent of all Intermediary Assets | | |
|---|---|---|---|---|
| | | 1970 | 1990 | 2009 |
| **Depository Institutions** | | | | |
| Commercial banks | $14,200 | 37.2% | 29.3% | 31.0% |
| Savings institutions | 1,398 | 18.8 | 12.1 | 3.1 |
| Credit unions | 877 | 1.3 | 1.9 | 1.9 |
| **Insurance Companies** | | | | |
| Life insurance | 4,552 | 14.8 | 12.1 | 10.0 |
| Property and casualty | 1,317 | 3.7 | 4.7 | 2.9 |
| **Pension Funds** | | | | |
| Private pension funds | 4,758 | 8.1 | 14.4 | 10.4 |
| Government pension funds | 3,587 | 4.4 | 6.5 | 7.8 |
| **Mutual Funds** | | | | |
| Money market funds | 3,584 | 0.0 | 4.4 | 7.8 |
| Stock and bond funds | 6,473 | 3.5 | 5.7 | 14.1 |
| **Finance Companies** | 1,777 | 4.7 | 5.4 | 3.9 |
| **Government-Sponsored Enterprises** | 3,224 | 3.4 | 3.7 | 7.0 |
| **Total Assets of All U.S. Financial Institutions in 2009 = $45.7 trillion** | | | | |

SOURCE: *Board of Governors of the Federal Reserve System, Flow of Funds of the United States, November 26, 2009, Tables L.109 to L.128.*

World, page 318), payday loan centers (see Your Financial World, page 295), rent-to-own centers, peer-to-peer lending firms (see In the News, pages 278–279), and even loan sharks.

Table 13.3 shows that depository institutions accounted for more than one-third of the $45.7 trillion in assets held by financial intermediaries in 2009. In the decades after 1970, the share of intermediation handled by banks fell until the crisis of 2007–2009 depressed the assets of many nonbanks. Insurance companies suffered a similar fate as their share of intermediation fell from 18.5 percent in 1970 to 12.9 percent in 2009. Meanwhile, mutual funds have been the big winners, growing from a 3.5 percent share in 1970 to over 20 percent in 2009. Pension funds increased in importance as well, rising from 12.5 percent of all assets in 1970 to more than 18 percent over the 39-year period.

Our goal in this section is to understand the role of each of these types of nondepository institution in our financial system. We will do so by focusing on the functions of each. Recall from Chapter 11 that the functions of financial institutions can be divided into five categories: (1) pooling the resources of small savers; (2) providing safekeeping and accounting services, which allow people to make payments and track their assets; (3) supplying liquidity by converting resources into means of payment whenever needed; (4) providing diversification services; and (5) collecting and processing information in order to reduce information costs. We will use the same system to classify nondepository institutions.

## Insurance Companies

Insurance companies began with long sea voyages. Centuries ago, transoceanic trade and exploration were fraught with risk, and that risk generated a demand for insurance. Over time, as long, risky voyages of discovery became the norm and the nature of sea travel changed, insurance changed with it. Modern forms of insurance can be traced back to around 1400, when wool merchants insured their overland shipments from London to Italy for 12 to 15 percent of their value. (Overseas shipments were even more expensive to insure.) The first insurance codes were developed in Florence in 1523. They specified the standard provisions for a general insurance policy, such as the beginning and end of the coverage period and the time frame for receipt of payment following a loss. They also stipulated procedures for handling fraudulent claims in an attempt to reduce the moral hazard problem.

In 1688, Lloyd's of London was established. Today, Lloyd's is famous for insuring singers' voices, dancers' legs, even food critics' taste buds, as well as more traditional assets like airplanes and ships. The best-known insurance company in the world, Lloyd's began in a small London coffeehouse whose proprietor, Edward Lloyd, catered to retired sea captains who had prospered in the East Indies spice trade. Having sailed many of the trade routes themselves, these captains possessed special knowledge of the hazards of sea voyages. They used their knowledge to assess the risks associated with particular routes and to dabble in marine insurance. The risks were not inconsequential. In the 17th century, a typical voyage to the Spice Islands (part of Indonesia) and back lasted three years. Only one in three ships returned with their cargo, and as few as one in eight sailors lived to tell of the adventure. The rewards of a successful voyage were coveted spices like nutmeg, a single sack of which could make a sea captain wealthy for the rest of his life.

To obtain insurance, a ship's owner would write the details of the proposed voyage on a piece of paper, together with the amount he was willing to pay for the service, and then circulate the paper among the patrons at Edward Lloyd's coffeehouse. Interested individuals would decide how much of the risk to accept and then sign their names under the description of the voyage. This customary way of doing business became the source of the term *underwriter*. Underwriting was open to anyone who wished to assume the risk associated with sea voyages. Because Lloyd's predated by several centuries the concept of limited liability, in which investors' losses were confined to the amount of their investment, underwriting implied unlimited liability. The saying was that an underwriter was liable down to his last cufflink.

**RISK**

Lloyd's may be thought of as an insurance market rather than as an insurance company. To participate in the market, individuals known as *names* join together in groups called syndicates. When a new insurance contract is offered, several syndicates sign up for a portion of the risk in return for a portion of the premiums.

Historically, becoming a name with Lloyd's has brought both reputation and risk. The risks were never more apparent than in the early 1990s, when Lloyd's racked up losses in excess of $10 billion as a result of claims on policies that protected firms against the legal damages associated with asbestos. The huge amount exceeded the estimated combined assets of all 34,000 Lloyd's names. Because of their unlimited liability, nearly 2,000 individuals were driven into personal bankruptcy; many of them filed lawsuits claiming that Lloyd's management had misled them. As a result, Lloyd's was reorganized. Today the firm provides insurance through the more conventional structure of a limited liability company. The losses of individual investors in a syndicate are limited to the amount of their initial investment, and no person is exposed to the possibility of financial ruin.

**Two Types of Insurance**    At their most basic level, all insurance companies operate like Lloyd's of London. They accept premiums from policyholders in exchange for the promise of compensation if certain events occur. A homeowner pays a premium in return for the promise that if the house burns down, the insurance company will pay to rebuild it. For the individual policyholder, then, insurance is a way to transfer risk. In terms of the financial system as a whole, insurance companies specialize in three of the five functions performed by intermediaries: They pool small premiums and make large investments with them; they diversify risks across a large population; and they screen and monitor policyholders to mitigate the problem of asymmetric information.

Insurance companies offer two types of insurance: life insurance and **property and casualty insurance**. Life insurers—companies like Prudential of America, Metropolitan Life, and John Hancock Mutual Life—sell policies that protect the insured against the loss of earnings from disability, retirement, or death. Property and casualty companies sell policies that protect households and businesses from losses arising from accident, fire, and natural disaster. Both types of intermediary allow individuals to transfer their risk to a group. While a single company may provide both kinds of insurance, the two businesses operate very differently.

Life insurance comes in two basic forms, called term and whole life insurance, as well as a variety of hybrids. **Term life insurance** provides a payment to the policyholder's beneficiaries in the event of the insured's death at any time during the policy's term. The premium depends on the very predictable proportion of people (of a given age) who will die. Term policies are generally renewable every year so long as the policyholder is less than 65 years old. Many people obtain term life insurance through their employers, an arrangement called group life insurance.

**Whole life insurance** is a combination of term life insurance and a savings account. The policyholder pays a fixed premium over his or her lifetime in return for a fixed benefit when the policyholder dies. Should the policyholder decide to discontinue the policy, its cash value will be refunded. As time passes and the policyholder ages, the emphasis of the whole life policy shifts from insurance to savings. Someone who lives to a ripe old age will have accumulated substantial savings in a whole life policy, which can be cashed in if the policyholder chooses. In fact, most whole life policies can be cashed in at any time. Whole life insurance tends to be an expensive way to save, though, so its use as a savings vehicle has declined markedly as people have discovered cheaper alternatives.

Most adults have experience with property and casualty insurance because driving a car without it is illegal. Auto insurance is a combination of property insurance on the car itself and casualty insurance on the driver, who is protected against liability for harm or injury to other people or their property. Holders of property and casualty insurance pay premiums in exchange for protection during the term of the policy.

On the balance sheets of insurance companies, these promises to policyholders show up as liabilities. While some claims may already be in process, most of them are future claims. On the asset side, insurance companies hold a combination of stocks and bonds. Property and casualty companies profit from the fees they charge for administering the policies they write; the claims are covered by the premiums. Because the assets are essentially reserves against sudden claims, they have to be liquid. A look at the balance sheet of a property and casualty insurer will show a preponderance of very short-term money-market instruments.

## YOUR FINANCIAL WORLD

### How Much Life Insurance Do You Need?

We discussed disability insurance in Chapter 3 and automobile insurance in Chapter 5. What about life insurance? How much should you buy? The first question is whether you should buy any at all. The purpose of life insurance is to take care of the people you are supporting should something unpleasant happen to you. Think of it as replacement income that will be there when you're not. People with young children are the ones who need life insurance the most. If a parent dies, someone will have to raise those children and put them through school, and a life insurance policy will pay the bills. Life insurance is *not* for a single college student with no obligations, so don't let anyone sell it to you if you don't need it.

If you think you need life insurance, the next step is to decide what kind. The best approach is to buy *term life insurance,* which will pay off only if you die. Because other kinds of life insurance include investment components, they are more costly. And because the people who need life insurance most are young families with limited incomes and big expenses, the more affordable the policy, the better. Making your insurance and investment decisions separately is also easier than trying to achieve all your goals with a single vehicle.*

Finally, how much life insurance should you buy? If you are married with two small children, most advisors recommend that you buy a term policy worth six to eight times your annual income. While that might cover your family's living expenses until the children are grown, consider carefully whether it will be enough to send them to college. If you and your spouse each earn $35,000 a year, each of you might need $400,000 worth of life insurance. For someone who is between 30 and 40 years old, a $400,000 policy costs about $500 a year, so out of your joint annual income of $70,000, you and your spouse would be spending $1,000 on term life insurance. That's expensive, so don't buy more than you need.

*Your parents and grandparents may have purchased whole life insurance policies for two reasons. First, in the past, individuals did not have access to all the investment choices that are available today. Second, tax laws were different; for some people, saving through a whole life insurance policy had tax advantages. But with the creation of tax-deferred savings vehicles like individual retirement accounts (IRAs), those benefits disappeared. Today, you would likely pay a life insurance company much more than the value of any tax benefits to you to administer a whole life insurance policy.

---

Life insurance companies hold assets of longer maturity than property and casualty insurers. Because most life insurance payments will be made well into the future, this better matches the maturity of the companies' assets and liabilities. Furthermore, while stocks may carry a relatively low degree of risk when held for periods of 25 years or more (recall the discussion in Chapter 8), insurance companies cannot risk the possibility that they may be forced to sell stocks when prices are low in order to pay policyholders' claims. As a result, life insurance companies hold mostly bonds.

**The Role of Insurance Companies**   Like life insurers, property and casualty insurers pool risks to generate predictable payouts. That is, they reduce risk by spreading it across many policies. Recall from Chapter 5 that a group of investments with uncorrelated returns is less risky than any individual investment. The same is true of insurance contracts. While there is no way to know exactly which policies will require payment—who will have an automobile accident, lose a house to fire, or die—the insurance company can estimate precisely the percentage of policyholders who will file claims. Doing so allows managers to compute accurately, with little uncertainty, how much the firm will need to pay out in any given year. From the point of view of policyholders, property and casualty insurance allows them to spread the risk of accident and damage across a large group of individuals.

In Chapter 11, we discussed the problem of asymmetric information in stock and bond finance. Recall that when a lender or investor cannot tell a good borrower or investment from a bad one, the tendency is for only the worst opportunities to present themselves. This phenomenon is adverse selection. Furthermore, once borrowers or entrepreneurs have received financing, they have less incentive to avoid risk than the lender or investor. That problem is called moral hazard.

While adverse selection and moral hazard create significant problems in the stock and bond markets, they create worse problems in the insurance market. A person who has terminal cancer surely has an incentive to buy life insurance for the largest amount possible—that's adverse selection. And without fire insurance, people would have more fire extinguishers in their houses. Fire insurance creates moral hazard, encouraging homeowners to be less careful in protecting their homes than they would otherwise. Insurance companies work hard to reduce both these problems. By screening applicants, they can reduce adverse selection. A person who wants to buy a life insurance policy must undergo a physical evaluation: weight, blood pressure, blood tests, and health history. Only those who pass the exam are allowed to purchase policies. And people who want automobile insurance must provide their driving records, including traffic citations and accident histories. While bad drivers may be allowed to buy car insurance, they will need to pay more for it. By screening drivers and adjusting their premiums accordingly, then, insurance companies can reduce their losses due to adverse selection.

Insurance companies have ways to reduce moral hazard as well. Policies usually include restrictive covenants that require the insured to engage or not to engage in certain activities. To qualify for fire insurance, a restaurant owner might be required to have the sprinkler system examined periodically; to obtain insurance against physical injury, a baseball or basketball player might be precluded from riding a motorcycle. Beyond such covenants, insurance policies often include *deductibles*, which require the insured to pay the initial cost of repairing accidental damage, up to some maximum amount. Or they may require *coinsurance*, in which the insurance company shoulders a percentage of the claim, perhaps 80 or 90 percent, and the insured assumes the rest of the cost.

It is interesting to speculate about the future of insurance in an age in which firms can collect more and more information at lower and lower cost. Remember that insurance is meant to shift risk from individuals to groups, not to shift the responsibility for events that are certain to happen. For example, no one expects an insurance company to sell life insurance to a person with a terminal disease.

Herein lies a potential problem. If, with the decoding of the human genome, tests become available whereby a person can determine their probability of developing a terminal disease, then they may be able to use this information to get a fairly good idea of their life expectancy and relative cost of health care. If applicants for health insurance were to withhold this information from insurance companies, the adverse

"We cannot write a life policy for your husband, Mrs. Blaine, because he is already dead. In insurance terms, that is considered a preëxisting condition."

SOURCE: © J.B. Handelsman/The New Yorker Collection/ www.cartoonbank.com.

## APPLYING THE CONCEPT
### REINSURANCE AND "CAT BONDS"

To get a mortgage on a home, you'll need insurance. Regardless of where you live, your lender will require you to have fire insurance, and in some places you may also need insurance against natural disasters like floods, earthquakes, or hurricanes. Without such insurance you won't get a mortgage, and without a mortgage you won't buy a house. Clearly, it's in everyone's interest for insurance companies to provide such insurance and spread the risk. But sometimes this kind of insurance isn't easy to obtain.

Imagine that an insurer is thinking of offering earthquake insurance in California. Unlike automobile accidents, when an earthquake hits, a large number of policyholders will all file claims at the same time. The result for the insurance company is a large, undiversified risk. To offer earthquake insurance and stay in business, a property and casualty insurance company must find some way to insure itself against catastrophic risks—large natural disasters that generate a significant number of payouts simultaneously.

*Reinsurance companies* offer a solution to this problem by providing insurance to insurance companies. Say the California insurer estimates that an earthquake would generate payments of $15 billion (the approximate loss in the 1994 earthquake in Northridge, Los Angeles). The company may have the resources to cover only the first $1 billion of policyholders' claims. To write the full $15 billion worth of insurance, the company will need to buy $14 billion of reinsurance.

Reinsurance companies are enormous; they operate all over the world. Their geographic spread allows them to diversify their risk, since earthquakes don't happen at the same time in both California and Japan. The fact that reinsurance companies can spread their risk globally gives them the ability to withstand individual losses, even if they are catastrophic. For this to work, reinsurers have to be big. So big, in fact, that they have become near monopolies, driving up the price of reinsurance in the process.

The rising cost of reinsurance has spurred the creation of a second solution to the problem of insuring catastrophic risk. Financial experts have designed catastrophic bonds, or *cat bonds,* which allow individual investors to share a very small portion of the reinsurance risk. It works like this. Through an investment bank, an insurance company will sell a substantial quantity of cat bonds, immediately investing proceeds in low-risk financial instruments like U.S. Treasury bonds. If a catastrophe occurs, the U.S. Treasury bonds are sold and the resulting funds used to pay the claims the insurance company faces. But if no earthquake, fire, or hurricane hits during the policy period, the cat bond owners receive a substantial return that can be as high as 10 percentage points above the yield on U.S. Treasury bonds of equal maturity.* This high level of compensation, coupled with a very low correlation with the return on most other investments, means that cat bonds can both improve the expected return and lower the risk of a typical investor's portfolio.

The existence of reinsurance and cat bonds has clear benefits. These mechanisms for transferring and spreading the risk of catastrophic disaster improve the risk-return trade-off for individual investors, enable insurance companies to offer more insurance than they could otherwise, and allow prospective homeowners to get the insurance they need—and the mortgage financing they want—to purchase a home.

*One of the first cat bonds to be issued was a $400 million offering in 1997 by the United Service Automobile Association (USAA), an insurer of current and past military personnel and their families. The bond agreement provided that if USAA's losses from a hurricane rated category 3, 4, or 5 exceeded $1 billion over the next year, bondholders would pay 80 percent of the next $500 million in claims.

selection problem could become severe enough to cause the industry to collapse. By contrast, if applicants chose to reveal this information, they might not be able to obtain insurance. Someone who has a high probability of getting heart disease at a young age will still be able to get automobile insurance, but getting life or health insurance will be very difficult.

The solution to this problem is not obvious, but it seems likely that any answer will involve government intervention. The government could either require insurance companies to provide coverage to everyone or act as an insurer of last resort.

## Pension Funds

Like an insurance company, a pension fund offers people the ability to make premium payments today in exchange for promised payments under certain future circumstances. Also like an insurance company, pension funds do not accept deposits.

They do help people to develop the discipline of saving regularly, getting them started early and helping them to stick with it. As we saw in Chapter 4, the earlier a person begins saving and the more disciplined he or she is, the better off that person will be later in life. Saving from an early age means enjoying a higher income at retirement. Pension plans not only provide an easy way to make sure that a worker saves and has sufficient resources in old age; they help savers to diversify their risk. By pooling the savings of many small investors, pension funds spread the risk, ensuring that funds will be available to investors in their old age.

People can use a variety of methods to save for retirement, including employer-sponsored plans and individual savings plans, both of which allow workers to defer income tax on their savings until they retire. Nearly everyone who works for a large corporation in the United States has an employer-administered pension plan. There are two basic types: defined-benefit (DB) pension plans and defined-contribution (DC) pension plans. Regardless of the type, many employer-sponsored plans require a person to work for a certain number of years before qualifying for benefits. This qualifying process is called **vesting**. Think of vesting as the point at which the contributions your employer has made to the pension plan on your behalf belong to you. Changing jobs before your pension contributions have been vested can be very costly.

Let's take a look at how the two types of pension plan work. **Defined-benefit plans** were once more common than they are today. Participants in DB plans receive a lifetime retirement income based on the number of years they worked at the company and their final salary. For example, someone who worked for the same company for 30 years and retired at a salary of $100,000 might receive 2 percent of that salary for each year of service, or $60,000 per year. That may seem good, but to reap such benefits, most people would need to work a very long time for the same firm.

**Defined-contribution plans** are replacing defined-benefit plans, and they are very different. These plans are sometimes referred to by names like "401(k)" after their designations in the Internal Revenue Service code. In a defined-contribution plan, the employee and employer both make contributions into an investment account that belongs to the employee. Unlike a defined-benefit plan, in a DC plan the employer takes no responsibility for the size of the employee's retirement income. Instead, at retirement the employee receives the accumulated funds in the account and must decide what to do with them. The options include accepting a lump sum, removing small amounts at a time, or converting the balance to a fixed monthly payment for life by purchasing an annuity (see Your Financial World: Annuities later in this chapter).

You can think of a pension plan as the opposite of life insurance. One pays off if you live, the other if you don't. The two vehicles are similar enough that the same institution often offers both. And not surprisingly, the balance sheets of pension funds look a lot like those of life insurance companies; both hold long-term assets like corporate bonds and stocks. The only difference is that life insurance companies hold only half the equities that pension funds do.[7]

Finally, it is worth noting that the U.S. government does provide insurance for private, defined-benefit pension systems. If a company goes bankrupt, the Pension Benefit Guaranty Corporation (PBGC) will take over the fund's liabilities. The PBGC currently guarantees some 29,000 pension funds covering 44 million workers and retirees. While the PBGC's insurance is capped, so that highly paid employees like

---

[7]The heavier emphasis on equities makes pension funds more risky. This is a risk that is potentially borne by the plans' participants. But as mentioned later in this section, defined-benefit pension plans are insured by the U.S. government, so in reality this is a risk borne broadly by everyone.

## APPLYING THE CONCEPT
### PUBLIC PENSIONS AND THE
### SOCIAL SECURITY SYSTEM

Providing for the elderly is a tremendous challenge for any society. Traditionally, children cared for their parents when they became old. But with the advent of modern industrial societies and an associated increase in geographic mobility, many elderly parents no longer live with their children. Today the expectation is that people will save enough while they are working to pay their own way when they retire. If they don't, the general view is that in a civilized society, government should care for the poor.

During the 20th century, the governments of many countries created pension systems that provided a guaranteed income to the elderly. These programs were financed by tax revenues paid by the young. As long as workers' incomes were growing quickly enough and the population itself was growing, the arrangement worked well. Around 1970, however, both economic growth and population growth began to slow in industrialized countries. At the same time, medical care was improving, raising the prospect of a longer life for everyone. Gradually the ratio of workers to retirees began to fall, so fewer and fewer working people were supporting more and more retirees.

Today, to remain financially viable, these systems must change. One solution—to raise the age at which full retirement benefits are received to 70 instead of 66—has so far been politically unpalatable. Failure to deal with the problem has set the stage for a crisis. In the United States, the Social Security system will eventually be unable to meet the obligations currently on its books.

Social Security is not a pension system in the traditional sense of the term. All U.S. workers pay Social Security tax (see the line labeled "FICA" on your pay stub); in return, the government promises to make payments to them when they retire. But with the Social Security taxes it collects from workers, the government can do only one of two things: it can give it to current retirees or spend it on general programs. As such, Social Security is a "pay-as-you-go" system that transfers revenues directly from current workers to current retirees.

This is a very different arrangement from a private pension fund, in which contributions accumulate and are invested for the long term and only after many years are paid out to retirees. Not only is the source of funds different but the allocation of risk differs too. In the current Social Security system, the responsibility to pay retirees belongs to younger generations. They foot the bill; they face the risk. If the economy does poorly, for example, wages of the young who are working will fall, making it more burdensome to pay the taxes required to honor promises to retirees. In contrast, in a private pension system, individuals' own savings provide their retirement incomes and they themselves face the risk that the return on their investments may be low.

The Social Security system's finances are in bad shape. According to the government's 2009 estimates, by 2037 tax income will be only sufficient to finance 76 percent of promised benefits. There are only a few ways the problem can be repaired. The government can reduce the benefits promised to future retirees, raise the tax rate that future workers pay, or convert the system into one that mirrors a private pension plan, with individual accounts. Most proposals to fix the system involve some combination of all three of these approaches. For example, suggestions to *privatize* the system involve reducing benefits to those who are currently working, raising their Social Security taxes, and placing new revenues into individual accounts similar to defined-contribution pension funds. In such a system, the government would continue to guarantee that the poor do not starve, but those who are well enough off to take care of themselves would have to do so.

At this point, all anyone knows is that the Social Security system will have to change and the faster the better. In evaluating the proposals to fix it, keep in mind two key questions: Who will pay the bills and who will shoulder the risks?

airline pilots are not fully protected, it still increases the incentive for a firm's managers to engage in risky behavior. To guard against this possibility, regulators monitor pension funds closely. Even so, some experts believe that PBGC could end up owing hundreds of billions of dollars in the not-too-distant future. Indeed, the spate of pension plan failures and investment setbacks in the financial crisis of 2007–2009 doubled the PBGC's deficit to $22 billion in fiscal 2009 compared with the prior year.

## Securities Firms: Brokers, Mutual Funds, and Investment Banks

The broad class of securities firms includes brokerages, investment banks, and mutual fund companies. In one way or another, these are all financial intermediaries. The primary services of brokerage firms are accounting (to keep track of customers' investment balances), custody services (to make sure valuable records such as stock certificates are safe), and access to secondary markets (in which customers can buy and sell financial instruments). Brokers also provide loans to customers who wish to purchase stock on margin. And they provide liquidity, both by offering check-writing privileges with their investment accounts and by allowing investors to sell assets quickly. Mutual-fund companies like Vanguard, Fidelity, and Dreyfus offer liquidity services as well; their money-market mutual funds are a key example. But the primary function of mutual funds is to pool the small savings of individuals in diversified portfolios that are composed of a wide variety of financial instruments.

All securities firms are very much in the business of producing information. But while brokers and mutual funds provide some investment advice to their retail customers, information is at the heart of the investment banking business. Investment banks like Goldman Sachs, Morgan Stanley, and JPMorgan Chase—all now divisions of bank holding companies—are the conduits through which firms raise funds in the capital markets. Through their **underwriting** services, these investment banks issue new stocks and a variety of other debt instruments. Most commonly, the underwriter guarantees the price of a new issue and then sells it to investors at a higher price, a practice called *placing the issue*. The underwriter profits from the difference between the price guaranteed to the firm that issues the security and the price at which the bond or stock is sold to investors. But since the price at which the investment bank sells the bonds or stocks in financial markets can turn out to be lower than the price guaranteed to the issuing company, there is some risk to underwriting. For most large issues, a group of investment banks will band together and spread the risk among themselves rather than one of them taking the risk alone.

INFORMATION

Information and reputation are central to the underwriting business. Underwriters collect information to determine the price of the new securities and then put their reputations on the line when they go out to sell the issues. A large, well-established investment bank will not underwrite issues indiscriminately. To do so would reduce the value of the bank's brand, along with the fees the bank can charge.

In addition to underwriting, investment banks provide advice to firms that want to merge with or acquire other firms. Investment bankers do the research to identify potential *mergers and acquisitions* and estimate the value of the new, combined company. The information they collect and the advice they give must be valuable because they are paid handsomely for them. In facilitating these combinations, investment banks perform a service to the economy. Mergers and acquisitions help to ensure that the people who manage firms do the best job possible. Managers who don't get the most out of the resources entrusted to them risk having their company purchased by executives who can do a better job. This threat of a takeover provides discipline in the management of individual companies and improves the allocation of resources across the economy.

## Finance Companies

Finance companies are in the lending business. They raise funds directly in the financial markets by issuing commercial paper and securities and then use them to make

# TOOLS OF THE TRADE
## Hedge Funds

**Hedge funds** are strictly for millionaires. These investment partnerships (sometimes referred to as *nontraditional investment funds*) bring together small groups of people who meet certain wealth requirements. To avoid various legal regulations, hedge funds come in two basic sizes: they can have a maximum of either 99 investors, each of whom has at least $1 million in net worth, or 499 investors, each of whom has at least $5 million in net worth. The larger hedge funds can also accept funds from institutional investors like pension funds, mutual funds, and insurance companies so long as their net worth is at least $25 million. The minimum investment in a hedge fund is usually $100,000. These really are millionaires' investment clubs.

Hedge funds are run by a general partner, or manager, who is in charge of day-to-day decisions. Managers are very well paid, receiving an annual fee of at least 2 percent of assets plus 20 percent of profits. In a year in which the fund's return on investment is 10 percent, the manager of an average-size fund of $500 million will receive $20 million in fees.

Because these funds are unregulated, finding out what their portfolios contain can be a challenge even for the fund's investors: the manager need not tell anyone. This secrecy creates the very real possibility of moral hazard. If a fund starts to incur losses, determining the reason for the fall in value is often impossible. To ensure that the manager's incentives match those of the investors, the manager is required to keep a large fraction of his or her own wealth in the fund. By and large, this requirement solves the problem of moral hazard; fraudulent behavior is extremely rare.

The name *hedge fund* may suggest that these funds employ the diversification techniques discussed in Chapter 5, but they do not. Hedging reduces risk by grouping together individual investments whose returns tend to move in opposite directions, but hedge funds are not low-risk enterprises. Because they are organized as private partnerships, hedge funds are not constrained in their investment strategies; they can trade in derivatives and borrow to create leverage.

A.W. Jones founded the first hedge fund in 1949. His fund combined leverage with short selling (the practice of borrowing a stock or bond whose price you believe will fall, selling it, and then buying it back at a lower price before repaying the lender). Jones divided the fund's equities into two groups: companies whose stock prices he thought would fall and companies whose stock prices he thought would rise. He sold the first group short and used the proceeds to buy shares in the second group. The term *hedge* in the name *hedge fund* comes from the fact that when the market in general went up or down, moving all stocks in the same direction, the fund would take losses on one group of stock but turn a profit on the second. It was hedged against movements in the market as a whole. Instead, Jones turned a profit when the stocks he sold short went down relative to the stocks he purchased. And those profits were substantial.

Today we would refer to Jones's fund as a "long-short hedge fund," since he was long on some stocks and short on others. More than 10,000 hedge funds are in existence today, and the long-short approach is only one of the strategies their managers follow. *Macro fund* managers take unhedged positions in the hope of benefiting from shifts in interest rates or national market conditions. *Global fund* managers engage in international stock picking. And the managers of *relative value funds* try to exploit small, transitory differences in the prices of related securities, such as U.S. Treasury bills and bonds. Long-Term Capital Management, the hedge fund that collapsed in September 1998 (see Chapter 9), was following this last strategy, trying to take advantage of price differences between U.S. Treasury bonds of slightly different maturities. Playing games with interest rates is what led the firm to amass $1.25 trillion in interest-rate swaps.

Regardless of the strategies they use, hedge fund managers typically strive to create returns that roughly equal those of the stock market (as measured by a comprehensive index like the S&P 500) but are uncorrelated with it. So while individual hedge funds are very risky—something like 10 percent of them close down every year—a portfolio that invests in a large number of these funds can expect returns equal to the stock market average with less risk. That is why people like hedge funds and why successful hedge fund managers are so well paid.

loans to individuals and corporations. Because these companies specialize in making loans, they are concerned largely with reducing the transactions and information costs that are associated with intermediated finance. And because of their narrow focus, finance companies are particularly good at screening potential borrowers' creditworthiness, monitoring their performance during the term of the loan, and seizing collateral in the event of a default.

## IN THE NEWS
### Fed's Tarullo Says Dividing Banks May Not Curb Too Big to Fail

**Bloomberg.com**

**By Craig Torres and Michael McKee**
**With assistance from Alison Vekshin**

November 10, 2009

Federal Reserve Governor Daniel Tarullo said proposals to separate trading from deposit taking and lending at the biggest banks probably wouldn't dispel the perception that some firms are too big to fail.

"Some very large institutions have in the past encountered serious difficulties through risky lending alone," the central bank governor said in remarks yesterday to the Money Marketeers of New York University.

U.S. legislators are drafting the most sweeping overhaul of financial regulation since the Great Depression after risky mortgage lending triggered more than $1.6 trillion in credit losses and writedowns at large financial institutions. Lawmakers are also debating whether they should give the government powers to break up or limit the size of firms whose failure could put the entire financial system at risk.

Congress redrew financial regulation in 1999 with the Gramm-Leach-Bliley Act, repealing Depression-era laws that separated commercial and investment banking. The legislation gave rise to financial conglomerates involved in insurance, stock brokerage and commodity trading.

The Obama administration wants to boost the Fed's ability to set stricter capital and liquidity standards at the biggest firms to curb systemic risk. Still, some economists say that big firms need to shrink.

[They] have advocated limiting or splitting some trading activities from commercial banking to limit risk.

...

Tarullo "was lobbying on behalf of the Fed's positions," said Ray Stone, a managing director at Stone & McCarthy Research Associates in Princeton, New Jersey, who attended the speech. "It comes down to capital requirements and liquidity requirements. Those are their main tools on the regulatory front."

Tarullo cited "massive failures" in risk management inside financial firms, and "serious deficiencies" in government regulation as causes of the crisis.

...

"As shown by Bear Stearns and Lehman, firms without commercial banking operations can now also pose a too-big-to-fail threat," he said. Lehman Brothers Holdings Inc. collapsed into bankruptcy in September 2008, and Bear Stearns Cos. was merged into JPMorgan Chase & Co. with Fed assistance.

---

Most finance companies specialize in one of three loan types: consumer loans, business loans, and what are called sales loans. Some also provide commercial and home mortgages. *Consumer finance* firms provide small installment loans to individual consumers. If you visit an appliance store to purchase a new refrigerator, you may be offered a deal that includes "no money down and no payments for six months." If you accept this loan offer, you'll be asked to fill out an application and to wait a few minutes while someone checks your credit. The credit is usually supplied not by the store but by a finance company like Wells Fargo. This kind of consumer credit allows people without sufficient savings to purchase appliances such as television sets, washing machines, and microwave ovens.

*Business finance* companies provide loans to businesses. If you want to start your own airline, for example, you will need to acquire some airplanes. That isn't as difficult as it may sound, because you don't need to shell out the entire $100 million price of a new plane. Airplanes, like automobiles, can be leased. That is, a business finance company buys the plane and then leases it back to you, an approach that significantly reduces the cost of starting your new enterprise. While this example is extreme, finance companies will purchase many types of equipment and lease them back to firms.

"Too-big-to-fail perceptions weaken normal market disciplinary forces," Tarullo said. Splitting apart commercial and investment banking activities "would seem unlikely to limit the too-big-to-fail problem to a significant degree."

...

Tarullo said an alternative to breaking apart banking and trading operations would be to limit the size of firms. Regulators would have to define how size increases systemic risk or perceptions of too-big-to-fail, a condition when investors and counterparties assume that the federal government must backstop a failing firm to save the overall financial system.

Tarullo said creating special charges for firms deemed systemically important, or developing rules that would require banks to build up capital in boom times, are concepts that have "substantial appeal" and may need further consideration.

Under a House proposal, the Fed would gain authority over the largest, most interconnected firms, while losing power to grant emergency bailout loans to individual companies.

...

The House bill would give the Fed power to tighten standards on capital, liquidity and leverage for companies posing a risk to the financial system. The Fed would gain authority to shrink financial firms that could destabilize markets and the economy....

The draft bill would also curb the emergency powers the Fed used during the crisis to bail out American International Group Inc. and finance $29 billion in troubled Bear Stearns assets to facilitate the broker's merger with JPMorgan Chase & Co.

...

### LESSONS OF THE ARTICLE

Following the financial crisis of 2007–2009, policymakers focused on how to prevent future crises. Proposed remedies included breaking up the largest financial firms, prohibiting certain risky activities, and charging a fee for risk taking. The article highlights the debate among policymakers about how to proceed and notes that limiting the activities of large intermediaries does not eliminate systemic risk (see Chapter 5, Lessons from the Crisis: Systemic Risk).

In addition to equipment leasing, business finance companies provide both inventory loans and accounts receivable loans. Inventory loans enable firms to keep their shelves stocked so that when a customer asks for a product, the firm can fill the order. Accounts receivable loans provide firms with immediate resources in anticipation of receipt of customers' payments. The purpose of both these loan types is to provide short-term liquidity to firms.

*Sales finance* companies specialize in larger loans for major purchases, such as automobiles. Car dealers customarily offer financing to people who are shopping for a new car. When you purchase a car, at a certain point in the negotiations the salesperson will ask how you intend to pay for it. Unless you have sizable savings or are buying a very cheap car, you will need to borrow. The car business is organized so that you don't need to leave the dealership to get your loan; someone there will take care of it for you. The financing is arranged through a finance company that specializes in making car loans. Until the auto industry bankruptcies of 2009, every major auto manufacturer owned a finance company. Most still do, as do large retailers like Target.

## Government-Sponsored Enterprises

You will not be surprised to learn that the U.S. government is directly involved in the financial intermediation system and that the risk taking of government-related intermediaries contributed importantly to the financial crisis of 2007–2009.

In some cases, the government provides loan guarantees; in others, it charters financial institutions to provide specific types of financing, such as home, farm, and student loans. In 1968, when Congress wanted to expand its support for mortgage lending to low- and moderate-income families, it privatized the Depression-era Federal National Mortgage Association (**Fannie Mae**) and, in 1970, issued a similar charter for a competing entity, the Federal Home Loan Mortgage Corporation (*Freddie Mac*). Each was thus chartered by the government as a corporation with a public purpose, a hybrid corporate form known as a government-sponsored enterprise (GSE). While the debt issued by Fannie and Freddie was not guaranteed by the government, market participants generally assumed that it would be in a crisis.

In 1968, Congress also established the Government National Mortgage Corporation (*Ginnie Mae*) as a GSE that is wholly owned by the federal government. The U.S. government explicitly guarantees Ginnie Mae debt. (To provide student loans, Congress in 1974 chartered the Student Loan Marketing Association—Sallie Mae—as a GSE but by 2004 had terminated the charter, making Sallie Mae a wholly private-sector firm).

At their founding, the financial GSEs had similar financial characteristics. They issued short-term bonds and used the proceeds to provide loans or guarantees of one form or another. Because of their explicit or implicit relationship to the government, they paid less than private borrowers for their liabilities and passed on some of these benefits in the form of subsidized mortgages and loans.

As the crisis of 2007–2009 highlighted, housing intermediation is by far the largest of these government-sponsored activities. In 2009, mortgage loans and mortgage guarantees issued by GSEs and other federal agencies surpassed $6 trillion, or more than half of the residential mortgage market of nearly $12 trillion. For comparison, outstanding Treasury securities—including bills, notes, and bonds—totaled about $7 trillion.

In the years preceding the 2007–2009 crisis, Fannie and Freddie had taken advantage of their implicit government backstop by operating on a slim capital cushion. Each had a leverage ratio (assets divided by capital) that was around three times higher than that of the average U.S. bank (recall the discussion in Chapter 12). In 2005, for example, their financial statements showed a leverage ratio of about 30 to 1. With such low levels of capital, these two massive GSEs could not withstand the surge of defaults when home prices began to decline nationwide in 2006.

Despite numerous public efforts to save them, a run on GSE debt in the summer of 2008 compelled the U.S. Treasury to place Fannie and Freddie into conservatorship—a bankruptcy procedure that allows them to operate despite insolvency. A year later, the Congressional Budget Office estimated that the government's commitments to those GSEs would add nearly $300 billion to the federal deficit in 2009, most of which reflected the value of their assets and liabilities when conservatorship began.[8]

In the crisis, Fannie and Freddie proved to be too big to fail—their demise probably would have toppled the entire financial system. This did *not* come as a surprise. In earlier years, many economists and policymakers had warned about the threat to the financial system posed by Fannie and Freddie. Yet, as of early 2010, it remains unclear

---

[8]See Congressional Budget Office, "An Overview of Federal Support for Housing," *Economic and Budget Issue Brief*, November 3, 2009.

**Table 13.4**   Summary of Financial Industry Structure

| Financial Intermediary | Primary Sources of Funds (Liabilities) | Primary Uses of Funds (Assets) | Services Provided |
|---|---|---|---|
| Depository Institution (Bank) | Checkable deposits<br>Savings and time deposits<br>Borrowing from other banks | Cash<br>Loans<br>Securities | • Pooling of small savings to provide large loans<br>• Diversified, liquid deposit accounts<br>• Access to payments system<br>• Screening and monitoring of borrowers |
| Insurance Company | Expected claims | Corporate bonds<br>Government bonds<br>Stocks<br>Mortgages | • Pooling of risk<br>• Screening and monitoring of policyholders |
| Securities Firm | Short-term loans | Commercial paper<br>Bonds | • Management of asset pools<br>• Clearing and settling trades |
| Investment Bank | | | • Immediate sale of assets<br>• Access to spectrum of assets, allowing diversification<br>• Evaluation of firms wishing to issue securities<br>• Research and advice for investors |
| Mutual-Fund Company | Shares sold to customers | Commercial paper<br>Bonds<br>Mortgages<br>Stocks<br>Real estate | • Pooling of small savings to provide access to large, diversified portfolios, which can be liquid |
| Finance Company | Bonds<br>Bank loans<br>Commercial paper | Mortgages<br>Consumer loans<br>Business loans | • Screening and monitoring of borrowers |
| Pension Fund | Policy benefits to be paid out to future retirees | Stocks<br>Government bonds<br>Corporate bonds<br>Commercial paper | • Pooling of employees' and employers' contributions<br>• Diversification of long-term investments to ensure future income for retirees |
| Government-Sponsored Enterprise | Commercial paper<br>Bonds<br>Loan guarantees | Mortgages<br>Farm loans<br>Guarantee payments | • Access to financing for borrowers who cannot obtain it elsewhere |

what the U.S. government will do with Fannie and Freddie. Will they be broken up into parts and privatized? Will they remain government owned and operated? Will the government act to prevent another GSE crisis in the future? You'll have to watch the financial news to find out.

Table 13.4 summarizes the characteristics and roles of financial intermediaries.

## YOUR FINANCIAL WORLD
Annuities

Most college students don't have to worry about annuities, at least not now. But it is very likely that when you retire, you will turn your retirement savings into an annuity. And, in the meantime, someone may try to sell you one. Here's what annuities are and how they work.

An annuity is a financial instrument in which a person (called the "annuitant") makes a payment in exchange for the promise of a series of future payments. Similar to a bond, annuities are typically sold by insurance companies, and they come in many forms and have many names. There are fixed-period versus lifetime annuities. A fixed-period annuity makes fixed monthly or annual payments for a specified period like 10 or 15 years. By contrast, a lifetime annuity guarantees periodic payments for the remainder of the annuitant's life (and possibly, that of the person's spouse as well). An annuity is the reverse of life insurance. A life insurance policyholder pays the insurance company each year or month, with the beneficiaries receiving a lump sum when he or she dies. An annuitant makes a lump-sum payment and then receives a stream of payments until death.

Then there are deferred versus immediate annuities. An immediate annuity starts right away, while with a deferred annuity, contributions are made and investment returns accrue for payment at a later date.

Once you realize that annuities are a type of investment, things get even more complicated. Insurance companies offer fixed versus variable annuities. Fixed annuities guarantee the principal value plus a minimum interest rate, like a bond. Variable annuities can be invested in a variety of mutual funds offered by the insurance company, and the growth depends on the performance of the funds. Variable annuities are complicated, and insurance companies will combine them with life insurance products.

Where does this leave us? Annuities are useful, but you should probably hold off buying one until you are ready to retire. Invest your retirement savings in index mutual funds with low expense ratios, and buy term life insurance. When the time comes to retire, then call an insurance company and buy an annuity. That's going to be the cheapest, easiest, and simplest way to go.

For more information on annuities, what they are and how they work, go to www.iii.org/individuals/annuities/.

## Terms

bank charter, 315
bank holding company, 318
defined-benefit pension plan, 330
defined-contribution pension plan, 330
dual banking system, 315
economies of scale, 323
economies of scope, 323
eurodollars, 321
Fannie Mae, 336
financial holding company, 322

hedge fund, 333
London Interbank Offered Rate (LIBOR), 322
property and casualty insurance, 326
term life insurance, 326
underwriting, 332
unit bank, 313
universal bank, 322
vesting, 330
whole life insurance, 326

## Chapter Lessons

1. The United States has a comparatively large but declining number of banks.
   a. The large number of banks in the United States is explained by restrictions on branching, both within and across state lines, that were imposed by the federal government in 1927.

www.mhhe.com/cecchetti3e

b. The large number of banks in the United States is a sign of an anticompetitive legal environment.

c. Since 1997, banks have been permitted to operate in more than one state. This change has increased competition and driven many small, inefficient banks out of business.

d. Between 1933 and 1999, banks were prohibited from engaging in the securities and insurance businesses.

e. Banking has been expanding not just across state boundaries but across international boundaries.

   i. Many U.S. banks operate abroad, and a large number of foreign banks do business in the United States.

   ii. Eurodollars—dollar deposits in foreign banks—play an important part in the international financial system.

f. The financial industry is constantly evolving. With changes in regulations, financial services can now be provided in two ways:

   i. through a large universal bank, which provides all the services anyone could possibly need.

   ii. through small specialized firms, which supply a limited number of services at a low price.

2. Nondepository institutions are playing an increasingly important role in the financial system. Five types of financial intermediary may be classified as nondepository institutions.

   a. Insurance companies.

      i. Life insurance companies insure policyholders against death through term life insurance and provide a vehicle for saving through whole life insurance.

      ii. Property and casualty companies insure individuals and businesses against losses arising from specific events, like accidents and fires.

      iii. The two primary functions of insurance companies are to:
      - allow policyholders to transfer risk.
      - screen and monitor policyholders to reduce adverse selection and moral hazard.

   b. Pension funds perform two basic services.

      i. They allow employees and employers to make payments today so that employees will receive an income after retirement.

      ii. They spread risk by ensuring that those employees who live longer than others will continue to receive an income. For this reason, pension funds may be thought of as the opposite of life insurance.

   c. Securities firms include three basic types of financial intermediary: brokers, mutual-fund companies, and investment banks.

      i. Brokers give customers access to the financial markets, allowing them to buy and sell securities.

      ii. Mutual-fund companies provide savers with small-denomination shares in large, diversified investment pools.

      iii. Investment banks screen and monitor firms before issuing their securities.

   d. Finance companies specialize in making loans to consumers and businesses for the purchase or lease of specific products, such as cars and business equipment.

   e. Government-sponsored enterprises supply direct financing and provide loan guarantees for low-interest mortgages, student loans, and agricultural loans.

# Conceptual Problems

1. For many years you have used your local, small-town bank. One day you hear that the bank is about to be purchased by Bank of America. From your vantage point as a retail bank customer, what are the costs and benefits of such a merger?

2. Why have technological advances hindered the enforcement of legal restrictions on bank branching?

3. How did the financial crisis of 2007–2009 affect the degree of concentration in the U.S. banking industry?

4. Banks have been losing their advantage over other financial intermediaries in attracting customers' funds. Why?

5. An industry with a large number of small firms is usually thought to be highly competitive. Is that supposition true of the banking industry? What are the costs and benefits to consumers of the current structure of the U.S. banking industry?

6.* What was the main rationale behind the separation of commercial and investment banking activities in the Glass-Steagall Act of 1933? Why was the act repealed?

7. Explain what the term "too-big-to-fail" means in reference to financial institutions. How did the policy responses to the financial crisis of 2007–2009 affect the too-big-to-fail problem?

8. Discuss the problems life insurance companies will face as genetic information becomes more widely available.

9. When the values of stocks and bonds fluctuate, they have an impact on the balance sheet of insurance companies. Why is that impact more likely to be a problem for life insurance companies than for property and casualty companies?

10.* As a current member of the workforce, what advantage to you would there be to privatizing part of the Social Security system to allow for individual private accounts? What do you see as the main potential problem?

11. What are the benefits of collaboration between a large appliance retailer and a finance company?

12. Why did government-sponsored enterprises (GSEs) such as Freddie Mac and Fannie Mae have substantially higher leverage ratios than the average U.S. bank in the years preceding the financial crisis of 2007–2009? Explain how this made the enterprises more vulnerable to the house-price declines that precipitated the crisis.

# Analytical Problems

13. Consider two countries with the following characteristics. Country A has no restrictions on bank branching and banks in Country A are permitted to offer investment and insurance products along with traditional banking services. In Country B, there are strict limits on branch banking and on the geographical

*Indicates more difficult problems

spread of a bank's business. In addition, banks in Country B are not permitted to offer investment or insurance services.

a. In which country do you think the banking system is more concentrated?

b. In which country do you think the banking system is more competitive?

c. In which country do you think, everything else being equal, banking products are cheaper?

Explain each of your choices.

14. You examine the balance sheet of an insurance company and note that its assets are made up mainly of U.S. Treasury bills and commercial paper. Is this more likely to be the balance sheet of a property and casualty insurance company or a life insurance company? Explain your answer.

15.* Statistically, teenage drivers are more likely to have an automobile accident than adult drivers. As a result, insurance companies charge higher insurance premiums for teenage drivers. Suppose one insurance company decided to charge teenagers and adults the same premium based on the average risk of an accident among both groups. Using your knowledge of the problems associated with asymmetric information, explain whether you think this insurance company will be profitable.

16. Use your knowledge of the problems associated with asymmetric information to explain why insurance companies often include deductibles as part of their policies.

17. Suppose you have a defined-contribution pension plan. As you go through your working life, in what order would you choose to have the following portfolio allocations: (a) 100 percent bonds and money-market instruments, (b) 100 percent stocks, (c) 50 percent bonds and 50 percent stocks?

18. As an employee, would you prefer to participate in a defined-benefit pension plan or a defined-contribution pension plan? Explain your answer.

19. In the aftermath of the financial crisis of 2007–2009, there have been calls to reinstate the separation of commercial and investment banking activities that was removed with the repeal of the Glass-Steagall Act. Do you think this is a good way to reduce systemic risk?

20. Suppose a well-known financial holding company agreed to be the underwriter for a new stock issue. After guaranteeing the price to the issuing company but before selling the stocks, a scandal surrounding the business practices of the financial holding company is revealed. How would you expect this scandal to affect (a) the financial holding company and (b) the issuing company?

# Chapter 14

## Regulating the Financial System

The painful effects of the global crisis of 2007–2009 brought home the importance of the financial system in our lives. Millions of people lost their jobs, their homes, and their wealth. Healthy firms needing to borrow temporarily to pay their employees or suppliers faced ruin. As the crisis peaked in the fall of 2008, the global economy suffered its deepest and broadest downturn since the Great Depression, and policymakers took unprecedented action to keep the crisis from precipitating a second Great Depression.

Although no financial crisis since the 1930s has matched the severity of the 2007–2009 episode, disruptions to the financial system are surprisingly frequent and widespread. In the quarter century preceding 2007, 93 countries experienced a total of 117 systemwide crises and 51 smaller disruptions in their financial systems. In other words, on average, roughly six countries experienced some financial disturbance every year of that period. And, virtually no part of the world has been spared; large industrialized countries have suffered along with smaller, less developed ones.

When financial crises occur, governments step in and put financial intermediaries back on track. They often do so by assuming responsibility for the banking system's liabilities so that depositors won't lose their savings. But the cleanup can also require the injection of capital into failed institutions. These crises not only were expensive to clean up, they had a dramatic impact on growth in the countries where they occurred.

Figure 14.1 plots information on the fiscal cost and economic impact of banking crises between 1970 and 2007. On the horizontal axis of the figure is a measure of the cost of the cleanup and on the vertical axis is the loss of economic output. The data show what one would expect: Bigger crises are worse for output.

Some degree of default is normal at every bank, including well-run ones. But in 1998, when 35 percent of all loans made by Korean banks defaulted at a cost of more than one-fourth the country's annual output, it was more than just bad luck. To put this percentage into perspective, in a normal year a country will invest 10 to 20 percent of its GDP, so the crisis cost Korea between one and two years' worth of business investment. Clearly, the Korean financial system was failing to perform one of its primary functions, the efficient channeling of resources from savers to borrowers so that credit goes to firms based on the merit of their proposed investments. Instead, borrowers who shouldn't have received loans got them, and projects that shouldn't have been funded went ahead. Because resources were wasted, Korea's growth and income were lower than they could have been.

Banking crises are not a recent phenomenon; the history of commercial banking over the last two centuries is replete with periods of turmoil and failure. By their very nature, financial systems are fragile and vulnerable to crisis. Unfortunately, when a country's financial system collapses, its economy goes with it, and with economic crisis comes the risk of violence and revolution. Keeping banks open and operating, then, is as essential to maintaining our way of life as a ready military defense. Because

**Figure 14.1**    Relationship between the Size of a Financial Crisis and the Loss of Economic Output, 1970-2007

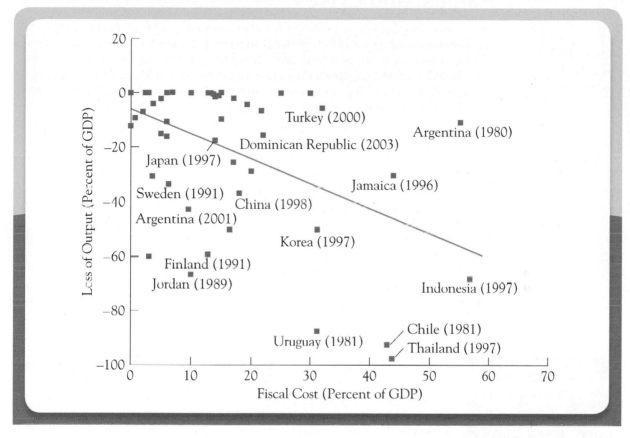

SOURCE: The loss of output is measured as the deviation from trend output. The data are from Luc Laeven and Fabian Valencia, "*Systemic Banking Crises: A New Database*," *IMF Working Paper WP/08/224*, November 2008. Used with permission.

a healthy financial system benefits everyone, governments are deeply involved in the way banks and other intermediaries function. As a result, the financial sector is subject to voluminous rules and regulations, and financial institutions must withstand constant scrutiny by official examiners. The importance of this government oversight in ensuring financial stability is hard to exaggerate. When government oversight fails, as it did in many countries in the years before the crisis of 2007–2009, the costs can be enormous.

The purpose of this chapter is threefold. First, we will look at the sources and consequences of financial fragility. By and large, financial crises are banking crises, so we will focus on that sector. Included in this group are **shadow banks** that, like banks, have liabilities that can be withdrawn at face value virtually without notice but are usually subject to less oversight than banks. Next, we will look at the institutional safeguards—for instance, deposit insurance—the government has built into the system in an attempt to avert financial crises. Third, we'll study the regulatory and supervisory environment of the banking industry. Finally, we'll examine emerging approaches to regulation that focus on the safety of the financial system rather than on individual institutions.

# The Sources and Consequences of Runs, Panics, and Crises

In a market-based economy, the opportunity to succeed is also an opportunity to fail. New restaurants open and others go out of business. Only one in 10 restaurants survives as long as three years. In principle, banks should be no different from restaurants: new ones should open and unpopular ones close. But few of us would want to live in a world where banks fail at the same rate as restaurants. Banks serve some essential functions in our economy: they provide access to the payments system, and they screen and monitor borrowers to reduce information problems. If your favorite restaurant closes suddenly, you can still eat, but if your bank closes, you lose your ability to make purchases and pay your rent. So while no one suggests that the government appoint officials to minimize restaurant closings, everyone expects the government to safeguard banks.

Banks' fragility arises from the fact that they provide liquidity to depositors. That is, they allow depositors to withdraw their balances on demand. If you want the entire amount in your checking account converted into cash, all you need to do is go to your bank and ask for it; the teller is obligated to give it to you. If a bank cannot meet this promise of withdrawal on demand because of insufficient liquid assets, it will fail.

Banks not only guarantee their depositors immediate cash on demand; they promise to satisfy depositors' withdrawal requests on a first-come, first-served basis. This commitment has some important implications. Suppose depositors begin to lose confidence in a bank's ability to meet their withdrawal requests. They have heard a rumor that one of the bank's largest loans has defaulted, so that the bank's assets may no longer cover its liabili-

ties. True or not, reports that a bank has become **insolvent** can spread fear that it will run out of cash and close its doors. Mindful of the bank's first-come, first-served policy, frenzied depositors may rush to the bank to convert their balances to cash before other customers arrive. Such a **bank run** can cause a bank to fail.

In short, a bank run can be the result of either real or imagined problems. No bank is immune to the loss of depositors' confidence just because it is profitable and sound. In practice, runs often start with shakier banks and then spread to healthier ones as confidence erodes.

The financial crisis of 2007–2009 is replete with examples of runs on banks and on the much less regulated shadow banks, which also provide liquidity to the financial system. The United Kingdom faced its first run on a large bank in more than a century when, in September 2007, depositors rushed to withdraw funds from Northern Rock, a major housing lender (see neighboring photos). Meanwhile, the largest savings bank in the United States, Washington Mutual, failed when depositors fled in September 2008. That same month, withdrawals from Wachovia Bank—at the time the fourth largest U.S. commercial bank—led to its emergency sale.

Quiet, invisible runs on shadow banks were even more dramatic, as they punctuated the peaks of the financial crisis. In March 2008, repo lenders and other creditors stopped lending to Bear Stearns, the fifth largest U.S. investment bank. The run halted only when the Federal Reserve Bank of New York stepped in to help the then-second

Crowds trying to get into the Northern Rock bank in Kingston upon Thames, United Kingdom, on September 17, 2007.

largest U.S. commercial bank, JPMorgan Chase, acquire Bear. A similar sudden stop in private lending led the U.S. government to take over Fannie Mae and Freddie Mac (the huge government-sponsored housing finance enterprises described in Chapter 13) in August 2008. The financial crisis peaked in September 2008 when a run on Lehman Brothers—the fourth largest U.S. investment bank—precipitated its bankruptcy. Shortly thereafter, losses on Lehman debt compelled a money-market mutual fund (MMMFs are described in Chapter 2) to "break the buck"—that is, to lower its share value below $1; that fixed value is traditionally promised by all MMMFs so that their customers can treat their shares as if they were bank deposits. Breaking the buck at one MMMF sparked runs at other MMMFs and thereby undermined a key component of the U.S. payments mechanism.

What matters during a bank run is not whether a bank is solvent, but whether it is liquid. Solvency means that the value of the bank's assets exceeds the value of its liabilities—that is, the bank has a positive net worth. Liquidity means that the bank has sufficient reserves and immediately marketable assets to meet depositors' demand for withdrawals. False rumors that a bank is *insolvent* can lead to a run that renders a bank **illiquid**. If people believe that a bank is in trouble, that belief alone can make it so.

When a bank fails, depositors may lose some or all of their deposits, and information about borrowers' creditworthiness may disappear. For these reasons alone, government officials work to ensure that all banks are operated in a way that minimizes their chance of failure. But that is not their main worry. The primary concern is that a single bank's failure might cause a small-scale bank run that could turn into a system-wide **bank panic**. This phenomenon of spreading panic on the part of depositors in banks (or of creditors to shadow banks) is called **contagion**. Contagion was powerful at the peak of the 2007–2009 financial crisis, as depositors and creditors grew anxious about the well-being of financial intermediaries around the world.

Information asymmetries are the reason that a run on a single bank can turn into a bank panic that threatens the entire financial system. Recall from Chapter 11 that if there is no way to tell a good used car from a bad one, the only used cars on the market will be lemons. What is true for cars is even truer for banks. Most of us are not in a position to assess the quality of a bank's balance sheet. In fact, because banks often make loans based on sophisticated statistical models, only an expert with knowledge of market conditions and access to all details about a bank's assets can estimate their worth. Depositors, then, are in the same position as uninformed buyers in the used car market: They can't tell the difference between a good bank and a bad bank. And who wants to make a deposit in a bank if there is even a small chance that it could be insolvent? So when rumors spread that a certain bank is in trouble, depositors and other creditors begin to worry about their own banks' financial condition. Concern about even one bank can create a panic that causes profitable banks throughout the nation to fail, leading to a complete collapse of the banking system.

INFORMATION

While banking panics and financial crises can easily result from false rumors, they can also occur for more concrete reasons. Because a bank's assets are a combination of loans and securities, anything that affects borrowers' ability to make their loan payments or drives down the market value of securities has the potential to imperil the bank's finances. The decline of U.S. housing prices and the resulting wave of mortgage defaults that began in 2006 set the stage for the crisis of 2007–2009 by lowering the value of assets on the balance sheets of intermediaries around the world. Recessions—widespread downturns in business activity—have a clear negative impact on a bank's balance sheet. When business slows, firms have a harder time paying their debts. People lose their jobs and suddenly can't make their loan payments. As default rates rise, bank assets lose value, and bank capital drops. With less capital, banks are forced to contract their balance sheets, making fewer loans. This decline in loans, in turn, means less business investment, which amplifies the downturn. Large asset price declines and deep recessions can lead to widespread failure of banks and shadow banks.

The history of banking in the United States shows clear evidence that downturns in the business cycle put pressure on banks, substantially increasing the risk of panics. To see this, we can look at the period from 1871 to 1914, prior to the creation of the Federal Reserve System. Over those four-plus decades, there were 11 business cycles—booms followed by recessions. Bank panics occurred during seven of them, five of which were very severe. The next series of severe bank panics occurred during the Great Depression of the 1930s, when output fell by roughly one-third. Bank panics usually start with real economic events, not just rumors.

Financial disruptions can also occur whenever borrowers' net worth falls, as it does during a deflation (see Applying the Concept: Deflation, Net Worth, and Information Costs in Chapter 11). Companies borrow a fixed number of dollars to invest in real assets like buildings and machines, whose values fall with deflation. So a drop in prices reduces companies' net worth (but not their loan payments). This decline in firms' net worth aggravates the adverse selection and moral hazard problems caused by information asymmetries, making loans more difficult to obtain. If these firms cannot get new financing, business investment will fall, reducing overall economic activity and raising the number of defaults on loans. As more and more borrowers default, banks' balance sheets deteriorate, compounding information problems and creating a full-blown crisis.

# The Government Safety Net

There are three reasons for the government to get involved in the financial system:

1. To protect investors.
2. To protect bank customers from monopolistic exploitation.
3. To safeguard the stability of the financial system.

First, the government is obligated to protect small investors, many of whom are unable to judge the soundness of their financial institutions. While competition is supposed to discipline all the institutions in the industry, in practice only the force of law can ensure a bank's integrity. As small investors, we rely on the government to protect us from mismanagement and malfeasance.

Second, the growing tendency for small firms to merge into large ones reduces competition, ultimately ending in monopolies. In general, monopolies exploit their customers, raising prices to earn unwarranted profits. Because monopolies are inefficient, the government intervenes to prevent the firms in an industry from becoming too large. In the financial system, that means ensuring that even large banks face competition.

STABILITY

Third, the combustible mix of liquidity risk and information asymmetries means that the financial system is inherently unstable. A financial firm can collapse much more quickly than an industrial company. For a steel corporation, an electronics manufacturer, or an automobile maker, failure occurs slowly as customers disappear one by one. But a financial institution can create and destroy the value of its assets in an astonishingly short period, and a single firm's failure can bring down the entire system.[1]

Government officials employ a combination of strategies to protect investors and ensure the stability of the financial system. First, they provide the safety net to insure small depositors. Authorities both operate as the *lender of last resort*, making loans to banks that face sudden deposit outflows, and provide *deposit insurance*, guaranteeing that depositors receive the full value of their accounts should an institution fail. But this safety net causes bank managers to take on too much risk, leading to the regulation and supervision that we will discuss later in the chapter.

This section will examine the unique role of depository institutions in our financial system. The point is that we need banks. While they are essential, they are also fragile. This leads to a discussion of the components of the safety net and the problems it creates. The next section will look at the government's responses to these problems.

## The Unique Role of Banks and Shadow Banks

As the key providers of liquidity, banks ensure a sufficient supply of the means of payment for the economy to operate smoothly and efficiently. This critical role and the problems associated with it make banks a key focus of attention for government regulators. Shadow banks are also major providers of liquidity, and following their role in the financial crisis of 2007–2009, they also have attracted intense attention from regulators.

We all rely heavily on these intermediaries for access to the payments system. If banks, MMMFs, and securities brokers were to disappear, we would no longer be able to transfer funds—at least not until someone stepped forward to take their place. Other financial institutions—insurance companies, pension funds, and the like—do not have this essential day-to-day function of facilitating payments.

Furthermore, because of their role in liquidity provision, banks and shadow banks are prone to runs. These intermediaries hold illiquid assets to back their liquid liabilities. In the case of banks, their promise of full and constant value to depositors is based on assets of uncertain value. The fixed-value shares of MMMFs are like bank deposits in all but name. The liabilities of other shadow banks are less similar but have important deposit-like characteristics. For example, repurchase agreements are usually overnight contracts, so a repo lender can refuse to roll over the loan to a securities broker at virtually any time, an action similar to a deposit withdrawal. In contrast, pension funds and insurance companies may hold illiquid assets, but their liability holders cannot withdraw funds whenever they want.

Moreover, banks and shadow banks are linked to one another both on their balance sheets and in their customers' minds. Take a quick look back at Table 12.1 (page 286) and you will see that in January 2010 interbank loans made up 1.8 percent of U.S.

---

[1]One culprit in creating this high degree of risk is derivatives. Like dynamite, when used properly derivatives are extremely beneficial, allowing the transfer of risk to those who can best bear it. But in the wrong hands, derivatives can bring down even the largest, most respected institutions. The failure of Barings Bank in 1995 is an example. One of the oldest and best-known banks in England, Barings collapsed in just two months after a single trader wiped out the bank's capital with losses of more than $1 billion on futures positions worth more than $17 billion. Bets like that can be made only using derivatives. And, because they can be made in ways that are extremely difficult for government regulators to detect, these high-risk actions have the potential to put the entire financial system at risk. In the crisis of 2007–2009, the most dramatic example of a system-threatening derivatives exposure was that of American International Group (AIG), the largest U.S. insurer. In September 2008, AIG became unable to meet the obligations arising from hundreds of billions of dollars of credit-default swaps (see pages 225–226).

"Yes, we do have the authority to regulate you."

commercial banking system assets—which was about one-sixth of all bank capital. Prior to the crisis, interbank lending had been substantially greater and represented roughly one-third of all bank capital. If a bank begins to fail, it will default on its loan payments to other banks and thereby transmit its financial distress to them. Similarly, MMMFs hold large volumes of commercial paper, most of which was issued by banks. And banks are among the key repo lenders to securities brokers. Banks and shadow banks are so interdependent that they are capable of initiating contagion throughout the financial system.

Other financial institutions also may pose such risks, but these intermediaries typically are very large and few in number (see footnote 1 regarding the derivatives exposure of AIG, the largest U.S. insurer). While the ramifications of a financial crisis outside the system of banks and shadow banks may be more limited, they are still damaging. As a result, the government also protects individuals who do business with finance companies, pension funds, and insurance companies.

For example, government regulations require insurance companies to provide proper information to policyholders and restrict the ways the companies manage their assets. The same is true for securities firms and pension funds, whose assets must be structured to ensure that they will be able to meet their obligations many years into the future.[2]

## The Government as Lender of Last Resort

The best way to stop a bank failure from turning into a bank panic is to make sure solvent institutions can meet their depositors' withdrawal demands. In 1873 the British economist Walter Bagehot suggested the need for a **lender of last resort** to perform this function. Such an institution could make loans to prevent the failure of solvent banks and could provide liquidity in sufficient quantities to prevent or end a financial panic. Specifically, Bagehot proposed that Britain's central bank should lend freely on good collateral at a high rate of interest. By lending freely he meant providing liquidity on demand to any bank that asked for it. Good collateral would ensure the bank's solvency, and the high interest rate would penalize the borrowing bank for failing to hold enough reserves or easily salable assets to meet deposit outflows.

The existence of a lender of last resort significantly reduces, but does not eliminate, contagion. The series of three bank panics that occurred during the Great Depression of the 1930s is one example of the failure of a lender of last resort. While the Federal Reserve had the capacity to operate as a lender of last resort in the 1930s, Figure 14.2 shows that banks did not take advantage of the opportunity to borrow when they needed to. In fact, their borrowing fell during panics, reaching levels well below normal compared to the boom years of the 1920s. So as banks became illiquid, the Federal Reserve's lending declined. The mere existence of a lender of last resort,

---

[2]All nondepository institutions are subject to some form of regulation. State regulators oversee insurance companies; the Pension Benefits Guaranty Corporation regulates private pension funds. Securities firms are overseen by a combination of the Securities and Exchange Commission, a government agency, and the Financial Industry Regulatory Authority. Finance companies are regulated by state agencies, as well as by the Federal Reserve if they are subsidiaries of bank holding companies.

## YOUR FINANCIAL WORLD
The Securities Investor Protection Corporation

Brokerage firms will advertise that they are members of the SIPC—that's the Securities Investor Protection Corporation. The SIPC provides insurance in the event that a brokerage firm fails, owing its customers cash and securities. It is insurance against fraud.

It is important to understand what SIPC insurance is and what it is not. If a bank accepts your deposits and uses the funds to make bad loans, your savings are protected by the FDIC against the bank's failure. By contrast, SIPC insurance replaces missing securities or cash that was supposed to be there—up to a limit of

$500,000. It does not compensate individuals for investments that lost value because market prices fell, nor will it cover individuals who were sold worthless securities. The SIPC protects against theft by a broker. One sizable SIPC payout in recent years was to the victims of Bernard Madoff's Ponzi scheme (see Chapter 11, Applying the Concept: The Madoff Scandal).

For more information on the SIPC, go to www.sipc.org For comprehensive information on investor rights, look at the National Association of Securities Dealer's Web site at www.nasd.com

then, will not keep the financial system from collapsing.

There is another flaw in the concept of a lender of last resort. For the system to work, central bank officials who approve the loan applications must be able to distinguish an illiquid from an insolvent institution. But during a crisis, computing the market value of a bank's assets is almost impossible, because there are no market prices. (If a bank could sell its marketable assets in the financial markets, it wouldn't need a loan from the central bank.) Because a bank will go to the central bank for a direct loan only after having exhausted all opportunities to sell its assets and borrow from other banks without collateral, its illiquidity and its need to seek a loan from the government raise the question of its solvency. Officials, anxious to keep the crisis from deepening, are likely to be generous in evaluating the bank's assets and to grant a loan even if they suspect the bank may be

**Figure 14.2**  Lending by the Federal Reserve to Commercial Banks, 1914–1940

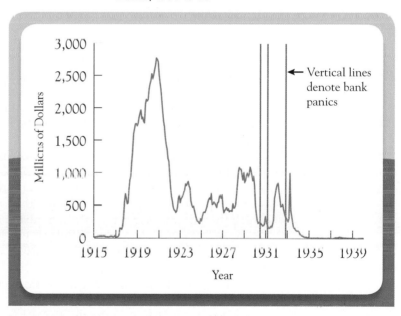

Figure shows discount loans to commercial banks from the Federal Reserve System.

SOURCE: Bank panic dates are from Milton Friedman and Anna J. Schwartz, A Monetary History of the United States: 1863 to 1960 (Princeton, NJ: Princeton University Press, 1963).

insolvent. Knowing this, bank managers will tend to take too many risks.

In other words, the central bank's difficulty in distinguishing a bank's insolvency from its illiquidity creates moral hazard for bank managers. It is important for a lender of last resort to operate in a manner that minimizes the tendency for bankers to take too much risk in their operations.

## APPLYING THE CONCEPT
### THE DAY THE BANK OF NEW YORK BORROWED $23 BILLION

While the existence of a lender of last resort may encourage bank managers to take too many risks, very few people would argue for abolishing the safeguard outright. There have been days when the system worked exactly as it should. November 20, 1985, was one of them. On that day the Bank of New York's computer system went haywire. BONY, as it was known, plays a central role in the U.S. Treasury securities market. The bank (now Bank of New York Mellon) acts as a clearinghouse, buying bonds from sellers and then reselling them to buyers.

On November 20, a software error prevented BONY from keeping track of its Treasury bond trades.* For 90 minutes transactions poured in, and the bank accumulated and paid for U.S. Treasury bonds, notes, and bills. Importantly, BONY promised to make payments without actually having the funds. But when the time came to deliver the securities and collect from the buyers, BONY

employees could not tell who the buyers and sellers were or what quantities and prices they had agreed to. The information had been erased. By the end of the day, the Bank of New York had bought and failed to deliver so many securities that it was committed to paying out $23 billion that it did not have.

Without a way to come up with $23 billion, BONY wasn't able to make payments to sellers who had delivered their securities. These sellers had made additional transactions in the expectation that they would be paid. Unless BONY found a way to make the promised payments, the problem would spread to other institutions. The Federal Reserve, as lender of last resort, stepped in and made a loan of $23 billion, preventing a computer problem at one very important bank from becoming a full-blown financial crisis.

*BONY's computers could store only 32,000 transactions at a time. When more transactions arrived than the computer could handle, the software's counter restarted at zero. Because the counter number was the key to where the trading information was stored, the information was effectively erased. (Had all the original transactions been processed before the counter restarted, there would have been no problem.)

Finally, as we learned in the crisis of 2007–2009, the U.S. lender-of-last-resort mechanism has not kept pace with the evolution of the financial system. Some intermediaries facing sudden flight by their very short-term creditors were not banks—to whom the Fed usually lends—but shadow banks, which do not normally have access to Fed loans. Only by using its emergency lending authority—something last done in the Great Depression of the 1930s—was the Fed able to lend to such nonbank intermediaries to stem the crisis.[3]

During the turmoil, the Fed utilized this emergency authority repeatedly when it needed to lend to securities brokers, MMMFs, insurers, other nonbank intermediaries, and even to nonfinancial firms. Based on this emergency authority, it developed a variety of new policy tools—including the Primary Dealer Credit Facility through which the authorities lent directly to nonbank securities dealers—to deliver liquidity where and when it was needed. While this ad hoc, reactive approach helped to both stem runs and counter their impact, it had limited value in preventing them in the first place.

Lending to nonbank intermediaries also added massively to the moral hazard usually associated with the lender of last resort. These intermediaries are not subject to regulation or supervision by the Federal Reserve, and the level of oversight they received from other agencies was typically less intense and intrusive than that applied to banks. Accordingly, in the absence of new oversight, the access to central bank loans granted by the Fed in the crisis will encourage these borrowers to take greater risks in the future.

[3]The Fed's authority to lend to nonbanks may be found in Section 13(3) of the Federal Reserve Act. Under this rule, the Board of Governors "in unusual and exigent circumstances" can authorize collateralized lending to any "individual, partnership, or corporation"—that is, to nonbanks. However, Congress is considering proposals that would limit this authority, for example, by requiring approval from the Secretary of the Treasury. You can view the Federal Reserve Act at http://www.federalreserve.gov/aboutthefed/fract.htm.

## Government Deposit Insurance

Congress's response to the Federal Reserve's inability to stem the bank panics of the 1930s was **deposit insurance**. The Federal Deposit Insurance Corporation guarantees that a depositor will receive the full account balance up to some maximum amount even if a bank fails. Bank failures, in effect, become the problem of the insurer; bank customers need not concern themselves with their bank's risk taking. So long as a bank has deposit insurance, customers' deposits are safe, even in the event of a run or bank failure.

Here's how the system works. When a bank fails, the FDIC resolves the insolvency either by closing the institution or by finding a buyer. The first approach, closing the bank, is called the *payoff method*. The FDIC pays off all the bank's depositors, then sells all the bank's assets in an attempt to recover the amount paid out. Under the pay-off method, depositors whose balances exceed the insurance limit, currently $250,000, suffer some losses.

In the second approach, called the *purchase-and-assumption method*, the FDIC finds a firm that is willing to take over the failed bank. Because the failed institution is insolvent—on the balance sheet, its liabilities exceed its assets—no purchaser will do so for free. In fact, the FDIC has to pay banks to purchase failed institutions. That is, the FDIC sells the failed bank at a negative price. Depositors prefer the purchase-and-assumption method to the payoff method because the transition is typically seamless, with the bank closing as usual at the end of the week and reopening on Monday morning under new ownership. In a purchase and assumption, no depositors, even those whose account balances exceed the deposit insurance limit, suffer a loss.

No private insurance fund can be big enough to withstand a run on all the banks it insures—but the FDIC is. Because the U.S. Treasury backs the FDIC, it can withstand virtually any crisis.

Since its inception, deposit insurance clearly helped to prevent runs on commercial banks. Even so, it did not prevent the crisis of 2007–2009 and the runs associated with it. The prime reason is that deposit insurance covers only depository institutions. But as the financial system developed, shadow banks—money market funds, securities brokers, and the like—gained importance. Those entities are sufficiently like banks that they, too, face the risk of runs by their short-term creditors. However, these non-banks lack the benefits of deposit insurance, and, until the latter part of the crisis, they had no access to a lender of last resort. Although some traditional banks suffered runs during the crisis—mostly by depositors whose balances exceeded the $100,000 insurance limit in effect at the time—most of the runs were against shadow banks.

## Problems Created by the Government Safety Net

We know that insurance changes people's behavior. Protected depositors have no incentive to monitor their bankers' behavior. Knowing this, bankers take on more risk than they would normally, because they get the benefits while the government assumes the costs. In protecting depositors, then, the government creates moral hazard. This is not just a theory. We can find evidence for this assertion by comparing bank balance sheets before and after the implementation of deposit insurance. Recall from Chapter 12 that commercial banks in the United States have significant leverage; their assets are about 9 times the size of their capital. In the 1920s, before the deposit insurance system was created, banks' ratio of assets to capital was about 4 to 1. Most economic and financial historians believe that government insurance led directly to the rise in risk.

## LESSONS FROM THE CRISIS
### SHOULD THE LENDER OF LAST RESORT ALSO SUPERVISE?

Who supervises the financial industry? How do the supervisors interact with the central bank as the *lender of last resort* (LOLR)? Different countries have answered these questions in different ways. Some have multiple regulators with overlapping jurisdictions. Others have only one regulator or a small number with little overlap. Some countries assign supervision to the central bank, but others do not.

The crisis exposed faults in every system. It also strengthened the case for making the central bank the leading financial supervisor. Let's take a brief but critical look at some examples.

At one end of the regulatory spectrum sits the United States with its large number of overlapping regulators. Table 14.1 (on page 356) lists the regulators of depository institutions as of early 2010. Additional agencies oversee other financial activities, such as the trading of securities and commodities and the sale of insurance. Although the Federal Reserve—the U.S. LOLR—supervises bank holding companies, which operate the largest banks, most intermediaries lie outside the Fed's supervisory sphere.

At the opposite end of the spectrum from the United States sits the United Kingdom, which has a unified financial regulator, the Financial Services Authority (FSA). The FSA is responsible not only for banks, but for the supervision of most financial institutions, markets, and exchanges in the country. However, the FSA is not the U.K. LOLR: that authority belongs to the Bank of England, the country's central bank.

The approach of countries in continental Europe is closer to that of their British neighbor than to that of the United States, but some of the national central banks nonetheless serve as bank supervisors. Importantly, the European Central Bank (ECB) has neither a regulatory nor a supervisory role as of this writing. However, its members—the euro area's national central banks—are the LOLR in their countries.*

The financial crisis of 2007–2009 tested all of these regulatory arrangements. Effective crisis management requires that policymakers act urgently to limit contagion from a weak financial institution, a loss of market function, or a threat to funding liquidity. Which structure was more likely to promptly detect and respond to systemic risks? How well did each arrangement fare in responding to the liquidity shortfall? How reliably were emergency lenders—each country's LOLR—able to distinguish between illiquid and insolvent intermediaries?

Unfortunately, none of the existing structures fared noticeably better than the others. The experience of 2007–2009 does not instill confidence in any of the regulatory approaches that existed before the crisis.

Multiple regulators complicated the U.S. response. The Federal Reserve had limited information about the firms that posed the most virulent systemic threats—Bear Stearns, Lehman Brothers, and AIG—because it had no supervisory role over those institutions. The Fed provided emergency liquidity to Bear and AIG but not to Lehman. Would better knowledge have prompted the Fed to address these threats differently or at an earlier stage? We can only speculate.

Looking at the United Kingdom, it is difficult to argue that the streamlined system facilitated rapid analysis and response. If anything, the British experience highlights the problems that arise when the central bank is not the financial supervisor. Ineffective coordination among the FSA, the Bank of England, and the U.K. Treasury in the summer of 2007 has been widely seen as a factor in the run on Northern Rock, the first run on a major U.K. bank in more than a century (see page 344).[†]

The lack of immediate, direct access to supervisory information also would seem to be a handicap for the ECB. Leading policymakers have emphasized the need to improve the information flow among euro-area financial regulators and the ECB. During the crisis, the ECB may have compensated for its information handicap by acting early to flood the euro-area system with liquidity.

---

*The European Commission (the executive branch of the European Union) has proposed the creation of a European Systemic Risk Board that would oversee *macro-prudential risks* (see pages 363–367). The proposal anticipates a prominent role for the ECB and the national central banks.

†See Stephen Cecchetti, "Why Central Banks Should Be Supervisors," *VOX*, November 30, 2007, http://www.voxeu.org/index.php?q=node/755.

---

And that is not the only problem. Government officials are especially worried about the largest institutions because they can pose a threat to the entire financial system. Although the failure of a community bank is unfortunate, the prospect of a large financial conglomerate going under is a regulator's worst nightmare. The financial havoc that could be caused by the collapse of an institution holding more than a trillion dollars in assets is too much for most people even to contemplate.

What this means is that some intermediaries are treated as *too big to fail* or *too interconnected to fail*. Putting such an institution through the usual mechanism for resolving a business failure—bankruptcy court—may force the bankruptcy of many

The idea that o
backed guarant
Only some cra
insurance make
dence is that it
posed to stabili
than good.

The problem
ior. Protected d
bankers' behav
on more risk th
the benefit of ri
assumes the c
depositors, the
In 1980, the de
was raised to $
the following te
tutions (banks,
than four time:
century since d
a vast majority
were small, the
$180 billion.

So, in an at
deposit insuran
bankers' excess
set up regulato
things, there ar

banks are not c
chartered and h
competition, sp
to hold a minir
balance sheet.

As we all kn
on an interstate
fast. Unless the
are worthless. T
structure in the
tors banks' com
ing world. The
practices confo

Banks are re
Federal Reserve
lapping nature
safeguard the so
choosing wheth
Federal Reserve

households, firms, and other intermediaries that have contracted with the failed institution. Thus, too big to fail really means too big or too complex to shut down or sell in an orderly fashion without large and painful spillovers. Regulators call such an institution *too big to resolve*.

Experience has led the managers of these too-big-to-fail intermediaries to expect that if their institutions begin to founder, the government will find a way to bail them out. Regulators allowed Lehman Brothers to fail in September 2008, but the painful financial and economic disruptions that ensued served only to reinforce the widespread expectation that government will bail out the largest and most interconnected financial institutions.

A bailout of a failed bank can take many forms. In most cases, the deposit insurer quickly finds a buyer; otherwise, the government, as lender of last resort, usually makes a loan to buy time to fashion a solution. Depositors whose balances do not exceed the insurance limit will be made whole. But in the crisis of 2007–2009, most of the creditors to banks were protected, not just the insured depositors. Following the Lehman failure, governments in Europe and the United States guaranteed all of the liabilities of their largest banks. In particular, they promised that the holders of bonds issued by the banks would not incur losses. Without these guarantees, the evaporation of funding liquidity probably would have led to a rapid cascade of failures because banks would be unable to fund themselves. In a number of cases, unlike in a normal bankruptcy, the managers of failing banks also kept their jobs.

During the crisis, governments also *recapitalized* some intermediaries—that is, gave them public money in return for partial ownership rights—to prevent a run by their creditors. In effect, governments declared recapitalized intermediaries to be too big to fail while they allowed smaller institutions to go under. In the United States, for example, the FDIC shut down 140 banks in 2009, the largest number since 1992. In these ways, the government, not the market, chose the winners and the losers.

Because it undermines the market discipline that depositors and creditors impose on banks and shadow banks, this **too-big-to-fail policy** is ripe for reform. Given the $250,000 insurance limit (set to return to $100,000 in 2014), a corporation with millions of dollars to deposit would normally be concerned about the quality and riskiness of the assets a bank holds. If the bank or MMMF were to fail, the corporation would face significant losses. Thus, the threat of withdrawal of these large balances restrains the bank or MMMF from taking on too much risk.[4] But for very large banks, the too-big-to-fail policy renders the deposit insurance ceiling meaningless. In the aftermath of the crisis of 2007–2009, everyone knew which banks were too big to fail and that the authorities would support them. With little threat that depositors will flee, bank managers can take whatever risks they like. The too-big-to-fail policy compounds the problem of moral hazard, encouraging managers of large banks to engage in extremely risky behavior (and putting small banks at a competitive disadvantage).

During the financial crisis, many shadow banks also received government bailouts and guarantees that foster moral hazard. Like their bank brethren, some of the largest shadow banks obtained government support because their failure was perceived as too costly in a crisis. And the problem is not limited to the too-big-to-fail class. The U.S.

---

[4]Intermediaries can suffer what is known as a *silent run* as when repo lenders refuse to roll over their loans to a securities broker or when investors electronically sell their shares in a MMMF rumored to be in trouble. Today, even traditional banks can suffer a silent run. If depositors with balances that exceed the insurance limit fear that their bank is in trouble, they needn't line up at the teller window to get their money. They can simply go online to initiate an electronic withdrawal.

## Terms

## Chapter Lessons

1. The collapse of banks and the banking system disrupts both the payments system and the screening and monitoring of borrowers.
   a. Intermediaries are insolvent when their liabilities exceed their assets.
   b. Because banks guarantee their depositors cash on demand on a first-come, first-served basis, they are subject to runs. Shadow banks like MMMFs and securities brokers also face runs because some of their liabilities can be withdrawn at face value without notice.
   c. A bank run can occur simply because depositors have become worried about a bank's soundness. Shadow banks also may face runs due to a loss of confidence.
   d. The inability of depositors to tell a sound from an unsound bank can turn a single bank's failure into a bank panic, causing even sound banks to fail through a process called contagion. Shadow banks face similar risks.
   e. A financial crisis in which the entire system of banks and shadow banks ceases to function can be caused by
      i. False rumors.
      ii. The actual deterioration of balance sheets for economic reasons.

2. The government is involved in every part of the financial system.
   a. Government officials may intervene in the financial system in order to
      i. Protect small depositors.
      ii. Protect bank customers from exploitation.
      iii. Safeguard the stability of the financial system.
   b. Most financial regulations apply to depository institutions, while shadow banks usually face less regulation.
   c. Intermediaries that are less prone to runs, such as pension funds and most insurers, face less intrusive government oversight than the banking industry.
   d. The U.S. government has established a two-part safety net to protect the nation's financial system.
      i. The Federal Reserve acts as the lender of last resort, providing liquidity to solvent institutions in order to prevent the failure of a single intermediary from becoming a systemwide panic.

ii. The Federal Deposit Insurance Corporation (FDIC) insures individual depositors helping to prevent bank runs by reducing depositors' incentive to flee at the first whiff of trouble.

e. The government's safety net encourages bank managers to take more risk than they would otherwise, increasing the problem of moral hazard.

3. Through regulation and supervision, government officials reduce the amount of risk banks can take, lowering their chances of failure. Regulators and supervisors
   a. Restrict competition.
   b. Restrict the types of assets banks can hold.
   c. Require banks to hold minimum levels of capital.
   d. Require banks to disclose their fees to customers and their financial indicators to investors.
   e. Monitor banks' compliance with government regulations.

4. Regulators use macro-prudential tools to limit systemic threats to the financial system. Such risks usually arise from externalities—costly spillovers from the behavior of intermediaries. These externalities have two sources: (1) *common exposure* of intermediaries to frail institutions or to underlying risks and (2) *pro-cyclicality* of the links between financial and economic activity, which amplifies boom and bust cycles.

# Conceptual Problems

1. Explain how a bank run can turn into a bank panic.

2. Current technology allows large bank depositors to withdraw their funds electronically at a moment's notice. They can do so all at the same time, without anyone's knowledge, in what is called a silent run. When might a silent run happen, and why?

3. Explain why financial institutions such as pension funds and insurance companies are not as vulnerable to runs as money-market mutual funds and securities dealers.

4. Explain the link between falling house prices and bank failures during the financial crisis of 2007–2009.

5. Discuss the regulations that are designed to reduce the moral hazard created by deposit insurance.

6. How does the lender of last resort function create moral hazard?

7. During the financial crisis of 2007–2009, the Federal Reserve used its emergency authority to lend to shadow banks. Explain how this extension of the lender of last resort function added to moral hazard.

8. Distinguish between illiquidity and insolvency. Why is it difficult for a lender of last resort to tell insolvency from illiquidity? Does the distinction matter?

9.* Why is the banking system much more heavily regulated than other areas of the economy?

*Indicates more difficult problems

10.* Explain why, in seeking to avoid financial crises, the government's role as regulator of the financial system does not imply it should protect individual institutions from failure.

11. Explain how macro-prudential regulations work to limit systemic risk in the financial system.

# Analytical Problems

12. Why do you think that runs on banks and shadow banks during the financial crisis of 2007–2009 were not limited to institutions with large exposures to subprime mortgage lending?

13. For each of the following events, state whether you think the immediate problem a typical bank is most likely to encounter is one of illiquidity or of insolvency. Explain your choice in each case.
    a. The government announces it is abolishing its deposit insurance program.
    b. The economy falls into recession and job losses are rampant.
    c. The central bank triples the reserve requirements, effective immediately.

14.* Do you think that the central bank, as lender of last resort, should also supervise the financial industry? Why or why not?

15. Suppose you have two deposits totaling $280,000 with a bank that has just been declared insolvent. Would you prefer that the FDIC resolve the insolvency under the "payoff method" or the "purchase and assumption" method? Explain your choice.

16.* How might the existence of the government safety net lead to increased concentration in the banking industry?

17. How do you think financial regulators should address the "too-big-to-fail" issue associated with large, systemically important financial institutions?

18. If banks' fragility arises from the fact that they provide liquidity to depositors, as a bank manager, how might you reduce the fragility of your institution?

19.* Why do you think bank managers are not always willing to pursue strategies to reduce the fragility of their institutions?

20. Regulators have traditionally required banks to maintain capital-asset ratios of a certain level to ensure adequate net worth based on the size and composition of the bank's assets on its balance sheet. Why might such capital adequacy requirements not be effective?

21. You are the lender of last resort and an institution approaches you for a loan. You assess that the institution has $800 million in assets, mostly in long-term loans, and $600 million in liabilities. The institution is experiencing unusually high withdrawal rates on its demand deposits and is requesting a loan to tide it over. Would you grant the loan?

22. You are a bank examiner and have concerns that the bank you are examining may have a solvency problem. On examining the bank's assets, you notice that the loan sizes of a significant portion of the bank's loans are increasing in relatively small increments each month. What do you think might be going on and what should you do about it?

# Part *IV*

## Central Banks, Monetary Policy, and Financial Stability

# Chapter 15

## Central Banks in the World Today

Beginning in the summer of 2007, the most severe and persistent financial crisis since the Great Depression shook intermediaries, markets, and economies around the globe. Some of the largest financial institutions failed, and the market disruptions triggered the worst global recession since the Second World War. The panic peaked after the September 2008 run on Lehman Brothers—the fourth largest U.S. investment bank—as investors around the globe sought to hold only the safest, most liquid assets they could find. Investors stopped lending to intermediaries, who stopped lending to each other. As the storm spread, the global financial system bordered on complete collapse for the first time in 75 years.

Central banks neither foresaw nor prevented the crisis of 2007–2009. Even long after the tempest began, they did not see how menacing it would become. Yet, as the expanding storm continuously poked new holes in the financial boat, policymakers developed new tools to plug the holes. When the financial hurricane finally reached its late-2008 crescendo, the world's leading central banks played a key role in bringing the financial system and the economy back to safe harbor. They acted in unprecedented fashion—on their own as well as with other central banks and with government finance ministries—to prevent the financial system from capsizing and, over time, to restore financial and economic stability.

The **central bank** of the United States is the Federal Reserve (widely known as the Fed for short). The people who work there are responsible for making sure that our financial system functions smoothly so that the average citizen can carry on without worrying about it. During the financial crisis, the Fed fell short of this goal. Nevertheless, it managed in 2008 to prevent the looming collapse of the financial system and to foster a vast improvement of financial conditions in 2009 that helped end the long, deep economic slump.

These watershed events will leave a lasting imprint on global economies, the financial system, and policymaking. Many changes are likely to prove permanent rather than temporary. As we saw in Chapters 12 and 13, the crisis has already transformed the structure of the financial industry in the United States, with further change on the horizon. Chapter 14 highlighted the new regulatory environment, especially new approaches to managing systemic risk.

In Part IV, we will study the evolving role of central banks. Central banks do not act only during times of crisis. Their work is vital to the day-to-day operation of any modern economy. Today there are roughly 170 central banks in the world: Virtually every country has one. Yet, despite the vast powers of these institutions and the constant news reports on their activities, most people have only a vague idea of what they are and what they do.

This chapter begins to explain the role of central banks in our economic and financial system. It describes the origins of modern central banking and examines the complexities policymakers now face in meeting their responsibilities. It also highlights a central question that has become politically controversial following the Fed's unprecedented actions in the crisis; namely, what is the proper relationship between a central bank and the government?

# The Basics: How Central Banks Originated and Their Role Today

The central bank started out as the government's bank and over the years added various other functions. A modern central bank not only manages the government's finances but provides an array of services to commercial banks. It is the bankers' bank. Let's see how this arrangement came about.

## The Government's Bank

Governments have financial needs of their own. Some rulers, like King William of Orange, created the central bank to finance wars. Others, like Napoléon Bonaparte, did it in an effort to stabilize their country's economic and financial system.[1]

While central banks have been around since the late 1600s, these early examples are really the exceptions, as central banking is largely a 20th-century phenomenon. In 1900, only 18 countries had central banks. Even the U.S. Federal Reserve did not begin operating until 1914.[2] As the importance of the government and the financial system grew, the need for a central bank grew along with it. Today it is hard to imagine not having one.

As the government's bank, the central bank occupies a privileged position: It has a monopoly on the issuance of currency. *The central bank creates money.* Historically, central bank money has been seen as more trustworthy than that issued by kings, queens, or emperors. Rulers have had a tendency to default on their debts, rendering their currencies worthless. By contrast, early central banks kept sufficient reserves to redeem their notes in gold. People must have faith in money if they are to use it, and experience tells us that this type of institutional arrangement creates that faith. Today the Federal Reserve has the sole legal authority to issue U.S. dollar bills.[3]

The ability to print currency means that the central bank can control the availability of money and credit in a country's economy. As we'll see in later chapters, most central banks go about this by adjusting short-term interest rates. This activity is what we usually refer to as **monetary policy.** In today's world, central banks use monetary policy to stabilize economic growth and inflation. An expansionary or accommodative policy, through lower interest rates, raises both growth and inflation over the short run, while tighter or restrictive policy reduces them. We will discuss the mechanics of monetary policy in more detail in later chapters.

Understanding why a country would want to have its own monetary policy is important. At its most basic level, printing paper money is a very profitable business. A $100 bill costs only a few cents to print, but it can be exchanged for $100 worth of

[1]The Bank of England was chartered in 1694 for the express purpose of raising taxes and borrowing to finance a war between Austria, England, and the Netherlands on one side and Louis XIV's France on the other. The Banque de France was created in 1800 in the aftermath of the deep recession and hyperinflation of the French Revolutionary period. For a more detailed discussion, see Glyn Davies' *The History of Money from Ancient Times to the Present Day* (Cardiff: University of Wales Press, 1994).

[2]For two short periods in the 19th century, the United States did have a national bank that served many of the functions of a central bank. Early American dislike for the centralization of power doomed these institutions, the First Bank of the United States (1791–1811) and the Second Bank of the United States (1816–1836). In the next chapter, we will see how industrial and financial development after the Civil War convinced people that they simply could not live without a central bank. See Michael F. Bryan and Bruce Champ's "Fear and Loathing of Central Banks in America," *Economic Commentary* of the Federal Reserve Bank of Cleveland, June 2002, for a brief description of this history.

[3]While once upon a time you could redeem dollar bills for gold, today all the Federal Reserve promises is that it will give you a crisp new dollar bill for a worn old one—and that is enough for the average person, given the public's faith in the Federal Reserve.

Finally, as we saw in our discussion of banking regulation, someone has to watch over commercial banks and nonbank financial institutions so that savers and investors can be confident they are sound. Those who monitor the financial system must have sensitive information. For example, they need to know the exact methods institutions use to make lending and credit decisions. Needless to say, such knowledge would be very useful to the institutions' competitors. Government examiners and supervisors are the only ones who can handle such information without conflict of interest. In some countries they are housed in the central bank, while in others they work in separate agencies. In the United States, as we saw in Chapter 14, the examiners work in various places, including the Federal Reserve.

As the government's bank and the bankers' bank, central banks are the biggest, most powerful players in a country's financial and economic system. Central bankers are supposed to use this power to stabilize the economy, making us all better off. And for the most part, that is what they do. But any institution with the power to ensure that the economic and financial systems run smoothly also has the power to create problems. By limiting its lending early in the financial crisis of 2007–2009, the Bank of England may have contributed to the first depositor run on a major British bank in more than a century. And the failure of the Bank of Russia to exert any control over the expansion of money and credit led to a very high inflation rate, contributing to the fact that the Russian economy shrank by nearly 50 percent during the 1990s.

Before we go on to examine the goals and objectives of central bankers in detail, it is essential that we understand what a modern central bank is *not*. First, a central bank does not control securities markets, though it may monitor and participate in bond and stock markets. Second, the central bank does not control the government's budget. In the United States, the budget is determined by Congress and the president through **fiscal policy**. The U.S. Treasury then administers the government, managing the collection of funds through the tax system and writing checks to pay for the government's expenditures. The Fed acts only as the Treasury's bank, providing a place for money paid to the government to be deposited, making good on the government's checks, and helping to borrow funds when they are needed. Not just in the United States but throughout the world, the common arrangement today is for the central bank to serve the government in the same way that a commercial bank serves a business or an individual. The treasury or finance ministry manages fiscal policy, and the central bank offers a set of services that make such management possible.

Table 15.1 lists the functions of a modern central bank.

---

**Table 15.1**   The Functions of a Modern Central Bank

1. *The Government's Bank*
   a. Manages the finances of the government.
   b. Through interest rates, controls the availability of money and credit.
2. *The Bankers' Bank*
   a. Guarantees that sound banks can do business by *lending* to them, even during crises.
   b. Operates a *payments system* for interbank payments.
   c. *Oversees* financial institutions to ensure confidence in their soundness.

# Stability: The Primary Objective of All Central Banks

The central bank is essentially part of the government.[6] Whenever we see an agency of the government involving itself in the economy, we need to ask why. What makes individuals incapable of doing what we have entrusted to the government? In the case of national defense and pollution regulation, the reasons are obvious. Most people will not voluntarily contribute their resources to the army. Nor will they spontaneously clean up their own air. To put it slightly differently, government involvement is justified by the presence of externalities or public goods; that is, when individuals do not pay the full costs or capture the complete benefits from their actions.

The rationale for the existence of a central bank is equally clear. While economic and financial systems may be fairly stable most of the time, when left on their own they are prone to episodes of extreme volatility. Prior to the advent of the Fed, the U.S. financial system was extremely unstable. It was plagued by numerous panics. Even with a central bank, these systems don't necessarily work well.

The historical record is filled with examples of failure, like the Great Depression of the 1930s, when the banking system collapsed, economic activity plunged by one-third, and, at its worst, one-quarter of Americans were unemployed for nearly a decade. Economic historians blame the Federal Reserve for the severity of that episode. The claim is that monetary policymakers failed to provide adequate money and credit, with the result that 10,000 of the country's 25,000 banks, accounting for 13 percent of all deposits, were closed. The Fed also bears considerable responsibility for the crisis of 2007–2009. It was largely passive as intermediaries took on increasing risk amid an unprecedented housing bubble, and it allowed the financial hurricane to intensify for more than a year after the storms began. Unlike the Great Depression, however, the Fed used all its emergency authority in historically unprecedented ways to steady the financial system when the crisis peaked in 2008. The Fed's tenacity and flexibility helped promote a huge recovery of financial conditions in 2009 and avoid a second Great Depression.

Central bankers work to reduce the volatility of the economic and financial systems by pursuing five specific objectives:

1. Low and stable inflation.
2. High and stable real growth, together with high employment.
3. Stable financial markets and institutions.
4. Stable interest rates.
5. A stable exchange rate.

STABILITY

It is important to realize that instability in any of these—inflation, growth, the financial system, interest rates, or exchange rates—poses an economywide risk that individuals can't diversify away. Recall from Chapter 5 that systematic risk, where everyone is affected, differs from idiosyncratic risk, which affects only a particular organization or individual. The job of the central bank is to improve general economic welfare by managing and reducing systematic risk. Keep in mind that it is probably

---

[6]Technically, the legal organization of central banks can be quite complex. Some are inside their country's government, some are private banks, and others are a combination. As we will see in Chapter 16, the Federal Reserve is in that last category, part government and part private bank. As a practical matter, since they all have a set of tasks that only they are allowed to perform, we will treat central banks as if they are a part of the government.

impossible to achieve all five of the central bank's objectives simultaneously. Trade-offs must be made. As we will see, stabilizing inflation may result in less stable growth, and stable interest rates may be inconsistent with all the other objectives.

## Low, Stable Inflation

In 2002, the director of research of the International Monetary Fund (the closest thing there is to a world central bank) summarized virtually every economist's view when he said, "Uncontrolled inflation strangles growth, hurting the entire populace, especially the indigent."[7] That is why many central banks take as their primary job the maintenance of **price stability**. That is, they strive to eliminate inflation. The consensus is that when inflation rises, the central bank is at fault.

The rationale for keeping the economy inflation free is straightforward. Standards, everyone agrees, should be standard. A pound should always weigh a pound, a cup should always hold a cup, and a yard should always measure a yard. Similarly, a dollar should always be worth a dollar. What is true for physical weights and measures should be true for the unit of account as well. The purchasing power of one dollar, one yen, or one euro should remain stable over long periods. Maintaining price stability enhances money's usefulness both as a unit of account and as a store of value.

Prices are central to everything that happens in a market-based economy. They provide the information individuals and firms need to ensure that resources are allocated to their most productive uses. When a seller can raise the price of a product, for example, that is supposed to signal that demand has increased, so producing more is worthwhile. But inflation degrades the information content of prices. When all prices are rising together, understanding the reasons becomes difficult. Did consumers decide they liked an item, shifting demand? Did the cost of producing the item rise, shifting supply? Or was inflation responsible for the jump in price? If the economy is to run efficiently, we need to be able to tell the difference.

**RISK**

If the inflation rate were predictable—say, 10 percent year in and year out—we might be able to adjust, eventually. But unfortunately, as inflation rises, it becomes less stable. If our best guess is that the rate of inflation will be 2 percent over the coming year, we can be fairly certain that the result will be a price level increase of between 1 and 3 percent. But experience tells us that when we expect the inflation rate to be around 10 percent, we shouldn't be surprised if it ends up anywhere between 8 and 12 percent. The higher inflation is, the less predictable it is, and the more systematic risk it creates.[8]

Moreover, high inflation is bad for growth. This fact is obvious in extreme cases, such as in 1985, when the inflation rate reached 11,000 percent in Bolivia, or in 1983, when it reached nearly 5,000 percent in Ukraine. In such cases of **hyperinflation**—when prices double every two to three months—prices contain virtually no information, and people use all their energy just coping with the crisis, so growth plummets. In Bolivia, growth went from more than plus 6 percent in the late 1970s to minus 5 percent during the hyperinflation. The Ukrainian economy shrank by more than 20 percent the year inflation peaked. Only when inflation was brought under control did these economies begin to grow again.

Because low inflation is the basis for general economic prosperity, most people agree that it should be the primary objective of monetary policy. But how low should

[7]Kenneth S. Rogoff, "An Open Letter to Joseph Stiglitz," International Monetary Fund, July 2, 2002.

[8]Inflation is costly for other reasons as well. They include the cost of going to the bank more often, the cost of changing prices more often, and distortions created by the way the tax rules are written.

## YOUR FINANCIAL WORLD
### Why Inflation Is Bad for You

If you ask most people why inflation is bad, they will say it is responsible for a decline in what they can purchase with their incomes. For them, inflation causes a drop in their standard of living: Prices have gone up, but their incomes, including their wages, haven't. Economists view inflation differently. To them, inflation is when everything that is denominated in dollars goes up proportionally—prices, incomes, savings account balances, everything. It is as if everything is suddenly measured in cents instead of dollars. How could this possibly make anyone worse off?

The problem is that high inflation tends to be more volatile than low inflation, so the higher inflation is, the greater the risk. When inflation is averaging 2 percent per year, chances are slim that it will more than double to 5 percent. Such an increase would mean that the central bank had lost control, at least temporarily. But if the rate of inflation is closer to 15 percent, an increase of 3 percentage points to 18 percent, a change of only one-fifth, could easily happen.

To see how this affects virtually everyone, recall from Chapter 6 that unpredictable inflation makes bonds risky.

Higher-than-expected inflation reduces the real return a bondholder receives. Because the real return is the nominal return minus expected inflation, if the nominal interest rate is 5 percent and inflation turns out to be 2 percent, then the real return drops to 3 percent. If the inflation rate ends up at 5 percent, the real return is zero. That's a risk. Because risk requires compensation, inflation risk drives up the interest rate required to entice investors to hold bonds.

Now think about two common financial transactions: getting a home mortgage and saving for retirement. When you buy a house, your goal is to get the lowest mortgage interest rate you can find. Inflation risk drives up mortgage interest rates, increasing your monthly payments and forcing you to purchase a less expensive house. Turning to your retirement savings, inflation risk makes it more difficult to know how much to save, because you are unsure what the purchasing power of your savings will be 40 or 50 years from now. Long-term planning is hard enough without the added burden of inflation risk.

inflation be? Zero is probably too low. There are a couple of reasons for this. First, if the central bank tries to keep the inflation rate at zero, there is a risk of deflation—a drop in prices. Deflation makes debts more difficult to repay, which increases the default rate on loans, affecting the health of banks. Recall from Chapter 11 that deflation increases the information problems lenders face, and may prevent some borrowers from obtaining loans. Second, if the inflation rate were zero, an employer wishing to cut labor costs would need to cut nominal wages, which is difficult to do. With a small amount of inflation, the employer can simply leave wages as they are, and workers' real wages will fall. So a small amount of inflation makes labor markets work better, at least from the employer's point of view.

## High, Stable Real Growth

When Ben S. Bernanke was sworn in as the 14th chairman of the Board of Governors of the Federal Reserve System, he said "Our mission, as set forth by the Congress, is a critical one: to preserve price stability, to foster maximum sustainable growth in output and employment, and to promote a stable and efficient financial system that serves all Americans well and fairly."[9] We just discussed the first of these; preserving price stability is analogous to keeping inflation low and stable. And we will look at financial stability in a moment. For now, let's examine the second item on Chairman Bernanke's list: to foster maximum sustainable growth in output and employment.

[9]Remarks by Chairman Ben S. Bernanke at the ceremonial swearing-in by President George W. Bush, Federal Reserve Board of Governors, Washington, D.C., February 6, 2006.

When central bankers talk like this, what they mean is that they are working to dampen the fluctuations of the business cycle. Booms are popular, but recessions are not. In recessions, people get laid off and businesses fail. Without a steady income, individuals struggle to make their auto, credit card, and mortgage payments. Consumers pull back, hurting businesses that rely on them to buy products. Reduced sales lead to more layoffs, and so on. The longer the downturn goes on, the worse it gets.

By adjusting interest rates, central bankers work to moderate these cycles and stabilize growth and employment. The idea is that there is some long-run *sustainable* level of production called **potential output** that depends on things like technology, the size of the capital stock, and the number of people who can work. Growth in these *inputs* leads to growth in *potential output*—**sustainable growth**. In the United States, growth usually runs around 3 percent per year. Over the short run, output may deviate from this potential level, and growth may deviate from its long-run sustainable rate. In recessions, the economy stalls, incomes stagnate, and unemployment rises. By lowering interest rates, monetary policymakers can moderate such declines.[10]

Similarly, there are times when growth rises above sustainable rates, and the economy overheats. These periods may seem to bring increased prosperity, but because they don't last forever, they are followed by reduced spending, lower business investment, and layoffs. A period of above-average growth has to be followed by a period of below-average growth. The job of the central bank during such periods is to raise interest rates and keep the economy from operating at unsustainable levels.

Importantly, in the long run, stability leads to higher growth. The reason is that unstable growth creates risk for which investors need to be compensated in the form of higher interest rates. With higher interest rates, businesses borrow less, which means that they have fewer resources to invest and grow. To understand how this works, think about getting a loan to buy a car. The more certain you are that you will have a good, steady job over the next few years, the larger the loan you will feel comfortable taking on. If you are nervous that you might lose your job, you will be cautious. What is true for you and your car loan is true for every person and every company. The greater the uncertainty about future business conditions, the more cautious people will be in making investments of all kinds. Stability leads to higher growth.[11]

The importance of keeping sustainable growth as high as possible is hard to overstate. The difference between an economy that grows at 4 percent per year and one that grows at 2 percent per year is the difference between an economy that doubles in size over 18 years and one that grows by less than 50 percent in the same period. (This calculation uses the rule of 72 described in Your Financial World: How Long Does Your Investment Take to Double? in Chapter 4.) Keeping employment high is equally important. In the same way that you can never get back the study time you lost when you went to the movies before an exam, it is impossible for the economy to recover what unemployed people would have produced had they been working during a downturn. You can't get the lost time back. Our hope is that policymakers can manage the country's affairs so that we will stay on a high and sustainable growth path.

The levels of growth and employment aren't the only things of importance, though. Stability matters too. Fluctuations in general business conditions are the primary

RISK

---

[10]Financial crises typically depress economic growth below their prior sustainable path for many years. In the most extreme U.S. example, the Great Depression, the U.S. economy did not regain its pre-1929 trend until 1942, when wartime production was in full swing.

[11]For a discussion on the relationship between the level and volatility of growth, both the evidence and the theory, see Garey Ramey and Valerie A. Ramey, "Cross-Country Evidence on the Link between Volatility and Growth," *American Economic Review* 85 (December 1995), pp. 1138–1151.

source of systematic risk, a kind of risk that can't be diversified away. As we have said a number of times, uncertainty about the future makes planning more difficult, so getting rid of uncertainty makes everyone better off.

## Financial System Stability

The Federal Reserve was founded to stop the financial panics that plagued the United States during the late 19th and early 20th centuries. It took a while to work out the kinks in the system. As we have seen, the U.S. financial system collapsed again in the early 1930s, as policymakers at the Federal Reserve watched. Between then and 2007, the Fed's track record in preventing or mitigating crises improved substantially. However, recent experience demonstrates that financial and economic catastrophes are not limited to history books. Accordingly, **financial system stability** is an integral part of every modern central banker's job. It is essential for policymakers to ensure that the markets for stocks, bonds, and the like continue to operate smoothly and efficiently.

If people lose faith in financial institutions and markets, they will rush to low-risk alternatives, and intermediation will stop. Savers will not lend and borrowers will not be able to borrow. Getting a car loan or a home mortgage becomes impossible, as does selling a bond to maintain or expand a business. When the financial system collapses, economic activity does, too.

The possibility of a severe disruption in the financial markets is a type of systematic risk. Nothing that a single individual does can eliminate it. Central banks must control this risk, making sure that the financial system remains in good working order. The *value at risk*, not the standard deviation, is the important measure here. Recall from Chapter 5 that value at risk measures the risk of the maximum potential loss. When thinking about financial stability, central bankers want to minimize the risk of a disaster and keep the chance of this maximum loss as small as possible. Their struggles in the crisis of 2007–2009 revealed just how difficult it can be to achieve these goals.

"*Personally, I liked this roller coaster a lot better before the Federal Reserve Board got hold of it.*"

SOURCE: © Robert Mankoff/The New Yorker Collection/ www.cartoonbank.com.

## Interest-Rate and Exchange-Rate Stability

If you ask them, most central bankers will tell you that they do their best to keep interest rates and exchange rates from fluctuating too much. They want to eliminate abrupt changes. But if you press them further, they will tell you that these goals are secondary to those of low inflation, stable growth, and financial stability. The reason for this hierarchy is that *interest-rate stability* and *exchange-rate stability* are means for achieving the ultimate goal of stabilizing the economy; they are not ends unto themselves.

It is easy to see why interest-rate volatility is a problem. First, most people respond to low interest rates by borrowing and spending more. Individuals take out loans to purchase cars, new appliances and the like, while corporations issue more bonds and use the proceeds to enlarge their operations. Conversely, when interest rates rise, people borrow and spend less. So, by raising expenditure when interest rates are low and reducing expenditure when interest rates are high, interest-rate volatility makes

| Table 15.2 | The Objectives of a Modern Central Bank |

STABILITY

| | |
|---|---|
| 1. *Low, stable inflation* | Inflation creates confusion and makes planning difficult. When inflation is high, growth is low. |
| 2. *High, stable growth* | Stable, predictable growth is higher than unstable, unpredictable growth. |
| 3. *Financial system stability* | Stable financial markets and institutions are a necessity for an economy to operate efficiently. |
| 4. *Stable interest rates* | Interest-rate volatility creates risk for both lenders and borrowers. |
| 5. *Stable exchange rates* | Variable exchange rates make the revenues from foreign sales and the cost of purchasing imported goods hard to predict. |

output unstable. Second, interest-rate volatility means higher risk—and a higher risk premium—on long-term bonds. (Remember from Chapter 7 that the long-term interest rate is the average of expected future short-term interest rates plus a risk premium that compensates for the volatility of short-term interest rates.) Risk makes financial decisions more difficult, lowering productivity and making the economy less efficient. Because central bankers control short-term interest rates, they are in a position to control this risk and stabilize the economy.

Stabilizing exchange rates is the last item on the list of central bank objectives. The value of a country's currency affects the cost of imports to domestic consumers and the cost of exports to foreign buyers. When the exchange rate is stable, the dollar price of a car produced in Germany is predictable, making life easier for the foreign automobile manufacturer, the domestic retailer, and the American car buyer. Planning ahead is easier for everyone.

Different countries have different priorities. While the Federal Reserve and the European Central Bank may not care much about exchange-rate stability, the heads of central banks in small, less developed, trade-oriented countries do. In *emerging-market countries* where exports and imports are central to the structure of the economy, officials might reasonably argue that good overall macroeconomic performance follows from a stable exchange rate.

Table 15.2 summarizes the five objectives of a modern central bank.

## Meeting the Challenge: Creating a Successful Central Bank

The past several decades were amazing in many ways. The Internet and cell phones came into widespread use. Overall economic conditions improved nearly everywhere, and especially in rapidly growing emerging economies, such as those of Brazil, China, and India. Growth was higher, inflation lower, and both more stable than in the 1980s. In the United States, the inflation rate fell from 6 percent to less than 2 percent at the end. Meanwhile, real growth rose from less than 3 percent to more than 4 percent, until the financial crisis began in 2007.

## LESSONS FROM THE CRISIS
### THREATS TO FED INDEPENDENCE

The Federal Reserve and the Treasury cooperated closely during the financial crisis of 2007–2009. At times, in working feverishly to restore financial stability, the Fed appeared to act as if it were an agent of the Treasury—"the government's bank" (see page 373).*

In doing so, did the Federal Reserve sacrifice its monetary policy independence and its objective of low, stable inflation? The crisis has fueled uncertainty about the economic and inflation outlook. However, the return to high and sustained inflation that some observers fear is far from inevitable.

To be sure, many Fed actions in the crisis were radical and precedent setting. Utilizing its emergency powers for the first time since the 1930s, the Fed lent directly to nonbanks (including Bear Stearns and AIG) and purchased commercial paper from nonfinancial firms. To counter the September 2008 liquidity crisis, the Fed doubled its assets in the space of two months. To lower mortgage costs, it acquired more than a trillion dollars of mortgage securities. And, of course, the Fed cut its policy rate to nearly zero for the first time.

Has the crisis made the Fed a slave of U.S. government policy wishes? Hardly. In a financial crisis, the policy goals of financial stability, stable growth, and stable prices may be mutually consistent. As a result, an independent central bank may wish to cooperate with fiscal authorities—which, in the U.S. case, is the Treasury—to promote financial stability and forestall deflation.

However, an independent central bank also must be prepared to reverse course when necessary to keep inflation low. A central bank balance sheet that *stays* bloated over the long term *eventually* leads to inflation (see Chapter 17). The central bank also needs the proper tools to reverse its emergency actions when the time is right (see the Chapter 18 discussion of paying interest on reserves).

If the central bank reverses course in a timely fashion, inflation need not result (see the Chapter 18 discussion of exit strategies from unconventional policy). The difficulty is judging when to exit. Given the uncertainties about the financial system and the economy, the chances of a policy misjudgment are high. Waiting too long to exit will lead to inflation. Exiting prematurely—as the Fed did in 1936 and as the Bank of Japan did in 1999—can undermine economic recovery.

Have Fed actions undermined its anti-inflation credibility? Not yet. As of spring 2010, professional forecasters and participants in the Treasury market seemed confident that the Fed will succeed at keeping inflation low over the long term. Surveys of forecasters and market prices of bonds point to average inflation of about 2 percent over the next decade, a rate not very different from pre-crisis expectations.

Perhaps the greatest threat to Fed independence is the popular backlash following the crisis bailouts of intermediaries like AIG. If heightened congressional scrutiny leads to political efforts to influence future monetary policy decisions, confidence in the Fed's commitment to low inflation could quickly erode.

---

*For example, in hurriedly arranging the emergency acquisition of Bear Stearns in March 2008, the Federal Reserve Bank of New York (FRBNY) had to accept collateral with highly uncertain market value. This action put U.S. taxpayers at risk of loss, a move that generally only the Treasury would undertake. The Treasury Secretary endorsed the action in a letter on March 17, 2008 (see http://finance.senate.gov/press/Bpress/2008press/prb040108a.pdf). One year later, the Treasury added that it would "seek to remove" these risky assets from the Fed's balance sheet or "to liquidate" them. In effect, the Fed had acted in a temporary, emergency capacity as "the government's bank" to address a systemic crisis until the Treasury gained the flexibility to respond.

---

Outside of the United States, improvements were even more dramatic. In 1980, nearly two-thirds of the countries in the world were experiencing an inflation rate in excess of 10 percent per year and nearly one in three was experiencing negative growth. Twenty-five years later, only one country in six had a two-digit inflation rate, while something like 150 countries were growing at rates in excess of 2 percent per year. And not only was inflation lower and growth higher, both were more stable, until the financial crisis struck.

What explains this long period of stability? A prime candidate is that technology sparked a boom just as central banks became better at their jobs. First, monetary policymakers realized that sustainable growth had gone up, so they could keep interest rates low without worrying about inflation. Second, central banks were redesigned. It wasn't just that new central banks were established, like the ones set up in the 15 republics of the former Soviet Union. The structure of existing central banks changed significantly. The Bank of England is more than three centuries old (its building in London has stood for more than 200 years) but its operating charter was completely rewritten in 1998. The same year brought major changes in the organizational structure of the Bank of Japan. Federal Reserve operations have changed, too. The first public announcement of a move in the federal funds rate was made on February 4, 1994. On January 19, 2002, the regular issuance of a statement explaining interest-rate decisions became an official part of Federal Reserve procedures.

Many people believe that improvements in economic performance during the 1990s were related at least in part to the policy followed by these restructured central banks. Improving monetary policy is not just a matter of finding the right person for the job. There is an ample supply of highly qualified people. In fact, in many countries there is a long history of central bankers who have tried but failed because they weren't free to pursue effective policies. Successful policymaking is as much a consequence of the institutional environment as of the people who work in the institutions. Nowhere is that more true than in central banking.

Today, in the aftermath of the financial crisis, economists are exploring how to improve financial regulation, and reconsidering the role that central banks should play in financial supervision. However, there remains a strong consensus among economists about the best way to design a central bank for making effective monetary policy. To be successful, a central bank must (1) be independent of political pressure, (2) make decisions by committee, (3) be accountable to the public and transparent in communicating its policy actions, and (4) operate within an explicit framework that clearly states its goals and makes clear the trade-offs among them.

## The Need for Independence

The idea of **central bank independence**—that central banks should be independent of political pressure—is a new one. After all, the central bank originated as the government's bank. It did the bidding first of the king or emperor and then of the democratically elected congress or parliament. Politicians rarely give up control over anything, much less something as important as monetary policy. But in the 1990s, nearly every government that hadn't already done so made the central bank independent of the finance ministry. The Banque de France became independent in 1993. Political control of the Bank of England and the Bank of Japan ended in 1998. And the new European Central Bank was independent from the day it opened on July 1, 1998.

Independence has two operational components. First, monetary policymakers must be free to control their own budgets. If politicians can starve the central bank of funding, then they can control the bank's decisions. Second, the bank's policies must not be reversible by people outside the central bank. Prior to 1998, policymakers at the Bank of England merely recommended interest-rate changes to the Chancellor of the Exchequer, a political official. That is, interest rate policy was ultimately decided by the British equivalent of the U.S. Secretary of the Treasury. Since 1998, the Bank of England's Monetary Policy Committee has made those decisions autonomously. The same is true in the United States, where the Federal Open Market Committee's decisions on when to raise or lower interest rates cannot be overridden by the president, Congress, or the Supreme Court.

Successful monetary policy requires a long time horizon. The impact of today's decisions won't be felt for a while—several years, in many instances. Democratically elected politicians are not a particularly patient bunch; their time horizon extends usually to the next election. The political system encourages members of Parliament and members of Congress to do everything they can for their constituents before the next election—including manipulating interest rates to bring short-term prosperity at the expense of long-term stability. The temptation to forsake long-term goals for short-term gains is difficult for most politicians to resist. Given the ability to choose, politicians are likely to select monetary policies that are overly accommodative. They will keep interest rates too low, raising output and employment quickly (before the election), but causing inflation to go up later (after the election). Low interest rates are very popular because there are more borrowers than lenders.

Knowing these tendencies, governments have moved responsibility for monetary policy into a separate, largely apolitical, institution. To insulate policymakers from the daily pressures faced by politicians, governments must give central bankers control of their budgets and authority to make irreversible decisions and must appoint them to long terms of office.

The Fed's extraordinary actions during the crisis of 2007–2009, however successful in stemming a second Great Depression, led to a political backlash in the United States against central bank independence. The consensus among economists is strongly in favor of central bank independence. Yet, the Fed's emergency actions in the crisis—including large bailouts and extraordinary credit provisions—may invite legislative interference in the day-to-day conduct of conventional monetary policy, making it less effective in keeping inflation low and stable. As the popular revulsion for bailouts grew in 2009, proposals to conduct government audits of all monetary policy decisions garnered widespread support in Congress. The lingering political question is whether Congress will choose to sacrifice the hard-won gains on the inflation front by weakening central bank independence. If so, it would be another costly legacy of the financial crisis (see Lessons from the Crisis: Threats to Fed Independence on page 383).

## Decision Making by Committee

Should important decisions be made by an individual or by a committee? Military planners know they can't have groups making decisions in the heat of a battle; someone has to be in charge. But monetary policy isn't war. Monetary policy decisions are made deliberately, after significant amounts of information are collected and examined. Occasionally a crisis does occur, and in those times someone does need to be in charge. But in the course of normal operations, it is better to rely on a committee than an individual. Though extraordinary individuals can be trusted to make policy as well as a committee, building an institution on the assumption that someone of exemplary ability will always be available to run it is unwise. And given the difficulty of removing a central bank governor—a feature that is built into the central bank system—the cost of putting the wrong person in charge can be very high.

The solution, then, is to make policy by committee. Pooling the knowledge, experience, and opinions of a group of people reduces the risk that policy will be dictated by an individual's quirks. Besides, in a democracy, vesting so much power in one individual poses a legitimacy problem. For these reasons, monetary policy decisions are made by committee in all major central banks in the world. As we will discuss in Chapter 16, the Federal Reserve has its Federal Open Market Committee, the European Central Bank its Governing Council, and the Bank of Japan its Monetary Policy Committee. The number of members varies from 9 in the United Kingdom and Japan to (currently) 22 at the ECB—but, crucially, it is always bigger than one.

**APPLYING THE CONCEPT**
INDEPENDENT CENTRAL BANKS DELIVER LOWER INFLATION

What drove politicians to give up control over monetary policy? It was the realization that independent central bankers would deliver lower inflation than they themselves could. Researchers noticed that the degree of control politicians can exert over central banks varies greatly across countries, and is related to inflation outcomes. Figure 15.1 shows an index of central bank independence* on the horizontal axis and average inflation rates from 1973 to 1988 on the vertical axis. Note that Germany and Switzerland, the two countries with the most independent central banks, had the lowest inflation, averaging around 3 percent per year over the 15-year period. Conversely, New Zealand and Spain, the two countries with the least independent central banks, had the highest inflation—between 7 and 9 percent. Even the politicians were convinced. They knew that the more control they had over the central bank, the more money they were likely to create. While printing more money relieves short-term fiscal problems, it eventually drives inflation higher. Politicians voluntarily tied their own hands, handing over control of monetary policy to an independent central bank.

The design of the European Central Bank (ECB) is a clear example of the logic that independence leads to lower inflation. Politicians in Spain, Italy, and France, where inflation had been running over 6 percent per year for several decades, wanted their economies to be more like Germany's. In hopes that the new institution would

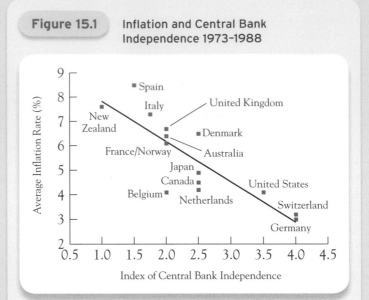

**Figure 15.1** Inflation and Central Bank Independence 1973–1988

SOURCE: "Central Bank Independence and Macroeconomic Performance: Some Comparative Evidence," *Journal of Money, Credit, and Banking* 25 (May 1993), pp. 151–162. Copyright 1993 The Ohio State University. Reproduced with permission.

deliver low inflation, they chose the German central bank, the Deutsche Bundesbank, as a model. By most accounts, the ECB is the most independent central bank in the world. And, as one would expect, inflation has been consistently low in the euro area.

*The index of central bank independence measures the ability of the central bank to use its policy tools without political interference. It is constructed using information on things like the length of the central bank governor's term, whether the governor can be fired, whether government representatives participate directly in monetary policy decisions, and whether the central bank is required to finance government deficits. The less the central bank is constrained by the government, the more independent it is.

## The Need for Accountability and Transparency

There is a big problem with central bank independence: It is inconsistent with representative democracy. The idea of putting appointed technocrats in charge of one of the most important government functions is inherently undemocratic.[12] Politicians answer to the voters; by design, independent central bankers don't. How can we have faith in our financial system if there are no checks on what the central bankers are doing? The economy will not operate efficiently unless we trust our policymakers.

[12]High courts, such as the U.S. Supreme Court, provide the leading example in democracies of an independent body of experts making key policy decisions. In Germany, where the Bundesbank was unusually powerful, the central bank was widely known as the "fourth branch of government."

Proponents of central bank independence realized they would need to solve this problem if their proposals were going to be adopted. Their solution was twofold. First, politicians would establish a set of goals; second, the policymakers would publicly report their progress in pursuing those goals. Explicit goals foster **accountability** and disclosure requirements create **transparency**. While central bankers are powerful, our elected representatives tell them what to do and then monitor their progress. That means requiring plausible explanations for their decisions, along with supporting data.

The institutional means for assuring accountability and transparency differ from one country to the next. In some cases, the government establishes an explicit numerical target for inflation, while in others the central bank defines the target. In the United Kingdom, the government sets a specific target each year; in the European Union, the central bank is asked only to pursue "price stability" as its primary objective; in the United States, the Federal Reserve is asked to deliver price stability as one of a number of objectives. Similar differences exist in the timing and content of information made public by central banks. Today every central bank announces its policy actions almost immediately, but the extent of the statements that accompany the announcement and the willingness to answer questions vary. The Federal Reserve's statements tend to be only a few sentences long, and no one answers questions. In contrast, the president and vice president of the European Central Bank hold a press conference to answer questions on a statement several pages in length.

It is difficult to know how important these differences in communications strategy are. Central bank statements are very different today than they were in the early 1990s. Until 1994, for example, the Federal Reserve didn't announce its policy decisions publicly. Secrecy, once the hallmark of central banking, is now understood to damage both the policymakers and the economies they are trying to manage. For monetary policy to be a stabilizing force, central bankers need to explain their actions in periodic public statements, like the ones that follow every Federal Open Market Committee meeting. In essence, the economy and financial markets should respond to information that everyone receives, not to speculation about what policymakers are doing. Thus, policymakers need to be as clear as possible about what they are trying to achieve and how they intend to achieve it. There really shouldn't be any surprises.

The crisis of 2007–2009 heightened the importance of transparency, both to make policy effective and to secure support for unprecedented actions. As we will see in Chapter 18, some unconventional monetary policies can be implemented only by communicating them. And transparency can help counter the uncertainties and anxieties that feed liquidity and deleveraging spirals (see Chapter 3, Lessons from the Crisis: Leverage).

INFORMATION

## The Policy Framework, Policy Trade-offs, and Credibility

We've seen that a modern central bank has a long list of objectives—low, stable inflation; high, stable growth; a stable financial system; and stable interest and exchange rates. To meet these objectives, central bankers must be independent, accountable, and good communicators. Together these qualities make up what we will call the **monetary policy framework**. The framework exists to resolve ambiguities that arise in the course of the central bank's work. Looking at the bank's objectives, we can see the problem. Setting a goal of low inflation is easy, but there are many ways to measure inflation. The central bank needs to decide which measure to use and then stick with it. Thus, the European Central Bank is explicit about the measure of inflation it uses in evaluating the success or failure of its policy. It is called the harmonized index of consumer prices, or HICP. More important than the details, though, is the fact that officials have told us what they are trying to do. Their statement helps people to plan at the same time that it holds officials accountable to the public.[13]

The monetary policy framework also clarifies the likely responses when goals conflict with one another. There is simply no way that policymakers can meet all their objectives at the same time. Aside from crisis episodes, they have only one instrument—the interest rate—with which to work, and it is impossible to use a single instrument to achieve a long list of objectives. To take a recent example, by mid-2004, the economy had recovered completely from the recession of 2001. Businesses were increasing production and hiring new workers. But, as the economy boomed, the inflation rate started to rise. And when this happens, the appropriate response is to tighten policy, raising interest rates. So, starting on June 30, 2004, the Federal Reserve's Federal Open Market Committee (FOMC) did just that. Seventeen times over the next two years policymakers raised the target interest rate—each time by 25 basis points. Obviously, if interest rates are changing every few months, they are not stable. More important, raising the interest rate means reducing the availability of money and credit at the risk of slowing growth. The goal of keeping inflation low and stable, then, can be inconsistent with the goal of avoiding a recession. By the end of 2006, inflation remained low while growth had slowed slightly. The financial crisis that erupted in August 2007 began more than a year after the Fed had stopped raising rates.

Central bankers face the trade-off between inflation and growth on a daily basis. In March 2008, with inflation soon to rise above 5 percent for the first time since 1991, the Federal Open Market Committee nevertheless cut its policy rate by an outsized 75 basis points to 2.25 percent and highlighted in its statement that "downside risks to growth remain." Although the committee members expressed concern about indications of rising inflation expectations, they judged that it was more important to cut the policy rate in an effort to halt the financial contagion that had resulted from the run on Bear Stearns, the fifth largest U.S. investment bank. As is often the case, policymakers were forced to choose among competing objectives amid great uncertainty. Indeed, two FOMC members dissented, preferring a less aggressive rate cut. As it turned out, when the financial crisis intensified later that year, inflation worries gave way to deflation fears and the prospect of the deepest recession since World War II.

Because policy goals often conflict, central bankers must make their priorities clear. The public needs to know whether policymakers are focusing primarily on price stability, as is the case in many countries, or whether they are willing to allow a modest rise in inflation to avoid a slowdown in economic activity. The public also needs to know the roles that interest-rate and exchange-rate stability play in policy deliberations. This important part of the policy framework limits the discretionary authority of the central bankers, ensuring that they will do the job they have been entrusted with. Thus, it is an essential part of the bank's communication responsibilities.

Finally, a well-designed policy framework helps policymakers establish **credibility**. For central bankers to achieve their objectives, everyone must trust them to do what they say they are going to do. This is particularly important when it comes to keeping inflation low. The reason is that most economic decisions are based on expectations about future inflation. We saw this relationship when we studied the determination of interest rates: The nominal interest rate equals the real interest rate plus expected

---

[13]In recent years, the Federal Reserve's Federal Open Market Committee has focused its attention on something called the "Personal Consumption Expenditure Price Index excluding food and energy." Every quarter, committee members provide three-year-ahead forecasts of inflation based on that index. At this writing, however, the committee has fallen short of adopting any explicit measure of inflation to evaluate its success in achieving its price stability objective.

| Table 15.3 | The Principles of Central Bank Design |
| --- | --- |

| | |
| --- | --- |
| 1. *Independence* | To keep inflation low, monetary decisions must be made free of political influence. |
| 2. *Decision making by committee* | Pooling the knowledge of a number of people yields better decisions than decision making by an individual. But effective crisis response requires a clear chain of command. |
| 3. *Accountability and transparency* | Policymakers must be held accountable to the public they serve and clearly communicate their objectives, decisions, and methods. |
| 4. *Policy framework* | Policymakers must clearly state their policy goals and the trade-offs among them. |

inflation. The same is true for wage and price decisions. Firms set prices based partly on what they believe inflation will be in the future. They make wage agreements with workers based on expected future inflation. The higher their expectations for future inflation, the higher prices, wages, and interest rates will be. Expected inflation creates inflation. Successful monetary policy, then, requires that inflation expectations be kept under control. The most straightforward way for the central bank to do so is to announce its objectives, show resolve in meeting them, and explain its actions clearly along the way.

Table 15.3 summarizes the principles of central bank design and can serve as a check list for evaluating the operation of any central bank we come across.

# Fitting Everything Together: Central Banks and Fiscal Policy

Before a European country can join the common currency area and adopt the euro, it is supposed to meet a number of conditions. Two of the most important are that the country's annual budget deficit—the excess of government spending over revenues each year—cannot exceed 3 percent of GDP and the government's total debt—its accumulated level of outstanding bonds and other borrowings—cannot exceed 60 percent of GDP.[14] Once a country gains membership in the monetary union, failure to maintain these standards can lead to pressure from other member countries and (in theory) even to substantial penalties.[15]

Remember that the central bank does not control the government's budget. Fiscal policy, the decisions about taxes and spending, are the responsibility of elected

[14]In practice, these limits were open to political interpretation, so countries that failed to meet them were allowed to join anyway. For example, in fall of 1998, Belgium's debt was 122 percent of its GDP—more than double the stated limit. But because the debt was forecasted to decline in the future, the requirement was waived.

[15]The "Stability and Growth Pact of 1997" dictated that "medium-term budgets" must be "close to balance or in surplus." That mechanism first came under significant strain in 2003. The previously agreed upon penalties that would be triggered by budget deficits in excess of 3 percent of GDP were not levied on the offending countries. In the aftermath of the 2007–2009 financial crisis, many countries far surpassed the deficit limit. The 2010 financing crisis facing Greece (and a few other euro-area countries) reflects worries about these large fiscal imbalances. In response, euro-area policymakers created a public facility for lending to member states facing borrowing problems. They also began considering reforms to restore regional fiscal discipline.

## IN THE NEWS
### Beware the Result of Outrage

The New York Times

By Andrew Ross Sorkin

November 24, 2009

The biggest news story of last week?

O.K., maybe it was Oprah Winfrey announcing she was going to call it quits with her daytime show in 2011.

But it's a close call. . . . [L]ast Thursday was an important day in Washington, too, with a couple of Winfrey-worthy aha! moments that could shake up the world of finance.

Representative Ron Paul of Texas won committee approval of a far-reaching amendment that would give Congress vast new authority over the Federal Reserve. The Fed has long enjoyed Lone Ranger autonomy, but that will quickly end if the final bill passes.

[In a separate amendment, other representatives] added their own bell-ringer for voters still outraged over bailouts: the next time the government has to step in and rescue a company, secured creditors will take a hit, too.

That would be a huge shift in the way bondholders are treated. Up to now, they've been kept whole, even as others have been asked to share the pain. Otherwise, some feared, creditors might get spooked, and lending might seize up.

. . .

[T]hese amendments, which are part of a 300-page bill to reform the financial industry that is making its way around the House of Representatives, are intended to help quiet some of the outrage over the bailout.

The Federal Reserve, which has printed money in exchange for assets from the nation's banks, has long operated opaquely. It is virtually impossible to size up its balance sheet.

So on its face, the Paul amendment seems well intended. After all, who can argue with a little more sunlight?

But consider these words of caution from Senator Judd Gregg, Republican of New Hampshire: "Congress has demonstrated time and again its inability to manage the nation's fiscal policy, illustrated by our staggering national debt in excess of $12 trillion. So how can anyone think that its involvement in monetary policy would be good for the country?"

So any unintended consequences of the amendment—what Senator Gregg calls "a dangerous move by this Congress to pander to the populist anger"—could indeed lead to less independence for the Federal Reserve, and the result ultimately may not be good for the economy.

That has been Fed Chairman Ben Bernanke's line all along. He does not want the Fed to be a puppet of Congress. And on that score, he is probably right. Could [the Fed] have raised interest rates in the early 1980s to nosebleed levels if Congress were pulling strings? What would happen in an election year? Interest rates would invariably go down, only to go up again later.

officials. But by specifying a range of "acceptable" levels of borrowing, Europeans are trying to restrict the fiscal policies that member countries enact. For the European Central Bank to do its job effectively, all the member countries' governments must behave responsibly.

While fiscal and monetary policymakers share the same ultimate goal—to improve the well-being of the population—conflicts can arise between them. Fiscal policymakers are responsible for providing national defense, educating children, building and maintaining transportation systems, and aiding the sick and poor. They need resources to pay for these services. Thus, funding needs create a natural conflict between monetary and fiscal policymakers. Central bankers, in their effort to stabilize prices and provide the foundation for high sustainable growth, take a long-term view, imposing limits on how fast the quantity of money and credit can grow. In contrast, fiscal policymakers tend to ignore the long-term inflationary effects of their actions and look for ways to spend resources today at the expense of prosperity tomorrow. For better or worse, their time horizon often extends only until the next election. Some fiscal

Representative Paul, of course, doesn't just want oversight of the Federal Reserve, he wants to dismantle it entirely. He has a dog in this fight and it is snarling: he has a book out called "End the Fed." In an interview with my colleague, Mr. Paul told him, "It's not pandering, it's listening."

"The people are angry because they are finding out what the Fed is doing," he added.

The other amendment is potentially even more controversial.

It calls for secured creditors of banks—the top creditors on the totem pole—to be entitled to receive only 80 percent, not 100 percent, of the money they put up if a bank is taken over in receivership or a conservatorship by the government.

That is a hot-button idea because, for the last year, many critics have asked why bondholders were protected by the government. Again, at a gut level, it seems fair for secured creditors to take a haircut if the taxpayer if going to bail them out.

Again, not so simple in practice. Because of the new risk, banks would find it more expensive to raise money—especially so when they run into problems.

Who wants to lend money to a bank when there is a chance the government is going to come in and take it over, so that even a secured creditor at the top of the food chain is going to lose something?

. . .

Indeed, there is an argument that the amendment will make the system more risky, not less so.

"Large systemically important firms would become more vulnerable to liquidity runs—of the sort seen last fall," [a] Barclays report said.

All these proposals are well intentioned, and with a bit of refining, they may ultimately be the right solutions. But as we learned with the bailouts, they may come with unintended consequences.

## LESSONS OF THE ARTICLE

The article highlights two points. First, popular fury over the crisis bailouts of large financial firms fueled a congressional attack on Fed independence. As of early 2010, it remains unclear whether Congress will enact legislation that weakens the Fed or instead, as the Obama administration has proposed, adds to its supervisory responsibilities. The second point is how regulatory reforms that aim to strengthen the financial system can have troublesome "unintended consequences." Partly as a result, fashioning an effective regulatory system probably will remain a work in progress for years to come.

policymakers resort to actions intended to get around restrictions imposed by the central bank, eroding what is otherwise an effective and responsible monetary policy.

In the earliest days of central banks, a government that needed money would simply order the bank to print some. Of course, the result was inflation and occasionally hyperinflation. That is what led to the evolution of the independent central banks. Today the central bank's autonomy leaves fiscal policymakers with two options for financing government spending. They can take a share of income and wealth from the country's citizens through taxes, or they can borrow by issuing bonds in the financial markets.

Because no one likes taxes, and officials fear angering the electorate, politicians often turn to borrowing in order to finance some portion of their spending. But a country can issue only so much debt. Beyond some limit, future tax revenues will not cover the payments that are due to lenders. At that point, the only solution is to turn to the central bank for the means to finance spending. As a technical matter, the government will "sell" new bonds directly to the central bank—bonds that no one else wants to buy. But doing so creates a monetary expansion, which leads to inflation.

In fact, if officials can't raise taxes and are having trouble borrowing, inflation is the only way out.

While central bankers hate it, inflation is a real temptation to shortsighted fiscal policymakers. It is a way to get resources in their hands. The mechanism is straightforward. The government forces the central bank to buy its bonds and then uses the proceeds to finance spending. But doing so increases the quantity of money in circulation, sparking inflation. While the rise in inflation may ultimately do great damage to the country's well-being, it also benefits fiscal policymakers: It reduces the value of the bonds the government has already sold, making them easier to repay. Inflation is a way for governments to default on a portion of the debt they owe.

U.S. fiscal and monetary policies to combat the crisis of 2007–2009 have led many observers to worry both about future inflation risks and about renewed financial instability. On the fiscal side, in 2009, the federal government's deficit neared 10 percent of GDP for the first time since World War II. On the monetary policy side, the Federal Reserve accumulated assets at an unprecedented pace as it sought to prevent a meltdown of the financial system.

At some stage, both these policies must be reversed to prevent a large future inflation. A failure to reverse them also eventually would undermine investor confidence in U.S. Treasuries.

While many politicians do act in their countries' long-term interests, there are plenty of examples of poor fiscal policymaking. Following the collapse of the Soviet Union, Russia had very few sources of revenue. Taxes were hard to collect and lenders were skeptical of the new government's ability to repay its loans, so interest rates were extremely high. Then there was the fact that almost everyone worked for the government. In short, expenses were high and revenue was low. Russian politicians turned to the Central Bank of Russia. The result was an inflation rate of more than 14 percent per *month* for five consecutive years.

In early 2002, Argentina's economy collapsed when banks refused to honor their depositors' withdrawal requests. Unemployment skyrocketed, output plummeted, and the president was forced to resign. The full story is complicated, but we can understand one aspect of it without much trouble. During 2001, Argentina's provincial governments (the equivalent of the state governments in the United States) began to experience significant budget problems. Their response was to start paying their employees with government bonds. But unlike the bonds we normally see, these were in small denominations—1, 2, 5, 10, 20 pesos, and so on. Not surprisingly, these small-denomination bonds were immediately used as means of payment, becoming money in effect. By mid-2002, this new form of money accounted for roughly 40 percent of the currency circulating in Argentina and the Central Bank of Argentina lost control over the amount of money circulating in the economy.

So, we see that the actions of fiscal policymakers can subvert the best efforts of central bankers. The Central Bank of Argentina was independent and its policymakers were well regarded. But if the government can shut down the banking system and issue its own money, then the central bank's independence is irrelevant. The Federal Reserve, the European Central Bank, the Bank of Japan, and 170 other central banks around the world are only independent for as long as their governments let them be. When faced with a fiscal crisis, politicians often look for the easiest way out. If that way is inflating the value of the currency today, they will worry about the consequences tomorrow.

This brings us back to the criteria for inclusion in the European Monetary Union. The founders of the system wanted to ensure that participating governments kept their fiscal houses in order so that none of them would be tempted to pressure the European Central Bank to create inflation and bail them out. Monetary policy can meet its objective of price stability only if the government lives within its budget and never forces the central bank to finance a fiscal deficit. In 2010, large fiscal deficits propelled government bond yields sharply higher in several euro-area countries and triggered a financing crisis in Greece, helping to weaken the euro. In response, euro-area governments created a facility for lending to member states that face difficulty borrowing in markets. As a condition of borrowing, a government would be required to restore fiscal discipline. As of this writing, the credibility and independence of the European Central Bank have kept euro-area inflation expectations low despite the region's fiscal problems.

In summary, responsible fiscal policy is essential to the success of monetary policy. Our discussions earlier in the chapter allowed us to conclude that there is no way for a poorly designed central bank to stabilize prices, output, the financial system, and interest and exchange rates, regardless of the government's behavior. To be successful, a central bank must operate in a particular way. It must be independent, accountable, and clear about its goals. It must have a well-articulated communications strategy and a sound decision-making mechanism. We turn in Chapter 16 to a detailed discussion of the structure of major central banks to see what makes them successful.

## Terms

accountability, 387

central bank, 372

central bank independence, 384

credibility, 388

financial system stability, 381

fiscal policy, 376

hyperinflation, 378

monetary policy, 373

monetary policy framework, 387

potential output, 380

price stability, 378

sustainable growth, 380

transparency, 387

## Chapter Lessons

1. The functions of a modern central bank are to
   a. Adjust interest rates and other tools to control the quantity of money and credit in the economy.
   b. Operate a payments system.
   c. Lend to sound banks during times of stress.
   d. Oversee the financial system.

2. The objective of a central bank is to reduce systematic risk in the economic and financial system. Specific objectives include
   a. Low and stable inflation.
   b. High and stable growth and employment.
   c. Stable financial markets and institutions.
   d. Stable interest rates.
   e. Stable exchange rates.

   Because these objectives often conflict, policymakers must have clear priorities.

3. The best central banks
   a. Are independent of political pressure.
   b. Make decisions by committee rather than by an individual.
   c. Are accountable to elected representatives and the public.
   d. Communicate their objectives, actions, and policy deliberations clearly to the public.
   e. Articulate clearly how they will act when their goals conflict.
   f. Are credible in their efforts to meet their objectives.

4. Fiscal policy can make the central bank's job impossible because
   a. Politicians tend to take a short-term view, ignoring the inflationary impact of their actions over the long term.
   b. Politicians are predisposed toward financing techniques that will create inflation.
   c. Inflation provides immediate revenue and reduces the value of the government's outstanding debt.
   d. Responsible fiscal policy is a precondition for successful monetary policy.
   e. Central banks remain independent at the pleasure of politicians.

# Conceptual Problems

1. In 1900, there were 18 central banks in the world; 100 years later, there were 174. Why does nearly every country in the world now have a central bank?

2. The power of a central bank is based on its monopoly over the issuance of currency. Economics teaches us that monopolies are bad and competition is good. Would competition among several central banks be better? Provide arguments both for and against.

3. Explain the costs of each of the following conditions and explain who bears them.
   a. Interest-rate instability
   b. Exchange-rate instability
   c. Inflation
   d. Unstable growth

4. Provide arguments for and against the proposition that a central bank should be allowed to set its own objectives.

5. Suggest one way in which the Federal Reserve contributed to the financial crisis of 2007–2009 and one way in which it helped contain the crisis.

6. The Maastricht Treaty, which established the European Central Bank, states that the governments of the countries in the European Monetary Union must not seek to influence the members of the central bank's decision-making bodies. Why is freedom from political influence crucial to the ECB's ability to maintain price stability?

7.* Explain why even the most independent central banks are still dependent on the support of the government to meet their policy objectives effectively?

*Indicates more difficult problems

8.  Explain how transparency helps eliminate the problems that are created by central bank independence.

9.  In what way did the financial crisis of 2007–2009 emphasize the importance of central bank transparency?

10.* While central bank transparency is widely accepted as desirable, too much openness may have disadvantages. Discuss what some of these drawbacks might be.

11.  Since 1993, the Bank of England has published a quarterly *Inflation Report*. Find a copy of the report on the bank's Web site, http://www.bankofengland.co.uk. Describe its contents, and explain why the bank might publish such a document.

## Analytical Problems

12.  Which do you think would be more harmful to the economy—an inflation rate that averages 5 percent a year and has a high standard deviation or an inflation rate of 7 percent that has a standard deviation close to zero?

13.  Suppose the central bank in your country has price stability as its primary goal. Faced with a choice of having monetary policy decisions made by a well-qualified individual with an extremely strong dislike of inflation or a committee of equally well-qualified people with a wide range of views, which choice would you recommend?

14.  Suppose the president of a newly independent country asks you for advice in designing the country's new central bank. For each of the following design features, choose which one you would recommend and briefly explain your choice:
    a. Central bank policy decisions that are irreversible or central bank policy decisions that can be overturned by the democratically elected government.
    b. The central bank has to submit a proposal for funding to the government each year or the central bank finances itself from the earnings on its assets and turns the balance over to the government.
    c. The central bank policymakers are appointed for periods of four years to coincide with the electoral cycle for the government or the central bank policymakers are appointed for 14-year terms.

15.  "A central bank should remain vague about the relative importance it places on its various objectives. That way, it has the freedom to choose which objective to follow at any point in time." Assess this statement in light of what you know about good central bank design.

16.* The long list of central bank goals includes the stability of interest rates and exchange rates. You look on the central bank Web site and note that they have increased interest rates at every one of their meetings over the last year. You read the financial press and see references to how the exchange rate has moved in response to these interest-rate changes. How could you reconcile this behavior with the central bank pursuing its objectives?

17.  Provide arguments for why you think the financial crisis of 2007–2009 did or did not compromise the independence of the Federal Reserve.

18. Suppose in an election year, the economy started to slow down. At the same time, clear signs of inflationary pressures were apparent. How might the central bank with a primary goal of price stability react? How might members of the incumbent political party who are up for re-election react?

19. Assuming that they could, which of the following governments do you think would be more likely to pursue policies that would seriously hinder the central bank's pursuit of low and stable inflation? Explain your choice.
    a. A government that is considered highly creditworthy both at home and abroad in a politically stable country with a well-developed tax system, or
    b. A government of a politically unstable country that is heavily indebted and considered an undesirable borrower in international markets.

20.* Suppose the government is heavily in debt. Why might it be tempting for the fiscal policymakers to sell additional bonds to the central bank in a move that it knows would be inflationary?

# Chapter 16

## The Structure of Central Banks: The Federal Reserve and the European Central Bank

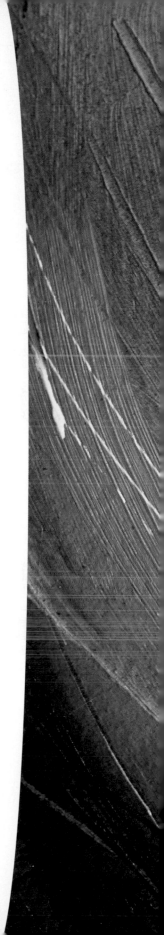

The instability and chaos that accompany financial panics damage more than just the banks that are directly involved. Fear of losing one's savings is a great disincentive to making deposits in banks, and making fewer deposits means smaller banks and fewer loans. Everyone is slow to regain confidence in the financial system after a panic, making it hard for anyone to get financing. New businesses can't get the resources they need to get started; established companies can't find the financing they need to expand. The more frequent the panics, the worse the situation gets, and the slower the economy grows.

That description sounds like the world after the financial crisis of 2007–2009. But it describes even more aptly the financial flaws of the United States during the late 19th and early 20th centuries. Between 1870 and 1907, the nation experienced 21 financial panics of varying severity. In the mostly agrarian economy of the time, a typical crisis began with either a crop failure that left farmers with nothing to sell or a bumper crop that drove prices down below costs. Either way, farmers defaulted on their loans. The losses damaged the balance sheets of rural banks, leading them to withdraw funds from larger banks in New York or Chicago, where they held deposits. If the rural banks' withdrawals were large enough, the urban banks would be forced to call in their own loans or to refuse renewal of loans that were coming due. As word of the financial difficulties spread, other banks would become concerned and begin to call in their loans as well. Finally, when average people (small depositors) heard of the problem, they would flock to their local banks, demanding to receive their balances in the form of currency or gold.[1]

Unless confidence in the system was restored quickly, such runs left bankers with no choice but to close their doors. During the Panic of 1907, an astonishing two-thirds of banks found themselves temporarily unable to redeem deposits in cash. The situation led one prominent German banker to observe that the U.S. banking system was at the same point in the early 1900s that Europe's had been in the 1400s. In the intervening centuries, Europeans had developed a system of central banks; Americans hadn't.

The prevailing philosophy of many 19th-century Americans was that centralized government of any form should be kept to a minimum. But the punishing effects of frequent financial panics led people to reconsider the merits of a powerful central bank. In 1913, Congress passed the Federal Reserve Act, which created the U.S. Federal Reserve System. As the central bank's knowledge of how policy mechanisms worked grew, its governance improved. By the 1990s, the Fed was widely recognized as a key promoter of low inflation and high sustainable growth.

---

[1]The process could also go the other way, from the big banks to the small ones. A large loan default in New York, for example, would force the large city bank to try to acquire reserves from the small country banks. The small banks would then be forced to start calling in loans, and the process would go on from there.

"I don't know a damn thing about monetary policy, but I know what I like."

SOURCE: © Robert Mankoff/The New Yorker Collection/ www.cartoonbank.com.

While central banking had stabilized European financial systems before 1900, the 20th century was another story. In that century, Europe experienced high inflation rates, low growth, high and volatile interest rates, and unstable exchange rates. After two world wars, governments' free spending led to unrelenting fiscal deficits. When European economies stagnated in the 1970s and 1980s, a consensus built that inflation was the fundamental problem and poor monetary policy was to blame. Leaders came to believe that the only way to ensure both political and economic stability was to forge closer ties among the continent's countries. They decided the best solution was a common currency and a single central bank. The result was the European monetary union, with its common currency, the euro, and its central bank, the *European Central Bank (ECB)*.

Europe's monetary union was the natural outgrowth of a decades-long process that established the free movement of goods, services, and capital throughout the continent of nearly 500 million people. Like the Fed, the ECB is based on principles that support the goal of price stability (principles we learned about in Chapter 15). We turn now to an examination of these two central banks to see how their structure helps them to meet their objectives.

# The Structure of the Federal Reserve System

The Federal Reserve Act, passed in 1913 and amended several times since then, establishes a system that is composed of three branches with overlapping responsibilities. There are 12 regional *Federal Reserve Banks*, distributed throughout the country; a central governmental agency, called the *Board of Governors of the Federal Reserve System*, located in Washington D.C.; and the *Federal Open Market Committee*. In addition, a series of advisory committees make recommendations to the board and the Federal Reserve Banks. Finally, there are the private banks that are members of the system. This complex structure diffuses power in a way that is typical of the U.S. government, creating a system of checks and balances that reduces the tendency for power to concentrate at the center.

All national banks (those chartered by the federal government) are required to belong to the Federal Reserve System. State banks that receive their charters from individual state banking authorities have the option of joining, but fewer than 20 percent take it. The original reason was cost. Prior to a change in the law in 1980, member banks were required to hold noninterest-bearing reserve deposits at the Fed, while nonmember banks could hold reserves in interest-bearing securities, such as U.S. Treasury bills. Today, members and nonmembers alike must hold reserve deposits at the Fed on which the Fed now pays interest, so there is no real distinction between them.

## The Federal Reserve Banks

In the heart of Wall Street, two blocks from the site where the World Trade Center towers once stood, sits a large, fortresslike building that is the home of the Federal

Reserve Bank of New York. Deep in the fourth subbasement is the largest gold vault in the world, stocked with many more bars than Fort Knox. All of this gold belongs to foreign countries and international organizations like the International Monetary Fund. It is stored there for free. You can take a tour to see the gold vault if you call ahead, but you won't get into the rest of the building without an invitation. When the bank was built, one of the vaults held cash, but today that vault is filled with excess furniture. Cash is stored across the Hudson River in New Jersey, in a three-story vault the size of a football field. People rarely enter the vault, and there are no tours—just thick walls, fences, security cameras, and guards with guns. (The cash is stored on pallets of about 160 shrink-wrapped blocks of 4,000 notes each. It is moved around entirely by small robotic forklifts.)

The Federal Reserve Bank of New York is the largest of the 12 **Federal Reserve Banks**, which, together with their branches, form the heart of the **Federal Reserve System**. (All 12 have cash vaults, but only New York has gold.) Figure 16.1 shows the location of the banks and the region or "district" each one serves. From a modern vantage point, this map looks very odd. Why is nearly one-third of the continental United States served by a single bank in San Francisco while the Philadelphia district is so small? And why are two of the 12 banks in Missouri?

One explanation is that the lines were drawn in 1914, so they represent the population density at the time. Then there was politics. Senator Carter Glass, one of the authors of the Federal Reserve Act, was from Richmond, Virginia, the headquarters of the

The gold vault at the Federal Reserve Bank of New York. It contains about one-fifth of official gold reserves in the world: more than 200 million troy ounces worth roughly $250 billion at May 2010 prices. A single gold bar in this picture weighs 400 ounces and is worth almost $500,000.

| Figure 16.1 | The Federal Reserve System |

The 12 Federal Reserve Banks and their districts.

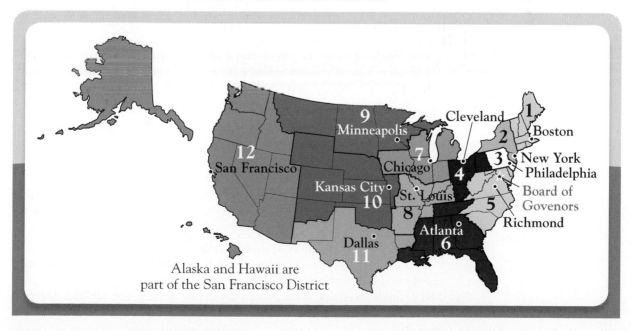

fifth district; Speaker of the House Champ Clark came from Missouri, the state with two Reserve Banks. But more important, politicians decided that no district should coincide with a single state. The Federal Reserve Bank of New York, for example, serves all of New York State as well as northern New Jersey (where the cash vault is), a small slice of southwestern Connecticut, Puerto Rico, and the Virgin Islands. The purpose of this arrangement is twofold: to ensure that every district contains as broad a mixture of economic interests as possible and that no person or group can obtain preferential treatment from the Reserve Bank.

STABILITY

Reserve Banks are strange creations, part public and part private. They are federally chartered banks and private, nonprofit organizations, owned by the commercial banks in their districts. As such, they are overseen by both their own boards of directors and the Board of Governors, an arm of the federal government. The method for choosing the nine members of the boards of directors ensures the inclusion of not only bankers but other business leaders and people who represent the public interest. Six directors are elected by the commercial bank members, and the remaining three are appointed by the Board of Governors. Though the range of views represented is wide, everyone has an interest in ensuring economic and financial stability.

Each Reserve Bank has a president who is appointed for a five-year term by the bank's board of directors with the approval of the Board of Governors. (All 12 presidents' terms run concurrently, starting and ending at exactly the same time.) Presidents tend to come from one of three groups. Some have worked their way up inside the Federal Reserve System and are experts on the business of the district banks. Others are academic economists who have studied the financial system. Then there are former bankers, people who were once customers of the Federal Reserve. Because the presidents work together, the fact that they come from diverse backgrounds means that collectively they have the experience to manage the wide-ranging responsibilities of the Federal Reserve Banks.

During the crisis of 2007–2009, government bailouts and other emergency credit provisions to the financial sector fed the perception that the Reserve Banks are too sympathetic to intermediaries. Partly as a result, some have proposed to reduce the influence of private member banks by changing the appointment process for the Reserve Bank presidents. One possibility would be to make them direct appointees of the U.S. president, subject to Senate confirmation.

The Reserve Banks conduct the day-to-day business of the central bank, serving as both the government's bank and the bankers' bank. Here is a brief list of the functions they perform:

1. As the bank for the U.S. government, they
   a. Issue new currency (Federal Reserve notes) and destroy old, worn currency.
   b. Maintain the U.S. Treasury's bank account and process electronic payments.
   c. Manage the U.S. Treasury's borrowings. That means issuing, transferring, and redeeming U.S. Treasury bonds, notes, and bills. But like you and your bank, the Treasury decides what it wants, and the Federal Reserve Banks just do it.

2. As the bankers' bank, they
   a. Hold deposits for the banks in their districts.
   b. Operate and ensure the integrity of a payments network for clearing paper checks and transferring funds electronically.
   c. Make funds available to commercial banks within the district through *discount loans* on which they charge interest at the *discount rate*.

> d. Supervise and regulate financial institutions in the district to ensure their safety and soundness, as well as evaluate proposed bank mergers and new operations.
>
> e. Collect and make available data on business conditions.

In addition to these duties, the Federal Reserve Bank of New York provides services to foreign central banks and to certain international organizations that hold accounts there. The Federal Reserve Bank of New York is also the system's point of contact with financial markets. It is where Treasury securities are auctioned, foreign currency is bought and sold, and the Federal Reserve's own portfolio is managed through what are called *open market operations*. In the financial crisis of 2007–2009, the Federal Reserve Bank of New York also operated a variety of special new *liquidity and credit facilities* that supplied funds to intermediaries and allowed the Fed to acquire a portfolio of non-Treasury assets, ranging from commercial paper to mortgage-backed securities (see Chapter 18 Tools of the Trade on page 465).

Finally, the Reserve Banks play an important part in formulating monetary policy. They do it both through their representation on the Federal Open Market Committee (FOMC), which makes interest-rate decisions and determines the size and composition of the Fed's balance sheet, and through their participation in setting the **discount rate**, the interest rate charged on loans to commercial banks. The Federal Reserve Act specifies that the discount rate is to be set by each of the Reserve Bank's board of directors, with the approval of the Board of Governors, and strictly speaking, it is. But the directors have virtually no say over the discount rate, because it is set automatically at a premium above the overnight interest rate that the FOMC controls. Once the FOMC makes its decision, there is nothing left for anyone else to do.[2] That's why in Figure 16.2 detailing the complex structure of the Federal Reserve System a solid line labeled "controls" runs from the FOMC to the discount rate. (We will learn more about this topic in Chapter 18.)

# The Board of Governors

The headquarters of the Federal Reserve System sits at the corner of 20th Street and Constitution Avenue in northwest Washington, D.C., a short walk from the White House in one direction and the State Department in the other. The seven members of the board, who are called governors, are appointed by the president and confirmed by the U.S. Senate for 14-year terms. The long terms are intended to protect the board from political pressure. The fact that the terms are staggered—one beginning every two years—limits any individual president's influence over the membership.[3] The board has a chairman and a vice chairman, appointed by the president from among the seven governors for four-year renewable terms. The board's membership usually includes academic economists, economic forecasters, and bankers. To ensure adequate regional representation on the board, no two governors can come from the same Federal Reserve district. The Federal Reserve Act explicitly requires "a fair representation of the financial, agricultural, industrial, and commercial interests."

---

[2]The only exception so far was during the financial crisis of 2007–2009, when the governors reduced the spread of the discount rate above the federal funds rate to encourage borrowing.

[3]In recent years, four out of every five governors have resigned prior to the end of their terms. Someone has been appointed to fill the remaining portion of the term. A person who has been appointed under those circumstances can be reappointed for a full term. (That is how Alan Greenspan, Ben Bernanke's famous predecessor, was able to remain chair for nearly 20 years.) A board member who serves a full term may not be reappointed, however.

**Figure 16.2** The Structure and Policy Organization of the Federal Reserve System

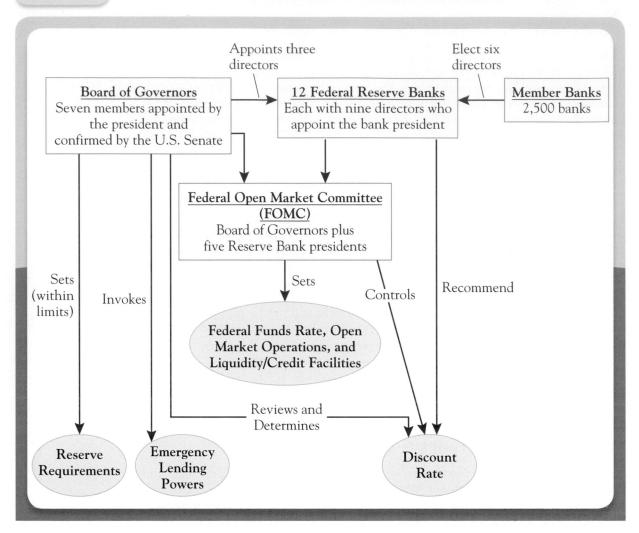

Together with a staff of several thousand, the **Board of Governors of the Federal Reserve System** performs the following duties:

- Sets the reserve requirement, which determines the level of reserves banks are required to hold.
- Approves or disapproves discount rate recommendations made by the Federal Reserve Banks.
- Administers consumer credit protection laws.
- Approves bank merger applications.
- Supervises and regulates the Reserve Banks, including their budgets and their presidents' salaries.
- Along with the Reserve Banks, regulates and supervises the banking system, examining individual banks for safety and soundness and for compliance with the law.

# YOUR FINANCIAL WORLD
Treasury Direct

The Federal Reserve takes care of the U.S. Treasury's banking needs. It is the government's banker, assisting the government by operating auctions for U.S. Treasury bonds when the government needs to borrow, keeping track of who owns the Treasury bonds, making interest payments on them every six months, and paying the principal when they mature. Although much of the Treasury's debt is bought and held by large financial institutions like banks, pension funds, and insurance companies, you can buy it yourself, without anyone's help, through *Treasury Direct*.

Treasury Direct lets you purchase as little as $1,000 worth of Treasury securities without paying any broker fees. All you need to do is fill out a few forms, write a check, and send them in. (You will have to use paper the first time, but after that you can do it electronically.) Everything you need to get started is available at the Bureau of Public Debt's Web site.

As a technical matter, buying a government bond means bidding at an auction that is held two or three times a week. How do you know what price to bid? Individuals aren't experts on bond pricing, so if they had to figure out how much to bid, Treasury Direct would never work. The solution is to place what is called a *noncompetitive bid*. This guarantees you will receive the bond you want at the average auction price, which is based on the bids of people who know what they are doing. Individuals send in checks to cover the face value of the bonds they want, and since the auction is normally designed so that the purchase price is less than face value, you get a small refund in the mail a few weeks later. The only complicated part of this is deciding exactly which bonds you want to buy.

Once you have bought the bonds, you will receive a notice of the interest payments, as well as periodic statements listing what you own. If you decide you want to sell the bonds, the Fed will do it for you at the highest market price available. Treasury Direct is by far the cheapest way to buy U.S. Treasury securities, especially in small amounts and for issues like Treasury Inflation Protection Securities (see the discussion of TIPS in *Your Financial World*, Chapter 6), which are difficult to purchase on the open market but easy to buy at auction.

- Invokes the **emergency powers** to lend to nonbanks when circumstances are deemed "unusual and exigent." These powers provided the authority for much of the Fed's emergency lending in the crisis of 2007–2009.
- Analyzes financial and economic conditions, both domestic and international.
- Collects and publishes detailed statistics about the system's activities and the economy at large. On the Federal Reserve Board's Web site, you can find information about the amount of money in the economy (M1 and M2), interest rates, exchange rates, the banking system's assets and liabilities, the level of production in U.S. industry, and the level of household wealth.

The seven governors do not have their own support staff. Instead, they request help and information from the managers of various departments, who assign individuals to specific tasks. The managers answer to the chair of the Board of Governors.

## The Federal Open Market Committee

When most people think about the Federal Reserve, what comes to mind is not the payments system or bank supervision but interest-rate setting. And when the business press discusses the Fed, its attention is really on the **Federal Open Market Committee (FOMC)**. This is the group that sets interest rates to control the availability of money and credit to the economy. The FOMC has been around since 1936 and has 12 voting members. These are the seven governors, the president of the Federal Reserve Bank of New York, and four Reserve Bank presidents. The chair of the Board of Governors chairs the FOMC as well, and the committee's vice chair is the president of the Federal Reserve Bank of New York. While only five of the 12 Reserve Bank presidents vote at any one time, all of them participate in the meeting.

The FOMC could control any interest rate, but the rate it chooses to control is the **federal funds rate**, the rate banks charge each other for overnight loans on their excess deposits at the Fed. We will discuss the details of this arrangement in the next two chapters. For now, keep in mind that the rate the FOMC controls is a nominal interest rate. Because inflation doesn't change quickly, however, the FOMC in effect controls the *real* interest rate. (Recall that the real interest rate equals the nominal interest rate minus expected inflation.) The real interest rate plays a central role in economic decisions. The higher the real interest rate, the more expensive borrowing is, and the less likely a company is to build a new factory or an individual is to purchase a new car. Furthermore, the lower the level of purchases by firms and households, the lower the level of growth will be. So by controlling the federal funds rate, the FOMC influences real growth. (The macroeconomic model that explains this mechanism is presented in Part V.)

The Board Room at the Federal Reserve in Washington, D.C., with its oblong table. This is the meeting place of the Federal Open Market Committee and Board of Governors of the Federal Reserve System.

The FOMC currently meets eight times a year, or roughly once every six weeks, in the Board Room at the Federal Reserve in Washington, D.C. During times of crisis, the committee can confer and change policy over the telephone. Because these "inter-meeting" policy shifts signal the financial markets that the FOMC believes conditions are dire, they are reserved for extraordinary times, like the aftermath of the terrorist attacks on the World Trade Center of September 2001. One measure of the financial crisis of 2007–2009 is that it prompted 12 unscheduled FOMC meetings, surpassing the cumulative total of recent decades!

Since 2009, all scheduled FOMC meetings have taken place over a two-day period, starting around 2 p.m. one afternoon, and finishing the next day at 1:00 p.m. In addition to the seven governors and 12 Reserve Bank presidents, numerous board staff members attend, along with at least one senior staff member from each Reserve Bank. In all, between 50 and 60 people are there. The primary purpose of the meeting is to decide on the target interest rate or, in response to the crisis of 2007–2009, on the scale and mix of assets to acquire. The FOMC itself does not engage in the financial market transactions that are required to keep the market federal funds rate near this target or to manage the Fed's portfolio. That job falls to the system open market account manager, who, together with his or her staff, works for the Federal Reserve Bank of New York. The policy directive simply instructs the New York Fed's staff to buy and sell securities so as to maintain the market federal funds rate at the target or to assemble the desired asset mix.

To figure out who really controls these key policy decisions, we need to look closely at how the FOMC works, focusing on the information that is distributed in advance and the mechanics of the meeting. Three important documents are distributed to all attendees prior to each meeting. Named for the colors of the covers of the old paper versions, they are the *beige book*, the *green book*, and the *blue book*. The beige book is a compilation of anecdotal information about current business activity, collected by the staffs of the Reserve Banks and published about two weeks before the meeting. This is the only FOMC document that is released to the public before the meeting.

The green book, containing the board staff's economic forecast for the next few years, and the blue book, with its discussion of financial markets and current policy options are distributed electronically during the week preceding the meeting. The green and blue books are treated as secret documents and are not released to the public until five years after the meeting.

An FOMC meeting is a formal proceeding that can be divided into two parts, each beginning with a staff report followed by a round of discussion that includes all of the meeting's participants (consisting of the 12 voting members and the remaining seven Reserve Bank presidents). Here's the order in which people speak:

1. The system open market account manager reports on financial market conditions and actions taken to maintain the target interest rate since the last meeting.

2. The director of the Division of International Finance comments on recent international economic developments.

3. The director of the Division of Research and Statistics at the Federal Reserve Board presents the staff's forecast (from the green book).

4. One at a time, committee members (including Reserve Bank presidents who are not currently voting) discuss their view of the economic outlook, including specific regional information. People speak for about five minutes each, in an order that changes from meeting to meeting. During the process, speakers also may comment in response to others' statements. The chair speaks at the end, concluding what is called the *economic go-round*.

5. The director of the Division of Monetary Affairs, who doubles as the secretary of the FOMC, describes the two or three policy options (from the blue book). One option is always to maintain the target interest rate at its current level.

6. Again, one at a time, the committee members comment on the policy options, with the chair speaking last.

7. A vote is taken, with the chair voting first, the vice chair second, and then the committee members in alphabetical order.

The staff may respond to questions following their presentations, but there is limited opportunity during the formal sessions for give-and-take among the FOMC members. One advantage of two-day meetings is that members also can engage each other informally—for example, over dinner on the first night. The meeting adjourns on the second day around 1:00 p.m., an hour or so prior to the 2:15 p.m. eastern time public release of the committee's decision, along with a brief explanatory statement. And three weeks later, detailed minutes summarizing the deliberations are released on the FOMC's public Web site.

To see where the committee's power lies and who controls interest-rate decisions, notice a few things (see Table 16.1). First, and foremost, the chair is the voice of the Federal Reserve System. He or she speaks to Congress and the public on behalf of the FOMC. Second, note that the governors make up a majority of the committee, and they work together daily at the headquarters of the Federal Reserve in Washington, D.C. Third, beyond the beige book, which is made available to the public, the most important information regularly distributed to all committee members before a meeting is the green book forecast and the blue book of policy options. These are both prepared by the Federal Reserve Board staff, which is controlled by the chair. In addition, in 2008, FOMC participants (i.e., the governors and all 12 of

**Table 16.1** A User's Guide to the Fed

The Federal Reserve System is complicated, so here is a list of the key players:

| | |
|---|---|
| *Chair of the Board of Governors.* | Most powerful person in the Federal Reserve System. Also chair of the FOMC. Effectively controls FOMC meetings and interest-rate policy. Appointed by the president to a four-year term, subject to U.S. Senate confirmation; must be one of the governors. |
| *Governors of the Board.* | Supervise and regulate an important portion of the financial industry. All are voting members of the FOMC. Appointed by the president to 14-year terms, subject to U.S. Senate confirmation. |
| *President of the Federal Reserve Bank of New York.* | Runs the biggest and most important of the Reserve Banks, where monetary policy operations are carried out and much of the Fed's work for the Treasury is done. Also provides services to commercial banks in the district. As with the presidents of the other Reserve Banks, appointed by the Bank's board of directors, with the approval of the Board of Governors, for a five-year term. Also vice chair of the FOMC. |
| *Presidents of the other 11 Federal Reserve Banks.* | Provide services to commercial banks in their districts. All participate in every FOMC meeting and four serve one-year terms as voting members of the FOMC on a rotating basis. |

The board and each of the Reserve Banks maintain Web sites that publish data, economic research, speeches, and information about customer services. In addition, the FOMC maintains a list of its meeting times on the board's Web site, along with links to the transcripts, minutes, and statements of the committee. The place to start is www.federalreserve.gov.

the Reserve Bank presidents) began distributing their own quarterly economic forecasts. Fourth, the chair sets the agenda for the FOMC meeting, determines the order in which people speak, and proposes the FOMC policy statement (see Tools of the Trade on page 407). Finally, though the votes are made public immediately after the meeting, committee members observe a blackout period from a week preceding an FOMC meeting to a week following the meeting, during which they do not speak publicly about the economic outlook or current monetary policy. Dissenters, who are identified immediately in the press release that comes the afternoon of the meeting, must wait a week to explain their views in public. And remember, the Board of Governors controls the Reserve Banks' budgets, as well as the salaries of their presidents.

Press reports, then, do give a good sense of where the FOMC's power lies. The chair of the Fed is the FOMC's most important member. So, if you want to know whether interest rates are likely to go up, down, or stay the same, that is the person you should listen to most closely. To have an impact on policy, governors or Reserve Bank presidents must build support for their positions through their statements at the meeting and in public speeches. While the chair is very powerful, the committee structure provides an important check on his or her power. Indeed, even two dissents on an FOMC vote are unusual, while three dissents—an outcome that has not occurred since the 1980s—would raise doubts about the chair's leadership.

# TOOLS OF THE TRADE
Decoding the FOMC Statement

As the financial crisis deepened in 2008, the range of FOMC policy actions broadened, and financial stability rose to the top of the Fed's agenda. Accordingly, the form of the **FOMC statement** released at the end of the FOMC's regularly scheduled meetings changed markedly. Nevertheless, some of the statement's familiar components remained:

- A clear statement of the committee's decision at the meeting regarding its target or target range for the federal funds rate (the interest rate that the FOMC controls)
- A summary of the committee's view of economic conditions, especially the inflation outlook.
- A description of how the outlook is expected to influence *future* policy.
- A description of the policy tools, in addition to the federal funds rate, that the Fed will use to achieve its objectives (to understand these, you have to follow current events very closely).
- A report of the voting.

Consider, for example, the following excerpt from the FOMC statement of December 16, 2008, when the committee first set the lower bound of its target range for the federal funds rate to zero:

*The Federal Open Market Committee decided today to establish a target range for the federal funds rate of 0 to 1/4 percent.*

*Since the Committee's last meeting [ . . . ] financial markets remain quite strained and credit conditions tight. Overall, the outlook for economic activity has weakened further.*

*Meanwhile, inflationary pressures have diminished appreciably [ . . . and] the Committee expects inflation to moderate further in coming quarters.*

*The Federal Reserve will employ all available tools to promote the resumption of sustainable economic growth and to preserve price stability. In particular, the Committee anticipates that weak economic conditions are likely to warrant exceptionally low levels of the federal funds rate for some time.*

*The focus of the Committee's policy going forward will be to support the functioning of financial markets and stimulate the economy through open market operations and other measures that sustain the size of the Federal Reserve's balance sheet at a high level. [ . . . ] The Federal Reserve will continue to consider ways of using its balance sheet to further support credit markets and economic activity.*

*Voting for the FOMC monetary policy action were: Ben S. Bernanke, Chairman; Christine M. Cumming; Elizabeth A. Duke; Richard W. Fisher; Donald L. Kohn; Randall S. Kroszner; Sandra Pianalto; Charles I. Plosser; Gary H. Stern; and Kevin M. Warsh.*

Interpreting these statements takes some practice, especially in such extraordinary circumstances as a financial crisis. A summary of the one here might go something like this: "The key threats to stability are the impairment of financial markets, the lack of credit and the decline of economic activity. Given the prospect of low and declining inflation pressures, the FOMC plans to keep interest rates near zero for an extended period to help stimulate the economy. In addition, the Federal Reserve is prepared to supply credit more directly to support economic activity when financial markets cannot."

By going to the FOMC's Web site at http://www.federalreserve.gov/fomc/, you can look at recent statements and see how they have been changing. What do you think the Fed will do next?

# Assessing the Federal Reserve System's Structure

In the last chapter, we developed a checklist for assessing a central bank's structure. We said that an effective central bank is one in which policymakers are independent of political influence, make decisions by committee, are accountable and transparent, and state their objectives clearly. Let's evaluate the Federal Reserve System using these criteria.

## Independence from Political Influence

We set out three criteria for judging a central bank's independence: budgetary independence, irreversible decisions, and long terms. The Fed meets each of these. It controls its own budget. The Fed's substantial revenue is a combination of interest on the government securities it holds and fees charged to banks for payments system services, including check clearing, electronic funds transfers, and the like. In fact, the Fed's income is so large that, in a typical year, 95 percent of it is returned to the U.S. Treasury.[4] Interest-rate changes are implemented immediately and can be changed only by the FOMC—no one else can reverse or change them. The terms of the governors are 14 years; the chair's term runs for four years; and the Reserve Bank presidents serve for five years (and they aren't even appointed by politicians).

Even though the structural elements required to maintain an independent monetary policy are in place, the Fed occasionally comes under political attack. As we have said, raising interest rates is never popular. In 2009, public outrage over the financial crisis and the bailouts of large intermediaries made the Fed a political target, posing the biggest threat to its independence in many years. Many legislators favored greater scrutiny of the Fed. And while the U.S. government proposed to enhance the Fed's supervisory powers because of the financial crisis, some in Congress sought to strip it of those powers altogether.

## Decision Making by Committee

The Fed clearly makes decisions by committee, because the FOMC *is* a committee. While the chair of the Board of Governors may dominate policy decisions, the fact that there are 12 voting members provides an important safeguard against arbitrary action by a single individual. In the Federal Reserve, no one person can become a dictator.

## Accountability and Transparency

The FOMC releases huge amounts of information to the public. Prior to each meeting, the committee publishes the beige book and makes it publicly available. Immediately after the meeting comes the announcement of the policy decision, together with the explanatory statement. Then, three weeks later, a detailed anonymous summary—the minutes—is published. After a five-year waiting period, the FOMC publishes the word-for-word transcript of a meeting. Each quarter, the FOMC now publishes the committee participants' outlook for economic growth and inflation over the next three years. Added to these documents is the Federal Reserve Board's twice-yearly "Monetary Policy Report to the Congress," which provides great detail about the outlook and the considerations behind policy setting. This report is accompanied by the chair's appearance before Congress to discuss the state of the nation's economy. Members of the FOMC also give frequent public speeches, and occasionally they testify before Congress. In an average year, the chair gives 15 to 20 speeches, and other governors and Reserve Bank presidents speak 5 to 10 times each. All of these communications—the

[4]The crisis year of 2009 was far from typical, because interest rates were extraordinarily low and because the Fed's balance sheet had expanded sharply. You can usually approximate the Fed's interest income by multiplying the value of its securities holdings—about $2 trillion—by the U.S. Treasury's one-year interest rate, roughly 0.25 percent in 2009. You'll get a number around $5 billion. (The same calculation in 2007 resulted in a figure of roughly $40 billion.) However, Fed net income actually hit a record $52 billion in 2009, because the Fed's extraordinary holdings of non-Treasury assets (mostly mortgage-backed securities) provided a higher yield than one-year Treasuries. The Fed returned $46 billion to the Treasury.

## APPLYING THE CONCEPT
### THE EVOLUTION OF FEDERAL RESERVE INDEPENDENCE

Like most large bureaucracies, the Federal Reserve moves very slowly and deliberately. Nevertheless, there have been some defining moments when the Fed's structure changed suddenly and significantly. The first one came in 1935, after the economywide financial failures that led to the Great Depression of the 1930s. To remove monetary policy from the political arena, the Secretary of the Treasury and the Comptroller of the Currency, two political appointees who served at the pleasure of the president, were kicked off the Federal Reserve Board, and the FOMC was created.

But independence in name is not independence in fact. During World War II, the Federal Reserve became part of the war effort, which meant ensuring a cheap source of funds for the Treasury. The Fed worked to keep interest rates low by making sure that bond prices remained high. Importantly, when the Treasury went to issue securities, to keep prices high the Fed would buy what the public refused to purchase. Early in 1951, the Secretary of the Treasury, who was under pressure to finance the new Korean War, tried to force the Fed to purchase significant quantities of bonds directly from the Treasury. Faced with rising inflation, the FOMC had announced its desire to curtail credit growth by reducing the rate at which it purchased government debt. President Truman was forced to step in and resolve the standoff. On March 4, 1951, the president, the secretary of the Treasury, and the Federal Reserve chair reached an "accord" and issued a joint announcement establishing the FOMC's independence in setting interest rates and controlling the rate of monetary expansion.*

These two events provided the foundation for the Federal Reserve's independence in forming monetary policy. Of course, the FOMC's ability to do its job still depends on the willingness of politicians to refrain from interference. The president and the secretary of the Treasury can make comments criticizing the FOMC's monetary policy decisions, and Congress does have the ability to revoke the Fed's independence. Following the financial crisis of 2007–2009, congressional criticism of the Fed became unusually intense, while proposals to limit Fed independence flourished. In contrast, the U.S. government proposed to expand the Fed's supervisory powers to help prevent another financial crisis.

*For a brief summary of this history, see Carl E. Walsh, "Federal Reserve Independence and the Accord of 1951," *Federal Reserve Bank of San Francisco Weekly Letter*, No. 93-21, May 28, 1993.

beige book, the statement, the minutes, the transcripts, the biannual report, the testimony, and the speeches—can be found on various Fed Web sites.

This avalanche of information certainly seems enough to give everyone a sense of what the FOMC is doing and why. But lots of information isn't always the right information. A few things are missing from the Fed's communications. First and foremost, there is no regular press conference, nor any real questioning of the chair on the FOMC's current policy stance. And there is the short period before and after the FOMC's meeting when no member will comment publicly on monetary policy. Second, the inputs into the decision-making process—documents like the staff forecast in the green book and the policy options in the blue book—and the meeting transcript are not made public until five years after the fact. In the financial crisis, the Fed also resisted the dissemination of information about the recipients of its loans because it was concerned about triggering a new run on a fragile—or even on a healthy—intermediary. That secrecy, however, fueled conspiracy theories about the supposed desire of the Fed to defend Wall Street firms rather than the U.S. economy. Finally, as we will discuss in a moment, the fact that the committee has been hesitant to state its objectives clearly and concisely hampers communication.

## Policy Framework

The Congress of the United States has set the Federal Reserve's objectives: "The Board of Governors of the Federal Reserve System and the Federal Open Market Committee shall maintain long run growth of the monetary and credit aggregates commensurate with the economy's long run potential to increase production, so as to

# YOUR FINANCIAL WORLD
### The Fed Can't Save You from a Stock-Market Crash

Will the Federal Reserve keep the stock market from crashing, helping us all to sleep better at night? We have already said that the central bank's job is to reduce systematic risk by stabilizing prices, output growth, and the financial system. But there is only so much that a central bank can, should, or will do. In the end, no one can save us from all the risks we face.

The history of the stock market in the late 1990s and early 2000s provides a stark illustration of the pressures central bankers face and the limits of their actions. As equity prices rose in 1998 and 1999, many investors came to believe that then Federal Reserve Board chairman Alan Greenspan would not let the stock market decline significantly. He and his colleagues on the FOMC would bail everyone out. Their reasoning went like this: Changes in wealth change consumption patterns. That is, the richer we all become, the more we spend; conversely, the poorer we are, the less we spend. A stock-market crash would reduce spending, sending the economy into a severe recession—something the "Greenspan Fed" would

not allow. For investors, this assumption meant that they could buy stocks without worrying about the downside; they need not fear a crash. While owning stock used to be risky, it wasn't anymore. Or so many people believed in 1999. And the lower the perceived risk, the smaller the risk premium became. This drove prices up even further. (Remember that the lower the risk, the more you will pay for a financial instrument.)

What happened? The answer is that the Fed doesn't control the stock market; it merely sets interest rates and ensures that banks have funds to honor their commitments. As the stock market declined through 2001 and 2002, the FOMC lowered its interest-rate target from 6 percent to 1 percent to avert a recession. Growth was sluggish for a few years, and inflation rose only slightly. But keeping stocks from falling from their unsustainable heights was beyond the Fed's control, even if members had wanted to do it. No one can eliminate the risk that is inherent in an investment—not even the most powerful central bank in the world.

*"I've called the family together to announce that, because of inflation, I'm going to have to let two of you go."*

SOURCE: © Joseph Farris/The New Yorker Collection/www.cartoonbank.com.

promote effectively the goals of maximum employment, stable prices, and moderate long-term interest rates."

What should we make of this vague statement? Some people see ambiguity as advantageous. Because laws are difficult to change, they argue, we wouldn't want the Fed's objectives to be extremely specific; the imprecision of the language means the Fed can essentially set its own goals. In the past, the FOMC has been unwilling to tell us exactly how it interprets this broad mandate and at this writing they still have not. But prior to becoming chairman, when he was a professor at Princeton University, Ben Bernanke argued that the best way to make monetary policy is to announce a specific numerical objective for inflation over some horizon. So far, under Chairman Bernanke, the FOMC has moved closer to this approach by publishing the committee participants' long-term inflation forecasts, which are probably close to their inflation objectives. However, the FOMC still does not publish a target that represents the committee's consensus. This choice may reflect concern about congressional objections to a policy framework that appears to give priority to stabilizing inflation over stabilizing employment.

# The European Central Bank

As recently as 1998, Romans shopped with *lire*, Berliners with *deutsche marks*, and Parisians with *francs*. The Banca d'Italia, Italy's central bank, controlled the number of lire that circulated, while the Bundesbank managed the quantity of deutsche marks and the Banque de France, the volume of francs. But on January 1, 1999, the majority of Western European countries adopted a common currency. Today, residents of Rome, Berlin, and Paris all make their purchases in euros, and monetary policy is the job of the **European Central Bank (ECB)**. In the same way that a dollar bill is worth a dollar everywhere in the United States, a euro note is worth a euro everywhere in the **euro area**. By 2010, the euro had become the currency of 16 countries (see the map in Figure 16.3).

The agreement to form a European monetary union was formalized in the Treaty of Maastricht, named for the Dutch city in which it was signed in 1992. The treaty initiated a lengthy process that led ultimately to the creation of the **European System of Central Banks (ESCB)**, which is composed of the European Central Bank (ECB) in Frankfurt, Germany, and the National Central Banks (NCBs) in the 27 countries in the European Union. The ECB and the NCBs of the 16 countries that participate in the monetary union make up what is known as the **Eurosystem**, which shares a common currency and common monetary policy. At this writing, Denmark, Sweden, and the United Kingdom, as well as 8 of the 12 countries that joined the European Union since May 1, 2004, remained outside the Eurosystem and retained control over their monetary policy.

A myriad of names and abbreviations are associated with central banking in Europe. To avoid confusion, we will refer to the institution that is responsible for monetary policy in the euro area as the European Central Bank. Our goal is to understand its basic organizational structure.[5] As we examine the ECB, keep in mind that, in economic terms, Europe is larger, and the euro area is only a bit smaller, than the United States.

## Organizational Structure

The Eurosystem mirrors the structure of the Federal Reserve System in several ways. There is the six-member **Executive Board of the ECB**, which is similar to the Board of Governors; the **National Central Banks**, which play many of the same roles as the Federal Reserve Banks; and the **Governing Council**, which formulates monetary policy, just as the FOMC does.[6] The Executive Board has a president (Jean-Claude Trichet of France until October 2011) and a vice president (Vítor Constâncio of Portugal until May 2018), who play the same role as the Fed's chair and vice chair. Executive Board members are appointed by a committee composed of the heads of state of the countries that participate in the monetary union (see Table 16.2 on page 413).

[5]Two publications are helpful in understanding European monetary policy. The first chief economist of the ECB, Otmar Issing, who also served on the ECB Executive Board in its first eight years, explains the evolution of ECB policies in *The Birth of the Euro* (Cambridge, UK: Cambridge University Press, 2008). *The Monetary Policy of the ECB* published by the ECB in 2004, provides a technical description of how things work.

[6]While the ECB may appear to be modeled after the Federal Reserve System, its structure is actually based on that of the Deutsche Bundesbank, the German central bank. Europeans uniformly viewed the Bundesbank as being successful in stabilizing the post-World War II German economy, so it was a natural model, but the real reason for the new structure was politics. The designers of the ECB had to find a way to create a common central bank that incorporated all of the existing national central banks. This meant adding a new central administration while retaining what was already there.

**Figure 16.3** The European System of Central Banks

Countries using the euro in 2010

European Union Member countries not using the euro in 2010

Countries that are not members of the European Union in 2010

The ECB and the NCBs together perform the traditional operational functions of a central bank, which we learned about in the last chapter. In addition to using interest rates to control the availability of money and credit in the economy, they are responsible for the smooth operation of the payments system and the issuance of currency. While the details differ from country to country, the National Central Banks continue to serve as bankers to the banks and governments in their countries, just as the Federal Reserve Banks do in the United States.

There are several important differences between the Fed and the ECB, however. Some exist by design and others as a result of the way the system came into being

| Table 16.2 | Key Aspects of the European Central Bank |
|---|---|

| | |
|---|---|
| European Central Bank (ECB) | The central authority in Frankfurt, Germany, that oversees monetary policy in the common currency area. (Established July 1, 1998.) |
| National Central Banks (NCBs) | The central banks of the countries that belong to the European Union. |
| European System of Central Banks (ESCB) | The ECB plus the NCBs of all the countries in the European Union, including those that do not participate in the monetary union. |
| Eurosystem | The ECB plus the NCBs of participating countries; together, they carry out the tasks of central banking in the euro area. |
| ECB Executive Board | The six-member body in Frankfurt that oversees the operation of the ECB and the Eurosystem. |
| Governing Council | The (currently) 22-member committee that makes monetary policy in the common currency area. |
| Euro | The currency used in the countries of the European Monetary Union. |
| Euro area | The countries that use the euro as their currency. |

(see Table 16.3). First, the ECB does not supervise and regulate financial institutions, although some of the NCBs do. Second, the implementation of monetary policy—the ECB's day-to-day interaction with the financial markets—is accomplished at all the national central banks, rather than being centralized as it is in the United States. Third, the ECB's budget is controlled by the National Central Banks, not the other way around. This arrangement means that the NCBs control the finances of the Executive Board and its headquarters in Frankfurt.

The focus of the ECB's activity is on the control of money and credit in the Eurosystem—that is, on monetary policy. The Governing Council, the equivalent of the Fed's FOMC, is composed of the six Executive Board members and the governors of the 16 (as of 2010) central banks in the euro area. Meetings to consider monetary policy actions are held monthly in Frankfurt, at the ECB's headquarters. Decisions are made by consensus; no formal votes are taken. The issue of voting has been a contentious one, but the ECB is adamant in its refusal to take votes (or to publicly admit to it). The rationale for this position is easy to understand. The Governing Council members are charged with setting policy for the euro area as a whole, regardless of economic conditions in the individual countries they come from. If votes were taken, they would ultimately become public. For the governor of the Banque de France to vote to raise interest rates at a time when the French economy is on its way into a recession would be difficult, even if it is the right thing to do for the euro area as a whole. Formal voting, as it is done at the FOMC, could get in the way of good policy.[7]

---

[7]An important difference between the ECB's Governing Council and the FOMC is that the governors of the Federal Reserve Board always hold the majority of the seats on the FOMC (7 out of 12) while the Executive Board members are always a minority on the Governing Council (6 out of a current 22). In the Eurosystem, power is less centralized than it is at the Fed.

**Table 16.3**  Comparing the FOMC to the ECB's Governing Council

| | FOMC | Governing Council |
|---|---|---|
| **Independence** | | |
| Budgetary control | Controlled by the Board of Governors. | Controlled by the NCBs. |
| Decisions irreversible | Yes. | Yes. |
| Terms of appointment | Governors 14 years, Reserve Bank presidents 5 years. | Executive Board members 8 years; heads of NCBs minimum of 5 years. |
| Threat of legislative change | Requires an act of Congress. | Requires agreement of all signatories to Treaty of Maastricht. |
| **Decision making** | | |
| | Committee of 19 members, 12 voting at one time. | Committee of 22 members, all participating equally. |
| **Accountability and Transparency** | | |
| Policy deliberations | Immediate release of target interest rate with a brief statement and the votes of the committee members. | Immediate release of target interest rate with an explanatory statement; the president and vice president answer questions. |
| | Minutes of the meeting released after three weeks. | Minutes of the meeting released after 20 years. |
| | Transcripts released after 5 years. | No transcripts. |
| Other information | Twice-yearly reports to Congress. | Quarterly report to the European Parliament. |
| | Public speeches of members. | Public speeches of members. |
| | Data collection and dissemination. | Data collection and dissemination. |
| | Publication of research reports, along with quarterly forecasts of inflation and growth. | Publication of research reports, along with twice-yearly forecasts of inflation and growth. |
| **Policy framework** | | |
| | Dual mandate of price stability and sustainable economic growth. No clear definition or statement of trade-offs between the two goals. | Price stability is paramount and defined numerically. All other goals are secondary. |
| **Cooperation with Fiscal Policymakers** | | |
| | No explicit mechanism. | Stated requirements for member countries' deficits and debt levels that are frequently violated. |

A number of important safeguards were included in the Treaty of Maastricht to ensure the central bank's independence. First, there are the terms of office: Executive Board members serve eight-year terms (without the possibility of reappointment), and member nations must appoint their central bank governors for a minimum of five years. Second, the ECB's financial interests must remain separate from any political organization. Third, the treaty states explicitly that the Governing Council cannot take instructions from any government, so its policy decisions are irreversible. The fact that the ECB is the product of a treaty agreed to by all of the countries of the European Union makes it extraordinarily difficult to change any of the terms under which it operates. People who study central banks generally agree that these provisions make the ECB the most independent central bank in the world.

Before we move on, it is worth noting that a number of additional European Union countries, particularly those in eastern Europe, may enter the monetary union in the coming years. As they do, some difficult decisions must be made. When it began in 1999, people already wondered how the ECB's initial 17-member Governing Council managed to make decisions. Imagine what could happen if membership were enlarged to 33—6 executive board members plus one representative from each of the 27 member countries! In anticipation of this problem, the Governing Council of the ECB has adopted a complex system of rotation (to be implemented when country membership reaches 19 states) that bears a passing resemblance to the system used by the FOMC. The Executive Board members will still have permanent places on the Governing Council, just as the Board of Governors of the Federal Reserve System does, while the remaining central bank governors will rotate. Over time, as the ECB gains popular legitimacy and council members face less risk of home-country criticism, an enlarged Governing Council may decide that voting will make their decision process more efficient.

## Accountability and Transparency

Like the Federal Reserve, the ECB distributes large volumes of information both on paper and on its Web site, in all of the ECB's official languages. Included are a weekly balance sheet; a monthly statistical bulletin; an analysis of current economic conditions; biannual forecasts of inflation and growth; research reports relevant to current policy; and an annual report. In addition, the president of the ECB appears before the European Parliament every quarter to report on monetary policy and answer questions, and Governing Council members speak regularly in public. But the most important aspect of the ECB's communication strategy concerns statements about the Governing Council's policy deliberations. (Like the FOMC, the Governing Council of the ECB targets a short-term interest rate on interbank loans.)

INFORMATION

Following each of the Governing Council's monthly meetings on monetary policy, the president and vice president of the ECB hold a news conference in Frankfurt. The proceedings begin with the president reading a several-page statement announcing the council's interest-rate decision, together with a brief report on current economic and financial conditions in the euro area. The president and vice president then answer questions. A transcript of all their remarks is posted on the ECB's Web site (www. ecb.int) soon afterward. This procedure contrasts starkly with the FOMC's practice of issuing a terse statement and refusing to answer questions immediately after its meetings. On the other hand, the FOMC issues minutes of its meetings within three weeks, while the ECB does not make its minutes public for 20 years. Minutes of the ECB's very first Governing Council meeting, which do not identify who said what, are not scheduled to be released until 2019. Furthermore, the Governing Council does not

# IN THE NEWS
## Fed Adopts De facto Inflation Target

FT

FINANCIAL
TIMES

## By Krishna Guha in Washington

### February 19, 2009

The U.S. Federal Reserve yesterday adopted a de facto inflation target of 2 percent or slightly less—closely mirroring the formal target at the European Central Bank.

The move came as Fed policymakers slashed their growth forecasts for this year and raised their forecasts for unemployment at the end of this year by more than a full percentage point relative to their estimates in October.

In a speech, Ben Bernanke, the Fed chairman, said recent economic data was "dismal" and pledged that the U.S. central bank would "continue to do everything possible within the limits of its authority to assist in restoring our nation to financial stability and economic prosperity as quickly as possible."

But he made no reference to potential purchases of Treasury securities, suggesting that the Fed intends for now to focus on targeted interventions that directly reduce private borrowing costs.

The "central tendency" Fed forecasts—which represent the mainstream view on the Federal open market committee—now see the economy contracting between 0.5 percent and 1.3 percent this year, with unemployment in the final quarter of the year between 8.5 percent and 8.8 percent.

Officials also marked down their inflation forecasts, with core inflation (excluding volatile food and energy prices) now seen between 0.9 percent and 1.1 percent this year and between 0.7 percent and 1.5 percent as late as 2011—suggesting increased risk of deflation.

The Fed released for the first time long-term forecasts for growth, unemployment and inflation. The forecasts show that mainstream Fed officials are seeking to achieve inflation of between 1.7 percent and 2 percent in the long run—very similar to the ECB, which aims for inflation close to but under 2 percent.

This long-term inflation forecast represents a de facto inflation target, as Mr. Bernanke explained in a speech yesterday. He said the inflation projection should be interpreted "as the rate of inflation that FOMC participants see as most consistent with the dual mandate given to it by Congress."

The Fed chairman said "increased clarity about the FOMC's views regarding longer-term inflation should help to better stabilize the public's inflation expectations, thus contributing to keeping actual inflation from rising too high or falling too low."

However, the de facto target still falls short of the formal inflation targets at most other leading central banks. It represents a range of individual targets rather than an agreed target range. Most officials target 2 percent, but some target 1.75 percent and others 1.5 percent. Moreover, the de facto target could drift over time as the composition of the FOMC changes.

Long-term forecasts for growth and unemployment, meanwhile, show the Fed thinks the trend growth rate in the U.S. is now between 2.5 percent and 2.7 percent, while the natural rate of unemployment is between 4.8 percent and 5 percent—considerably higher than at the low point of the past cycle.

SOURCE: Copyright © 2009 by *The Financial Times Limited*. Reprinted with permission.

## LESSONS OF THE ARTICLE

As an economics professor at Princeton University, Ben Bernanke wrote about the virtues of central banks adopting inflation targets. But the adoption of a new policy framework depends on building political support both among the members of the FOMC and in the U.S. Congress, which oversees the Fed. Under Chairman Bernanke, the FOMC gradually adjusted its procedures to become more like those of an inflation-targeting central bank, but there remained important differences. Has the FOMC announced an explicit inflation target?

keep verbatim transcripts of meetings. While observers generally sympathize with the view that transcripts eliminate spontaneity from a meeting, the same cannot be said of minutes. It is hard to justify such a long lag in making public an anonymous summary of the Governing Council's deliberations.

In assessing whether the ECB's communications strategy is sufficient, we need to ask two questions. First, does the information that is released minimize the extent to which people will be surprised by future policy actions? Second, does it hold policymakers accountable for their decisions? On the first issue, the primary problem turns out to be that often a number of conflicting opinions are expressed. While confusion in communication was a problem when the ECB first got started, the Governing Council now knows the importance of providing a unified public front, and its members' public statements are more consistent. On the second issue, indications are that the system is working and that there is accountability. The ECB is forced to justify its actions to the euro-area public, explaining its policies and responding to criticisms in more than a dozen languages.

## The Price Stability Objective and Monetary Policy Strategy

STABILITY

The Treaty of Maastricht states, "The primary objective of the European System of Central Banks [ESCB] shall be to maintain price stability. Without prejudice to the objective of price stability, the ESCB shall support the general economic policies in the [European] Community," including the objective of sustainable and noninflationary growth. Like the Fed's legislatively dictated objectives, this statement is quite vague. However, the treaty is widely understood to place priority on price stability as the top objective for the ECB, while the Fed's mandate does not. The Governing Council's response has been to explain its interpretation of the statement and describe the factors that guide its policy decisions. Before assuming operational responsibility on January 1, 1999, the council prepared a press release entitled "A Stability-Oriented Monetary Policy Strategy." The strategy has two parts. First, there is a numerical definition of price stability. Second, the Governing Council announces its intention to focus on a broad-based assessment of the outlook for future prices, with money playing a prominent role.[8]

The ECB's Governing Council defines price stability as an inflation rate of close to, but less than, 2 percent, based on a euro-area-wide measure of consumer prices. The index, called the harmonized index of consumer prices (HICP), is similar to the U.S. consumer price index (CPI). The HICP is an average of retail price inflation in all the countries of the monetary union, weighted by the size of their gross domestic products. So inflation in Germany, where more than one-fourth of the total economic activity in the euro area occurs, is much more important to policy decisions than inflation in Ireland, whose economy is about one-fifteenth the size of Germany's. This arrangement has important implications for monetary policy operations, because there will surely be times when the proper policy for Ireland is to raise interest rates but the proper policy for Germany is to lower them. Given Ireland's relative size, a change in inflation or growth there has little impact on the euro area as a whole. The same is true for a number of other small countries in the union.

The fact that the economically large countries matter much more than the small ones can affect the dynamics of the Governing Council's policymaking. Remember

---

[8]The ECB refers to this statement as its "two-pillar" strategy. Observers have been critical of the way money is included in the policy framework. If the goal is to stabilize prices, why isn't money growth just one of a wide range of indicators that are factored into policy decisions?

## LESSONS FROM THE CRISIS
### GOVERNMENT FUNDING IN THE EURO AREA

The designers of the ECB wished to ensure that it would never sacrifice price stability to finance a fiscal deficit. They introduced a rule—the so-called *no-bailout* clause of the Maastricht Treaty—that forbids the ECB from directly helping a government facing financial distress.

Following the financial crisis of 2007–2009, that rule came as close as ever to a test. In early 2010, investor worries about the very large fiscal deficits of several euro-area governments led to a widening of yield spreads of their debt over German debt, which enjoys low yields as the regional benchmark. As we saw in Chapter 7, sovereign yield spreads usually reflect default risk.

Euro-area policymakers recognized a serious threat. The funding liquidity of a government can evaporate, just as it did in the crisis for many banks, households, and businesses. The history of sovereign borrowing is replete with examples of such disruptions. Think of the crises in Russia (1998) and Argentina (2001).

If some euro-area countries became unable to borrow, the economic fallout would probably spread across the region. The economies of the euro area are closely linked through trade and through the cross-border operations of many companies. These linkages encourage solidarity among euro-area policymakers.

Given the no-bailout rule governing the ECB, the burden of preventing a disruption of sovereign borrowing falls on euro-area fiscal leaders. What can they do to limit the risk of a government funding crisis in a member country? One approach would be to have other euro-area countries lend to that distressed government. Another approach would be to guarantee its debt Issues (just as many governments guaranteed the new debt issuance of their banks at the height of the financial crisis).

However, policymakers understand that a euro-area safety net for weaker sovereign borrowers would diminish the incentive of those borrowers to improve their budgets. Over time, it could lead to a broader fiscal deterioration in the euro area. That moral hazard is comparable to the problem caused by the government safety net for banks, which encourages them to take too much risk (see Chapter 14).

In the spring of 2010, after posting the second largest budget deficit of any euro-area country, the Greek government experienced significant problems borrowing. The investor focus on rising sovereign debt also led to a sharp further widening of bond yield spreads of several other euro-area countries.

To stem the burgeoning crisis, euro-area nations teamed up with the International Monetary Fund (IMF) to offer Greece large-scale loans at a cost below market yields, provided that the Greek government implement a set of stringent budget reforms proposed by the IMF. The action—which was quite unpopular in lender countries as well as in Greece—meant that the burden of funding Greek deficits was shared by euro-area taxpayers. In addition, euro-area governments created a separate public lending facility should member states other than Greece face difficulties borrowing in markets. The ECB also played a role in stemming the crisis, accepting Greek debt as collateral even as its rating fell below investment grade, and purchasing the debt of member states for the first time. While the conditional lending programs and ECB actions broadened the toolkit that euro-area leaders could use in confronting a fiscal crisis, it remains to be seen how successful these new and controversial mechanisms will be in securing long-run stability in the region.

that a group including the heads of all the euro-area national central banks, as well as the members of the Executive Board, makes interest-rate decisions. While the Governing Council's job is to stabilize prices in the euro area as a whole, one wonders whether the smaller countries might have undue influence on its policy decisions. To understand this concern, imagine what would happen if all the Governing Council's members pressed for actions appropriate to their own countries. The result would be a policy appropriate to the median country. And because there are only three large countries in the ECB—Germany, France, and Italy—the median country is likely to be fairly small. The custom of drawing half the Executive Board members from the large countries and half from the small ones is not a foolproof counterweight to this tendency.

These potential shortcomings notwithstanding, evidence strongly suggests that the ECB is doing the job it is supposed to do. That is, the Governing Council's policy has been appropriate to the euro area; it has not been skewed toward smaller countries' concerns. The specificity of the price stability objective set forth in the Treaty of Maastricht holds policymakers accountable, limiting discretion in their decision making.[9]

[9] Strong evidence for the effectiveness and credibility of the ECB can be found in Stephen Cecchetti and Kermit Schoenholtz, "How Central Bankers See It: The First Decade of ECB Policy and Beyond," NBER Working Paper 14489, November 2008.

# Terms

# Chapter Lessons

1. The Federal Reserve System is the central bank of the United States. Its decentralized structure comprises three primary elements:
   a. Twelve Federal Reserve Banks, each with its own board of directors, that
      i. Serve as the government's bank, issuing currency, maintaining the U.S. Treasury's bank account, and handling the Treasury's securities.
      ii. Serve as the bankers' bank, holding deposits, operating a payments system, making loans, and evaluating the safety and soundness of financial institutions in their districts.
   b. The seven-member Board of Governors in Washington, D.C., including the chair
      i. Regulates and supervises the financial system.
      ii. Oversees the Federal Reserve Banks.
      iii. Publishes economic data.
   c. The Federal Open Market Committee
      i. Makes monetary policy by setting interest rates or altering the balance sheet.
      ii. Has 12 voting members, including the seven governors and five of the 12 Reserve Bank presidents.
      iii. Meets eight times a year.
      iv. Is controlled largely by the chair.

2. The FOMC's success in meeting its objectives is enhanced by
   a. Its independence, which comes from its members' long terms, budgetary autonomy, and the irreversibility of its policy decisions.
   b. Clear communication of its policy decisions through an explanatory statement that is distributed immediately and minutes that are published following the next meeting.
   c. Regular public appearances of the committee's members.

   It is impaired by
   a. Its unwillingness to define exactly what it means by the stated goals of price stability and sustainable economic growth.
   b. Its unwillingness to respond to questions about its policy stance in a more timely manner.

3. The European Central Bank (ECB) is the central bank for the countries that participate in the European Monetary Union.
   a. The ECB is composed of three distinct parts:
      i. The National Central Banks (NCBs) provide services to the banks and governments in their countries.
      ii. The European Central Bank in Frankfurt, with its six-member Executive Board, oversees the monetary system.
      iii. The Governing Council makes monetary policy decisions.
   b. The ECB's primary objective is to stabilize prices in the common currency area.
   c. The ECB's success in meeting its policy objectives is aided by the timely announcement of policy decisions, press conferences in which top ECB officials respond to questions, and the release of twice-yearly forecasts.
   d. The ECB's success is impaired by the fact that the minutes of its policy meetings are not published for 20 years.

# Conceptual Problems

1. What are the Federal Reserve's goals? How are Fed officials held accountable for meeting them?

2. Go to the Federal Reserve Board's Web site and locate the FOMC's most recent statement. What did the committee members say at their last meeting regarding the Federal funds target and the two goals of price stability and sustainable economic growth? Does the statement make any reference to the financial stability goal?

3. Some people have argued that the high inflation of the late 1970s was a consequence of the fact that Federal Reserve Board Chairman Arthur Burns did what President Richard Nixon wanted him to do. Explain the connection.

4. How might the financial crisis of 2007–2009 lead to a change in the appointment process of presidents of the regional Federal Reserve banks?

5.* How did the political climate in the early 1900s influence the structure of the Federal Reserve System?

6. While the chair of the Federal Reserve Board has only one of 12 votes on the FOMC, he is never in the minority. What gives him the power to control the committee?

7. What are the goals of the ECB? How are its officials held accountable for meeting them?

8. Go to the ECB's Web site and locate the most recent introductory statement made by the president of the ECB at the press conference following a Governing Council meeting. What was the Governing Council's policy decision? How was it justified? Is there any reference to financial stability measures?

9. Do you think the FOMC has an easier or a harder time agreeing on monetary policy than the Governing Council of the ECB? Why?

10.* What are the two most important factors in ensuring that power is decentralized in the Eurosystem?

*Indicates more difficult problems

11. Why did the "no-bailout" clause of the Maastricht Treaty come under stress during and after the financial crisis of 2007–2009?

12. The Monetary Policy Committee (MPC) of the Bank of England is responsible for setting interest rates in the United Kingdom. Go to the bank's Web site at http://www.bankofengland.co.uk, and get as much information about the MPC as you can. How big is it? Who are its members? How often does it meet? What sort of announcements and publications does it offer? Is it independent of the United Kingdom's Parliament?

## Analytical Problems

13. Do you think the current procedures for appointing members to the Board of Governors are consistent with the principles of good central bank design? Explain your answer.

14.* Currently, all the national central banks in the Eurosystem are involved with the implementation of monetary policy. What do you think the advantage would be of centralizing the conduct of these day-to-day interactions with financial markets at the ECB in Frankfurt? Are there any disadvantages you can think of?

15. If you were charged with redrawing the boundaries of the Federal Reserve districts, what criteria would you use to complete the task?

16. In February 2009, the Federal Reserve released for the first time a long-run forecast for inflation. Do you think this move will help the Federal Reserve control inflation? Do you think it is equivalent to announcing a formal inflation target?

17. Do you think the members of the ECB's Governing Council should take formal votes? Why or why not? If they do vote, how do you think the votes should be allocated?

18. If members of the ECB's Governing Council do decide to take formal votes on monetary policy decisions, do you think these votes should be published? Why or why not?

19. Why do you think the statement released after each Federal Open Market Committee meeting retains the same basic structure?

20. Do you think, in the interest of transparency, the chair of the Federal Reserve Board should explain in detail the subtleties surrounding policy decisions? Why or why not?

21.* If you were asked to design a new central bank, what two institutional design features of (a) the Federal Reserve System and (b) the ECB would you adopt? Explain your choices.

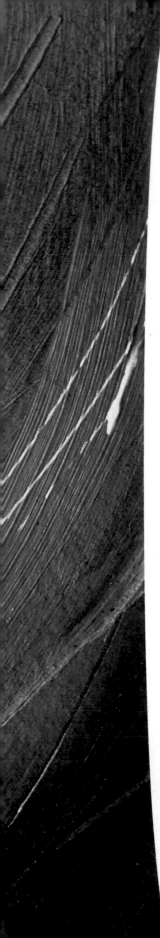

# Chapter 18

## Monetary Policy: Stabilizing the Domestic Economy

Central bankers have a long list of goals and a short list of tools they can use to achieve them. They are supposed to stabilize prices, output, the financial system, exchange rates, and interest rates, yet the only real power they have comes from their control over their own balance sheet and their monopoly on the supply of currency and reserves. To achieve their goals, policymakers can change the size of the monetary base by buying and selling assets—primarily government securities—and by making loans to banks. They can also alter the mix of assets they hold.

In practice, central banks choose a target for the market interest rate on overnight interbank loans and adjust the scale of the monetary base to hit that target. The rate on interbank loans, known as the federal funds rate, is the rate at which U.S. banks make overnight loans to each other. Through what is known as a "channel" or "corridor" system, the Fed limits the deviations of the market federal funds rate from the target by adjusting the rate they charge for discount loans to banks in need of funds (*the discount rate*, which sets a ceiling on the market federal funds rate) and the rate they pay on excess reserves banks hold at the central bank (*the deposit rate*, which puts a floor under the market federal funds rate). These three interest rates—the federal funds rate, the discount rate, and the deposit rate—are the primary tools of monetary policy during normal times.[1] In a financial crisis, however, when key markets do not function properly, central banks also may adjust the size and composition of their balance sheet to compensate temporarily for the market malfunction.

Interest rates play a central role in all of our lives. They are the cost of borrowing for those of us who need resources and the reward for lending to those of us with savings. Higher interest rates tend to restrict the growth of credit, making it harder for businesses to get financing and for individuals to find or keep jobs. Little wonder that everyone is preoccupied with interest rates and that the business press is constantly speculating about whether the Federal Open Market Committee will change its target.

Between September 2007 and December 2008, the FOMC lowered its target for the federal funds rate 10 times, including once between normally scheduled meetings, taking it from 5.25 percent to a range of 0 to 0.25 percent. This marked the first time since the 1930s that the Fed hit the **zero bound** on the nominal federal funds rate. Because banks can always hold cash—which pays zero interest—they will never choose to lend their reserves at a negative nominal interest rate. Therefore, the nominal policy rate faces a zero bound—it can never fall below zero.

The Fed's extraordinary reduction of the federal funds rate was a direct consequence of policymakers' belief that real economic activity was plunging amid the worst global financial crisis since the Great Depression. From the start of 2008, real GDP fell in five of the succeeding six quarters. When it hit bottom in the spring of 2009, GDP was

---

[1]As we will see, the Fed has a fourth conventional policy tool, reserve requirements, but that instrument has taken a back seat to the other three in macroeconomic management.

nearly 4 percent lower than a year earlier, the largest drop in more than 60 years. The unemployment rate climbed nearly 6 percentage points—a post–World War II record—from its trough of 4.4 percent to a peak above 10 percent. For a few months in mid-2008 during an oil-related inflation spike, the Fed's rate-cutting briefly paused, but as the deep recession lowered inflation, policy rates resumed their march to the zero bound.

Remarkably, even setting the federal funds rate target at essentially zero wasn't enough to stabilize the economy! The crisis had undermined the willingness and ability of major financial intermediaries to lend. It had disrupted the function of key financial markets, including those for interbank loans, commercial paper, home mortgages, and even municipal bonds. Healthy nonfinancial firms that had always been able to borrow short term in order to pay their employees, purchase materials for production, and the like suddenly couldn't find access to funds and faced ruin. At the same time, fears of deflation (akin to Japan's experience in the 1990s) threatened to keep the real interest rate (the nominal interest rate minus the expected inflation rate) from falling as the Fed eased. As we will see in Chapter 21, it is the real interest rate that drives economic activity.

In this environment, the Federal Reserve moved to substitute itself for dysfunctional intermediaries and markets. To do that, policymakers undertook the most dramatic alteration of the Fed's balance sheet in history (see Figure 18.1). Beginning

**Figure 18.1**    U.S. Federal Reserve Assets (billions of U.S. dollars), July 2007–January 2010

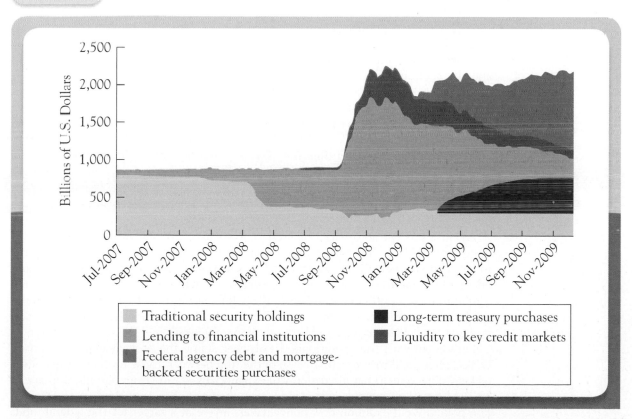

SOURCE: *Federal Reserve Bank of Cleveland.*

with the Bear Stearns rescue in March 2008, the Fed lent massively to fragile financial institutions. Then, after the September 2008 failure of Lehman Brothers, the Fed's balance sheet exploded in unprecedented fashion (see Chapter 17, Table 17.1, and Figure 18.1). Authorities created a variety of new programs aimed at supplying funds directly to key financial markets by directly or indirectly purchasing a wide variety of financial instruments. At various points during 2008 and 2009, the Fed lent more than $100 billion through the discount window, offered nearly $500 billion of credit at auction, acquired more than $300 billion of long-term Treasury securities and $1 trillion of mortgage-backed securities, and had net holdings of commercial paper (CP) in excess of $300 billion. Over time, as financial conditions normalized and the economy bottomed, the Fed's discount lending and its interventions in the CP market wound down.

The Federal Reserve has been widely accused of failing to anticipate the financial crisis and even of contributing to it. Yet, its aggressive actions to restore financial and economic stability following the crisis won wide praise as an example of effective monetary policy stabilization. In an unprecedented move, *Time* magazine made an economist—Federal Reserve Chairman Ben Bernanke—its Person of the Year because "his creative leadership helped ensure that 2009 was a period of weak recovery rather than catastrophic depression."

We have emphasized on several occasions that the economy relies on the central bank to ensure the stability of the financial system when it is under stress. In Chapter 17, we saw that the Federal Reserve reacted to the terrorist attacks of September 11, 2001, by temporarily flooding the banking system with reserves through discount window loans. Looking back from the perspective of the Fed's response to the crisis of 2007–2009, the September 11 episode seems remarkably small, brief, and contained.

To sum up, the financial crisis of 2007–2009 and the ensuing recession were the most severe and enduring since the Great Depression. To steady the financial system and the economy, the Fed utilized its three principal **conventional policy tools**—the federal funds rate target, the rate for discount window lending, and the deposit rate—to the fullest possible extent to support economic activity, including lowering its federal funds target rate essentially to zero. Policymakers then proceeded to develop and use a variety of **unconventional policy tools**—including commitments to keep interest rates low over time and massive purchases of risky assets in thin, fragile markets. To be able to lend to a wide range of institutions, the Fed—for the first time since the 1930s—invoked its emergency powers to lend to nonbanks (see Chapter 15, Lessons from the Crisis). These unconventional measures added meaningfully to the conventional actions.

Against this extraordinary background, *Time* magazine called the Fed "the most important and least understood force shaping the American—and global—economy." In this chapter, we will see how the Fed uses its policy tools, both conventional and unconventional, to achieve economic stability. We will see that those tools are quite similar to those of other central banks. We will focus on three links: the link between the central bank's balance sheet and its policy tools; between the policy tools and monetary policy objectives; and between monetary policy and the real economy.

Let's begin with the operational details that define the tools available to central banks. Then we'll turn to a discussion of the link between those tools and the policymakers' objectives. That discussion will explain why—aside from periods of financial crisis or near-zero interest rates—modern monetary policy is equivalent to interest-rate policy. We'll examine how policymakers arrive at a target for the federal funds rate. Finally, we'll turn to a discussion of a number of unconventional policy tools that were used in the crisis of 2007–2009 and explain how they augment conventional policy. We'll also look briefly at how central banks can exit from unconventional policy accommodation (just as they exit from conventional policy easing by hiking interest rates).

To keep the discussion manageable, we'll focus on monetary policy in large economies like that of the United States (where trade is a relatively small part of GDP) and of the euro area (a more "open" economy—i.e., where trade is a larger part of GDP). Chapter 19 will discuss exchange rates and other issues that are important to central banks in small, open economies.

# The Federal Reserve's Conventional Policy Toolbox

Like all central banks, the Federal Reserve can, if policymakers wish, control the quantity of reserves that commercial banks hold. Reserves are injected into the banking system through an increase in the size of the Fed's balance sheet, either because of a decision by the Fed to buy securities or because of a bank's decision to borrow from the Fed. Besides the quantity of reserves, the central bank can control either the size of the monetary base or the price of its components. Like most modern central banks, the Fed has chosen to focus its attention on prices. The three prices it concentrates on are the interest rate at which banks borrow and lend reserves overnight, the interest rate at which banks can borrow reserves from the Fed, and the interest rate that the Fed pays on excess reserves that banks hold at the central bank.[2]

In examining day-to-day monetary policy, understanding the institutional structure of the central bank and financial markets is essential. What is true in one country may or may not be true elsewhere. Because cataloging the structure and tools of monetary policy around the world is too big a task, we will begin with the Federal Reserve and financial markets in the United States. In the next section, we will look at the ECB's operating procedures to see how they differ.

The Federal Reserve has four conventional monetary policy tools, also known as *monetary policy instruments* (see Table 18.1).

1. The **target federal funds rate,** the interest rate at which banks make overnight loans to each other.
2. The **discount rate,** the interest rate the Fed charges on the loans it makes to banks and that forms a ceiling for the market federal funds rate.
3. The **deposit rate,** the interest rate that the Fed pays on excess reserves that banks hold in their accounts at the central bank and that puts a floor under the market federal funds rate.
4. The **reserve requirement,** the level of balances a bank is required to hold either as vault cash or on deposit or at a Federal Reserve Bank.

We will examine these four tools in detail. As we do, keep in mind that each has multiple purposes. That is, these tools are related to several of the central bank's functions and objectives.

---

[2]In October 2008, at the peak of the financial crisis, Congress authorized the Fed to pay interest on reserves, and it began to do so immediately. This authority brought the Fed's set of conventional policy tools in line with that of other major central banks like the ECB. Later in this chapter, we will see how important this tool can be.

**Table 18.1**    The Tools of U.S. Monetary Policy

|  | What Is It? | How Is It Controlled? | What Is Its Impact? |
|---|---|---|---|
| **Target Federal Funds Rate** | Interest rate charged on overnight loans between banks. | Supply of reserves adjusted through open market operations to meet expected demand at the target rate. | Changes interest rates throughout the economy. |
| **Discount Rate** | Interest rate charged by the Federal Reserve on loans to commercial banks. | Set at a premium over the target federal funds rate. | Ceiling on market federal funds rate. Means to provide liquidity to banks in times of crisis. |
| **Deposit Rate** | Interest rate paid by the Federal Reserve on excess reserves held by banks. | Set at a spread below the target funds rate. | Sets a floor under the market federal funds rate. |
| **Reserve Requirement** | Fraction of deposits that banks must keep either on deposit at the Federal Reserve or as cash in their vaults. | Set by the Federal Reserve Board within a legally imposed range. | Stabilizes the demand for reserves. |

## The Target Federal Funds Rate and Open Market Operations

The target federal funds rate is the Federal Open Market Committee's primary policy instrument. Financial market participants are constantly speculating about movements in this rate. FOMC meetings always end with a decision on the target level, and the statement released after the meeting begins with an announcement of that decision. To a large extent, this is U.S. monetary policy. But because the federal funds rate is the rate at which banks lend reserves to each other overnight, it is determined in the market, not controlled by the Fed. With this qualification in mind, we will distinguish between the *target* federal funds rate set by the FOMC and the **market federal funds rate**, at which transactions between banks take place.[3]

The name *federal funds* comes from the fact that the funds banks trade are their deposit balances at Federal Reserve Banks. On any given day, banks target the level of reserves they would like to hold at the close of business. But as the day goes by, the normal flow of business may leave them with more or less reserves than they want to hold. This discrepancy between actual and desired reserves gives rise to a market for reserves, with some banks lending out their excess funds and others borrowing to cover a shortfall. Without this market, banks would need to hold substantial quantities of excess reserves as insurance against shortfalls. While transactions are often made through brokers (third parties who bring buyers and sellers together), they are all bilateral agreements between two banks. Because the loans are unsecured—there is no collateral to fall back on in the event of nonpayment—the borrowing bank must be creditworthy in the eyes of the lending bank, or the loan cannot be made.

[3]The market federal funds rate is often referred to as the "effective" federal funds rate. Published daily by the Fed, it is the average of the interest rates on market transactions in federal funds weighted by the size of the transactions.

If the Fed wanted to, it could force the market federal funds rate to equal the target rate all the time by participating directly in the market for overnight reserves, both as a borrower and as a lender. However, policymakers believe that the federal funds market provides valuable information about the health of specific banks. When a bank cannot get an overnight loan from any other bank, it's a key sign of trouble. Accordingly, as mentioned earlier in the chapter, the Fed allows the federal funds rate to fluctuate around its target in a channel or corridor defined by the discount rate and the deposit rate.

MARKETS

Operationally, the discount rate is set at a spread above the target federal funds rate, and the deposit rate is set at a spread below the target federal funds rate. When the market federal funds rate climbs to the discount rate, banks may borrow from the Fed at the discount rate. When the market federal funds rate falls to the deposit rate, banks can deposit their excess reserves at the Fed at the deposit rate. Consequently, the discount rate functions as a cap on the market federal funds rate and the deposit rate as a floor beneath the market federal funds rate. The Fed can adjust the width of the so-called channel or corridor around the target federal funds rate when it wishes to allow a wider or narrower range of fluctuations in the market federal funds rate (see Applying the Concept on page 462).

The Fed's approach places it in a somewhat awkward position. It targets an interest rate at the same time that it wants to allow an interbank lending market to flourish. Instead of adopting a strategy that would fix the interest rate at the target directly, the Fed chooses to control the federal funds rate by manipulating the quantity of reserves. Using *open market operations*, the Fed adjusts the supply of reserves, with the goal of keeping the market federal funds rate close to the target rate. That is, the Fed buys or sells securities to add or drain reserves as required to meet the expected demand for reserves at the target rate.

We can use a standard supply-and-demand diagram to analyze the market in which banks borrow and lend reserves. The demand curve for reserves is downward sloping. At higher market interest rates, holding reserves that pay only the Fed's deposit rate is more costly than at lower market rates. However, when the federal funds rate in the market drops to the deposit rate, banks are willing to hold any amount of reserves supplied beyond this level, so the demand curve turns flat. As described above, keeping the market federal funds rate at the target means balancing supply and demand for reserves at that target rate. The staff of the Open Market Trading Desk does this by first estimating the demand for reserves at the target rate each morning, and then supplying that quantity for the day. This means the daily supply for reserves is vertical. That is, it is vertical until the market federal funds rate reaches the discount rate; at that point banks will borrow from the Fed rather than paying a higher interest rate in the market.

All of this is pictured in Figure 18.2: the reserve demand curve slopes down

**Figure 18.2**   The Market for Bank Reserves

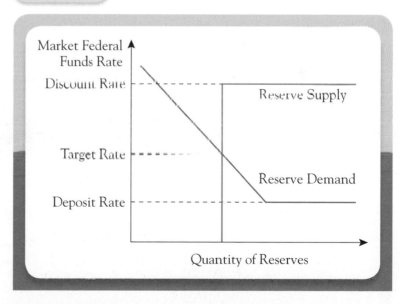

Reserve demand generally slopes down because the higher the market funds rate, the more costly it is to hold reserves paying the deposit rate. Reserve demand turns flat at the deposit rate, because banks face no better alternative to holding reserves at that rate. For levels of the market federal funds rate below the discount rate, reserve supply is vertical at the point that the open market trading desk estimates reserve demand will equal the target funds rate. At the discount rate, reserve supply becomes horizontal.

**Figure 18.3** The Market for Bank Reserves

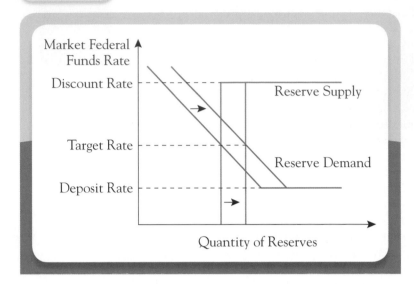

An increase in reserve demand is met by an open market purchase that increases reserve supply, thereby keeping the market federal funds rate at the target.

and turns flat at the deposit rate, while the reserve supply curve is vertical until it reaches the discount rate, at which point it becomes horizontal. Within a day, the federal funds rate can fluctuate in a range from the deposit rate to the discount rate. But as the reserve demand curve shifts from day to day, or when the FOMC decides to raise or lower their federal funds rate target, the Fed staff will use open market operations to shift the daily reserve supply curve to accommodate the change, thereby ensuring that the market federal funds rate stays near the target. Figure 18.3 shows a case in which, through open market purchases that increase reserve supply, the Federal Reserve's staff maintains the market federal funds rate at its target following an increase in reserve demand.

Let's take a moment to compare the FOMC's target rate with the market rate over the last two decades, to see how well the Fed's staff has met its objective. Figure 18.4 plots both the target federal funds rate (the dark line that moves stepwise) and the market federal funds rate (the orange line that jumps around) beginning in 1992. As you can see, the market interest rate

**Figure 18.4** Target Federal Funds Rate and Daily Market Rate, 1992-2009

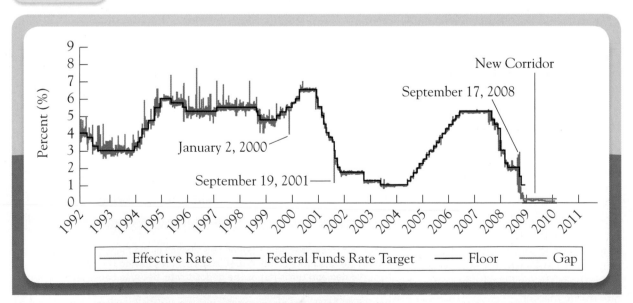

SOURCE: *Board of Governors of the Federal Reserve.*

was close to the target on most days after the year 2000. Changes in the reserve ac-counting rules in 1998 (described later in the chapter), combined with improvements in information systems both within banks and at the Fed, made it easier for the Open Market Trading Desk to estimate reserve demand. The use of the discount rate as a daily cap on the funds rate after 2002 appears to have stabilized the market rate even further.

However, the financial crisis of 2007–2009 introduced new targeting errors. The loss of liquidity in the interbank lending market in September 2008 made it extremely difficult for Fed officials to hit their target. The result is the spikes we see in the graph. At the end of 2008, the FOMC announced a range for the funds rate—shown as a floor and a cap—rather than a specific target. As liquidity conditions normalized, the spikes largely disappeared.

## Discount Lending, the Lender of Last Resort, and Crisis Management

When a central bank extends credit to commercial banks, its balance sheet changes. So by controlling the quantity of loans it makes, a central bank can control the size of reserves, the size of the monetary base, and ultimately interest rates. While the Fed could take this approach (and did for the first decade of its existence in the early 20th century), today it does not. Lending by Federal Reserve Banks to commercial banks, called **discount lending**, is usually small aside from crisis periods. During a normal week, the entire Federal Reserve System makes only a few hundred million dollars in loans. Yet, discount lending is the Fed's primary tool for ensuring short-term financial stability, eliminating bank panics, and preventing the sudden collapse of institutions that are experiencing financial difficulties. When there is a crisis, dis-count lending explodes. On Wednesday, September 12, 2001, the first business day after the collapse of the World Trade Center, banks borrowed $45.5 billion from the Fed! In the preceding week, borrowing had averaged just over $100 million per day. Similarly, in the month after Lehman failed in September 2008, discount lending rose by about $90 billion, while total lending surged by roughly $400 billion!

Recall that crises were the primary impetus for the creation of the Federal Reserve in the first place. The idea was that some central government authority should be capable of providing funds to sound banks to keep them from failing during finan-cial panics. The knowledge that the central bank would not allow solvent banks to become illiquid—that depositors could always get their funds—became one of the important safeguards against bank runs. The central bank, then, is the **lender of last resort**, making loans to banks when no one else will or can. But a bank is supposed to show that it is sound to get a loan in a crisis. This means having assets that the central bank is willing to take as collateral, because the central bank does not make uncollateralized loans. A bank that does not have assets it can use as collateral for a discount loan is a bank that should probably fail. Indeed, this is the principal reason that Fed officials gave when they explained why they could not prevent Lehman's failure in September 2008.

For most of its history, the Federal Reserve loaned reserves to banks at a rate *below* the target federal funds rate. Borrowing from the Fed was cheaper than borrowing from another bank. Even so, no one borrowed, because the Fed required banks to exhaust all other sources of funding before they applied for a loan. Moreover, banks that used discount loans regularly faced the possibility of being denied loans in the

## YOUR FINANCIAL WORLD
### What the Federal Funds Rate Means to You

On learning that the FOMC controls the federal funds rate, most people's reaction is, "I'm not a bank and I don't borrow overnight, so why should I care?" What they do care about is the interest rate they pay on student loans, or auto loans, or home mortgages. But because interest rates often move together, people who care about long-term interest rates must care about short-term interest rates.

Remember from our discussion of the term structure of interest rates in Chapter 7 that the long-term interest rate is the average of expected future short-term interest rates. Thus, the rate charged on a 30-year, fixed-rate home mortgage is the average of the expected one-year rates for the next 30 years. Those one-year interest rates, in turn, are averages of the expected one-day interest rates for the next 365 days. Unless everyone expects the FOMC to keep interest rates at the same level for a very long time, the interest rates you care about will move—by less than the target federal funds rate, but they will move.

To see how important this is, we can look at the example of a 30-year mortgage. In early 2004, with the federal funds rate target at 1 percent, the interest rate on a 30-year, fixed-rate mortgage was 5½ percent, and the monthly payment on a $100,000 loan was roughly $570. By July 2006, the FOMC had raised the federal funds rate target to 5¼ percent, and the mortgage interest rate had risen to 6¾ percent. At the higher interest rate, the monthly payment on a $100,000 mortgage was something like $650—more than $80 a month higher!

future. Needless to say, these rules created quite a disincentive to borrow from the Fed. Almost everyone was willing to pay high rates in the marketplace rather than ask the Fed for a loan; only banks with nowhere else to go went to the Fed. But by severely discouraging banks from borrowing, the Fed destabilized the interbank market for reserves causing some of the upward spikes that you can see in Figure 18.4. Eventually, officials decided to make the process more rational. In 2002, they instituted the discount lending procedures that are in place today.

In addition to providing a mechanism for stabilizing the financial system, the current discount lending procedures also help the Fed meet its interest-rate stability objective. To see how this all works, we need to look at the details of how lending functions. The Federal Reserve makes three types of loans, called *primary credit*, *secondary credit*, and *seasonal credit*. As with the target federal funds rate, the Fed controls the interest rate on these loans, not the quantity of credit extended. The banks decide how much to borrow, and the rules are not very complicated. Let's look at each one in turn.

**Primary Credit**    **Primary credit** is extended on a very short-term basis, usually overnight, to institutions that the Fed's bank supervisors deem to be sound (as measured by the standardized ratings they produce).[4] Banks seeking to borrow must post acceptable collateral to back the loan.[5] The interest rate on primary credit is set at a spread *above* the federal funds target rate. This is called the **primary discount rate**.[6] The term *discount rate* usually refers to this primary discount rate.

As long as a bank qualifies and is willing to pay the penalty interest rate, it can get the loan. The rules allow a borrowing bank to lend the funds again if it wishes. Primary credit is designed to provide additional reserves at times when the open market staff's

[4]Banks with CAMELS ratings of 1 or 2 qualify for primary credit. The ratings are described in Chapter 14.

[5]The list of acceptable collateral is fairly broad, including not only government securities and investment-grade corporate bonds but consumer loans, commercial and agricultural loans, and some mortgage obligations.

[6]In the case of a financial emergency resulting from an act of war, military or terrorist attack, natural disaster, or other catastrophic event, the primary discount rate can be reduced to the target federal funds rate.

forecasts are off and so the day's reserve supply falls short of the banking system's demand. In that case, the market federal funds rate will rise above the FOMC's target. Providing a facility through which banks can borrow at a penalty rate above the target puts a cap on the market federal funds rate. Banks will go to the discount window and borrow reserves from the Fed rather than go into the federal funds market and pay a rate above the primary discount rate. So the system is designed both to provide liquidity in times of crisis, ensuring financial stability, and to keep reserve shortages from causing spikes in the market federal funds rate. By restricting the range over which the market federal funds rate can move, this system helps to maintain interest-rate stability.

**Secondary Credit**    Secondary credit is available to institutions that are not sufficiently sound to qualify for primary credit. Because secondary credit is provided to banks that are in trouble, the **secondary discount rate** is set above the primary discount rate. There are two reasons a bank might seek secondary credit. The first is the standard one: a temporary shortfall in reserves. But short-run secondary borrowing is highly unusual. Banks that request secondary credit from the Fed are banks that can't borrow from anyone else. By offering to pay a rate above the primary discount rate, a bank signals other banks that it doesn't qualify for primary credit. By paying the Fed the secondary discount rate for funds, the bank advertises that it is in trouble. It is hard to see any but the most desperate banker doing this. Indeed, even during the crisis of 2007–2009, secondary credit did not exceed $1 billion.

So who is secondary credit for, anyway? It is for banks that are experiencing longer-term problems that they need some time to work out. There are times when banks have serious financial difficulty that they can resolve without failing. A bank that takes a large loss from poor lending decisions will become undercapitalized, but it may be able to raise funds to continue operating if it is given enough time. Such a bank has nothing to lose by requesting secondary credit. Without it, it will fail anyway. But before the Fed makes the loan, it has to believe there is a good chance the bank will be able to survive. You can see why secondary credit is rare.

**Seasonal Credit**    Seasonal credit is used primarily by small agricultural banks in the Midwest to help in managing the cyclical nature of farmers' loans and deposits.[7] Historically, these banks had poor access to national money markets, so the Fed stepped in to provide credit, charging them a market-based interest rate.[8] In recent years, however, there has been a move to eliminate seasonal credit. While the Fed still extends several hundred million dollars of seasonal credit during the summer months, there seems little justification for the practice any longer. Banks that used seasonal credit in the past now have easy access to longer-term loans from large commercial banks.

## Reserve Requirements

Reserve requirements are the fourth tool in the monetary policymaker's toolbox. Since 1935, the Federal Reserve Board has had the authority to set the reserve requirements,

---

[7]During spring and summer, as farmers plant and cultivate their crops, the demand for loans rises and deposits decline, driving down bank reserves. Harvests and crop sales bring repayment of loans and increases in deposits, raising bank reserves.

[8]The interest rate charged on seasonal credit is the average of the market (effective) federal funds rate and market rate on 90-day negotiable certificates of deposit, both averaged over the previous two weeks.

the minimum level of reserves banks must hold either as vault cash or on deposit at the Fed.[9] Required reserves equal the required reserve ratio times the level of deposits to which the requirement is applied. (In Chapter 17, we wrote this relationship as $RR = r_D D$.) As we saw in the last chapter, changes in the reserve requirement affect the money multiplier and the quantity of money and credit circulating in the economy. Increasing it reduces the deposit expansion potential of the banking system, lowering the level of money supported by a given monetary base. So, by adjusting the reserve requirement, the central bank can influence economic activity. Unfortunately, the reserve requirement turns out not to be very useful. One reason is that small changes in the reserve requirement have a large—really, too large—impact on the level of deposits. But there are other reasons it isn't a good way to control the quantity of money. To see why, we need to look at the details.

The method for computing required reserves is complex. Everything is based on two-week averages. The reserve requirement is applied to two-week average balances in accounts with unlimited checking privileges—*transaction deposits*. This reserve computation period ends every second Monday. The reserves a bank must hold are also averaged over a two-week period, called the *maintenance period*, which begins on the third Thursday after the end of the computation period. That may sound a bit complicated, but really it isn't. What it means is that the banks and the Fed both know exactly what level of reserves every bank is required to hold during a given maintenance period well *before* the period starts. All banks have 16 days to figure out their deposit balances before they even need to start holding reserves. This procedure is called *lagged-reserve accounting*, and it makes the demand for reserves more predictable.

In 1980, the Monetary Control Act changed the rules slightly so that the Fed can now set the reserve requirement ratio between 8 percent and 14 percent of these so-called transactions deposits. Now that interest is paid on reserves, the reserve requirement is not very costly to banks. Yet, to help small banks, the law specifies a graduated reserve requirement that is similar to the graduated income tax. The first few million dollars in deposits are exempt; then the reserve requirement ratio rises to 3 percent for the next $50 million or so in deposits. For everything above that level, the rate is 10 percent.[10] The accounting rules allow banks to carry small amounts of excess reserves forward and backward one maintenance period to meet their reserve requirements.

The purpose of the reserve requirement has changed over the years. In the beginning, reserves were required to ensure banks were sound and to reassure depositors that they could withdraw currency on demand. With the advent of deposit insurance, the rationale for requiring reserves changed. Today, the reserve requirement exists primarily to stabilize the demand for reserves and help the Fed to maintain the market federal funds rate close to target. A critical element in the Fed's daily open market operations is an estimate of the reserve demand for the day. The better the forecast, the easier it is to keep the market federal funds rate close to the FOMC's target. Changes in the reserve accounting rules over the years have made the open market operations staff's job of estimating reserve demand easier. Before August 1998, the computation and maintenance periods overlapped. Banks had to manage their deposits and reserves

---

[9]Originally, the requirements were specified in the Federal Reserve Act and could not be changed. For a concise history of reserve requirements, see Joshua N. Feinman, "Reserve Requirements: History, Current Practice, and Potential Reform," *Federal Reserve Bulletin* 79, no. 6 (June 1993), pp. 569–589.

[10]The level at which the higher reserve requirement kicks in changes every year, based on the amount of demand deposits in the banking system. In 2010, the reserve requirement was zero for the first $10.7 million in deposits, 3 percent for deposits up to $55.2 million, and 10 percent above that.

at the same time, and the result was a volatile market federal funds rate. Since summer 1998, with the implementation of the lagged-reserve accounting system, things calmed down quite a bit. As you can see from Figure 18.4, except on the occasion of crises, the market federal funds rate now stays much closer to the target.

The case against using the reserve requirement as a direct policy tool is persuasive. An example will help to illustrate the pitfalls of using the reserve requirement as a policy tool. Following the banking crises of the Great Depression, U.S. banks began accumulating excess reserves. By the beginning of 1936, less than half of the $5.6 billion of reserves held in the banking system were required; the rest were excess reserves. The Federal Reserve Board was puzzled and became concerned that the high level of excess reserves could be used to support a rapid expansion of deposits and loans, which would lead to inflation. To head off the possibility, beginning in August 1936 the Fed used its newly acquired powers and in three steps doubled the reserve requirement. Suddenly, $3 billion in excess reserves was reduced to $1 billion. Bank executives were not happy. They spent the next year rebuilding their reserve balances until excess reserves were back to the level where they had been before the reserve requirement was raised. The consequences for the economy were grim. While the monetary base remained relatively stable, the money multiplier plummeted, driving M1 and M2 down. As monetary aggregates fell, the economy went along with them. From its peak in spring 1937 to its trough less than a year later, real GDP fell more than 10 percent.

# Operational Policy at the European Central Bank

Like the Federal Reserve's, the ECB's monetary policy toolbox contains an overnight interbank rate (equivalent to the federal funds rate), a rate at which the central bank lends to commercial banks (equivalent to the discount rate), a reserve deposit rate, and a reserve requirement. While the conventional toolkit is the same, the details are different, so let's have a look at them.

## The ECB's Target Interest Rate and Open Market Operations

While the ECB occasionally engages in outright purchases of securities, it provides reserves to the European banking system primarily through what are called *refinancing operations*. The main refinancing operation is a weekly auction of two-week **repurchase agreements (repo)** in which the ECB, through the National Central Banks, provides reserves to banks in exchange for securities and then reverses the transaction two weeks later. The policy instrument of the ECB's Governing Council is the minimum interest rate allowed at these refinancing auctions, which is called the main refinancing operations **minimum bid rate**. This is the European equivalent of the Fed's target federal funds rate, so we will refer to it as the *target refinancing rate*. In normal times, the main refinancing operations provide banks with virtually all their reserves. However, in the crisis of 2007–2009, the ECB sought to steady financial markets by providing most reserves through longer-term refinancing. Together, these operations accounted for more than one-third of the ECB's balance sheet in early 2010.

## APPLYING THE CONCEPT
### THE CHANNEL SYSTEM AND THE FUTURE OF MONETARY POLICY

It is their monopoly over the supply of currency and reserves—the monetary base—that gives central banks influence over the economic and financial system. As a practical matter, modern policymakers chose to use this monopoly power to influence the price of reserves in overnight markets. That's the federal funds rate in the United States. But numerous innovations are reducing the demand for the monetary base. Innovations in payments systems have reduced our demand for currency and the use of information technology has lowered reserve requirements as banks sweep client funds from checking to savings accounts. Being a monopolist is great, but only if there is demand for your product. As the demand for the reserves disappears, will monetary policy go with it?

To see, we can look at the cases of Australia, Canada, and New Zealand. Central bankers there have eliminated reserve requirements entirely, but retain monetary policy control. They do it through what is called a "channel" or "corridor" system that involves setting not only a target interest rate, but also a lending and deposit rate—just as the Fed and the ECB do. The lending rate is the rate charged on discount loans, while the deposit rate is the rate paid by the central bank on commercial bank reserve deposits. As reserve demand fluctuates during the day, the overnight interest rate stays between these two bounds.

Figure 18.5 shows the reserve market with a channel system. Recall that reserve demand slopes down because the higher the market interest rate, the more costly it is to hold reserves. In the channel system, reserve demand becomes flat when the interbank market rate falls to the deposit rate, because banks have no better alternative than the deposit rate. Reserve supply is a step function: vertical at the level of reserves the central bank initially chooses to supply and horizontal at the lending rate.

The channel system has important implications for the behavior of overnight market interest rates. At the beginning of the day, central bank staff estimates that reserve demand will be at $RD_0$, so they supply the quantity of reserves that they believe will yield the target rate. But as the day progresses, reserve demand turns out to be different from what was expected. If demand rises significantly to $RD_1$ the overnight rate will start to rise. But once it gets to the lending rate, banks can simply borrow from the central bank, capping the rate. If reserve demand falls to $RD_2$ then banks will deposit reserves in the central bank, putting a floor under the overnight rate.

Now let's go back to the question we started with: What happens as reserve demand goes to zero? The answer is that this system still works. Banks in need of funds will never be willing to pay more than the central bank's lending rate and those that have excess funds will never be willing to lend at a rate below the central bank's deposit rate. Overnight interest rates will always be inside the corridor, giving monetary policymakers a tool to influence the economy.

While the ECB's refinancing operations are broadly similar to the Fed's daily open market operations, there are some differences. The most important one is that these operations are done at all the National Central Banks (NCBs) simultaneously. In 2010, there were 16 locations (and as the Eurosystem expands to include more countries, the number will grow). In the United States, everything is done at the Federal Reserve Bank of New York. And while the Fed solicits prices from a short list of 18 securities dealers in the course of its normal operations, literally hundreds of European banks participate in the ECB's weekly auctions. Finally, because of the differences in financial structure in different countries, the collateral that is accepted in refinancing operations differs from country to country. Under normal circumstances, the Fed takes U.S. government securities (although the range of accepted collateral widened during the crisis of 2007–2009). In contrast, some of the National Central Banks in the Eurosystem accept a broad range of collateral, including not only government-issued bonds but also privately issued bonds and bank loans. And when the rating on government bonds of one euro-area country fell below investment grade in 2010, the ECB continued to accept them as collateral.

In addition to the weekly main refinancing operations, the ECB engages in both monthly long-term refinancing operations, in which it offers reserves for three months, and infrequent small operations that occur between the main refinancing operations, when policymakers want to fine-tune reserve levels. During the financial crisis, the ECB offered some reserves for up to a year.

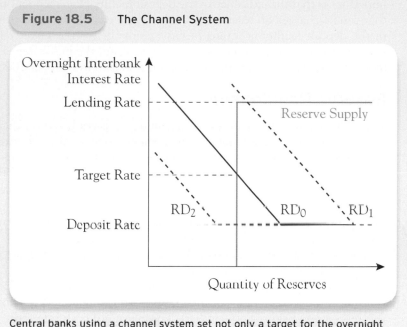

**Figure 18.5**   The Channel System

Central banks using a channel system set not only a target for the overnight interbank interest rate, but also a lending rate that they change for reserve loans and a deposit rate that they pay when banks' reserve accounts contain excess reserves. As a result, as the demand for reserves fluctuates, the overnight interest rate always remains between the two limits.

## The Marginal Lending Facility

The **ECB's Marginal Lending Facility** is the analog to the Federal Reserve's primary credit facility. Through this facility, the ECB provides overnight loans to banks at a rate that is normally well *above* the target-refinancing rate. The spread between the marginal lending rate and the target refinancing rate is set by the Governing Council and was 75 basis points in early 2010. As in the case of discount borrowing from the Fed, commercial banks initiate these borrowing transactions when they face a reserve deficiency that they cannot satisfy more cheaply in the marketplace. Banks do borrow regularly, and on occasion the amounts they borrow are large. The similarity between this procedure and the Federal Reserve's primary credit facility is no accident, because the ECB's system (which is itself based on the German Bundesbank's) was the model for the 2002 redesign of the Fed's discount window.

## The Deposit Facility

Banks with excess reserves at the end of the day can deposit them overnight in the **ECB's Deposit Facility** at an interest rate substantially *below* the target-refinancing rate. Again, the spread is determined by the Governing Council and was 75 basis points in early 2010. While they are usually small, these deposits can be substantial, because they include all the excess reserves in the Eurosystem's banks. But what is important is that the existence of the deposit facility places a floor on the interest rate that can be charged on reserves. Because a bank can always deposit its excess reserves in the deposit facility at a rate 75 basis points below the target refinancing rate, it will never make a loan at a lower rate. Once again, the ECB's deposit facility was the model for the Fed's deposit rate that was introduced in October 2008.

## Reserve Requirements

The ECB requires that banks hold minimum reserves based on the level of their liabilities. The reserve requirement of 2 percent is applied to checking accounts and some other short-term deposits. Deposit levels are averaged over a month, and reserve levels must be held over the following month. Like the Fed, the ECB pays interest on required reserves; the rate is based on the interest rate from the weekly refinancing auctions, averaged over a month, which is designed to be very close to the overnight interbank rate. As a result, the cost of meeting the reserve requirement is relatively low, and banks do not go out of their way to escape it.

MARKETS

The European system is designed to give the ECB tight control over the short-term money market in the euro area. And it usually works well. Figure 18.6 shows the target refinancing rate, which is the minimum bid rate in the weekly auctions, as the red line running through the center of the graph, with the marginal lending rate above and the deposit rate below (both in blue). The **overnight cash rate** is the European analog to the market federal funds rate, the rate banks charge each other for overnight loans. As you can see, this rate fluctuates quite a bit. And, during the crisis of 2007–2009, it stayed below the main refinancing rate for most of the period, as the ECB flooded the system with liquidity. Yet, even in this period, the overnight cash rate remained within the band formed by the marginal lending rate and the deposit rate.

**Figure 18.6** Euro-Area Overnight Cash Rate and ECB Interest Rates, 1999–2009

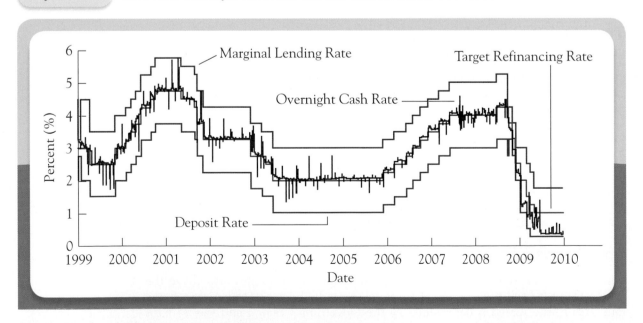

SOURCE: *European Central Bank.*

# TOOLS OF THE TRADE
Some Unconventional Policy Tools

To stabilize the financial system and the economy during the crisis of 2007–2009, the Fed undertook a range of unprecedented policy actions, both in scale and scope. We saw earlier that the target federal funds rate dropped to the zero bound, while the Fed's balance sheet ballooned. We also saw that the authorities purchased a large volume of assets with credit risk, while cutting traditional holdings of short-term Treasuries (Figure 18.1).

These extraordinary policy interventions were made possible by the introduction of a wide variety of new policy tools. In this chapter, we have discussed four *conventional* tools: the target federal funds rate, the discount rate, the deposit rate, and reserve requirements. In addition to these, the Federal Reserve officially recognizes several other unconventional tools, or facilities, which are

described in Table 18.2. Several of these facilities involved lending to nonbanks, something the Fed can do only by invoking its emergency powers in "unusual and exigent circumstances." Look for updates of the Fed's toolkit at http://www.federalreserve.gov/monetarypolicy/.

Note that Table 18.2 leaves out several important mechanisms that the Fed used extensively in the crisis. For example, in 2009, it purchased more than $1 trillion of mortgage-backed securities to help lower the cost of mortgages in a thin market. The volume of that "credit easing" exceeded the entire Fed balance sheet prior to the crisis! The Fed also committed to keeping its policy rate low for an extended period in order to influence long-term interest rate expectations. Such a "policy duration commitment" is discussed later in this chapter.

**Table 18.2    Some Unconventional Policy Tools**

| Policy Tool | Description |
|---|---|
| Term Auction Facility (TAF) | The Fed auctions a fixed volume of funds at maturities less than three months against collateral to depository institutions. |
| Primary Dealer Credit Facility (PDCF) | The Fed lends overnight to primary dealers (including nonbanks) against a broad range of collateral. |
| Term Securities Lending Facility (TSLF) | The Fed provides Treasury securities in exchange for a broad range of collateral in order to promote market liquidity. |
| Asset-backed Commercial Paper (ABCP) Money-Market Mutual Fund (MMMF) Liquidity Facility | The Fed lends to depositories and bank holding companies to finance purchases of ABCP from MMMFs. |
| Commercial Paper Funding Facility (CPFF) | The Federal Reserve Bank (FRB) of New York finances the purchase of commercial paper from eligible issuers via primary dealers. |
| Money-Market Investor Funding Facility (MMIFF) | The FRB New York funds investment vehicles that purchase assets from MMMFs. |
| Term Asset-Backed Securities Loan Facility (TALF) | The FRB New York lends to holders of high-rated newly issued asset-backed securities (ABS), using the ABS as collateral. |

This pattern contrasts starkly with that of the U.S. market federal funds rate before 2002. Looking back at Figure 18.4, we can see that the market federal funds rate occasionally moves more than 100 basis points above or below the target. In fact, over the first 10 years plotted there, the funds rate was more than 100 basis points away from the target 28 times, or nearly three times a year. As the Federal Reserve gradually introduced a version of the ECB's conventional policy toolkit, the funds rate was more than 100 basis points away from the target on only three occasions between 2002 and early 2010, all of which occurred during the crisis of 2007–2009. The European system is clearly more successful in keeping the short-term rate close to target.

# Linking Tools to Objectives: Making Choices

Monetary policymakers use the various tools they have to meet the objectives society gives them. Their goals—low and stable inflation, high and stable growth, a stable financial system, stable interest and exchange rates—are (or should be) given to them by their elected officials. But day-to-day policy is left to the technicians, who must then decide which tools are the best for the job.

STABILITY

Over the years, a consensus has developed among monetary policy experts, both inside and outside central banks, that (1) the reserve requirement is not useful as an operational instrument, (2) central bank lending is necessary to ensure financial stability, and (3) short-term interest rates are the tool to use to stabilize short-term fluctuations in prices and output. Later in this chapter, we will see how exceptional conditions—such as dysfunctional financial markets or nominal short-term interest rates at zero—favor the use of unconventional policy tools, but even those tools aim to influence some market interest rate. The logic of this conclusion is straightforward. To follow it, let's start by listing the features that distinguish good policy instruments from bad ones.

## Desirable Features of a Policy Instrument

A good monetary policy instrument has three features.

1. It is easily *observable* by everyone.
2. It is *controllable* and quickly changed.
3. It is tightly *linked* to the policymakers' objectives.

These features seem obvious. After all, a policy tool wouldn't be very useful if you couldn't observe it, control it, or predict its impact on your objectives. But beyond the obvious, it is important that a policy instrument be easily observable to ensure transparency in policymaking, which enhances accountability. Controllability is important in both the short term and the long term. An instrument that can be adjusted quickly in the face of a sudden change in economic conditions is clearly more useful than one that takes time to adjust. And the more predictable the impact of an instrument, the easier it will be for policymakers to meet their objectives.

Requiring that a monetary policy instrument be observable and controllable leaves us with only a few options to choose from. The reserve requirement won't work. Because banks cannot adjust their balance sheets quickly, changes need to be announced some time in advance. Then there are the components of the central bank's balance sheet—commercial bank reserves, the monetary base, loans, and foreign exchange reserves—as well as their prices—various interest rates and the exchange rate. (Exchange rate policy is discussed in the next chapter.) But how do we choose between controlling quantities and controlling prices? Over the years, central banks have switched from one to the other. For example, from 1979 to 1982, the Fed did try targeting bank reserves, with an eye toward reducing the inflation rate from double-digit levels. Inflation fell quickly, so in a sense the policy was a success. But one side effect of choosing to control reserves was that interest rates became highly variable, rising from 14 percent to over 20 percent and then falling to less than 9 percent, all in a period of less than six months.

The consensus today is that the Fed's strategy of targeting reserves rather than interest rates in the period from 1979 to 1982 was a way of driving interest rates to levels that would not have been politically acceptable had they been announced as targets. Even in an environment of double-digit inflation rates, the FOMC could not explicitly raise the target federal funds rate to 20 percent. By saying they were targeting the quantity of reserves, the committee members escaped responsibility for the high interest rates. When inflation had fallen and interest rates came back down, the FOMC reverted to targeting the federal funds rate. And that is what it has done ever since. (Further details of this episode are discussed in Chapter 20.)

Appearances and politics aside, there is a very good reason the vast majority of central banks in the world today choose to target an interest rate rather than some quantity on their balance sheet. To understand it, let's look at what would happen if the FOMC chose to target the quantity of reserves in the banking system. Targeting the quantity of reserves requires holding supply constant at the target level. That means supply is vertical not only each day (as in Figure 18.2) but that it is fixed over much longer periods of weeks or possibly even months. The consequences of this are easy to see. With reserve supply fixed, a shift in reserve demand changes the federal funds rate. When reserve demand increases, the market federal funds rate will go up and when reserve demand falls, the market federal funds rate will go down. If the Fed chooses to target the quantity of reserves, it gives up control of the federal funds rate. Figure 18.7 shows what can happen: as reserve demand increases and falls, the market federal funds rate fluctuates over a range that is determined by the intersection of supply and demand.

From the discussion in Chapter 15 we can infer that, in order to meet their objectives, central bankers will tend to adopt operating procedures

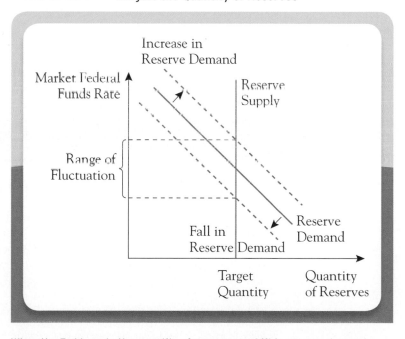

**Figure 18.7**    The Market for Bank Reserves when the Fed Targets the Quantity of Reserves

When the Fed targets the quantity of reserves, a shift in reserve demand causes the market federal funds to move. An increase in reserve demand forces the interest rate up, while a fall in reserve demand forces the interest rate down.

## APPLYING THE CONCEPT
### INFLATION TARGETING

If you can focus central bankers' attention clearly on a well-articulated objective, you will get better policy. The problem is how to do it. During the 1990s, a number of countries adopted a policy framework called **inflation targeting** in an effort to improve monetary policy performance. And it seems to have worked. Countries that embraced inflation targeting achieved both lower inflation and higher real growth.

Inflation targeting bypasses intermediate targets and focuses directly on the objective of low inflation. It is a monetary policy strategy that involves the public announcement of a numerical inflation target, together with a commitment to make price stability the central bank's primary objective to which all other objectives are subordinated. This approach creates an environment in which everyone believes policymakers will keep the inflation rate low, so long-term expectations of inflation remain low, anchoring long-term interest rates and promoting growth. As we saw in Chapter 15, one of the keys to any successful central bank policy is for policymakers to convince the public that they will keep inflation low. Their commitment must be credible. Inflation targeting is designed to convince people that monetary policy will deliver low inflation.

Central banks that employ inflation targeting operate under what has been described as a *hierarchical mandate,* in which inflation comes first and everything else comes second. The United Kingdom, Australia, Chile, and South Africa are among the roughly two dozen countries that target inflation. Most observers put the ECB in the group as well. This approach contrasts with the Federal Reserve's *dual mandate,* in which inflation and growth are on an equal footing. Because of this dual mandate, the Fed has shied away from adopting inflation targeting.

To understand how inflation targeting works, let's look at the British example. The Bank of England Act of 1998 both granted the Bank of England independence and dictated its objective: to deliver price stability, as defined by the government's inflation target. A nine-member Monetary Policy Committee meets monthly to determine short-term interest rates in an effort to meet this objective, which has been defined as consumer price inflation of 2.0 percent. Because transparency is a crucial part of inflation targeting, the Bank of England publishes the minutes of its Monetary Policy Committee's meetings, as well as quarterly forecasts of inflation in its *Inflation Report.*

By focusing on a clearly defined and easily observable numerical inflation statistic and requiring frequent communication with the public, inflation targeting increases policymakers' accountability and helps to establish their credibility. Not only do central bankers know what they are supposed to do, but everyone else does, too. The result is not just lower and more stable inflation but—usually—higher and more stable growth as well. However, as we saw in the global crisis of 2007–2009, inflation targeting is not sufficient to prevent financial disruptions that undermine economic stability.

that keep interest rates from becoming volatile. Interest rates are the primary linkage between the financial system and the real economy, so stabilizing growth means keeping interest rates from being overly volatile. In the context of choosing an operating target, that means keeping unpredictable changes in reserve demand from influencing interest rates and feeding into the real economy. The best way to do this is to target interest rates.[11]

## Operating Instruments and Intermediate Targets

Before continuing, we should pause to consider some terms and concepts that often crop up in discussions of central banking. Central bankers sometimes use the terms *operating instrument* and *intermediate target.* Operating instruments refer to actual tools of policy. These are instruments that the central bank controls directly. Every central

---

[11]More than 40 years ago, William Poole first observed that the decision to target either interest rates, or an aggregate like reserves or the monetary base, depends on what is less predictable. Is it the money multiplier that links the monetary base to monetary aggregates? Or is it the linkage between money and the real economy? (This is the velocity of money which we will discuss in Chapter 20.) Poole showed that if the money multiplier is less predictable, policymakers should target interest rates, otherwise, it is better to target the monetary base. See William Poole, "Optimal Choice of Monetary Policy Instruments in a Simple Stochastic Macro Model," *Quarterly Journal of Economics* 84, no. 2 (1970), pp. 197–216.

**Figure 18.8**   Instruments, Targets, and Objectives

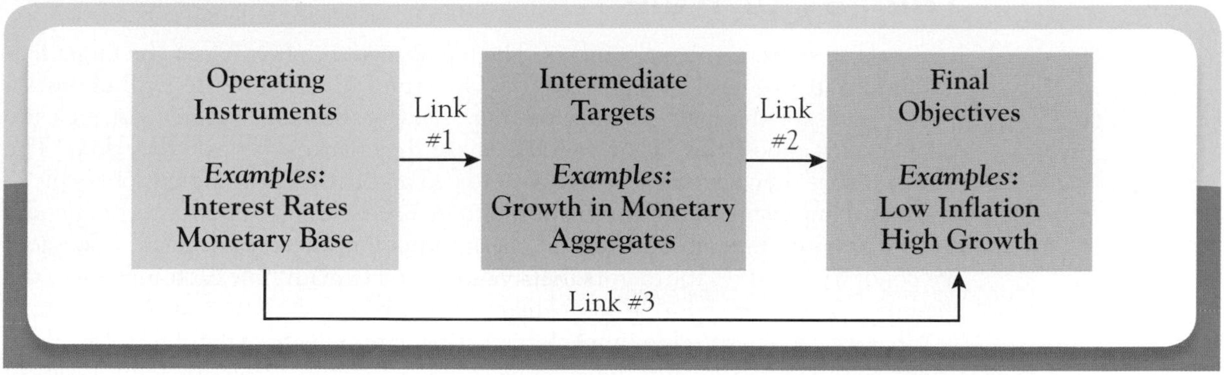

| Operating Instruments<br><br>*Examples:*<br>Interest Rates<br>Monetary Base | Link #1 → | Intermediate Targets<br><br>*Examples:*<br>Growth in Monetary Aggregates | Link #2 → | Final Objectives<br><br>*Examples:*<br>Low Inflation<br>High Growth |

Link #3

bank can control the size of its balance sheet, for instance. It can choose to use this power to control the monetary base if it wishes, or to control the interest rate in the market for reserves, as the FOMC does. These are the operating instruments.

Central bankers use the term **intermediate targets** to refer to instruments that are not directly under their control but lie instead somewhere between their policymaking tools and their objectives (see Figure 18.8). The monetary aggregates are a prime example of intermediate targets. The idea behind targeting M2, for example, is that changes in the monetary base, or reserves, affect the monetary aggregates before they influence inflation or output. So in targeting M2, central bankers can more effectively meet their objectives. They don't actually care about money growth itself, in other words; it is just a useful indicator. And announcing targets for money growth that can be monitored by the public increases policymakers' accountability.

Over the last two decades of the 20th century, central bankers largely abandoned intermediate targets, having realized that they didn't make much sense. There may be something special about monetary aggregates, and it may be particularly helpful in forecasting future economic developments and in guiding policy. But then again, it may not be helpful. More important, circumstances may change in ways that make an intermediate target unworkable. Link #1, between the operating instruments and the intermediate target, may shift (this is the problem described at the end of Chapter 17) or link #2, between money growth and the final inflation and growth objectives, may change (we will discuss this in Chapter 20). If either of these happened, the central bank would need to explain why it was changing its target and it would look as if policymakers don't know what they are doing.[12] So while people still do discuss intermediate targets, it is hard to justify using them. Instead, policymakers focus on how their actions directly affect their target objectives—link #3. A recent example of this is the practice of *inflation targeting*, which is discussed in Applying the Concept.

[12]Something similar happened to the Deutsche Bundesbank at the time of German reunification in 1990. The West German government decided to exchange East German currency at a rate roughly five times the black market exchange rate. The result was a huge increase in the quantity of money circulating in the reunified nation. This created a problem for the German central bank. For 20 years or so, policymakers had kept inflation under control with a very public policy focused on restraining money growth. Now money growth had exploded for political reasons, and there was nothing they could do about it. They had missed their targets for reasons outside their control and were forced to make excuses.

# A Guide to Central Bank Interest Rates: The Taylor Rule

Interest-rate setting is about numbers. The members of the FOMC set the target federal funds rate at 3 or 4 or 5 percent; the Governing Council of the ECB chooses a specific level for the main refinancing rate. These policymakers don't just pick the number, they choose the day on which to make the changes. How do they do it? The answer is that they have large staffs—at the Fed and the ECB, hundreds of people—who distill huge amounts of information into manageable sets of policy recommendations. Committee members digest all the information, meet, and reach a decision. We could try to list all the factors they consider and explain how each influences the committee's decision, but that would take another book.

What we can do is study a simple formula that approximates what the FOMC does. Called the **Taylor rule** after the economist who created it, Professor John Taylor of Stanford University, it tracks the actual behavior of the target federal funds rate and relates it to the real interest rate, inflation, and output.[13] The formula is

$$\text{Target fed funds rate} = 2 + \text{Current inflation} + \tfrac{1}{2}(\text{Inflation gap}) + \tfrac{1}{2}(\text{Output gap}) \quad (1)$$

This expression assumes a long-term real interest rate of 2 percent, which is added to current inflation, the inflation gap, and the output gap. The inflation gap is current inflation minus an inflation target, both measured as percentages; the output gap is current GDP minus its potential level—that is, the percentage deviation of current output from potential output. (As Chapter 21 discusses in detail, potential output is what the economy is capable of producing when its resources are being used at normal rates.) When inflation exceeds the target level, the inflation gap is positive; when current output is above potential output, the output gap is positive.

The Taylor rule says that the target federal funds rate should be set equal to the current level of inflation plus a 2 percent real interest rate, plus a factor related to the deviation of inflation and output from their target levels. For example, if inflation is currently 3 percent, the target rate is 2 percent, and GDP equals its potential level so there is no output gap, then the target federal funds rate should be set at $2 + 3 + \tfrac{1}{2} = 5\tfrac{1}{2}$ percent.

This rule makes intuitive sense: When inflation rises above its target level, the response is to raise interest rates; when output falls below the target level, the response is to lower interest rates. If inflation is currently on target and there is no output gap (current GDP equals potential GDP), then the target federal funds rate should be set at its neutral rate of target inflation plus 2.

The Taylor rule has some interesting properties. Consider what happens if inflation rises by 1 percentage point, from 2 percent to 3 percent, and the inflation target is 2 percent (assume that everything else remains the same). What happens to the target federal funds rate? The increase in inflation affects two terms in the Taylor rule, current inflation and the inflation gap. Because the inflation target doesn't change, both these terms rise 1 percentage point. The increase in current inflation feeds one for one into the target federal funds rate, but the increase in the inflation gap is halved. *A 1 percentage point increase in the inflation rate raises the target federal funds rate 1½ percentage points.*

---

[13]The Taylor rule first appeared in "Discretion versus Policy Rules in Practice," *Carnegie-Rochester Conference Series on Public Policy* 39 (1993), pp. 195–214.

Significantly, the Taylor rule tells us that for each percentage point increase in inflation, the real interest rate, which is equal to the nominal interest rate minus expected inflation, goes up half a percentage point. Because economic decisions depend on the real interest rate, this means that higher inflation leads policymakers to raise the inflation-adjusted cost of borrowing, thereby slowing the economy and ultimately reducing inflation. If central banks failed to do this, if they allowed the real interest rate to fall following an increase in inflation, the result would be further increases in production and further increases in inflation.

The Taylor rule also states that for each percentage point output is above potential—that is, for each percentage point in the output gap—interest rates will go up half a percentage point.

The fractions that precede the terms for the inflation and output gaps—the halves in equation (1)—depend both on how sensitive the economy is to interest-rate changes and on the preferences of central bankers. The more central bankers care about inflation, the bigger the multiplier for the inflation gap and the lower the multiplier for the output gap. It is not unusual for central banks to raise the target interest rate by twice the increase in inflation while virtually ignoring the output gap.

Returning to the United States, we see that implementing the Taylor rule requires four inputs: (1) the constant term, set at 2 in equation (1); (2) a measure of inflation; (3) a measure of the inflation gap; and (4) a measure of the output gap. The constant is a measure of the long-term risk-free real interest rate, which is about 1 percentage point below the economy's growth rate. Because the U.S. economy has been growing at a rate of about 3 percent per year, we set this term at 2. But the number can and does change.

Next we need to add measures of current inflation and the inflation gap. What index should we use? While the CPI is widely known, economists and central bankers believe that the personal consumption expenditure (PCE) index is a more accurate measure of inflation. The PCE index comes from the national income accounts and is based on the "C" in "Y = C + I + G + X − M." As for the inflation target to use in measuring the inflation gap, we will follow Taylor and use 2 percent, so the neutral target federal funds rate is 4 percent (2 plus 2). For the output gap, the natural choice is the percentage by which GDP deviates from a measure of its trend, or potential.

Figure 18.9 (see page 474) plots the FOMC's actual target federal funds rate, together with the rate predicted by the Taylor rule. The result is striking: The two lines are reasonably close to each other. The FOMC changed the target federal funds rate when the Taylor rule predicted it should. While the rule didn't match policy exactly, it did predict what policymakers would do in a general way. And what is really remarkable is that Professor Taylor created his rule around 1992, at the beginning of the period shown in the graph.

Before we get carried away and replace the FOMC with an equation, or begin betting in the financial markets based on the Taylor rule's predictions, we should recognize some caveats. First, at times the target rate does deviate from the Taylor rule, and with good reason. The Taylor rule is too simple to take account of sudden threats to financial stability, such as the terrorist attacks of September 11, 2001.

# IN THE NEWS
## Fed May Take Chance End to Debt Purchases Won't Hurt Housing

Bloomberg.com

### By Steve Matthews and Vivien Lou Chen

January 27, 2010

The Federal Reserve may take a chance the housing market can stage a comeback without its support by announcing today it will stick to the plan to end a $1.25 trillion program of mortgage-debt purchases in March.

Fed Chairman Ben S. Bernanke and other policy makers meet after the sixth straight monthly gain in home prices in November added to signs housing is stabilizing. With financial markets rebounding, the central bank has said it plans to end emergency aid to bond dealers and money markets by Feb. 1.

The Fed will probably acknowledge growth accelerated last quarter while noting that tight credit and unemployment near a 26-year high still pose risks to the recovery. Officials are likely to maintain a pledge to keep interest rates low for "an extended period" as they look for evidence of a sustained expansion that will create jobs without raising inflation expectations, former Fed governor Lyle Gramley said.

"The Fed wants to sit still until the smoke clears," said Gramley, a senior economic adviser to Potomac Research Group. "To change the 'extended period' language would send a signal to markets that a tightening is not far off, and I don't think the Fed wants to do that," Gramley said. He doesn't expect a rate increase for at least six months.

Regional Fed presidents have differed over whether to continue buying mortgage-backed securities after March 31, with James Bullard of St. Louis saying the central bank should create such an option and Philadelphia's Charles Plosser saying the purchases should end as scheduled.

The Fed plans to buy $1.25 trillion of mortgage-backed securities sold by government-backed, housing-finance firms Fannie Mae, Freddie Mac and federal agency Ginnie Mae, along with $175 billion of corporate debt issued by Fannie, Freddie and the government-chartered Federal Home Loan Banks. During the current meeting "the real discussion will be when they end the MBS program," said former Atlanta

---

Indeed, we can learn from the periods in which the policy rate deviates from the Taylor rule. For example, why did the FOMC set the federal funds rate target below the Taylor rule in 1992–1993, 2002–2005, and 2008–2009 (see Figure 18.9)? The answer is that these periods were characterized by at least one of two factors: (1) unusually stringent conditions across an array of financial markets or (2) deflationary worries that arose as nominal interest rates approached their zero bound.

When financial conditions are much stronger or much weaker than usual, policymakers seeking to stabilize the economy may set an interest rate target that differs substantially from the Taylor rule. We can think of financial conditions as a measure that combines the state of a broad array of markets, including both the prices of assets and the volume of transactions in these assets. Euphoric conditions are often associated both with high prices and volumes in asset trading and with easy access to credit, while depressed conditions are linked with the opposite states (see Chapter 8

Fed research director Robert Eisenbeis, using the acronym for mortgage-backed securities.

"You don't want to risk cutting off the recovery in housing by essentially pulling the rug from under it."

The Fed's purchases have helped reduce mortgage rates by a range of a 25 basis points to 75 basis points, Boston Fed President Eric Rosengren said through a spokesman. A basis point is 0.01 percentage point. Rates won't increase by an equal amount after the end of purchases because the Fed will continue to hold a large portfolio of mortgage-backed securities, Rosengren said.

Eisenbeis disagreed, saying mortgage rates could rise by 75 basis points to 100 basis points.

The rate for 30-year fixed U.S. home loans, which reached a record low of 4.71 percent last month, was 4.99 percent in the week ended Jan. 21, according to mortgage finance company Freddie Mac.

U.S. central bankers, after reducing the main interest rate to a range from zero to 0.25 percent, switched last year to asset purchases and credit programs as the primary policy tools. The Fed has expanded its balance sheet to $2.24 trillion at the end of 2009 from $879 billion at the start of 2007. Since March, the FOMC has said "exceptionally low" rates are likely warranted for "an extended period."

Policy makers will likely note continued "slack" in labor markets following last month's unexpected loss of 85,000 jobs. The FOMC projects the unemployment rate will be between 9.3 percent and 9.7 percent in the fourth quarter of this year, according to forecasts released after its November meeting.

"It's still too early to expect a dramatic announcement with regard to the Fed's exit strategy because the economy is still finding its footing," said Alan Skrainka, chief market strategist for Edward Jones & Co. in St. Louis [. . .].

"It's a delicate balancing act," he said. "If the Fed pulls back too soon, the economy falters. If the Fed waits too long, the inflation risk grows."

### LESSONS OF THE ARTICLE

Setting monetary policy to deliver low, stable inflation and high, stable growth is never easy. However, it was particularly challenging following the financial crisis of 2007-2009, because the Fed had no prior experience with many of its unconventional policy tools. The central bank's purchase of more than $1 trillion of mortgage-backed securities was perhaps the most important example. At the time this article appeared in early 2010, many observers worried that the housing market and the economy would suffer if the FOMC were to halt buying of MBS, as planned, in March 2010, well after nationwide house prices had stopped falling. The FOMC executed its plan as scheduled.

for a discussion of asset bubbles). Although the policy target rate influences financial conditions, the link is a loose one: financial conditions can and do vary substantially, even in the absence of any changes in the policymakers' target interest rate.

Financial conditions affect policy choices because they alter prospects for private spending and for inflation. Lax or easy conditions mean that households and firms are more readily able to borrow, to spend out of wealth, and to invest. Plunging asset prices and the loss of credit work in the opposite direction. Consequently, a tightening or easing in financial conditions is a signal to policymakers about the future path of economic activity and inflation, and this affects their evaluation of appropriate levels of the interest rate and the Taylor rule.

An interesting example of this interaction arose in 2004–2006, when Federal Reserve policymakers chose to raise the target federal funds rate in an effort to moderate economic growth and inflation risks. However, from the perspective of broad financial

## Policy Duration Commitment

The simplest unconventional approach is for a central bank to make a commitment today about *future* policy target rates. For example, if policymakers believe that inflation will stay well below their objective (see Applying the Concept: Inflation Targeting on page 468), they might promise to keep their policy target rate low for an extended period. If such a *policy duration commitment* is stated to last for an indefinite period, we call it an *unconditional* commitment, because it depends only on the passage of time. Alternatively, a central bank can make a *conditional* commitment to keep interest rates low until some stated economic conditions change (say, an upturn in business activity or a rise of employment).

How do policy duration commitments influence the economy and inflation? If it works, a policy commitment will lower the long-term interest rates that affect private spending. As Chapter 7 highlights, long-term bond yields depend in part on expectations about future short-term rates, which the central bank has the power to alter. Consequently, what central bankers say about their future plans can matter greatly. However, to be effective, a policy duration commitment needs to be credible. Otherwise, long-term market interest rates may not respond as a central bank hopes.

In the past, policymakers used several mechanisms to make their commitments about future policy credible. For example, from the late 1930s until 1951, the Fed purchased long-term Treasury bonds with the objective of capping their interest rates at an artificially low level.[16] However, exiting from such intervention can be disruptive because investors face the prospect of immediate capital losses when yields rise. Consequently, if bondholders fear that the central bank will stop intervening, they may sell immediately. In such circumstances, the only way to sustain the cap on long-term interest rates would be for the central bank to buy *all* the bonds.

Today, many economists advocate policy frameworks like inflation targeting that are designed to enhance the credibility of a duration commitment. If a central bank targets inflation, a commitment to keep interest rates low will be most credible precisely when inflation is expected to stay below target for some time.

How has the Federal Reserve used policy duration commitments? In 2002–2004, the FOMC believed that inflation would sink undesirably low and even worried about the possibility of deflation. The FOMC issued an unconditional commitment in which it indicated that its target funds rate would stay low for the "foreseeable future" or for a "considerable period." And when the Fed began to tighten in 2004, it assured markets that the withdrawal of accommodation would occur at a "measured pace" to avoid fears of sharp rate hikes. However, the subsequent rise of inflation suggests that this commitment kept U.S. monetary policy too easy for too long.

In 2008, the FOMC adopted a conditional approach as the financial crisis deepened and deflation concerns resurfaced. Policymakers announced that "weak economic conditions are likely to warrant exceptionally low levels of the federal funds rate for some time."[17] The statement shows that economic conditions, rather than the passage of time, would determine how long policy rates stay low.

Although policy duration commitments can be effective, the Fed's experience suggests that they are difficult to calibrate and can have disturbing side effects. Consequently, they remain tools for extraordinary circumstances—when the conventional policy toolbox is largely empty.

[16] The 10-year Treasury bond rate remained close to 2 percent in this period.

[17] Statement of the Federal Open Market Committee, December 16, 2008. See http://www.federalreserve.gov/newsevents/press/monetary/20081216b.htm.

# Quantitative Easing

*Quantitative easing* (QE) is perhaps the most well-known mechanism to relax the monetary stance when the policy target rate is close to zero. QE occurs when the central bank expands the supply of aggregate reserves to the banking system *beyond* the level that would be needed to maintain its policy rate target. The central bank uses the proceeds from this reserve expansion to buy assets, thereby expanding its overall balance sheet. In the example in Table 18.3, the central bank adds $1 billion to commercial bank reserves held in their accounts at the Fed and acquires $1 billion in Treasury bonds.

Figure 18.10 illustrates the impact of QE on supply and demand in the federal funds market. At a market federal funds rate of zero, an addition to aggregate reserves no longer reduces the funds rate. The reason is that banks will hold cash (which pays zero interest) rather than lend in the federal funds market at a rate below zero. As a result, the Fed can add limitlessly to reserves—and to the assets on its balance sheet—without depressing the market federal funds rate below zero. The amount of QE is the volume of reserves in excess of the level needed to keep the policy rate at its target, in this case zero. In Figure 18.10, it is the gap between points A and B.

A simple thought experiment shows that QE *can* shape the path of economic growth and inflation, even if the financial system is impaired. Imagine that the central bank expands reserves to the point where it purchases *all* of the goods and services produced in the economy. For QE to be ineffective, it would imply that the central bank could purchase the entire economy without influencing the level of prices! This nonsensical outcome means that QE, applied with sufficient vigor, can alter economic and inflation prospects.

Nonetheless, it is difficult to predict the effects of QE. Limited experience means that we have little data on which to base such a forecast. Moreover, the mechanism by which QE affects economic prospects is not clear. When interest rates are at zero, banks are indifferent between holding cash, reserve deposits at the central bank, and short-term government debt. All of these assets are riskless, so an

### Table 18.3   How Quantitative Easing Affects the Central Bank Balance Sheet

| Assets | Liabilities |
| --- | --- |
| Treasury bonds (+$1 billion) | Reserves (+$1 billion) |

### Figure 18.10   Quantitative Easing

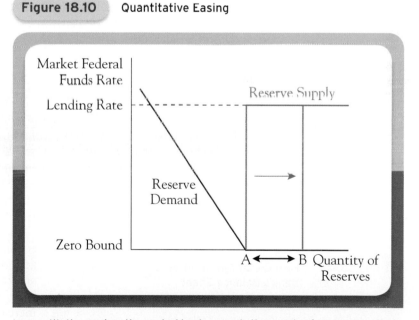

In quantitative easing, the central bank expands the supply of reserves so that the vertical portion of the supply curve lies to the right of the level needed to keep the market funds rate at its target (in this case, zero). The market federal funds rate remains at zero because banks have no better alternative than holding more reserves. The amount of QE is the volume of reserves beyond the level needed to keep the market funds rate at its target (the gap between points A and B).

increase in the supply of reserves (QE) may simply lead banks to hold more of them rather than provide additional loans to households and firms.

Such claims of QE's ineffectiveness were common when the Bank of Japan undertook the practice in the late 1990s. Japanese banks accumulated massive excess reserves, but lending continued to decline. We can see why this happened. After sustaining devastating losses, banks sought to rebuild their financial positions by *deleveraging*—that is, their objective was to lower the ratio of their assets to bank capital (recall Chapter 3, Lessons from the Crisis: Leverage).

How, then, might QE succeed (short of a central bank acquiring a large portion of the goods and services in an economy to alter the price level)? One mechanism is that it can add credibility to a policymaker's promise to keep interest rates low. Suppose that investors believe that a central bank will keep its policy rate at the zero floor until after it will have exited from QE. Then, announcements of an expansion of aggregate reserves (QE) could lower bond yields by extending the time horizon over which bondholders expect a zero policy rate. In this way, QE may reinforce the impact of a policy duration commitment.

A key problem with QE is that central banks do not know how much is needed to be effective. They can only calibrate the appropriate level of reserves by experimentation. As the central bank boosts aggregate reserves (and expands its balance sheet), it can observe the impact on financial conditions and the economy. Naturally, this lack of predictability makes policymakers uncomfortable because the experiment might result in an undesirable pickup of inflation. Nevertheless, when conventional policy tools have been exhausted, QE can be a powerful tool for central bankers to prevent a sustained deflation.

How has the Federal Reserve used QE? Its first and only application since the Great Depression occurred after the Lehman failure in September 2008 (see how the Fed's balance sheet jumped in Figure 18.1). Partly as a result, policymakers remain highly uncertain about the appropriate dosage of QE. They also lack experience in exiting from QE.

## Credit Easing

In contrast to quantitative easing, which increases the *size* of the central bank's balance sheet, *credit easing* (CE) shifts the *composition* of the balance sheet away from risk-free assets and toward risky assets. Typically, these risky assets involve credit risk in which the borrower can default.

A simple example of CE would be for the central bank to sell short-term U.S. Treasury bills and buy mortgage-backed securities (MBS, see page 49) of similar maturity. As seen in Table 18.4, this shift leaves the size of the balance sheet unchanged. Only the mix of default-free and credit-risk assets is altered.

How does CE alter the outlook for the economy and inflation? The central bank's actions can influence both the *cost* and *availability* of credit. When the central bank acquires an asset, such as MBS, it increases the overall demand for the asset. Increased demand tends to boost its price while driving its yield down. In the absence of private demand for the risky asset, the central bank's purchase makes credit available where none existed.

**Table 18.4**  How Credit Easing Affects the Central Bank's Balance Sheet

| Assets | Liabilities |
|---|---|
| 3-month Treasury bills (−$1 billion) | |
| Mortgage-backed securities (+$1 billion) | |

The impact of CE is likely to be greater in thin, illiquid markets. Under such conditions, even small interventions can have a magnified effect on market prices. The impact of CE is also likely to be larger the bigger the difference between the yield on the asset that the central bank buys and the yield on the asset that the central bank sells. Assets with similar yields and risk characteristics are usually *close substitutes*. Assets with different risk characteristics and yields are less substitutable. By altering the relative supply of such assets to private investors, CE narrows their interest-rate differences.

The Federal Reserve's shift to CE in the financial crisis was unprecedented. In Figure 18.1, assets with default risk (those other than the assets labeled "Traditional security holdings" and "Long-term Treasury purchases") became the largest component of the Fed's balance sheet. Aside from direct lending to financial institutions, the boldest example of CE during the crisis was the Fed's acquisition of more than $1 trillion of MBS. The goal was to lower mortgage yields and support the housing market.

Like QE, CE is significantly more unwieldy for central bankers than conventional interest-rate policy. A central bank cannot reliably anticipate the impact of CE on the cost of credit. And CE poses concerns that need not arise with QE. For example, like fiscal policy, CE favors some users of credit over others. The special access that the Fed provided to issuers of commercial paper during the crisis is one example. In normal times, using conventional policy techniques, a central bank typically avoids such direct allocation of credit, promoting market competition rather than picking winners. CE purposely deviates from such *asset neutrality* in order to influence relative prices.

Exiting from CE probably also is more difficult than unwinding QE. Risky assets are generally harder to sell—that is, they are less liquid—than Treasuries, so the central bank may not be able to get rid of them exactly when it wants. In addition, political influences can become important if powerful users of credit and their government representatives seek to hinder the Fed from selling specific assets for fear of raising the costs of a particular class of borrowers.

## Making an Effective Exit

When central banks pursue conventional interest-rate targets, officials think about the policy choices they face every six to eight weeks. Deliberations are continuous, forming a *strategy* that influences expectations about the future path of their instrument and their objective. Decisions are not a series of one-time, unrelated choices. We can think of central bankers setting interest rates as participating in a complicated game—like chess—that requires them to make moves today while keeping in mind moves they may need to make far in the future.

The introduction of and exit from unconventional policies—such as duration commitments, quantitative easing, and credit easing—also require looking into the future. Without a consistent and credible approach, policymakers may be unable to keep inflation expectations close to their inflation objective. And, if they fail, unstable inflation expectations could lead to broader economic instability.

Compared with conventional policy, exiting from QE and CE poses additional obstacles that appear technical but have important implications. The key question is whether a central bank that wishes to raise interest rates in order to tighten policy conditions will be able to do so as quickly as desired. With conventional policy, the answer is yes. In the case of QE and CE, the answer depends on the size and composition of the central bank's balance sheet and on the toolset available to the policymakers.

With conventional policy, a central bank that wishes to hike the policy rate can do so by modestly trimming the aggregate reserves that it supplies to the banking system.

A central bank may hold enough short-term risk-free assets (such as Treasury bills) to reduce the supply of reserves merely by allowing some of these assets to mature. If necessary, the authorities also could sell a portion of these assets, which are among the most liquid.

What happens when QE and CE have vastly expanded the amount of reserves and assets on the central bank's balance sheet? The answer is that the central bank may need to sell a large volume of assets to reduce reserve supply sufficiently to raise the policy rate target. But QE and CE assets are typically more difficult to sell (less liquid) than Treasury bills. Moreover, the value of any CE assets that default will plunge. In these circumstances, a central bank may be unable to sell assets and withdraw reserves from the banking system rapidly enough to hike the policy interest rate when it desires. So what can authorities do?

Following the financial crisis of 2007–2009, many people worried that the swollen balance sheets of the Fed and other central banks would lead to runaway inflation. Everybody knows that a timely exit from QE and CE is necessary to keep inflation low. But will it be possible?

The answer is yes. In fact, central banks like the Fed have several policy options that allow them to tighten without having to sell their assets. The most important one is that policymakers can employ a conventional tool in an unconventional way: namely, they can raise the deposit rate that the central bank pays on reserves. Figure 18.11 shows an example in which the Fed raises its deposit rate from zero to a new positive rate $X$. The deposit rate sets a floor for the market federal funds rate, even if the Fed does not reduce its supply of reserves. The reason is that, once the market funds rate falls to the deposit rate, banks have no better alternative than to hold additional reserves on deposit at the central bank. Their reserve demand shifts from $RD_0$

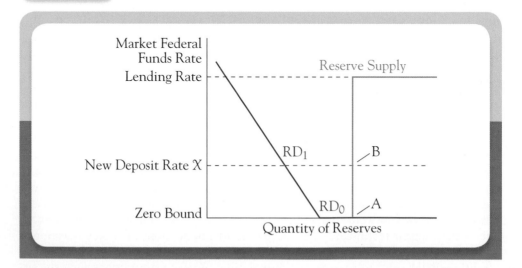

**Figure 18.11**    Exiting Quantitative Easing by Hiking the Deposit Rate

By hiking the deposit rate from zero to $X$, the central bank changes reserve demand from $RD_0$ to $RD_1$. $RD_1$ turns flat at the new deposit rate $X$ (dashed red line), because banks have no better alternative to holding reserves when the market funds rate falls to $X$. By hiking the deposit rate, the central bank raises the floor for the market funds rate without reducing the supply of reserves. The equilibrium in reserve supply and demand moves from point A to point B.

# YOUR FINANCIAL WORLD
## Economic History Is Constantly Changing

The publication of new economic growth data makes head-lines. Every three months, the Department of Commerce's Bureau of Economic Analysis publishes information on GDP for the preceding quarter. So at the end of April, we get the first estimate of growth for January through March, and news reporters trumpet it. Such attention would make sense except for the fact that the data are then revised numerous times. Only the initial estimates come out in April; in May, June, and July, they are revised as government statisticians slowly accumulate more in-formation about what actually happened. And every July for the next three years they are revised again. By July 2005, GDP for the first quarter of 2002 had been revised six times! Every five years after that, the data are revised yet again as new surveys of the population and business activity become available.

These revisions would be irrelevant if they were small, but they are not. An example will show how large the change can be. Figure 18.12 plots the progression of es-timates of GDP growth for the third quarter of 1990, the

trough of a mild recession.* The initial estimate, published in October 1990, suggested that the economy had grown +1.8 percent. The economy had been doing poorly, so this news was welcome. But as the data were revised, the story changed. Growth estimates dropped to −1.9 percent for a while, finally settling at about zero percent in 2009.

What this means is that history is constantly changing. Our view of what really happened in the economy must be adjusted regularly. So when you see a headline announcing the publication of data on recent growth in GDP, remem-ber that today's figure is just a rough estimate. Five years or more will pass before economists know what actually happened.

*These data come from a real-time database maintained by the Federal Reserve Bank of Philadelphia. For a description of the data, see Dean Croushore and Tom Stark, "A Funny Thing Hap-pened on the Way to the Data Bank: A Real-Time Data Set for Macroeconomists," *Business Review* of the Federal Reserve Bank of Philadelphia, September/October 2000, pp. 15–27.

**Figure 18.12** Revisions to Third-Quarter 1990 GDP Growth

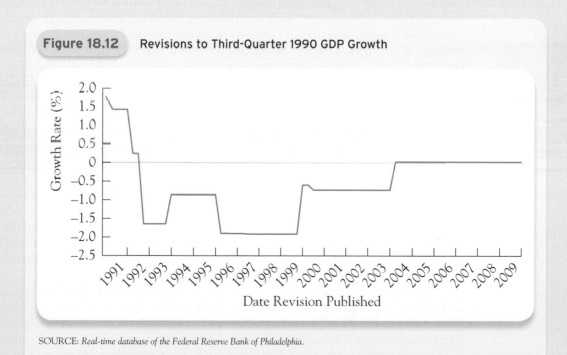

SOURCE: *Real-time database of the Federal Reserve Bank of Philadelphia.*

to $RD_1$ in the figure, moving the equilibrium of reserve demand and supply from point A to point B.

So, by hiking the deposit rate, the Fed can raise the target federal funds rate without reducing the level of reserve supply or changing the composition of its balance sheet! Paying interest on reserves allows a central bank to use two powerful policy tools independently of one another: (1) it can adjust the target rate for interbank loans without changing the size or composition of its balance sheet, and (2) it can adjust the size and composition of its balance sheet without changing the target rate for interbank loans.

This flexibility means that the central bank can change its balance sheet in a fashion consistent with financial stability while keeping inflation under control. Specifically, if they wish to hike the target interest rate, policymakers holding large quantities of illiquid assets can avoid a fire sale by simply raising the deposit rate that they pay on reserves. Central bankers are unlikely to acquire illiquid assets except in extreme circumstances, but their toolbox allows them to do it without sacrificing inflation credibility—provided, that is, that they can adjust the rate that they pay on reserves (the deposit rate) when necessary. Today, leading central banks like the Fed and the ECB have this authority and use it.

# Concluding Remarks

In truth, central bankers have a nearly impossible job. They are supposed to stabilize the economy and financial system at the same time that they provide services to commercial banks and the government. To perform this task, we give them control over their own balance sheet, allowing them to buy and sell securities in the financial markets and make loans to banks. As we know, monopolists can choose between controlling the quantity of the product they sell or the price at which they sell it. Because the central bank is the monopoly supplier of currency and reserves, policymakers can control either the quantity or the price. In normal times, they choose to control the price, which is an interest rate. Because movements in interest rates affect the entire economic system, control over interest rates usually gives monetary policymakers the leverage they need to stabilize inflation rates, growth rates, and the financial system. As we will see in detail in Part V, higher interest rates slow inflation and growth by reducing the availability of credit; lower interest rates stimulate economic activity by making credit cheaper and easier to get.

Over the years, central bankers have learned from their mistakes. They understand the importance of keeping the financial system running smoothly and have refined their ability to lend quickly in times of crisis. And because everyone understands the importance of keeping inflation low, we have designed our central banks to deliver price stability. The outcome is that the inflation rate is lower now than it was from 1970 to 1995.

Today we have a set of principles that tells us how central banks should be designed and how they should use interest rates to stabilize their economy. But central bankers cannot do the job alone. Sound monetary policy must be combined with responsible fiscal policy to build a healthy economic and financial system. Moreover, with the fading economic importance of national borders, the time has passed when even large central banks could avoid taking international conditions into account. To fill this hole in our analysis, we turn in Chapter 19 to a study of exchange rate management and the international financial system.

# Terms

conventional policy tools, 452

credit easing, 475

deposit rate, 453

discount lending, 457

discount rate, 453

ECB's Deposit Facility, 463

ECB's Marginal Lending Facility, 463

inflation targeting, 468

intermediate targets, 469

lender of last resort, 457

market federal funds rate, 454

minimum bid rate, 461

overnight cash rate, 464

policy duration commitment, 475

primary credit, 458

primary discount rate, 458

quantitative easing, 475

repurchase agreement (repo), 461

reserve requirement, 453

secondary discount rate, 459

target federal funds rate, 453

Taylor rule, 470

unconventional policy tools, 452

zero bound, 450

# Chapter Lessons

1. The Federal Reserve has four conventional monetary policy tools.
   a. The target federal funds rate is the primary instrument of monetary policy.
      i. Open market operations are used to control the federal funds rate.
      ii. The Fed forecasts the demand for reserves each day and then supplies the amount needed to meet the demand at the target rate.
   b. The discount lending rate is used to supply funds to banks, particularly during crises.
      i. The Fed sets the primary lending rate at a spread above the target federal funds rate.
      ii. In setting the primary lending rate above the target federal funds rate, the Fed is attempting to stabilize the market interest rate on overnight interbank lending. The primary lending rate is the cap for the market rate on overnight interbank loans.
      iii. The Fed also makes loans to banks in distress and to banks in need of seasonal liquidity.
   c. The deposit rate is the rate that the Fed pays on excess reserves held by banks at the central bank.
      i. The deposit rate is set at a spread below the target federal funds rate.
      ii. The deposit rate determines the floor for the market rate on overnight interbank loans.
   d. Reserve requirements are used to stabilize the demand for reserves.
      i. Banks are required to hold reserves against certain deposits.
      ii. Banks can hold either deposits at Federal Reserve Banks that earn interest or vault cash.
      iii. Reserves are accounted for in such a way that everyone knows the level of reserves required several weeks before banks must hold them.

2. The European Central Bank's primary objective is price stability.
   a. The ECB provides liquidity to the banking system through weekly auctions called refinancing operations.

    b. The minimum bid rate on the main refinancing operations, also known as the target refinancing rate, is the target interest rate controlled by the Governing Council.

    c. The ECB allows banks to borrow from the marginal lending facility at an interest rate that is set above the target refinancing rate.

    d. Banks with excess reserves can deposit them at national central banks and receive interest at a spread below the target refinancing rate.

    e. European banks are required to hold reserves; they receive an interest rate on their balances that is equal to the average of the rate in recent refinancing operations.

3. Monetary policymakers use several tools to meet their objectives.
    a. The best tools are observable, controllable, and tightly linked to objectives.
    b. Short-term interest rates are the primary tools for monetary policymaking.
    c. Modern central banks do not use intermediate targets like money growth.

4. The Taylor rule is a simple equation that describes movements in the federal funds target rate. It suggests that
    a. When inflation rises, the FOMC raises the target interest rate by 1½ times the increase.
    b. When output rises above potential by 1 percent, the FOMC raises the target interest rate half a percentage point.

5. Unconventional monetary policy can supplement conventional policy when a zero policy rate is not low enough to stabilize the economy or when an impaired financial system prevents conventional interest-rate policy from working. The three principal unconventional tools of the central bank are:
    a. Policy duration commitment: promising to keep rates low in the future.
    b. Quantitative easing: supplying aggregate reserves beyond the quantity needed to lower the policy rate to zero.
    c. Credit easing: changing the mix of assets at the central bank to alter their relative prices.

6. Unconventional monetary policy is unpredictable and potentially disruptive, so it is used only in those extraordinary circumstances when the conventional toolkit is insufficient to stabilize the economy. One conventional policy tool—the payment of interest on reserves—can help a central bank exit smoothly from unconventional monetary policy.

## Conceptual Problems

1. Explain how the Federal Reserve limits deviations of the market federal funds rate from its target through use of the "corridor" system.

2. Suppose the demand for reserves became less stable. How would monetary policy be affected?

3. From 1979 to 1982, the FOMC used money growth as an intermediate target. To do so, the committee instructed the Open Market Trading Desk to target the level of reserves in the banking system. What was the justification for doing so? Explain why the result was unstable interest rates. Would you advocate a return to reserve targeting? Why or why not?

4. The Web site of the Federal Reserve Bank of New York contains information on the target federal funds rate. Find the data and describe the changes that have occurred since June 2006. Comparing recent developments with earlier patterns in the target, what strikes you as unusual?

5. Go to the Web site of the Federal Reserve Board at www.federalreserve.gov and find the section describing monetary policy tools. Which unconventional tools employed during the financial crisis of 2007–2009 has the Fed stopped using? What do you think determined the order in which various facilities were shut down? Which, if any, of the tools still remain in operation?

6.* Use your knowledge of the problems associated with asymmetric information to explain why, prior to the change in the Federal Reserve's discount lending facility in 2002, banks were extremely unlikely to borrow from the facility despite funds being available at a rate below the target federal funds rate.

7. The European Central Bank's Web site contains information on the interest rates under the bank's control. At what levels are the interest rates now and when did they last change? At the press conference held at the time of the last change, how did the Governing Council justify the action?

8. The ECB pays a market-based interest rate on required reserves and a lower rate on excess reserves. Explain why the system is structured this way.

9.* Explain why both the Federal Reserve and the ECB use an overnight interest rate rather than a longer-term interest rate as their policy tool.

10.* Outline and compare the ways in which the Federal Reserve and the ECB added to or adjusted their monetary policy tools in response to the financial crisis of 2007–2009.

11. How might the Federal Reserve exit from the unconventional policies it employed during the financial crisis of 2007–2009 without causing inflationary problems?

## Analytical Problems

12. The central bank of a country facing economic and financial market difficulties asks for your advice. The bank hit the zero bound with its policy interest rate, but it wasn't enough to stabilize the economy. Drawing on the actions taken by the Federal Reserve during the financial crisis of 2007–2009, what might you advise this central bank to do?

13. Suppose the demand for reserves is stable. Use a graph of the Market for Bank Reserves to show how the Open Market Trading Desk would implement a decision by the FOMC to raise the target federal funds rate. You should assume that the discount and deposit rates are adjusted so that the spreads between them and the target federal funds rate are maintained.

14. Suppose, one morning, the Open Market Trading Desk drastically underestimates the demand for reserves when deciding the quantity of reserves to supply to the market. Use the graph of the Market for Bank Reserves to show why the

*Indicates more difficult problems

market federal funds rate will not exceed the discount rate regardless of how large the gap between estimated and actual reserve demand.

15. Consider a situation where reserve requirements were binding and the Federal Reserve decided to reduce the requirements. Use the graph of the Market for Bank Reserves to illustrate how the Open Market Trading Desk would react to this change assuming the demand for excess reserves remains unchanged.

16. Suppose the Federal Reserve did not pay interest on excess reserves. How would the reserve demand curve differ from that in Figure 18.2?

17. Using a graph for overnight interbank loans in Europe, show how, in early 2010, the overnight interbank rate could not have not fallen more than 75 basis points below the minimum bid rate regardless of how much demand for reserves fell.

18.* Suppose ECB officials ask your opinion about their operational framework for monetary policy. You respond by commenting on their success at keeping short-term interest rates close to target but also express concern about the complexity of their process for managing the supply of reserves. What specific changes would you suggest the ECB should make to its system in the future?

19. Use the following Taylor rule to calculate what would happen to the real interest rate if inflation increased by 3 percentage points.

Target federal funds rate $= 2 +$ Current inflation $+ \frac{1}{2}$(Inflation gap) $+ \frac{1}{2}$(Output gap)

20.* The Taylor rule in question 19 is thought to be a reasonably good description of policy behavior in the United States in the absence of unusual financial market conditions or deflationary worries. Taking into account what you know about the policy goals of the ECB and that the average growth rate tends to be lower in Europe than in the United States, how would you amend the Taylor rule to better approximate policymaking behavior by the ECB?

# Chapter 23

## Modern Monetary Policy and the Challenges Facing Central Bankers

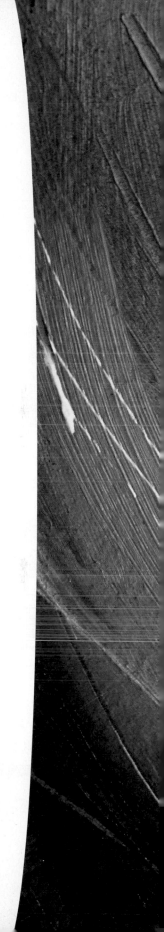

As we saw earlier, the financial crisis of 2007–2009 and the recession it triggered were by far the most widespread and costly since the Great Depression. And, although the financial disruptions began in the United States, they spread to almost all corners of the global economy. Indeed, the peak-to-trough decline of GDP was greater in many countries than in the United States (see Panel A of Figure 23.1).

The response of monetary policymakers was likewise unprecedented. Interbank lending rates—the target of central bank policy—plunged toward zero in the United States, Japan, and much of Europe (see Panel B of Figure 23.1). And many central banks deployed unconventional monetary policy tools—including policy duration commitments, quantitative easing, and credit easing—to compensate for the collapse of intermediation and the fragility of financial markets. Although monetary policies failed to prevent the crisis, they nevertheless helped to contain it. Around mid-2009, the worldwide plunge in GDP bottomed out, and most economies began growing again. Some, like China's, had regained strength even earlier, partly because of an extraordinary fiscal expansion.

Yet, many observers worried that the aftermath of the financial crisis would dim the economic outlook for years to come. Some of the concerns stemmed from the deterioration of fiscal conditions—a number of countries racked up record fiscal deficits and surges in government debt in reaction to the crisis. But the damage to the global financial system posed at least as big and pervasive a problem.

Deep, long recessions are typically followed by unusually sharp and long-lived economic rebounds. But the experience of previous financial crises—especially the Great Depression and the 1990s breakdown in Japan—led policymakers to worry that the rebound from the crisis of 2007–2009 would be weaker than the norm. They expected that anxious banks would make credit expensive and difficult to obtain, that investors would be cautious about buying securitized assets, and that U.S. households would prefer to save more and borrow less. Policymakers also made clear that a period of increased regulation lay ahead, which added to the hesitancy among intermediaries.

The aggregate demand and supply framework described in Chapter 21 helps us understand many sources of inflation and fluctuations in the business cycle as well as how stabilization policy works. But it does not explain why policymakers in many countries doubted that conventional monetary policy would be sufficient to counter the crisis of 2007–2009. And it does not explain their worries about the possibility of prolonged economic stagnation in the aftermath of the financial crisis. To understand these concerns, we must return to the question of *how* monetary policy affects the economy.

Chapter 17 showed that central banks influence the economy by controlling their balance sheet. Chapter 18 described how, in normal times, monetary policymakers use their balance sheet to control the interest rate banks charge each other for overnight loans. We learned that the real interest rate is the nominal interest rate minus the rate

**Figure 23.1** Economic Activity and Policy Rates in the Financial Crisis of 2007–2009

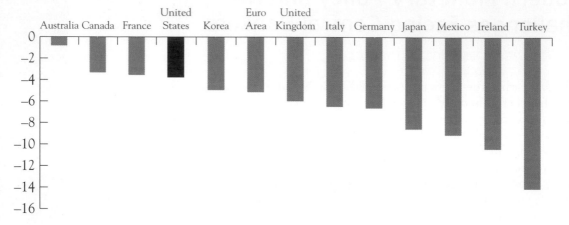

A. Peak-to-Trough Percent Change of Real GDP During Financial Crisis of 2007–2009

Note: The U.S. peak and trough occurred in fourth quarter 2007 and second quarter 2009, respectively. In the other countries, the dates differed somewhat, but the troughs occurred by third quarter 2009.

SOURCE: OECD *and authors' calculations*.

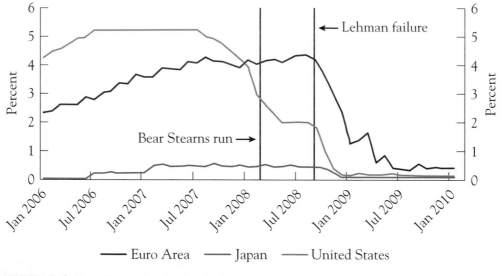

B. Overnight Interbank Lending Rates, 2006–2010

SOURCES: *Bank of Japan, European Central Bank, and Federal Reserve Board.*

of expected inflation. Because the expected rate of inflation generally changes only slowly, changing the target for the policy interest rate also changes the short-run real interest rate. In Chapter 21, we saw that the components of aggregate expenditure are sensitive to the real interest rate, so by changing the real interest rate, policymak-ers can influence real economic activity. Yet, the 2007–2009 experience (as well as that of Japan in the 1990s) suggests that conventional interest-rate policy does not always work. To see why not, we need to look at all the ways that monetary policy actions affect real economic activity—that is, all the channels through which monetary policy is transmitted.

Examining the transmission mechanism of monetary policy is the first of this chapter's two main topics. The second topic is the question of why, in the aftermath of the financial crisis of 2007–2009, monetary policy and the challenges facing central bankers are especially difficult.

# The Monetary Policy Transmission Mechanism

Any time the central bank alters the size of its balance sheet, the effects ripple through the economy, changing nearly everyone's behavior. Households adjust their spending on houses and cars. Companies rethink their decisions about how much and how fast to grow. Exchange rates change, bond and stock prices move, and banks adjust their balance sheets. In fact, we would be challenged to find a financial or economic decision that is unaffected. To fully appreciate how conventional monetary policy works, then, we need to examine the various ways in which changes in the policy-controlled interest influence the quantity of aggregate output demanded in the economy as a whole. These are referred to collectively as the channels of the **monetary policy transmission mechanism**. We will begin with the traditional **interest-rate** and **exchange-rate channels**. Next we will study the role of banks and finally the importance of stock price movements.

## The Traditional Channels: Interest Rates and Exchange Rates

Central banks, such as the Federal Reserve, the European Central Bank, and the Bank of Japan, target a very short-term (usually overnight) interest rate. In the Fed's case, for example, a change of conventional policy is a change in the target federal funds rate. And as we saw in Chapter 21, a change in the monetary policymakers' target interest rate represents a change in the real interest rate, which has a direct effect on total spending. The lower the real interest rate, the higher investment, consumption, and net exports will be.

Let's review this process. As the real interest rate falls, financing becomes less expensive, so firms become more likely to undertake investment projects and families more likely to purchase new cars. Changes in the real interest rate also affect the exchange rate. When the real interest rate falls, investor demand for U.S. assets falls with it, lowering the demand for and increasing the supply of dollars, reducing its value (see Chapter 19, Figure 19.2). That is, an easing of monetary policy—by which we mean a decrease in the target nominal interest rate, which lowers the real interest rate—leads to a depreciation of the dollar. A less valuable dollar, in turn, drives up the cost of imported goods and services, reducing imports from abroad. At the same time, however, the lower value of the dollar makes U.S. goods and services cheaper to foreigners, so they will buy more of them. Together, lower imports and higher exports mean higher net exports, or an increase in total spending.

# TOOLS OF THE TRADE

## Correlation Does Not Imply Causality

Suppose we notice that the higher the crime rate in a neighborhood, the more often police are present. Should we infer that the police are causing crime? Surely not. Nor should we conclude from the fact that hospitals are filled with doctors that doctors make people ill. A fundamental principal of sound logical reasoning is that correlation does not imply causality. The fact that two events happened together does not indicate a causal link.

In the physical sciences, where researchers can conduct controlled experiments, establishing a causal link is not a serious challenge. We know from scientific trials that antibiotic drugs really do eliminate infections. It's not just chance that the people who take them feel better. But in economics, establishing a causal relationship is much more difficult. How can we be sure that monetary policy affects real economic activity? Our theories tell us that when policymakers raise the nominal interest rate, the real interest rate goes up, depressing aggregate expenditure and lowering real economic activity. But do we have any hard-and-fast evidence of this relationship?

The answer is that we do have some evidence that higher interest rates are associated with lower levels of real growth. Look back at Figure 21.17 (page 571), and you'll see the pattern: when interest rates rise, growth falls. But does that mean that increases in the interest rate cause recessions? What if, simultaneously, an increase in oil prices depresses real growth, causing policymakers to raise the interest rate in order to head off rising inflation?

That is, what if some third factor drives up the interest rate, forcing growth down at the same time? In that case, the interest rate becomes another implication of the fundamental cause of recession, an increase in oil prices.

How can we eliminate this problem and determine the extent to which monetary policy actually causes economic fluctuations? The answer is that we need to look for clear evidence that particular monetary policy actions are unrelated to this sort of third factor. Some years ago, Christina Romer and David Romer of the University of California at Berkeley read through the records of the Federal Reserve's interest-rate decisions since 1946. They identified a series of dates on which FOMC members stated unambiguously that they were raising interest rates to combat inflation. Each of these episodes was followed by a recession. Romer and Romer argued that, because the intention in each of these instances was to fight inflation, the FOMC's actions were not the result of the level of GDP at the time. Instead, it was monetary policy actions that were the fundamental cause.* With hard work and ingenuity, economists are ultimately able to distinguish causality from correlation.

*See Christina D. Romer and David H. Romer, "Does Monetary Policy Matter? A New Test in the Spirit of Friedman and Schwartz," in O. J. Blanchard and S. Fischer, eds., *NBER Macroeconomic Annual* (Cambridge, MA: MIT Press, 1989), pp. 121–170.

INFORMATION

While these traditional channels of monetary policy transmission make sense theoretically, they present a practical problem. Though changes in monetary policy do influence firms' decisions to purchase new equipment and build new buildings, the interest-rate channel is not very powerful. That is, data suggest that the investment component of total spending isn't very sensitive to interest rates, which should not be a surprise to us. At the end of our discussion of financial intermediation in Chapter 11, we saw that information problems often make external financing too difficult and costly for firms to undertake, either directly in the financial markets or indirectly through institutions. As a result, the vast majority of investments are financed by businesses themselves, through their own funds. While a small change in the interest rate does change the cost of external financing, it doesn't have much of an effect on investment decisions.

The impact of short-term interest rates on household decisions is also rather modest. The problem is that people's decisions to purchase cars or houses depend on longer-term interest rates rather than the policymakers' short-run target rate. So household consumption decisions will change only to the extent that changing the target interest rate affects long-term interest rates. And the overall effect isn't that large.

As for the effect of monetary policy on the exchange rate, once again, theory and practice differ. In the real world, the policy-controlled interest rate is just one of many factors that shift the demand and supply for the dollar on foreign exchange markets. The rather long list, described in Chapter 10, includes a change in the riskiness of domestic investment relative to foreign investment; a change in the preference of U.S. consumers for foreign-produced goods and services; and a change in foreigners' income and wealth. The influence of these other factors may overwhelm the impact of monetary policy on the exchange rate and net exports.

Thus, after careful analysis, we must conclude that the traditional channels of monetary policy transmission aren't very powerful. Yet evidence shows that monetary policy *is* effective. When policy-controlled interest rates go up, the quantity of aggregate output demanded does go down. The dynamic aggregate demand curve slopes down. Something else must be amplifying the impact of monetary policy changes on real economic activity. Otherwise, no one would care about the central bank's periodic policy statements. To figure out what that link might be, we turn now to a discussion of two alternative transmission channels: the stock and real estate markets, and the behavior of banks.

## Bank-Lending and Balance-Sheet Channels

Four times a year the Federal Reserve conducts an opinion survey on bank-lending practices. Addressed to the senior loan officers who oversee lending policies at the 60 or so largest banks in the country, the survey contains questions about both the demand for and the supply of loans. On the demand side, the questions have to do with the quantity and quality of loan applications. On the supply side, they have to do with the relative difficulty of getting a loan, as well as the rates borrowers must pay. This survey provides important information to monetary policymakers. Without it, they would not be able to tell whether a change in the quantity of new loans granted resulted from a shift in supply or a shift in demand. Was a drop in the quantity of new loans the result of fewer applications or a tightening of credit standards? Did interest-rate spreads climb because the quality of borrowers declined or because banks became more risk averse? Policymakers at the Fed care about the answers to these questions because if banks stop making loans, some businesses can't borrow to finance their investment projects, and economic growth slows.

The fact is that banks are essential to the operation of a modern industrial economy. They direct resources from savers to investors and solve problems caused by information asymmetries. Financial intermediaries specialize in screening borrowers to ensure they are creditworthy and in monitoring loan recipients to guarantee that they use borrowed funds as they said they would. But banks are not only the hub of the financial system; they are also the conduit through which monetary policy is transmitted to the economy. When policymakers change the size of the central bank's balance sheet, their action has an immediate impact on commercial bank balance sheets because it affects the level of reserves they hold. To understand monetary policy changes completely, then, we need to look carefully at how they affect the banking system. That means we need to examine the impact of policy changes on banks and bank lending.

**Banks and Bank Lending**   For the vast majority of individuals and firms, the cost of issuing either stocks or bonds is prohibitive. These borrowers do not have access to direct capital market financing; instead, they must go to banks, which step in to reduce the information costs small borrowers face. A small business that is denied

## YOUR FINANCIAL WORLD

Don't Count on Inflation to Bail You Out

When policymakers lower interest rates, their aim is to encourage people to borrow. Central bankers know that low-interest mortgages make it possible for people to buy homes they otherwise couldn't afford. And low-interest car loans allow them to buy a new car earlier than they would otherwise. In lowering interest rates, the FOMC is counting on a surge in borrowing to drive output higher. But while the increase in debt may help the economy as a whole, it can be dangerous for some individuals. They may borrow too much and end up with more debt than they can manage.

The problem with debt is that it must be repaid. Making sure you can repay your debts means carefully calculating what you can afford—not just now but over the entire term of the loan. To avoid overextending yourself, don't borrow on the assumption that your income is going to rise rapidly. While you will typically receive annual increases in your real wage (adjusted for inflation), they are likely to be fairly modest. In fact, for the economy as a whole, pay raises tend to match the rate of productivity growth, which is usually between 2 and 3 percent. So don't be tempted into thinking that, though your budget may be tight when you take out a loan, future salary raises will remedy the problem.

The strategy of counting on salary increases to help eliminate debt amounts to counting on inflation to bail you out. It's true that inflation can be helpful to people who are in debt because it reduces the burden of repayment. But if policymakers at the Fed are doing their job, which is to keep inflation low, hoping inflation will help you pay off your loans is a strategy that is likely to backfire.

a bank loan has nowhere else to turn, so the project it wishes to undertake goes unfunded. When banks stop lending, then, a large class of borrowers simply can't obtain financing. Thus, bank lending is an important channel through which monetary policy affects the economy.[1] By altering the supply of funds to the banking system, policymakers can affect banks' ability and willingness to lend. This policy mechanism is referred to as the **bank-lending channel** of monetary policy transmission.

To see how the banking-lending channel works, think about the immediate consequences of an open market purchase (see Figure 17.2 on page 430). Recall that an open market operation involves an exchange of securities for reserves between the banking system and the central bank. When the central bank purchases securities from commercial banks, it pays for them with reserves. So after an open market purchase, banks have fewer securities and more reserves that usually bear lower interest. Unless bank managers do something, their revenues will fall. The natural reaction of the banks is to lend the new funds. These new loans work their way through the banking system through the process of multiple deposit creation, increasing the supply of loans throughout the economy. (Take a look back at the section on the deposit expansion multiplier in Chapter 17, pages 433 to 439.) In short, an open market purchase has a direct impact on the supply of loans, increasing their availability to those who depend on banks for financing.

Monetary policymakers are not the only people who can influence bank-lending practices. Financial regulators can, too. Changes in financial regulations, such as an increase or decrease in the amount of capital banks are required to hold when they make certain types of loans, will have an impact on the amount of bank lending as well. In 1980, for example, President Jimmy Carter authorized the Federal Reserve to impose a series of credit controls in an attempt to reduce bank lending and, with it,

[1]Studies of how and why monetary policy is transmitted through bank lending and balance sheets include Ben Bernanke and Mark Gertler, "Inside the Black Box: The Credit Channel of Monetary Policy Transmission," *Journal of Economic Perspectives* 9 (Fall 1995), pp. 27–45.

| Figure 23.2 | Survey Measures of Changing Credit Conditions by Firm Size |

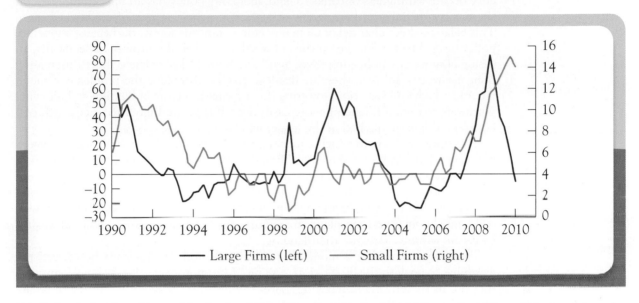

Note: For large firms, credit conditions are tightening when the figure is above zero and easing when it is below zero. For small firms, a higher figure indicates that the net share of firms concerned about credit availability is greater than before.

SOURCES: *For large businesses, Federal Reserve Board's survey of senior loan officers at selected banks; for small businesses, survey of firms by the National Federation of Independent Business. Permission to use data from the National Federation of Independent Business.*

the level of output and inflation. A mild recession followed. In the early 1990s, the economy failed to make a strong recovery from the recession after the first Gulf War. Careful examination of the historical record suggests that the disappointing economic performance was a direct consequence of a slowdown in bank lending. At the time, bank balance sheets were very weak, having been eroded by large loan losses during the banking crises of the 1980s. When an increase in capital requirements was added to the banks' already heavy burden, the result was a reduction in lending.

Figure 23.2 plots two surveys of how credit conditions for large and small nonfarm businesses vary over time. One line shows the net share of banks tightening standards for loans to large firms (at least $50 million in annual sales); the other shows the share of small firms that view credit as harder to obtain (than three months earlier) minus the share that view credit as easier to obtain. In both cases, credit conditions typically tighten in recessions and ease in booms. Note, however, that small firms— which depend more on bank loans than large firms—sometimes face tight credit conditions even in economic recoveries.[2] The figure shows that happening in 1992 and again in the aftermath of the financial crisis of 2007–2009. A cutback in lending to creditworthy small firms that want to expand or to qualified households that wish to buy a home creates "financial headwinds" that limit the pace of national economic growth during recovery. This is a key reason policymakers worry that the recovery from a recession caused by a financial crisis may be weaker than the recovery from a recession caused by other factors.

---

[2]Small firms are critical to private, nonfarm U.S. economic activity and employment: they account for about half of output and generate up to 80 percent of net new jobs each year (see Traci L. Mach and John D. Wolken, "Financial Services Used by Small Businesses: Evidence from the 2003 Survey of Small Business Finances," *Federal Reserve Bulletin*, October 2006, pp. A167–A195).

### Firms' Balance Sheets and Household Net Worth

Besides its influence on the willingness of banks to lend, monetary policy has an important effect on the creditworthiness of borrowers—or at least on their perceived creditworthiness. This **balance-sheet channel** of monetary policy transmission works because monetary policy has a direct influence on the net worth of potential borrowers. Specifically, an easing of monetary policy improves firms' and households' balance sheets, increasing their net worth. In turn, these increases in net worth reduce the problems of moral hazard and adverse selection, lowering the information costs of lending and allowing borrowers to obtain financing more easily. Recall that the higher the net worth of a borrower, the more likely that the lender will be repaid.

There are two ways in which a monetary policy expansion can improve borrowers' net worth. First, as we have already discussed, an expansionary policy drives up asset prices, increasing the value of firms and the wealth of households. Higher equity and property prices mean higher net worth, which implies lower information costs and greater ease in obtaining financing. The increase in home equity loans that follows a real estate boom is an example of this process. With an increase in household wealth, banks are willing to step up their lending.

The second way that a monetary policy expansion can improve borrowers' net worth has to do with the drop in interest rates. Most borrowers already have loans that they are in the process of repaying; lower interest rates reduce the burden of repayment. For a firm, the drop in the cost of financing increases the difference between revenues and expenses, raising profits and increasing the firm's value. Something similar happens for individuals. When interest rates fall, people who hold variable-rate loans enjoy lower interest payments. This drop in the cost of their financing reduces the information problems that plague the lending relationship. Why? To evaluate a borrower's creditworthiness, banks look at the percentage of a person's income that is devoted to loan payments. At lower interest rates, that percentage will be lower, so individuals will qualify for larger loans. The conclusion is that *as interest rates fall, the supply of loans increases.*

It is worth pausing to emphasize that information is the driving force in the bank-lending and balance-sheet channels of monetary policy transmission. Information services are central to banks' role in the financial system because they help to address the problems of adverse selection and moral hazard. The primacy of information in banking has some important implications for our understanding of the link between the financial system and the real economy. It means that financial instability, which is characterized by large and unpredictable moves in asset prices, accompanied by widespread bankruptcy, will reduce lenders' willingness to supply financing. It also means that accounting scandals, such as the ones that plagued U.S. companies in 2001 and 2002, will have an effect on the economy as a whole. When bankers are worried about the accuracy of accounting information, they will be less willing to make loans to anyone. Inferior information leads to an increase in adverse selection, reducing bank lending, lowering investment, and ultimately depressing the quantity of aggregate output demanded.

The channels of monetary policy transmission depend on the structure of the financial system. To the extent that banks are unimportant sources of funds for firms and individuals, the bank-lending channel is not tremendously important. As we will see at the end of this chapter, with the growth of loan brokers and asset-backed securities, the bank-lending channel has become less important than it once was. But information problems and the balance-sheet effects they create seem likely to persist for some time. While technology has made the processing of increasing amounts of information easier and cheaper, it seems unlikely to solve the problems of adverse selection and moral hazard, which make net worth such an important determinant of a borrower's creditworthiness.

## Asset-Price Channels: Wealth and Investment

When the interest rate moves, so do stock prices. Specifically, a fall in the interest rate tends to push stock prices up. This relationship between the interest rate and the stock market is referred to as the **asset-price channel** of monetary policy transmission. To understand it, we must first figure out why a change in the interest rate might cause a movement in stock prices. Then we must explain how a change in stock prices can influence the quantity of aggregate output demanded.

To see how the interest rate influences stock prices, recall that the fundamental value of a stock is the present value of the stream of its future dividends. The lower the interest rate is, the higher the present value is and, therefore, the higher the stock price will be. Added to this relationship is the fact that an easing of monetary policy might well improve consumer and business confidence in the prospects for future growth. More growth means more revenue and higher profits and that, too, will drive up stock prices. In fact, because current stock prices are based largely on expectations of future growth and future interest rates, they tend to move in anticipation of a cut in interest rates.

Monetary policy affects real estate markets in the same way that it influences stock markets. The mechanism is straightforward. When policymakers reduce their interest-rate target, it drives the mortgage rate down. Lower mortgage rates mean higher demand for residential housing, driving up the prices of existing homes.

In short, when the central bank reduces its target interest rate, the stock and real estate markets are likely to boom. Then what? Stock and property prices affect both individual consumption and business investment. For individuals, a rise in stock and real estate prices means an increase in wealth. The richer people become, the more they will consume. If stock values go high enough, shareholders can actually buy the luxury cars they have been wanting, or take the fancy vacations they've been dreaming of, or maybe both. The conclusion is that higher asset prices mean increased wealth and consumption.

Just as consumption is affected by stock price movements, so is investment. As stock prices rise, firms find it easier to raise funds by issuing new shares. That is, they gain access to financing in the primary capital market. To see why, think of a simple example in which the price of a company's stock suddenly increases. In the meantime, nothing has happened to the cost of a new investment and hence to its internal rate of return. But at the higher stock price, financing is now cheaper. This story should sound familiar. Recall the way in which the traditional *interest-rate channel* influences investment: a lower real interest rate means a lower cost of financing, which raises the profitability of investment projects. As a result, borderline investment projects suddenly become profitable when real interest rates fall. The same thing happens when stock prices rise. As financing becomes less expensive, more investments become profitable. In short, when asset markets boom, so does business investment in new equipment and buildings.[3]

---

[3]This line of reasoning, known as *Tobin's q-theory*, was originally developed by the Nobel Prize-winning economist James Tobin. Tobin pointed out that the question of whether or not a firm invests should depend on the ratio of the market value of its shares to the replacement cost of its plant and equipment, which he called *q*. When q is greater than one—that is, when a firm's stock-market value exceeds its cost of rebuilding—investment in new plant and equipment is cheap relative to the value placed on it in the financial markets. When q is less than one, embarking on new investments isn't worthwhile.

**Table 23.1**    The Monetary Policy Transmission Mechanism

| Channel | Mechanism |
|---|---|
| Interest rates (traditional channel) | Lower interest rates reduce the cost of investment, making more projects profitable. |
| Exchange rates (traditional channel) | Lower interest rates reduce the attractiveness of domestic investment, depressing the value of the currency and increasing net exports. |
| Bank lending | An easing of monetary policy raises the level of bank reserves and bank deposits, increasing the supply of funds. |
| Firms' balance sheets | Lower interest rates raise firms' profits, increasing their net worth and reducing the problems of adverse selection and moral hazard. |
| Household net worth | Lower interest rates raise individuals' net worth, improving their creditworthiness and allowing them to increase their borrowing. |
| Asset prices | Higher stock prices and real estate values fuel an increase in both business investment and household consumption. |

Overall, changes in monetary policy influence aggregate expenditure in the economy through a variety of channels that are summarized in Table 23.1. Each of the transmission mechanisms works slightly differently, but they all lead us to the same conclusion: When interest rates rise, the quantity of aggregate output demanded falls so the dynamic aggregate demand curve slopes down.

## Financial Crisis Obstructs Monetary Policy Transmission

We have seen that monetary policy is transmitted to the economy through financial intermediaries and through asset prices. Yet, financial conditions deteriorated through much of the crisis of 2007–2009, even as central bankers were cutting interest rates aggressively. What prevented policy easing from being transmitted as usual to the real economy?

The answer is that the crisis intensified the fundamental problems of asymmetric information—adverse selection and moral hazard—that affect the provision of credit in a modern economy. In general, a reduction in the quality of information about potential borrowers makes it more difficult for them to borrow. In the financial crisis, the widespread losses at intermediaries in general and the heightened uncertainty about the damage suffered by specific intermediaries reduced confidence in their ability to repay loans and thus virtually shut off the availability of credit to many of them. The hesitancy to lend in this episode was not unlike the common reluctance of buyers to acquire a used car when it might be a lemon (see pages 268–269). In short, funding liquidity dried up. As for households and nonfinancial firms, their net worth fell substantially, which greatly reduced their ability to borrow, so they responded by cutting spending. The result of this was a destabilizing feedback loop between worsening economic prospects and the deterioration of financial conditions that influence spending.

The process started in 2006 with the downturn in U.S. housing prices that led to widespread mortgage defaults. Major lenders—particularly in the United States and

Europe—faced enormous and growing losses. Insufficient screening and monitoring had resulted in too many risky mortgages (see Chapter 11, Lessons from the Crisis: Information Asymmetry and Securitization). Losses from U.S. mortgage-backed securities and related financial instruments sharply depressed the capital in the financial system (see Chapter 12, Lessons from the Crisis: Insufficient Bank Capital). As a result, intermediaries were compelled to deleverage (see Chapter 3, Lessons from the Crisis: Leverage). They even stopped lending to each other—especially in the aftermath of the Lehman failure in September 2008—because they doubted the solvency of their counterparties (see Chapter 3, Lessons from the Crisis: Interbank Lending) or were simply uncertain about who would bear the losses (recall the Chapter 9 discussion of credit-default swaps).

The result was an intense scramble for funding that led to a near collapse of the financial system as a whole. Only the aggressive supply of reserves from central banks and of new capital from governments made it possible to restore the basic function of financial intermediaries and markets. With the usual policy transmission mechanism obstructed during the crisis, the Federal Reserve and other central banks also used unconventional policy mechanisms to directly influence key financial conditions that affect spending in the economy. The Fed's acquisitions of mortgage-backed securities and commercial paper stand out in this regard. Over time, central bank promises to keep interest rates low over an extended period (a policy duration commitment) also influenced the willingness of investors to purchase other important assets, like equities and private-sector debt.

The bottom line: when the policy transmission mechanism is obstructed, central banks cannot assume that a cut in their target policy rate will ease the financial conditions that influence the economy. Indeed, through most of the crisis of 2007–2009, rate cuts did not even halt the deterioration of financial conditions, let alone improve them. And when the policy rate hits zero, as it essentially did in the United States at the end of 2008, cutting it further is no longer a policy option.

Likewise, when central banks hike rates to slow an economy, their success will depend on whether financial conditions respond. If an asset price bubble is under way, as it was in the United States in 2004–2006, the economic impact of central bank policy tightening probably will be smaller than usual. As a result, central banks must always take into account the workings of the monetary policy transmission mechanism in order to achieve their goals of economic and price stability.

# The Challenges Modern Monetary Policymakers Face

The financial crisis of 2007–2009 was a "game changer" for the practitioners and theorists of monetary policy. Surely no one assumes now that monetary policy is a hard and fast science—that a few equations coupled with some statistical analysis and the help of a big computer will suffice. To do their job well, central bankers need a detailed understanding of how both the financial system and the real economy will react to their policy changes.

That job would be tough enough in a world that is standing still, but the dynamism that is such a pervasive and desirable feature of today's economy makes the job all the more difficult. In fact, modern monetary policymakers face a series of daunting challenges. In this section, we will look at three that grew more prominent thanks to the financial crisis of 2007–2009. First, stock prices and property

## APPLYING THE CONCEPT
### WHAT HAPPENED IN JAPAN?

After decades of strong economic growth, the Japanese economy ground to a halt in the 1990s. Why did the Japanese economy fail to respond to the Bank of Japan's long sequence of interest-rate reductions? Solving the mystery requires that we look at various channels of monetary policy transmission—in this case, asset prices and bank lending.

Figure 23.3 provides the first piece of the puzzle, the collapse of the Japanese stock market. From a peak of nearly 40,000 at the end of 1989, the Nikkei 225 index (the Japanese equivalent to the S&P 500) fell by more than half, to 16,000 in 1992. Property prices fell even more sharply, with commercial land prices in the largest cities plunging by nearly 90 percent! The impact of this decline in asset prices was severe. Beyond its direct effects on consumption and investment, both of which collapsed, the crash did considerable damage to both the creditworthiness of borrowers and banks' balance sheets. Borrowers' net worth fell with the collapse of equity and property values, worsening information problems and depressing aggregate expenditure even further.

When real growth slowed to a standstill, firms were no longer able to repay their loans. The quantity of nonperforming loans skyrocketed, eroding bank capital and causing loan officers to become extremely wary of extending new loans. By 2000, bad loans accounted for 14 percent of outstanding loans, up from 3 percent in 1993. Bank capital fell from a relatively low 5¼ percent of assets early in the 1990s to less than 2½ percent in 2000.*

The dramatic rise in the number of nonperforming loans was compounded by the fact that many were backed by assets whose value had collapsed. As a result, some banks had virtually no capital left. They should have been shut down but, for political reasons, closing them was impossible. So they were allowed to continue operating.†

Given the large numbers of both bankrupt firms and impaired banks, it was no wonder that the Bank of Japan's monetary policy had virtually no impact. The fact that the interest rate was zero simply didn't matter, because the channels through which interest-rate reductions would normally have influenced real economic activity were almost completely blocked. There was no way for borrowers to obtain

*For a thorough discussion of the problems in the Japanese financial system during the 1990s, see Anil K. Kashyap, "Sorting Out Japan's Financial Crisis," Economic Perspectives of the Federal Reserve Bank of Chicago, 2000, 4th Quarter, pp. 42–55.

†A striking feature of the Japanese experience in the 1990s is that regulators and supervisors failed to enforce prudential regulations that would have forced many banks to close for lack of adequate capital. The reasons for their "regulatory forbearance" are complex, but two are particularly noteworthy. First, without a fully developed deposit insurance system, it was unclear to regulators how depositors would be compensated when banks were liquidated. Second, and possibly more important, shutting the doors on banks would have meant foreclosing on defaulted borrowers. and, thereby, throwing many workers out of their jobs. See Mitsuhiro Fukao, "Japan's Lost Decade and Its Financial System," The World Economy 26, no. 5 (March 2003), pp. 365–384.

values have a tendency to go through boom and bust cycles. Second, policymakers' options are limited, as we have seen by the fact the nominal interest rate cannot fall below zero. Third, the structures of the economy and the financial system are constantly evolving, and the latter may be affected greatly by changing regulation in the years ahead.

## Booms and Busts in Property and Equity Prices

Nearly everyone agrees that we would all be better off without skyrocketing increases in property and stock prices followed by sudden collapses. The unprecedented surge and collapse in U.S. housing prices was the ultimate source of the financial crisis of 2007–2009. Since the Great Depression of the 1930s, housing prices had declined nationwide in only three years, and then only slightly. Real house prices had been reasonably stable, because inflation offset the trend rise of nominal house prices. The spike in house prices in the years preceding the crisis was spectacularly unprecedented (see Figure 23.4). At the time, some argued that it was a bubble and therefore must burst and cause severe economic damage. Others said that housing fundamentals—growing household income, lower mortgage rates, and the like—had boosted affordability,

**Figure 23.3** The Nikkei 225 Index, 1984-2010

SOURCE: *The Bank of Japan.*

financing. Thus, policymakers had little ability to shift the dynamic aggregate demand curve or even to influence its slope. To clean up the mess, the banking system would need to be put back on a solid footing.

Not all asset bubbles have such devastating impact. When the Internet bubble burst in 2000, the U.S. economy did not follow the same path as Japan's. Though Americans suffered many of the same consequences as the Japanese—their wealth declined, reducing consumption and investment and damaging borrowers' balance sheets—U.S. banks were better capitalized and were able to continue lending. A healthy financial system makes all the difference.

**Figure 23.4** U.S. Real Housing Price Index, 1890-2009 (1890 = 100)

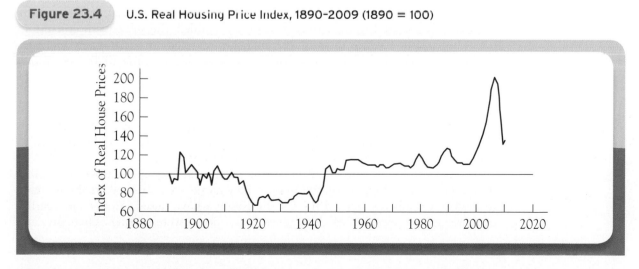

SOURCE: From *Irrational Exuberance*, 2/e. Princeton, 2005. Reprinted with permission by Robert J. Schiller. Updates from: http://www.econ.yale.edu/~schiller/data/Fig2-1.xls.

**Figure 23.5**     The Nasdaq Composite Index, 1984-2010

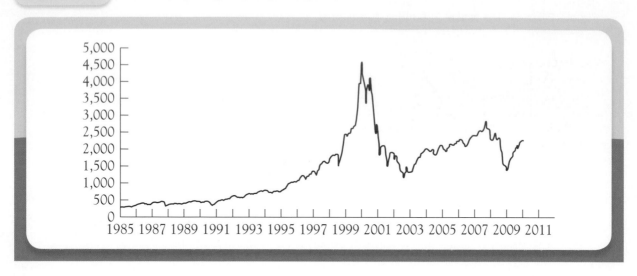

SOURCE: Used with permission from *finance.yahoo.com*.

which both justified the price surge and made it sustainable.[4] The ensuing collapse in home prices settled the debate, bringing on a financial and economic contraction more severe and widespread than even most pessimists expected.

Abrupt changes in asset prices, like the U.S. house price bubble, affect virtually every aspect of economic activity. Looking back at the first part of this chapter, we can see that changes in asset prices have a direct impact on both consumption and investment. Bubbles—which are identified after the fact by a sharp rise then a sharp decline in prices—are particularly damaging because the wealth effects they create cause consumption to surge and then contract just as rapidly. Equity bubbles—like the boom in the Internet sector in the late 1990s—allow firms to finance new projects more easily, causing investment to boom and then bust (see Figure 23.5). Because the collateral that is used to back these loans is overvalued, the subsequent collapse in prices impairs the balance sheets of the financial intermediaries that made the loans. Whether the economic impact is severe—as it was in Japan in the 1990s (see Applying the Concept on page 618) and in the global crisis of 2007–2009—depends on how much damage there is to the financial system. The collapse of the Internet bubble of the late 1990s had a relatively minor impact because intermediaries faced limited credit exposure and remained well capitalized. In contrast, as we saw earlier in this chapter, the loss of capital in the financial system in 2007–2009 could have led to catastrophe without extraordinary government actions.

The devastating worldwide effects of the reversal in U.S. house prices beginning in 2006 has focused renewed attention on how monetary policymakers should react to asset price bubbles. Should the Federal Reserve have raised interest rates earlier or more aggressively in 2003–2006 when house prices were soaring? There are, and

---

[4]For a review of the debate, see Jane Dokko et al., "Monetary Policy and the Housing Bubble," Federal Reserve Board, Finance and Economics Discussion Series 2009-49, December 2009.

were, arguments on both sides.[5] Proponents of a policy of "leaning against bubbles" say that stabilizing inflation and real growth means raising interest rates to discourage bubbles from developing in the first place. If successful, this policy would reduce the consumption and investment booms that accompany bubbles, along with the busts that inevitably follow.

Opponents of this interventionist view claim that bubbles are too difficult to identify when they are developing. They point to the debate about U.S. housing prices in 2004 and 2005 as evidence that views were not unanimous. However, the fact that an economic phenomenon is difficult to measure is no excuse for ignoring it. Indeed, we have no choice: as we saw in the discussion of monetary policy transmission, macroeconomic forecasts rest on estimates of future wealth and stock prices. Without them, there is no way to forecast either consumption or investment.

Opponents of leaning against bubbles used to argue that central banks should simply wait until the bubble bursts and only then react aggressively to limit the fallout on the economy by cleaning up the mess. They pointed to the Great Depression and the 1990s in Japan as examples of what can happen if the central bank attempts to prick a bubble with interest-rate policy. Critics of an activist response also pointed to the mild U.S. recession in 2001—despite the collapse of the bubble for Internet stocks—as a successful instance of how policy can stabilize inflation and the economy in the face of a burst asset price bubble.

The crisis of 2007–2009 undermined the rosy view that policymakers can sit back and clean up after a bubble bursts. Having seen financial conditions collapse even with the policy rate set at zero, and having experienced the deepest global downturn since World War II, few central bankers remain sanguine about using conventional interest-rate policy to limit the fallout from asset price bubbles after they burst. However, central bankers still worry that interest rates are only a blunt tool and that pricking an asset price bubble could require rate hikes so severe that they would bludgeon the economy and reduce the likelihood of hitting a central bank's objective for inflation. If the rate hikes were applied more cautiously to halt, say, a housing price bubble, it would be, as one economist put it, "like adding a grain of sand a day to a scale that is weighing a car."

Today, there is a more nuanced case against using interest rates to prick asset price bubbles: namely, that the proper policy toolkit for addressing bubbles is not interest rates but the macroprudential regulatory tools that we discussed in Chapter 14. According to this view, bubbles are a major threat, particularly when they are associated with an expansion of credit that exposes the financial system to the eventual collapse of asset prices. As a result, the best response would be to adjust regulatory rules—such as procyclical capital requirements, systemic capital surcharges, and fees for insuring the capital of banks—to inhibit intermediaries from extending such risky credits in economic booms. The macroprudential regulatory approach would thus help avoid the more destructive option of having to tighten interest rates across the whole economy to address a bubble in a specific asset. Yet, this approach still depends on the foresight and judgment of regulators to limit the buildup of a menacing asset price bubble.

---

[5]An early example of the case for intervention may be found in Stephen G. Cecchetti, Hans Genberg, and Sushil Wadhwani, "Asset Prices in a Flexible Inflation Targeting Framework," in William C. Hunter, George G. Kaufman, and Michael Pomerleano, Eds., *Asset Price Bubbles: Implications for Monetary, Regulatory and International Policies* (Cambridge, MA: MIT Press: 2002), pp. 427–444. For an early version of the case against, see Ben Bernanke and Mark Gertler, "Should Central Banks Respond to Movements in Asset Prices?" *American Economic Review*, May 2001, pp. 253–257.

## YOUR FINANCIAL WORLD
Know the Level of Inflation

By now, you're probably convinced that inflation is bad for everyone, including yourself. Nevertheless, we all have to face at least some inflation. The first step in dealing with it is to become informed. You need to know the current inflation rate for any number of reasons. For example, it is essential in figuring out whether a nominal wage increase represents a real wage increase. And while any business news source will tell you the nominal interest rate, without a measure of inflation, you can't compute the real interest rate. Making informed economic and financial decisions requires that you know the inflation rate.

Casual observation of the prices we pay from day to day is an unreliable way to evaluate inflation, because most of us have fairly selective memories and are prone to remember price changes on goods that we buy frequently (such as food and gasoline) rather than on important infrequent purchases (such as autos, cameras, and computers). Surveys indicate that most people overestimate inflation. So economic statistics are more reliable. The Bureau of Labor Statistics, the government agency that computes the consumer price index, provides information about inflation on its Web site, www.bls.gov/cpi/.

What should you look for on the BLS Web site? First, don't pay much attention to monthly measures of inflation; they aren't very reliable as indicators of the long-term inflation trend. Instead, focus on 12-month changes, especially measures that exclude food and energy. These so-called core measures of inflation omit parts of the price index that tend to be extremely volatile, making sharp movements that are likely to be reversed in a few months. Because gasoline prices rise and fall from one month to the next, for example, removing them smoothes inflation, making the core measure more representative of the long-term trend.

Knowing the level of inflation is essential to managing your finances. If you don't know the level of inflation, you won't know whether the interest rate you receive on your savings is high or low, or whether the interest rate you are paying on your loans is high or low. Nor will you be able to evaluate properly the next raise you receive. Stay informed about inflation so that you can adjust for it. Know the real interest rate you receive or pay and how much your real wage is changing.

While the crisis of 2007–2009 has not settled this debate, it has advanced the discussion substantially.[6] Many policymakers still resist the idea of using interest rates to address asset bubbles, but they no longer rule it out. Using interest rates to combat asset price bubbles now is more likely to be viewed as a backup approach for extreme circumstances, if the first-best methods of macroprudential regulation fail to limit a systemic threat.

## Deflation and the Zero Nominal-Interest-Rate Bound

In Chapter 18, we noted that nominal interest rates cannot be negative—that there is a **zero nominal-interest-rate bound**. The reason is that investors can always hold cash, so bonds must have positive yields to attract bondholders. While this point may strike you as something only investors should worry about, it is not. The fact that nominal interest rates can't fall below zero places a significant restriction on what monetary policymakers can do. Look back at Panel B of Figure 23.1 and you will see that the policy target rate in 2009 was virtually zero in Japan and the United States, and only modestly higher in the euro area. Even though the global economy was sinking, policymakers had no scope to lower rates further. The risk of becoming caught in

[6]For one view of how the financial crisis should alter monetary policy practices more generally, see Olivier Blanchard, Giovanni Dell'Ariccia, and Paulo Mauro, "Rethinking Macroeconomic Policy," IMF Staff Position Note, February 12, 2010, SPN/10/03.

precisely such a predicament has concerned central bankers around the world at least since Japan's experience with the zero bound in the 1990s.

The problem posed by the zero nominal-interest-rate bound is a serious one. To understand why, we can do an exercise based on the macroeconomic model presented in Chapters 21 and 22. Think about the consequences of a shock that depresses aggregate expenditure. The shock could be caused by a decline in investment due to a fall in business prospects; by an appreciation of the dollar due to a deteriorating investment climate abroad, which has increased foreign demand for dollars; or by a decline in individuals' confidence in the future. Regardless of the source, the slowdown drives spending down at every level of inflation and the real interest rate, shifting the dynamic aggregate demand curve to the left. The immediate consequence of this drop in the quantity of aggregate output demanded is that real output falls below potential output, creating a recessionary output gap that puts downward pressure on inflation. Under normal circumstances, monetary policymakers would react to the decline in inflation by cutting the nominal interest rate enough to lower the real interest rate. Their action would increase spending, raise real output, and eliminate the output gap.

Now let's make a small adjustment to this story and assume that, when the shock occurs, inflation is zero and the target nominal interest rate that central bankers control is close to zero. Under these conditions, the decline in aggregate demand still drives real output below potential output, placing downward pressure on inflation. But when inflation falls, it drops below zero so that on average, prices are falling. The result is **deflation**.

Deflation isn't necessarily a problem, unless the shock that moves the economy away from its long-run equilibrium is big enough to drive output down to such a low level that policymakers can't bring it up, even by setting their nominal interest rate target to zero. At that point, we have arrived at one of the central banker's worst nightmares: a nominal interest rate of zero accompanied by deflation and real output that is below potential. The recessionary output gap places further downward pressure on prices, driving deflation down even more. Because the nominal interest rate is already zero, policymakers cannot counter the worsening deflation by lowering it. Instead, the real interest rate rises, reducing spending, shifting the dynamic aggregate demand curve to the left, and expanding the recessionary output gap even more. The result is a *deflationary spiral* in which deflation grows worse and worse.

Recall that deflation aggravates information problems in ways that inflation does not. Deflation makes it more difficult for businesses to obtain financing for new projects. Without financing there is no investment; without investment there is no growth. The primary reason this happens is that debt is measured in fixed dollars, and deflation makes those dollars more valuable. Thus, deflation increases the real value of a firm's liabilities without affecting the real value of its assets. At a lower net worth, companies are suddenly less creditworthy.

In short, deflation and the zero nominal-interest-rate bound can have a devastating impact on growth by short-circuiting the process that

*"I had no idea our marriage was so interest-rate sensitive."*

SOURCE: © Robert Mankoff/The New Yorker Collection/ www.cartoonbank.com.

normally stabilizes the economy so that it is no longer self-correcting. Concern about the instabilities of a deflationary spiral helped to animate the central bank response to the crisis of 2007–2009, even though the crisis began with inflation above desirable levels. Policymakers were concerned that the deep recession itself could lower inflation expectations sharply and raise real interest rates in a destabilizing manner.

Can policymakers do anything to avoid this pitfall? The answer is yes; there are ways to minimize the chances of this sort of catastrophe. Policymakers can choose from three strategies. First, they can set their inflation objective with the perils of deflation in mind; second, they can act boldly when there is even a hint of deflation; and third, they can utilize the unconventional policy tools that we discussed in Chapter 18.

The difficulties posed by the zero nominal-interest-rate bound arise only when central bankers have achieved their objective of low, stable inflation. When inflation is high, so is the nominal interest rate; chances are therefore remote that the interest rate will hit the zero bound. This observation suggests that central bankers should set their inflation objective high enough to minimize the possibility of a deflationary spiral. The consensus is that an inflation objective of 2 to 3 percent gives policymakers enough latitude to avoid the problems caused by deflation.

Reducing the interest rate significantly and rapidly when faced with the possibility of hitting the zero nominal-interest-rate bound is another approach to avoiding deflation. Central bankers call this strategy "acting preemptively," which means working hard to avoid ever reaching the point where interest rates hit zero. Acting preemptively was one reason why the FOMC reduced the target federal funds rate by 5.25 percentage points to the zero bound in a series of 10 cuts between September 2007 and December 2008. Dramatic actions of that sort are meant to ensure that the economy will recover before deflation can take hold.

Finally, as we saw in Chapter 18, central bankers have at their disposal a range of unconventional policy tools that they can employ when the traditional interest-rate target, an overnight rate, hits zero.[7] These include policy duration commitments, quantitative easing, and credit easing—all of which were actively employed by central bankers in the financial crisis of 2007–2009. The mechanics are straightforward. Central bankers use policy duration commitments to influence long-term bond yields, which depend in part on expectations about future policy rates. They use quantitative easing and credit easing to control the size of their balance sheet and the mix of assets that they hold. During normal times, policymakers control the supply of their reserve liabilities in order to meet a target interest rate. But even if the short-run target rate drops to zero, monetary policymakers retain their ability to expand their balance sheet. They can continue to purchase securities to increase the size of the monetary base.

Everyone agrees that unconventional policy options are feasible. And we have seen their effective use in the crisis of 2007–2009. Nevertheless, central bankers are very reluctant to use such tools and, when used, are eager to exit as soon as improvements in the economy make it safe for them to do so. One reason for this aversion to unconventional tools is the lack of experience using them. Monetary policymaking rests on quantitative estimates of the impact of a change in the target interest rate on

---

[7]For an early discussion of unconventional monetary policy options, see the speech by then-Federal Reserve Board governor, now chairman, Ben S. Bernanke, "Deflation: Making Sure 'It' Doesn't Happen Here," remarks before the National Economists Club, Washington, D.C., November 21, 2001. The speech is available on the Federal Reserve Board's Web site at www.federalreserve.gov.

the central bank's objectives. Policymakers have some idea of how a reduction of 25 or 50 basis points in the federal funds rate would affect output and inflation over the next year or two. But they have much less experience in knowing what the quantitative impact of an unconventional policy option will be. What is the effect on prices, consumption, and investment if the supply of reserves increases by a factor of 100 (as it did in the United States in September–October 2008) or if the central bank doubles its assets by purchasing $1 trillion of mortgage-backed securities (as the Fed did in 2009)?

Beyond the uncertainty that comes from a lack of experience, another key reason for keeping unconventional policy tools unconventional is that policy exit—reducing the size of the balance sheet and restoring the mix of securities to a conventional portfolio of shorter-term government instruments—may be difficult. As we saw in Chapter 18, the ability to pay interest on reserves allows a central bank to tighten policy—by hiking the deposit rate that forms the floor for the overnight lending rate—even if policymakers choose temporarily not to sell the unconventional assets on the balance sheet. Nevertheless, central banks prefer assets that are liquid and that do not tilt the playing field in favor of specific private borrowers. And although they may wish to sell assets acquired in unconventional policy moves—including bonds with default risk and long-term bonds—in doing so they may suffer a loss. If a central bank faced sufficient losses, it might need to ask the government to replenish its capital. Such reliance on government could add to inflation expectations if it were viewed as a threat to central bank independence.

## The Evolving Structure of the Financial System

Monetary policy works through its effects on the financial system. Thus, differences in financial structure across countries may help explain differences in the effectiveness of monetary policy. By extension, changes in financial structure will change the impact of monetary policy. Recall from the first part of this chapter that one of the primary channels through which monetary policy influences real output and inflation is its impact on the supply of bank loans. By influencing bank lending, policymakers can affect the ease with which individuals and firms obtain financing.

Banks are crucial to this mechanism. As the nature of banking changes, we would expect the importance of this channel of monetary policy transmission to change along with it, and that has been the case. In the United States, for example, banks are no longer as important a source of financing as they once were. Thirty years ago, they accounted for virtually all the credit in the U.S. economy. At the time the crisis of 2007–2009 hit, direct bank loans had fallen to less than 60 percent of total credit extended.

The shift away from bank financing and toward direct financing in the capital markets means that the bank-lending channel of monetary policy became less important in the decades before the financial crisis that began in 2007. The decline of banks as a source of finance was accompanied by a corresponding rise in the importance of securities markets and of shadow banks—including securities brokers, money-market mutual funds, and government-sponsored enterprises (GSEs). Recall the asset-backed securities discussed in Chapter 3. Mortgage-backed and other asset-backed securities surged in volume over the past 30 years. In 1980, mortgage-backed securities accounted for only $0.1 trillion of the $1.5 trillion in U.S. mortgages outstanding. By 2009, they surpassed half of the nearly $15 trillion in mortgages outstanding.

To create mortgage-backed securities, a broker bundles together a large number of home mortgages and then sells shares in the pool. Investors in mortgage-backed

## IN THE NEWS
### Bernanke's How-To on Rate Increase Lacks a When

**The New York Times**

By Sewell Chan

February 11, 2010

Washington—"At some point." "At the appropriate time." "When the time comes."

On Wednesday, the Federal Reserve's chairman, Ben S. Bernanke, outlined a strategy—but not a timetable—for scaling back the extraordinary measures it began taking in 2007 to prop up the economy as financial markets teetered on collapse.

The Federal Reserve has eased borrowing by lowering short-term interest rates to nearly zero and built up a $2.2 trillion balance sheet by scooping up assets like mortgage-backed securities and even vast sums of Treasury bonds and notes.

Eventually, to avoid inflation, both actions will have to be reined in. But Mr. Bernanke, in a 10-page statement, provided few hints as to how long that period will be.

"[A]t some point the Federal Reserve will need to tighten financial conditions by raising short-term interest rates and reducing the quantity of bank reserves outstanding," he wrote.

Mr. Bernanke, however, did provide new details of a major concern: how, as the recovery proceeds, to gradually shrink the balance sheet.

Mr. Bernanke suggested that a new policy tool—the interest rate on excess reserves, which the Fed began paying in October 2008—would be a vital part of the Fed's strategy.

Increasing that interest rate, he said, will have the effect of pushing up other short-term interest rates, including the benchmark fed funds rate—the rate at which banks lend to each other overnight.

It is even possible, Mr. Bernanke said, that the Fed "could for a time use the interest rate paid on reserves, in combination with targets for reserve quantities," to communicate its policy stance to the markets. Since 1994, the fed funds rate has been the much-watched centerpiece of statements by the Federal Open Market Committee, the Fed's crucial policy-making arm.

For days, economists have been trying to forecast what Mr. Bernanke would say about the sequence of steps and the combination of tools the Fed will use to tighten credit. On that subject, Mr. Bernanke offered only hints of his thinking.

"One possible sequence would involve the Federal Reserve continuing to test its tools for draining reserves on a limited basis" he wrote.

"As the time for the removal of policy accommodation draws near, those operations could be scaled up to drain more significant volumes of reserve balances to provide tighter control over short-term interest rates. The actual firming of policy would then be implemented through an increase in the interest rate paid on reserves."

But Mr. Bernanke suggested that "if economic and financial developments were to require a more rapid exit from the current highly accommodative policy"—that is, if fears emerge about inflation—the Fed "could increase the interest rate paid on reserves at about the same time it commences significant draining operations."

Along with raising the interest rate on reserves, Mr. Bernanke discussed three other options for draining reserves. The first involves reverse repurchase agreements, in

securities purchase shares in the revenue from the underlying financial instruments—in this case, the mortgage payments made by homebuyers. Although their home purchase began with a bank loan, homebuyers in this way ultimately obtain a form of financing that is almost equivalent to direct capital market financing. Over the years, securitization—the process of pooling streams of revenue from loans and other receivables into marketable securities—has expanded in scope and size; it now includes car loans, credit card debt, student loans, equipment leases, and even movie box-office receipts.

Yet, the financial crisis that ended in 2009 is having a greater impact on the shape of the financial system than any event since the Great Depression. For example, it has interrupted the trend toward direct finance: securitization has declined or slowed which the Fed would sell securities from its portfolio with an agreement to repurchase them at a later date.

The second involves term deposits—similar to certificates of deposit—to banks. That would convert part of the banks' reserves into deposits that could not be used for short-term liquidity needs and would not be counted as reserves.

A third tool involves redeeming or selling securities. That strategy could carry risk, as the Fed's large portfolio of mortgage-backed securities is helping to prop up the housing market and keep mortgage-interest rates low.

As part of its special lending programs to inject liquidity into the market, the Fed modified its discount window—the traditional program for direct lending to banks—to make terms more generous and to make nonbanks eligible for borrowing. That effort is winding down, and Mr. Bernanke said that "before long, we expect to consider a modest increase in the spread" between the discount rate—the rate at which the Fed directly lends to banks—and the fed funds rate. He emphasized that the change "should not be interpreted as signaling any change in the outlook for monetary policy."

Mr. Bernanke's statement elicited mixed views from economists.

Laurence J. Kotlikoff, an economist at Boston University, said that despite Mr. Bernanke's efforts to be reassuring, the prospect for serious inflation was real. "We could go from here to hyperinflation, basically overnight, because we've increased the basic supply of money by a factor of three," he said.

Mr. Kotlikoff also was skeptical about Mr. Bernanke's proposed solution. "The Fed printed more than $1 trillion in new money and then went out and handed it to the banks, and now they're trying to bribe those banks not to actually release it into the public stream—that's what these interest rates on reserves are," he said.

Mr. Bernanke did note that the balance sheet would shrink on its own, over time, as assets like mortgage-backed securities are prepaid or mature. "In the long run, the Federal Reserve anticipates that its balance sheet will shrink toward more historically normal levels and that most or all of its security holdings will be Treasury securities," he wrote.

SOURCE: Copyright © 2010 by *The New York Times Co.* Reprinted with permission.

---

### LESSONS OF THE ARTICLE

By early 2010, the Fed had presented the public with considerable detail about the tools that it would use—"at the appropriate time"—to tighten monetary policy and exit from the unconventional policies that it had implemented during the financial crisis of 2007–2009. The large size and unusual composition of the Fed's post-crisis balance sheet meant that the procedures for tightening would be different than in normal periods. By raising the interest rate that it pays on reserves, the Fed is able to tighten policy without shrinking its balance sheet. When the Fed tightens, see if you can detect the shift by examining its assets and liabilities, which are reported each week in Federal Reserve Statistical Release H.4.1 (Factors Affecting Reserve Balances: http://www.federalreserve.gov/releases/h41/).

---

since 2006. The volume of asset-backed commercial paper in the United States, which approached $1 trillion in 2007, plummeted to only about one-third of that level in 2009. The volume of securities backed by U.S. government agencies and the GSEs stagnated in 2009, even though the Federal Reserve purchased nearly $1 trillion of the issues. When the housing-related GSEs themselves failed in 2008, they were placed under the direct control of the federal government, which has had to inject massive amounts of capital to restore the GSEs' positive net worth. Their future is highly uncertain, with many observers calling for them to be dismantled.[8]

[8]See, for example, "Towards a New Architecture for U.S. Mortgage Markets: The Future of the Government-Sponsored Enterprises," in NYU Stern Working Group on Financial Reform, *Real-time Recommendations for Financial Reform, December 2009*, pp. 60–62, http://govtpolicyrecs.stern.nyu.edu/docs/whitepapers_ebook_full.pdf.

However, it is far too soon to say exactly how the post-crisis financial system will change. Will the trend toward direct finance resume? In part, that will depend on how regulatory policy evolves in coming years as regulators seek to prevent another crisis or minimize its potential impact. A macroprudential regulator—of the kind that we discussed in Chapter 14—will try to limit intermediaries' incentives for taking systemic risk. High on the list of such incentives were the low capital requirements that applied to some mortgage-backed securities prior to the financial crisis of 2007–2009.

Will macroprudential regulation prevent the restoration of securitization? Probably not: regulators are aware that effective securitization can lead to a better diversification of risk. But unlike the incomplete securitization that prevailed earlier, effective securitization must avoid leaving concentrations of securitized assets on the balance sheets of intermediaries that make them vulnerable to collapsing asset price bubbles. Consequently, macroprudential regulation will tend to slow the future pace of securitization, especially compared to the boom years preceding the financial crisis.

However the financial system evolves, the pattern will be a critical one for central bankers, who need to know the quantitative impact their policies are likely to have. As the structure of the financial system changes, the effect of a 25- or 50-basis-point move in the federal funds rate will doubtless change with it. The changing effectiveness of conventional monetary policy likely will require central bankers to update their unconventional policy tools, too. Central bankers will always have to assess how the financial system is altering the monetary transmission mechanism.

The changing nature of the financial system is important for individuals as well as policymakers. As the characteristics of money, banks, and loans evolve, we will all adjust how we pay for our purchases, how we hold our wealth, and how we obtain credit. Our use of currency will likely continue to decline. U.S. banks that now receive interest on their reserves may continue to hold far more of them than before the financial crisis. No one can predict exactly when or to what extent these changes will occur, but now that you have reached the end of this book, you know how to think about them. You understand the economic role of financial institutions as well as what a central bank is and how it operates. Together with the aggregate demand–aggregate supply model, this knowledge gives you a framework with which to comprehend the evolution of the financial system, its effects on monetary policy, and its effects on you personally.

## Terms

asset-price channel, 615
balance-sheet channel, 614
bank-lending channel, 612
deflation, 623
exchange-rate channel, 609

interest-rate channel, 609
monetary policy transmission
   mechanism, 609
zero nominal-interest-rate
   bound, 622

# Chapter Lessons

1. Monetary policy influences the economy through several channels.
   a. The traditional channels of monetary policy transmission are interest rates and exchange rates.
      i. Interest rates influence consumption and investment.
      ii. Exchange rates affect net exports.
   b. Monetary policy affects the supply of bank loans, changing the availability of bank financing to firms and individuals.
   c. Monetary policy can change firms' and households' net worth, affecting their creditworthiness as borrowers.
   d. The asset-price channel of monetary policy transmission works through stock and real estate prices.
      i. Stock and property prices influence household wealth and consumption.
      ii. Stock prices also affect businesses' ability and incentive to raise funds and make investments.
2. Monetary policymakers face significant challenges. To be successful, they require
   a. Accurate estimates of potential GDP, even when its growth trend is shifting.
   b. An understanding of how to cope with the problems created by the zero nominal-interest-rate bound and the possibility of deflation.
   c. A knowledge of how and when to react to the possibility of a stock or real estate boom (and bust).
   d. An awareness of the changing structure of the financial system and a knowledge of how to react to it.

# Conceptual Problems

1. Explain in detail how monetary policy influences banks' lending behavior. Show how an open market purchase affects the banking system's balance sheet, and discuss the impact on the supply of bank loans. (You may wish to refer to Chapter 17 in answering this question.)

2. Explain why you might expect the recovery from the 2007–2009 recession to be weaker than normal?

3.* Explain why the traditional interest-rate channel of monetary policy transmission from monetary policy actions to changes in investment and consumption decisions may be relatively weak.

4. Explain why monetary policymakers' actions in cutting the Federal Funds rate to almost zero were not sufficient to boost economic activity during the recession of 2007–2009.

5. When monetary policymakers hit the zero nominal-interest-rate bound with their policy rate, they have the option to turn to unconventional tools of monetary policy. How do these unconventional tools work, and why are policymakers reluctant to use them except in very difficult circumstances?

6. During the financial crisis of 2007–2009, the Federal Reserve took many extraordinary measures to support the economy. As the economy recovers, what actions might the Fed take to tighten financial conditions?

*Indicates more difficult problems

7.  The government decides to place limits on the interest rates banks can pay their depositors. Seeing that alternative investments pay higher interest rates, depositors withdraw their funds from banks and place them in bonds. Will their action have an impact on the economy? If so, how?

8.  New developments in information technology have simplified the assessment of individual borrowers' creditworthiness. What are the likely consequences for the structure of the financial system? For monetary policy?

9.* Describe the theory of the exchange-rate channel of the monetary transmission mechanism. How, through the exchange rate, does an interest rate increase influence output? Why is this link difficult to find in practice?

10. Many economists have argued that Japan's economic problems during the 1990s were caused largely by bank failures and the refusal of the Japanese government to clean up the banking system. Explain how a collapse of the banking system could cause a fall in real output. Can monetary policymakers do anything to revive the economy under such circumstances?

11. Why might the zero nominal-interest-rate bound lead policymakers to raise their inflation objective?

## Analytical Problems

12. Considering the role of the U.S. house price bubble in the financial crisis of 2007–2009, how do you think monetary policymakers should respond to bubbles in asset markets?

13. For each of the following, explain whether the response is theoretically consistent with a tightening of monetary policy and identify which of the traditional channels of monetary policy is at work:
    a. Firms become more likely to undertake investment projects.
    b. Households become less likely to purchase refrigerators and washing machines.
    c. Net exports fall.

14. Suppose in Country A, changes in short-term interest rates translate quickly into changes in long-term interest rates, while in Country B long-term interest rates do not respond much to changes in short-term rates. In which country would you expect the interest-rate channel of monetary policy to be stronger? Explain your answer.

15. Consider a situation where central bank officials repeatedly express concern that output exceeds potential output and that the economy is overheating. Although they haven't implemented any policy moves as yet, the data show that consumption of luxury goods has begun to slow. Explain how this behavior could reflect the asset-price channel of monetary policy at work.

16. Do you think the balance-sheet channel of monetary policy would be stronger or weaker if
    a. Firms' balance sheets in general are very healthy?
    b. Firms have a lot of existing variable-rate debt?

17. In the wake of the financial crisis of 2007–2009, would you anticipate the bank-lending channel becoming more or less important in the United States in the near future? Explain your answer.

18.* Suppose there is an unexpected slowdown in the rate of productivity growth in the economy so that forecasters consistently overestimate the growth rate of GDP. If the central bank bases its policy decisions on the consensus forecast, what would be the likely consequences for inflation assuming it maintains its existing inflation target?

19. Suppose the policy interest rate controlled by the central bank and the inflation rate were both zero. Explain in terms of the aggregate demand–aggregate supply framework how the economy could fall into a deflationary spiral if it were hit by a negative aggregate demand shock.

20.* Use the aggregate demand–aggregate supply framework to show how a boom in equity prices might affect inflation and output in the short run. In the absence of any policy change by the central bank, what would the long-run impact be on inflation and output?

21. Compare the impact of a given change in monetary policy in two economies that are similar in every way except that, in Economy A, the financial system is very evolved with a large shadow banking system providing many alternatives to bank financing, while in Economy B, bank loans account for almost all of the financing in the economy.

# Glossary

Note: The number in parentheses at the end of each entry is the number of the chapter in which the term is introduced.

## A

**accommodative monetary policy** A policy that is aimed at increasing output and raising inflation, usually a lowering of the central bank's interest-rate target. (15)

**accountability** The idea that central bankers should be held responsible for their policies. (15)

**adverse selection** The problem of distinguishing a good risk from a bad one before making a loan or providing insurance; it is caused by asymmetric information. (11)

**aggregate expenditure** The total demand for the economy's production; the sum of consumption, investment, government purchases, and net exports. (21)

**American option** An option that can be exercised any time up to the expiration date, in contrast to a *European option*. (9)

**appreciation of a currency** The increase in the value of a country's currency relative to the value of another country's currency. (10)

**arbitrage** The practice of simultaneously buying and selling financial instruments to benefit from temporary price differences; eliminates a riskless profit opportunity. (9)

**asset** Something of value that can be owned; a financial claim or property that serves as a store of value. (3)

**asset-backed securities** Shares in the returns or payments arising from a specific asset or pool of assets, such as home mortgages or student loans. (3)

**asset-price channel** The channel of the monetary policy transmission mechanism where changes in policy affect aggregate expenditure through their impact on stock prices and the value of real estate. (23)

**asymmetric information** The fact that the two parties to a transaction have unequal knowledge about each other. A borrower, for example, has more information about his or her abilities and prospects than a lender. (11)

**at-the-money option** An option whose strike price equals the current market price for the underlying instrument. (9)

**automated clearinghouse (ACH) transaction** The most common form of electronic funds transfers. (2)

**average** See *expected value*. (5)

## B

**balance of payments** An accounting system for tracking both the flow of goods and services and the flow of assets across international boundaries. (19)

**balance sheet** The list of assets and liabilities that shows an individual's or firm's financial position. (3)

**balance-sheet channel** The channel of the monetary policy transmission mechanism where changes in policy affect aggregate expenditure through their impact on household and firm balance sheets. (23)

**bank** See *depository institution*. (12)

**bank capital** Bank assets minus bank liabilities. The net worth of the bank. The value of the bank to its owners. (12)

**bank charter** The license authorizing the operation of a bank. (13)

**bank holding company** A company that owns one or more banks and possibly other nonbank subsidiaries. (13)

**bank-lending channel** The channel of the monetary policy transmission mechanism in which changes in policy affect aggregate expenditure through their impact on banks' willingness to make loans. (23)

**bank panic** The simultaneous failure of many banks during a financial crisis. (14)

**bank run** An event when depositors lose confidence in a bank and make withdrawals, exhausting the bank's reserves. (14)

**bank supervision** Government oversight of commercial banks; see also *supervision*. (14)

**Basel Accord** An agreement requiring internationally active banks to hold capital equal to or greater than a specified share (8% or as agreed by regulators) of their risk-adjusted assets. (14)

**basis point** One one-hundredth of a percentage point. (4)

**benchmark** The performance of a group of experienced investment advisors or money managers. (5)

**benchmark bond** A low-risk bond, usually a U.S. Treasury bond, to which the yield on a risky bond is compared to assess its risk. (7)

**Big Mac index** The index used to estimate whether currencies are under- or overvalued that is based on the price of the Big Mac in various countries. (10)

**Board of Governors of the Federal Reserve System** The seven-member board that oversees the Federal Reserve System, including participation in both monetary policy and financial regulatory decisions. (16)

**bond** A financial instrument that promises a series of future payments on specific dates. Also known as a *fixed-income security*. (4)

**bond market** A financial market in which debt instruments with a maturity of more than one year are traded. (3)

**bond principal value** The final payment made to the holder of a bond; also known as the *par value* and the *face value*. (4)

**Bretton Woods system** The international monetary system in place from 1945 to 1971, in which exchange rates were fixed to the U.S. dollar, and the dollar was convertible into gold at $35 per ounce. (19)

**British pound** The name of the currency used in the United Kingdom. (10)

**brokerage firm** Financial intermediary that provides accounting and custody services, access to secondary markets, liquidity, loans, and advice. (13)

**bubble** A persistent and expanding gap between actual asset prices and those warranted by the fundamentals; usually created by mass enthusiasm. (8)

**business cycles** The periodic fluctuations in aggregate economic output. (1)

## C

**call option** A contract that confers the right, but not the obligation, to purchase a financial instrument at a predetermined price on or prior to an agreed upon date. (9)

**call reports** The detailed financial reports banks are required to file every three months. Officially known as the *Consolidated Reports of Conditions and Income*. (14)

**callable bond** A bond that the issuer has the option of repaying before the maturity date. (6)

**CAMELS** The system used by U.S. bank examiners to summarize their evaluation of a bank's health. The acronym stands for Capital adequacy, Asset quality, Management, Earnings, Liquidity, and Sensitivity to risk. (14)

**capital account** The part of the balance of payments accounts that measures the flow of assets among countries; also called the *financial account*. (10)

**capital account deficit/surplus** A country's capital inflows minus its capital outflows. (10)

**capital controls** Government-imposed barriers to investment across international boundaries; restrictions on the ability of foreigners to buy and sell domestic assets. (19)

**capital gain** The difference between the price that has been paid for an asset and the higher price at which it is sold; contrasts with a *capital loss*, where the price paid exceeds the price at which the asset is sold. (6)

**capital inflow controls** Government restrictions that restrict the flow of funds into a country to purchase domestic assets. (19)

**capital loss** The difference between the price that has been paid for an asset and the lower price at which it is sold; contrasts with *capital gain*. (6)

**capital market** See *bond market* and *equity market*. (8)

**capital outflow controls** Government restrictions on the flow of funds out of a country to purchase foreign assets. (19)

**cash items in process of collection** Checks and transfers due to a bank that have not yet been collected; a bank asset. (12)

**central bank** The financial institution that manages the government's finances, controls the availability of money and credit in the economy, and serves as the bank to commercial banks. (1, 15)

**central bank independence** The central bank's freedom from political pressure. (15)

**central bank's balance sheet** The statement of the assets and liabilities of the central bank. (17)

**centralized counterparty (CCP)** An entity that interposes itself between the two sides of a transaction, becoming the buyer to every seller and the seller to every buyer. (9)

**centralized exchange** A financial market in which financial instruments are traded in a single physical location. (3)

**check** An instruction to the bank to take funds from one account and transfer them to another. (2)

**clearing corporation** The institution that acts as the counterparty to both sides of all futures market transactions, guaranteeing that the parties to the contract will meet their obligations. (9)

**collateral** Assets pledged to pay for a loan in the event that the borrower doesn't make the required payments. (3, 11)

**commercial banks** Financial intermediaries that provide banking services to businesses and households, allowing them to deposit funds safely and borrow them when necessary. (2)

**commercial paper** Short-term, privately issued zero-coupon debt that is low risk and very liquid and usually has a maturity of less than 270 days. (7)

**commodity money** Precious metals or other items with intrinsic value that are used as money. (2)

**common exposure** Exposure of many financial institutions to the same risk factor. (14)

**common stock** Ownership shares in a firm; also called just *stock* and *equity*. (8)

**compound interest** The interest you get on interest as it accumulates over time. (4)

**consol or perpetuity** A coupon bond in which the issuer makes regular interest payments forever, never repaying the principal; a coupon bond with infinite time to maturity. (6)

**consumption** Spending by individuals for items like food, clothing, housing, transportation, entertainment, and education. (21)

**contagion** When the failure of one bank causes a run on other banks. (14)

**conventional (monetary) policy tools** The federal funds rate target, the rate for discount window lending, and the deposit rate. (18)

**counterparty** The person or institution that is on the other side of a financial contract. (3)

**coupon bond** A bond offering annual coupon payments at regular intervals until the maturity date, at which time the principal is repaid. (4)

**coupon payment** Yearly payment made to the holder of a coupon bond. (4)

**coupon rate** Annual interest rate equal to the yearly coupon payment divided by the face value of a coupon bond. (4)

**credibility** The idea that everyone trusts central bankers to do what they say they are going to do. (15)

**credit card** A promise by a bank to lend the cardholder money in order to make purchases. (2)

**credit-default swap (CDS)** A credit derivative that makes a payment if a borrower defaults; allows lenders to insure themselves against the risk that a borrower will default. (9)

**credit easing** An unconventional monetary policy in which the central bank alters the mix of assets on its balance sheet in order to change their relative prices (interest rates) in a way that stimulates economic activity. (18)

**credit risk** The probability that a borrower will not repay a loan; see also *default risk*. (12)

**credit union** A nonprofit depository institution that is owned by people with a common bond, such as members of police associations, union members, university students, and employees. (12)

**currency** Paper money; for example, dollar bills or euro notes. (2)

**currency board** A fixed-exchange-rate system in which the central bank commits to holding enough foreign currency assets (often dollars) to back domestic currency liabilities at a fixed rate. (19)

**currency in the hands of the public** The quantity of dollar bills held by the nonbank public; part of M1. (2)

**currency-to-deposit ratio** The ratio of publicly held currency to demand deposits held at commercial banks. (17)

**current account** The part of the balance-of-payments account that measures the flow of currently produced goods and services among countries. (10)

**current account deficit/surplus** A country's goods and services exports minus its goods and services imports. (10)

**current output** The level of goods and services currently being produced in an economy. (21)

**current yield** A bond's yearly coupon payment divided by its current market price. (6)

## D

**debit card** A card that provides instructions to the bank to transfer funds from the cardholder's account directly to a merchant's account. (2)

**debt** A loan obligating the borrower to make payments to the lender. (2)

**debt market** A financial market where bonds, loans, and mortgages are traded. (3)

**default** Failure to meet an obligation; in the case of a debt, the failure of the borrower to make required payments to the lender. (5)

**default risk** The probability that a borrower will not repay a loan; see also *credit risk*. (6)

**defined-benefit pension plan** A pension plan in which beneficiaries receive a lifetime retirement income based on the number of years they worked at the company and their final salary. (13)

**defined-contribution pension plan** A pension plan in which beneficiaries make payments into an account and then receive the accumulation, plus the investment income, on retirement, at which time they must decide what to do with the funds. The options include accepting a lump sum, removing small amounts at a time, or converting the balance to a fixed monthly payment for life by purchasing an annuity. (13)

**deflation** A sustained fall in the general price level; the opposite of *inflation*. (11, 23)

**demand deposits** Standard checking accounts that pay no interest; part of M1. (2)

**demand for dollars** Dollars demanded in the foreign exchange market as a function of the nominal exchange rate. (10)

**demand shock** An unexpected change in aggregate expenditure, such as a rise or fall in consumer confidence, that shifts the dynamic aggregate demand curve. (22)

**deposit expansion multiplier** The formula for the increase in commercial bank deposits following a one-dollar increase in reserves. (17)

**deposit insurance** The government guarantee that depositors will receive the full value of their accounts (up to a legal limit) should a bank fail. (14)

**depository institution** A financial institution that accepts deposits and makes loans. (12)

**deposit rate** The interest rate paid by the Federal Reserve to depository institutions on the balances they hold in their reserve accounts that exceed the amount required by the central bank. (18)

**depreciation** The decrease in the value of a country's currency relative to the value of another country's currency. (10)

**derivative** See *derivative instrument*. (9)

**derivative instrument** A financial instrument, such as a futures contract or an option, whose value and payoff are "derived from" the behavior of underlying instruments. (3)

**direct finance** Financing in which borrowers sell securities directly to lenders in the financial markets. (3)

**discount lending** Lending by the Federal Reserve, usually to commercial banks. (18)

**discount loan** A loan from the Federal Reserve, usually to a commercial bank. (12, 17)

**discount rate** The interest rate at which the Federal Reserve makes discount loans to commercial banks. (16, 18)

**disinflation** The term used to describe declines in inflation. (22)

**diversification** Splitting wealth among a variety of assets to reduce risk. (5)

**dividend-discount model** The theory that the fundamental value of a stock equals the present value of expected future dividend payments. (8)

**dividends** The payments made to a company's stockholders when the company makes a profit. (8)

**dollarization** One country's formal adoption of the currency of another country for use in all its financial transactions. (19)

**Dow Jones Industrial Average** The best-known index of stock market performance, it measures the average price of a single share in 30 very large and well-known American companies. (8)

**dual banking system** The system in the United States in which banks supervised by federal government and state government authorities coexist. (13)

**dynamic aggregate demand (AD) curve** The graph of the relationship between inflation and the quantity of spending on domestically produced goods and services. (21)

# E

**ECB's Deposit Facility** Where euro-area banks with excess reserves can deposit them overnight and earn interest. (18)

**ECB's Main Refinancing Operations** The weekly auction of two-week repurchase agreements in which the ECB, through the National Central Banks, provides reserves to banks in exchange for securities. (18)

**ECB's Marginal Lending Facility** The facility through which the ECB provides overnight loans to banks; the analog to the Federal Reserve's primary credit facility. (18)

**economies of scale** When the average cost of producing a good or service falls as the quantity produced increases. (13)

**economies of scope** When the average cost of producing a good or service falls as the number of different types of goods produced increases. (13)

**electronic communications networks (ECNs)** Financial markets organized as an electronic network, such as Arca or Instinet. (3)

**electronic funds transfer (EFT)** Movements of funds directly from one account to another over an electronic network. (2)

**emergency powers** The Federal Reserve's extraordinary authority to lend to nonbanks when circumstances are deemed "unusual and exigent." (16)

**e-money** Private money, as represented by a claim on the issuer, which is (1) stored on an electronic device, (2) issued on receipt of funds, and (3) accepted as a means of payment by persons other than the issuer. (2)

**equation of exchange** The equation stating that nominal income equals the quantity of money times the velocity of money; $MV = PY$. (20)

**equity** Ownership shares in a firm; also called *stock* and *common stock*. (8)

**equity market** A financial market where stocks are bought and sold. (3)

**euro** The name of the currency used in the countries of the European Monetary Union. (10)

**euro area** The countries in Europe that use the euro as their common currency. (16)

**eurodollars** Dollar-denominated deposits outside the U.S. (13)

**European Central Bank (ECB)** The central authority, located in Frankfurt, Germany, which oversees monetary policy in the common currency area. (16)

**European option** An option that can be exercised only on the expiration date, not before, in contrast with an *American option*. (9)

**European System of Central Banks (ESCB)** The European Central Bank plus the National Central Banks of all the countries in the European Union, including those that do not participate in the monetary union. (1, 16)

**Eurosystem** The European Central Bank plus the National Central Banks of participating countries; together, they carry out the tasks of central banking in the euro area. (16)

**examination (of banks)** The formal process by which government specialists evaluate a bank's financial condition. (14)

**excess reserves** Reserves in excess of required reserves. (12, 17)

**excess reserve-to-deposit ratio** The ratio of banks' excess reserves to their demand deposit liabilities. (17)

**exchange rate** See *nominal exchange rate*. (10)

**exchange-rate channel** The channel of the monetary policy transmission mechanism where changes in policy affect aggregate expenditure through their impact on exchange rates. (23)

**exchange-rate stability** One of the objectives of the central bank is to reduce exchange-rate fluctuations making it stable. (15)

**Executive Board of the ECB** The six-member body in Frankfurt that oversees the operation of the European Central Bank and the Eurosystem. (16)

**exercise price** The predetermined price at which a call or put option specifies that the underlying asset can be bought (call) or sold (put); also called the *strike price*. (9)

**expansionary output gap** When current output exceeds potential output; the gap puts upward pressure on inflation. (21)

**expectations hypothesis of the term structure** The proposition that long-term interest rates are the average of expected future short-term interest rates. (7)

**expected return** The probability-weighted sum of possible returns to an investment. (5)

**expected value** The probability-weighted sum of possible values of an investment; also known as the *mean* or *average*. (5)

**externality** Spillover impact from an activity of one party on to other parties who are not compensated (such as may occur when a firm creates pollution or systemic risk). (14)

# F

**face value** See *bond principal value*. (4)

**fallen angel** A low-grade bond that was initially a high-grade bond but whose issuer fell on hard times. (7)

**Fannie Mae** The Federal National Mortgage Association; a government-sponsored entity that aids in the financing of home mortgages. (13)

**federal funds market** The market where banks lend their excess reserves to other banks; the loans are unsecured. (12)

**federal funds rate** The interest rate banks charge each other for overnight loans on their excess deposits at the Fed; the interest rate targeted by the FOMC. (16)

**Federal Open Market Committee (FOMC)** The 12-member committee that makes monetary policy decisions in the United States. Members include the seven members of the Board of Governors, the president of the Federal Reserve Bank of New York, and the presidents of four Federal Reserve Banks. (16)

**Federal Reserve Banks** The 12 regional banks in the Federal Reserve System. (1, 16)

**Federal Reserve System** The central bank responsible for monetary policy in the United States. (1, 16)

**fiat money** Currency with no intrinsic value, it has value as a consequence of government decree. (2)

**finance company** A nondepository financial institution that raises funds directly in financial markets to provide loans to businesses and households. (13)

**financial holding company** A company that owns a variety of financial intermediaries. (13)

**financial institutions** Firms, such as banks and insurance companies, that provide access to the financial markets, both to savers who wish to purchase financial instruments directly and to borrowers who want to issue them; also known as *financial intermediaries*. (1, 3)

**financial instrument** The written legal obligation of one party to transfer something of value (usually money) to another party at some future date, under certain conditions. (1, 3)

**financial market** The part of the financial system that allows people to buy and sell financial instruments quickly and cheaply. (1, 3)

**financial system** The system that allows people to engage in economic transactions. It is composed of six parts: money, financial instruments, financial markets, financial institutions, regulatory agencies, and central banks. (1)

**financial system stability** One objective of the central bank is to eliminate financial system volatility, ensuring that it remains stable. (15)

**fiscal policy** The government's tax and expenditure policies, usually formulated by elected officials. (15)

**fixed-payment loan** A type of loan that requires a fixed number of equal payments at regular intervals; home mortgages and car loans are examples. (4)

**fixed-rate payer** The party to an interest-rate swap that is making fixed payments. (9)

**flexible-rate payer** The party to an interest-rate swap that is making variable payments. Also called *floating-rate payer*. (9)

**flight to quality** An increase in the demand for low-risk government bonds, coupled with a decrease in the demand for virtually every risky investment. (7)

**float** A loan from the Federal Reserve to the commercial banking system that is the result of the workings of the check-clearing process. (17)

**floating-rate payer** See *flexible-rate payer*. (9)

**FOMC statement** The press release that immediately follows every FOMC meeting; usually contains an announcement of the federal funds rate target, an evaluation of the current economic environment, and a statement of the risks to the economy. (16)

**forbearance** Willingness of regulators to allow banks with insufficient capital to continue to operate. (14)

**foreign exchange intervention** The purchase or sale of foreign exchange by government officials with the intention of moving the nominal exchange rate. (17, 19)

**foreign exchange reserves** Assets of the central bank denominated in foreign currency. (17)

**foreign exchange risk** The risk arising from holding assets denominated in one currency and liabilities denominated in another. (12)

**forward contract** An agreement to exchange an asset for money in the future at a currently agreed upon price. (9)

**free rider** Someone who doesn't pay the cost but still gets the benefit of a good or service. (11)

**fundamental value** The present value of the expected future returns to owning an asset, which equals the asset's price in an efficient market. (8)

**funding liquidity** The ability to borrow money. (2)

**future value** The value on some future date of an investment made today. (4)

**futures contract** A standardized agreement specifying the delivery of an underlying asset (commodity or financial instrument) at a given future date for a currently agreed-upon price. (9)

# G

**gold standard** A fixed-exchange-rate regime in which the currencies of participating countries are directly convertible into gold. (19)

**Governing Council of the ECB** The (currently) 22-member committee that makes monetary policy in the euro area. (16)

**government purchases** Spending on goods and services by federal, state, and local governments. (21)

**government-sponsored enterprises (GSEs)** Federal credit agencies that provide loans directly for farm and home mortgages as well as guaranteeing programs that insure the loans made by private lenders. (3)

**gross domestic product (GDP)** The market value of final goods and services produced in the economy during a year. (2)

# H

**hard peg** An exchange-rate system in which the central bank implements an institutional mechanism that ensures its ability to convert a domestic currency into the foreign currency to which it is pegged. (19)

**hedge funds** Private, largely unregulated, investment partnerships that bring together small groups of people who meet certain (high) wealth requirements. (13)

**hedger** Someone who uses financial instruments, like derivatives, to reduce risk. (9)

**hedging** Reducing overall risk by investing in two assets with opposing payoffs. (5)

**high-powered money** See *monetary base*. (17)

**holding period return** The return from purchasing and selling a bond (applies to bonds sold before or at maturity). (6)

**hyperinflation** Very high inflation; when prices double every two to three months. (15)

# I

**idiosyncratic risk** Risk affecting a small number of people (a specific firm or industry). (5)

**illiquid** The inability to meet immediate payment obligations. For a bank, reserves are insufficient to honor current withdrawal requests. (14)

**in-the-money option** An option that would yield a profit if exercised immediately. A call option is in the money when the strike price is less than the current market price for the underlying instrument. (9)

**indirect finance** An institution like a bank stands between the lender and the borrower, borrowing from the lender and providing the funds to the borrower. (3)

**inflation** A sustained rise in the general price level; the opposite of *deflation*. (2)

**inflation-indexed bonds** A bond whose yield equals a fixed real interest rate plus realized (as opposed to expected) inflation. (6)

**inflation persistence** A term used to describe the phenomenon that when inflation is low one year, it tends to be low the next, and when it is high, it tends to stay high. (21)

**inflation rate** The measurement of inflation. (2)

**inflation risk** The risk that the real value of the payments from owning a bond will be different from what was expected; that the real interest rate on a bond will differ from what was expected. (2, 6)

**inflation targeting** A monetary policy strategy that involves the public announcement of a numerical inflation target, together with a commitment to make price stability the central bank's primary objective to which all other objectives are subordinated. (18)

**information** A collection of facts. The basis for the third core principle of money and banking: Information is the basis for decisions. (1)

**information costs** The costs lenders must pay to screen potential borrowers to determine their creditworthiness and monitor how they use the loans. (3)

**insolvent** When the value of a firm's or bank's assets is less than the value of its liabilities; negative net worth. (14)

**insurance company** A financial intermediary that accepts premiums, which it invests in securities and real estate (its assets) in return for promising compensation to policyholders should certain events occur (its liabilities). (3)

**interest rate** The cost of borrowing and the reward to lending. See also *yield*. (4)

**interest-rate channel** The traditional channel of the monetary policy transmission mechanism where changes in policy affect aggregate expenditure through their impact on interest rates. (23)

**interest-rate risk** 1. The risk that the interest rate will change, causing the price of a bond to change with it. (6) 2. The risk that changes in interest rates will affect a financial intermediary's net worth. It arises from a mismatch in the maturity of assets and liabilities. (12)

**interest-rate spread** 1. The difference between the interest rate a bank receives on its assets and the interest rate it pays to obtain liabilities. (12) 2. Can also be used as a synonym for *risk spread*. (7, 12)

**interest-rate stability** One of the objectives of the central bank is to reduce interest-rate fluctuations keeping it stable. (15)

**interest-rate swap** A contract between two counterparties specifying the exchange of interest payments on a series of future dates. (9)

**intermediate targets** Variables that are not directly under the central bank's control but lie somewhere between the tools policymakers do control and their objectives; the quantity of money is an example. (18)

**internal rate of return** The interest rate that equates the present value of an investment with its cost. (4)

**International Monetary Fund (IMF)** The international organization created to administer the Bretton Woods system of fixed exchange rates, provide technical assistance helping countries to design their financial and economic systems, and make loans to countries in crisis. (18)

**inverted yield curve** When the term structure of interest rates slopes down. (7)

**investment** Spending by firms for additions to the physical capital they use to produce goods and services; also includes construction of new houses. (21)

**investment bank** A financial intermediary that issues (underwrites) stocks and bonds for corporate customers and advises customers. (3)

**investment-grade bond** Bond with low default risk; Moody's rating of Baa or higher; and Standard & Poor's rating of BBB or higher. (7)

**investment horizon** The length of time an investor plans on holding an asset. (6)

## J

**junk bond** A bond with a high risk of default. Also called a *high-yield bond*. (7)

## L

**lagged-reserve accounting** The procedure where a bank's reserve requirement is computed based on the level of deposits several weeks earlier. (18)

**large certificates of deposit** Certificates of deposit that exceed $100,000 in face value. They can be bought and sold in financial markets. (12)

**law of one price** The principle that two identical goods should sell for the same price regardless of location. (10)

**lender of last resort** The ultimate source of credit to banks during a panic. A role for the central bank. (14, 18)

**letter of credit** A financial guarantee provided for a fee, usually by a bank, that insures a payment by one of its customers. (12)

**leverage** Borrowing to finance part of an investment; increases expected return and risk. (5)

**liability** Something you owe. (3)

**life insurance** Insurance that makes payment on the death of the policyholder; see *term life insurance* and *whole life insurance*. (13)

**limited liability** The provision that even if a company fails completely, the maximum amount that shareholders can lose is their initial investment. (8)

**liquidity** A measure of the ease with which an asset can be turned into a means of payment. (2)

**liquidity premium theory of the term structure** The proposition that long-term interest rates equal the average of expected short-term interest rates plus a risk premium that rises with the time to maturity. (7)

**liquidity risk** The risk that a financial institution's liability holders will suddenly seek to cash in their claims; for a bank this is the risk that depositors will unexpectedly withdraw deposit balances. (12)

**loan commitment** A line of credit, similar to an individual's credit card limit, provided by a bank or other lender that gives a firm the ability to borrow whenever necessary. (12)

**loan loss reserves** A portion of a bank's capital that is set aside to cover potential losses from defaulted loans. (12)

**London Interbank Offered Rate (LIBOR)** The interest rate at which banks lend eurodollars to other banks. (13)

**long futures position** The position held by a buyer of a futures contract. (9)

**long-run aggregate supply curve (LRAS)** The quantity of output supplied in the long run at any level of inflation; the LRAS curve is vertical at potential output. (21)

**long-run real interest rate** The real interest rate that equates aggregate demand with potential output. (21)

**Lucas critique** Economist Robert Lucas's observation that changes in policymakers' behavior will change people's expectations, altering their behavior and the observed relationships among economic variables. (20)

## M

**M1** The narrowest monetary aggregate, which measures the most liquid means of payment available: currency, travelers' checks, demand deposits, and other checkable deposits. (2)

**M2** The monetary aggregate most commonly used in the United States, it includes M1 plus somewhat less liquid financial instruments: small-denomination time deposits, savings deposits, money-market deposit accounts, and retail money-market mutual fund shares. (2)

**macro-prudential (regulation)** Aimed at limiting systemic risks in the financial system. (14)

**margin** 1. A minimum down payment legally required to purchase a stock. 2. A deposit placed by the buyer and seller of a futures contract with the clearing corporation. (9)

**marked to market** Accounting rule in which a financial instrument is repriced and funds transferred from the loser to the winner at the end of every day. (9)

**market capitalization** The total market value of a company; the price of a share of stock times the total number of shares outstanding. (8)

**market federal funds rate** The overnight interest rate at which lending between banks takes place in the market; differs from the federal funds rate target set by the FOMC. (18)

**market liquidity** The ability to sell assets. (2)

**markets** A virtual or physical place where goods, services, and financial instruments are purchased and sold. The basis for the fourth core principle of money and banking: Markets set prices and allocate resources. (1)

**matched-sale purchase (reverse repo)** A short-term arrangement in which the Federal Reserve's Open Market Trading Desk sells a security and agrees to repurchase it in the near future. (18)

**maturity date** The time to the expiration of a debt instrument; the time until a bond's last promised payment is made. (4)

**mean** See *expected value*. (5)

**means of payment** Something that can be used to purchase goods and services; one of the functions of money. (2)

**micro-prudential (regulation)** Aimed at limiting the risks within intermediaries in order to reduce the probability of an individual institution's failure. (14)

**minimum bid rate** The minimum interest rate that banks can bid for reserves in the ECB's weekly refinancing operation; the European equivalent of the Fed's target federal funds rate; also known as the *target refinancing rate*. (18)

**monetary aggregates** Measures of the quantity of money; M1 and M2. (2)

**monetary base** The currency in the hands of the public plus reserves in the banking system; the central bank's liabilities. (17)

**monetary policy** The central bank's management of money, credit, and interest rates. (15)

**monetary policy framework** A structure in which central bankers clearly state their goals and the trade-offs among them. (15)

**monetary policy reaction curve** The relationship between the real interest rate set by the central bank and the level of inflation. (21)

**monetary policy transmission mechanism** The channels through which changes in the central bank balance sheet influence real economic activity. (23)

**money** An asset that is generally accepted as payment for goods and services or repayment of debt, acts as a unit of account, and serves as a store of value. (1, 2)

**money market** A market in which debt instruments with a maturity of less than one year are traded. (3)

**money-market deposit accounts** Accounts that pay interest and offer limited check-writing privileges; part of M2. (2)

**money-market mutual fund shares** Shares in funds that collect relatively small sums from individuals, pool them together, and invest them in short-term marketable debt issued by large corporations; retail shares are part of M2. (2)

**money multiplier** The ratio between the quantity of money and the monetary base; the quantity of money (M) equals the money multiplier (m) times the monetary base (MB). $M = m \times MB$. (17)

**moral hazard** The risk that a borrower or someone who is insured will behave in a way that is not in the interest of the lender or insurer; it is caused by asymmetric information. (11)

**mortgage-backed security** A financial instrument that provides its owner with a share of the mortgage payments from a large pool of mortgages. (3)

**multiple deposit creation** Part of the money supply process whereby a $1 increase in the quantity of reserves works its way through the banking system, increasing the quantity of money by more than $1. (17)

**municipal bonds** Bonds issued by state and local governments to finance public projects; the coupon payments are exempt from federal and state income taxes. Also called *tax-exempt bonds*. (7)

**mutual fund** A fund that pools the resources of a large number of small investors and invests them in portfolios of bonds, stocks, and real estate; managed by professional managers. (8)

**mutual fund company** Financial intermediary that pools the resources of a large number of small investors and invests them in portfolios of bonds, stocks, and real estate. (3)

## N

**Nasdaq Composite Index** The value-weighted index of more than 5,000 companies traded on the over-the-counter (OTC) market through the National Association of Securities Dealers Automatic Quotations service; the index is composed mainly of smaller, newer firms and in recent years has been dominated by technology and Internet companies. (8)

**National Central Banks (NCBs)** The central banks of the countries that belong to the European Union. (16)

**net exports** Exports minus imports, it represents an addition to the demand for domestically produced goods. (21)

**net interest income** A bank's interest income minus its interest expenses. (12)

**net interest margin** A bank's interest income minus its interest expenses divided by total bank assets; net interest income as a percentage of total bank assets. (12)

**net worth** The difference between a firm's or household's assets and liabilities. (11)

**nominal exchange rate** The value of one unit of a country's currency in terms of another country's currency. (10)

**nominal gross domestic product** The market value of final goods and services produced in the economy during a year measured at current (dollar) prices. (20)

**nominal interest rate** An interest rate expressed in dollar terms; the real interest rate plus expected inflation. (4)

**nondepository institution** A financial intermediary that does not issue deposit liabilities. (12)

**notional principal** The amount upon which the interest payments in an interest-rate swap are based. (9)

## O

**off-balance-sheet activities** Bank activities, such as trading in derivatives and issuing loan commitments, that are neither assets nor liabilities on the bank's balance sheet. (12)

**open market operations** When the central bank buys or sells a security in the open market; also includes central bank *repurchase agreements*. (17)

**open market purchase** The purchase of a security by the central bank. (17)

**open market sale** The sale of a security by the central bank. (17)

**open market trading desk** The group of people at the Federal Reserve Bank of New York who purchase and sell securities for the Fed's System Open Market Account. (18)

**operating instruments** The policy instruments that the central bank controls directly; the federal funds rate is an example. (18)

**operational risk** The risk a financial institution faces from computer hardware or software failure, natural disaster, terrorist attacks, and the like. (12)

**organized exchange** See *centralized exchange*. (3)

**out-of-the money option** An option that would not yield a profit if exercised immediately. A call option is out of the money when the strike price is more than the current market price for the underlying instrument. (9)

**output gap** The difference between current output and potential output. (21)

**overnight cash rate** The overnight interest rate on interbank loans in Europe; the European analog to the market federal funds rate. (18)

**over-the-counter (OTC) market** A financial market in which trades occur through networks of dealers connected together electronically. (3)

**overvalued currency** A country's currency when it is worth more than purchasing power parity implies. (10)

# P

**par value** See *bond principal value*. (4)

**payments system** The web of arrangements that allow for the exchange of goods and services, as well as assets, among different people. (2)

**payoff** The amount an investor receives in return for an investment. (5)

**payoff method** Where the Federal Deposit Insurance Corporation sells or pays off a failed bank's depositors and then sells the failed bank's assets in an attempt to recover the amount paid out. (14)

**pension fund company** Financial intermediary that invests individual and company contributions into stocks, bonds, and real estate (its assets) in order to provide payments to retired workers (its liabilities). (3)

**perpetuity** See *consol*. (6)

**policy directive** The instructions from the FOMC to the System Open Market Account manager specifying the federal funds rate target. (16)

**policy duration commitment** Promise by the central bank to maintain the current policy interest rate for a period of time or until a specified condition arises. (18)

**portfolio** A collection or group of investments held by a person or company. (3)

**portfolio demand for money** The theory of the demand for money based on the use of money as a store of value; the theory that treats money as an asset analogous to a bond. (20)

**potential output** What the economy is capable of producing when its resources are used at normal rates; also called sustainable output. (15, 21)

**precautionary demand for money** The theory of the demand for money based on the idea that people hold money to ensure they have resources when faced with unexpected events. (20)

**present discounted value** See *present value*. (4)

**present value** The value today (in the present) of a payment that is promised to be made in the future. (4)

**price stability** One objective of the central bank is to keep inflation low so that prices are stable on average. (15)

**price-weighted average** An index based on the average price of a collection of individual stocks. Price-weighted averages give greater weight to shares with higher prices. (8)

**primary credit** The term used to describe short-term, usually overnight, discount loans made by the Federal Reserve to commercial banks. (18)

**primary discount rate** The interest rate charged by the Federal Reserve on primary credit; also known as the discount rate, it is set at a spread above the target federal funds rate. (18)

**primary financial market** A financial market in which a borrower obtains funds from a lender by selling newly issued securities. (3)

**prime-grade commercial paper** Commercial paper with a low risk of default. (7)

**principal** See *bond principal value*. (4)

**probability** A measure of the likelihood that an event will occur. (5)

**pro-cyclicality** Refers to the mutually reinforcing interaction between financial and economic activity that amplifies economic booms and busts Note: the more general term *pro-cyclical* means moving in tandem with the swings of the business cycle. (14)

**prompt corrective action** Regulators' closing of failing banks, mandated by bank regulations. (14)

**property and casualty insurance** Insurance against damage from events like automobile accidents, fire, and theft. (13)

**purchase-and-assumption method** Where Federal Deposit Insurance Corporation finds a firm that is willing to take over a failed bank. (14)

**purchasing power parity (PPP)** The principle that a unit of currency will purchase the same basket of goods anywhere in the world. (10)

**pure discount bond** See *zero-coupon bond*. (6)

**put option** A contract that confers the right, but not the obligation, to sell a financial instrument at a predetermined price on or prior to an agreed upon date. (9)

# Q

**quantitative easing** Unconventional monetary policy action by the central bank to supply aggregate reserves beyond the quantity needed to lower the policy rate to zero. (18)

**quantity theory of money** The theory that changes in nominal income are determined by changes in the quantity of money. (20)

# R

**rating** A measure of the default risk associated with a company's debt; normally a series of letters going from AAA for bonds with the lowest risk of default to D for bonds that have defaulted. (7)

**rating downgrade** When a bond-rating agency lowers the rating of a company, signaling that its bonds have an increased risk of default. (7)

**rating upgrade** When a bond-rating agency raises the rating of a company, signaling that its bonds have a reduced risk of default. (7)

**real business-cycle theory** The theory that prices and wages are flexible, so inflation adjusts rapidly, current output always equals potential output, and all business-cycle fluctuations arise from changes in potential output. (22)

**real exchange rate** The exchange rate at which one can exchange the goods and services from one country for goods and services from another country. (10)

**real interest rate** The interest rate measured in terms of constant (real) dollars; the nominal interest rate minus expected inflation. (4)

**recession** A decline in overall economic activity, as defined by the National Bureau of Economic Research. (22)

**recessionary output gap** When current output is below potential output, the gap puts downward pressure on inflation. (21)

**regulation (financial)** A set of specific rules imposed by the government that the managers of financial institutions and participants in financial markets must follow. (1, 14)

**regulatory agencies** Entities responsible for making sure that the elements of the financial system operate in a safe and reliable manner. (1)

**regulatory competition** A situation where more than one regulatory agency works to safeguard the soundness of a bank. (14)

**reinsurance company** A very large company that provides insurance to insurance companies. (13)

**repurchase agreement (repo)** A short-term collateralized loan in which a security is exchanged for cash, with the agreement that the parties will reverse the transaction on a specific future date, as soon as the next day. (12, 18)

**required reserve ratio** The ratio of required reserves to demand deposit liabilities. (17)

**required reserves** Reserves that a bank must hold to meet the requirements set by regulators. In the United States, the requirements are established by the Federal Reserve. (12, 17)

**reserve requirement** Regulation obligating depository institutions to hold a certain fraction of their demand deposits as either vault cash or deposits at the central bank. (18)

**reserves** A bank's vault cash plus the balance in its account at the Federal Reserve. (12, 17)

**residual claimant** The final person to be paid. Stockholders are residual claimants; if the company runs into financial trouble, only after all other creditors have been paid will they receive what is left, if anything. (8)

**return on assets (ROA)** Bank net profits after taxes divided by total bank assets; a measure of bank profitability. (12)

**return on equity (ROE)** Bank net profits after taxes divided by bank capital; a measure of the return to the bank's owners. (12)

**risk** A measure of uncertainty about the future payoff to an investment, measured over some time horizon and relative to a benchmark. The basis for the second core principle of money and banking: Risk requires compensation. (1, 5)

**risk-averse investor** Someone who prefers an investment with a certain return to one with the same expected return but any amount of uncertainty. (5)

**risk-free asset** An investment whose future value is known with certainty. (5)

**risk-free rate of return** The rate of return on a risk-free asset. (5)

**risk-neutral investor** Someone who is indifferent between investments with different risks but the same expected return. (5)

**risk premium** The expected return minus the risk-free rate of return; the payment to the buyer of an asset for taking on risk. (5)

**risk sharing** The ability of individuals to combine and share the financial risks that they face; one of the services provided by a financial intermediary. (11)

**risk spread** The yield over and above that on a low-risk bond such as a U.S. Treasury with the same time to maturity, it is a measure of the compensation investors require for the risk they are bearing. Also called a *default risk premium*. (7)

**risk structure of interest rates** The relationship among the yields of bonds with the same time to maturity but different levels of risk. (7)

**rule of 72** The rule that allows you to find out how many years it will take for the value of an investment to double; divide 72 by the annual interest rate. (4)

# S

**savings deposits** The general term used to describe interest-bearing deposits that may have limited withdrawal privileges, but have no expiration date. (2)

**seasonal credit** Discount lending made in response to local, seasonal liquidity needs; used primarily by small agricultural banks in the Midwest to help manage the cyclical nature of farmers' loans and deposits. (18)

**secondary credit** Discount lending to banks that are not sufficiently sound to qualify for primary credit. (18)

**secondary discount rate** The interest rate charged on secondary credit; it is usually 50 basis points above the primary discount rate. (18)

**secondary financial market** A financial market in which previously issued securities are bought and sold. (3)

**secondary reserves** Short-term U.S. Treasury securities held as bank assets. (12)

**securities** Financial instruments representing ownership or debt; stocks, bonds, and derivatives. (3)

**shadow bank** Institution with liabilities that, like bank deposits, can be withdrawn at face value with little or no notice but that are usually subject to less oversight than banks. (14)

**short futures position** The position held by the seller of a futures contract. (9)

**short-run aggregate supply curve (SRAS)** The quantity of output supplied in the short run at any level of inflation; the SRAS curve is upward-sloping with inflation. (21)

**sovereign risk** The risk that a foreign borrower will not repay a loan because its government prohibits it from doing so. (12)

**speculative attack** A crisis in which financial market participants believe the government will become unable to maintain its exchange rate at the current fixed level, so they sell the currency, forcing an immediate devaluation. (19)

**speculator** Someone who takes risks for the purpose of making a profit. (9)

**spot price** The market price paid for immediate delivery of a commodity or financial instrument. (9)

**spread over Treasuries** The difference between the yield on a bond and that on a U.S. Treasury with the same time to maturity; a measure of the riskiness of the bond. (7)

**spreading risk** Reducing overall risk by investing in assets whose payoffs are unrelated. (5)

**stability** Steady and lacking in variation. The basis for the fifth core principle of money and banking: Stability improves welfare. (1)

**stabilization policy** Monetary and fiscal policies designed to stabilize output and inflation. (22)

**Standard & Poor's 500 Index** A stock-market index that is based on the value of 500 of the largest firms in the U.S. economy. (8)

**standard deviation** Square root of the variance measure of risk; measures the dispersion of possible outcomes. (5)

**sterilized foreign exchange intervention** A foreign exchange intervention that alters the composition of the central bank's assets but leaves the size of its liabilities unchanged. (19)

**stock** Ownership shares in a firm; also called *common stock* and *equity*. (3)

**stock market** The market where the prices of common stock are determined. (8)

**stock-market indexes** Index numbers that provide a sense of whether the value of the stock market is going up or down. (8)

**store of value** Allows movement of purchasing power into the future; one of the functions of money. (2)

**stored-value card** A card that can be used to make purchases after money is transferred from a cardholder's account. (2)

**strike price** See *exercise price*. (9)

**stripped bond** A bond whose principal and coupon payments are traded separately. (6)

**supervision (financial)** General government oversight of financial institutions. (1, 14)

**supply of dollars** The number of dollars supplied in the foreign exchange market as a function of the nominal exchange rate. (10)

**supply shock** An unexpected change in the costs of production, such as a rise or fall in oil prices, that shifts the short-run aggregate supply curve. (22)

**sustainable growth** When the economy is growing at the rate dictated by potential output. (15)

**swap** A financial contract obligating one party to exchange one set of payments for a second set of payments made by a counterparty. (9)

**swap spread** The difference between the benchmark interest rate and the swap rate, it is a measure of risk. (9)

**System Open Market Account (SOMA)** The official name for the securities holdings of the Federal Reserve System. (18)

**systematic risk** Economywide risk that affects everyone and cannot be diversified. (5)

# T

**T-account** A simplified balance sheet in the form of a T that shows the changes in assets on one side and the changes in liabilities on the other. (17)

**target federal funds rate** The Federal Open Market Committee's target for the interest rate at which banks make overnight loans to each other; the FOMC's primary policy instrument. (18)

**taxable bond** A bond whose coupon payments are not exempt from income tax. (7)

**tax-exempt bonds** See *municipal bonds*. (7)

**Taylor rule** A rule of thumb for explaining movements in the federal funds rate; the monetary policy rule developed by economist John Taylor. (18)

**term life insurance** Insurance that provides a payment to the policyholder's beneficiaries in the event of the insured's death at any time during the policy's term. (13)

**term spread** The gap between yields to maturity on a long- and a short-term bond (usually free of default risk); see also *yield curve*. (7)

**term structure of interest rates** The relationship among bonds with the same risk characteristics but different maturities. (7)

**term to maturity** The length of time until a bond's final payment. (4)

**theory of efficient markets** The notion that the prices of all financial instruments, including stocks, reflect all available information. (8)

**time** A measurable period during which something can happen. The basis for the first core principle of money and banking: time has value. (1)

**time deposits** Deposits that cannot be withdrawn before a specified date. Small-denomination time deposits are part of M2. (2)

**time value (of an option)** The price the buyer of an option pays to the seller that is in excess of the value of the option if it were immediately exercised. (9)

**too-big-to-fail policy** The idea that some financial institutions are so large that government officials cannot allow them to fail because their failure will put the entire financial system at risk. (14)

**trading or market risk** The risk that traders who work for a bank will create losses on the bank's own account. (12)

**transactions costs** The costs, including time, associated with buying and selling financial instruments, as well as goods and services. (3)

**transactions demand for money** The demand for money based on the use of money as a means of payment, for transactions purposes. (20)

**transmission mechanism of monetary policy** The way changes in central bank policy influence the real economy. (23)

**transparency** The central bank's communication of its policy decisions and how they are made clearly to the financial markets and the public. (15)

**travelers' checks** Issued by travel companies, banks, and credit card companies, they are guaranteed by the issuer and usually work just like cash; part of M1. (2)

**Treasury Direct** The system that allows individuals to purchase U.S. Treasury securities directly from the government without the use of a broker. (16)

# U

**unconventional (monetary) policy tools** Policy mechanisms (including policy duration commitments, quantitative easing, and credit easing) that are usually reserved for extraordinary episodes when conventional interest rate policy is insufficient for economic stabilization. (18)

**underlying instrument** A financial instrument used by savers/lenders to transfer resources directly to investors/borrowers; also known as a *primitive security*. (3)

**undervalued currency** A country's currency when it is worth less than purchasing power parity implies. (10)

**underwriter** A financial intermediary that sells a firm's stocks or bonds to the public, guaranteeing the price the issuer will receive. (11)

**underwriting** The process through which an investment bank guarantees the price of a new security to a corporation and then sells it to the public. (13)

**unit bank** A bank without branches. (13)

**unit of account** The units (like dollars) used to quote prices and other financial quantities; one of the functions of money. (2)

**universal bank** An institution that engages in all aspects of financial intermediation, including banking, insurance, real estate, brokerage services, and investment banking. (13)

**unsecured loan** A loan that is not guaranteed by collateral. (11)

**unsterilized foreign exchange intervention** A foreign exchange intervention that both alters the composition and changes the size of the central bank's balance sheet. (19)

**U.S. Treasury bill** A zero-coupon bond in which the U.S. government agrees to pay the bondholder a fixed dollar amount on a specific future date; has a maturity of less than one year. (6)

**U.S. Treasury bond** A coupon bond issued by the U.S. Treasury to finance government activities. (6)

# V

**value at risk** The worst possible loss over a specific time horizon at a given probability; a measure of risk. (5)

**value-weighted index** An index that is based on the value of the firms, like the S&P 500. Value-weighted indexes give greater weight to larger firms. (8)

**variance** The probability-weighted sum of the squared deviations of the possible outcomes from their expected value. (5)

**vault cash** Currency that is physically held inside a bank's vaults and automated teller machines (ATMs). (12, 17)

**velocity of money** The average number of times each unit of money is used per unit of time. (20)

**venture capital firm** A financial intermediary that specializes in investing in risky new "ventures" in return for a stake in the ownership and a share of the profits. (11)

**vesting** When the contributions your employer has made to the pension plan on your behalf belong to you. (13)

# W

**wealth** The total value of all assets; the net worth of an individual. (2)

**whole life insurance** A combination of term life insurance and a savings account in which a policyholder pays a fixed premium over his or her lifetime in return for a fixed benefit when the policyholder dies. (13)

**Wilshire 5000** The most broadly based value-weighted stock index in use. It covers the roughly 6,500 publicly traded stocks in the United States. (8)

# Y

**yen** The currency used in Japan. (10)

**yield** The interest rate that equates the price of a bond with the present value of its payments. (4)

**yield curve** A plot showing the yields to maturity of different bonds of the same riskiness against the time to maturity. (7)

**yield on a discount basis** The return to holding a bond; differs from yield to maturity because it divides the difference between the face value and the price by the face value and because it uses a 360-day year. (6)

**yield to maturity** The yield bondholders receive if they hold the bond to its maturity when the final principal payment is made. (6)

**yuan** The currency used in China. (10)

# Z

**zero bound** The term for the fact that a nominal interest rate, including the monetary policy rate, cannot fall below zero. (18, 23)

**zero-coupon bond** A promise to pay the face value of the bond on a specific future date, with no coupon payments. (6)

**zero nominal-interest-rate bound** See zero bound. (18, 23)